Avizandum Legislation on

The Scots Law of Obligations

Fifth edition

Editor

Laura J Macgregor LLM, Solicitor
Senior lecturer in commercial law,
University of Edinburgh

Avizandum Publishing Ltd
Edinburgh
2011

Published by
Avizandum Publishing Ltd
58 Candlemaker Row
Edinburgh EH1 2QE

First published 2003
2nd edition   2005
3rd edition   2007
4th edition   2009
5th edition   2011

ISBN 1-904968-48-1

British Library Cataloguing in Publication Data
A catalogue record for this book is available from the British Library

Typeset by AFS Image Setters Ltd, Glasgow
Printed and bound by Bell & Bain Ltd, Glasgow

EDITOR'S PREFACE

The aim of *Avizandum Legislation on the Scots Law of Obligations* remains unchanged: it has been produced for the use of students at undergraduate level studying obligations as part of a law degree in Scotland.

Even the most cursory glance through this volume will illustrate to the reader that the law of obligations is a fragmented and difficult subject. The task of deciding what to include is not made easier by the fact that, in such a vast subject, different academic institutions focus on different parts of obligations law in their courses. As with the previous editions, one of the guiding principles has been keeping the length, and therefore the cost to the student, to a minimum. With this in mind, another difficult task is to decide how much or how little of a particular statute to reproduce. Again, the approach is unchanged from previous editions; the most important statutes are reproduced in full and, in other cases, only selected provisions of statutes are included. In this way the student is provided with a comprehensive picture of the relevant legislation.

This volume has a companion title: *Avizandum Statutes on Scots Commercial and Consumer Law*. As a general rule, statutes appear either in this volume or in the companion volume and not in both. There are exceptions; certain statutes, such as the Sale of Goods Act 1979, are so important as to merit a place in both volumes. A debate on which pieces of legislation are part of the law of obligations and which are part of commercial law would ultimately be a fruitless one. As a general rule, legislation which has a consumer-protection flavour has been reproduced in the *Commercial and Consumer Law Statutes*, reflecting the fact that consumer law tends to be taught as part of a commercial law course.

As stated above, the volume is for the use of undergraduate students. More specifically, it is intended for use principally at ordinary rather than honours level. It has, however, been possible to include some material which facilitates the study of obligations at a deeper level, including certain international 'codes' such as the UNIDROIT Principles of International Commercial Contracts 2010.

This edition, like the previous one, includes a selection of material from the Draft Common Frame of Reference ('DCFR'), or, to give it its formal title, 'Principles, Definitions, and Model Rules of European Private Law'. At the time of going to press, an Expert Group has prepared a feasibility study on a draft instrument on European Contract Law (see http://ec.europa.eu/justice/contract/files/feasibility-study_en.pdf). It seems clear that the eventual common frame of reference will be more limited in scope than the DCFR. The DCFR nevertheless exists as a point of reference for comparative lawyers generally, and also for Scots lawyers analysing some of the out-dated parts of Scots law. Indeed, the Scottish Law Commission is currently subjecting Scots contract law to a 'health check' by reference to the DCFR (see http://www.scotlawcom.gov.uk/law-reform-projects/contract-law-in-light-of-the-draft-common-frame-of-reference-dcf/). For these reasons, the DCFR merits inclusion in this set of statutes, not-withstanding the fact that the eventual common frame of reference may differ significantly from the draft. The selection of material from this source has been made with a view to allowing students to consult quickly the relevant article of the DCFR on their chosen part of contract law, for example, enforcement or withholding of performance. Students wishing to carry out more detailed problem-solving exercises using the DCFR as a basis should consult the full version.

This edition also continues the approach of previous editions in choosing to incorporate Bills produced by the Scottish Law Commission and the Law Commission. One such example is the Unfair Contract Terms Bill – an innovative piece of legislation which seeks to tackle a fiendishly complex area of law.

Grateful thanks must go primarily to Margaret Cherry, whose hard work and patience have enabled this volume, and the others in the series, to be produced. I would also like to express my thanks to academic colleagues throughout Scotland, particularly Gordon Cameron, Dundee University and Dot Reid, Glasgow University, for their comments. These have proved very helpful in the planning of this edition. Further comments are most welcome, and should be sent to L.Macgregor@ed.ac.uk.

Materials are in general up to date to 31 July 2011.

Laura Macgregor
University of Edinburgh
August 2011

CONTENTS

PART I

STATUTES

LAWBURROWS ACT 1429
(1429, c 20)

Item It is statute ande ordanit that gif ony of the kingis liegis haf ony doute of his life outhir be dede or manance or violent presumpcioun ande he ask souerte of thaim that he doutis the schiref sal tak souerte of the party that the complante is maid apoun sa that the party playntife mak prufe of the dede or of manance or of the violent presumpcioun maid or done till hym [. . .].

LAWBURROWS ACT 1581
(1581, c 22)

Oure souerane lord with aduise of his thre estatis in this present parliament Ordanis that all letteris of lawborrowis salbe direct in tyme cuming at the instance of the pairteis complenand chargeing the personis complenit vpoun to find sicker souertie and lawborrowis that the complenaris thair wyffis bairnis tenentis and seruandis salbe harmeles and skaithles in thair bodeis landis takkis possessionis guidis and geir and on na wayis to be molestit or trublit thairin be the personis complenit vpoun nor na vtheris of thair causing sending hunding out resetting command assistance and ratihabitioun quhome thai may stop or let direclie or indireclie vthirwayis nor be the ordoure of law and justice vnder greit panes to be modifeit be the [. . .] ordinar Judges Be quhome in caise the said lawborrowis salbe dewlie tryit to be brokin the ane half of the pane sall pertene to oure souerane lord and the vthair half to the pairte grevit according to the effect and meaning of the said act maid to that effect of befoir.

COMPENSATION ACT 1592
(1592, c 61)

Oure Sourane Lord and estaitis of parliament statutis and Ordanis that ony debt de liquido ad liquidum instantlie verifiet be wreit or aith of the partie befoir the geving of decreit be admittit be all Jugis within this realme be way of exceptioun Bot nocht eftir the geving thairof In the suspensioun or in reductioun of the same decreit.

PARLIAMENTARY PAPERS ACT 1840
(3 & 4 Vict, c 9)

1 Proceedings, criminal or civil, against persons for publication of papers printed by order of Parliament, to be stayed upon delivery of a certificate and affidavit to the effect that such publication is by order of either House of Parliament
It shall and may be lawful for any person or persons who now is or are, or here-after shall be, a defendant or defendants in any civil or criminal proceeding com-

menced or prosecuted in any manner soever, for or on account or in respect of the publication of any such report, paper, votes, or proceedings by such person or persons, or by his, her, or their servant or servants, by or under the authority of either House of Parliament, to bring before the court in which such proceeding shall have been or shall be so commenced or prosecuted, or before any judge of the same (if one of the superior courts at Westminster), first giving twenty-four hours notice of his intention so to do to the prosecutor or plaintiff in such proceeding, a certificate under the hand of [the Speaker of the House of Lords], or of the clerk of the Parliaments, or of the speaker of the House of Commons, or of the clerk of the same house, stating that the report, paper, votes, or proceedings, as the case may be, in respect whereof such civil or criminal proceeding shall have been commenced or prosecuted, was published by such person or persons, or by his, her, or their servant or servants, by order or under the authority of the House of Lords or of the House of Commons, as the case may be, together with an affidavit verifying such certificate; and such court or judge shall thereupon immediately stay such civil or criminal proceeding; and the same, and every writ or process issued therein, shall be and shall be deemed and taken to be finally put an end to, determined, and superseded by virtue of this Act.

2   Proceedings to be stayed when commenced in respect of a copy of an authenticated report, &c

And be it enacted, that in case of any civil or criminal proceeding hereafter to be commenced or prosecuted for or on account or in respect of the publication of any copy of such report, paper, votes, or proceedings, it shall be lawful for the defendant or defendants at any stage of the proceedings to lay before the court or judge such report, paper, votes, or proceedings, and such copy, with an affidavit verifying such report, paper, votes, or proceedings, and the correctness of such copy, and the court or judge shall immediately stay such civil or criminal proceeding; and the same, and every writ or process issued therein, shall be and shall be deemed and taken to be finally put an end to, determined, and superseded by virtue of this Act.

3   In proceedings for printing any extract or abstract of a paper, it may be shewn that such extract was bonâ fide made

And be it enacted, that it shall be lawful in any civil or criminal proceeding to be commenced or prosecuted for printing any extract from or abstract of such report, paper, votes, or proceedings, to give in evidence [. . .] such report, paper, votes, or proceedings, and to show that such extract or abstract was published bonâ fide and without malice; and if such shall be the opinion of the jury, a verdict of not guilty shall be entered for the defendant or defendants.

4   Act not to affect the privileges of Parliament

Provided always, and it is hereby expressly declared and enacted, that nothing herein contained shall be deemed or taken, or held or construed, directly or indirectly, by implication or otherwise, to affect the privileges of Parliament in any manner whatsoever.

TRESPASS (SCOTLAND) ACT 1865
(1865, c lvi)

1 Short Title
This Act may be cited for all Purposes as 'The Trespass (Scotland) Act, 1865.'

2 Interpretation of Terms
In this Act the following Words shall have the Meanings hereby assigned to them:
'Premises' shall mean and include any House, Barn, Stable, Shed, Loft, Granary, Outhouse, Garden, Stackyard, Court, Close, or inclosed Place:
'Magistrate' shall mean and include the [sheriff principal and sheriff], or any One or more Justice or Justices of the Peace, or any One or more Magistrate or Magistrates, having Jurisdiction respectively in the County or Burgh where any Offence against the Provisions of this Act is committed, or where any Person charged with such Offence is found or brought to Trial:
'Procurator Fiscal' shall mean and include the Procurator Fiscal of the Court having such Jurisdiction.
['Road' shall mean and include any way, other than—
    (a)   a waterway; or
    (b)   without prejudice to section 100(c) (damage to roads by fire) or 129(4) (camping in a road) of the Roads (Scotland) Act 1984, a road within the meaning of that Act.]

3 Parties lodging in Premises or encamping on Land, without Permission, guilty of an Offence
[(1)]   Every Person who lodges in any Premises, or occupies or encamps on any Land, being private Property, without the Consent and Permission of the Owner or legal Occupier of such Premises or Land, and every Person who encamps or lights a Fire on or near any [. . .] Road or inclosed or cultivated Land, or in or near any Plantation, without the Consent and Permission of the Owner or Legal Occupier of such Road, Land, or Plantation, [. . .] shall be guilty of an Offence punishable as herein-after provided.
   [(2)   Subsection (1) above does not extend to anything done by a person in the exercise of the access rights created by the Land Reform (Scotland) Act 2003 (asp 2).]

4 Apprehension and Punishment of Offenders
Every Person who commits any Offence against the Provisions of this Act may, if found in the Act of committing the same by any Officer of Police or Constable, be apprehended by such Officer or Constable, and detained in any Prison, Police Station, Lock-up, or other Place of safe Custody, and not later than in the course of the next lawful Day after he shall have been so taken into Custody shall be brought before a Magistrate; and every Person charged with the Commission of any such Offence may, if not so taken into Custody, or if he shall have been liberated on Bail or Pledge, be summoned to appear before a Magistrate [; and every person committing an offence against the provisions of this Act shall be liable, on summary conviction, to a fine not exceeding level 1 on the standard scale.]

5 As to Prosecutions under Act
Every Prosecution for an Offence against the Provisions of this Act shall be raised and proceeded in at the Instance of the Procurator Fiscal, and shall be heard and determined by One or more Magistrate or Magistrates in a summary Form; and every such Prosecution shall be commenced within One Month after the Offence has been committed.

BILLS OF EXCHANGE ACT 1882
(1882, c 61)

3 Bill of exchange defined

(1) A bill of exchange is an unconditional order in writing, addressed by one person to another, signed by the person giving it, requiring the person to whom it is addressed to pay on demand or at a fixed or determinable future time a sum certain in money to or to the order of a specified person, or to bearer.

(2) An instrument which does not comply with these conditions, or which orders any act to be done in addition to the payment of money, is not a bill of exchange.

(3) An order to pay out of a particular fund is not unconditional within the meaning of this section; but an unqualified order to pay, coupled with (a) an indication of a particular fund out of which the drawee is to re-imburse himself or a particular account to be debited with the amount, or (b) a statement of the transaction which gives rise to the bill, is unconditional.

(4) A bill is not invalid by reason—

    (a) That it is not dated;

    (b) That it does not specify the value given, or that any value has been given therefor;

    (c) That it does not specify the place where it is drawn or the place where it is payable.

73 Cheque defined

A cheque is a bill of exchange drawn on a banker payable on demand. Except as otherwise provided in this Part, the provisions of this Act applicable to a bill of exchange payable on demand apply to a cheque.

83 Promissory note defined

(1) A promissory note is an unconditional promise in writing made by one person to another signed by the maker, engaging to pay, on demand, or at a fixed or determinable future time, a sum certain in money, to, or to the order of, a specified person or to bearer.

(2) An instrument in the form of a note payable to maker's order is not a note within the meaning of this section unless and until it is indorsed by the maker.

(3) A note is not invalid by reason only that it contains also a pledge of collateral security with authority to sell or dispose thereof.

(4) A note which is, or on the face of it purports to be, both made and payable within the British Islands is an inland note. Any other note is a foreign note.

FACTORS ACT 1889
(1889, c 45)

Preliminary

1 Definitions

For the purposes of this Act—

(1) The expression 'mercantile agent' shall mean a mercantile agent having in the customary course of his business as such agent authority either to sell goods or to consign goods for the purpose of sale, or to buy goods, or to raise money on the security of goods:

(2) A person shall be deemed to be in possession of goods or of the documents of title to goods, where the goods or documents are in his actual custody or are held by any other person subject to his control or for him or on his behalf:

(3) The expression 'goods' shall include wares and merchandise:

(4) The expression 'document of title' shall include any bill of lading, dock warrant, warehouse-keeper's certificate, and warrant or order for the delivery of

goods, and any other document used in the ordinary course of business as proof of the possession or control of goods, or authorising or purporting to authorise, either by endorsement or by delivery, the possessor of the document to transfer or receive goods thereby represented:

(5) The expression 'pledge' shall include any contract pledging, or giving a lien or security on, goods, whether in consideration of an original advance or of any further or continuing advance or of any pecuniary liability:

(6) The expression 'person' shall include any body of persons corporate or unincorporate.

Dispositions by mercantile agents

2 Powers of mercantile agent with respect to disposition of goods

(1) Where a mercantile agent is, with the consent of the owner, in possession of goods or of the documents of title to goods, any sale, pledge, or other disposition of the goods, made by him when acting in the ordinary course of business of a mercantile agent, shall, subject to the provisions of this Act, be as valid as if he were expressly authorised by the owner of the goods to make the same; provided that the person taking under the disposition acts in good faith, and has not at the time of the disposition notice that the person making the disposition has not authority to make the same.

(2) Where a mercantile agent has, with the consent of the owner, been in possession of goods or of the documents of title to goods, any sale, pledge, or other disposition, which would have been valid if the consent had continued, shall be valid notwithstanding the determination of the consent; provided that the person taking under the disposition has not at the time thereof notice that the consent has been determined.

(3) Where a mercantile agent has obtained possession of any documents of title to goods by reason of his being or having been, with the consent of the owner, in possession of the goods represented thereby, or of any other documents of title to the goods, his possession of the first-mentioned documents shall, for the purposes of this Act, be deemed to be with the consent of the owner.

(4) For the purposes of this Act the consent of the owner shall be presumed in the absence of evidence to the contrary.

3 Effect of pledges of documents of title

A pledge of the documents of title to goods shall be deemed to be a pledge of the goods.

4 Pledge for antecedent debt

Where a mercantile agent pledges goods as security for a debt or liability due from the pledgor to the pledgee before the time of the pledge, the pledgee shall acquire no further right to the goods than could have been enforced by the pledgor at the time of the pledge.

5 Rights acquired by exchange of goods or documents

The consideration necessary for the validity of a sale, pledge, or other disposition of goods, in pursuance of this Act, may be either a payment in cash, or the delivery or transfer of other goods, or of a document of title to goods, or of a negotiable security, or any other valuable consideration; but where goods are pledged by a mercantile agent in consideration of the delivery or transfer of other goods, or of a document of title to goods, or of a negotiable security, the pledgee shall acquire no right or interest in the goods so pledged in excess of the value of the goods, documents, or security when so delivered or transferred in exchange.

6 Agreements through clerks, &c

For the purposes of this Act an agreement made with a mercantile agent through a clerk or other person authorised in the ordinary course of business to make contracts of sale or pledge on his behalf shall be deemed to be an agreement with the agent.

7 Provisions as to consignors and consignees

(1) Where the owner of goods has given possession of the goods to another person for the purpose of consignment or sale, or has shipped the goods in the name of another person, and the consignee of the goods has not had notice that such person is not the owner of the goods, the consignee shall, in respect of advances made to or for the use of such person, have the same lien on the goods as if such person were the owner of the goods, and may transfer any such lien to another person.

(2) Nothing in this section shall limit or affect the validity of any sale, pledge, or disposition, by a mercantile agent.

Dispositions by sellers and buyers of goods

8 Disposition by seller remaining in possession

Where a person, having sold goods, continues, or is, in possession of the goods or of the documents of title to the goods, the delivery or transfer by that person, or by a mercantile agent acting for him, of the goods or documents of title under any sale, pledge, or other disposition thereof, or under any agreement for sale, pledge, or other disposition thereof, to any person receiving the same in good faith and without notice of the previous sale, shall have the same effect as if the person making the delivery or transfer were expressly authorised by the owner of the goods to make the same.

9 Disposition by buyer obtaining possession

Where a person, having bought or agreed to buy goods, obtains with the consent of the seller possession of the goods or the documents of title to the goods, the delivery or transfer, by that person or by a mercantile agent acting for him, of the goods or documents of title under any sale, pledge, or other disposition thereof, or under any agreement for sale, pledge, or other disposition thereof, to any person receiving the same in good faith and without notice of any lien or other right of the original seller in respect of the goods, shall have the same effect as if the person making the delivery or transfer were a mercantile agent in possession of the goods or documents of title with the consent of the owner.

[For the purposes of this section—

(i) the buyer under a conditional sale agreement shall be deemed not to be a person who has bought or agreed to buy goods, and

(ii) 'conditional sale agreement' means an agreement for the sale of goods which is a consumer credit agreement within the meaning of the Consumer Credit Act 1974 under which the purchase price or part of it is payable in instalments, and the property in the goods is to remain in the seller (notwithstanding that the buyer is to be in possession of the goods) until such conditions as to the payment of instalments or otherwise as may be specified in the agreement are fulfilled.]

10 Effect of transfer of documents on vendor's lien or right of stoppage in transitu

Where a document of title to goods has been lawfully transferred to a person as a buyer or owner of the goods, and that person transfers the document to a person who takes the document in good faith and for valuable consideration, the last-mentioned transfer shall have the same effect for defeating any vendor's lien or right of stoppage in transitu as the transfer of a bill of lading has for defeating the right of stoppage in transitu.

Supplemental

11 Mode of transferring documents

For the purposes of this Act, the transfer of a document may be by endorsement, or, where the document is by custom or by its express terms transferable by delivery or makes the goods deliverable to the bearer, then by delivery.

12 Saving for rights of true owner

(1) Nothing in this Act shall authorise an agent to exceed or depart from his authority as between himself and his principal, or exempt him from any liability, civil or criminal, for so doing.

(2) Nothing in this Act shall prevent the owner of goods from recovering the goods from any agent or his trustee in bankruptcy at any time before the sale or pledge thereof, or shall prevent the owner of goods pledged by an agent from having the right to redeem the goods at any time before the sale thereof, on satisfying the claim for which the goods were pledged, and paying to the agent, if by him required, any money in respect of which the agent would by law be entitled to retain the goods or the documents of title thereto, or any of them, by way of lien as against the owner, or from recovering from any person with whom the goods have been pledged any balance of money remaining in his hands as the produce of the sale of the goods after deducting the amount of his lien.

(3) Nothing in this Act shall prevent the owner of goods sold by an agent from recovering from the buyer the price agreed to be paid for the same, or any part of that price, subject to any right of set off on the part of the buyer against the agent.

13 Saving for common law powers of agent

The provisions of this Act shall be construed in amplification and not in derogation of the powers exercisable by an agent independently of this Act.

[. . .]

16 Extent of Act

This Act shall not extend to Scotland.

17 Short title

This Act may be cited as the Factors Act, 1889.

FACTORS (SCOTLAND) ACT 1890
(1890, c 40)

1 Application of 52 & 53 Vict c 45 to Scotland

Subject to the following provisions, the Factors Act, 1889, shall apply to Scotland:—

(1) The expression 'lien' shall mean and include right of retention; the expression 'vendor's lien' shall mean and include any right of retention competent to the original owner or vendor; and the expression 'set off' shall mean and include compensation.

(2) In the application of section five of the recited Act, a sale, pledge, or other disposition of goods shall not be valid unless made for valuable consideration.

2 Short title

This Act may be cited as the Factors (Scotland) Act, 1890.

LAW REFORM (MISCELLANEOUS PROVISIONS) (SCOTLAND) ACT 1940
(1940, c 42)

1 Amendment of the law as to enforcement of decrees ad factum praestandum

(1) No person shall be apprehended or imprisoned on account of his failure to

comply with a decree ad factum praestandum except in accordance with the following provisions—

(i) On an application by the person in right of such a decree (hereinafter referred to as the applicant) to the court by which the decree was granted, the court may, if it is satisfied that the person against whom such decree was granted (hereinafter referred to as the respondent) is wilfully refusing to comply with the decree, grant warrant for his imprisonment for any period not exceeding six months;

(ii) Where the court is satisfied that a person undergoing imprisonment in pursuance of a warrant granted under this section has complied, or is no longer wilfully refusing to comply, with the decree, the court shall, notwithstanding any period specified in the warrant, order the immediate liberation of such person, and it shall be the duty of the applicant, as soon as he is satisfied that the decree has been complied with, forthwith to inform the clerk of the court of such compliance;

(iii) Imprisonment under a warrant granted under this subsection shall not operate to extinguish the obligation imposed by the decree on which the application proceeds;

(iv) The person on whose application a warrant for imprisonment has been granted under this subsection shall not be liable to aliment, or to contribute to the aliment of, the respondent while in prison.

(2) On any application in pursuance of the foregoing subsection, the court may, in lieu of granting warrant for imprisonment, recall the decree on which the application proceeds and make an order for the payment by the respondent to the applicant of a specified sum or make such other order as appears to the court to be just and equitable in the circumstances, including, in the case where the decree on which the application proceeds is a decree for delivery of corporeal moveables, a warrant to officers of court to search any premises in the occupation of the respondent or of such other person as may be named in the warrant, and to take possession of, and deliver to the applicant, any such moveables which may be found in such premises.

(3) Any warrant granted under the last foregoing subsection shall be deemed to include authority to open shut and lockfast places for the purpose of carrying the warrant into lawful execution.

3 Contribution among joint wrongdoers

(1) Where in any action of damages in respect of loss or damage arising from any wrongful acts or negligent acts or omissions two or more persons are, in pursuance of the verdict of a jury or the judgment of a court found jointly and severally liable in damages or expenses, they shall be liable *inter se* to contribute to such damages or expenses in such proportions as the jury or the court, as the case may be, may deem just: Provided that nothing in this subsection shall affect the right of the person to whom such damages or expenses have been awarded to obtain a joint and several decree therefor against the persons so found liable.

(2) Where any person has paid any damages or expenses in which he has been found liable in any such action as aforesaid, he shall be entitled to recover from any other person who, if sued, might also have been held liable in respect of the loss or damage on which the action was founded, such contribution, if any, as the court may deem just.

(3) Nothing in this section shall—

(a) apply to any action in respect of loss or damage suffered before the commencement of this Act; or

(b) affect any contractual or other right of relief or indemnity or render enforceable any agreement for indemnity which could not have been enforced if this section had not been enacted.

LAW REFORM (CONTRIBUTORY NEGLIGENCE) ACT 1945
(1945, c 28)

1 Apportionment of liability in case of contributory negligence

(1) Where any person suffers damage as the result partly of his own fault and partly of the fault of any other person or persons, a claim in respect of that damage shall not be defeated by reason of the fault of the person suffering the damage, but the damages recoverable in respect thereof shall be reduced to such extent as the court thinks just and equitable having regard to the claimant's share in the responsibility for the damage:

Provided that—

(a)   this subsection shall not operate to defeat any defence arising under a contract;

(b)   where any contract or enactment providing for the limitation of liability is applicable to the claim, the amount of damages recoverable by the claimant by virtue of this subsection shall not exceed the maximum limit so applicable.

(2)   Where damages are recoverable by any person by virtue of the foregoing subsection subject to such reduction as is therein mentioned, the court shall find and record the total damages which would have been recoverable if the claimant had not been at fault.

[. . .]

(4)   Where any person dies as the result partly of his own fault and partly of the fault of any other person or persons, a claim by any dependant of the first mentioned person for damages or solatium in respect of that person's death shall not be defeated by reason of his fault, but the damages or solatium recoverable shall be reduced to such extent as the court thinks just and equitable having regard to the share of the said person in the responsibility for his death.

(5)   Where, in any case to which subsection (1) of this section applies, one of the persons at fault avoids liability to any other such person or his personal representative by pleading the Limitation Act, 1939, or any other enactment limiting the time within which proceedings may be taken, he shall not be entitled to recover any damages [or contributions] from that other person or representative by virtue of the said subsection.

(6)   Where any case to which subsection (1) of this section applies is tried with a jury, the jury shall determine the total damages which would have been recoverable if the claimant had not been at fault and the extent to which those damages are to be reduced.

[. . .]

3 Saving for Maritime Conventions Act, 1911, and past cases

(1)   This Act shall not apply to any claim to which section one of the Maritime Conventions Act, 1911, applies and that Act shall have effect as if this Act had not passed.

(2)   This Act shall not apply to any case where the acts or omissions giving rise to the claim occurred before the passing of this Act.

4 Interpretation

The following expressions have the meanings hereby respectively assigned to them, that is to say—

'court' means, in relation to any claim, the court or arbitrator by or before whom the claim falls to be determined;

'damage' includes loss of life and personal injury;

[. . .]

'fault' means negligence, breach of statutory duty or other act or omission which gives rise to a liability in tort or would, apart from this Act, give rise to the defence of contributory negligence.

5 Application to Scotland

In the application of this Act to Scotland—

(a) the expression 'dependant' means, in relation to any person, any person who would in the event of such first mentioned person's death through the fault of a third party be entitled to sue that third party for damages or solatium; and the expression 'fault' means wrongful act, breach of statutory duty or negligent act or omission which gives rise to liability in damages, or would apart from this Act, give rise to the defence of contributory negligence;

[(b) section 3 of the Law Reform (Miscellaneous Provisions) (Scotland) Act 1940 (contribution among joint wrongdoers) shall apply in any case where two or more persons are liable, or would if they had all been sued be liable, by virtue of section 1(1) of this Act in respect of the damage suffered by any person;]

(c) [substitutes s 1(4) above]

6 [Northern Ireland provisions]

7 Short title and extent

This Act may be cited as the Law Reform (Contributory Negligence) Act, 1945.

DEFAMATION ACT 1952
(1952, c 66)

3 Actions for verbal injury

In any action for verbal injury it shall not be necessary for the pursuer to aver or prove special damage if the words on which the action is founded are calculated to cause pecuniary damage to the pursuer.

[. . .]

5 Justification

In an action for libel or slander in respect of words containing two or more distinct charges against the plaintiff, a defence of justification shall not fail by reason only that the truth of every charge is not proved if the words not proved to be true do not materially injure the plaintiff's reputation having regard to the truth of the remaining charges.

6 Fair comment

In an action for libel or slander in respect of words consisting partly of allegations of fact and partly of expression of opinion, a defence of fair comment shall not fail by reason only that the truth of every allegation or fact is not proved if the expression of opinion is fair comment having regard to such of the facts alleged or referred to in the words complained of as are proved.

[. . .]

9 Extension of certain defences to broadcasting

(1) Section three of the Parliamentary Papers Act, 1840 (which confers protection in respect of proceedings for printing extracts from or abstracts of parliamentary papers) shall have effect as if the reference to printing included a reference to broadcasting by means of wireless telegraphy.

[. . .]

10 Limitation on privilege at elections

A defamatory statement published by or on behalf of a candidate in any election to a local government authority [, to the National Assembly for Wales, to the Scottish Parliament] or to Parliament shall not be deemed to be published on a privileged occasion on the ground that it is material to a question in issue in the election, whether or not the person by whom it is published is qualified to vote at the election.

11   Agreements for indemnity
An agreement for indemnifying any person against civil liability for libel in respect of the publication of any matter shall not be unlawful unless at the time of the publication that person knows that the matter is defamatory, and does not reasonably believe that there is a good defence to any action brought upon it.

12   Evidence of other damages recovered by plaintiff
In any action for libel or slander the defendant may give evidence in mitigation of damages that the plaintiff has recovered damages, or has brought actions for damages, for libel or slander in respect of the publication of words to the same effect as the words on which the action is founded, or has received or agreed to receive compensation in respect of any such publication.

14   Application of Act to Scotland
This Act shall apply to Scotland subject to the following modifications, that is to say—
    (a)   sections one, two, eight and thirteen shall be omitted;
    (b)   [*substitute s 3 for Scotland*]
    [. . .]
    (d)   for any reference to libel, or to libel or slander, there shall be substituted a reference to defamation; the expression 'plaintiff' means pursuer; the expression 'defendant' means defender; for any reference to an affidavit made by any person there shall be substituted a reference to a written declaration signed by that person; for any reference to the High Court there shall be substituted a reference to the Court of Session or, if an action of defamation is depending in the sheriff court in respect of the publication in question, the sheriff; the expression 'costs' means expenses; and for any reference to a defence of justification there shall be substituted a reference to a defence of veritas.

16   Interpretation
    (1)   Any reference in this Act to words shall be construed as including a reference to pictures, visual images, gestures and other methods of signifying meaning.
[. . .]

INTEREST ON DAMAGES (SCOTLAND) ACT 1958
(1958, c 61)

1   Power of courts to grant interest on damages
    (1)   [Where a court pronounces an interlocutor decerning for payment by any person of a sum of money as damages, the interlocutor may include decree for payment by that person of interest, at such rate or rates as may be specified in the interlocutor, on the whole or any part of that sum for the whole or any part of the period between the date when the right of action arose and the date of the interlocutor.]
    [(1A)   Where a court pronounces an interlocutor decerning for payment of a sum which consists of or includes damages or solatium in respect of personal injuries sustained by the pursuer or any other person, then (without prejudice to the exercise of the power conferred by subsection (1) of this section in relation to any part of that sum which does not represent such damages or solatium) the court shall exercise that power so as to include in that sum interest on those damages and on that solatium or on such part of each as the court considers appropriate, unless the court is satisfied that there are reasons special to the case why no interest should be given in respect thereof.
    (1B)   For the avoidance of doubt, it is hereby declared that where, in any action in which it is competent for the court to award interest under this Act, a tender is made in the course of the action, the tender shall, unless otherwise stated therein,

be in full satisfaction of any claim to interest thereunder by any person in whose favour the tender is made; and in considering in any such action whether an award is equal to or greater than an amount tendered in the action, the court shall take account of the amount of any interest awarded under this Act, or such part of that interest as the court considers appropriate.]

(2)   Nothing in this section shall—

(a)   authorise the granting of interest upon interest, or

(b)   prejudice any other power of the court as to the granting of interest, or

(c)   affect the running of any interest which apart from this section would run by virtue of any enactment or rule of law.

[. . .]

3   Citation, interpretation, extent and commencement

(1)   This Act may be cited as the Interest on Damages (Scotland) Act, 1958.

(2)   [In this Act, 'personal injuries' includes any disease and any impairment of a person's physical or mental condition.]

(3)   This Act shall extend to Scotland only, and shall not apply to any action commenced against any person before the passing of this Act.

OCCUPIERS' LIABILITY (SCOTLAND) ACT 1960
(1960, c 30)

1   Variation of rules of common law as to duty of care owed by occupiers

(1)   The provisions of the next following section of this Act shall have effect, in place of the rules of the common law, for the purpose of determining the care which a person occupying or having control of land or other premises (in this Act referred to as an 'occupier of premises') is required, by reason of such occupation or control, to show towards persons entering on the premises in respect of dangers which are due to the state of the premises or to anything done or omitted to be done on them and for which he is in law responsible.

(2)   Nothing in those provisions shall be taken to alter the rules of the common law which determine the person on whom in relation to any premises a duty to show care as aforesaid towards persons entering thereon is incumbent.

(3)   Those provisions shall apply, in like manner and to the same extent as they do in relation to an occupier of premises and to persons entering thereon,—

(a)   in relation to a person occupying or having control of any fixed or moveable structure, including any vessel, vehicle or aircraft, and to persons entering thereon; and

(b)   in relation to an occupier of premises or a person occupying or having control of any such structure and to property thereon, including the property of persons who have not themselves entered on the premises or structure.

2   Extent of occupier's duty to show care

(1)   The care which an occupier of premises is required, by reason of his occupation or control of the premises, to show towards a person entering thereon in respect of dangers which are due to the state of the premises or to anything done or omitted to be done on them and for which the occupier is in law responsible shall, except in so far as he is entitled to and does extend, restrict, modify or exclude by agreement his obligations towards that person, be such care as in all the circumstances of the case is reasonable to see that that person will not suffer injury or damage by reason of any such danger.

(2)   Nothing in the foregoing subsection shall relieve an occupier of premises of any duty to show in any particular case any higher standard of care which in that case is incumbent on him by virtue of any enactment or rule of law imposing special standards of care on particular classes of persons.

(3)   Nothing in the foregoing provisions of this Act shall be held to impose on an occupier any obligation to a person entering on his premises in respect of risks which that person has willingly accepted as his; and any question whether a risk was so accepted shall be decided on the same principles as in other cases in which one person owes to another a duty to show care.

3   Landlord's liability by virtue of responsibility for repairs

(1)   Where premises are occupied or used by virtue of a tenancy under which the landlord is responsible for the maintenance or repair of the premises, it shall be the duty of the landlord to show towards any persons who or whose property may from time to time be on the premises the same care in respect of dangers arising from any failure on his part in carrying out his responsibility aforesaid as is required by virtue of the foregoing provisions of this Act to be shown by an occupier of premises towards persons entering on them.

(2)   Where premises are occupied or used by virtue of a subtenancy, the foregoing subsection shall apply to any landlord who is responsible for the maintenance or repair of the premises comprised in the sub-tenancy.

(3)   Nothing in this section shall relieve a landlord of any duty which he is under apart from this section.

(4)   For the purposes of this section, any obligation imposed on a landlord by any enactment by reason of the premises being subject to a tenancy shall be treated as if it were an obligation imposed on him by the tenancy, 'tenancy' includes a statutory tenancy which does not in law amount to a tenancy and includes also any contract conferring a right of occupation, and 'landlord' shall be construed accordingly.

(5)   This section shall apply to tenancies created before the commencement of this Act as well as to tenancies created after its commencement.

4   Application to Crown

This Act shall bind the Crown, but as regards the liability of the Crown for any wrongful or negligent act or omission giving rise to liability in reparation shall not bind the Crown any further than the Crown is made liable in respect of such acts or omissions by the Crown Proceedings Act, 1947, and that Act and in particular section two thereof shall apply in relation to duties under section two or section three of this Act as statutory duties.

5   Short title, extent and commencement

(1)   This Act may be cited as the Occupiers' Liability (Scotland) Act 1960, and shall extend to Scotland only.

(2)   This Act shall come into operation at the end of the period of three months beginning with the day on which it is passed.

<h2 style="text-align:center">HIRE-PURCHASE ACT 1964
(1964, c 53)</h2>

[PART III
TITLE TO MOTOR VEHICLES ON HIRE-PURCHASE OR CONDITIONAL SALE

27   Protection of purchasers of motor vehicles

(1)   This section applies where a motor vehicle has been bailed or (in Scotland) hired under a hire-purchase agreement, or has been agreed to be sold under a conditional sale agreement, and, before the property in the vehicle has become vested in the debtor, he disposes of the vehicle to another person.

(2)   Where the disposition referred to in subsection (1) above is to a private purchaser, and he is a purchaser of the motor vehicle in good faith without notice of the hire-purchase or conditional sale agreement (the 'relevant agreement') that disposition shall have effect as if the creditor's title to the vehicle has been vested in the debtor immediately before that disposition.

(3)   Where the person to whom the disposition referred to in subsection (1) above is made (the 'original purchaser') is a trade or finance purchaser, then if the person who is the first private purchaser of the motor vehicle after that disposition (the 'first private purchaser') is a purchaser of the vehicle in good faith without notice of the relevant agreement, the disposition of the vehicle to the first private purchaser shall have effect as if the title of the creditor to the vehicle had been vested in the debtor immediately before he disposed of it to the original purchaser.

(4)   Where, in a case within subsection (3) above—

(a)   the disposition by which the first private purchaser becomes a purchaser of the motor vehicle in good faith without notice of the relevant agreement is itself a bailment or hiring under a hire-purchase agreement, and

(b)   the person who is the creditor in relation to that agreement disposes of the vehicle to the first private purchaser, or a person claiming under him, by transferring to him the property in the vehicle in pursuance of a provision in the agreement in that behalf, the disposition referred to in paragraph (b) above (whether or not the person to whom it is made is a purchaser in good faith without notice of the relevant agreement) shall as well as the disposition referred to in paragraph (a) above, have effect as mentioned in subsection (3) above.

(5)   The preceding provisions of this section apply—

(a)   notwithstanding anything in [section 21 of the Sale of Goods Act 1979] (sale of goods by a person not the owner), but

(b)   without prejudice to the provisions of the Factors Acts (as defined by [section 61(1) of the said Act of 1979]) or any other enactment enabling the apparent owner of goods to dispose of them as if he were the true owner.

(6)   Nothing in this section shall exonerate the debtor from any liability (whether criminal or civil) to which he would be subject apart from this section; and, in a case where the debtor disposes of the motor vehicle to a trade or finance purchaser, nothing in this section shall exonerate—

(a)   that trade or finance purchaser, or

(b)   any other trade or finance purchaser who becomes a purchaser of the vehicle and is not a person claiming under the first private purchaser,

from any liability (whether criminal or civil) to which he would be subject apart from this section.

28   Presumptions relating to dealings with motor vehicles

(1)   Where in any proceedings (whether criminal or civil) relating to a motor vehicle it is proved—

(a)   that the vehicle was bailed or (in Scotland) hired under a hire-purchase agreement, or was agreed to be sold under a conditional sale agreement, and

(b)   that a person (whether a party to the proceedings or not) became a private purchaser of the vehicle in good faith without notice of the hire-purchase or conditional sale agreement (the 'relevant agreement'), this section shall have effect for the purposes of the operation of section 27 of this Act in relation to those proceedings.

(2)   It shall be presumed for those purposes unless the contrary is proved, that the disposition of the vehicle to the person referred to in subsection (1)(b) above (the 'relevant purchaser') was made by the debtor.

(3)   If it is proved that that disposition was not made by the debtor, then it shall be presumed for those purposes, unless the contrary is proved—

(a)   that the debtor disposed of the vehicle to a private purchaser purchasing in good faith without notice of the relevant agreement, and

(b)   that the relevant purchaser is or was a person claiming under the person to whom the debtor so disposed of the vehicle.

(4)   If it is proved that the disposition of the vehicle to the relevant purchaser was not made by the debtor, and that the person to whom the debtor disposed of

the vehicle (the 'original purchaser') was a trade or finance purchaser, then it shall be presumed for those purposes, unless the contrary is proved—

(a)   that the person who, after the disposition of the vehicle to the original purchaser, first became a private purchaser of the vehicle was a purchaser in good faith without notice of the relevant agreement, and

(b)   that the relevant purchaser is or was a person claiming under the original purchaser.

(5)   Without prejudice to any other method of proof, where in any proceedings a party thereto admits a fact, that fact shall, for the purposes of this section, be taken as against him to be proved in relation to those proceedings.

29   Interpretation of Part III

(1)   In this Part of this Act—

'conditional sale agreement' means an agreement for the sale of goods under which the purchase price or part of it is payable by instalments, and the property in the goods is to remain in the seller (notwithstanding that the buyer is to be in possession of the goods) until such conditions as to the payment of instalments or otherwise as may be specified in the agreement are fulfilled;

'creditor' means the person by whom goods are bailed or (in Scotland) hired under a hire-purchase agreement or as the case may be, the seller under a conditional sale agreement, or the person to whom his rights and duties have passed by assignment or operation of law;

'disposition' means any sale or contract of sale (including a conditional sale agreement), any bailment or (in Scotland) hiring under a hire-purchase agreement and any transfer of the property of goods in pursuance of a provision in that behalf contained in a hire-purchase agreement, and includes any transaction purporting to be a disposition (as so defined), and 'dispose of' shall be construed accordingly;

'hire-purchase agreement' means an agreement, other than a conditional sale agreement, under which—

(a)   goods are bailed or (in Scotland) hired in return for periodical payments by the person to whom they are bailed or hired, and

(b)   the property in the goods will pass to that person if the terms of the agreement are complied with and one or more of the following occurs—

(i)   the exercise of an option to purchase by that person,

(ii)   the doing of any other specified act by any party to the agreement,

(iii)   the happening of any other specified events; and

'motor vehicle' means a mechanically propelled vehicle intended or adapted for use on roads to which the public has access.

(2)   In this Part of this Act 'trade or finance purchaser' means a purchaser who, at the time of the disposition made to him, carries on a business which consists, wholly or partly—

(a)   of purchasing motor vehicles for the purpose of offering or exposing them for sale, or

(b)   of providing finance by purchasing motor vehicles for the purpose of bailing or (in Scotland) hiring them under hire-purchase agreements or agreeing to sell them under conditional sale agreements,

and 'private purchaser' means a purchaser who, at the time of the disposition made to him, does not carry on any such business.

(3)   For the purposes of this Part of this Act a person becomes a purchaser of a motor vehicle if, and at the time when, a disposition of the vehicle is made to him; and a person shall be taken to be a purchaser of a motor vehicle without notice of a hire-purchase agreement or conditional sale agreement if, at the time of the disposition made to him, he has no actual notice that the vehicle is or was the subject of any such agreement.

(4)   In this Part of this Act the 'debtor' in relation to a motor vehicle which has

been bailed or hired under a hire-purchase agreement, or, as the case may be, agreed to be sold under a conditional sale agreement, means the person who at the material time (whether the agreement has before that time been terminated or not) either—

(a) is the person to whom the vehicle is bailed or hired under that agreement, or

(b) is, in relation to the agreement, the buyer,

including a person who at that time is, by virtue of section 130(4) of the Consumer Credit Act 1974 treated as a bailee or (in Scotland) a custodier of the vehicle.

(5) In this Part of this Act any reference to the title of the creditor to a motor vehicle which has been bailed or (in Scotland) hired under a hire-purchase agreement or agreed to be sold under a conditional sale agreement, and is disposed of by the debtor, is a reference to such title (if any) to the vehicle as, immediately before that disposition, was vested in the person who then was the creditor in relation to the agreement.]

EMPLOYER'S LIABILITY (DEFECTIVE EQUIPMENT) ACT 1969
(1969, c 37)

1 Extension of employer's liability for defective equipment

(1) Where after the commencement of this Act—

(a) an employee suffers personal injury in the course of his employment in consequence of a defect in equipment provided by his employer for the purposes of the employer's business; and

(b) the defect is attributable wholly or partly to the fault of a third party (whether identified or not),

the injury shall be deemed to be also attributable to negligence on the part of the employer (whether or not he is liable in respect of the injury apart from this subsection), but without prejudice to the law relating to contributory negligence and to any remedy by way of contribution or in contract or otherwise which is available to the employer in respect of the injury.

(2) In so far as any agreement purports to exclude or limit any liability of an employer arising under subsection (1) of this section, the agreement shall be void.

(3) In this section—

'business' includes the activities carried on by any public body;

'employee' means a person who is employed by another person under a contract of service or apprenticeship and is so employed for the purposes of a business carried on by that other person, and 'employer' shall be construed accordingly;

'equipment' includes any plant and machinery, vehicle, aircraft and clothing;

'fault' means negligence, breach of statutory duty or other act or omission which gives rise to liability in tort in England and Wales or which is wrongful and gives rise to liability in damages in Scotland; and

'personal injury' includes loss of life, any impairment of a person's physical or mental condition and any disease.

(4) This section binds the Crown, and persons in the service of the Crown shall accordingly be treated for the purposes of this section as employees of the Crown if they would not be so treated apart from this subsection.

EMPLOYER'S LIABILITY (COMPULSORY INSURANCE) ACT 1969
(1969, c 57)

1 Insurance against liability for employees

(1) Except as otherwise provided by this Act, every employer [. . .] shall insure, and maintain insurance, under one or more approved policies with an authorised insurer or insurers against liability for bodily injury or disease sustained by [those of his relevant employees who are employed by him for work on or from an off-

shore installation, or on or from an associated structure in the course of an activity undertaken on or in connection with an offshore installation, and arising out of and in the course of their employment for that work.]

(2) Regulations may provide that the amount for which an employer is required by this Act to insure and maintain insurance shall, either generally or in such cases or classes of case as may be prescribed by the regulations, be limited in such manner as may be so prescribed.

2 Employees to be covered

(1) For the purposes of this Act the term 'employee' means an individual who has entered into or works under a contract of service or apprenticeship with an employer whether by way of manual labour, clerical work or otherwise, whether such contract is expressed or implied, oral or in writing.

(2) This Act shall not require an employer to insure—

(a) in respect of an employee of whom the employer is the husband, wife, [civil partner,] father, mother, grandfather, grandmother, step-father, step-mother, son, daughter, grandson, granddaughter, stepson, stepdaughter, brother, sister, half-brother, half-sister.

SUPPLY OF GOODS (IMPLIED TERMS) ACT 1973
(1973, c 13)

8 Implied terms as to title

[(1) In every hire-purchase agreement, other than one to which subsection (2) below applies, there is—

(a) an implied term on the part of the creditor that he will have a right to sell the goods at the time when the property is to pass; and

(b) an implied term that—

(i) the goods are free, and will remain free until the time when the property is to pass, from any charge or encumbrance not disclosed or known to the person to whom the goods are bailed or (in Scotland) hired before the agreement is made, and

(ii) that person will enjoy quiet possession of the goods except so far as it may be disturbed by any person entitled to the benefit of any charge or encumbrance so disclosed or known.

(2) In a hire-purchase agreement, in the case of which there appears from the agreement or is to be inferred from the circumstances of the agreement an intention that the creditor should transfer only such title as he or a third person may have, there is—

(a) an implied term that all charges or encumbrances known to the creditor and not known to the person to whom the goods are bailed or hired have been disclosed to that person before the agreement is made; and

(b) an implied term that neither—

(i) the creditor; nor

(ii) in a case where the parties to the agreement intend that any title which may be transferred shall be only such title as a third person may have, that person; nor

(iii) anyone claiming through or under the creditor or that third person not otherwise than under a charge or encumbrance disclosed or known to the person to whom the goods are bailed or hired, before the agreement is made;

will disturb the quiet possession of the person to whom the goods are bailed or hired.

(3) As regards England and Wales and Northern Ireland, the term implied by subsection (1)(a) above is a condition and the terms implied by subsections (1)(b), (2)(a) and (2)(b) above are warranties.]

9   Bailing or hiring by description

(1)   [Where under a hire-purchase agreement goods are bailed or (in Scotland) hired by description, there is an implied term that the goods will correspond with the description, and if under the agreement the goods are bailed or hired by reference to a sample as well as a description, it is not sufficient that the bulk of the goods corresponds with the sample if the goods do not also correspond with the description.]

[(1A)   As regards England and Wales and Northern Ireland, the term implied by subsection (1) above is a condition.]

(2)   [Goods shall not be prevented from being bailed or hired by description by reason only that, being exposed for sale, bailment or hire, they are selected by the person to whom they are bailed or hired.]

10   Implied undertakings as to quality or fitness

(1)   [Except as provided by this section and section 11 below and subject to the provisions of any other enactment, including any enactment of the Parliament of Northern Ireland or the Northern Ireland Assembly, there is no implied term as to the quality or fitness for any particular purpose of goods bailed or (in Scotland) hired under a hire-purchase agreement.]

(2)   [Where the creditor bails or hires goods under a hire-purchase agreement in the course of a business, there is an implied term that the goods supplied under the agreement are of satisfactory quality.]

[(2A)   For the purposes of this Act, goods are of satisfactory quality if they meet the standard that a reasonable person would regard as satisfactory, taking account of any description of the goods, the price (if relevant) and all the other relevant circumstances.

(2B)   For the purposes of this Act, the quality of goods includes their state and condition and the following (among others) are in appropriate cases aspects of the quality of goods—

(a)   fitness for all the purposes for which goods of the kind in question are commonly supplied,

(b)   appearance and finish,

(c)   freedom from minor defects,

(d)   safety, and

(e)   durability.

(2C)   The term implied by subsection (2) above does not extend to any matter making the quality of goods unsatisfactory—

(a)   which is specifically drawn to the attention of the person to whom the goods are bailed or hired before the agreement is made,

(b)   where that person examines the goods before the agreement is made, which that examination ought to reveal, or

(c)   where the goods are bailed or hired by reference to a sample, which would have been apparent on a reasonable examination of the sample.

(2D)   If the person to whom the goods are bailed or hired deals as consumer or, in Scotland, if the goods are hired to a person under a consumer contract, the relevant circumstances mentioned in subsection (2A) above include any public statements on the specific characteristics of the goods made about them by the creditor, the producer or his representative, particularly in advertising or on labelling.

(2E)   A public statement is not by virtue of subsection (2D) above a relevant circumstance for the purposes of subsection (2A) above in the case of a contract of hire-purchase, if the creditor shows that—

(a)   at the time the contract was made, he was not, and could not reasonably have been, aware of the statement,

(b)   before the contract was made, the statement had been withdrawn in public or, to the extent that it contained anything which was incorrect or misleading, it had been corrected in public, or

(c)   the decision to acquire the goods could not have been influenced by the statement.

(2F)   Subsections (2D) and (2E) above do not prevent any public statement from being a relevant circumstance for the purposes of subsection (2A) above (whether or not the person to whom the goods are bailed or hired deals as consumer or, in Scotland, whether or not the goods are hired to a person under a consumer contract) if the statement would have been such a circumstance apart from those subsections.]

(3)   Where the creditor bails or hires goods under a hire-purchase agreement in the course of a business and the person to whom the goods are bailed or hired, expressly or by implication, makes known—

(a)   to the creditor in the course of negotiations conducted by the creditor in relation to the making of the hire-purchase agreement, or

(b)   to a credit-broker in the course of negotiations conducted by that broker in relation to goods sold by him to the creditor before forming the subject matter of the hire-purchase agreement,

any particular purpose for which the goods are being bailed or hired, there is an implied term that the goods supplied under the agreement are reasonably fit for that purpose, whether or not that is a purpose for which such goods are commonly supplied, except where the circumstances show that the person to whom the goods are bailed or hired does not rely, or that it is unreasonable for him to rely, on the skill or judgment of the creditor or credit-broker.

(4)   An implied term as to quality or fitness for a particular purpose may be annexed to a hire-purchase agreement by usage.

(5)   The preceding provisions of this section apply to a hire-purchase agreement made by a person who in the course of a business is acting as agent for the creditor as they apply to an agreement made by the creditor in the course of a business, except where the creditor is not bailing or hiring in the course of a business and either the person to whom the goods are bailed or hired knows that fact or reasonable steps are taken to bring it to the notice of that person before the agreement is made.

(6)   In subsection (3) above and this subsection—

(a)   'credit-broker' means a person acting in the course of a business of credit brokerage;

(b)   'credit brokerage' means the effecting of introductions of individuals desiring to obtain credit—

(i)   to persons carrying on any business so far as it relates to the provision of credit, or

(ii)   to other persons engaged in credit brokerage.

(7)   As regards England and Wales and Northern Ireland, the terms implied by subsections (2) and (3) above are conditions.

[(8)   In Scotland, 'consumer contract' in this section has the same meaning as in section 12A(3) below.]

11   Samples

[(1)   Where under a hire-purchase agreement goods are bailed or (in Scotland) hired by reference to a sample, there is an implied term—

(a)   that the bulk will correspond with the sample in quality; and

(b)   that the person to whom the goods are bailed or hired will have a reasonable opportunity of comparing the bulk with the sample; and

(c)   that the goods will be free from any defect, making their quality unsatisfactory, which would not be apparent on reasonable examination of the sample.

(2)   As regards England and Wales and Northern Ireland, the term implied by subsection (1) above is a condition.]

[12   Exclusion of implied terms

An express term does not negative a term implied by this Act unless inconsistent with it.]

[12A   Remedies for breach of hire-purchase agreement as respects Scotland

(1)   Where in a hire-purchase agreement the creditor is in breach of any term of the agreement (express or implied), the person to whom the goods are hired shall be entitled—

(a)   to claim damages, and

(b)   if the breach is material, to reject any goods delivered under the agreement and treat it as repudiated.

(2)   Where a hire-purchase agreement is a consumer contract, then, for the purposes of subsection (1) above, breach by the creditor of any term (express or implied)—

(a)   as to the quality of the goods or their fitness for a purpose,

(b)   if the goods are, or are to be, hired by description, that the goods will correspond with the description,

(c)   if the goods are, or are to be, hired by reference to a sample, that the bulk will correspond with the sample in quality,

shall be deemed to be a material breach.

(3)   In subsection (2) above 'consumer contract' has the same meaning as in section 25(1) of the Unfair Contract Terms Act 1977; and for the purposes of that subsection the onus of proving that a hire-purchase agreement is not to be regarded as a consumer contract shall lie on the creditor.

(4)   This section applies to Scotland only.]

[. . .]

14   Special provisions as to conditional sale agreements

[(1)   Section 11(4) of the Sale of Goods Act 1979 (whereby in certain circumstances a breach of a condition in a contract of sale is treated only as a breach of warranty) shall not apply to [a conditional sale agreement] where the buyer deals as consumer within Part I of the Unfair Contract Terms Act 1977 or, in Scotland, the agreement is a consumer contract within Part II of that Act.]

15   Supplementary

[(1)   In sections 8 to 14 above and this section—

'business' includes a profession and the activities of any government department (including a Northern Ireland department), [or local or public authority];

'buyer' and 'seller' includes a person to whom rights and duties under a conditional sale agreement have passed by assignment or operation of law;

'conditional sale agreement' means an agreement for the sale of goods under which the purchase price or part of it is payable by instalments, and the property in the goods is to remain in the seller (notwithstanding that the buyer is to be in possession of the goods) until such conditions as to the payment of instalments or otherwise as may be specified in the agreement are fulfilled;

['consumer sale' has the same meaning as in section 55 of the Sale of Goods Act 1979 (as set out in paragraph 11 of Schedule 1 to that Act)];

'creditor' means the person by whom the goods are bailed or (in Scotland) hired under a hire-purchase agreement or the person to whom his rights and duties under the agreement have passed by assignment or operation of law; and

'hire-purchase agreement' means an agreement, other than conditional sale agreement, under which—

(a)   goods are bailed or (in Scotland) hired in return for periodical payments by the person to whom they are bailed or hired, and

(b)   the property in the goods will pass to that person if the terms of the agreement are complied with and one or more of the following occurs—

(i)   the exercise of an option to purchase by that person,

(ii)   the doing of any other specified act by any party to the agreement,

(iii)   the happening of any other specified event.

['producer' means the manufacturer of goods, the importer of goods into the

European Economic Area or any person purporting to be a producer by placing his name, trade mark or other distinctive sign on the goods;]

(3) In section 14(2) above 'corresponding hire-purchase agreement' means, in relation to a conditional sale agreement, a hire-purchase agreement relating to the same goods as the conditional sale agreement and made between the same parties and at the same time and in the same circumstances and, as nearly as may be, in the same terms as the conditional sale agreement.

(4) Nothing in sections 8 to 13 above shall prejudice the operation of any other enactment including any enactment of the Parliament of Northern Ireland or the Northern Ireland Assembly or any rule of law whereby any term, other than one relating to quality or fitness, is to be implied in any hire-purchase agreement.]

PRESCRIPTION AND LIMITATION (SCOTLAND) ACT 1973
(1973 c 52)

PART I
PRESCRIPTION

Positive prescription

[1 Validity of right

(1) If land has been possessed by any person, or by any person and his successors, for a continuous period of ten years openly, peaceably and without any judicial interruption and the possession was founded on, and followed—

(a) the recording of a deed which is sufficient in respect of its terms to constitute in favour of that person a real right in—

(i) that land; or

(ii) land of a description *habile* to include that land; or

(b) registration of a real right in that land, in favour of that person, in the Land Register of Scotland, subject to an exclusion of indemnity under section 12(2) of the Land Registration (Scotland) Act 1979 (c 33),

then, as from the expiry of that period, the real right so far as relating to that land shall be exempt from challenge.

(2) Subsection (1) above shall not apply where—

(a) possession was founded on the recording of a deed which is invalid *ex facie* or was forged; or

(b) possession was founded on registration in the Land Register of Scotland proceeding on a forged deed and the person appearing from the Register to have the real right in question was aware of the forgery at the time of registration in his favour.

(3) In subsection (1) above, the reference to a real right is to a real right which is registrable in the Land Register of Scotland or a deed relating to which can competently be recorded; but this section does not apply to [real burdens,] servitudes or public rights of way.

[. . .]

(5) Where, in any question involving any foreshore or any salmon fishings, this section is pled against the Crown as owner of the regalia, subsection (1) above shall have effect as if for the words 'ten years' there were substituted 'twenty years'.

(6) This section is without prejudice to section 2 of this Act.]

[2 Special cases

(1) If—

(a) land has been possessed by any person, or by any person and his successors, for a continuous period of twenty years openly, peaceably and without any judicial interruption; and

(b)   the possession was founded on, and followed the execution of, a deed (whether recorded or not) which is sufficient in respect of its terms to constitute in favour of that person a real right in that land, or in land of a description *habile* to include that land, then, as from the expiry of that period, the real right so far as relating to that land shall be exempt from challenge except on the ground that the deed is invalid *ex facie* or was forged.

(2)   This section applies—

(a)   to the real right of the lessee under a lease; and

(b)   to any other real right in land, being a real right of a kind which, under the law in force immediately before the commencement of this Part of this Act, was sufficient to form a foundation for positive prescription without the deed constituting the title to the real right having been recorded,

but does not apply to servitudes or public rights of way.

(3)   This section is without prejudice to section 1 of this Act or to section 3(3) of the Land Registration (Scotland) Act 1979 (c 33).]

3   Positive servitudes and public rights of way

(1)   If in the case of a positive servitude over land—

(a)   the servitude has been possessed for a continuous period of twenty years openly, peaceably and without any judicial interruption, and

(b)   the possession was founded on, and followed the execution of, a deed which is sufficient in respect of its terms (whether expressly or by implication) to constitute the servitude,

then, as from the expiration of the said period, the validity of the servitude as so constituted shall be exempt from challenge except on the ground that the deed is invalid *ex facie* or was forged.

(2)   If a positive servitude over land has been possessed for a continuous period of twenty years openly, peaceably and without judicial interruption, then, as from the expiration of that period, the existence of the servitude as so possessed shall be exempt from challenge.

(3)   If a public right of way over land has been possessed by the public for a continuous period of twenty years openly, peaceably and without judicial interruption, then, as from the expiration of that period, the existence of the right of way as so possessed shall be exempt from challenge.

(4)   References in subsections (1) and (2) of this section to possession of a servitude are references to possession of the servitude by any person in possession of the relative dominant tenement.

(5)   This section is without prejudice to the operation of section 7 of this Act.

4   Judicial interruption of periods of possession for purposes of sections 1, 2 and 3

(1)   In sections 1, 2 and 3 of this Act references to a judicial interruption, in relation to possession, are references to the making in appropriate proceedings, by any person having a proper interest to do so, of a claim which challenges the possession in question.

(2)   In this section 'appropriate proceedings' means—

(a)   any proceedings in a court of competent jurisdiction in Scotland or elsewhere, except proceedings in the Court of Session initiated by a summons which is not subsequently called;

(b)   any arbitration in Scotland [in respect of which an arbitrator (or panel of arbitrators) has been appointed];

(c)   any arbitration in a country other than Scotland, being an arbitration an award in which would be enforceable in Scotland.

(3)   The date of a judicial interruption shall be taken to be—

(a)   where the claim has been made in an arbitration [the date when the arbitration begins];

(b)   in any other case, the date when the claim was made.

[(4)　An arbitration begins for the purposes of this section—

(a)　when the parties to the arbitration agree that it begins, or

(b)　in the absence of such agreement, in accordance with rule 1 of the Scottish Arbitration Rules (see section 7 of, and schedule 1 to, the Arbitration (Scotland) Act 2010.]

5　Further provisions supplementary to sections 1, 2 and 3

(1)　In sections 1, 2 and 3 of this Act 'deed' includes a judicial decree; and for the purposes of the said sections any of the following, namely an instrument of sasine, a notarial instrument and a notice of title, which narrates or declares that a person has a [right in land shall be treated as a deed sufficient to constitute that right].

[. . .]

Negative prescription

6　Extinction of obligations by prescriptive periods of five years

(1)　If, after the appropriate date, an obligation to which this section applies has subsisted for a continuous period of five years—

(a)　without any relevant claim having been made in relation to the obligation, and

(b)　without the subsistence of the obligation having been relevantly acknowledged,

then as from the expiration of that period the obligation shall be extinguished:

Provided that in its application to an obligation under a bill of exchange or a promissory note this subsection shall have effect as if paragraph (b) thereof were omitted.

(2)　Schedule 1 to this Act shall have effect for defining the obligations to which this section applies.

(3)　In subsection (1) above the reference to the appropriate date, in relation to an obligation of any kind specified in Schedule 2 to this Act is a reference to the date specified in that Schedule in relation to obligations of that kind, and in relation to an obligation of any other kind is a reference to the date when the obligation became enforceable.

(4)　In the computation of a prescriptive period in relation to any obligation for the purposes of this section—

(a)　any period during which by reason of—

(i)　fraud on the part of the debtor or any person acting on his behalf, or

(ii)　error induced by words or conduct of the debtor or any person acting on his behalf,

the creditor was induced to refrain from making a relevant claim in relation to the obligation, and

(b)　any period during which the original creditor (while he is the creditor) was under legal disability,

shall not be reckoned as, or as part of, the prescriptive period:

Provided that any period such as is mentioned in paragraph (a) of this subsection shall not include any time occurring after the creditor could with reasonable diligence have discovered the fraud or error, as the case may be, referred to in that paragraph.

(5)　Any period such as is mentioned in paragraph (a) or (b) of subsection (4) of this section shall not be regarded as separating the time immediately before it from the time immediately after it.

7　Extinction of obligations by prescriptive periods of twenty years

(1)　If, after the date when any obligation to which this section applies has become enforceable, the obligation has subsisted for a continuous period of twenty years—

(a)   without any relevant claim having been made in relation to the obligation, and

(b)   without the subsistence of the obligation having been relevantly acknowledged,

then as from the expiration of that period the obligation shall be extinguished:

Provided that in its application to an obligation under a bill of exchange or a promissory note this subsection shall have effect as if paragraph (b) thereof were omitted.

(2)   This section applies to an obligation of any kind (including an obligation to which section 6 of this Act applies), not being an obligation [to which section 22A of this Act applies or an obligation] specified in Schedule 3 to this Act as an imprescriptible obligation [or an obligation to make reparation in respect of personal injuries within the meaning of Part II of this Act or in respect of the death of any person as a result of such injuries.]

8   Extinction of other rights relating to property by prescriptive periods of twenty years

(1)   If, after the date when any right to which this section applies has become exercisable or enforceable, the right has subsisted for a continuous period of twenty years unexercised by or unenforced, and without any relevant claim in relation to it having been made, then as from the expiration of that period the right shall be extinguished.

(2)   This section applies to any right relating to property, whether heritable or moveable, not being a right specified in Schedule 3 to this Act as an imprescriptible right or falling within section 6 or 7 of this Act as being a right correlative to an obligation to which either of those sections applies.

[8A   Extinction of obligations to make contribution between wrongdoers

(1)   If any obligation to make a contribution by virtue of section 3(2) of the Law Reform (Miscellaneous Provisions) (Scotland) Act 1940 in respect of any damages or expenses has subsisted for a continuous period of 2 years after the date on which the right to recover the contribution became enforceable by the creditor in the obligation—

(a)   without any relevant claim having been made in relation to the obligation; and

(b)   without the subsistence of the obligation having been relevantly acknowledged;

then as from the expiration of that period the obligation shall be extinguished.

(2)   Subsections (4) and (5) of section 6 of this Act shall apply for the purposes of this section as they apply for the purposes of that section.]

9   Definition of 'relevant claim' for purposes of sections 6, 7 and 8

(1)   In sections 6 [, 7 and 8A] of this Act the expression 'relevant claim', in relation to an obligation, means a claim made by or on behalf of the creditor for implement or part-implement of the obligation, being a claim made—

(a)   in appropriate proceedings, or

[(b)   by the presentation of, or the concurring in, a petition for sequestration or by the submission of a claim under section 22 or 48 of the Bankruptcy (Scotland) Act 1985 [. . .]; or

(c)   by a creditor to the trustee acting under a trust deed as defined in section 5(2)(c) of the Bankruptcy (Scotland) Act 1985; or

(d)   by the presentation of, or the concurring in, a petition for the winding up of a company or by the submission of a claim in a liquidation in accordance with rules made under section 411 of the Insolvency Act 1986;]

and for the purposes of the said sections 6 [, 7 and 8A] the execution by or on behalf of the creditor in an obligation of any form of diligence directed to the enforcement of the obligation shall be deemed to be a relevant claim in relation to the obligation.

(2) In section 8 of this Act the expression 'relevant claim', in relation to a right, means a claim made in appropriate proceedings by or on behalf of the creditor to establish the right or to contest any claim to a right inconsistent therewith.

(3) Where a claim which, in accordance with the foregoing provisions of this section, is a relevant claim for the purposes of section 6, 7[, 8 or 8A] of this Act is made in an arbitration, [the date when the arbitration begins] shall be taken for those purposes to be the date of the making of the claim.

(4) In this section the expression 'appropriate proceedings' and, in relation to an arbitration, the expression ['the date when the arbitration begins'] have the same meanings as in section 4 of this Act.

10 Relevant acknowledgement for purposes of sections 6 and 7

(1) The subsistence of an obligation shall be regarded for the purposes of sections 6 [, 7 and 8A] of this Act as having been relevantly acknowledged if, and only if, either of the following conditions is satisfied, namely—

(a) that there has been such performance by or on behalf of the debtor towards implement of the obligation as clearly indicates that the obligation still subsists;

(b) that there has been made by or on behalf of the debtor to the creditor or his agent an unequivocal written admission clearly acknowledging that the obligation still subsists.

(2) Subject to subsection (3) below, where two or more persons are bound jointly by an obligation so that each is liable for the whole, and the subsistence of the obligation has been relevantly acknowledged by or on behalf of one of those persons then—

(a) if the acknowledgment is made in the manner specified in paragraph (a) of the foregoing subsection it shall have effect for the purposes of the said sections 6 [, 7 and 8A] as respects the liability of each of those persons, and

(b) if it is made in the manner specified in paragraph (b) of that subsection it shall have effect for those purposes only as respects the liability of the person who makes it.

(3) Where the subsistence of an obligation affecting a trust has been relevantly acknowledged by or on behalf of one two or more co-trustees in the manner specified in paragraph (a) or (b) of subsection (1) of this section, the acknowledgment shall have effect for the purposes of the said sections 6 [, 7 and 8A] as respects the liability of the trust estate and any liability of each of the trustees.

(4) In this section references to performance in relation to an obligation include, where the nature of the obligation so requires, references to refraining from doing something and to permitting or suffering something to be done or maintained.

11 Obligations to make reparation

(1) Subject to subsections (2) and (3) below, any obligation (whether arising from any enactment, or from any rule of law or from, or by reason of any breach of, a contract or promise) to make reparation for loss, injury or damage caused by an act, neglect or default shall be regarded for the purposes of section 6 of this Act as having become enforceable on the date when the loss, injury or damage occurred.

(2) Where as a result of a continuing act, neglect or default loss, injury or damage has occurred before the cessation of the act, neglect or default the loss, injury or damage shall be deemed for the purposes of subsection (1) above to have occurred on the date when the act, neglect or default ceased.

(3) In relation to a case where on the date referred to in subsection (1) above (or, as the case may be, that subsection as modified by subsection (2) above) the

creditor was not aware, and could not with reasonable diligence have been aware, that loss, injury or damage caused as aforesaid had occurred, the said subsection (1) shall have effect as if for the reference therein to that date there were substituted a reference to the date when the creditor first became, or could with reasonable diligence have become, so aware.

(4) Subsections (1) and (2) above (with the omission of any reference therein to subsection (3) above) shall have effect for the purposes of section 7 of this Act as they have effect for the purposes of section 6 of this Act.

12 Savings

(1) Where by virtue of any enactment passed or made before the passing of this Act a claim to establish a right or enforce implement of an obligation may be made only within a period of limitation specified in or determined under the enactment, and, by the expiration of a prescriptive period determined under section 6, 7 or 8 of this Act the right or obligation would, apart from this subsection, be extinguished before the expiration of the period of limitation, the said section shall have effect as if the relevant prescriptive period were extended so that it expires—

(a) on the date when the period of limitation expires, or

(b) if on that date any such claim made within that period has not been finally disposed of, on the date when the claim is so disposed of.

(2) Nothing in section 6, 7 or 8 of this Act shall be construed so as to exempt any deed from challenge at any time on the ground that it is invalid *ex facie* or was forged.

13 Prohibition of contracting out

Any provision in any agreement purporting to provide in relation to any right or obligation that section 6, 7 [, 8 or 8A] of this Act shall not have effect shall be null.

General

14 Computation of prescriptive periods

(1) In the computation of a prescriptive period for the purposes of any provision of this Part of this Act—

(a) time occurring before the commencement of this Part of this Act shall be reckonable towards the prescriptive period in like manner as time occurring thereafter, but subject to the restriction that any time reckoned under this paragraph shall be less than the prescriptive period;

(b) any time during which any person against whom the provision is pled was under legal disability shall (except so far as otherwise provided by [subsection (4) of section 6 of this Act including that subsection as applied by section 8A of this Act] be reckoned as if the person were free from that disability;

(c) if the commencement of the prescriptive period would, apart from this paragraph, fall at a time in any day other than the beginning of the day, the period shall be deemed to have commenced at the beginning of the next following day;

(d) if the last day of the prescriptive period would, apart from this paragraph, be a holiday, the period shall, notwithstanding anything in the said provision, be extended to include any immediately succeeding day which is a holiday, any further immediately succeeding days which are holidays, and the next succeeding day which is not a holiday;

(e) save as otherwise provided in this Part of this Act regard shall be had to the like principles as immediately before the commencement of this Part of this Act were applicable to the computation of periods of prescription for the purposes of the Prescription Act 1617.

(2) In this section 'holiday' means a day of any of the following descriptions,

namely, a Saturday, a Sunday and a day which, in Scotland, is a bank holiday under the Banking and Financial Dealings Act 1971.

15   Interpretation of Part I

(1)   In this Part of this Act, unless the context otherwise requires, the following expressions have the meanings hereby assigned to them, namely—

'bill of exchange' has the same meaning as it has for the purposes of the Bills of Exchange Act 1882;

'date of execution', in relation to a deed executed on several dates, means the last of those dates;

'enactment' includes an order, regulation, rule or other instrument having effect by virtue of an Act;

'holiday' has the meaning assigned to it by section 14 of this Act;

'land' includes heritable property of any description;

'lease' includes a sub-lease;

'legal disability' means legal disability by reason of nonage or unsoundness of mind;

'possession' includes civil possession, and 'possessed' shall be construed accordingly;

'prescriptive period' means a period required for the operation of section 1, 2, 3, 6, 7 [, 8 or 8A] of this Act;

'promissory note' has the same meaning as it has for the purposes of the Bills of Exchange Act 1882;

'trustee' includes any person holding property in fiduciary capacity for another and, without prejudice to that generality, includes a trustee within the meaning of the Trusts (Scotland) Act 1921; and 'trust' shall be construed accordingly;

and references to the recording of a deed are references to the recording thereof in the General Register of Sasines.

(2)   In this Part of this Act, unless the context otherwise requires, any reference to an obligation or to a right includes a reference to the right or, as the case may be, to the obligation (if any), correlative thereto.

(3)   In this Part of this Act any reference to an enactment shall, unless the context otherwise requires, be construed as a reference to that enactment as amended or extended, and as including a reference thereto as applied, by or under any other enactment.

16   Amendments and repeals related to Part I

(1)   The enactment specified in Part I of Schedule 4 to this Act shall have effect subject to the amendment there specified, being an amendment related to this Part of this Act.

(2)   Subject to the next following subsection, the enactments specified in Part I of Schedule 5 to this Act (which includes certain enactments relating to the limitation of proof) are hereby repealed to the extent specified in column 3 of that Schedule.

(3)   Where by virtue of any Act repealed by this section the subsistence of an obligation in force at the date of the commencement of this Part of this Act was immediately before that date, by reason of the passage of time, provable only by the writ or oath of the debtor the subsistence of the obligation shall [(notwithstanding anything in sections 16(1) and 17(2)(a) of the Interpretation Act 1978, which relates to the effect of repeals)] as from that date be provable as if the said repealed Act had not passed.

PART II

LIMITATION OF ACTIONS

[16A   Part II not to extend to product liability

This Part of this Act does not apply to any action to which section 22B or 22C of this Act applies.]

[17 Actions in respect of personal injuries not resulting in death

(1) This section applies to an action of damages where the damages claimed consist of or include damages in respect of personal injuries, being an action (other than an action to which section 18 of this Act applies) brought by the person who sustained the injuries or any other person.

(2) Subject to subsection (3) below and section 19A of this Act, no action to which this section applies shall be brought unless it is commenced within a period of 3 years after—

(a) the date on which the injuries were sustained or, where the act or omission to which the injuries were attributable was a continuing one, that date or the date on which the act or omission ceased, whichever is the later; or

(b) the date (if later than any date mentioned in paragraph (a) above) on which the pursuer in the action became, or on which, in the opinion of the court, it would have been reasonably practicable for him in all the circumstances to become, aware of all the following facts—

(i) that the injuries in question were sufficiently serious to justify his bringing an action of damages on the assumption that the person against whom the action was brought did not dispute liability and was able to satisfy a decree;

(ii) that the injuries were attributable in whole or in part to an act or omission; and

(iii) that the defender was a person to whose act or omission the injuries were attributable in whole or in part or the employer or principal of such a person.

(3) In the computation of the period specified in subsection (2) above there shall be disregarded any time during which the person who sustained the injuries was under legal disability by reason of nonage or unsoundness of mind.

18 Actions where death has resulted from personal injuries

(1) This section applies to any action in which, following the death of any person from personal injuries, damages are claimed in respect of the injuries or the death.

(2) Subject to subsections (3) and (4) below and section 19A of this Act, no action to which this section applies shall be brought unless it is commenced within a period of 3 years after—

(a) the date of death of the deceased; or

(b) the date (if later than the date of death) on which the pursuer in the action became, or on which, in the opinion of the court, it would have been reasonably practicable for him in all the circumstances to become, aware of both of the following facts—

(i) that the injuries of the deceased were attributable in whole or in part to an act or omission; and

(ii) that the defender was a person to whose act or omission the injuries were attributable in whole or in part or the employer or principal of such a person.

(3) Where the pursuer is a relative of the deceased, there shall be disregarded in the computation of the period specified in subsection (2) above any time during which the relative was under legal disability by reason of nonage or unsoundness of mind.

(4) Subject to section 19A of this Act, where an action of damages has not been brought by or on behalf of a person who has sustained personal injuries within the period specified in section 17(2) of this Act and that person subsequently dies in consequence of those injuries, no action to which this section applies shall be brought in respect of those injuries or the death from those injuries.

(5) In this section 'relative' has the same meaning as in [the Damages (Scotland) Act 2011].

[18A   Limitation of defamation and other actions

(1)   Subject to subsections (2) and (3) below and section 19A of this Act, no action for defamation shall be brought unless it is commenced within a period of 3 years after the date when the right of action accrued.

(2)   In the computation of the period specified in subsection (1) above there shall be disregarded any time during which the person alleged to have been defamed was under legal disability by reason of nonage or unsoundness of mind.

(3)   Nothing in this section shall affect any right of action which accrued before the commencement of this section.

(4)   In this section—

(a)   'defamation' includes *convicium* and malicious falsehood, and 'defamed' shall be construed accordingly; and

(b)   references to the date when a right of action accrued shall be construed as references to the date when the publication or communication in respect of which the action for defamation is to be brought first came to the notice of the pursuer.

18B   Actions of harassment

(1)   This section applies to actions of harassment (within the meaning of section 8 [or section 8A] of the Protection from Harassment Act 1997) which include a claim for damages.

(2)   Subject to subsection (3) below and to section 19A of this Act, no action to which this section applies shall be brought unless it is commenced within a period of 3 years after—

(a)   the date on which the alleged harassment ceased; or

(b)   the date (if later than the date mentioned in paragraph (a) above) on which the pursuer in the action became, or on which, in the opinion of the court, it would have been reasonably practicable for him in all the circumstances to have become, aware, that the defender was a person responsible for the alleged harassment or the employer or principal of such a person.

(3)   In the computation of the period specified in subsection (2) above there shall be disregarded any time during which the person who is alleged to have suffered the harassment was under legal disability by reason of nonage or unsoundness of mind.]

[. . .]

[19A   Power of court to override time-limits etc

(1)   Where a person would be entitled, but for any of the provisions of sections 17, [18, 18A or 18B] of this Act, to bring an action, the court may, if it seems to it equitable to do so, allow him to bring the action notwithstanding that provision.

(2)   The provisions of subsection (1) above shall have effect not only as regards rights of action accruing after the commencement of this section but also as regards those, in respect of which a final judgment has not been pronounced, accruing before such commencement.

(3)   In subsection (2) above, the expression 'final judgment' means an interlocutor of a court of first instance which, by itself, or taken along with previous interlocutors, disposes of the subject matter of a cause notwithstanding that judgment may not have been pronounced on every question raised or that the expenses found due may not have been modified, taxed or decerned for; but the expression does not include an interlocutor dismissing a cause by reason only of a provision mentioned in subsection (1) above.

(4)   An action which would not be entertained but for this section shall not be tried by jury.]

. . .

[19D   Interruption of limitation period: arbitration

(1)   Any period during which an arbitration is ongoing in relation to a matter is to be disregarded in any computation of the period specified in section 17(2), 18(2), 18A(1) or 18B(2) of this Act in relation to that matter.

(2)   In this section, 'arbitration' means—

(a)   any arbitration in Scotland,

(b)   any arbitration in a country other than Scotland, being an arbitration an award in which would be enforceable in Scotland.]

[. . .]

[22   Interpretation of Part II and supplementary provisions

(1)   In this Part of this Act—

'the court' means the Court of Session or the sheriff court; and

'personal injuries' includes any disease and any impairment of a person's physical or mental condition.

(2)   Where the pursuer in an action to which section 17, 18 [or 18A] of this Act applies is pursuing the action by virtue of the assignation of a right of action, the reference in subsection (2)(b) of the said section 17 or, [of the said section, or, as the case may be, subsection (4)(b) of the said section 18A] to the pursuer in the action shall be construed as a reference to the assignor of the right of action.

(3)   For the purposes of the said subsection (2)(b) knowledge that any act or omission was or was not, as a matter of law, actionable, is irrelevant.

(4)   An action which would not be entertained but for the said subsection (2)(b) shall not be tried by jury.]

[PART IIA

PRESCRIPTION OF OBLIGATIONS AND LIMITATION OF ACTIONS UNDER PART I OF THE CONSUMER PROTECTION ACT 1987

Prescription of obligations

[22A   Ten years' prescription of obligations

(1)   An obligation arising from liability under section 2 of the 1987 Act (to make reparation for damage caused wholly or partly by a defect in a product) shall be extinguished if a period of 10 years has expired from the relevant time, unless a relevant claim was made within that period and has not been finally disposed of, and no such obligation shall come into existence after the expiration of the said period.

(2)   If, at the expiration of the period of 10 years mentioned in subsection (1) above, a relevant claim has been made but has not been finally disposed of, the obligation to which the claim relates shall be extinguished when the claim is finally disposed of.

(3)   In this section a claim is finally disposed of when—

(a)   a decision disposing of the claim has been made against which no appeal is competent;

(b)   an appeal against such a decision is competent with leave, and the time limit for leave has expired and no application has been made or leave has been refused;

(c)   leave to appeal against such a decision is granted or is not required, and no appeal is made within the time limit for appeal; or

(d)   the claim is abandoned;

'relevant claim' in relation to an obligation means a claim made by or on behalf of the creditor for implement or part implement of the obligation, being a claim made—

(a)   in appropriate proceedings within the meaning of section 4(2) of this Act; or

(b)   by the presentation of, or the concurring in, a petition for sequestration or by the submission of a claim under section 22 or 48 of the Bankruptcy (Scotland) Act 1985; or

(c)   by the presentation of, or the concurring in, a petition for the winding up of a company or by the submission of a claim in a liquidation in accordance with the rules made under section 411 of the Insolvency Act 1986; 'relevant time' has the meaning given in section 4(2) of the 1987 Act.

(4)   Where a relevant claim is made in an arbitration, [the date when the arbitration begins (within the meaning of section 4(4) of this Act)] shall be taken for those purposes to be the date of the making of the claim.]

Limitation of actions

[22B   3 year limitation of actions

(1)   This section shall apply to an action to enforce an obligation arising from liability under section 2 of the 1987 Act (to make reparation for damage caused wholly or partly by a defect in a product), except where section 22C of this Act applies.

(2)   Subject to subsection (4) below, an action to which this section applies shall not be competent unless it is commenced within the period of 3 years after the earliest date on which the person seeking to bring (or a person who could at an earlier date have brought) the action was aware, or on which, in the opinion of the court, it was reasonably practicable for him in all the circumstances to become aware, of all the facts mentioned in subsection (3) below.

(3)   The facts referred to in subsection (2) above are—

(a)   that there was a defect in a product;

(b)   that the damage was caused or partly caused by the defect;

(c)   that the damage was sufficiently serious to justify the pursuer (or other person referred to in subsection (2) above) in bringing an action to which this section applies on the assumption that the defender did not dispute liability and was able to satisfy a decree;

(d)   that the defender was a person liable for the damage under the said section 2.

(4)   In the computation of the period of 3 years mentioned in subsection (2) above, there shall be disregarded any period during which the person seeking to bring the action was under legal disability by reason of nonage or unsoundness of mind.

(5)   The facts mentioned in subsection (3) above do not include knowledge of whether particular facts and circumstances would or would not, as a matter of law, result in liability for damage under the said section 2.

(6)   Where a person would be entitled, but for this section, to bring an action for reparation other than one in which the damages claimed are confined to damages for loss of or damage to property, the court may, if it seems to it equitable to do so, allow him to bring the action notwithstanding this section.

22C   Actions under the 1987 Act where death has resulted from personal injuries

(1)   This section shall apply to an action to enforce an obligation arising from liability under section 2 of the 1987 Act (to make reparation for damage caused wholly or partly by a defect in a product) where a person has died from personal injuries and the damages claimed include damages for those personal injuries or that death.

(2)   Subject to subsection (4) below, an action to which this section applies shall not be competent unless it is commenced within the period of 3 years after the later of—

(a)   the date of death of the injured person;

(b)   the earliest date on which the person seeking to make (or a person who could at an earlier date have made) the claim was aware, or on which, in the opinion of the court, it was reasonably practicable for him in all the circumstances to become aware—

    (i)   that there was a defect in the product;

    (ii)   that the injuries of the deceased were caused (or partly caused) by the defect; and

    (iii)   that the defender was a person liable for the damage under the said section 2.

(3)   Where the person seeking to make the claim is a relative of the deceased, there shall be disregarded in the computation of the period mentioned in subsection (2) above any period during which that relative was under legal disability by reason of nonage or unsoundness of mind.

(4)   Where an action to which section 22B of this Act applies has not been brought within the period mentioned in subsection (2) of that section and the person subsequently dies in consequence of his injuries, an action to which this section applies shall not be competent in respect of those injuries or that death.

(5)   Where a person would be entitled, but for this section, to bring an action for reparation other than one in which the damages claimed are confined to damages for loss of or damage to property, the court may, if it seems to it equitable to do so, allow him to bring the action notwithstanding this section.

(6)   In this section 'relative' has the same meaning as in the [Damages (Scotland) Act 2011].

(7)   For the purposes of subsection (2)(b) above there shall be disregarded knowledge of whether particular facts and circumstances would or would not, as a matter of law, result in liability for damage under the said section 2.]

[22CA   Interruption of limitation period for 1987 Act actions: arbitration

(1)   Any period during which an arbitration is ongoing in relation to a matter is to be disregarded in any computation of the period specified in section 22B(2) or 22C(2) of this Act in relation to that matter.

(2)   In this section, 'arbitration' means—

(a)   any arbitration in Scotland,

(b)   any arbitration in a country, other than Scotland, being an arbitration an award in which would be enforceable in Scotland.]

Supplementary

[22D   Interpretation of this Part

(1)   Expressions used in this Part and in Part I of the 1987 Act shall have the same meanings in this Part as in the said Part I.

(2)   For the purposes of section 1(1) of the 1987 Act, this Part shall have effect and be construed as if it were contained in Part I of that Act.

(3)   In this Part, 'the 1987 Act' means the Consumer Protection Act 1987.]

[. . .]

[23A   Private international law application

(1)   Where the substantive law of a country other than Scotland falls to be applied by a Scottish court as the law governing an obligation, the court shall apply the relevant rules of law of that country relating to the extinction of the obligations or the limitation of time within which proceedings may be brought to enforce the obligation to the exclusion of any corresponding rule of Scots law.

(2)   This section shall not apply where it appears to the court that the application of the relevant foreign rule of law would be incompatible with the principles of public policy applied by the court.

(3)   This section shall not apply in any case where the application of the corresponding rule of Scots law has extinguished the obligation, or barred the bringing of proceedings prior to the coming into force of the Prescription and Limitation (Scotland) Act 1984.]

[(4)   This section shall not apply in any case where the law of a country other than Scotland falls to be applied by virtue of any choice of law rule contained in the Rome II Regulation.

(5)   In subsection (4) 'the Rome II Regulation' means Regulation (EC) No 864/2007 of the European Parliament and of the Council on the law applicable to non-contractual obligations (Rome II), including that Regulation as applied by regulation 4 of the Law Applicable to Non-Contractual Obligations (Scotland) Regulations 2008 (conflicts falling within Article 25(2) of Regulation (EC) No 864/2007).]

24   The Crown
This Act binds the Crown.

25   Short title, commencement and extent
(1)   This Act may be cited as the Prescription and Limitation (Scotland) Act 1973.

(2)   This Act shall come into operation as follows—

(a)   Parts II and III of this Act, Part II of Schedule 4 to this Act and Part II of Schedule 5 to this Act shall come into operation on the date on which this Act is passed;

(b)   except as aforesaid this Act shall come into operation on the expiration of three years from the said date.

[. . .]

(4)   This Act extends to Scotland only.

SCHEDULES

<table>
<tr><td>Section 6</td><td>SCHEDULE 1</td></tr>
</table>

OBLIGATIONS AFFECTED BY PRESCRIPTIVE PERIODS OF FIVE YEARS
UNDER SECTION 6

1.   Subject to paragraph 2 below, section 6 of this Act applies—

(a)   to any obligation to pay a sum of money due in respect of a particular period—

(i)   by way of interest;

(ii)   by way of an instalment of an annuity;

[. . .]

(v)   by way of rent or other periodical payment under a lease;

(vi)   by way of a periodical payment in respect of the occupancy or use of land, not being an obligation falling within any other provision of this sub-paragraph;

(vii)   by way of a periodical payment under a [title condition], not being an obligation falling within any other provision of this sub-paragraph;

[(aa)   to any obligation to make a compensatory payment ('compensatory payment' being construed in accordance with section 8(1) of the Abolition of Feudal Tenure etc (Scotland) Act 2000 (asp 5), including that section as read with section 56 of that Act);

(aa)   to any obligation to pay compensation by virtue of section 2 of the Leasehold Casualties (Scotland) Act 2001 (asp 5);

(ab)   to any obligation arising by virtue of a right—

(i)   of reversion under the third proviso to section 2 of the School Sites Act 1841 (4 & 5 Vict c 38) (or of reversion under that proviso as applied by virtue of any other enactment);

(ii) to petition for a declaration of forfeiture under section 7 of the Entail Sites Act 1840 (3 & 4 Vict c 48);

(ac) to any obligation to pay a sum of money by way of costs to which section 12 of the Tenements (Scotland) Act 2004 (asp 11) applies;]

(b) to any obligation based on redress of unjustified enrichment, including without prejudice to that generality any obligation of restitution, repetition or recompense;

(c) to any obligation arising from *negotiorum gestio*;

(d) to any obligation arising from liability (whether arising from any enactment or from any rule of law) to make reparation;

[(dd) to any obligation arising by virtue of section 7A(1) of the Criminal Injuries Compensation Act 1995 (recovery of compensation from offenders: general);]

(e) to any obligation under a bill of exchange or a promissory note;

(f) to any obligation of accounting, other than accounting for trust funds;

(g) to any obligation arising from, or by reason of any breach of, a contract or promise, not being an obligation falling within any other provision of this paragraph.

2. Notwithstanding anything in the foregoing paragraph, section 6 of this Act does not apply—

(a) to any obligation to recognise or obtemper a decree of court, an arbitration award or an order of a tribunal or authority exercising jurisdiction under any enactment;

(b) to any obligation arising from the issue of a bank note;

[. . .]

(d) to any obligation under a contract of partnership or of agency, not being an obligation remaining, or becoming prestable on or after the termination of the relationship between the parties under the contract;

(e) except as provided in paragraph 1(a)[, (aa) or (ac)] of this Schedule, to any obligation relating to land (including an obligation to recognise a servitude);

[(ee) so as to extinguish, before the expiry of the continuous period of five years which immediately follows the coming into force of section 88 of the Title Conditions (Scotland) Act 2003 (asp 9) (prescriptive period for obligations arising by virtue of 1841 Act or 1840 Act), an obligation mentioned in sub-paragraph (ab) of paragraph 1 of this Schedule;]

(f) to any obligation to satisfy any claim to [. . .] legitim, jus relicti or jus relictae, or to any prior right of a surviving spouse under section 8 or 9 of the Succession (Scotland) Act 1964;

(g) to any obligation to make reparation in respect of personal injuries within the meaning of Part II of this Act or in respect of the death of any person as a result of such injuries;

[(gg) to any obligation to make reparation or otherwise make good in respect of defamation within the meaning of section 18A of this Act;

(ggg) to any obligation arising from liability under section 2 of the Consumer Protection Act 1987 (to make reparation for damage caused wholly or partly by a defect in a product);]

(h) to any obligation specified in Schedule 3 to this Act as an imprescriptible obligation.

[. . .]

[4. In this Schedule, 'title condition' shall be construed in accordance with section 122(1) of the Title Conditions (Scotland) Act 2003 (asp 9).]

Section 6   SCHEDULE 2
APPROPRIATE DATES FOR CERTAIN OBLIGATIONS FOR PURPOSES OF
SECTION 6

1—(1) This paragraph applies to any obligation, not being part of a banking transaction, to pay money in respect of—

(a) goods supplied on sale or hire, or

(b) services rendered,

in a series of transactions between the same parties (whether under a single contract or under several contracts) and charged on continuing account.

(2) In the foregoing sub-paragraph—

(a) any reference to the supply of goods on sale includes a reference to the supply of goods under a hire-purchase agreement, a credit-sale agreement or a conditional sale agreement as defined (in each case) by section 1 of the Hire-Purchase (Scotland) Act 1965; and

(b) any reference to services rendered does not include the work of keeping the account in question.

(3) Where there is a series of transactions between a partnership and another party, the series shall be regarded for the purposes of this paragraph as terminated (without prejudice to any other mode of termination) if the partnership (in the further provisions of this sub-paragraph referred to as 'the old partnership') is dissolved and is replaced by a single new partnership having among its partners any person who was a partner in the old partnership, then, for the purposes of this paragraph, the new partnership shall be regarded as if it were identical with the old partnership.

(4) The appropriate date in relation to an obligation to which this paragraph applies is the date on which payment for the goods last supplied, or, as the case may be, the services last rendered, became due.

2—(1) This paragraph applies to any obligation to repay the whole, or any part of, a sum of money lent to, or deposited with, the debtor under a contract of loan or, as the case may be, deposit.

(2) The appropriate date in relation to an obligation to which this paragraph applies is—

(a) if the contract contains a stipulation which makes provision with respect to the date on or before which repayment of the sum or, as the case may be, the part thereof is to be made, the date on or before which, in terms of that stipulation, the sum or part thereof is to be repaid; and

(b) if the contract contains no such stipulation, but a written demand for repayment of the sum, or, as the case may be, the part thereof, is made by or on behalf of the creditor to the debtor, the date when such demand is made or first made.

3—(1) This paragraph applies to any obligation under a contract of partnership or of agency, being an obligation remaining, or becoming, prestable on or after the termination of the relationship between the parties under the contract.

(2) The appropriate date in relation to an obligation to which this paragraph applies is—

(a) if the contract contains a stipulation which makes provision with respect to the date on or before which performance on the obligation is to be due, the date on or before which, in terms of that stipulation, the obligation is to be performed; and

(b) in any other case the date when the said relationship terminated.

4—(1) This paragraph applies to any obligation—

(a) to pay an instalment of a sum of money payable by instalments,

(b) to execute any instalment of work due to be executed by instalments, not being an obligation to which any of the foregoing paragraphs applies.

(2) The appropriate date in relation to an obligation to which this paragraph

applies is the date on which the last of the instalments is due to be paid or, as the case may be, to be executed.

Sections 7 & 8: Schedule 1   SCHEDULE 3
RIGHTS AND OBLIGATIONS WHICH ARE IMPRESCRIPTIBLE FOR THE
PURPOSES OF SECTIONS 7 AND 8 AND SCHEDULE 1

The following are imprescriptible rights and obligations for the purposes of sections 7(2) and 8(2) of, and paragraph 2(h) of Schedule 1 to, this Act, namely—
(a)   any real right of ownership in land;
(b)   the right in land of the lessee under a recorded lease;
(c)   any right exercisable as a *res merae facultatis*;
(d)   any right to recover property *extra commercium*;
(e)   any obligation of a trustee—
(i)   to produce accounts of the trustee's intromissions with any property of the trust;
(ii)   to make reparation or restitution in respect of any fraudulent breach of trust to which the trustee was a party or was privy;
(iii)   to make furthcoming to any person entitled thereto any trust property, or the proceeds of any such property, in the possession of the trustee, or to make good the value of any such property previously received by the trustee and appropriated to his own use;
(f)   any obligation of a third party to make furthcoming to any person entitled thereto any trust property received by the third party otherwise then in good faith and in his possession;
(g)   any right to recover stolen property from the person by whom it was stolen or from any person privy to the stealing thereof;
(h)   any right to be served as heir to an ancestor or to take any steps necessary for making up or completing title to any [real right] in land.

GUARD DOGS ACT 1975
(1975, c 50)

1   Control of guard dogs
(1)   A person shall not use or permit the use of a guard dog at any premises unless a person ('the handler') who is capable of controlling the dog is present on the premises and the dog is under the control of the handler at all times while it is being so used except while it is secured so that it is not at liberty to go freely about the premises.
(2)   The handler of a guard dog shall keep the dog under his control at all times while it is being used as a guard dog at any premises except—
(a)   while another handler has control over the dog; or
(b)   while the dog is secured so that it is not at liberty to go freely about the premises.
(3)   A person shall not use or permit the use of a guard dog at any premises unless a notice containing a warning that a guard dog is present is clearly exhibited at each entrance to the premises.

DANGEROUS WILD ANIMALS ACT 1976
(1976, c 38)

7   Interpretation
(1)   Subject to subsection (2) of this section, for the purposes of this Act a person is a keeper of an animal if he has it in his possession; and if at any time an animal ceases to be in the possession of a person, any person who immediately

before that time was a keeper thereof by virtue of the preceding provisions of this subsection continues to be a keeper of the animal until another person becomes a keeper thereof by virtue of those provisions.

(2)   Where an animal is in the possession of any person for the purpose of—

(a)   preventing it from causing damage,

(b)   restoring it to its owner,

(c)   undergoing veterinary treatment, or

(d)   being transported on behalf of another person,

the person having such possession shall not by virtue only of that possession be treated for the purposes of this Act as a keeper of the animal.

(3)   In this Act expressions cognate with 'keeper' shall be construed in accordance with subsections (1) and (2) of this section.

(4)   In this Act, unless the context otherwise requires, the following expressions have the meanings hereby respectively assigned to them, that is to say—

'circus' includes any place where animals are kept or introduced wholly or mainly for the purpose of performing tricks or manoeuvres;

'damage' includes the death of, or injury to, any person;

'dangerous wild animal' means any animal of a kind for the time being specified in the first column of the Schedule to this Act;

'local authority' means in relation to England [. . .] a district council, a London borough council or the Common Council of the City of London [, in relation to Wales, a county council or county borough council] and, in relation to Scotland, [a council constituted under section 2 of the Local Government etc (Scotland) Act 1994];

'premises' includes any place;

'veterinary practitioner' means a person who is for the time being registered in the supplementary veterinary register;

'veterinary surgeon' means a person who is for the time being registered in the register of veterinary surgeons;

[. . .]

(5)   The second column of the Schedule to this Act is included by way of explanation only; in the event of any dispute or proceedings, only the first column is to be taken into account.

SCHEDULE*   Section 7

KINDS OF DANGEROUS WILD ANIMALS

NOTE: See section 7(5) of this Act for the effect of the second column of this Schedule.

Scientific name of kind	Common name or names
MAMMALS	
Marsupials	
Family *Dasyuridae*: The species *Sarcophilus laniarius*.	The Tasmanian devil.
Family *Macropodidae*: The species *Macropus fuliginosus, Macropus giganteus, Macropus robustus* and *Macropus rufus*.	The western and eastern grey kangaroos, the wallaroo and the red kangaroo

Schedule substituted by the Dangerous Wild Animals Act 1976 (Modification) (Scotland) Order 2008 (SSI2008/302)

Scientific name of kind	Common name or names
Primates	
Family *Cebidae*: All species except those of the genera *Aotus*, *Callicebus* and *Saimiri*.	New-world monkeys (including capuchin, howler, saki, uacari, spider and woolly monkeys). *Exceptions*: Night monkeys (also known as owl monkeys), titi monkeys and squirrel monkeys.
Family *Cercopithecidae*.	Old-world monkeys (including baboons, the drill, colobus monkeys, the gelada, guenons, langurs, leaf monkeys, macaques, the mandrill, mangabeys, the patas monkey, the proboscis monkey and the talapoin).
Family *Hominidae*: All species except those of the genus *Homo*	Anthropoid apes (including the chimpanzee, the bonobo, the orang-utan and gorillas). *Exception*: Man.
Family *Hylobatidae*: All species.	Gibbons and Siamangs.
Family *Indriidae*: All species except those of the genus *Avahi*.	Leaping lemurs (including the indri and sifakas). *Exception*: Woolly lemurs.
Family *Lemuridae*: All species except those of the genus *Hapalemur*.	Large lemurs. *Exceptions*: Bamboo lemurs (also known as gentle lemurs).
Edentates	
Family *Dasypodidae*: The species *Priodontes maximus*.	The giant armadillo.
Family *Myrmecophagidae*: The species *Myrmecophaga tridactyla*.	The giant anteater.
Carnivores	
Family *Canidae*: All species except— (a) those of the genera *Alopex*, *Cerdocyon*, *Dusicyon*, *Otocyon*, *Pseudalopex*, *Urocyon*, *Vulpes* and *Nyctereutes* (b) *Canis familiaris*, other than the subspecies *Canis familiaris dingo*.	Canids (including wild dogs, wolves, jackals, the maned wolf, the dhole, the bush dog, and the dingo) other than the excepted species. *Exceptions*: (a) foxes, culpeo, grey zorro, raccoon dogs (b) domestic dogs.

Scientific name of kind	Common name or names

Family *Felidae*: All species except—
(a) Felis silvestris (including the subspecies *Felis silvestris catus*), *Felis margarita*, *Felis nigripes*, *Otocolobus manul*, *Leopardus tigrinus*, *Leopardus geoffroyi* (also known as *Oncifelis geoffroyi*), *Leopardus guigna* (also known as *Oncifelis guigna*), *Catopuma badia* (also known as *Pardofelis badia*) and *Prionailurus rubiginosus*
(b) a hybrid descended exclusively from two or more of the species described in paragraph (a)
(c) a hybrid of which—
  (i) one parent is *Felis silvestris catus*, and
  (ii) the other parent is a first generation hybrid of *Felis silvestris catus* and any species not described in paragraph (a)
(d) a hybrid descended exclusively from hybrid cats as described in paragraph (c) (ignoring, for the purpose of determining exclusivity of descent, the parents and remoter ancestors of any hybrid within that paragraph)
(e) a hybrid descended exclusively from *Felis silvestris catus* and any one or more hybrid cat as described in paragraph (c) (ignoring, for the purpose of determining exclusivity of descent, the parents and remoter ancestors of any hybrid within that paragraph).
	Cats (including the bobcat, caracal, cheetah, jaguar, leopard, lion, lynx, ocelot, puma, serval and tiger) other than the excepted species.
	
	Exceptions:
	(a) the wild cat (including the domestic cat), the sand cat, the black-footed cat, the pallas cat (also known as the manul), the little spotted cat (also known as the oncilla or tiger cat), the Geoffroy's cat, the kodkod (also known as the guina), the bay cat (also known as the Borneo cat), and the rusty-spotted cat
	(b) a cat descended exclusively from two or more of the species described in paragraph (a)
	(c) a cat of which one parent is a domestic cat and the other parent is a first generation hybrid of a domestic cat and a cat that is a dangerous wild animal
	(d) a cat descended exclusively from hybrid cats described in paragraph (c)
	(e) a cat descended exclusively from the domestic cat and hybrid cats described in paragraph (c).

Family *Hyaenidae*: All species except *Proteles cristatus*.	Hyenas. *Exception*: Aardwolf.
Family *Mustelidae*: (a) all species of the genera *Arctonyx, Melogale, Mydaus, Taxidea, Pteronura, Aonyx, Enhydra* and *Lontra* (b) the genus *Lutra* except the species *Lutra lutra* (c) the species *Eira barbara, Gulo gulo, Martes pennanti* and *Mellivora capensis*.	(a) the hog badger, the ferret badger, the stink badger, the American badger, the giant otter, the African clawless otter, the oriental small-clawed otter, the sea otter, the river otters, and the marine otter; (b) the hairy-nosed otter (c) the tayra, the wolverine, the fisher (also known as the peken or fisher cat) and the honey badger. *Exception*: European otter.
Family *Ursidae*: All species including the species *Ailuropoda melanoleuca* and *Ailurus fulgens*.	All bears including the giant panda and the red panda.

Scientific name of kind	Common name or names
Family *Viverridae*: (a) all species of the genera *Civettictis* and *Viverra* (b) the species *Cryptoprocta ferox*.	(a) civets (including the African civet, the large-spotted civets, the Malayan civet and the Indian civets) (b) the fossa.
Pinnipedes	
Family *Odobenidae*: All species.	The walrus.
Family *Otariidae*: All species.	Eared seals.
Family *Phocidae*: All species except *Phoca vitulina* and *Halichoerus grypus*.	True seals (also known as earless seals) other than the excepted species. *Exceptions*: Common seal (also known as the harbour seal). Grey seal.
Elephants	
Family *Elephantidae*: All species.	Elephants.
Aardvark	
Family *Orycteropodidae*: The species *Orycteropus afer*.	The aardvark.
Odd-toed ungulates	
Family *Equidae*: All species except *Equus asinus* and *Equus caballus*.	Horses, wild asses, zebras. *Exceptions*: Donkey (also known as the ass), domestic horse.
Family *Rhinocerotidae*: All species.	Rhinoceroses.
Family *Tapiridae*: All species.	Tapirs.
Even-toed ungulates	
Family *Antilocapridae*: The species *Antilocapra Americana*.	The pronghorn.
Family *Bovidae*: All species except domestic forms of the genera *Bos*, *Bubalus*, *Capra* and *Ovis*.	Antelopes, bison, buffalo, gazelles, goats and sheep. *Exceptions*: Domestic cattle, domestic buffalo, domestic goats, domestic sheep.
Family *Camelidae*: All species of the genera *Camelus*.	Camels.
Family *Cervidae*: All species of the genera *Alces* and *Rangifer*, except domestic forms of the species *Rangifer tarandus*.	Moose (also known as the elk) Caribou (also known as the reindeer). *Exception*: Domestic reindeer.
Family *Giraffidae*: All species.	The giraffe and the okapi.
Family *Hippopotamidae*: All species.	The hippopotamus and the pygmy hippopotamus.
Family *Suidae*: All species, except domestic forms of the species *Sus scrofa* other than farmed wild boar.	Old-world pigs other than animals of the excepted kind. *Exception*: Domestic pig, other than farmed wild boar.

Scientific name of kind	Common name or names
Family *Tayassuidae*: All species.	New-world pigs (otherwise known as peccaries).
Hybrids	
A hybrid of a mammal specified in the first column of this Schedule where one parent is, or both parents are, of a kind so specified, but not including an excepted hybrid of the Family *Felidae*.	A hybrid animal with a dangerous wild animal as a parent. *Exception*: A cat hybrid that is not a dangerous wild animal.
BIRDS	
Cassowaries	
Family *Casuariidae*: All species.	Cassowaries
Ostrich	
Family *Struthionidae*: All species.	The ostrich.
REPTILES	
Crocodilians	
Family *Alligatoridae*: All species.	Alligators and caimans.
Family *Crocodylidae*: All species.	Crocodiles and the false gharial.
Family *Gavialidae*: All species.	The gharial (also known as the gavial).
Lizards and snakes	
Family *Atractaspididae*: All species of the genera *Atractaspis*.	Burrowing asps (also known as mole vipers, or burrowing vipers). Stiletto snakes.
Family *Colubridae*: (a) all species of the genera *Malpolon* and *Thelotornis* (b) the species *Dispholidus typus, Rhabdophis subminiatus, Rhabdophis tigrinus, Elapomorphus lemniscatus, Philodryas olfersii, Tachymenis peruviana, Xenodon severus.*	(a) all rear-fanged venomous colubrid snakes of the specified genera (including montpellier snakes, the false cobra, and twig or bird snakes) (b) the boomslang, the red-necked keelback, the tiger keelback (also known as the yamakagashi or the Japanese tiger-snake), the Argentine black-headed snake, the South American green racer, the Peruvian racer (also known as the Peru slender snake), the Amazon false viper (also known as the false fer-de-lance).
Family *Elapidae*: All species.	Front-fanged venomous snakes of the specified family (including cobras, coral snakes, kraits, mambas, whipsnakes, death adders and all other Australian poisonous snakes).
Family *Hydrophiidae*: All species.	Sea snakes.
Family *Helodermatidae*: All species.	The gila monster and the Mexican beaded lizard.

Scientific name of kind	Common name or names
Family *Viperidae*: All species.	Front-fanged venomous snakes of the specified family (including adders, the barba amarilla, the bushmaster, the fer-de-lance, moccasins, rattlesnakes and vipers).
INVERTEBRATES	
Spiders	
Family *Ctenidae*: All species of the genus *Phoneutria*.	Wandering spiders.
Family *Hexathelidae*: All species of the genus *Atrax*.	The Sydney funnel-web spider and its close relatives.
Family *Sicariidae*: All species of the genus *Loxosceles*.	Brown recluse spiders (also known as violin spiders).
Family *Theridiidae*: All species of the genus *Latrodectus*.	The widow spiders and close relatives.
Scorpions	
Family *Buthidae*: All species.	Buthid scorpions.
Family *Hemioscorpiidae*: The species *Hemiscorpius lepturus*.	Middle Eastern thin-tailed scorpion.

DIVORCE (SCOTLAND) ACT 1976
(1976, c 39)

10 Right of husband to cite paramour as a co-defender and to sue for damages abolished

(1)   After the commencement of this Act the following rights of a husband shall be abolished, that is to say—

(a)   the right to cite a paramour of his wife as a co-defender in an action for divorce, and

(b)   the right to claim or to obtain damages (including solatium) from a paramour by way of reparation.

(2)   Nothing in the provisions of the foregoing subsection shall preclude the court from awarding the expenses of the action for or against the paramour or alleged paramour in accordance with the practice of the court.

[. . .]

UNFAIR CONTRACT TERMS ACT 1977
(1977, c 50)

PART II
AMENDMENT OF LAW FOR SCOTLAND

15   Scope of Part II

(1)   This Part of this Act [. . .] is subject to Part III of this Act and does not affect the validity of any discharge or indemnity given by a person in consideration of the receipt by him of compensation in settlement of any claim which he has.

(2)   Subject to subsection (3) below, sections 16 to 18 of this Act apply to any contract only to the extent that the contract—

(a)   relates to the transfer of the ownership or possession of goods from one person to another (with or without work having been done on them);

(b)   constitutes a contract of service or apprenticeship;

(c)   relates to services of whatever kind, including (without prejudice to the foregoing generality) carriage, deposit and pledge, care and custody, mandate, agency, loan and services relating to the use of land;

(d)   relates to the liability of an occupier of land to persons entering upon or using that land;

(e)   relates to a grant of any right or permission to enter upon or use land not amounting to an estate or interest in the land.

(3)   Notwithstanding anything in subsection (2) above, sections 16 to 18—

(a)   do not apply to any contract to the extent that the contract—

(i)   is a contract of insurance (including a contract to pay an annuity on human life);

(ii)   relates to the formation, constitution or dissolution of any body corporate or unincorporated association or partnership;

(b)   apply to—

a contract of marine salvage or towage;

a charter party of a ship or hovercraft;

a contract for the carriage of goods by ship or hovercraft; or

a contract to which subsection (4) below relates,

only to the extent that—

(i)   both parties deal or hold themselves out as dealing in the course of a business (and then only in so far as the contract purports to exclude or restrict liability for breach of duty in respect of death or personal injury); or

(ii)   the contract is a consumer contract (and then only in favour of the consumer).

(4)   This subsection relates to a contract in pursuance of which goods are carried by ship or hovercraft and which either—

(a)   specifies ship or hovercraft as the means of carriage over part of the journey to be covered; or

(b)   makes no provision as to the means of carriage and does not exclude ship or hovercraft as that means,

in so far as the contract operates for and in relation to the carriage of the goods by that means.

16   Liability for breach of duty

(1)   [Subject to subsection (1A) below,] where a term of a contract [, or a provision of a notice given to persons generally or to particular persons,] purports to exclude or restrict liability for breach of duty arising in the course of any business or from the occupation of any premises used for business purposes of the occupier, that term [or provision]—

(a)   shall be void in any case where such exclusion or restriction is in respect of death or personal injury;

(b)   shall, in any other case, have no effect if it was not fair and reasonable to incorporate the term in the contract [or, as the case may be, if it is not fair and reasonable to allow reliance on the provision].

[(1A) Nothing in paragraph (b) of subsection (1) above shall be taken as implying that a provision of a notice has effect in circumstances where, apart from that paragraph, it would not have effect.]

(2) Subsection (1)(a) above does not affect the validity of any discharge and indemnity given by a person, on or in connection with an award to him of compensation for pneumoconiosis attributable to employment in the coal industry, in respect of any further claim arising from his contracting that disease.

(3) Where under subsection (1) above a term of a contract [or a provision of a notice] is void or has no effect, the fact that a person agreed to, or was aware of, the term [or provision] shall not of itself be sufficient evidence that he knowingly and voluntarily assumed any risk.

17 Control of unreasonable exemptions in consumer or standard form contracts

(1) Any term of a contract which is a consumer contract or a standard form contract shall have no effect for the purpose of enabling a party to the contract—

(a) who is in breach of a contractual obligation, to exclude or restrict any liability of his to the consumer or customer in respect of the breach;

(b) in respect of a contractual obligation, to render no performance, or to render a performance substantially different from that which the consumer or customer reasonably expected from the contract;
if it was not fair and reasonable to incorporate the term in the contract.

(2) In this section 'customer' means a party to a standard form contract who deals on the basis of written standard terms of business of the other party to the contract who himself deals in the course of a business.

18 Unreasonable indemnity clauses in consumer contracts

(1) Any term of a contract which is a consumer contract shall have no effect for the purpose of making the consumer indemnify another person (whether a party to the contract or not) in respect of liability which that other person may incur as a result of breach of duty or breach of contract, if it was not fair and reasonable to incorporate the term in the contract.

(2) In this section 'liability' means liability arising in the course of any business or from the occupation of any premises used for business purposes of the occupier.

19 'Guarantee' of consumer goods

(1) This section applies to a guarantee—

(a) in relation to goods which are of a type ordinarily supplied for private use or consumption; and

(b) which is not a guarantee given by one party to the other party to a contract under or in pursuance of which the ownership or possession of the goods to which the guarantee relates is transferred.

(2) A term of a guarantee to which this section applies shall be void in so far as it purports to exclude or restrict liability for loss or damage (including death or personal injury)—

(a) arising from the goods proving defective while—

(i) in use otherwise than exclusively for the purposes of a business; or

(ii) in the possession of a person for such use; and

(b) resulting from the breach of duty of a person concerned in the manufacture or distribution of the goods.

(3) For the purposes of this section, any document is a guarantee if it contains or purports to contain some promise or assurance (however worded or presented) that defects will be made good by complete or partial replacement, or by repair, monetary compensation or otherwise.

20   Obligations implied by law in sale and hire-purchase contracts
(1)   Any term of a contract which purports to exclude or restrict liability for breach of the obligations arising from—
(a)   section 12 of the Sale of Goods Act [1979] (seller's implied undertakings as to title etc);
(b)   section 8 of the Supply of Goods (Implied Terms) Act 1973 (implied terms as to title in hire-purchase agreements),
shall be void.
(2)   Any term of a contract which purports to exclude or restrict liability for breach of the obligations arising from—
(a)   section 13, 14 or 15 of the said Act of [1979] (seller's implied undertakings as to conformity of goods with description or sample, or as to their quality or fitness for a particular purpose);
(b)   section 9, 10 or 11 of the said Act of 1973 (the corresponding provisions in relation to hire-purchase),
shall—
(i)   in the case of a consumer contract, be void against the consumer;
(ii)   in any other case, have no effect if it was not fair and reasonable to incorporate the term in the contract.

21   Obligations implied by law in other contracts for the supply of goods
(1)   Any term of a contract to which this section applies purporting to exclude or restrict liability for breach of an obligation—
(a)   such as is referred to in subsection (3)(a) below—
(i)   in the case of a consumer contract, shall be void against the consumer, and
(ii)   in any other case, shall have no effect if it was not fair and reasonable to incorporate the term in the contract;
(b)   such as is referred to in subsection (3)(b) below, shall have no effect if it was not fair and reasonable to incorporate the term in the contract.
(2)   This section applies to any contract to the extent that it relates to any such matter as is referred to in section 15(2)(a) of this Act, but does not apply to—
(a)   a contract of sale of goods or a hire-purchase agreement; or
(b)   a charterparty of a ship or hovercraft unless it is a consumer contract (and then only in favour of the consumer).
(3)   An obligation referred to in this subsection is an obligation incurred under a contract in the course of a business and arising by implication of law from the nature of the contract which relates—
(a)   to the correspondence of goods with description or sample, or to the quality or fitness of goods for any particular purpose; or
(b)   to any right to transfer ownership or possession of goods, or to the enjoyment of quiet possession of goods.
[(3A)   Notwithstanding anything in the foregoing provisions of this section, any term of a contract which purports to exclude or restrict liability for breach of the obligations arising under section 11B of the Supply of Goods and Services Act 1982 (implied terms about title, freedom from encumbrances and quiet possession in certain contracts for the transfer of property in goods) shall be void.]
[. . .]

22   Consequence of breach
For the avoidance of doubt, where any provision of this Part of this Act requires that the incorporation of a term in a contract must be fair and reasonable for that term to have effect—
(a)   if that requirement is satisfied, the term may be given effect to notwithstanding that the contract has been terminated in consequence of breach of that contract;

(b)   for the term to be given effect to, that requirement must be satisfied even where a party who is entitled to rescind the contract elects not to rescind it.

23   Evasion by means of secondary contract

Any term of any contract shall be void which purports to exclude or restrict, or has the effect of excluding or restricting—

(a)   the exercise, by a party to any other contract, of any right or remedy which arises in respect of that other contract in consequence of breach of duty, or of obligation, liability for which could not by virtue of the provisions of this Part of this Act be excluded or restricted by a term of that other contract;

(b)   the application of the provisions of this Part of this Act in respect of that or any other contract.

24   The 'reasonableness' test

(1)   In determining for the purposes of this Part of this Act whether it was fair and reasonable to incorporate a term in a contract, regard shall be had only to the circumstances which were, or ought reasonably to have been, known to or in the contemplation of the parties to the contract at the time the contract was made.

(2)   In determining for the purposes of section 20 or 21 of this Act whether it was fair and reasonable to incorporate a term in a contract, regard shall be had in particular to the matters specified in Schedule 2 to this Act; but this sub-section shall not prevent a court or arbiter from holding in accordance with any rule of law, that a term which purports to exclude or restrict any relevant liability is not a term of the contract.

[(2A)   In determining for the purposes of this Part of this Act whether it is fair and reasonable to allow reliance on a provision of a notice (not being a notice having contractual effect), regard shall be had to all the circumstances obtaining when the liability arose or (but for the provision) would have arisen.]

(3)   Where a term in a contract [or a provision of a notice] purports to restrict liability to a specified sum of money, and the question arises for the purposes of this Part of this Act whether it was fair and reasonable to incorporate the term in the contract [or whether it is fair and reasonable to allow reliance on the provision], then, without prejudice to subsection (2) above [in the case of a term in a contract], regard shall be had in particular to—

(a)   the resources which the party seeking to rely on that term [or provision] could expect to be available to him for the purpose of meeting the liability should it arise;

(b)   how far it was open to that party to cover himself by insurance.

(4)   The onus of proving that it was fair and reasonable to incorporate a term in a contract [or that it is fair and reasonable to allow reliance on a provision of a notice] shall lie on the party so contending.

25   Interpretation of Part II

(1)   In this Part of this Act—

'breach of duty' means the breach—

(a)   of any obligation, arising from the express or implied terms of a contract, to take reasonable care or exercise reasonable skill in the performance of the contract;

(b)   of any common law duty to take reasonable care or exercise reasonable skill;

(c)   of the duty of reasonable care imposed by section 2(1) of the Occupiers' Liability (Scotland) Act 1960;

'business' includes a profession and the activities of any government department or local or public authority;

'consumer' has the meaning assigned to that expression in the definition in this section of 'consumer contract';

'consumer contract' means [subject to subsections (1A) and (1B) below] a contract [. . .] in which—

    (a)   one party to the contract deals, and the other party to the contract ('the consumer') does not deal or hold himself out as dealing, in the course of a business, and

    (b)   in the case of a contract such as is mentioned in section 15(2)(a) of this Act, the goods are of a type ordinarily supplied for private use or consumption; and for the purposes of this Part of this Act the onus of proving that a contract is not to be regarded as a consumer contract shall lie on the party so contending;

'goods' has the same meaning as in the Sale of Goods Act [1979];

'hire-purchase agreement' has the same meaning as in section 189(1) of the Consumer Credit Act 1974;

['notice' includes an announcement, whether or not in writing, and any other communication or pretended communication;]

'personal injury' includes any disease and any impairment of physical or mental condition.

[(1A)   Where the consumer is an individual, paragraph (b) in the definition of 'consumer contract' in subsection (1) must be disregarded.

(1B)   The expression of 'consumer contract' does not include a contract in which—

    (a)   the buyer is an individual and the goods are second hand goods sold by public auction at which individuals have the opportunity of attending in person; or

    (b)   the buyer is not an individual and the goods are sold by auction or competitive tender.]

(2)   In relation to any breach of duty or obligation, it is immaterial for any purpose of this Part of this Act whether the act or omission giving rise to that breach was inadvertent or intentional or whether liability for it arises directly or vicariously.

(3)   In this Part of this Act, any reference to excluding or restricting any liability includes—

    (a)   making the liability or its enforcement subject to any restrictive or onerous conditions;

    (b)   excluding or restricting any right or remedy in respect of the liability, or subjecting a person to any prejudice in consequence of his pursuing any such right or remedy;

    (c)   excluding or restricting any rule of evidence or procedure;

    [. . .]

(5)   In section 15 and 16 and 19 to 21 of this Act, any reference to excluding or restricting liability for breach of any obligation or duty shall include a reference to excluding or restricting the obligation or duty itself.

PART III
PROVISIONS APPLYING TO WHOLE OF UNITED KINGDOM

26 International supply contracts

(1)   The limits imposed by this Act on the extent to which a person may exclude or restrict liability by reference to a contract term do not apply to liability arising under such a contract as is described in subsection (3) below.

(2)   The terms of such a contract are not subject to any requirement of reasonableness under section 3 or 4: and nothing in Part II of this Act should require the incorporation of the terms of such a contract to be fair and reasonable for them to have effect.

(3)   Subject to subsection (4), that description of contract is one whose characteristics are the following—

(a)   either it is a contract of sale of goods or it is one under or in pursuance of which the possession of ownership of goods passes, and

(b)   it is made by parties whose places of business (or, if they have none, habitual residences) are in the territories of different States (the Channel Islands and the Isle of Man being treated for this purpose as different States from the United Kingdom).

(4)   A contract falls within subsection (3) above only if either—

(a)   the goods in question are, at the time of the conclusion of the contract, in the course of carriage, or will be carried, from the territory of one State to the territory of another; or

(b)   the acts constituting the offer and acceptance have been done in the territories of different States; or

(c)   the contract provides for the goods to be delivered to the territory of a state other than that within whose territory those acts were done.

27   Choice of law clauses

(1)   Where the [law applicable to] a contract is the law of any part of the United Kingdom only by choice of the parties (and apart from that choice would be the law of some country outside the United Kingdom) sections 2 to 7 and 16 to 21 of this Act do not operate as part [of the law applicable to the contract].

(2)   This Act has effect notwithstanding any contract term which applies or purports to apply the law of some country outside the United Kingdom, where (either or both)—

(a)   the term appears to the court, or arbitrator or arbiter to have been imposed wholly or mainly for the purpose of enabling the party imposing it to evade the operation of this Act; or

(b)   in the making of the contract one of the parties dealt as consumer, and he was then habitually resident in the United Kingdom, and the essential steps necessary for the making of the contract were taken there, whether by him or by others on his behalf.

29   Saving for other relevant legislation

(1)   Nothing in this Act removes or restricts the effect of, or prevents reliance upon, any contractual provision which—

(a)   is authorised or required by the express terms or necessary implication of an enactment; or

(b)   being made with a view to compliance with an international agreement to which the United Kingdom is a party, does not operate more restrictively than is contemplated by the agreement.

(2)   A contract term is to be taken—

(a)   for the purposes of Part I of this Act, as satisfying the requirement of reasonableness . . .

if it is incorporated or approved by, or incorporated pursuant to a decision or ruling of, a competent authority acting in the exercise of any statutory jurisdiction or function and is not a term in a contract to which the competent authority is itself a party.

(3)   In this section—

'competent authority' means any court, arbitrator or arbiter, government department or public authority;

'enactment' means any legislation (including subordinate legislation) of the United Kingdom or Northern Ireland and any instrument having effect by virtue of such legislation; and

'statutory' means conferred by an enactment.

. . .

SCHEDULE 2
'GUIDELINES' FOR APPLICATION OF REASONABLENESS TEST

Sections 11(2) and 24(2)

The matters to which regard is to be had in particular for the purposes of sections 6(3), 7(3) and (4), 20 and 21 are any of the following which appear to be relevant—

(a)   the strength of the bargaining positions of the parties relative to each other, taking into account (among other things) alternative means by which the customer's requirements could have been met;

(b)   whether the customer received an inducement to agree to the terms, or in accepting it had an opportunity of entering into a similar contract with other persons, but without having to accept similar terms;

(c)   whether the customer knew or ought reasonably to have known of the existence and extent of the term (having regard, among other things, to any customs of the trade and any previous course of dealing between the parties);

(d)   where the term excludes or restricts any relevant liability if some condition is not complied with, whether it was reasonable at the time of the contract to expect that compliance with that condition would be practicable;

(e)   whether the goods were manufactured, processed or adapted to the special order of the customer.

SALE OF GOODS ACT 1979
(1979, c 54)

PART I
CONTRACTS TO WHICH ACT APPLIES

1   Contracts to which Act applies

(1)   This Act applies to contracts of sale of goods made on or after (but not to those made before) 1 January 1894.

(2)   In relation to contracts made on certain dates, this Act applies subject to the modification of certain of its sections as mentioned in Schedule 1 below.

(3)   Any such modification is indicated in the section concerned by a reference to Schedule 1 below.

(4)   Accordingly, where a section does not contain such a reference, this Act applies in relation to the contract concerned without such modification of the section.

PART II
FORMATION OF THE CONTRACT

Contract of sale

2   Contract of sale

(1)   A contract of sale of goods is a contract by which the seller transfers or agrees to transfer the property in goods to the buyer for a money consideration, called the price.

(2)   There may be a contract of sale between one part owner and another.

(3)   A contract of sale may be absolute or conditional.

(4)   Where under a contract of sale the property in the goods is transferred from the seller to the buyer the contract is called a sale.

(5)   Where under a contract of sale the transfer of the property in the goods is to take place at a future time or subject to some condition later to be fulfilled the contract is called an agreement to sell.

(6)   An agreement to sell becomes a sale when the time elapses or the conditions are fulfilled subject to which the property in the goods is to be transferred.

3   Capacity to buy and sell

(1)   Capacity to buy and sell is regulated by the general law concerning capacity to contract and to transfer and acquire property.

(2)   Where necessaries are sold and delivered [. . .] to a person who by reason of mental incapacity or drunkenness is incompetent to contract, he must pay a reasonable price for them.

(3)   In subsection (2) above 'necessaries' means goods suitable to the condition in life of the [. . .] person concerned and to his actual requirements at the time of the sale and delivery.

Formalities of contract

4   How contract of sale is made

(1)   Subject to this and any other Act, a contract of sale may be made in writing (either with or without seal), or by word of mouth, or partly in writing and partly by word of mouth, or may be implied from the conduct of the parties.

(2)   Nothing in this section affects the law relating to corporations.

Subject matter of contract

5   Existing or future goods

(1)   The goods which form the subject of a contract of sale may be either existing goods, owned or possessed by the seller, or goods to be manufactured or acquired by him after the making of the contract of sale, in this Act called future goods.

(2)   There may be a contract for the sale of goods the acquisition of which by the seller depends on a contingency which may or may not happen.

(3)   Where by a contract of sale the seller purports to effect a present sale of future goods, the contract operates as an agreement to sell the goods.

6   Goods which have perished

Where there is a contract for the sale of specific goods, and the goods without the knowledge of the seller have perished at the time when a contract is made, the contract is void.

7   Goods perishing before sale but after agreement to sell

Where there is an agreement to sell specific goods and subsequently the goods, without any fault on the part of the seller or buyer, perish before the risk passes to the buyer, the agreement is avoided.

The price

8   Ascertainment of price

(1)   The price in a contract of sale may be fixed by the contract, or may be left to be fixed in a manner agreed by the contract, or may be determined by the course of dealing between the parties.

(2)   Where the price is not determined as mentioned in subsection (1) above the buyer must pay a reasonable price.

(3)   What is a reasonable price is a question of fact dependent on the circumstances of each particular case.

9 Agreement to sell at valuation

(1) Where there is an agreement to sell goods on the terms that the price is to be fixed by the valuation of a third party, and he cannot or does not make the valuation, the agreement is avoided; but if the goods or any part of them have been delivered to and appropriated by the buyer he must pay a reasonable price for them.

(2) Where the third party is prevented from making the valuation by the fault of the seller or buyer, the party not at fault may maintain an action for damages against the party at fault.

[Implied terms etc]

10 Stipulations about time

(1) Unless a different intention appears from the terms of the contract, stipulations as to time of payment are not of the essence of a contract of sale.

(2) Whether any other stipulation as to time is or is not of the essence of the contract depends on the terms of the contract.

(3) In a contract of sale 'month' prima facie means calendar month.

11 *[Does not apply to Scotland.]*

12 Implied terms about title, etc

(1) In a contract of sale, other than one to which subsection (3) below applies, there is an implied [term] on the part of the seller that in the case of a sale he has a right to sell the goods, and in the case of an agreement to sell he will have such a right at the time when the property is to pass.

(2) In a contract of sale, other than one to which subsection (3) below applies, there is also an implied [term] that—

(a) the goods are free, and will remain free until the time when the property is to pass, from any charge or encumbrance not disclosed or known to the buyer before the contract is made, and

(b) the buyer will enjoy quiet possession of the goods except so far as it may be disturbed by the owner or other person entitled to the benefit of any charge or encumbrance so disclosed or known.

(3) This subsection applies to a contract of sale in the case of which there appears from the contract or is to be inferred from its circumstances an intention that the seller should transfer only such title as he or a third person may have.

(4) In a contract to which subsection (3) above applies there is an implied [term] that all charges or encumbrances known to the seller and not known to the buyer have been disclosed to the buyer before the contract is made.

(5) In a contract to which subsection (3) above applies there is also an implied [term] that none of the following will disturb the buyer's quiet possession of the goods, namely—

(a) the seller;

(b) in a case where the parties to the contract intend that the seller should transfer only such title as a third person may have, that person;

(c) anyone claiming through or under the seller or that third person otherwise than under a charge or encumbrance disclosed or known to the buyer before the contract is made.

[(5A) As regards England and Wales and Northern Ireland, the term implied by subsection (1) above is a condition and the terms implied by subsections (2), (4) and (5) above are warranties.]

(6) Paragraph 3 of Schedule 1 below applies in relation to a contract made before 18 May 1973.

13   Sale by description

(1)   Where there is a contract for the sale of goods by description, there is an implied [term] that the goods will correspond with the description.

[(1A)   As regards England and Wales and Northern Ireland, the term implied by subsection (1) above is a condition.]

(2)   If the sale is by sample as well as by description it is not sufficient that the bulk of the goods corresponds with the sample if the goods do not also correspond with the description.

(3)   A sale of goods is not prevented from being a sale by description by reason only that, being exposed for sale or hire, they are selected by the buyer.

(4)   Paragraph 4 of Schedule 1 below applies in relation to a contract made before 18 May 1973.

14   Implied terms about quality or fitness

(1)   Except as provided by this section and section 15 below and subject to any other enactment, there is no implied [term] about the quality or fitness for any particular purpose of goods supplied under a contract of sale.

(2)   [Where the seller sells goods in the course of a business, there is an implied term that the goods supplied under the contract are of satisfactory quality.]

[(2A)   For the purposes of this Act, goods are of satisfactory quality if they meet the standard that a reasonable person would regard as satisfactory, taking account of any description of the goods, the price (if relevant) and all the other relevant circumstances.

(2B)   For the purposes of this Act, the quality of goods includes their state and condition and the following (among others) are in appropriate cases aspects of the quality of goods—

(a)   fitness for all the purposes for which goods of the kind in question are commonly supplied,

(b)   appearance and finish,

(c)   freedom from minor defects,

(d)   safety, and

(c)   durability.

(2C)   The term implied by subsection (2) above does not extend to any matter making the quality of goods unsatisfactory—

(a)   which is specifically drawn to the buyer's attention before the contract is made,

(b)   where the buyer examines the goods before the contract is made, which that examination ought to reveal, or

(c)   in the case of a contract for sale by sample, which would have been apparent on a reasonable examination of the sample.

(2D)   If the buyer deals as consumer or, in Scotland, if a contract of sale is a consumer contract, the relevant circumstances mentioned in subsection (2A) above include any public statements on the specific characteristics of the goods made about them by the seller, the producer or his representative, particularly in advertising or on labelling.

(2E)   A public statement is not by virtue of subsection (2D) above a relevant circumstance for the purposes of subsection (2A) above in the case of a contract of sale, if the seller shows that—

(a)   at the time the contract was made, he was not, and could not reasonably have been, aware of the statement,

(b)   before the contract was made, the statement had been withdrawn in public or, to the extent that it contained anything which was incorrect or misleading, it had been corrected in public, or

(c)   the decision to buy the goods could not have been influenced by the statement.

(2F)   Subsections (2D) and (2E) above do not prevent any public statement from being a relevant circumstance for the purposes of subsection (2A) above (whether or not the buyer deals as consumer or, in Scotland, whether or not the contract of sale is a consumer contract) if the statement would have been such a circumstance apart from those subsections.]

(3)   Where the seller sells goods in the course of a business and the buyer, expressly or by implication, makes known—

(a)   to the seller, or

(b)   where the purchase price or part of it is payable by instalments and the goods were previously sold by a credit-broker to the seller, to that credit-broker,

any particular purpose for which the goods are being bought, there is an implied [term] that the goods supplied under the contract are reasonably fit for that purpose, whether or not that is a purpose for which such goods are commonly supplied, except where the circumstances show that the buyer does not rely, or that it is unreasonable for him to rely, on the skill or judgment of the seller or credit-broker.

(4)   An implied [term] about quality or fitness for a particular purpose may be annexed to a contract of sale by usage.

(5)   The preceding provisions of this section apply to a sale by a person who in the course of a business is acting as agent for another as they apply to a sale by a principal in the course of a business, except where that other is not selling in the course of a business and either the buyer knows that fact or reasonable steps are taken to bring it to the notice of the buyer before the contract is made.

[(6)   As regards England and Wales and Northern Ireland, the terms implied by subsections (2) and (3) above are conditions.]

(7)   Paragraph 5 of Schedule 1 below applies in relation to a contract made on or after 18 May 1973 and before the appointed day, and paragraph 6 in relation to one made before 18 May 1973.

(8)   In subsection (7) above and paragraph 5 of Schedule 1 below references to the appointed day are to the day appointed for the purposes of those provisions by an order of the Secretary of State made by statutory instrument.

Sale by sample

15   Sale by sample

(1)   A contract of sale is a contract for sale by sample where there is an express or implied term to that effect in the contract.

(2)   In the case of a contract for sale by sample there is an implied [term]—

(a)   that the bulk will correspond with the sample in quality;

[. . .]

(c)   that the goods will be free from any defect, making their quality unsatisfactory, which would not be apparent on reasonable examination of the sample.

[(3)   As regards England and Wales and Northern Ireland, the term implied by subsection (2) above is a condition.]

(4)   Paragraph 7 of Schedule 1 below applies in relation to a contract made before 18 May 1973.

Miscellaneous

15A   [*Does not apply to Scotland.*]

[15B   Remedies for breach of contract as respects Scotland

(1)   Where in a contract of sale the seller is in breach of any term of the contract (express or implied), the buyer shall be entitled—

(a)   to claim damages, and

(b)   if the breach is material, to reject any goods delivered under the contract and treat it as repudiated.

(2)　Where a contract of sale is a consumer contract, then, for the purposes of subsection (1)(b) above, breach by the seller of any term (express or implied)—

(a)　as to the quality of the goods or their fitness for a purpose,

(b)　if the goods are, or are to be, sold by description, that the goods will correspond with the description,

(c)　if the goods are, or are to be, sold by reference to a sample, that the bulk will correspond with the sample in quality,

shall be deemed to be a material breach.

(3)　This section applies to Scotland only.]

PART III
EFFECTS OF THE CONTRACT

Transfer of property as between seller and buyer

16　Goods must be ascertained

[Subject to section 20A below] where there is a contract for the sale of unascertained goods no property in the goods is transferred to the buyer unless and until the goods are ascertained.

17　Property passes when intended to pass

(1)　Where there is a contract for the sale of specific or ascertained goods the property in them is transferred to the buyer at such time as the parties to the contract intend it to be transferred.

(2)　For the purpose of ascertaining the intention of the parties regard shall be had to the terms of the contract, the conduct of the parties and the circumstances of the case.

18　Rules for ascertaining intention

Unless a different intention appears, the following are rules for ascertaining the intention of the parties as to the time at which the property in the goods is to pass to the buyer.

Rule 1.—Where there is an unconditional contract for the sale of specific goods in a deliverable state the property in the goods passes to the buyer when the contract is made, and it is immaterial whether the time of payment or the time of delivery, or both, be postponed.

Rule 2.—Where there is a contract for the sale of specific goods and the seller is bound to do something to the goods for the purpose of putting them into a deliverable state, the property does not pass until the thing is done and the buyer has notice that it has been done.

Rule 3.—Where there is a contract for the sale of specific goods in a deliverable state but the seller is bound to weigh, measure, test, or do some other act or thing with reference to the goods for the purpose of ascertaining the price, the property does not pass until the act or thing is done and the buyer has notice that it has been done.

Rule 4.—When goods are delivered to the buyer on approval or on sale or return or other similar terms the property in the goods passes to the buyer:—

(a)　when he signifies his approval or acceptance to the seller or does any other act adopting the transaction;

(b)　if he does not signify his approval or acceptance to the seller but retains the goods without giving notice of rejection, then, if a time has been fixed for the return of the goods, on the expiration of that time, and, if no time has been fixed, on the expiration of a reasonable time.

Rule 5.—(1)　Where there is a contract for the sale of unascertained or future goods by description, and goods of that description and in a deliverable state are unconditionally appropriated to the contract, either by the seller with the assent of the buyer or by the buyer with the assent of the seller, the property in the goods then passes to the buyer; and the assent may be express or implied, and may be given either before or after the appropriation is made.

(2) Where, in pursuance of the contract, the seller delivers the goods to the buyer or to a carrier or other bailee or custodier (whether named by the buyer or not) for the purpose of transmission to the buyer, and does not reserve the right of disposal, he is to be taken to have unconditionally appropriated the goods to the contract.

[(3) Where there is a contract for the sale of a specified quantity of unascertained goods in a deliverable state forming part of a bulk which is identified either in the contract or by subsequent agreement between the parties and the bulk is reduced to (or to less than) that quantity, then, if the buyer under that contract is the only buyer to whom goods are then due out of the bulk—

(a)   the remaining goods are to be taken as appropriated to that contract at the time when the bulk is so reduced; and

(b)   the property in those goods then passes to that buyer.

(4)   Paragraph (3) above applies also (with the necessary modifications) where a bulk is reduced to (or to less than) the aggregate of the quantities due to a single buyer under separate contracts relating to that bulk and he is the only buyer to whom goods are then due out of that bulk.]

19   Reservation of right of disposal

(1)   Where there is a contract for the sale of specific goods or where goods are subsequently appropriated to the contract, the seller may, by the terms of the contract or appropriation, reserve the right of disposal of the goods until certain conditions are fulfilled; and in such a case, notwithstanding the delivery of the goods to the buyer, or to a carrier or other bailee or custodier for the purpose of transmission to the buyer, the property in the goods does not pass to the buyer until the conditions imposed by the seller are fulfilled.

(2)   Where goods are shipped, and by the bill of lading the goods are deliverable to the order of the seller or his agent, the seller is prima facie to be taken to reserve the right of disposal.

(3)   Where the seller of goods draws on the buyer for the price, and transmits the bill of exchange and bill of lading to the buyer together to secure acceptance or payment of the bill of exchange, the buyer is bound to return the bill of lading if he does not honour the bill of exchange, and if he wrongfully retains the bill of lading the property in the goods does not pass to him.

20   [Passing of risk]

(1)   Unless otherwise agreed, the goods remain at the seller's risk until the property in them is transferred to the buyer, but when the property in them is transferred to the buyer the goods are at the buyer's risk whether delivery has been made or not.

(2)   But where delivery has been delayed through the fault of either buyer or seller the goods are at the risk of the party at fault as regards any loss which might not have occurred but for such fault.

(3)   Nothing in this section affects the duties or liabilities of either seller or buyer as a bailee or custodier of the goods of the other party.

[(4)   In a case where the buyer deals as consumer or, in Scotland, where there is a consumer contract in which the buyer is a consumer, subsections (1) to (3) above must be ignored and the goods remain at the seller's risk until they are delivered to the consumer.]

[20A   Undivided shares in goods forming part of a bulk

(1)   This section applies to a contract for the sale of a specified quantity of unascertained goods if the following conditions are met—

(a)   the goods or some of them form part of a bulk which is identified either in the contract or by subsequent agreement between the parties; and

(b)   the buyer has paid the price for some or all of the goods which are the subject of the contract and which form part of the bulk.

(2)   Where this section applies, then (unless the parties agree otherwise), as soon as the conditions specified in paragraphs (a) and (b) of subsection (1) above are met or at such later time as the parties may agree—

(a)   property in an undivided share in the bulk is transferred to the buyer; and

(b)   the buyer becomes an owner in common of the bulk.

(3)   Subject to subsection (4) below, for the purposes of this section, the undivided share of a buyer in a bulk at any time shall be such share as the quantity of goods paid for and due to the buyer out of the bulk bears to the quantity of goods in the bulk at that time.

(4)   Where the aggregate of the undivided shares of buyers in a bulk determined under subsection (3) above would at any time exceed the whole of the bulk at that time, the undivided share in the bulk of each buyer shall be reduced proportionately so that the aggregate of the undivided shares is equal to the whole bulk.

(5)   Where a buyer has paid the price for only some of the goods due to him out of a bulk, any delivery to the buyer out of the bulk shall, for the purposes of this section, be ascribed in the first place to the goods in respect of which payment has been made.

(6)   For the purpose of this section payment of part of the price for any goods shall be treated as payment for a corresponding part of the goods.]

[20B   Deemed consent by co-owner to dealings in bulk goods

(1)   A person who has become an owner in common of a bulk by virtue of section 20A above shall be deemed to have consented to—

(a)   any delivery of goods out of the bulk to any other owner in common of the bulk, being goods which are due to him under his contract;

(b)   any removal, dealing with, delivery or disposal of goods in the bulk by any other person who is an owner in common of the bulk in so far as the goods fall within that co-owner's undivided share in the bulk at the time of the removal, dealing, delivery or disposal.

(2)   No cause of action shall accrue to anyone against a person by reason of that person having acted in accordance with paragraph (a) or (b) of subsection (1) above in reliance on any consent deemed to have been given under that subsection.

(3)   Nothing in this section or section 20A above shall—

(a)   impose an obligation on a buyer of goods out of a bulk to compensate any other buyer of goods out of that bulk for any shortfall in the goods received by that other buyer;

(b)   affects any contractual arrangement between buyers of goods out of a bulk for adjustments between themselves; or

(c)   affect the rights of any buyer under his contract.]

Transfer of title

21   Sale by person not the owner

(1)   Subject to this Act, where goods are sold by a person who is not their owner, and who does not sell them under the authority or with the consent of the owner, the buyer acquires no better title to the goods than the seller had, unless the owner of the goods is by his conduct precluded from denying the seller's authority to sell.

(2)   Nothing in this Act affects—

(a)   the provisions of the Factors Acts or any enactment enabling the apparent owner of goods to dispose of them as if he were their true owner;

(b)   the validity of any contract of sale under any special common law or statutory power of sale or under the order of a court of competent jurisdiction.

22   [*Does not apply to Scotland.*]

23   Sale under voidable title
When the seller of goods has a voidable title to them, but his title has not been avoided at the time of the sale, the buyer acquires a good title to the goods, provided he buys them in good faith and without notice of the seller's defect of title.

24   Seller in possession after sale
Where a person having sold goods continues or is in possession of the goods, or of the documents of title to the goods, the delivery or transfer by that person, or by a mercantile agent acting for him, of the goods or documents of title under any sale, pledge, or other disposition thereof, to any person receiving the same in good faith and without notice of the previous sale, has the same effect as if the person making the delivery or transfer were expressly authorised by the owner of the goods to make the same.

25   Buyer in possession after sale
(1)   Where a person having bought or agreed to buy goods obtains, with the consent of the seller, possession of the goods or the documents of title to the goods, the delivery or transfer by that person, or by a mercantile agent acting for him, of the goods or documents of title, under any sale, pledge, or other disposition thereof, to any person receiving the same in good faith and without notice of any lien or other right of the original seller in respect of the goods, has the same effect as if the person making the delivery or transfer were a mercantile agent in possession of the goods or documents of title with the consent of the owner.

(2)   For the purposes of subsection (1) above—

(a)   the buyer under a conditional sale agreement is to be taken not to be a person who has bought or agreed to buy goods, and

(b)   'conditional sale agreement' means an agreement for the sale of goods which is a consumer credit agreement within the meaning of the Consumer Credit Act 1974 under which the purchase price or part of it is payable by instalments, and the property in the goods is to remain in the seller (notwithstanding that the buyer is to be in possession of the goods) until such conditions as to the payment of instalments or otherwise as may be specified in the agreement are fulfilled.

(3)   Paragraph 9 of Schedule 1 below applies in relation to a contract under which a person buys or agrees to buy goods and which is made before the appointed day.

(4)   In subsection (3) above and paragraph 9 of Schedule 1 below references to the appointed day are to the day appointed for the purposes of those provisions by an order of the Secretary of State made by statutory instrument.

26   Supplementary to sections 24 and 25
In sections 24 and 25 above 'mercantile agent' means a mercantile agent having in the customary course of his business as such agent authority either—

(a)   to sell goods, or

(b)   to consign goods for the purpose of sale, or

(c)   to buy goods, or

(d)   to raise money on the security of goods.

PART IV
PERFORMANCE OF THE CONTRACT

27 Duties of seller and buyer

It is the duty of the seller to deliver the goods, and of the buyer to accept and pay for them, in accordance with the terms of the contract of sale.

28 Payment and delivery are concurrent conditions

Unless otherwise agreed, delivery of the goods and payment of the price are concurrent conditions, that is to say, the seller must be ready and willing to give possession of the goods to the buyer in exchange for the price and the buyer must be ready and willing to pay the price in exchange for possession of the goods.

29 Rules about delivery

(1)   Whether it is for the buyer to take possession of the goods or for the seller to send them to the buyer is a question depending in each case on the contract, express or implied, between the parties.

(2)   Apart from any such contract, express or implied, the place of delivery is the seller's place of business if he has one, and if not, his residence; except that, if the contract is for the sale of specific goods, which to the knowledge of the parties when the contract is made are in some other place, then that place is the place of delivery.

(3)   Where under the contract of sale the seller is bound to send the goods to the buyer, but no time for sending them is fixed, the seller is bound to send them within a reasonable time.

(4)   Where the goods at the time of sale are in the possession of a third person, there is no delivery by seller to buyer unless and until the third person acknowledges to the buyer that he holds the goods on his behalf; but nothing in this section affects the operation of the issue or transfer of any document of title to goods.

(5)   Demand or tender of delivery may be treated as ineffectual unless made at a reasonable hour, and what is a reasonable hour is a question of fact.

(6)   Unless otherwise agreed, the expenses of and incidental to putting the goods into a deliverable state must be borne by the seller.

30 Delivery of wrong quantity

(1)   Where the seller delivers to the buyer a quantity of goods less than he contracted to sell, the buyer may reject them, but if the buyer accepts the goods so delivered he must pay for them at the contract rate.

(2)   Where the seller delivers to the buyer a quantity of goods larger than he contracted to sell, the buyer may accept the goods included in the contract and reject the rest, or he may reject the whole.

. . .

(2C)   Subsections (2A) and (2B) above do not apply to Scotland.

(2D)   Where the seller delivers a quantity of goods—

(a)   less than he contracted to sell, the buyer shall not be entitled to reject the goods under subsection (1) above,

(b)   larger than he contracted to sell, the buyer shall not be entitled to reject the whole under subsection (2) above,

unless the shortfall or excess is material.

(2E)   Subsection (2D) above applies to Scotland only.]

(3)   Where the seller delivers to the buyer a quantity of goods larger than he contracted to sell and the buyer accepts the whole of the goods so delivered he must pay for them at the contract rate.

[. . .]

(5)   This section is subject to any usage of trade, special agreement, or course of dealing between the parties.

31 Instalment deliveries

(1) Unless otherwise agreed, the buyer of goods is not bound to accept delivery of them by instalments.

(2) Where there is a contract for the sale of goods to be delivered by stated instalments, which are to be separately paid for, and the seller makes defective deliveries in respect of one or more instalments, or the buyer neglects or refuses to take delivery of or pay for one or more instalments, it is a question in each case depending on the terms of the contract and the circumstances of the case whether the breach of contract is a repudiation of the whole contract or whether it is a severable breach giving rise to a claim for compensation but not to a right to treat the whole contract as repudiated.

32 Delivery to carrier

(1) Where, in pursuance of a contract of sale, the seller is authorised or required to send the goods to the buyer, delivery of the goods to a carrier (whether named by the buyer or not) for the purpose of transmission to the buyer is prima facie deemed to be delivery of the goods to the buyer.

(2) Unless otherwise authorised by the buyer, the seller must make such contact with the carrier on behalf of the buyer as may be reasonable having regard to the nature of the goods and the other circumstances of the case; and if the seller omits to do so, and the goods are lost or damaged in course of transit, the buyer may decline to treat the delivery to the carrier as a delivery to himself or may hold the seller responsible in damages.

(3) Unless otherwise agreed, where goods are sent by the seller to the buyer by a route involving sea transit, under circumstances in which it is usual to insure, the seller must give such notice to the buyer as may enable him to insure them during their sea transit, and if the seller fails to do so, the goods are at his risk during such sea transit.

[(4) In a case where the buyer deals as consumer or, in Scotland, where there is a consumer contract in which the buyer is a consumer, subsections (1) to (3) above must be ignored, but if in pursuance of a contract of sale the seller is authorised or required to send the goods to the buyer, delivery of the goods to the carrier is not delivery of the goods to the buyer.]

33 Risk where goods are delivered at distant place

Where the seller of goods agrees to deliver them at his own risk at a place other than that where they are when sold, the buyer must nevertheless (unless otherwise agreed) take any risk of deterioration in the goods necessarily incident to the course of transit.

34 Buyer's right of examining the goods

[Unless otherwise agreed, when the seller tenders delivery of goods to the buyer, he is bound on request to afford the buyer a reasonable opportunity of examining the goods for the purpose of ascertaining whether they are in conformity with the contract and, in the case of a contract for sale by sample, of comparing the bulk with the sample.]

35 Acceptance

(1) The buyer is deemed to have accepted the goods [subject to subsection (2) below—

(a) when he intimates to the seller that he has accepted them, or

(b) when the goods have been delivered to him and he does any act in relation to them which is inconsistent with the ownership of the seller.

(2) Where goods are delivered to the buyer, and he has not previously examined them, he is not deemed to have accepted them under subsection (1) above until he has had a reasonable opportunity of examining them for the purpose—

(a)   of ascertaining whether they are in conformity with the contract, and

(b)   in the case of a contract for sale by sample, of comparing the bulk with the sample.

(3)   Where the buyer deals as consumer or (in Scotland) the contract of sale is a consumer contract, the buyer cannot lose his right to rely on subsection (2) above by agreement, waiver or otherwise.

(4)   The buyer is also deemed to have accepted the goods when after the lapse of a reasonable time he retains the goods without intimating to the seller that he has rejected them.

(5)   The questions that are material in determining for the purposes of subsection (4) above whether a reasonable time has elapsed include whether the buyer has had a reasonable opportunity of examining the goods for the purpose mentioned in subsection (2) above.

(6)   The buyer is not by virtue of this section deemed to have accepted the goods merely because—

(a)   he asks for, or agrees to, their repair by or under an arrangement with the seller, or

(b)   the goods are delivered to another under a sub-sale or other disposition.

(7)   Where the contract is for the sale of goods making one or more commercial units, a buyer accepting any goods included in a unit is deemed to have accepted all the goods making the unit; and in this subsection 'commercial unit' means a unit division of which would materially impair the value of the goods or the character of the unit.

(8)]   Paragraph 10 of Schedule 1 below applies in relation to a contract made before 22 April 1967 or (in the application of this Act to Northern Ireland) 28 July 1967.

[35A   Right of partial rejection

(1)   If the buyer—

(a)   has the right to reject the goods by reason of a breach on the part of the seller that affects some or all of them, but

(b)   accepts some of the goods, including, where there are any goods unaffected by the breach, all such goods,

he does not by accepting them lose his right to reject the rest.

(2)   In the case of a buyer having the right to reject an instalment of goods, subsection (1) above applies as if references to the goods were references to the goods comprised in the instalment.

(3)   For the purposes of subsection (1) above, goods are affected by a breach if by reason of the breach they are not in conformity with the contract.

(4)   This section applies unless a contrary intention appears in, or is to be implied from, the contract.]

36   Buyer not bound to return rejected goods

Unless otherwise agreed, where goods are delivered to the buyer, and he refuses to accept them, having the right to do so, he is not bound to return them to the seller, but it is sufficient if he intimates to the seller that he refuses to accept them.

37   Buyer's liability for not taking delivery of goods

(1)   When the seller is ready and willing to deliver the goods, and requests the buyer to take delivery, and the buyer does not within a reasonable time after such request take delivery of the goods, he is liable to the seller for any loss occasioned by his neglect or refusal to take delivery, and also for a reasonable charge for the care and custody of the goods.

(2)   Nothing in this section affects the rights of the seller where the neglect or refusal of the buyer to take delivery amounts to a repudiation of the contract.

PART V
RIGHTS OF UNPAID SELLER AGAINST THE GOODS

Preliminary

38 Unpaid seller defined

(1)   The seller of goods is an unpaid seller within the meaning of this Act—

(a)   when the whole of the price has not been paid or tendered;

(b)   when a bill of exchange or other negotiable instrument has been received as conditional payment, and the condition on which it was received has not been fulfilled by reason of the dishonour of the instrument or otherwise.

(2)   In this Part of this Act 'seller' includes any person who is in the position of a seller, as, for instance, an agent of the seller to whom the bill of lading has been indorsed, or a consignor or agent who has himself paid (or is directly responsible for) the price.

39 Unpaid seller's rights

(1)   Subject to this and any other Act, notwithstanding that the property in the goods may have passed to the buyer, the unpaid seller of goods, as such, has by implication of law—

(a)   a lien on the goods or right to retain them for the price while he is in possession of them;

(b)   in the case of the insolvency of the buyer, a right of stopping the goods in transit after he has parted with the possession of them;

(c)   a right of re-sale as limited by this Act.

(2)   Where the property in goods has not passed to the buyer, the unpaid seller has (in addition to his other remedies) a right of withholding delivery similar to and coextensive with his rights of lien or retention and stoppage in transit where the property has passed to the buyer.

[. . .]

Unpaid seller's lien

41 Seller's lien

(1)   Subject to this Act, the unpaid seller of goods who is in possession of them is entitled to retain possession of them until payment or tender of the price in the following cases:—

(a)   where the goods have been sold without any stipulation as to credit;

(b)   where the goods have been sold on credit but the term of credit has expired;

(c)   where the buyer becomes insolvent.

(2)   The seller may exercise his lien or right of retention notwithstanding that he is in possession of the goods as agent or bailee or custodier for the buyer.

42 Part delivery

Where an unpaid seller has made part delivery of the goods, he may exercise his lien or right of retention on the remainder, unless such part delivery has been made under such circumstances as to show an agreement to waive the lien or right of retention.

43 Termination of lien

(1)   The unpaid seller of goods loses his lien or right of retention in respect of them—

(a)   when he delivers the goods to a carrier or other bailee or custodier for the purpose of transmission to the buyer without reserving the right of disposal of the goods;

(b)   when the buyer or his agent lawfully obtains possession of the goods;

(c)   by waiver of the lien or right of retention.

(2)   An unpaid seller of goods who has a lien or right of retention in respect of them does not lose his lien or right of retention by reason only that he has obtained judgment or decree for the price of the goods.

Stoppage in transit

44   Right of stoppage in transit
Subject to this Act, when the buyer of goods becomes insolvent the unpaid seller who has parted with the possession of the goods has the right of stopping them in transit, that is to say, he may resume possession of the goods as long as they are in course of transit, and may retain them until payment or tender of the price.

45   Duration of transit
(1)   Goods are deemed to be in course of transit from the time when they are delivered to a carrier or other bailee or custodier for the purpose of transmission to the buyer, until the buyer or his agent in that behalf takes delivery of them from the carrier or other bailee or custodier.

(2)   If the buyer or his agent in that behalf obtains delivery of the goods before their arrival at the appointed destination, the transit is at an end.

(3)   If, after the arrival of the goods at the appointed destination, the carrier or other bailee or custodier acknowledges to the buyer or his agent that he holds the goods on his behalf and continues in possession of them as bailee or custodier for the buyer or his agent, the transit is at an end, and it is immaterial that a further destination for the goods may have been indicated by the buyer.

(4)   If the goods are rejected by the buyer, and the carrier or other bailee or custodier continues in possession of them, the transit is not deemed to be at an end, even if the seller has refused to receive them back.

(5)   When goods are delivered to a ship chartered by the buyer it is a question depending on the circumstances of the particular case whether they are in the possession of the master as a carrier or as agent to the buyer.

(6)   Where the carrier or other bailee or custodier wrongfully refuses to deliver the goods to the buyer or his agent in that behalf, the transit is deemed to be at an end.

(7)   Where part delivery of the goods has been made to the buyer or his agent in that behalf, the remainder of the goods may be stopped in transit, unless such part delivery has been made under such circumstances as to show an agreement to give up possession of the whole of the goods.

46   How stoppage in transit is effected
(1)   The unpaid seller may exercise his right of stoppage in transit either by taking actual possession of the goods or by giving notice of his claim to the carrier or other bailee or custodier in whose possession the goods are.

(2)   The notice may be given either to the person in actual possession of the goods or to his principal.

(3)   If given to the principal, the notice is ineffective unless given at such time and under such circumstances that the principal, by the exercise of reasonable diligence, may communicate it to his servant or agent in time to prevent a delivery to the buyer.

(4)   When notice of stoppage in transit is given by the seller to the carrier or other bailee or custodier in possession of the goods, he must re-deliver the goods to, or according to the directions of, the seller; and the expenses of the re-delivery must be borne by the seller.

Re-sale etc by buyer

47 Effect of sub-sale etc by buyer

(1) Subject to this Act, the unpaid seller's right of lien or retention or stoppage in transit is not affected by any sale or other disposition of the goods which the buyer may have made, unless the seller has assented to it.

(2) Where a document of title to goods has been lawfully transferred to any person as buyer or owner of the goods, and that person transfers the document to a person who takes it in good faith and for valuable consideration, then—

(a) if the last-mentioned transfer was by way of sale the unpaid seller's right of lien or retention or stoppage in transit is defeated; and

(b) if the last-mentioned transfer was made by way of pledge or other disposition for value, the unpaid seller's right of lien or retention of stoppage in transit can only be exercised subject to the rights of the transferee.

Rescission: and re-sale by seller

48 Rescission: and re-sale by seller

(1) Subject to this section, a contract of sale is not rescinded by the mere exercise by an unpaid seller of his right of lien or retention or stoppage in transit.

(2) Where an unpaid seller who has exercised his right of lien or retention or stoppage in transit re-sells the goods, the buyer acquires a good title to them as against the original buyer.

(3) Where the goods are of a perishable nature, or where the unpaid seller gives notice to the buyer of his intention to re-sell, and the buyer does not within a reasonable time pay or tender the price, the unpaid seller may re-sell the goods and recover from the original buyer damages for any loss occasioned by his breach of contract.

(4) Where the seller expressly reserves the right of re-sale in case the buyer should make default, and on the buyer making default re-sells the goods, the original contract of sale is rescinded but without prejudice to any claim the seller may have for damages.

[PART VA
ADDITIONAL RIGHTS OF BUYER IN CONSUMER CASES

48A Introductory

(1) This section applies if—

(a) the buyer deals as consumer or, in Scotland, there is a consumer contract in which the buyer is a consumer, and

(b) the goods do not conform to the contract of sale at the time of delivery.

(2) If this section applies, the buyer has the right—

(a) under and in accordance with section 48B below, to require the seller to repair or replace the goods, or

(b) under and in accordance with section 48C below—

(i) to require the seller to reduce the purchase price of the goods to the buyer by an appropriate amount, or

(ii) to rescind the contract with regard to the goods in question.

(3) For the purposes of subsection (1)(b) above goods which do not conform to the contract of sale at any time within the period of six months starting with the date on which the goods were delivered to the buyer must be taken not to have so conformed at that date.

(4) Subsection (3) above does not apply if—

(a) it is established that the goods did so conform at that date;

(b) its application is incompatible with the nature of the goods or the nature of the lack of conformity.

48B   Repair or replacement of the goods

(1)   If section 48A above applies, the buyer may require the seller—

    (a)   to repair the goods, or

    (b)   to replace the goods.

(2)   If the buyer requires the seller to repair or replace the goods, the seller must—

    (a)   repair or, as the case may be, replace the goods within a reasonable time but without causing significant inconvenience to the buyer;

    (b)   bear any necessary costs incurred in doing so (including in particular the cost of any labour, materials or postage).

(3)   The buyer must not require the seller to repair or, as the case may be, replace the goods if that remedy is—

    (a)   impossible, or

    (b)   disproportionate in comparison to the other of those remedies, or

    (c)   disproportionate in comparison to an appropriate reduction in the purchase price under paragraph (a), or rescission under paragraph (b), of section 48C(1) below.

(4)   One remedy is disproportionate in comparison to the other if the one imposes costs on the seller which, in comparison to those imposed on him by the other, are unreasonable, taking into account—

    (a)   the value which the goods would have if they conformed to the contract of sale,

    (b)   the significance of the lack of conformity, and

    (c)   whether the other remedy could be effected without significant inconvenience to the buyer.

(5)   Any question as to what is a reasonable time or significant inconvenience is to be determined by reference to—

    (a)   the nature of the goods, and

    (b)   the purpose for which the goods were acquired.

48C   Reduction of purchase price or rescission of contract

(1)   If section 48A above applies, the buyer may—

    (a)   require the seller to reduce the purchase price of the goods in question to the buyer by an appropriate amount, or

    (b)   rescind the contract with regard to those goods,

if the condition in subsection (2) below is satisfied.

(2)   The condition is that—

    (a)   by virtue of section 48B(3) above the buyer may require neither repair nor replacement of the goods; or

    (b)   the buyer has required the seller to repair or replace the goods, but the seller is in breach of the requirement of section 48B(2)(a) above to do so within a reasonable time and without significant inconvenience to the buyer.

(3)   For the purposes of this Part, if the buyer rescinds the contract, any reimbursement to the buyer may be reduced to take account of the use he has had of the goods since they were delivered to him.

48D   Relation to other remedies etc

(1)   If the buyer requires the seller to repair or replace the goods the buyer must not act under subsection (2) until he has given the seller a reasonable time in which to repair or replace (as the case may be) the goods.

(2)   The buyer acts under this subsection if—

    (a)   in England and Wales or Northern Ireland he rejects the goods and terminates the contract for breach of condition;

    (b)   in Scotland he rejects any goods delivered under the contract and treats it as repudiated;

    (c)   he requires the goods to be replaced or repaired (as the case may be).

48E Powers of the court

(1)   In any proceedings in which a remedy is sought by virtue of this Part the court, in addition to any other power it has, may act under this section.

(2)   On the application of the buyer the court may make an order requiring specific performance or, in Scotland, specific implement by the seller of any obligation imposed on him by virtue of section 48B above.

(3)   Subsection (4) applies if—

(a)   the buyer requires the seller to give effect to a remedy under section 48B or 48C above or has claims to rescind under section 48C, but

(b)   the court decides that another remedy under section 48B or 48C is appropriate.

(4)   The court may proceed—

(a)   as if the buyer had required the seller to give effect to the other remedy, or if the other remedy is rescission under section 48C; or

(b)   as if the buyer had claimed to rescind the contract under that section.

(5)   If the buyer has claimed to rescind the contract the court may order that any reimbursement to the buyer is reduced to take account of the use he has had of the goods since they were delivered to him.

(6)   The court may make an order under this section unconditionally or on such terms and conditions as to damages, payment of the price and otherwise as it thinks just.

48F Conformity with the contract

For the purposes of this Part, goods do not conform to a contract of sale if there is, in relation to the goods, a breach of an express term of the contract or a term implied by section 13, 14 or 15 above.]

PART VI
ACTIONS FOR BREACH OF THE CONTRACT

Seller's remedies

49 Action for price

(1)   Where, under a contract of sale, the property in the goods has passed to the buyer and he wrongfully neglects or refuses to pay for the goods according to the terms of the contract, the seller may maintain an action against him for the price of the goods.

(2)   Where, under a contract of sale, the price is payable on a day certain irrespective of delivery and the buyer wrongfully neglects or refuses to pay such price, the seller may maintain an action for the price, although the property in goods has not passed and the goods have not been appropriated to the contract.

(3)   Nothing in this section prejudices the right of the seller in Scotland to recover interest on the price from the date of tender of the goods, or from the date on which the price was payable, as the case may be.

50 Damages for non-acceptance

(1)   Where the buyer wrongfully neglects or refuses to accept and pay for the goods, the seller may maintain an action against him for damages for non-acceptance.

(2)   The measure of damages is the estimated loss directly and naturally resulting in the ordinary course of events, from the buyer's breach of contract.

(3)   Where there is an available market for the goods in question the measure of damages is prima facie to be ascertained by the difference between the contract price and the market or current price at the time or times when the goods ought to have been accepted or (if no time was fixed for acceptance) at the time of the refusal to accept.

Buyer's remedies

51   Damages for non-delivery

(1)   Where the seller wrongfully neglects or refuses to deliver the goods to the buyer, the buyer may maintain an action against the seller for damages for non-delivery.

(2)   The measure of damages is the estimated loss directly and naturally resulting, in the ordinary course of events, from the seller's breach of contract.

(3)   Where there is an available market for the goods in question the measure of damages is prima facie to be ascertained by the difference between the contract price and the market or current price of the goods at the time or times when they ought to have been delivered or (if no time was fixed) at the time of the refusal to deliver.

52   Specific performance

(1)   If any action for breach of contract to deliver specific or ascertained goods the court may, if it thinks fit, on the plaintiff's application, by its judgment or decree direct that the contract shall be performed specifically, without giving the defendant the option of retaining the goods on payment of damages.

(2)   The plaintiff's application may be made at any time before judgment or decree.

(3)   The judgment or decree may be unconditional, or on such terms and conditions as to damages, payment of the price and otherwise as seem just to the court.

(4)   The provisions of this section shall be deemed to be supplementary to, and not in derogation of, the right of specific implement in Scotland.

53   [*Does not apply to Scotland.*]

[53A   Measure of damages as respects Scotland

(1)   The measure of damages for the seller's breach of contract is the estimated loss directly and naturally resulting, in the ordinary course of events, from the breach.

(2)   Where the seller's breach consists of the delivery of goods which are not of the quality required by the contract and the buyer retains the goods, such loss as aforesaid is prima facie the difference between the value of the goods at the time of delivery to the buyer and the value they would have had if they had fulfilled the contract.

(3)   This section applies to Scotland only.]

Interest, etc

54   Interest, etc

Nothing in this Act affects the right of the buyer or the seller to recover interest or special damages in any case where by law interest or special damages may be recoverable, or to recover money paid where the consideration for the payment of it has failed.

PART VII
SUPPLEMENTARY

55   Exclusion of implied terms

(1)   Where a right, duty or liability would arise under a contract of sale of goods by implication of law, it may (subject to the Unfair Contract Terms Act 1977) be negatived or varied by express agreement, or by the course of dealing between the parties, or by such usage as binds both parties to the contract.

(2)   An express [term] does not negative a [term] implied by this Act unless inconsistent with it.

(3)   Paragraph 11 of Schedule 1 below applies in relation to a contract made on or after 18 May 1973 and before 1 February 1978, and paragraph 12 in relation to one made before 18 May 1973.

56   Conflict of laws

Paragraph 13 of Schedule 1 below applies in relation to a contract made on or after 18 May 1973 and before 1 February 1978, so as to make provision about conflict of laws in relation to such a contract.

57   Auction sales

(1)   Where goods are put up for sale by auction in lots, each lot is prima facie deemed to be the subject of a separate contract of sale.

(2)   A sale by auction is complete when the auctioneer announces its completion by the fall of the hammer, or in other customary manner; and until the announcement is made any bidder may retract his bid.

(3)   A sale by auction may be notified to be subject to a reserve or upset price, and a right to bid may also be reserved expressly by or on behalf of the seller.

(4)   Where a sale by auction is not notified to be subject to a right to bid by or on behalf of the seller, it is not lawful for the seller to bid himself or to employ any person to bid at the sale, or for the auctioneer knowingly to take any bid from the seller or any such person.

(5)   A sale contravening subsection (4) above may be treated as fraudulent by the buyer.

(6)   Where, in respect of a sale by auction, a right to bid is expressly reserved (but not otherwise) the seller or any one person on his behalf may bid at the auction.

58   Payment into court in Scotland

In Scotland where a buyer has elected to accept goods which he might have rejected, and to treat a breach of contract as only giving rise to a claim for damages, he may, in an action by the seller for the price, be required, in the discretion of the court before which the action depends, to consign or pay into court the price of the goods, or part of the price, or to give other reasonable security for its due payment.

59   Reasonable time a question of fact

Where a reference is made in this Act to a reasonable time the question what is a reasonable time is a question of fact.

60   Rights etc enforceable by action

Where a right, duty or liability is declared by this Act, it may (unless otherwise provided by this Act) be enforced by action.

61   Interpretation

(1)   In this Act, unless the context or subject matter otherwise requires,—

'action' includes counterclaim and set-off, and in Scotland condescendence and claim and compensation;

['bulk' means a mass or collection of goods of the same kind which—

(a)   is contained in a defined space or area; and

(b)   is such that any goods in the bulk are interchangeable with any other goods therein of the same number or quantity;]

'business' includes a profession and the activities of any government department (including a Northern Ireland department) or local or public authority;

'buyer' means a person who buys or agrees to buy goods;

['consumer contract' has the same meaning as in section 25(1) of the Unfair Contract Terms Act 1977; and for the purposes of this Act the onus of proving that a contract is not to be regarded as a consumer contract shall lie on the seller;]

'contract of sale' includes an agreement to sell as well as a sale;

'credit-broker' means a person acting in the course of a business of credit brokerage carried on by him, that is a business of effecting introductions of individuals desiring to obtain credit—

(a)   to persons carrying on any business so far as it relates to the provision of credit, or

(b)   to other persons engaged in credit brokerage;

'defendant' includes in Scotland defender, respondent, and claimant in a multiplepoinding;

'delivery' means voluntary transfer of possession from one person to another; [except that in relation to sections 20A and 20B above it includes such appropriation of goods to the contract as results in property in the goods being transferred to the buyer;]

'document of title to goods' has the same meaning as it has in the Factors Acts;

'Factors Acts' means the Factors Act 1889, the Factors (Scotland) Act 1890, and any enactment amending or substituted for the same;

'fault' means wrongful act or default;

'future goods' means goods to be manufactured or acquired by the seller after the making of the contract of sale;

'goods' includes all personal chattels other than things in action and money, and in Scotland all corporeal moveables except money; and in particular 'goods' includes emblements, industrial growing crops, and things attached to or forming part of the land which are agreed to be severed before sale or under the contract of sale; [and includes an undivided share in goods;]

'plaintiff' includes pursuer, complainer, claimant in a multiplepoinding and defendant or defender counter-claiming;

['producer' means the manufacturer of goods, the importer of goods into the European Economic Area or any person purporting to be a producer by placing his name, trade mark or other distinctive sign on the goods;]

'property' means the general property in goods, and not merely a special property;

['repair' means, in cases where there is a lack of conformity in goods for the purposes of section 48F of this Act, to bring the goods into conformity with the contract;]

'sale' includes a bargain and sale as well as a sale and delivery;

'seller' means a person who sells or agrees to sell goods;

'specific goods' means goods identified and agreed on at the time a contract of sale is made; [and includes an undivided share, specified as a fraction or percentage, of goods identified and agreed on as aforesaid;]

'warranty' (as regards England and Wales and Northern Ireland) means an agreement with reference to goods which are the subject of a contract of sale, but collateral to the main purpose of such contract, the breach of which gives rise to a claim for damages, but not to a right to reject the goods and treat the contract as repudiated.

[. . .]

(3)   A thing is deemed to be done in good faith within the meaning of this Act when it is in fact done honestly, whether it is done negligently or not.

(4)   A person is deemed to be insolvent within the meaning of this Act if he has either ceased to pay his debts in the ordinary course of business or he cannot pay his debts as they become due, [. . .]

(5)   Goods are in a deliverable state within the meaning of this Act when they are in such a state that the buyer would under the contract be bound to take delivery of them.

[(5A)   References in this Act to dealing as consumer are to be construed in accordance with Part I of the Unfair Contract Terms Act 1977; and, for the purposes of this Act, it is for a seller claiming that the buyer does not deal as consumer to show that he does not.]

(6) As regards the definition of 'business' in subsection (1) above, paragraph 14 of Schedule 1 below applies in relation to a contract made on or after 18 May 1973 and before 1 February 1978, and paragraph 15 in relation to one made before 18 May 1973,

62 Savings: rules of law etc

(1) The rules in bankruptcy relating to contracts of sale apply to those contracts, notwithstanding anything in this Act.

(2) The rules of the common law, including the law merchant, except in so far as they are inconsistent with the provisions of this Act, and in particular the rules relating to the law of principal and agent and the effect of fraud, misrepresentation, duress or coercion, mistake, or other invalidating cause, apply to contracts for the sale of goods.

(3) Nothing in this Act or the Sale of Goods Act 1893 affects the enactments relating to bills of sale, or any enactment relating to the sale of goods which is not expressly repealed or amended by this Act or that.

(4) The provisions of this Act about contracts of sale do not apply to a transaction in the form of a contract of sale which is intended to operate by way of mortgage, pledge, charge, or other security.

[. . .]

64 Short title and commencement

(1) This Act may be cited as the Sale of Goods Act 1979.

(2) This Act comes into force on 1 January 1980.

CIVIL AVIATION ACT 1982
(1982, c 16)

Trespass by aircraft and aircraft nuisance, noise, etc

76 Liability of aircraft in respect of trespass, nuisance and surface damage

(1) No action shall lie in respect of trespass or in respect of nuisance, by reason only of the flight of an aircraft over any property at a height above the ground which, having regard to wind, weather and all the circumstances of the case is reasonable, or the ordinary incidents of such flight, so long as the provisions of any Air Navigation Order and of any orders under section 62 above have been duly complied with and there has been no breach of section 81 below.

(2) Subject to subsection (3) below, where material loss or damage is caused to any person or property on land or water by, or by a person in, or an article, animal or person falling from, an aircraft while in flight, taking off or landing, then unless the loss or damage was caused or contributed to by the negligence of the person by whom it was suffered, damages in respect of the loss or damage shall be recoverable without proof of negligence or intention or other cause of action, as if the loss or damage had been caused by the wilful act, neglect, or default of the owner of the aircraft.

(3) Where material loss or damage is caused as aforesaid in circumstances in which—

(a) damages are recoverable in respect of the said loss or damage by virtue only of subsection (2) above, and

(b) a legal liability is created in some person other than the owner to pay damages in respect of the said loss or damage,

the owner shall be entitled to be indemnified by that other person against any claim in respect of the said loss or damage.

Rights etc in relation to aircraft

86   Power to provide for the mortgaging of aircraft

(1)   Her Majesty may by Order in Council make provision for the mortgaging of aircraft registered in the United Kingdom or capable of being so registered.

(2)   Without prejudice to the generality of the powers conferred by subsection (1) above, an Order in Council under this section may, in particular—

(a)   include provisions which correspond (subject to such modifications as appear to Her Majesty in Council to be necessary or expedient) to any of the provisions of the Merchant Shipping Act [1995] relating to the mortgaging of ships;

(b)   make provision as respects the rights and liabilities of mortgagors and mortgagees of such aircraft as are mentioned in subsection (1) above, and as respects the priority inter se of such rights and the relationship of such rights to other rights in or over such aircraft, including possessory liens for work done to such aircraft and rights under section 88 below or under regulations made by virtue of [section 83 of the Transport Act 2000 (detention and sale of aircraft)];

(c)   make provision as respects the operation, in relation to such aircraft as aforesaid, of any of the enactments in force in any part of the United Kingdom relating to bills of sale or the registration of charges on the property or undertaking of companies;

(d)   provide for the rights of mortgagees of such aircraft to be exercisable, in such circumstances as may be specified in the Order, in relation to payments for the use of the aircraft;

(e)   confer on courts in the United Kingdom powers in respect of any register maintained in pursuance of the Order and in respect of transactions affecting aircraft registered therein;

(f)   make provision for enabling the mortgage of an aircraft to extend to any store of spare parts for that aircraft and for applying, for that purpose, to any such spare parts provisions such as are mentioned in the preceding paragraphs of this subsection;

(g)   make provision specifying, subject to the consent of the Treasury, the fees to be paid in respect of the making or deletion of entries in any such register as aforesaid and in respect of any other matters in respect of which it appears to Her Majesty in Council to be expedient for the purposes of the Order to charge fees;

(h)   provide for the imposition of penalties in respect of the making of false statements in connection with matters dealt with in the Order and in respect of the forgery of documents relating to such matters.

SUPPLY OF GOODS AND SERVICES ACT 1982
(1982, c 29)

[PART IA
SUPPLY OF GOODS AS RESPECTS SCOTLAND

Contracts for the transfer of property in goods

11A The contracts concerned

(1) In this Act in its application to Scotland a 'contract for the transfer of goods' means a contract under which one person transfers or agrees to transfer to another the property in goods, other than an excepted contract.

(2) For the purposes of this section an excepted contract means any of the following—

(a) a contract of sale of goods;

(b) a hire-purchase agreement;

[. . .]

(d) a transfer or agreement to transfer for which there is no consideration;

(e) a contract intended to operate by way of mortgage, pledge, charge or other security.

(3) For the purposes of this Act in its application to Scotland a contract is a contract for the transfer of goods whether or not services are also provided or to be provided under the contract, and (subject to subsection (2) above) whatever is the nature of the consideration for the transfer or agreement to transfer.

11B Implied terms about title, etc

(1) In a contract for the transfer of goods, other than one to which subsection (3) below applies, there is an implied term on the part of the transferor that in the case of a transfer of the property in the goods he has a right to transfer the property and in the case of an agreement to transfer the property in the goods he will have such a right at the time when the property is to be transferred.

(2) In a contract for the transfer of goods, other than one to which subsection (3) below applies, there is also an implied term that—

(a) the goods are free, and will remain free until the time when the property is to be transferred, from any charge or encumbrance not disclosed or known to the transferee before the contract is made, and

(b) the transferee will enjoy quiet possession of the goods except so far as it may be disturbed by the owner or other person entitled to the benefit of any charge or encumbrance so disclosed or known.

(3) This subsection applies to a contract for the transfer of goods in the case of which there appears from the contract or is to be inferred from its circumstances an intention that the transferor should transfer only such title as he or a third person may have.

(4) In a contract to which subsection (3) above applies there is an implied term that all charges or encumbrances known to the transferor and not known to the transferee have been disclosed to the transferee before the contract is made.

(5) In a contract to which subsection (3) above applies there is also an implied term that none of the following will disturb the transferee's quiet possession of the goods, namely—

(a) the transferor;

(b) in a case where the parties to the contract intend that the transferor should transfer only such title as a third person may have, that person;

(c) anyone claiming through or under the transferor or that third person otherwise than under a charge or encumbrance disclosed or known to the transferee before the contract is made.

(6) [*amends Unfair Contract Terms Act 1977*]

11C Implied terms where transfer is by description

(1)   This section applies where, under a contract for the transfer of goods, the transferor transfers or agrees to transfer the property in the goods by description.

(2)   In such a case there is an implied term that the goods will correspond with the description.

(3)   If the transferor transfers or agrees to transfer the property in the goods by reference to a sample as well as by description it is not sufficient that the bulk of the goods corresponds with the sample if the goods do not also correspond with the description.

(4)   A contract is not prevented from falling within subsection (1) above by reason only that, being exposed for supply, the goods are selected by the transferee.

11D Implied terms about quality or fitness

(1)   Except as provided by this section and section 11E below and subject to the provisions of any other enactment, there is no implied term about the quality or fitness for any particular purpose of goods supplied under a contract for the transfer of goods.

(2)   Where, under such a contract, the transferor transfers the property in goods in the course of a business, there is an implied term that the goods supplied under the contract are of satisfactory quality.

(3)   For the purposes of this section and section 11E below, goods are of satisfactory quality if they meet the standard that a reasonable person would regard as satisfactory, taking account of any description of the goods, the price (if relevant) and all the other relevant circumstances.

[(3A)   If the contract for the transfer of goods is a consumer contract, the relevant circumstances mentioned in subsection (3) above include any public statements on the specific characteristics of the goods made about them by the transferor, the producer or his representative, particularly in advertising or on labelling.

(3B)   A public statement is not by virtue of subsection (3A) above a relevant circumstance for the purposes of subsection (3) above in the case of a contract for the transfer of goods, if the transferor shows that—

(a)   at the time the contract was made, he was not, and could not reasonably have been, aware of the statement,

(b)   before the contract was made, the statement had been withdrawn in public or, to the extent that it contained anything which was incorrect or misleading, it had been corrected in public, or

(c)   the decision to acquire the goods could not have been influenced by the statement.

(3C)   Subsections (3A) and (3B) above do not prevent any public statement from being a relevant circumstance for the purposes of subsection (3) above (whether or not the contract for the transfer of goods is a consumer contract) if the statement would have been such a circumstance apart from those subsections.]

(4)   The term implied by subsection (2) above does not extend to any matter making the quality of goods unsatisfactory—

(a)   which is specifically drawn to the transferee's attention before the contract is made,

(b)   where the transferee examines the goods before the contract is made, which that examination ought to reveal, or

(c)   where the property in the goods is, or is to be, transferred by reference to a sample, which would have been apparent on a reasonable examination of the sample.

(5)   Subsection (6) below applies where, under a contract for the transfer of goods, the transferor transfers the property in goods in the course of a business and the transferee, expressly or by implication, makes known—

(a)   to the transferor, or

(b)   where the consideration or part of the consideration for the transfer is a sum payable by instalments and the goods were previously sold by a credit-broker to the transferor, to that credit-broker,

any particular purpose for which the goods are being acquired.

(6)   In that case there is (subject to subsection (7) below) an implied term that the goods supplied under the contract are reasonably fit for the purpose, whether or not that is a purpose for which such goods are commonly supplied.

(7)   Subsection (6) above does not apply where the circumstances show that the transferee does not rely, or that it is unreasonable for him to rely, on the skill or judgment of the transferor or credit-broker.

(8)   An implied term about quality or fitness for a particular purpose may be annexed by usage to a contract for the transfer of goods.

(9)   The preceding provisions of this section apply to a transfer by a person who in the course of a business is acting as agent for another as they apply to a transfer by a principal in the course of a business, except where that other is not transferring in the course of a business and either the transferee knows that fact or reasonable steps are taken to bring it to the transferee's notice before the contract concerned is made.

[(10)   For the purposes of this section, 'consumer contract' has the same meaning as in section 11F(3) below.]

11E   Implied terms where transfer is by sample

(1)   This section applies where, under a contract for the transfer of goods, the transferor transfers or agrees to transfer the property in the goods by reference to a sample.

(2)   In such a case there is an implied term—

(a)   that the bulk will correspond with the sample in quality;

(b)   that the transferee will have a reasonable opportunity of comparing the bulk with the sample; and

(c)   that the goods will be free from any defect, making their quality unsatisfactory, which would not be apparent on reasonable examination of the sample.

(3)   For the purposes of this section a transferor transfers or agrees to transfer the property in goods by reference to a sample where there is an express or implied term to that effect in the contract concerned.

11F   Remedies for breach of contract

(1)   Where in a contract for the transfer of goods a transferor is in breach of any term of the contract (express or implied), the other party to the contract (in this section referred to as 'the transferee') shall be entitled—

(a)   to claim damages; and

(b)   if the breach is material, to reject any goods delivered under the contract and treat it as repudiated.

(2)   Where a contract for the transfer of goods is a consumer contract and the transferee is the consumer, then, for the purposes of subsection (1)(b) above, breach by the transferor of any term (express or implied)—

(a)   as to the quality of the goods or their fitness for a purpose;

(b)   if the goods are, or are to be, transferred by description, that the goods will correspond with the description;

(c)   if the goods are, or are to be, transferred by reference to a sample, that the bulk will correspond with the sample in quality,

shall be deemed to be a material breach.

(3)   In subsection (2) above, 'consumer contract' has the same meaning as in section 25(1) of the 1977 Act; and for the purposes of that subsection the onus of

proving that a contract is not to be regarded as a consumer contract shall lie on the transferor.

Contracts for the hire of goods

11G   The contracts concerned

(1)   In this Act in its application to Scotland a 'contract for the hire of goods' means a contract under which one person ('the supplier') hires or agrees to hire goods to another, other than [a hire purchase agreement].

[. . .]

(3)   For the purposes of this Act in its application to Scotland a contract is a contract for the hire of goods whether or not services are also provided or to be provided under the contract, and [. . .] whatever is the nature of the consideration for the hire or agreement to hire.

11H   Implied terms about right to transfer possession etc

(1)   In a contract for the hire of goods there is an implied term on the part of the supplier that—

(a)   in the case of a hire, he has a right to transfer possession of the goods by way of hire for the period of the hire; and

(b)   in the case of an agreement to hire, he will have such a right at the time of commencement of the period of the hire.

(2)   In a contract for the hire of goods there is also an implied term that the person to whom the goods are hired will enjoy quiet possession of the goods for the period of the hire except so far as the possession may be disturbed by the owner or other person entitled to the benefit of any charge or encumbrance disclosed or known to the person to whom the goods are hired before the contract is made.

(3)   The preceding provisions of this section do not affect the right of the supplier to repossess the goods under an express or implied term of the contract.

11I   Implied terms where hire is by description

(1)   This section applies where, under a contract for the hire of goods, the supplier hires or agrees to hire the goods by description.

(2)   In such a case there is an implied term that the goods will correspond with the description.

(3)   If under the contract the supplier hires or agrees to hire the goods by reference to a sample as well as by description it is not sufficient that the bulk of the goods corresponds with the sample if the goods do not also correspond with the description.

(4)   A contract is not prevented from falling within subsection (1) above by reason only that, being exposed for supply, the goods are selected by the person to whom the goods are hired.

11J   Implied terms about quality or fitness

(1)   Except as provided by this section and section 11K below and subject to the provisions of any other enactment, there is no implied term about the quality or fitness for any particular purpose of goods hired under a contract for the hire of goods.

(2)   Where, under such a contract, the supplier hires goods in the course of a business, there is an implied term that the goods supplied under the contract are of satisfactory quality.

(3)   For the purposes of this section and section 11K below, goods are of satisfactory quality if they meet the standard that a reasonable person would regard as satisfactory, taking account of any description of the goods, the consideration for the hire (if relevant) and all the other relevant circumstances.

[(3A)   If the contract for the transfer of goods is a consumer contract, the relevant circumstances mentioned in subsection (3) above include any public statements on the specific characteristics of the goods made about them by the transferor, the producer or his representative, particularly in advertising or on labelling.

(3B) A public statement is not by virtue of subsection (3A) above a relevant circumstance for the purposes of subsection (3) above in the case of a contract for the transfer of goods, if the transferor shows that—

(a) at the time the contract was made, he was not, and could not reasonably have been, aware of the statement,

(b) before the contract was made, the statement had been withdrawn in public or, to the extent that it contained anything which was incorrect or misleading, it had been corrected in public, or

(c) the decision to acquire the goods could not have been influenced by the statement.

(3C) Subsections (3A) and (3B) above do not prevent any public statement from being a relevant circumstance for the purposes of subsection (3) above (whether or not the contract for the transfer of goods is a consumer contract) if the statement would have been such a circumstance apart from those subsections.]

(4) The term implied by subsection (2) above does not extend to any matter making the quality of goods unsatisfactory—

(a) which is specifically drawn to the attention of the person to whom the goods are hired before the contract is made, or

(b) where that person examines the goods before the contract is made, which that examination ought to reveal; or

(c) where the goods are hired by reference to a sample, which would have been apparent on reasonable examination of the sample.

(5) Subsection (6) below applies where, under a contract for the hire of goods, the supplier hires goods in the course of a business and the person to whom the goods are hired, expressly or by implication, makes known—

(a) to the supplier in the course of negotiations conducted by him in relation to the making of the contract; or

(b) to a credit-broker in the course of negotiations conducted by that broker in relation to goods sold by him to the supplier before forming the subject matter of the contract,

any particular purpose for which the goods are being hired.

(6) In that case there is (subject to subsection (7) below) an implied term that the goods supplied under the contract are reasonably fit for that purpose, whether or not that is a purpose for which such goods are commonly supplied.

(7) Subsection (6) above does not apply where the circumstances show that the person to whom the goods are hired does not rely, or that it is unreasonable for him to rely, on the skill or judgment of the hirer or credit-broker.

(8) An implied term about quality or fitness for a particular purpose may be annexed by usage to a contract for the hire of goods.

(9) The preceding provisions of this section apply to a hire by a person who in the course of a business is acting as agent for another as they apply to a hire by a principal in the course of a business, except where that other is not hiring in the course of a business and either the person to whom the goods are hired knows that fact or reasonable steps are taken to bring it to that person's notice before the contract concerned is made.

[(10) For the purposes of this section, 'consumer contract' has the same meaning as in section 11F(3) above.]

11K Implied terms where hire is by sample

(1) This section applies where, under a contract for the hire of goods, the supplier hires or agrees to hire the goods by reference to a sample.

(2) In such a case there is an implied term—

(a) that the bulk will correspond with the sample in quality; and

(b)   that the person to whom the goods are hired will have a reasonable opportunity of comparing the bulk with the sample; and
(c)   that the goods will be free from any defect, making their quality unsatisfactory, which would not be apparent on reasonable examination of the sample.
(3)   For the purposes of this section a supplier hires or agrees to hire goods by reference to a sample where there is an express or implied term to that effect in the contract concerned.

Exclusion of implied terms, etc

11L   Exclusion of implied terms etc
(1)   Where a right, duty or liability would arise under a contract for the transfer of goods or a contract for the hire of goods by implication of law, it may (subject to subsection (2) below and the 1977 Act) be negatived or varied by express agreement, or by the course of dealing between the parties, or by such usage as binds both parties to the contract.
(2)   An express term does not negative a term implied by the preceding provisions of this Part of this Act unless inconsistent with it.
(3)   Nothing in the preceding provisions of this Part of this Act prejudices the operation of any other enactment or any rule of law whereby any term (other than one relating to quality or fitness) is to be implied in a contract for the transfer of goods or a contract for the hire of goods.]

[PART IB
ADDITIONAL RIGHTS OF TRANSFEREE IN CONSUMER CASES

11M   Introductory
(1)   This section applies if—
(a)   the transferee deals as consumer or, in Scotland, there is a consumer contract in which the transferee is a consumer, and
(b)   the goods do not conform to the contract for the transfer of goods at the time of delivery.
(2)   If this section applies, the transferee has the right—
(a)   under and in accordance with section 11N below, to require the transferor to repair or replace the goods, or
(b)   under and in accordance with section 11P below—
(i)   to require the transferor to reduce the amount to be paid for the transfer by the transferee by an appropriate amount, or
(ii)   to rescind the contract with regard to the goods in question.
(3)   For the purposes of subsection (1)(b) above, goods which do not conform to the contract for the transfer of goods at any time within the period of six months starting with the date on which the goods were delivered to the transferee must be taken not to have so conformed at that date.
(4)   Subsection (3) above does not apply if—
(a)   it is established that the goods did so conform at that date;
(b)   its application is incompatible with the nature of the goods or the nature of the lack of conformity.
(5)   For the purposes of this section, 'consumer contract' has the same meaning as in section 11F(3) above.

11N   Repair or replacement of the goods
(1)   If section 11M above applies, the transferee may require the transferor—
(a)   to repair the goods, or
(b)   to replace the goods.
(2)   If the transferee requires the transferor to repair or replace the goods, the transferor must—

(a)   repair or, as the case may be, replace the goods within a reasonable time but without causing significant inconvenience to the transferee;

(b)   bear any necessary costs incurred in doing so (including in particular the cost of any labour, materials or postage).

(3)   The transferee must not require the transferor to repair or, as the case may be, replace the goods if that remedy is—

(a)   impossible,

(b)   disproportionate in comparison to the other of those remedies, or

(c)   disproportionate in comparison to an appropriate reduction in the purchase price under paragraph (a), or rescission under paragraph (b), of section 11P(1) below.

(4)   One remedy is disproportionate in comparison to the other if the one imposes costs on the transferor which, in comparison to those imposed on him by the other, are unreasonable, taking into account—

(a)   the value which the goods would have if they conformed to the contract for the transfer of goods,

(b)   the significance of the lack of conformity to the contract for the transfer of goods, and

(c)   whether the other remedy could be effected without significant inconvenience to the transferee.

(5)   Any question as to what is a reasonable time or significant inconvenience is to be determined by reference to—

(a)   the nature of the goods, and

(b)   the purpose for which the goods were acquired.

11P   Reduction of purchase price or rescission of contract

(1)   If section 11M above applies, the transferee may—

(a)   require the transferor to reduce the purchase price of the goods in question to the transferee by an appropriate amount, or

(b)   rescind the contract with regard to those goods,

if the condition in subsection (2) below is satisfied.

(2)   The condition is that—

(a)   by virtue of section 11N(3) above the transferee may require neither repair nor replacement of the goods, or

(b)   the transferee has required the transferor to repair or replace the goods, but the transferor is in breach of the requirement of section 11N(2)(a) above to do so within a reasonable time and without significant inconvenience to the transferee.

(3)   If the transferee rescinds the contract, any reimbursement to the transferee may be reduced to take account of the use he has had of the goods since they were delivered to him.

11Q   Relation to other remedies etc

(1)   If the transferee requires the transferor to repair or replace the goods the transferee must not act under subsection (2) until he has given the transferor a reasonable time in which to repair or replace (as the case may be) the goods.

(2)   The transferee acts under this subsection if—

(a)   in England and Wales or Northern Ireland he rejects the goods and terminates the contract for breach of condition;

(b)   in Scotland he rejects any goods delivered under the contract and treats it as repudiated; or

(c)   he requires the goods to be replaced or repaired (as the case may be).

11R   Powers of the court

(1)   In any proceedings in which a remedy is sought by virtue of this Part the court, in addition to any other power it has, may act under this section.

(2)   On the application of the transferee the court may make an order requiring

specific performance or, in Scotland, specific implement by the transferor of any obligation imposed on him by virtue of section 11N above.

(3)   Subsection (4) applies if—

(a)   the transferee requires the transferor to give effect to a remedy under section 11N or 11P above or has claims to rescind under section 11P, but

(b)   the court decides that another remedy under section 11N or 11P is appropriate.

(4)   The court may proceed—

(a)   as if the transferee had required the transferor to give effect to the other remedy, or if the other remedy is rescission under section 11P,

(b)   as if the transferee had claimed to rescind the contract under that section.

(5)   If the transferee has claimed to rescind the contract the court may order that any reimbursement to the transferee is reduced to take account of the use he has had of the goods since they were delivered to him.

(6)   The court may make an order under this section unconditionally or on such terms and conditions as to damages, payment of the price and otherwise as it thinks just.

11S   Conformity with the contract

(1)   Goods do not conform to a contract for the supply or transfer of goods if—

(a)   there is, in relation to the goods, a breach of an express term of the contract or a term implied by section 3, 4 or 5 above or, in Scotland, by section 11C, 11D or 11E above, or

(b)   installation of the goods forms part of the contract for the transfer of goods, and the goods were installed by the transferor, or under his responsibility, in breach of the term implied by section 13 below or (in Scotland) in breach of any term implied by any rule of law as to the manner in which the installation is carried out.]

<h1 style="text-align:center">ADMINISTRATION OF JUSTICE ACT 1982
(1982, c 53)</h1>

8   Services rendered to injured person

(1)   Where necessary services have been rendered to the injured person by a relative in consequence of the injuries in question, then, unless the relative has expressly agreed in the knowledge that an action for damages has been raised or is in contemplation that no payment should be made in respect of those services, the responsible person shall be liable to pay to the injured person by way of damages such sum as represents reasonable remuneration for those services and repayment of reasonable expenses incurred in connection therewith.

[(2)   The injured person shall be under an obligation to account to the relative for any damages recovered from the responsible person under subsection (1) above.

(3)   Where, at the date of an award of damages in favour of the injured person, it is likely that necessary services will, after that date, be rendered to him by a relative in consequence of the injuries in question, then, unless the relative has expressly agreed that no payment shall be made in respect of those services, the responsible person shall be liable to pay to the injured person by way of damages such sum as represents—

(a)   reasonable remuneration for those services; and

(b)   reasonable expenses which are likely to be incurred in connection therewith.

(4)   The relative shall have no direct right of action in delict against the responsible person in respect of any services or expenses referred to in this section.]

9   Services to injured person's relative

(1)   The responsible person shall be liable to pay to the injured person a

reasonable sum by way of damages in respect of the inability of the injured person
to render the personal services referred to in subsection (3) below.

[(1A)   In assessing the amount of damages payable by virtue of subsection (1)
above to an injured person whose date of death is expected to be earlier than had
the injuries not been sustained, the court is to assume that the person will live
until the date when death would have been expected had the injuries not been
sustained.]

[. . .]

(3)   The personal services referred to in [subsection 1] above are personal
services—

(a)   which were or might have been expected to have been rendered by the
injured person before the occurrence of the act or omission giving rise to
liability,

(b)   of a kind which, when rendered by a person other than a relative, would
ordinarily be obtainable on payment, and

(c)   which the injured person but for the injuries in question might have been
expected to render gratuitously to a relative.

(4)   Subject to [section 6(1) of the Damages (Scotland) Act 2011 (asp 7) (relative's loss of personal services)], the relative shall have no direct right of action in
delict against the responsible person in respect of the personal services mentioned
in subsection (3) above.

10   Assessment of damages for personal injuries

Subject to any agreement to the contrary, in assessing the amount of damages payable to the injured person in respect of personal injuries there shall not be taken
into account so as to reduce that amount—

(a)   any contractual pension or benefit (including any payment by a friendly
society or trade union);

(b)   any pension or retirement benefit payable from public funds other than any
pension or benefit to which section 2(1) of the Law Reform (Personal Injuries) Act
1948 applies;

(c)   any benefit payable from public funds, in respect of any period after the
date of the award of damages, designed to secure to the injured person or any
relative of his a minimum level of subsistence;

(d)   any redundancy payment under the [Employment Rights Act 1996], or
any payment made in circumstances corresponding to those in which a right
to a redundancy payment would have accrued if section 135 of that Act had
applied;

(e)   any payment made to the injured person or to any relative of his by the
injured person's employer following upon the injuries in question where the recipient is under an obligation to reimburse the employer in the event of damages
being recovered in respect of those injuries;

(f)   subject to paragraph (iv) below, any payment of a benevolent character
made to the injured person or to any relative of his by any person following upon
the injuries in question;

but there shall be taken into account—

(i)   any remuneration or earnings from employment;

(ii)   any [contribution-based jobseeker's allowance (payable under the
Jobseekers Act 1995)];

(iii)   any benefit referred to in paragraph (c) above payable in respect of any
period prior to the date of the award of damages;

(iv)   any payment of a benevolent character made to the injured person or to
any relative of his by the responsible person following on the injuries in
question, where such a payment is made directly and not through a trust or
other fund from which the injured person or his relatives have benefited or may
benefit.

11   Maintenance at public expense to be taken into account in assessment of damages: Scotland

In an action for damages for personal injuries (including any such action arising out of a contract) any saving to the injured person which is attributable to his maintenance wholly or partly at public expense in—

(a)   a hospital [. . .] or other institution

[(b)   accommodation provided by a care home service (as defined by section 2(3) of the Regulation of Care (Scotland) Act 2001 (asp 8)).]

shall be set off against any income lost by him as a result of the injuries.

12   Award of provisional damages for personal injuries: Scotland

(1)   This section applies to an action for damages for personal injuries in which—

(a)   there is proved or admitted to be a risk that at some definite or indefinite time in the future the injured person will, as a result of the act or omission which gave rise to the cause of the action, develop some serious disease or suffer some serious deterioration in his physical or mental condition; and

(b)   the responsible person was, at the time of the act or omission giving rise to the cause of the action,

(i)   a public authority or public corporation; or

(ii)   insured or otherwise indemnified in respect of the claim.

(2)   In any case to which this section applies, the court may, on the application of the injured person, order—

(a)   that the damages referred to in subsection (4)(a) below be awarded to the injured person; and

(b)   that the injured person may apply for the further award of damages referred to in subsection (4)(b) below,

and the court may, if it considers it appropriate, order that an application under paragraph (b) above may be made only within a specified period.

(3)   Where an injured person in respect of whom an award has been made under subsection (2)(a) above applies to the court for an award under subsection (2)(b) above, the court may award to the injured person the further damages referred to in subsection (4)(b) below.

(4)   The damages referred to in subsections (2) and (3) above are—

(a)   damages assessed on the assumption that the injured person will not develop the disease or suffer the deterioration in his condition; and

(b)   further damages if he develops the disease or suffers the deterioration.

(5)   Nothing in this section shall be construed—

(a)   as affecting the exercise of any power relating to expenses including a power to make rules of court relating to expenses; or

(b)   as prejudicing any duty of the court under any enactment or rule of law to reduce or limit the total damages which would have been recoverable apart from any such duty.

(6)   The Secretary of State may, by order, provide that categories of defenders shall, for the purposes of paragraph (b) of subsection (1) above, become or cease to be responsible persons, and may make such modifications of that paragraph as appear to him to be necessary for the purpose.

And an order under this subsection shall be made by statutory instrument subject to annulment in pursuance of a resolution of either House of Parliament.

13   Supplementary

(1)   In this Part of this Act, unless the context otherwise requires—

['personal injuries' means—

(a)   any disease, and

(b)   any impairment of a person's physical or mental condition;]

'relative', in relation to the injured person, means—

(a)   the spouse or divorced spouse;

[(aa) the civil partner or former civil partner,]

(b) any person, not being the spouse of the injured person, who was, at the time of the act or omission giving rise to liability in the responsible person, living with the injured person as husband or wife;

(c) any ascendant or descendant;

(d) any brother, sister, uncle or aunt; or any issue of any such person;

(e) any person accepted by the injured person as a child of his family.

In deducing any relationship for the purposes of the foregoing definition—

(a) any relationship by affinity shall be treated as a relationship by consanguinity; any relationship of the half blood shall be treated as a relationship of the whole blood; and the stepchild of any person shall be treated as his child; and

(b) [section 1(1) of the Law Reform (Parent and Child) (Scotland) Act 1986 shall apply; and any reference (however expressed) in this Part of this Act to a relative shall be construed accordingly.]

[(ba) any person, not being the civil partner of the injured person, who was, at the time of the act or omission giving rise to liability in the responsible person, living with the injured person as the civil partner of the injured person.]

(2) Any reference in this Part of this Act to a payment, benefit or pension shall be construed as a reference to any such payment, benefit or pension whether in cash or in kind.

(3) This Part of this Act binds the Crown.

LAW REFORM (HUSBAND AND WIFE) (SCOTLAND) ACT 1984
(1984, c 15)

Abolition of actions of breach of promise of marriage, adherence and enticement

1 Promise of marriage not an enforceable obligation

(1) No promise of marriage or agreement between two persons to marry one another shall have effect under the law of Scotland to create any rights or obligations; and no action for breach of any such promise or agreement may be brought in any court in Scotland, whatever the law applicable to the promise or agreement.

(2) This section shall have effect in relation to any promise made or agreement entered into before it comes into force, but shall not affect any action commenced before it comes into force.

2 Actions of adherence and enticement abolished

(1) No spouse shall be entitled to apply for a decree from any court in Scotland ordaining the other spouse to adhere.

(2) No person shall be liable in delict to any person by reason only of having induced the spouse of that person to leave or remain apart from that person.

(3) This section shall not affect any action commenced before this Act comes into force.

LAW REFORM (MISCELLANEOUS PROVISIONS) (SCOTLAND) ACT 1985
(1985, c 73)

Provisions relating to leases

. . .

4 Irritancy clauses etc relating to monetary breaches of lease

(1) A landlord shall not, for the purpose of treating a lease as terminated or terminating it, be entitled to rely—

(a) on a provision in the lease which purports to terminate it, or to enable him to terminate it, in the event of a failure of the tenant to pay rent, or to make any other payment, on or before the due date therefor or such later date or within such period as may be provided for in the lease; or

(b)   on the fact that such a failure is, or is deemed by a provision of the lease to be, a material breach of contract,
unless subsection (2) or (5) below applies.

(2)   This subsection applies if—

(a)   the landlord has, at any time after the payment of rent or other payment mentioned in subsection (1) above has become due, served a notice on the tenant—

(i)   requiring the tenant to make payment of the sum which he has failed to pay together with any interest thereon in terms of the lease within the period specified in the notice; and

(ii)   stating that, if the tenant does not comply with the requirement mentioned in sub-paragraph (i) above, the lease may be terminated; and

(b)   the tenant has not complied with that requirement.

(3)   The period to be specified in any such notice shall be not less than—

(a)   a period of 14 days immediately following the service of the notice; or

(b)   if any period remaining between the service of the notice and the expiry of any time provided for in the lease or otherwise for the late payment of the sum which the tenant has failed to pay is greater than 14 days, that greater period.

(4)   Any notice served under subsection (2) above shall be sent by recorded delivery and shall be sufficiently served if it is sent to the tenant's last business or residential address in the United Kingdom known to the landlord or to the last address in the United Kingdom provided to the landlord by the tenant for the purpose of such service.

(5)   This subsection applies if the tenant does not have an address in the United Kingdom known to the landlord and has not provided an address in the United Kingdom to the landlord for the purpose of service.

5   Irritancy clauses etc not relating to monetary breaches of leases

(1)   Subject to subsection (2) below, a landlord shall not, for the purpose of treating a lease as terminated or terminating it, be entitled to rely—

(a)   on a provision in the lease which purports to terminate it, or to enable the landlord to terminate it, in the event of an act or omission by the tenant (other than such a failure as is mentioned in section 4(1)(a) of this Act) or of a change in the tenant's circumstances; or

(b)   on the fact that such act or omission or change is, or is deemed by a provision of the lease to be, a material breach of contract,
if in all the circumstances of the case a fair and reasonable landlord would not seek so to rely.

(2)   No provision of a lease shall of itself, irrespective of the particular circumstances of the case, be held to be unenforceable by virtue of subsection (1) above.

(3)   In the consideration, for the purposes of subsection (1)(a) or (b) above, of the circumstances of a case where—

(a)   an act, omission or change is alleged to constitute a breach of a provision of the lease or a breach of contract; and

(b)   the breach is capable of being remedied in reasonable time,
regard shall be had to whether a reasonable opportunity has been afforded to the tenant to enable the breach to be remedied.

6   Supplementary and transitional provisions relating to sections 4 and 5

(1)   The parties to a lease shall not be entitled to disapply any provision of section 4 or 5 of this Act from it.

(2)   Where circumstances have occurred before the commencement of sections 4 and 5 of this Act which would have entitled a landlord to terminate a lease in reliance on a provision in the lease or on the ground that the circumstances constituted a material breach of contract, but the landlord has not before such com-

mencement given written notice to the tenant of his intention to terminate the lease in respect of those circumstances, he shall, after such commencement, be entitled to terminate the lease in respect of those circumstances only in accordance with the provisions of section 4 or 5 (as the case may be) of this Act.

(3)　Nothing in section 4 or 5 of this Act shall apply in relation to any payment which has to be made, or any other condition which has to be fulfilled, before a tenant is entitled to entry under a lease.

7　Interpretation of sections 4 to 6

(1)　In sections 4 to 6 of this Act 'lease' means a lease of land, whether entered into before or after the commencement of those sections, but does not include a lease of land—

(a)　used wholly or mainly for residential purposes;

(b)　comprising [. . .] a croft, the subject of a cottar or the holding of a landholder or a statutory small tenant [; or

(c)　where the lease is an agricultural lease.]

(2)　In subsection (1) above—

['agricultural lease' means a lease constituting a 1991 Act tenancy within the meaning of the Agricultural Holdings (Scotland) Act 2003 (asp 11) or a lease constituting a short limited duration tenancy or a limited duration tenancy (within the meaning of that Act);]

'cottar' has the same meaning as in section 28(4) of the Crofters (Scotland) Act 1955;

'croft' has the same meaning as in section 3 of the Crofters (Scotland) Act 1955; and

'holding' (in relation to a landholder or statutory small tenant), 'landholder' and 'statutory small tenant' have the same meanings as in the Small Landholders (Scotland) Acts 1886 to 1931.

Provisions relating to other contracts and obligations

8　Rectification of defectively expressed documents

(1)　Subject to section 9 of this Act, where the court is satisfied, on an application made to it, that—

(a)　a document intended to express or to give effect to an agreement fails to express accurately the common intention of the parties to the agreement at the date when it was made; or

(b)　a document intended to create, transfer, vary or renounce a right, not being a document falling within paragraph (a) above, fails to express accurately the intention of the grantor of the document at the date when it was executed,

it may order the document to be rectified in any manner that it may specify in order to give effect to that intention.

(2)　For the purposes of subsection (1) above, the court shall be entitled to have regard to all relevant evidence, whether written or oral.

(3)　Subject to section 9 of this Act, in ordering the rectification of a document under subsection (1) above (in this subsection referred to as 'the original document'), the court may, at its own instance or on an application made to it, order the rectification of any other document intended for any of the purposes mentioned in paragraph (a) or (b) of subsection (1) above which is defectively expressed by reason of the defect in the original document.

(4)　Subject to section 9(4) of this Act, a document ordered to be rectified under this section shall have effect as if it had always been so rectified.

(5)　Subject to section 9(5) of this Act, where a document recorded in the Register of Sasines is ordered to be rectified under this section and the order is likewise recorded, the document shall be treated as having been always so recorded as rectified.

[(5A)   Subsection (5) above applies in relation to documents registered in the Register of Floating Charges as it applies in relation to a document recorded in the Register of Sasines (and the references to recording are to be read accordingly).]

(6)   Nothing in this section shall apply to a document of a testamentary nature.

(7)   It shall be competent to register in the Register of Inhibitions [. . .] a notice of an application under this section for the rectification of a deed relating to land, being an application in respect of which authority for service or citation has been granted; and the land to which the application relates shall be rendered litigious as from the date of registration of such a notice.

(8)   A notice under subsection (7) above shall specify the names and designations of the parties to the application and the date when authority for service or citation was granted and contain a description of the land to which the application relates.

(9)   In this section and section 9 of this Act 'the court' means the Court of Session or the sheriff court.

9   Provisions supplementary to section 8: protection of other interest

(1)   The court shall order a document to be rectified under section 8 of this Act only where it is satisfied—

(a)   that the interests of a person to whom this section applies would not be adversely affected to a material extent by the rectification; or

(b)   that that person has consented to the proposed rectification.

(2)   Subject to subsection (3) below, this section applies to a person (other than a party to the agreement or the grantor of the document) who has acted or refrained from acting in reliance on the terms of the document or on the title sheet of an interest in land registered in the Land Register of Scotland being an interest to which the document relates, with the result that his position has been affected to a material extent.

(3)   This section does not apply to a person—

(a)   who, at the time when he acted or refrained from acting as mentioned in subsection (2) above, knew, or ought in the circumstances known to him at that time to have been aware, that the document or (as the case may be) the title sheet failed accurately to express the common intention of the parties to the agreement or, as the case may be, the intention of the grantor of the document; or

(b)   whose reliance on the terms of the document or on the title sheet was otherwise unreasonable.

(4)   Notwithstanding subsection (4) of section 8 of this Act and without prejudice to subsection (5) below, the court may, for the purpose of protecting the interests of a person to whom this section applies, order that the rectification of a document shall have effect as at such date as it may specify, being a date later than that as at which it would have effect by virtue of the said subsection (4).

(5)   Notwithstanding subsection (5) of section 8 of this Act and without prejudice to subsection (4) above, the court may, for the purpose of protecting the interests of a person to whom this section applies, order that a document as rectified shall be treated as having been recorded as mentioned in the said subsection (5) at such date as it may specify, being a date later than that as at which it would be treated by virtue of that subsection as having been so recorded.

(6)   For the purposes of subsection (1) above, the court may require the Keeper of the Registers of Scotland to produce such information as he has in his possession relating to any persons who have asked him to supply details with regard to a title sheet mentioned in subsection (2) above; and any expense incurred by the Keeper under this subsection shall be borne by the applicant for the order.

(7)   Where a person to whom this section applies was unaware, before a document was ordered to be rectified under section 8 of this Act, that an application had been made under that section for the rectification of the document, the Court

of Session, on an application made by that person within the time specified in sub-section (8) below, may—

(a)   reduce the rectifying order; or

(b)   order the applicant for the rectifying order to pay such compensation to that person as it thinks fit in respect of his reliance on the terms of the document or on the title sheet.

(8)   The time referred to in subsection (7) above is whichever is the earlier of the following—

(a)   the expiry of 5 years after the making of the rectifying order;

(b)   the expiry of 2 years after the making of that order first came to the notice of the person referred to in that subsection.

10   Negligent misrepresentation

(1)   A party to a contract who has been induced to enter into it by negligent misrepresentation made by or on behalf of another party to the contract shall not be disentitled, by reason only that the misrepresentation is not fraudulent, from recovering damages from the other party in respect of any loss or damage he has suffered as a result of the misrepresentation; and any rule of law that such damages cannot be recovered unless fraud is proved shall cease to have effect.

(2)   Subsection (1) applies to any proceedings commenced on or after the date on which it comes into force, whether or not the negligent misrepresentation was made before or after that date, but does not apply to any proceedings commenced before that date.

ANIMALS (SCOTLAND) ACT 1987
(1987, c 9)

1   New provisions as to strict liability for injury or damage caused by animals

(1)   Subject to subsection (4) and (5) below and section 2 of this Act, a person shall be liable for any injury or damage caused by an animal if—

(a)   at the time of the injury or damage complained of, he was a keeper of the animal;

(b)   the animal belongs to a species whose members generally are by virtue of their physical attributes or habits likely (unless controlled or restrained) to injure severely or kill persons or animals, or damage property to a material extent; and

(c)   the injury or damage complained of is directly referable to such physical attributes or habits.

(2)   In this section 'species' includes—

(a)   a form or variety of the species or a sub-division of the species, or the form or variety, identifiable by age, sex or such other criteria as are relevant to the behaviour of animals; and

(b)   a kind which is the product of hybridisation.

(3)   For the purposes of subsection (1)(b) above—

(a)   dogs, and dangerous wild animals within the meaning of section 7(4) of the Dangerous Wild Animals Act 1976, shall be deemed to be likely (unless con-trolled or restrained) to injure severely or kill persons or animals by biting or otherwise savaging, attacking or harrying; and

(b)   any of the following animals in the course of foraging, namely—

cattle, horses, asses, mules, hinnies, sheep, pigs, goats and deer,

shall be deemed to be likely (unless controlled or restrained) to damage to a material extent land or the produce of land, whether harvested or not.

(4)   Subsection (1) above shall not apply to any injury caused by an animal where the injury consists of disease transmitted by means which are unlikely to cause severe injury other than disease.

(5)   Subsection (1) above shall not apply to injury or damage caused by the mere fact that an animal is present on a road or in any other place.

(6)   For the purposes of the Law Reform (Contributory Negligence) Act 1945, any injury or damage for which a person is liable under this section shall be treated as due to his fault as defined in that Act.

(7)   Subsections (1) and (2) of section 3 of the Law Reform (Miscellaneous Provisions) (Scotland) Act 1940 (contribution among joint wrongdoers) shall, subject to any necessary modifications, apply in relation to an action of damages in respect of injury or damage which is brought in pursuance of this section as they apply in relation to an action of damages in respect of loss or damage arising from any wrongful acts or omissions; but nothing in this subsection shall affect any contractual, or (except as aforesaid) any other, right of relief or indemnity.

(8)   The foregoing provisions of this section and section 2 of this Act replace—
(a)   any rule of law which imposes liability, without proof of a negligent act or omission, on the owner or possessor of an animal for injury or damage caused by that animal on the ground that the animal is *ferae naturae* or is otherwise known to be dangerous or harmful;
(b)   the Winter Herding Act 1686;
(c)   section 1(1) and (2) of the Dogs Act 1906 (injury to cattle or poultry).

2   Exceptions from liability under section 1

(1)   A person shall not be liable under section 1(1) of this Act if—
(a)   the injury or damage was due wholly to the fault of—
(i)   the person sustaining it; or
(ii)   in the case of injury sustained by an animal, a keeper of the animal;
(b)   the person sustaining the injury or damage or a keeper of the animal sustaining the injury willingly accepted the risk of it as his; or
(c)   subject to subsection (2) below, the injury or damage was sustained on, or in consequence of the person or animal sustaining the injury or damage coming on to, land which was occupied by a person who was a keeper, or by another person who authorised the presence on the land, of the animal which caused the injury or damage; and, either—
(i)   the person sustaining the injury or damage was not authorised or entitled to be on that land; or (as the case may be)
(ii)   no keeper of the animal sustaining the injury was authorised or entitled to have the animal present on that land.

(2)   A person shall not be exempt from liability by virtue of subsection (1)(c) above if the animal causing the injury or damage was kept on the land wholly or partly for the purpose of protecting persons or property, unless the keeping of the animal there, and the use made of the animal, for that purpose was reasonable, and, if the animal was a guard dog within the meaning of the Guard Dogs Act 1975, unless there was compliance with section 1 of that Act.

(3)   In subsection (1) above—
(a)   in paragraph (a) 'fault' has the same meaning as in the Law Reform (Contributory Negligence) Act 1945;
(b)   in paragraph (c) 'authorised' means expressly or impliedly authorised.

3   Detention of straying animals

(1)   Without prejudice to section 98 of the Roads (Scotland) Act 1984, where an animal strays on to any land and is not then under the control of any person, the occupier of the land may detain the animal for the purpose of preventing injury or damage by it.

(2)   Part VI of the Civic Government (Scotland) Act 1982 (lost and abandoned property) shall apply in relation to an animal, other than a stray dog, detained under subsection (1) above as it applies in relation to any property taken possession of under section 67 of that Act subject to the omission from section 74 of the words from 'or livestock' to '129 of this Act' and to any other necessary

modifications; and section 4 of the Dogs Act 1906 shall, subject to any necessary modifications, apply to a stray dog detained under subsection (1) above as it applies to a stray dog taken possession of under that section.

4 Killing of, or injury to, animals attacking or harrying persons or livestock

(1) Subject to subsection (2) below, in any civil proceedings against a person for killing or causing injury to an animal, it shall be a defence for him to prove—

    (a) that he acted—

        (i) in self-defence;

        (ii) for the protection of any other person; or

        (iii) for the protection of any livestock and was one of the persons mentioned in subsection (3) below; and

    (b) that within 48 hours after the killing or injury notice thereof was given by him or on his behalf at a police station or to a constable.

(2) There shall be no defence available under subsection (1) above to a person killing or causing injury to an animal where the killing or injury—

    (a) occurred at or near a place where the person was present for the purpose of engaging in a criminal activity; and

    (b) was in furtherance of that activity.

(3) The persons referred to in subsection (1)(a)(iii) above are—

    (a) a person who, at the time of the injury or killing complained of, was a keeper of the livestock concerned;

    (b) the owner or occupier of the land where the livestock was present; and

    (c) a person authorised (either expressly or impliedly) to act for the protection of the livestock by such a keeper of the livestock or by the owner or occupier of the land where the livestock was present.

(4) A person killing or causing injury to an animal ('the defender') shall be regarded, for the purposes of this section, as acting in self defence or for the protection of another person or any livestock if, and only if—

    (a) the animal is attacking him or that other person or that livestock and (whether or not the animal is under the control of anyone) the defender has reasonable grounds for believing that there are no other practicable means of ending the attack; or

    (b) the defender has reasonable grounds for believing—

        (i) that the animal is about to attack him, such person or livestock and that (whether or not the animal is under the control of anyone) there are no other practicable means of preventing the attack; or

        (ii) that the animal has been attacking a person or livestock, is not under the control of anyone and has not left the vicinity where the attack took place, and that there are no other practicable means of preventing a further attack by the animal while it is still in that vicinity.

(5) In subsection (4) above 'attack' or 'attacking' includes 'harry' or 'harrying'.

(6) In this section—

'livestock' means any animal of a domestic variety (including in particular sheep, cattle and horses) and, while they are in captivity, any other animals.

5 Meaning of a keeper of an animal

(1) Subject to subsection (2) below, for the purposes of this Act a person is a keeper of an animal if—

    (a) he owns the animal or has possession of it; or

    (b) he has actual care and control of a child under the age of 16 who owns the animal or has possession of it.

(2) For the purposes of this section—

    (a) a person shall not be regarded as having possession of an animal by reason only that he is detaining it under section 3 of this Act or is otherwise temporarily detaining it for the purpose of protecting it or any person or other animal or of restoring it as soon as is reasonably practicable to its owner or a possessor of it;

(b)   if an animal has been abandoned or has escaped, a person who at the time of the abandonment or escape was the owner of it or had it in his possession shall remain its owner or shall be regarded as continuing to have possession of it until another person acquires its ownership or (as the case may be) comes into possession of it; and

(c)   the Crown shall not acquire ownership of an animal on its abandonment.

6   Application to Crown
This Act binds the Crown, but this section shall not authorise proceedings to be brought against Her Majesty in her private capacity.

7   Interpretation
In this Act, unless the context otherwise requires—
   'animal' does not include viruses, bacteria, algae, fungi or protozoa;
   'harry' includes chase in such a way as may be likely to cause injury or suffering; and 'harrying' shall be construed accordingly;
   'injury' includes death, any abortion or other impairment of physical or mental condition and any loss of or diminution in the produce of an animal and, subject to section 1(4) of this Act, disease.

8   Transitional provision and repeals
(1)   This Act shall apply only in relation to injury or damage caused after the commencement of the Act.

(2)   The enactments mentioned in the Schedule to this Act are hereby repealed to the extent specified in the third column of that Schedule.

9   Short title, commencement and extent
(1)   This Act may be cited as the Animals (Scotland) Act 1987.

(2)   This Act shall come into force at the end of a period of 2 months beginning with the date on which it is passed.

(3)   This Act extends to Scotland only.

CONSUMER PROTECTION ACT 1987
(1987, c 43)

PART I
PRODUCT LIABILITY

1   Purpose and construction of Part I
(1)   This Part shall have effect for the purpose of making such provision as is necessary in order to comply with the product liability Directive and shall be construed accordingly.

(2)   In this Part, except in so far as the context otherwise requires—
[. . .]
   'dependant' and 'relative' have the same meaning as they have in, respectively, the Fatal Accidents Act 1976 and the [Damages (Scotland) Act 2011];
   'producer', in relation to a product, means—
      (a)   the person who manufactured it;
      (b)   in the case of a substance which has not been manufactured but has been won or abstracted, the person who won or abstracted it;
      (c)   in the case of a product which has not been manufactured, won or abstracted but essential characteristics of which are attributable to an industrial or other process having been carried out (for example, in relation to agricultural produce), the person who carried out that process;
   'product' means any goods or electricity and (subject to subsection (3) below)

includes a product which is comprised in another product, whether by virtue of being a component part or raw material or otherwise; and

'the product liability Directive' means the Directive of the Council of the European Communities, dated 25th July 1985, (No 85/374/EEC) on the approximation of the laws, regulations and administrative provisions of the member States concerning liability for defective products.

(3)   For the purposes of this Part a person who supplies any product in which products are comprised, whether by virtue of being component parts or raw materials or otherwise, shall not be treated by reason only of his supply of that product as supplying any of the products so comprised.

2   Liability for defective products

(1)   Subject to the following provisions of this Part, where any damage is caused wholly or partly by a defect in a product, every person to whom subsection (2) below applies shall be liable for the damage.

(2)   This subsection applies to—

(a)   the producer of the product;

(b)   any person who, by putting his name on the product or using a trade mark or other distinguishing mark in relation to the product, has held himself out to be the producer of the product;

(c)   any person who has imported the product into a member State from a place outside the member States in order, in the course of any business of his, to supply it to another.

(3)   Subject as aforesaid, where any damage is caused wholly or partly by a defect in a product, any person who supplied the product (whether to the person who suffered the damage, to the producer of any product in which the product in question is comprised or to any other person) shall be liable for the damage if—

(a)   the person who suffered the damage requests the supplier to identify one or more of the persons (whether still in existence or not) to whom subsection (2) above applies in relation to the product;

(b)   that request is made within a reasonable period after the damage occurs and at a time when it is not reasonably practicable for the person making the request to identify all those persons; and

(c)   the supplier fails, within a reasonable period after receiving the request, either to comply with the request or to identify the person who supplied the product to him.

[. . .]

(5)   Where two or more persons are liable by virtue of this Part for the same damage, their liability shall be joint and several.

(6)   This section shall be without prejudice to any liability arising otherwise than by virtue of this Part.

3   Meaning of 'defect'

(1)   Subject to the following provisions of the section, there is a defect in a product for the purposes of this Part if the safety of the product is not such as persons generally are entitled to expect; and for those purposes 'safety', in relation to a product, shall include safety with respect to products comprised in that product and safety in the context of risks of damage to property, as well as in the context of risks of death or personal injury.

(2)   In determining for the purposes of subsection (1) above what persons generally are entitled to expect in relation to a product all the circumstances shall be taken into account, including—

(a)   the manner in which, and purposes for which, the product has been marketed, its get-up, the use of any mark in relation to the product and any instructions for, or warnings with respect to, doing or refraining from doing anything with or in relation to the product;

(b)   what might reasonably be expected to be done with or in relation to the product; and

(c)   the time when the product was supplied by its producer to another;

and nothing in this section shall require a defect to be inferred from the fact alone that the safety of a product which is supplied after that time is greater than the safety of the product in question.

4 Defences

(1)   In any civil proceedings by virtue of this Part against any person ('the person proceeded against') in respect of a defect in a product it shall be a defence for him to show—

(a)   that the defect is attributable to compliance with any requirement imposed by or under any enactment or with any Community obligation; or

(b)   that the person proceeded against did not at any time supply the product to another; or

(c)   that the following conditions are satisfied, that is to say—

(i)   that the only supply of the product to another by the person proceeded against was otherwise than in the course of a business of that person's; and

(ii)   that section 2(2) above does not apply to that person or applies to him by virtue only of things done otherwise than with a view to profit; or

(d)   that the defect did not exist in the product at the relevant time; or

(e)   that the state of scientific and technical knowledge at the relevant time was not such that a producer of products of the same description as the product in question might be expected to have discovered the defect if it had existed in his products while they were under his control; or

(f)   that the defect—

(i)   constituted a defect in a product ('the subsequent product') in which the product in question had been comprised; and

(ii)   was wholly attributable to the design of the subsequent product or to compliance by the producer of the product in question with instructions given by the producer of the subsequent product.

(2)   In this section 'the relevant time', in relation to electricity, means the time at which it was generated, being a time before it was transmitted or distributed, and in relation to any other product, means—

(a)   if the person proceeded against is a person to whom subsection (2) of section 2 above applies in relation to the product, the time when he supplied the product to another;

(b)   if that subsection does not apply to that person in relation to the product, the time when the product was last supplied by a person to whom that subsection does apply in relation to the product.

5 Damage giving rise to liability

(1)   Subject to the following provisions of this section, in this Part 'damages' means death or personal injury or any loss of or damage to any property (including land).

(2)   A person shall not be liable under section 2 above in respect of any defect in a product for the loss of or any damage to the product itself or for the loss of or any damage to the whole or any part of any product which has been supplied with the product in question comprised in it.

(3)   A person shall not be liable under section 2 above for any loss of or damage to any property which, at the time it is lost or damaged, is not—

(a)   of a description of property ordinarily intended for private use, occupation or consumption; and

(b)   intended by the person suffering the loss or damage mainly for his own private use, occupation or consumption.

(4)   No damages shall be awarded to any person by virtue of this Part in

respect of any loss of or damage to any property if the amount which would fall to be so awarded to that person, apart from this subsection and any liability for interest, does not exceed £275.

. . .

(8)   Subsections (5) to (7) above shall not extend to Scotland.

6   Application of certain enactments etc

(1)   Any damage for which a person is liable under section 2 above shall be deemed to have been caused—

(a)   for the purposes of the Fatal Accidents Act 1976, by that person's wrongful act, neglect or default;

(b)   for the purposes of section 3 of the Law Reform (Miscellaneous Provisions) (Scotland) Act 1940 (contribution among joint wrongdoers), by that person's wrongful act or negligent act or omission;

(c)   for the purposes of [sections 3 to 6 of the Damages (Scotland) Act 2011] (rights of relatives of a deceased), by that person's act or omission, and

(d)   for the purposes of Part II of the Administration of Justice Act 1982 (damages for personal injuries, etc—Scotland), by an act or omission giving rise to liability in that person to pay damages.

(2)   Where—

(a)   a person's death is caused wholly or partly by a defect in a product, or a person dies after suffering damage which has been so caused;

(b)   a request such as mentioned in paragraph (a) of subsection (3) of section 2 above is made to a supplier of the product by that person's personal representatives or, in the case of a person whose death is caused wholly or partly by the defect, by any dependant or relative of that person; and

(c)   the conditions specified in paragraphs (b) and (c) of that subsection are satisfied in relation to that request,

this Part shall have effect for the purposes of the Law Reform (Miscellaneous Provisions) Act 1934, the Fatal Accidents Acts 1976 and the [Damages (Scotland) Act 2011] as if liability of the supplier to that person under that subsection did not depend on that person having requested the supplier to identify certain persons or on the said conditions having been satisfied in relation to a request made by that person.

(3)   Section 1 of the Congenital Disabilities (Civil Liability) Act 1976 shall have effect for the purposes of this Part as if—

(a)   a person were answerable to a child in respect of an occurrence caused wholly or partly by a defect in a product if he is or has been liable under section 2 above in respect of any effect of the occurrence on a parent of the child, or would be so liable if the occurrence caused a parent of the child to suffer damage;

(b)   the provisions of this Part relating to liability under section 2 above applied in relation to liability by virtue of paragraph (a) above under the said section 1; and

(c)   subsection (6) of the said section 1 (exclusion of liability) were omitted.

(4)   Where any damage is caused partly by a defect in a product and partly by the fault of the person suffering the damage, the Law Reform (Contributory Negligence) Act 1945 and section 5 of the Fatal Accidents Act 1976 (contributory negligence) shall have effect as if the defect were the fault of every person liable by virtue of this Part for the damage caused by the defect.

(5)   In subsection (4) above 'fault' has the same meaning as in the said Act of 1945.

(6)   Schedule 1 to this Act shall have effect for the purpose of amending the Limitation Act 1980 and the Prescription and Limitation (Scotland) Act 1973 in their application in relation to the bringing of actions by virtue of this Part.

(7)   It is hereby declared that liability by virtue of this Part is to be treated as

liability in tort for the purposes of any enactment conferring jurisdiction on any court with respect to any matter.

(8)   Nothing in this Part shall prejudice the operation of section 12 of the Nuclear Installations Act 1965 (rights to compensation for certain breaches of duties confined to rights under that Act).

7   Prohibition on exclusions from liability

The liability of a person by virtue of this Part to person who has suffered damage caused wholly or partly by a defect in a product, or to a dependant or relative of such a person, shall not be limited or excluded by any contract term, by any notice or by any other provision.

8   Power to modify Part I

(1)   Her Majesty may by Order in Council make such modifications of this Part and of any other enactment (including an enactment contained in the following Parts of this Act, or in an Act passed after this Act) as appear to Her Majesty in Council to be necessary or expedient in consequence of any modification of the product liability Directive which is made at any time after the passing of this Act.

(2)   An Order in Council under subsection (1) above shall not be submitted to Her Majesty in Council unless a draft of the Order has been laid before, and approved by a resolution of, each House of Parliament.

9   Application of Part I to Crown

(1)   Subject to subsection (2) below, this Part shall bind the Crown.

(2)   The Crown shall not, as regards the Crown's liability by virtue of this Part, be bound by this Part further than the Crown is made liable in tort or in reparation under the Crown Proceedings Act 1947, as that Act has effect from time to time.

45   Interpretation

(1)   In this Act, except in so far as the context otherwise requires—

'aircraft' includes gliders, balloons and hovercraft;

'business' includes a trade or profession and the activities of a professional or trade association or of a local authority or other public authority;

'conditional sale agreement', 'credit-sale agreement' and 'hire-purchase agreement' have the same meanings as in the Consumer Credit Act 1974 but as if in the definitions in that Act 'goods' had the same meaning as in this Act;

'contravention' includes a failure to comply and cognate expressions shall be construed accordingly;

'enforcement authority' means the Secretary of State, any other Minister of the Crown in charge of a Government department, any such department and any authority, council or other person on whom functions under this Act are conferred by or under section 27 above;

'gas' has the same meaning as in Part I of the Gas Act 1986;

'goods' includes substances, growing crops and things comprised in land by virtue of being attached to it and any ship, aircraft or vehicle;

'information' includes accounts, estimates and returns;

'magistrates' court', in relation to Northern Ireland, means a court of summary jurisdiction;

'modifications' includes additions, alterations and omissions, and cognate expressions shall be construed accordingly;

'motor vehicle' has the same meaning as in the Road Traffic Act [1988];

'notice' means a notice in writing;

'notice to warn' means a notice under section 13(1)(b) above;

'officer', in relation to an enforcement authority, means a person authorised in writing to assist the authority in carrying out its functions under or for the purposes of the enforcement of any of the safety provisions or of any of the provisions made by or under Part III of this Act;

'personal injury' includes any disease and any other impairment of a person's physical or mental condition;

'premises' includes any place and any ship, aircraft or vehicle;

'prohibition notice' means a notice under section 13(1)(a) above;

'records' includes any books or documents and any records in non-documentary form;

'safety provision' means [. . .] any provision of safety regulations, a prohibition notice or a suspension notice;

'safety regulations' means regulations under section 11 above;

'ship' includes any boat and any other description of vessel used in navigation;

'subordinate legislation' has the same meaning as in the Interpretation Act 1978;

'substance' means any natural or artificial substance, whether in solid, liquid or gaseous form or in the form of a vapour, and includes substances that are comprised in or mixed with other goods;

'supply' and cognate expressions shall be construed in accordance with section 46 below;

'suspension notice' means a notice under section 14 above.

(2)   Except in so far as the context otherwise requires, references in this Act to a contravention of a safety provision shall, in relation to any goods, include references to anything which would constitute such a contravention if the goods were supplied to any person.

(3)   References in this Act to any goods in relation to which any safety provision has been or may have been contravened shall include references to any goods which it is not reasonably practicable to separate from any such goods.

[. . .]

(5)   In Scotland, any reference in this Act to things comprised in land by virtue of being attached to it is a reference to moveables which have become heritable by accession to heritable property.

COURT OF SESSION ACT 1988
(1988, c 36)

46   Specific relief may be granted in interdict proceedings
Where a respondent in any application or proceedings in the Court, whether before or after the institution of such proceedings or application, has done any act which the Court might have prohibited by interdict, the Court may ordain the respondent to perform any act which may be necessary for reinstating the petitioner in his possessory right, or for granting specific relief against the illegal act complained of.

47   Interim interdict and other interim orders
(1)   In any cause containing a conclusion or a crave for interdict or liberation, the Division of the Inner House or the Lord Ordinary (as the case may be) may, on the motion of any party to the cause, grant interim interdict or liberation; and it shall be competent for the Division of the Inner House or the Lord Ordinary before whom any cause in which interim interdict has been granted is pending to deal with any breach of the interim interdict without the presentation of a petition and complaint.

(2)   In any cause in dependence before the Court, the Court may, on the motion of any party to the cause, make such order regarding the interim possession of any property to which the cause relates, or regarding the subject matter of the cause, as the Court may think fit.

(3)   Every interim act, warrant and decree granted during the dependence of a cause in the Court shall, unless the Court otherwise directs, be extractible *ad interim*.

ENVIRONMENTAL PROTECTION ACT 1990
(1990, c 43)

79 Statutory nuisances and inspections therefor

(1) [Subject to subsections [(1ZA)] to (6A) below], the following matters constitute 'statutory nuisances' for the purposes of this Part, that is to say—

  (a)   any premises in such a state as to be prejudicial to health or a nuisance;

  (b)   smoke emitted from premises so as to be prejudicial to health or a nuisance;

  (c)   fumes or gases emitted from premises so as to be prejudicial to health or a nuisance;

  (d)   any dust, steam, smell or other effluvia arising on industrial, trade or business premises and being prejudicial to health or a nuisance;

  (e)   any accumulation or deposit which is prejudicial to health or a nuisance;

  [(ea)   any water covering land or land covered with water which is in such a state as to be prejudicial to health or a nuisance;]

  (f)   any animal kept in such a place or manner as to be prejudicial to health or a nuisance;

  [(faa)   any insects emanating from premises and being prejudicial to health or a nuisance;]

  [(fba)   artificial light emitted from—

      (i)   premises;

      (ii)   any stationary object,

so as to be prejudicial to health or a nuisance;]

  (g)   noise emitted from premises so as to be prejudicial to health or a nuisance;

  [(ga)   noise that is prejudicial to health or a nuisance and is emitted from or caused by a vehicle, machinery or equipment in a street [or in Scotland, road];]

  (h)   any other matter declared by any enactment to be a statutory nuisance;

and it shall be the duty of every local authority to cause its area to be inspected from time to time to detect any statutory nuisances which ought to be dealt with under section 80 below [or sections 80 and 80A below] and, where a complaint of a statutory nuisance is made to it by a person living within its area, to take such steps as are reasonably practicable to investigate the complaint.

  [(1ZA)   The Scottish Ministers may by regulations—

  (a)   amend this section so as to—

      (i)   prescribe additional matters which constitute statutory nuisances for the purposes of this Part;

      (ii)   vary the description of any matter which constitutes a statutory nuisance;

  (b)   in relation to an amendment under paragraph (a), amend this Act and any other enactment to make such incidental, supplementary, consequential, transitory, transitional or saving provision as the Scottish Ministers consider appropriate.]

  [(1ZB)   Before making regulations under subsection (1ZA) above, the Scottish Ministers must consult, in so far as it is reasonably practicable to do so, the persons mentioned in subsection (1ZC) below.]

  [(1ZC)   Those persons are—

  (a)   such associations of local authorities; and

  (b)   such other persons,

as the Scottish Ministers consider appropriate.]

  [(1A)   No matter shall constitute a statutory nuisance to the extent that it consists of, or is caused by, any land being in a contaminated state.]

  [(1B)   Land is in a 'contaminated state' for the purposes of subsection (1A) above if, and only if, it is in such a condition, by reason of substances in, on or under the land, that—

(a)   significant harm is being caused or there is a significant possibility of such harm being caused; or

(b)   significant pollution of the water environment is being caused or there is a significant possibility of such pollution being caused;

and in this subsection 'harm', 'pollution' in relation to the water environment, 'substance' and 'the water environment' have the same meanings as in Part IIA of this Act.]

(2)   Subsection (1)(b) [, (fba)] and (g) above do not apply in relation to premises [(or, in respect of paragraph (fba)(ii) above, a stationary object located on premises)]—

(a)   occupied on behalf of the Crown for naval, military or air force purposes or for the purposes of the department of the Secretary of State having responsibility for defence, or

(b)   occupied by or for the purposes of a visiting force;

and 'visiting force' means any such body, contingent or detachment of the forces of any country as is a visiting force for the purposes of any of the provisions of the Visiting Forces Act 1952.

(3)   Subsection (1)(b) above does not apply to—

(i)   smoke emitted from a chimney of a private dwelling within a smoke control area,

(ii)   dark smoke emitted from a chimney of a building or a chimney serving the furnace of a boiler or industrial plant attached to a building or for the time being fixed to or installed on any land,

(iii)   smoke emitted from a railway locomotive steam engine, or

(iv)   dark smoke emitted otherwise than as mentioned above from industrial or trade premises.

(4)   Subsection (1)(c) above does not apply in relation to premises other than private dwellings.

(5)   Subsection (1)(d) above does not apply to steam emitted from a railway locomotive engine.

[(5ZA)   For the purposes of subsection (1)(ea) above, 'land'—

(a)   includes structures (other than buildings) in, on or over land;

(b)   does not include—

(i)   mains or other pipes used for carrying a water supply;

(ii)   any part of the public sewerage system;

(iii)   any other sewers, drains or other pipes used for carrying sewage;

(iv)   the foreshore, that is to say, the land between the high and low water marks of ordinary spring tides;

(v)   the seabed.

[(5ZB)   In subsection (5ZA) above—

'drain', 'sewage' and 'sewer' have the meanings given by section 59 of the Sewerage (Scotland) Act 1968;

'main' has the meaning given by section 109(1) of the Water (Scotland) Act 1980;

'pipe' includes a service pipe within the meaning of that section of that Act;

'public sewerage system' has the meaning given by section 29 of the Water Services etc (Scotland) Act 2005.]

[(5AA)   Subsection (1)(faa) above does not apply to insects that are wild animals included in Schedule 5 to the Wildlife and Countryside Act 1981.]

[(5AB)   For the purposes of subsection (1)(faa) above, 'premises' does not include—

(a)   a site of special scientific interest (within the meaning of section 3(6) of the Nature Conservation (Scotland) Act 2004);

(b)   such other place (or type of place) as may be prescribed in regulations made by the Scottish Ministers.]

[(5AC)   Before making regulations under subsection (5AB)(b) above, the Scottish

Ministers must consult, in so far as it is reasonably practicable to do so, the persons mentioned in subsection (5AD) below.]

[(5AD)   Those persons are—
    (a)   such associations of local authorities; and
    (b)   such other persons,
as the Scottish Ministers consider appropriate.]

[(5BA)   Subsection (1)(fba) above does not apply to artificial light emitted from a lighthouse (within the meaning of Part 8 of the Merchant Shipping Act 1995.]

(6)   Subsection (1)(g) above does not apply to noise caused by aircraft other than model aircraft.

[(6A)   Subsection (1)(ga) above does not apply to noise made—
    (a)   by traffic,
    (b)   by any naval, military or air force of the Crown or by a visiting force (as defined in subsection (2) above), or
    (c)   by a political demonstration or a demonstration supporting or opposing a cause or campaign.]

(7)   In this Part—
'chimney' includes structures and openings of any kind from or through which smoke may be emitted;
'dust' does not include dust emitted from a chimney as an ingredient of smoke;
['equipment' includes a musical instrument;]
'fumes' means any airborne solid matter smaller than dust;
'gas' includes vapour and moisture precipitated from vapour;
'industrial, trade or business premises' means premises used for any industrial, trade or business purposes or premises not so used on which matter is burnt in connection with any industrial, trade or business process, and premises are used for industrial purposes where they are used for the purposes of any treatment or process as well as where they are used for the purposes of manufacturing;
'local authority' means [. . .]—
    (a)   in Greater London, a London borough council, the Common Council of the City of London and, as respects the Temples, the Sub-Treasurer of the Inner Temple and the Under-Treasurer of the Middle Temple respectively;
    (b)   [in England and Wales] outside Greater London, a district council; . . .
    [(bb)   in Wales, a county council or county borough council;]
    (c)   the Council of the Isles of Scilly; [and
    (d)   in Scotland, a district or islands council or a council constituted under section 2 of the Local Government etc (Scotland) Act 1994;]
'noise' includes vibration;
['person responsible'—
    (a)   in relation to a statutory nuisance, means the person to whose act, default or sufferance the nuisance is attributable;
    (b)   in relation to a vehicle, includes the person in whose name the vehicle is for the time being registered under [the Vehicle Excise and Registration Act 1994] and any other person who is for the time being the driver of the vehicle;
    (c)   in relation to machinery or equipment, includes any person who is for the time being the operator of the machinery or equipment;]
'prejudicial to health' means injurious, or likely to cause injury, to health;
'premises' includes land [(subject to subsection (5AB) above)] and, subject to subsection (12) [and [, in relation to England and Wales,] section 81A(9)] below, any vessel;
'private dwelling' means any building, or part of a building, used or intended to be used, as a dwelling;
['road' has the same meaning as in Part IV of the New Roads and Street Works Act 1991;]
'smoke' includes soot, ash, grit and gritty particles emitted in smoke;

['street' means a highway and any other road, footway, square or court that is for the time being open to the public;]
and any expressions used in this section and in [the Clean Air Act 1993] have the same meaning in this section as in that Act and [section 3 of the Clean Air Act 1993] shall apply for the interpretation of the expression 'dark smoke' and the operation of this Part in relation to it.

(8)   Where, by an order under section 2 of the Public Health (Control of Disease) Act 1984, a port health authority has been constituted for any port health district, [. . .] the port health authority [. . .] shall have by virtue of this subsection, as respects its district, the functions conferred or imposed by this Part in relation to statutory nuisances other than a nuisance falling within paragraph (g) [or (ga)] of subsection (1) above and no such order shall be made assigning those functions; and 'local authority' and 'area' shall be construed accordingly.

(9)   In this Part 'best practicable means' is to be interpreted by reference to the following provisions—

(a)   'practicable' means reasonably practicable having regard among other things to local conditions and circumstances, to the current state of technical knowledge and to the financial implications;

(b)   the means to be employed include the design, installation, maintenance and manner and periods of operation of plant and machinery, and the design, construction and maintenance of buildings and structures;

(c)   the test is to apply only so far as compatible with any duty imposed by law;

(d)   the test is to apply only so far as compatible with safety and safe working conditions, and with the exigencies of any emergency or unforeseeable circumstances;

and, in circumstances where a code of practice under section 71 of the Control of Pollution Act 1974 (noise minimisation) is applicable, regard shall also be had to guidance given in it.

(10)   A local authority shall not without the consent of the Secretary of State institute summary proceedings under this Part in respect of a nuisance falling within paragraph (b), (d) [, (e) or (g) and, in relation to Scotland, [paragraph (ga)],] of subsection (1) above if proceedings in respect thereof might be instituted under Part I [of the Alkali &c Works Regulation Act 1906 or section 5 of the Health and Safety at Work etc Act 1974 or under regulations under section 2 of the Pollution Prevention and Control Act 1999.]

(11)   The area of a local authority which includes part of the seashore shall also include for the purposes of this Part the territorial sea lying seawards from that part of the shore; and subject to subsection (12) [and [, in relation to England and Wales,] section 81A(9)] below, this Part shall have effect, in relation to any area included in the area of a local authority by virtue of this subsection—

(a)   as if references to premises and the occupier of premises included respectively a vessel and the master of a vessel; and

(b)   with such other modifications, if any, as are prescribed in regulations made by the Secretary of State.

(12)   A vessel powered by steam reciprocating machinery is not a vessel to which this Part of this Act applies.

AGE OF LEGAL CAPACITY (SCOTLAND) ACT 1991
(1991, c 50)

1   Age of legal capacity

(1)   As from the commencement of this Act—

(a)   a person under the age of 16 years shall, subject to section 2 below, have no legal capacity to enter into any transaction;

(b)   a person of or over the age of 16 years shall have legal capacity to enter into any transaction.

(2)   Subject to section 8 below, any reference in any enactment to a pupil (other than in the context of education or training) or to a person under legal disability or incapacity by reason of nonage shall, insofar as it relates to any time after the commencement of this Act, be construed as a reference to a person under the age of 16 years.

(3)   Nothing in this Act shall—

(a)   apply to any transaction entered into before the commencement of this Act;

(b)   confer any legal capacity on any person who is under legal disability or incapacity other than by reason of nonage;

(c)   affect the delictual or criminal responsibility of any person;

(d)   affect any enactment which lays down an age limit expressed in years for any particular purpose;

(e)   prevent any person under the age of 16 years from receiving or holding any right, title or interest;

(f)   affect any existing rule of law or practice whereby—

(i)   any civil proceedings may be brought or defended, or any step in civil proceedings may be taken, in the name of a person under the age of 16 years [in relation to whom there is no person entitled to act as his legal representative (within the meaning of Part I of the Children (Scotland) Act 1995), or where there is such a person,] is unable (whether by reason of conflict of interest or otherwise) or refuses to bring or defend such proceedings or take such step;

(ii)   the court may, in any civil proceedings, appoint a curator ad litem to a person under the age of 16 years;

(iii)   the court may, in relation to the approval of an arrangement under section 1 of the Trusts (Scotland) Act 1961, appoint a curator ad litem to a person of or over the age of 16 years but under the age of 18 years;

(iv)   the court may appoint a curator bonis to any person;

(g)   prevent any person under the age of 16 years from [exercising parental responsibilities and parental rights (within the meaning of sections 1(3) and 2(4) respectively of the Children (Scotland) Act 1995) in relation to any child of his.]

(4)   Any existing rule of law relating to the legal capacity of minors and pupils which is inconsistent with the provisions of this Act shall cease to have effect.

(5)   Any existing rule of law relating to reduction of a transaction on the ground of minority and lesion shall cease to have effect.

2   Exceptions to general rule

(1)   A person under the age of 16 years shall have legal capacity to enter into a transaction—

(a)   of a kind commonly entered into by persons of his age and circumstances, and

(b)   on terms which are not unreasonable.

(2)   A person of or over the age of 12 years shall have testamentary capacity, including legal capacity to exercise by testamentary writing any power of appointment.

(3)   A person of or over the age of 12 years shall have legal capacity to consent to the making of an adoption order in relation to him. [. . .]

(4)   A person under the age of 16 years shall have legal capacity to consent on his own behalf to any surgical, medical or dental procedure or treatment where, in the opinion of a qualified medical practitioner attending him, he is capable of understanding the nature and possible consequences of the procedure or treatment.

[(4ZA)   For the purposes of subsection (4), the storage of gametes in accordance with the Human Fertilisation and Embryology Act 1990 is to be treated as a medical procedure.

(4ZB)   A person under the age of 16 years shall have legal capacity to consent to the use of the person's human cells in accordance with Schedule 3 to the Human Fertilisation and Embryology Act 1990 for the purposes of a project of research where the person is capable of understanding the nature of the research; and in this subsection 'human cells' has the same meaning as in that Schedule.]

[(4A)   A person under the age of sixteen years shall have legal capacity to instruct a solicitor, in connection with any civil matter, where that person has a general understanding of what it means to do so; and without prejudice to the generality of this subsection a person twelve years of age or more shall be presumed to be of sufficient age and maturity to have such understanding.

(4B)   A person who by virtue of subsection (4A) above has legal capacity to instruct a solicitor shall also have legal capacity to sue, or to defend, in any civil proceedings.

(4C)   Subsections (4A) and (4B) above are without prejudice to any question of legal capacity arising in connection with any criminal matter.]

(5)   Any transaction—

(a)   which a person under the age of 16 years purports to enter into after the commencement of this Act, and

(b)   in relation to which that person does not have legal capacity by virtue of this section,

shall be void.

3   Setting aside of transactions

(1)   A person under the age of 21 years ('the applicant') may make application to the court to set aside a transaction which he entered into while he was of or over the age of 16 years but under the age of 18 years and which is a prejudicial transaction.

(2)   In this section 'prejudicial transaction' means a transaction which—

(a)   an adult, exercising reasonable prudence, would not have entered into in the circumstances of the applicant at the time of entering into the transaction, and

(b)   has caused or is likely to cause substantial prejudice to the applicant.

(3)   Subsection (1) above shall not apply to—

(a)   the exercise of testamentary capacity;

(b)   the exercise by testamentary writing of any power of appointment;

(c)   the giving of consent to the making of an adoption order;

(d)   the bringing or defending of, or the taking of any step in, civil proceedings;

(e)   the giving of consent to any surgical, medical or dental procedure or treatment;

(f)   a transaction in the course of the applicant's trade, business or profession;

(g)   a transaction into which any other party was induced to enter by virtue of any fraudulent misrepresentation by the applicant as to age or other material fact;

(h)   a transaction ratified by the applicant after he attained the age of 18 years and in the knowledge that it could be the subject of an application to the court under this section to set it aside; or

(j)   a transaction ratified by the court under section 4 below.

(4)   Where an application to set aside a transaction can be made or could have been made under this section by the person referred to in subsection (1) above, such application may instead be made by that person's executor, trustee in bankruptcy, trustee acting under a trust deed for creditors or curator bonis at any time prior to the date on which that person attains or would have attained the age of 21 years.

(5)   An application under this section to set aside a transaction may be made—

(a)   by an action in the Court of Session or the sheriff court, or

(b)   by an incidental application in other proceedings in such court,

and the court may make an order setting aside the transaction and such further order, if any, as seems appropriate to the court in order to give effect to the rights of the parties.

4 Ratification by court of proposed transaction

(1)   Where a person of or over the age of 16 years but under the age of 18 years proposes to enter into a transaction which, if completed, could be the subject of an application to the court under section 3 above to set aside, all parties to the proposed transaction may make a joint application to have it ratified by the court.

(2)   The court shall not grant an application under this section if it appears to the court that an adult, exercising reasonable prudence and in the circumstances of the person referred to in subsection (1) above, would not enter into the transaction.

(3)   An application under this section shall be made by means of a summary application—

(a)   to the sheriff of the sheriffdom in which any of the parties to the proposed transaction resides, or

(b)   where none of the said parties resides in Scotland, to the sheriff at Edinburgh,

and the decision of the sheriff on such application shall be final.

5 Guardians of persons under 16

(1)   Except insofar as otherwise provided in Schedule 1 to this Act, as from the commencement of this Act any reference in any rule of law, enactment or document to the tutor [. . .] of a pupil child shall be construed as a reference to [a person entitled to act as a child's legal representative (within the meaning of Part I of the Children (Scotland) Act 1995) and any reference to the tutory of such a child shall be construed as a reference to the entitlement to act as a child's legal representative enjoyed by a person, by, under or by virtue of the said Part I.]

(2)   Subject to section 1(3)(f) above, as from the commencement of this Act no guardian of a person under the age of 16 years shall be appointed as such except under [section 7 of the Children (Scotland) Act 1995.]

(3)   As from the commencement of this Act, no person shall, by reason of age alone, be subject to the curatory of another person.

(4)   As from the commencement of this Act, no person shall be appointed as factor loco tutoris.

6 Attainment of age

(1)   The time at which a person attains a particular age expressed in years shall be taken to be the beginning of the relevant anniversary of the date of his birth.

(2)   Where a person has been born on 29th February in a leap year, the relevant anniversary in any year other than a leap year shall be taken to be 1st March.

(3)   The provisions of this section shall apply only to a relevant anniversary which occurs after the commencement of this Act.

[. . .]

8 Transitional provision

Where any person referred to in section 6(4)(b), 17(3), 18(3) or 18A(2) of the Prescription and Limitation (Scotland) Act 1973 as having been under legal disability by reason of nonage was of or over the age of 16 years but under the age of 18 years immediately before the commencement of this Act, any period prior to such commencement shall not be reckoned as, or as part of, the period of 5 years, or (as the case may be) 3 years, specified respectively in section 6, 17, 18 or 18A of that Act.

9 Interpretation

In this Act, unless the context otherwise requires—

'existing' means existing immediately before the commencement of this Act;

[. . .]

'transaction' means a transaction having legal effect, and includes—

(a)   any unilateral transaction;

(b)   the exercise of testamentary capacity;

(c)   the exercise of any power of appointment;

(d)   the giving by a person of any consent having legal effect;

(e)   the bringing or defending of, or the taking of any step in, civil proceedings;

(f)   acting as arbiter or trustee;

(g)   acting as an instrumentary witness.

10 Amendments and repeals

(1)   The enactments mentioned in Schedule 1 to this Act shall have effect subject to the amendments therein specified.

(2)   The enactments specified in Schedule 2 to this Act are repealed to the extent specified in the third column of that Schedule.

11 Short title, commencement and extent

(1)   This Act may be cited as the Age of Legal Capacity (Scotland) Act 1991.

(2)   This Act shall come into force at the end of the period of two months beginning with the date on which it is passed.

(3)   This Act shall extend to Scotland only.

CARRIAGE OF GOODS BY SEA ACT 1992
(1992, c 50)

1 Shipping documents etc to which Act applies

(1)   This Act applies to the following documents, that is to say—

(a)   any bill of lading;

(b)   any sea waybill; and

(c)   any ship's delivery order.

(2)   References in this Act to a bill of lading—

(a)   do not include references to a document which is incapable of transfer either by indorsement or, as a bearer bill, by delivery without indorsement; but

(b)   subject to that, do include references to a received for shipment bill of lading.

(3)   References in this Act to a sea waybill are references to any document which is not a bill of lading but—

(a)   is such a receipt for goods as contains or evidences a contract for the carriage of goods by sea; and

(b)   identifies the person to whom delivery of the goods is to be made by the carrier in accordance with that contract.

(4)   References in this Act to a ship's delivery order are references to any document which is neither a bill of lading nor a sea waybill but contains an undertaking which—

(a)   is given under or for the purposes of a contract for the carriage by sea of the goods to which the document relates, or of goods which include those goods; and

(b)   is an undertaking by the carrier to a person identified in the document to deliver the goods to which the document relates to that person.

(5)   The Secretary of State may by regulations make provision for the application of this Act to cases where an electronic communications network or any other information technology is used for effecting transactions corresponding to—

(a)   the issue of a document to which this Act applies;

(b)   the indorsement, delivery or other transfer of such a document; or

(c)   the doing of anything else in relation to such a document.

(6)   Regulations under subsection (5) above may—

(a)   make such modifications of the following provisions of this Act as the Secretary of State considers appropriate in connection with the application of this Act to any case mentioned in that subsection; and

(b)   contain supplemental, incidental, consequential and transitional provision;

and the power to make regulations under that subsection shall be exercisable by statutory instrument subject to annulment in pursuance of a resolution of either House of Parliament.

2   Rights under shipping documents

(1)   Subject to the following provisions of this section, a person who becomes—

(a)   the lawful holder of a bill of lading;

(b)   the person who (without being an original party to the contract of carriage) is the person to whom delivery of the goods to which a sea waybill relates is to be made by the carrier in accordance with that contract; or

(c)   the person to whom delivery of the goods to which a ship's delivery order relates is to be made in accordance with the undertaking contained in the order,

shall (by virtue of becoming the holder of the bill or, as the case may be, the person to whom delivery is to be made) have transferred to and vested in him all rights of suit under the contract of carriage as if he had been a party to that contract.

(2)   Where, when a person becomes the lawful holder of a bill of lading, possession of the bill no longer gives a right (as against the carrier) to possession of the goods to which the bill relates, that person shall not have any rights transferred to him by virtue of subsection (1) above unless he becomes the holder of the bill—

(a)   by virtue of a transaction effected in pursuance of any contractual or other arrangements made before the time when such a right to possession ceased to attach to possession of the bill; or

(b)   as a result of the rejection to that person by another person of goods or documents delivered to the other person in pursuance of any such arrangements.

(3)   The rights vested in any person by virtue of the operation of subsection (1) above in relation to a ship's delivery order—

(a)   shall be so vested subject to the terms of the order; and

(b)   where the goods to which the order relates form a part only of the goods to which the contract of carriage relates, shall be confined to rights in respect of the goods to which the order relates.

(4)   Where, in the case of any document to which this Act applies—

(a)   a person with any interest or right in or in relation to goods to which the document relates sustains loss or damage in consequence of a breach of the contract of carriage; but

(b)   subsection (1) above operates in relation to that document so that rights
of suit in respect of that breach are vested in another person,
the other person shall be entitled to exercise those rights for the benefit of the
person who sustained the loss or damage to the same extent as they could have
been exercised if they had been vested in the person for whose benefit they are
exercised.

(5)   Where rights are transferred by virtue of the operation of subsection (1)
above in relation to any document, the transfer for which that subsection provides
shall extinguish any entitlement to those rights which derives—

(a)   where that document is a bill of lading, from a person's having been an
original party to the contract of carriage; or

(b)   in the case of any document to which this Act applies, from the previous
operation of that subsection in relation to that document;
but the operation of that subsection shall be without prejudice to any rights which
derive from a person's having been an original party to the contract contained in,
or evidenced by, a sea waybill and, in relation to a ship's delivery order, shall be
without prejudice to any rights deriving otherwise than from the previous operation of that subsection in relation to that order.

3   Liabilities under shipping documents

(1)   Where subsection (1) of section 2 of this Act operates in relation to any
document to which this Act applies and the person in whom rights are vested by
virtue of that subsection—

(a)   takes or demands delivery from the carrier of any of the goods to which
the document relates;

(b)   makes a claim under the contract of carriage against the carrier in respect
of any of those goods; or

(c)   is a person who, at a time before those rights were vested in him, took or
demanded delivery from the carrier of any of those goods,
that person shall (by virtue of taking or demanding delivery or making the claim
or, in a case falling within paragraph (c) above, of having the rights vested in him)
become subject to the same liabilities under that contract as if he had been a party
to that contract.

(2)   Where the goods to which a ship's delivery order relates form a part only
of the goods to which the contract of carriage relates, the liabilities to which any
person is subject by virtue of the operation of this section in relation to that order
shall exclude liabilities in respect of any goods to which the order does not relate.

(3)   This section, so far as it imposes liabilities under any contract on any person,
shall be without prejudice to the liabilities under the contract of any person as an
original party to the contract.

4   Representations in bills of lading

A bill of lading which—

(a)   represents goods to have been shipped on board a vessel or to have been
received for shipment on board a vessel; and

(b)   has been signed by the master of the vessel or by a person who was not the
master but had the express, implied or apparent authority of the carrier to sign
bills of lading,
shall, in favour of a person who has become the lawful holder of the bill, be conclusive evidence against the carrier of the shipment of the goods or, as the case
may be, of their receipt for shipment.

5   Interpretation etc

(1)   In this Act—
'bill of lading', 'sea waybill' and 'ship's delivery order' shall be construed in
accordance with section 1 above;
'the contract of carriage'—

(a)   in relation to a bill of lading or sea waybill, means the contract contained in or evidenced by that bill or waybill; and

(b)   in relation to a ship's delivery order, means the contract under or for the purposes of which the undertaking contained in the order is given;

'holder', in relation to a bill of lading, shall be construed in accordance with subsection (2) below;

'information technology' includes any computer or other technology by means of which information or other matter may be recorded or communicated without being reduced to documentary form; [. . .]

(2)   References in this Act to the holder of a bill of lading are references to any of the following persons, that is to say—

(a)   a person with possession of the bill who, by virtue of being the person identified in the bill, is the consignee of the goods to which the bill relates;

(b)   a person with possession of the bill as a result of the completion, by delivery of the bill, of any indorsement of the bill or, in the case of a bearer bill, of any other transfer of the bill;

(c)   a person with possession of the bill as a result of any transaction by virtue of which he would have become a holder falling within paragraph (a) or (b) above had not the transaction been effected at a time when possession of the bill no longer gave a right (as against the carrier) to possession of the goods to which the bill relates;

and a person shall be regarded for the purposes of this Act as having become the lawful holder of a bill of lading wherever he has become the holder of the bill in good faith.

(3)   References in this Act to a person's being identified in a document include references to his being identified by a description which allows for the identity of the person in question to be varied, in accordance with the terms of the document, after its issue; and the reference in section 1(3)(b) of this Act to a document's identifying a person shall be construed accordingly.

(4)   Without prejudice to sections 2(2) and 4 above, nothing in this Act shall preclude its operation in relation to a case where the goods to which a document relates—

(a)   cease to exist after the issue of the document; or

(b)   cannot be identified (whether because they are mixed with other goods or for any other reason);

and references in this Act to the goods to which a document relates shall be construed accordingly.

(5)   The preceding provisions of this Act shall have effect without prejudice to the application, in relation to any case, of the rules (the Hague-Visby Rules) which for the time being have the force of law by virtue of section 1 of the Carriage of Goods by Sea Act 1971.

6   Short title, repeal, commencement and extent

(1)   This Act may be cited as the Carriage of Goods by Sea Act 1992.

(2)   The Bills of Lading Act 1855 is hereby repealed.

(3)   This Act shall come into force at the end of the period of two months beginning with the day on which it is passed; but nothing in this Act shall have effect in relation to any document issued before the coming into force of this Act.

(4)   This Act extends to Northern Ireland.

REQUIREMENTS OF WRITING (SCOTLAND) ACT 1995
(1995, c 7)

1 Writing required for certain contracts, obligations, trusts, conveyances and wills

(1) Subject to subsection (2) below and any other enactment, writing shall not be required for the constitution of a contract, unilateral obligation or trust.

(2) Subject to [subsections (2A) and (3)] below, a written document complying with section 2 of this Act shall be required for—

(a) the constitution of—

(i) a contract or unilateral obligation for the creation, transfer, variation or extinction of [a real right] in land;

(ii) a gratuitous unilateral obligation except an obligation undertaken in the course of business; and

(iii) a trust whereby a person declares himself to be sole trustee of his own property or any property which he may acquire;

(b) the creation, transfer, variation or extinction of [a real right] in land otherwise than by the operation of a court decree, enactment or rule of law; and

(c) the making of any will, testamentary trust disposition and settlement or codicil.

[(2A) An electronic document complying with section 2A shall be valid for—

(a) the constitution of a contract or unilateral obligation for the creation, transfer, variation or extinction of a real right in land;

(b) the constitution of a gratuitous unilateral obligation; and

(c) the creation, transfer, variation or extinction of a real right in land.

(2B) In this section, 'electronic document' means a document created as an electronic communication within the ARTL system.]

(3) Where a contract, obligation or trust mentioned in [subsections (2)(a) or (2A)] above is not constituted in a written document complying with section 2 [or, as the case may be, an electronic document complying with section 2A], of this Act but one of the parties to the contract, a creditor in the obligation or a beneficiary under the trust ('the first person') has acted or refrained from acting in reliance on the contract, obligation or trust with the knowledge and acquiescence of the other party to the contract, the debtor in the obligation or the truster ('the second person')—

(a) the second person shall not be entitled to withdraw from the contract, obligation or trust; and

(b) the contract, obligation or trust shall not be regarded as invalid, on the ground that it is not so constituted, if the condition set out in subsection (4) below is satisfied.

(4) The condition referred to in subsection (3) above is that the position of the first person—

(a) as a result of acting or refraining from acting as mentioned in that subsection has been affected to a material extent; and

(b) as a result of such a withdrawal as is mentioned in that subsection would be adversely affected to a material extent.

(5) In relation to the constitution of any contract, obligation or trust mentioned in [subsections (2)(a) or (2A)] above, subsections (3) and (4) above replace the rules of law known as *rei interventus* and homologation.

(6) This section shall apply to the variation of a contract, obligation or trust as it applies to the constitution thereof but as if in subsections (3) and (4) for the references to acting or refraining from acting in reliance on the contract, obligation or trust and withdrawing therefrom there were substituted respectively references to acting or refraining from acting in reliance on the variation of the contract, obligation or trust and withdrawing from the variation.

(7) In this section ['real right in land' means any real] right in or over land,

including any right to occupy or to use land or to restrict the occupation or use of land, but does not include—

(a) a tenancy;
(b) a right to occupy or use land; or
(c) a right to restrict the occupation or use of land,

if the tenancy or right is not granted for more than one year, unless the tenancy or right is for a recurring period or recurring periods and there is a gap of more than one year between the beginning of the first, and the end of the last, such period.

(8) For the purposes of subsection (7) above 'land' does not include—

(a) growing crops; or
(b) a moveable building or other moveable structure.

2 Type of writing required for formal validity of certain documents

(1) No document required by section 1(2) of this Act shall be valid in respect of the formalities of execution unless it is subscribed by the granter of it or, if there is more than one granter, by each granter, but nothing apart from such subscription shall be required for the document to be valid as aforesaid.

(2) A contract mentioned in section 1(2)(a)(i) of this Act may be regarded as constituted or varied (as the case may be) if the offer is contained in one or more documents and the acceptance is contained in another document or other documents, and each document is subscribed by the granter or granters thereof.

(3) Nothing in this section shall prevent a document which has not been subscribed by the granter or granters of it from being used as evidence in relation to any right or obligation to which the document relates.

(4) This section is without prejudice to any other enactment which makes different provision in respect of the formalities of execution of a document to which this section applies.

[2A Formalities of execution of electronic documents

(1) An electronic document shall be valid in respect of the formalities of execution if that document has been authenticated by the granter, or if there is more than one granter by each granter, in accordance with subsection (2).

(2) An electronic document is authenticated by a person if the digital signature of that person—

(a) is incorporated into or logically associated with the electronic document;
(b) was created by the person by whom it purports to have been created;
(c) was created in accordance with such requirements as may be set out in directions made by the Keeper of the Registers of Scotland; and
(d) is certified in accordance with—
(i) subsection (3); and
(ii) such requirements as may be set out in directions made by the Keeper of the Registers of Scotland.

(3) For the purpose of this section a digital signature incorporated into or logically associated with an electronic document is certified by any person if that person (whether before or after the creation of the electronic document) has made a statement confirming that—

(a) the signature;
(b) a means of producing, communicating or verifying the signature; or
(c) a procedure applied to the signature,

is (either alone or in combination with other factors) a valid means of establishing the authenticity of the document, the integrity of the document or both.

2B Directions by the Keeper of the Registers of Scotland

A direction made by the Keeper of the Registers of Scotland under section 2A—

(a) shall be published in such manner as the Keeper considers appropriate for the purpose of bringing it to the attention of the persons affected by it;

(b)   may make different provision for different purposes;
(c)   may include incidental, supplementary, saving and transitional provisions; and
(d)   may be varied or revoked by a subsequent direction.

2C   Authentication of an electronic document by a person granting in more than one capacity
Where a person grants an electronic document in more than one capacity authentication of that document by that person in accordance with this Act shall be sufficient to bind that person in all such capacities.]

3   Presumption as to granter's subscription or date or place of subscription
(1)   Subject to subsections (2) to (7) below, where—
(a)   a document bears to have been subscribed by a granter of it;
(b)   the document bears to have been signed by a person as a witness of that granter's subscription and the document, or the testing clause or its equivalent, bears to state the name and address of the witness; and
(c)   nothing in the document, or in the testing clause or its equivalent, indicates—
(i)   that it was not subscribed by that granter as it bears to have been so subscribed; or
(ii)   that it was not validly witnessed for any reason specified in paragraphs (a) to (e) of subsection (4) below,
the document shall be presumed to have been subscribed by that granter.
(2)   Where a testamentary document consists of more than one sheet, it shall not be presumed to have been subscribed by a granter as mentioned in subsection (1) above unless, in addition to it bearing to have been subscribed by him and otherwise complying with that subsection, it bears to have been signed by him on every sheet.
(3)   For the purposes of subsection (1)(b) above—
(a)   the name and address of a witness may be added at any time before the document is—
(i)   founded on in legal proceedings; or
(ii)   registered for preservation in the Books of Council and Session or in sheriff court books; and
(b)   the name and address of a witness need not be written by the witness himself.
(4)   Where, in any proceedings relating to a document in which a question arises as to a granter's subscription, it is established—
(a)   that a signature bearing to be the signature of the witness of that granter's subscription is not such a signature, whether by reason of forgery or otherwise;
(b)   that the person who signed the document as the witness of that granter's subscription is a person who is named in the document as a granter of it;
(c)   that the person who signed the document as the witness of that granter's subscription, at the time of signing—
(i)   did not know the granter;
(ii)   was under the age of 16 years; or
(iii)   was mentally incapable of acting as a witness;
(d)   that the person who signed the document, purporting to be the witness of that granter's subscription, did not witness such subscription;
(e)   that the person who signed the document as the witness of that granter's subscription did not sign the document after him or that the granter's subscription or, as the case may be, acknowledgement of his subscription and the person's signature as witness of that subscription were not one continuous process;
(f)   that the name or address of the witness of that granter's subscription was

added after the document was founded on or registered as mentioned in sub-section (3)(a) above or is erroneous in any material respect; or

(g)   in the case of a testamentary document consisting of more than one sheet, that a signature on any sheet bearing to be the signature of the granter is not such a signature, whether by reason of forgery or otherwise,

then, for the purposes of those proceedings, there shall be no presumption that the document has been subscribed by that granter.

(5)   For the purposes of subsection (4)(c)(i) above, the witness shall be regarded as having known the person whose subscription he has witnessed at the time of witnessing if he had credible information at that time of his identity.

(6)   For the purposes of subsection (4)(e) above, where—

(a)   a document is granted by more than one granter; and

(b)   a person is the witness to the subscription of more than one granter,

the subscription or acknowledgement of any such granter and the signature of the person witnessing that granter's subscription shall not be regarded as not being one continuous process by reason only that, between the time of that subscription or acknowledgement and that signature, another granter has subscribed the document or acknowledged his subscription.

(7)   For the purposes of the foregoing provisions of this section a person witnesses a granter's subscription of a document—

(a)   if he sees the granter subscribe it; or

(b)   if the granter acknowledges his subscription to that person.

(8)   Where—

(a)   by virtue of subsection (1) above a document to which this subsection applies is presumed to have been subscribed by a granter of it;

(b)   the document, or the testing clause or its equivalent, bears to state the date or place of subscription of the document by that granter; and

(c)   nothing in the document, or in the testing clause or its equivalent, indicates that that statement as to date or place is incorrect,

there shall be a presumption that the document was subscribed by that granter on the date or at the place as stated.

(9)   Subsection (8) above applies to any document other than a testamentary document.

(10)   Where—

(a)   a testamentary document bears to have been subscribed and the document, or the testing clause or its equivalent, bears to state the date or place of subscription (whether or not it is presumed under subsections (1) to (7) above to have been subscribed by a granter of it); and

(b)   nothing in the document, or in the testing clause or its equivalent, indicates that that statement as to date or place is incorrect,

there shall be a presumption that the statement as to date or place is correct.

[3A   Presumption as to the authentication of electronic documents
Where an electronic document bears to have been authenticated by the granter and nothing in the document or in the authentication indicates that it was not so authenticated the document shall be presumed to have been authenticated by the granter.]

4   Presumption as to granter's subscription or date or place of subscription when established in court proceedings
(1)   Where a document bears to have been subscribed by a granter of it, but there is no presumption under section 3 of this Act that the document has been subscribed by that granter, then, if the court, on an application being made to it by any person who has an interest in the document, is satisfied that the document was subscribed by that granter, it shall—

(a)   cause the document to be endorsed with a certificate to that effect; or

(b)   where the document has already been registered in the Books of Council and Session or in sheriff court books, grant decree to that effect.

(2)   Where a document bears to have been subscribed by a granter of it, but there is no presumption under section 3 of this Act as to the date or place of subscription, then, if the court, on an application being made to it by any person who has an interest in the document, is satisfied as to the date or place of subscription, it shall—

(a)   cause the document to be endorsed with a certificate to that effect; or

(b)   where the document has already been registered in the Books of Council and Session or in sheriff court books, grant decree to that effect.

(3)   On an application under subsection (1) or (2) above evidence shall, unless the court otherwise directs, be given by affidavit.

(4)   An application under subsection (1) or (2) above may be made either as a summary application or as incidental to and in the course of other proceedings.

(5)   The effect of a certificate or decree—

(a)   under subsection (1) above shall be to establish a presumption that the document has been subscribed by the granter concerned;

(b)   under subsection (2) above shall be to establish a presumption that the statement in the certificate or decree as to date or place is correct.

(6)   In this section 'the court' means—

(a)   in the case of a summary application—

(i)   the sheriff in whose sheriffdom the applicant resides; or

(ii)   if the applicant does not reside in Scotland, the sheriff at Edinburgh; and

(b)   in the case of an application made in the course of other proceedings, the court before which those proceedings are pending.

5   Alterations to documents: formal validity and presumptions

(1)   An alteration made to a document required by section 1(2) of this Act—

(a)   before the document is subscribed by the granter or, if there is more than one granter, by the granter first subscribing it, shall form part of the document as so subscribed;

(b)   after the document is so subscribed shall, if the alteration has been signed by the granter or (as the case may be) by all the granters, have effect as a formally valid alteration of the document as so subscribed,

but an alteration made to such a document otherwise than as mentioned in paragraphs (a) and (b) above shall not be formally valid.

(2)   Subsection (1) above is without prejudice to—

(a)   any rule of law enabling any provision in a testamentary document to be revoked by deletion or erasure without authentication of the deletion or erasure by the testator;

(b)   the Erasures in Deeds (Scotland) Act 1836 and section 54 of the Conveyancing (Scotland) Act 1874.

(3)   The fact that an alteration to a document was made before the document was subscribed by the granter of it, or by the granter first subscribing it, may be established by all relevant evidence, whether written or oral.

(4)   Where a document bears to have been subscribed by the granter or, if there is more than one granter, by all the granters of it, then, if subsection (5) or (6) below applies, an alteration made to the document shall be presumed to have been made before the document was subscribed by the granter or, if there is more than one granter, by the granter first subscribing it, and to form part of the document as so subscribed.

(5)   This subsection applies where—

(a)   the document is presumed under section 3 of this Act to have been subscribed by the granter or granters (as the case may be);

(b)   it is stated in the document, or in the testing clause or its equivalent, that the alteration was made before the document was subscribed; and

(c)   nothing in the document, or in the testing clause or its equivalent, indicates that the alteration was made after the document was subscribed.

(6)   This subsection applies where subsection (5) above does not apply, but the court is satisfied, on an application being made to it, that the alteration was made before the document was subscribed by the granter or, if there is more than one granter, by the granter first subscribing it, and causes the document to be endorsed with a certificate to that effect or, where the document has already been registered in the Books of Council and Session or in sheriff court books, grants decree to that effect.

(7)   Subsections (3), (4) and (6) of section 4 of this Act shall apply in relation to an application under subsection (6) above as they apply in relation to an application under subsection (1) of that section.

(8)   Where an alteration is made to a document after the document has been subscribed by a granter, Schedule 1 to this Act (presumptions as to granter's signature and date and place of signing in relation to such alterations) shall have effect.

[(9)   This section shall have no application as regards an electronic document.]

6 Registration of documents

(1)   Subject to subsection (3) below [and section 6A of this Act], it shall not be competent—

(a)   to record a document in the Register of Sasines; or

(b)   to register a document for execution or preservation in the Books of Council and Session or in sheriff court books,

unless subsection (2) below applies in relation to the document.

(2)   This subsection applies where—

(a)   the document is presumed under section 3 or 4 of this Act to have been subscribed by the granter; or

(b)   if there is more than one granter, the document is presumed under section 3 or 4 or partly under the one section and partly under the other to have been subscribed by at least one of the granters.

(3)   Subsection (1) above shall not apply in relation to—

(a)   the recording of a document in the Register of Sasines or the registration of a document in the Books of Council and Session or in sheriff court books, if such recording or registration is required or expressly permitted under any enactment;

(b)   the recording of a court decree in the Register of Sasines;

(c)   the registration in the Books of Council and Session or in sheriff court books of—

(i)   a testamentary document;

(ii)   a document which is directed by the Court of Session or (as the case may be) the sheriff to be so registered;

(iii)   a document whose formal validity is governed by a law other than Scots law, if the Keeper of the Registers of Scotland or (as the case may be) the sheriff clerk is satisfied that the document is formally valid according to the law governing such validity;

(iv)   a court decree granted under section 4 or 5 of this Act in relation to a document already registered in the Books of Council and Session or in sheriff court books (as the case may be); or

(d)   the registration of a court decree in a separate register maintained for that purpose.

(4)   A document may be registered for preservation in the Books of Council and Session or in sheriff court books without a clause of consent to registration.

[6A   Registration for preservation and execution of electronic standard securities

(1)   This section applies where an electronic document, which creates a standard security over a real right in land, is presumed under section 3A of this Act to have been authenticated by the granter.

(2)   An office copy of the electronic document may be registered for preservation and execution in the Books of Council and Session or in the sheriff court books.

(3)   An office copy so registered is to be treated for the purposes of executing any diligence (including, for the avoidance of doubt, for the purposes of sections 1 and 2 of the Writs Execution (Scotland) Act 1877 (c 40)) as if—

(a)   the standard security were created by a document to which section 6(2) of his Act applies, and

(b)   the office copy were that document.]

7   Subscription and signing

(1)   Except where an enactment expressly provides otherwise, a document is subscribed by a granter of it if it is signed by him at the end of the last page (excluding any annexation, whether or not incorporated in the document as provided for in section 8 of this Act).

(2)   Subject to paragraph 2(2) of Schedule 2 to this Act, a document, or an alteration to a document, is signed by an individual natural person as a granter or on behalf of a granter of it if it is signed by him—

(a)   with the full name by which he is identified in the document or in any testing clause or its equivalent; or

(b)   with his surname, preceded by at least one forename (or an initial or abbreviation or familiar form of a forename); or

(c)   except for the purposes of section 3(1) to (7) of this Act, with a name (not in accordance with paragraph (a) or (b) above) or description or an initial or mark if it is established that the name, description, initial or mark—

(i)   was his usual method of signing, or his usual method of signing documents or alterations of the type in question; or

(ii)   was intended by him as his signature of the document or alteration.

(3)   Where there is more than one granter, the requirement under subsection (1) above of signing at the end of the last page of a document shall be regarded as complied with if at least one granter signs at the end of the last page and any other granter signs on an additional page.

(4)   Where a person grants a document in more than one capacity, one subscription of the document by him shall be sufficient to bind him in all such capacities.

(5)   A document, or an alteration to a document, is signed by a witness if it is signed by him—

(a)   with the full name by which he is identified in the document or in any testing clause or its equivalent; or

(b)   with his surname, preceded by at least one forename (or an initial or abbreviation or familiar form of a forename),

and if the witness is witnessing the signature of more than one granter, it shall be unnecessary for him to sign the document or alteration more than once.

(6)   This section is without prejudice to any rule of law relating to the subscription or signing of documents by members of the Royal Family, by peers or by the wives or the eldest sons of peers.

(7)   Schedule 2 to this Act (special rules relating to subscription and signing of documents etc by partnerships, companies, [limited liability partnerships,] local authorities, other bodies corporate and Ministers) shall have effect.

8   Annexations to documents

(1)   Subject to subsection (2) below and except where an enactment expressly

otherwise provides, any annexation to a document shall be regarded as incorporated in the document if it is—

    (a)   referred to in the document; and

    (b)   identified on its face as being the annexation referred to in the document,

without the annexation having to be signed or subscribed.

(2)   Where a document relates to land and an annexation to it describes or shows all or any part of the land to which the document relates, the annexation shall be regarded as incorporated in the document if and only if—

    (a)   it is referred to in the document; and

    (b)   it is identified on its face as being the annexation referred to in the document; and

    (c)   it is signed on—

        (i)   each page, where it is a plan, drawing, photograph or other representation; or

        (ii)   the last page, where it is an inventory, appendix, schedule or other writing.

(3)   Any annexation referred to in subsection (2) above which bears to have been signed by a granter of the document shall be presumed to have been signed by the person who subscribed the document as that granter.

(4)   Section 7(2) of this Act shall apply in relation to any annexation referred to in subsection (2) above as it applies in relation to a document as if for any reference to a document (except the reference in paragraph (a)) there were substituted a reference to an annexation.

(5)   It shall be competent to sign any annexation to a document at any time before the document is—

    (a)   founded on in legal proceedings;

    (b)   registered for preservation in the Books of Council and Session or in sheriff court books;

    (c)   recorded in the Register of Sasines;

    (d)   registered in the Land Register of Scotland.

(6)   Where there is more than one granter, the requirement under subsection (2)(c)(ii) above of signing on the last page shall be regarded as complied with (provided that at least one granter signs at the end of the last page) if any other granter signs on an additional page.

9 Subscription on behalf of blind granter or granter unable to write

(1)   Where a granter of a document makes a declaration to a relevant person that he is blind or unable to write, the relevant person—

    (a)   having read the document to that granter; or

    (b)   if the granter makes a declaration that he does not wish him to do so, without having read it to the granter,

shall, if authorised by the granter, be entitled to subscribe it and, if it is a testamentary document, sign it as mentioned in section 3(2) of this Act, on the granter's behalf.

(2)   Subscription or signing by a relevant person under subsection (1) above shall take place in the presence of the granter.

(3)   This Act shall have effect in relation to subscription or signing by a relevant person under subsection (1) above subject to the modifications set out in Schedule 3 to this Act.

(4)   A document subscribed by a relevant person under subsection (1) above which confers on the relevant person or his spouse, son or daughter a benefit in money or money's worth (whether directly or indirectly) shall be invalid to the extent, but only to the extent, that it confers such benefit.

(5)   This section and Schedule 3 to this Act apply in relation to the signing of—

    (a)   an annexation to a document as mentioned in section 8(2) of this Act;

    (b)   an alteration made to a document or to any such annexation to a document, as they apply in relation to the subscription of a document; and for that purpose, any reference to reading a document includes a reference to describing a plan, drawing, photograph or other representation in such an annexation or in an alteration to such an annexation.

(6)   In this Act 'relevant person' means a solicitor who has in force a practising certificate as defined in section 4(c) of the Solicitors (Scotland) Act 1980, an advocate, a justice of the peace or a sheriff clerk and, in relation to the execution of documents outwith Scotland, includes a notary public or any other person with official authority under the law of the place of execution to execute documents on behalf of persons who are blind or unable to write.

(7)   Nothing in this section shall prevent the granter of a document who is blind from subscribing or signing the document as mentioned in section 7 of this Act.

10 Forms of testing clause

(1)   Without prejudice to the effectiveness of any other means of providing information relating to the execution of a document, this information may be provided in such form of testing clause as may be prescribed in regulations made by the Secretary of State.

(2)   Regulations under subsection (1) above shall be made by statutory instrument which shall be subject to annulment in pursuance of a resolution of either House of Parliament and may prescribe different forms for different cases or classes of case.

11 Abolition of proof by writ or oath, reference to oath and other common law rules

(1)   Any rule of law and any enactment whereby the proof of any matter is restricted to proof by writ or by reference to oath shall cease to have effect.

(2)   The procedure of proving any matter in any civil proceedings by reference to oath is hereby abolished.

(3)   The following rules of law shall cease to have effect—

(a)   any rule whereby certain contracts and obligations and any variations of those contracts and obligations, and assignations of incorporeal moveables, are required to be in writing; and

(b)   any rule which confers any privilege—

(i)   on a document which is holograph or adopted as holograph; or

(ii)   on a writ *in re mercatoria.*

(4)   Subsections (1) and (2) above shall not apply in relation to proceedings commenced before the commencement of this Act.

12 Interpretation

(1)   In this Act, except where the context otherwise requires—

'alteration' includes interlineation, marginal addition, deletion, substitution, erasure or anything written on erasure;

'annexation' includes any inventory, appendix, schedule, other writing, plan, drawing, photograph or other representation annexed to a document;

['ARTL System' means the computer system managed and controlled by the Keeper of the Registers of Scotland to enable creation of electronic documents and the electronic generation and communication of an application for registration of a dealing affecting an interest in land registered in the Land Register of Scotland and automated registration in respect of that interest;]

'authorised' means expressly or impliedly authorised and any reference to a person authorised to sign includes a reference to a person authorised to sign generally or in relation to a particular document;

['company' has the meaning given by section 1(1) of the Companies Act 2006;]

['dealing' means a transaction or event capable of affecting the title to an interest in land registered in the Land Register of Scotland;]

'decree' includes a judgment or order, or an official certified copy, abbreviate or extract of a decree;

['digital signature' means data in electronic form which serves as a method of authentication and which is—

(i) uniquely linked to the signatory;

(ii) capable of identifying the signatory;

(iii) created using a signature-creation device that the signatory can maintain under the signatory's sole control; and

(iv) linked to the data to which it relates in such a manner that any subsequent change of data is detectable;]

'director' includes any person occupying the position of director, by whatever name he is called;

'document' includes any annexation which is incorporated in it under section 8 of this Act and any reference, however expressed, to the signing of a document includes a reference to the signing of an annexation;

['electronic communication' has the same meaning as in the Electronic Communications Act 2000;

'electronic document' has the meaning given by section 1(2B);]

'enactment' includes an enactment contained in a statutory instrument [and an enactment comprised in, or in an instrument made under, an Act of the Scottish Parliament];

'governing board', in relation to a body corporate to which paragraph 5 of Schedule 2 to this Act applies, means any governing body, however described;

'local authority' means a local authority within the meaning of section 235(1) of the Local Government (Scotland) Act 1973 and a council constituted under section 2 of the Local Government etc. (Scotland) Act 1994;

'Minister' has the same meaning as 'Minister of the Crown' has in section 8 of the Ministers of the Crown Act 1975 [and also includes a Member of the Scottish Executive];

'office-holder' does not include a Minister but, subject to that, means—

(a) the holder of an office created or continued in existence by a public general Act of Parliament;

(b) the holder of an office the remuneration in respect of which is paid out of money provided by Parliament [or out of the Scottish Consolidated Fund];

(c) the registrar of companies [. . .];

'officer'—

(a) in relation to a Minister, means any person in the civil service of the Crown who is serving in his Department [or as the case may be, as a member of the staff of the Scottish Ministers or the Lord Advocate];

(b) in relation to an office-holder, means any member of his staff, or any person in the civil service of the Crown who has been assigned or appointed to assist him in the exercise of his functions;

'proper officer', in relation to a local authority, has the same meaning as in section 235(3) of the Local Government (Scotland) Act 1973; and

'secretary' means, if there are two or more joint secretaries, any one of them.

['signature-creation data' means unique data (including, but not limited to, codes or private cryptographic keys) which are used by the signatory to create an electronic signature; and

'signature-creation device' means configured software or hardware used to implement the signature-creation data.]

(2) Any reference in this Act to subscription or signing by a granter of a document or an alteration made to a document, in a case where a person is subscribing or signing under a power of attorney on behalf of the granter, shall be construed as a reference to subscription or signing by that person of the document or alteration.

[(3) In a case where a person is authenticating an electronic document on behalf of a granter, any reference in this Act to authentication by a granter of an electronic document shall be construed as a reference to authentication by that person.]

13 Application of Act to Crown

(1) Nothing in this Act shall—

(a) prevent Her Majesty from authenticating—

(i) a document by superscription; or

(ii) a document relating to her private estates situated or arising in Scotland in accordance with section 6 of the Crown Private Estates Act 1862;

(b) prevent authentication under the Writs Act 1672 of a document passing the seal appointed by the Treaty of Union to be kept and used in Scotland in place of the Great Seal of Scotland formerly in use; or

(c) prevent any document mentioned in paragraph (a) or (b) above authenticated as aforesaid from being recorded in the Register of Sasines or registered for execution or preservation in the Books of Council and Session or in sheriff court books.

(2) [. . .]

(3) Subject to subsections (1) and (2) above, this Act binds the Crown.

14 Minor and consequential amendments, repeals, transitional provisions and savings

(1) The enactments mentioned in Schedule 4 to this Act shall have effect subject to the minor and consequential amendments specified in that Schedule.

(2) The enactments mentioned in Schedule 5 to this Act are hereby repealed to the extent specified in the third column of that Schedule.

(3) Subject to subsection (4) below and without prejudice to subsection (5) below and section 11(4) of this Act, nothing in this Act shall—

(a) apply to any document executed or anything done before the commencement of this Act; or

(b) affect the operation, in relation to any document executed before such commencement, of any procedure for establishing the authenticity of such a document.

(4) In the repeal of the Blank Bonds and Trusts Act 1696 (provided for in Schedule 5 to this Act), the repeal of the words from 'And farder' to the end—

(a) shall have effect in relation to a deed of trust, whether executed before or after the commencement of this Act; but

(b) notwithstanding paragraph (a) above, shall not have effect in relation to proceedings commenced before the commencement of this Act in which a question arises as to the deed of trust.

(5) The repeal of certain provisions of the Lyon King of Arms Act 1672 (provided for in Schedule 5 to this Act) shall not affect any right of a person to add a territorial designation to his signature or the jurisdiction of the Lord Lyon King of Arms in relation to any such designation.

(6) For the purposes of this Act, if it cannot be ascertained whether a document was executed before or after the commencement of this Act, there shall be a presumption that it was executed after such commencement.

15 Short title, commencement and extent

(1) This Act may be cited as the Requirements of Writing (Scotland) Act 1995.

(2) This Act shall come into force at the end of the period of three months beginning with the date on which it is passed.

(3) This Act extends to Scotland only.

SCHEDULES

SCHEDULE 1
ALTERATIONS MADE TO A DOCUMENT AFTER IT HAS BEEN SUBSCRIBED

Presumption as to granter's signature or date or place of signing

1.—(1) Subject to sub-paragraphs (2) to (7) below, where—

(a) an alteration to a document bears to have been signed by a granter of the document;

(b) the alteration bears to have been signed by a person as a witness of that granter's signature and the alteration, or the testing clause or its equivalent, bears to state the name and address of the witness; and

(c) nothing in the document or alteration, or in the testing clause or its equivalent, indicates—

(i) that the alteration was not signed by that granter as it bears to have been so signed; or

(ii) that it was not validly witnessed for any reason specified in paragraphs (a) to (e) of sub-paragraph (4) below,

the alteration shall be presumed to have been signed by that granter.

(2) Where an alteration to a testamentary document consists of more than one sheet, the alteration shall not be presumed to have been signed by a granter as mentioned in sub-paragraph (1) above unless, in addition to it bearing to have been signed by him on the last sheet and otherwise complying with that sub-paragraph, it bears to have been signed by him on every other sheet.

(3) For the purposes of sub-paragraph (1)(b) above—

(a) the name and address of a witness may be added at any time before the alteration is—

(i) founded on in legal proceedings; or

(ii) registered for preservation in the Books of Council and Session or in sheriff court books; and

(b) the name and address of a witness need not be written by the witness himself.

(4) Where, in any proceedings relating to an alteration to a document in which a question arises as to a granter's signature, it is established—

(a) that a signature bearing to be the signature of the witness of that granter's signature is not such a signature, whether by reason of forgery or otherwise;

(b) that the person who signed the alteration as the witness of that granter's signature is a person who is named in the document as a granter of the document;

(c) that the person who signed the alteration as the witness of that granter's signature, at the time of signing—

(i) did not know the granter;

(ii) was under the age of 16 years; or

(iii) was mentally incapable of acting as a witness;

(d) that the person who signed the alteration, purporting to be the witness of that granter's signature, did not witness such signature;

(e) that the person who signed the alteration as the witness of that granter's signature did not sign the alteration after him or that the signing of the alteration by the granter or, as the case may be, the granter's acknowledgement of his signature and the signing by the person as witness were not one continuous process;

(f) that the name or address of the witness of that granter's signature was added after the alteration was founded on or registered as mentioned in sub-paragraph (3)(a) above or is erroneous in any material respect; or

(g) in the case of an alteration to a testamentary document consisting of more than one sheet, that a signature on any sheet of the alteration bearing to be the signature of the granter is not such a signature, whether by reason of forgery or otherwise,

then, for the purposes of those proceedings, there shall be no presumption that the alteration has been signed by that granter.

(5) For the purposes of sub-paragraph (4)(c)(i) above, the witness shall be regarded as having known the person whose signature he has witnessed at the time of witnessing if he had credible information at that time of his identity.

(6) For the purposes of sub-paragraph (4)(e) above, where—

(a) an alteration to a document is made by more than one granter; and

(b) a person is the witness to the signature of more than one granter,

the signing of the alteration by any such granter or the acknowledgement of his signature and the signing by the person witnessing that granter's signature shall not be regarded as not being one continuous process by reason only that, between the time of signing or acknowledgement by that granter and of signing by that witness, another granter has signed the alteration or acknowledged his signature.

(7) For the purposes of the foregoing provisions of this paragraph a person witnesses a granter's signature of an alteration—

(a) if he sees the granter sign it; or

(b) if the granter acknowledges his signature to that person.

(8) Where—

(a) by virtue of sub-paragraph (1) above an alteration to a document to which this sub-paragraph applies is presumed to have been signed by a granter of the document;

(b) the alteration, or the testing clause or its equivalent, bears to state the date or place of signing of the alteration by that granter; and

(c) nothing in the document or alteration, or in the testing clause or its equivalent, indicates that that statement as to date or place is incorrect,

there shall be a presumption that the alteration was signed by that granter on the date or at the place as stated.

(9) Sub-paragraph (8) above applies to any document other than a testamentary document.

(10) Where—

(a) an alteration to a testamentary document bears to have been signed and the alteration, or the testing clause or its equivalent, bears to state the date or place of signing (whether or not it is presumed under sub-paragraphs (1) to (7) above to have been signed by a granter of the document); and

(b) nothing in the document or alteration, or in the testing clause or its equivalent, indicates that that statement as to date or place is incorrect,

there shall be a presumption that the statement as to date or place is correct.

Presumption as to granter's signature or date or place of signing when established in court proceedings

2.—(1) Where an alteration to a document bears to have been signed by a granter of the document, but there is no presumption under paragraph 1 above that the alteration has been signed by that granter, then, if the court, on an application being made to it by any person having an interest in the document, is satisfied that the alteration was signed by that granter, it shall—

(a) cause the document to be endorsed with a certificate to that effect; or

(b) where the document has already been registered in the Books of Council and Session or in sheriff court books, grant decree to that effect.

(2) Where an alteration to a document bears to have been signed by a granter of the document, but there is no presumption under paragraph 1 above as to the date or place of signing, then, if the court, on an application being made to it by

any person having an interest in the document, is satisfied as to the date or place of signing, it shall—

    (a)   cause the document to be endorsed with a certificate to that effect; or

    (b)   where the document has already been registered in the Books of Council and Session or in sheriff court books, grant decree to that effect.

    (3)   In relation to an application under sub-paragraph (1) or (2) above evidence shall, unless the court otherwise directs, be given by affidavit.

    (4)   An application under sub-paragraph (1) or (2) above may be made either as a summary application or as incidental to and in the course of other proceedings.

    (5)   The effect of a certificate or decree—

    (a)   under sub-paragraph (1) above shall be to establish a presumption that the alteration has been signed by the granter concerned;

    (b)   under sub-paragraph (2) above shall be to establish a presumption that the statement in the certificate or decree as to date or place is correct.

    (6)   In this paragraph 'the court' means—

    (a)   in the case of a summary application—

        (i)   the sheriff in whose sheriffdom the applicant resides; or

        (ii) if the applicant does not reside in Scotland, the sheriff at Edinburgh; and

    (b)   in the case of an application made in the course of other proceedings, the court before which those proceedings are pending.

SCHEDULE 2

SUBSCRIPTION AND SIGNING: SPECIAL CASES

General

1.   Any reference in this Act to subscription or signing by a granter of a document or an alteration to a document, in a case where the granter is a person to whom any of paragraphs 2 to 6 of this Schedule applies shall, unless the context otherwise requires, be construed as a reference to subscription or, as the case may be, signing of the document or alteration by a person in accordance with that paragraph.

Partnerships

2.—(1)   Except where an enactment expressly provides otherwise, where a granter of a document is a partnership, the document is signed by the partnership if it is signed on its behalf by a partner or by a person authorised to sign the document on its behalf.

    (2)   A person signing on behalf of a partnership under this paragraph may use his own name or the firm name.

    (3)   Sub-paragraphs (1) and (2) of this paragraph apply in relation to the signing of an alteration made to a document as they apply in relation to the signing of a document.

    (4)   In this paragraph 'partnership' has the same meaning as in section 1 of the Partnership Act 1890.

Companies

3.—(1)   Except where an enactment expressly provides otherwise, where a granter of a document is a company, the document is signed by the company if it is signed on its behalf by a director, or by the secretary, of the company or by a person authorised to sign the document on its behalf.

    (2)   This Act is without prejudice to—

    (a)   [sections 270(3) and 274 of the Companies Act 2006]; and

(b)   paragraph 9 of Schedule 1, paragraph 9 of Schedule 2, and paragraph 7 of Schedule 4, to the Insolvency Act 1986.

(3)   Sub-paragraphs (1) and (2) of this paragraph apply in relation to the signing of an alteration made to a document as they apply in relation to the signing of a document.

(4)   Where a granter of a document is a company, section 3 of and Schedule 1 to this Act shall have effect subject to the modifications set out in sub-paragraphs (5) and (6) below.

(5)   In section 3—

(a)   for subsection (1) there shall be substituted the following subsections—

'(1)   Subject to subsections (1A) to (7) below, where—

(a)   a document bears to have been subscribed on behalf of a company by a director, or by the secretary, of the company or by a person bearing to have been authorised to subscribe the document on its behalf;

(b)   the document bears to have been signed by a person as a witness of the subscription of the director, secretary or other person subscribing on behalf of the company and to state the name and address of the witness; and

(c)   nothing in the document, or in the testing clause or its equivalent, indicates—

(i)   that it was not subscribed on behalf of the company as it bears to have been so subscribed; or

(ii)   that it was not validly witnessed for any reason specified in paragraphs (a) to (e) of subsection (4) below,

the document shall be presumed to have been subscribed by the company.

(1A)   Where a document does not bear to have been signed by a person as a witness of the subscription of the director, secretary or other person subscribing on behalf of the company it shall be presumed to have been subscribed by the company if it bears to have been subscribed on behalf of the company by—

(a)   two directors of the company; or

(b)   a director and secretary of the company; or

(c)   two persons bearing to have been authorised to subscribe the document on its behalf.

(1B)   For the purposes of subsection (1)(b) above, the name and address of the witness may bear to be stated in the document itself or in the testing clause or its equivalent.

(1C)   A presumption under subsection (1) or (1A) above as to subscription of a document does not include a presumption—

(a)   that a person bearing to subscribe the document as a director or the secretary of the company was such director or secretary; or

(b)   that a person subscribing the document on behalf of the company bearing to have been authorised to do so was authorised to do so.';

(b)   in subsection (4) after paragraph (g) there shall be inserted the following paragraph—

'(h)   if the document does not bear to have been witnessed, but bears to have been subscribed on behalf of the company by two of the directors of the company, or by a director and secretary of the company, or by two authorised persons, that a signature bearing to be the signature of a director, secretary or authorised person is not such a signature, whether by reason of forgery or otherwise;'.

(6)   In paragraph 1 of Schedule 1—

(a)   for sub-paragraph (1) there shall be substituted the following sub-paragraphs—

'(1)   Subject to sub-paragraphs (1A) to (7) below, where—

(a)   an alteration to a document bears to have been signed on behalf of a company by a director, or by the secretary, of the company or by a person bearing to have been authorised to sign the alteration on its behalf;

(b)   the alteration bears to have been signed by a person as a witness of the signature of the director, secretary or other person signing on behalf of the company and to state the name and address of the witness; and

(c)   nothing in the document or alteration, or in the testing clause or its equivalent, indicates—

(i)   that the alteration was not signed on behalf of the company as it bears to have been so signed; or

(ii)   that the alteration was not validly witnessed for any reason specified in paragraphs (a) to (e) of sub-paragraph (4) below,

the alteration shall be presumed to have been signed by the company.

(1A)   Where an alteration does not bear to have been signed by a person as a witness of the signature of the director, secretary or other person signing on behalf of the company it shall be presumed to have been signed by the company if it bears to have been signed on behalf of the company by—

(a)   two directors of the company; or

(b)   a director and secretary of the company; or

(c)   two persons bearing to have been authorised to sign the alteration on its behalf.

(1B)   For the purposes of sub-paragraph (1)(b) above, the name and address of the witness may bear to be stated in the alteration itself or in the testing clause or its equivalent.

(1C)   A presumption under sub-paragraph (1) or (1A) above as to signing of an alteration to a document does not include a presumption—

(a)   that a person bearing to sign the alteration as a director or the secretary of the company was such director or secretary; or

(b)   that a person signing the alteration on behalf of the company bearing to have been authorised to do so was authorised to do so.';

(b)   in sub-paragraph (4) after paragraph (g) there shall be inserted the following paragraph—

'(h)   if the alteration does not bear to have been witnessed, but bears to have been signed on behalf of the company by two of the directors of the company, or by a director and secretary of the company, or by two authorised persons, that a signature bearing to be the signature of a director, secretary or authorised person is not such a signature, whether by reason of forgery or otherwise;'.

[Limited liability partnerships

3A.   (1)   Except where an enactment expressly provides otherwise, where a granter of a document is a limited liability partnership, the document is signed by the limited liability partnership if it is signed on its behalf by a member of the limited liability partnership.

(2)   This Act is without prejudice to paragraph 9 of Schedule 1, paragraph 9 of Schedule 2, and paragraph 7 of Schedule 4, to the Insolvency Act 1986.

(3)   Sub-paragraphs (1) and (2) of this paragraph apply in relation to the signing of an alteration made to a document as they apply in relation to the signing of a document.

(4)   Where a granter of a document is a limited liability partnership, section 3 of and Schedule 1 to this Act shall have effect subject to the modifications set out in sub-paragraphs (5) and (6) below.

(5)   In section 3—

(a) for subsection (1) there shall be substituted the following sub-sections—

'(1) Subject to subsections (1A) to (7) below, where—

(a) a document bears to have been subscribed on behalf of a limited liability partnership by a member of the limited liability partnership;

(b) the document bears to have been signed by a person as a witness of the subscription of the member of the limited (c)#nothing in the document, or in the testing clause or its equivalent, indicates—

(i) that it was not subscribed on behalf of the limited liability partnership as it bears to have been so subscribed; or

(ii) that it was not validly witnessed for any reason specified in paragraphs (a) to (e) of subsection (4) below,

the document shall be presumed to have been subscribed by the limited liability partnership.

(1A) Where a document does not bear to have been signed by a person as a witness of the subscription of the member of the limited liability partnership it shall be presumed to have been subscribed by the limited liability partnership if it bears to have been subscribed on behalf of the limited liability partnership by two members of the limited liability partnership.

(1B) A presumption under subsection (1) or (1A) above as to subscription of a document does not include a presumption that a person bearing to subscribe the document as a member of the limited liability partnership was such member.'

(b) in subsection (4) after paragraph (g) there shall be inserted the following paragraph—

'(h) if the document does not bear to have been witnessed, but bears to have been subscribed on behalf of the limited liability partnership by two of the members of the limited liability partnership, that a signature bearing to be the signature of a member is not such a signature, whether by reason of forgery or otherwise;'

(6) In paragraph 1 of Schedule 1—

(a) for sub-paragraph (1) there shall be substituted the following sub-paragraphs—

'(1) Subject to sub-paragraphs (1A) to (7) below, where—

(a) an alteration to a document bears to have been signed on behalf of a limited liability partnership by a member of the limited liability partnership;

(b) the alteration bears to have been signed by a person as a witness of the signature of the member of the limited liability partnership and to state the name and address of the witness; and

(c) nothing in the document or alteration, or in the testing clause or its equivalent, indicates—

(i) that the alteration was not signed on behalf of the limited liability partnership as it bears to have been so signed; or

(ii) that the alteration was not validly witnessed for any reason specified in paragraphs (a) to (e) of sub-paragraph (4) below,

the alteration shall be presumed to have been signed by the limited liability partnership.

(1A) Where an alteration does not bear to have been signed by a person as a witness of the signature of the member of the limited liability partnership it shall be presumed to have been signed by the limited liability partnership if it bears to have been signed on behalf of the limited liability partnership by two members of the limited liability partnership.

(1B) For the purposes of sub-paragraph (1)(b) above, the name and address of the witness may bear to be stated in the alteration itself or in the testing clause or its equivalent.

(1C) A presumption under sub-paragraph (1) or (1A) above as to signing of an alteration to a document does not include a presumption that a person bearing to sign the alteration as a member of the limited liability partnership was such member';

(b) in sub-paragraph (4) after paragraph (g) there shall be inserted the following—

'; or

(h) if the alteration does not bear to have been witnessed, but bears to have been signed on behalf of the limited liability partnership by two of the members of the limited liability partnership, that a signature bearing to be the signature of a member is not such a signature, whether by reason of forgery or otherwise;']

Local authorities

4.—(1) Except where an enactment expressly provides otherwise, where a granter of a document is a local authority, the document is signed by the authority if it is signed on their behalf by the proper officer of the authority.

(2) For the purposes of the signing of a document under this paragraph, a person purporting to sign on behalf of a local authority as an officer of the authority shall be presumed to be the proper officer of the authority.

(3) Sub-paragraphs (1) and (2) of this paragraph apply in relation to the signing of an alteration made to a document as they apply in relation to the signing of a document.

(4) Where a granter of a document is a local authority, section 3 of and Schedule 1 to this Act shall have effect subject to the modifications set out in sub-paragraphs (5) to (8) below.

(5) For section 3(1) there shall be substituted the following subsections—

'(1) Subject to subsections (1A) to (7) below, where—

(a) a document bears to have been subscribed on behalf of a local authority by the proper officer of the authority;

(b) the document bears—

(i) to have been signed by a person as a witness of the proper officer's subscription and to state the name and address of the witness; or

(ii) (if the subscription is not so witnessed), to have been sealed with the common seal of the authority; and

(c) nothing in the document, or in the testing clause or its equivalent, indicates—

(i) that it was not subscribed on behalf of the authority as it bears to have been so subscribed; or

(ii) that it was not validly witnessed for any reason specified in paragraphs (a) to (e) of subsection (4) below or that it was not sealed as it bears to have been sealed or that it was not validly sealed for the reason specified in subsection (4)(h) below,

the document shall be presumed to have been subscribed by the proper officer and by the authority.

(1A) For the purposes of subsection (1)(b)(i) above, the name and address of the witness may bear to be stated in the document itself or in the testing clause or its equivalent.'.

(6) In section 3(4) after paragraph (g) there shall be inserted the following paragraph—

'(h) if the document does not bear to have been witnessed, but bears to have been sealed with the common seal of the authority, that it was sealed by a person without authority to do so or was not sealed on the date on which it was subscribed on behalf of the authority;'.

(7)   For paragraph 1(1) of Schedule 1 there shall be substituted the following sub-paragraphs—

'(1)   Subject to sub-paragraphs (1A) to (7) below, where—

(a)   an alteration to a document bears to have been signed on behalf of a local authority by the proper officer of the authority;

(b)   the alteration bears—

(i)   to have been signed by a person as a witness of the proper officer's signature and to state the name and address of the witness; or

(ii) · (if the signature is not so witnessed), to have been sealed with the common seal of the authority; and

(c)   nothing in the document or alteration, or in the testing clause or its equivalent, indicates—

(i)   that the alteration was not signed on behalf of the authority as it bears to have been so signed; or

(ii)   that the alteration was not validly witnessed for any reason specified in paragraphs (a) to (e) of sub-paragraph (4) below or that it was not sealed as it bears to have been sealed or that it was not validly sealed for the reason specified in sub-paragraph (4)(h) below,

the alteration shall be presumed to have been signed by the proper officer and by the authority.

(1A)   For the purposes of sub-paragraph (1)(b)(i) above, the name and address of the witness may bear to be stated in the alteration itself or in the testing clause or its equivalent.'.

(8)   In paragraph 1(4) of Schedule 1 after paragraph (g) there shall be inserted the following paragraph—

'(h)   if the alteration does not bear to have been witnessed, but bears to have been sealed with the common seal of the authority, that it was sealed by a person without authority to do so or was not sealed on the date on which it was signed on behalf of the authority;'.

Other bodies corporate

5.—(1)   This paragraph applies to any body corporate other than a company or a local authority.

(2)   Except where an enactment expressly provides otherwise, where a granter of a document is a body corporate to which this paragraph applies, the document is signed by the body if it is signed on its behalf by—

(a)   a member of the body's governing board or, if there is no governing board, a member of the body;

(b)   the secretary of the body by whatever name he is called; or

(c)   a person authorised to sign the document on behalf of the body.

(3)   Sub-paragraphs (1) and (2) of this paragraph apply in relation to the signing of an alteration made to a document as they apply in relation to the signing of a document.

(4)   Where a granter of a document is a body corporate to which this paragraph applies, section 3 of and Schedule 1 to this Act shall have effect subject to the modifications set out in sub-paragraphs (5) to (8) below.

(5)   For section 3(1) there shall be substituted the following subsections—

'(1)   Subject to subsections (1A) to (7) below, where—

(a)   a document bears to have been subscribed on behalf of a body corporate to which paragraph 5 of Schedule 2 to this Act applies by—

(i)   a member of the body's governing board or, if there is no governing board, a member of the body;

(ii)   the secretary of the body; or

(iii)   a person bearing to have been authorised to subscribe the document on its behalf;

(b)   the document bears—

(i)   to have been signed by a person as a witness of the subscription of the member, secretary or other person signing on behalf of the body and to state the name and address of the witness; or

(ii)   (if the subscription is not so witnessed), to have been sealed with the common seal of the body; and

(c)   nothing in the document, or in the testing clause or its equivalent, indicates—

(i)   that it was not subscribed on behalf of the body as it bears to have been so subscribed; or

(ii)   that it was not validly witnessed for any reason specified in paragraphs (a) to (e) of subsection (4) below or that it was not sealed as it bears to have been sealed or that it was not validly sealed for the reason specified in subsection (4)(h) below,

the document shall be presumed to have been subscribed by the member, secretary or authorised person (as the case may be) and by the body.

(1A)   For the purposes of subsection (1)(b)(i) above, the name and address of the witness may bear to be stated in the document itself or in the testing clause or its equivalent.

(1B)   A presumption under subsection (1) above as to subscription of a document does not include a presumption—

(a)   that a person bearing to subscribe the document as a member of the body's governing board, a member of the body or the secretary of the body was such member or secretary; or

(b)   that a person subscribing the document on behalf of the body bearing to have been authorised to do so was authorised to do so.'.

(6)   In section 3(4) after paragraph (g) there shall be inserted the following paragraph—

'(h)   if the document does not bear to have been witnessed, but bears to have been sealed with the common seal of the body, that it was sealed by a person without authority to do so or was not sealed on the date on which it was subscribed on behalf of the body;'.

(7)   For paragraph 1(1) of Schedule 1 there shall be substituted the following sub-paragraphs—

'(1) Subject to sub-paragraphs (1A) to (7) below, where—

(a)   an alteration to a document bears to have been signed on behalf of a body corporate to which paragraph 5 of Schedule 2 to this Act applies by—

(i)   a member of the body's governing board or, if there is no governing board, a member of the body;

(ii)   the secretary of the body; or

(iii)   a person bearing to have been authorised to sign the alteration on its behalf,

(b)   the alteration bears—

(i)   to have been signed by a person as a witness of the signature of the member, secretary or other person signing on behalf of the body and to state the name and address of the witness; or

(ii)   (if the signature is not so witnessed), to have been sealed with the common seal of the body; and

(c)   nothing in the document or alteration, or in the testing clause or its equivalent, indicates—

(i)   that the alteration was not signed on behalf of the body as it bears to have been so signed; or

(ii)   that the alteration was not validly witnessed for any reason specified in paragraphs (a) to (e) of sub-paragraph (4) below or that it was not sealed as it bears to have been sealed or that it was not validly sealed for the reason specified in sub-paragraph (4)(h) below,
the alteration shall be presumed to have been signed by the member, secretary or authorised person (as the case may be) and by the body.

(1A)   For the purposes of sub-paragraph (1)(b)(i) above, the name and address of the witness may bear to be stated in the alteration itself or in the testing clause or its equivalent.

(1B)   A presumption under sub-paragraph (1) above as to signing of an alteration to a document does not include a presumption—

(a)   that a person bearing to sign the alteration as a member of the body's governing board, a member of the body or the secretary of the body was such member or secretary; or

(b)   that a person signing the alteration on behalf of the body bearing to have been authorised to do so was authorised to do so.'.

(8)   In paragraph 1(4) of Schedule 1 after paragraph (g) there shall be inserted the following paragraph—

'(h)   if the alteration does not bear to have been witnessed, but bears to have been sealed with the common seal of the body, that it was sealed by a person without authority to do so or was not sealed on the date on which it was signed on behalf of the body;'.

Ministers of the Crown and office-holders

6.—(1)   Except where an enactment expressly provides otherwise, where a granter of a document is a Minister or an office-holder, the document is signed by the Minister or office-holder if it is signed—

(a)   by him personally; or

(b)   in a case where by virtue of any enactment or rule of law a document by a Minister may be signed by an officer of his or by any other Minister, by that officer or by that other Minister as the case may be; or

(c)   in a case where by virtue of any enactment or rule of law a document by an office-holder may be signed by an officer of his, by that officer; or

(d)   by any other person authorised to sign the document on his behalf.

(2)   For the purposes of the signing of a document under this paragraph, a person purporting to sign—

(a)   as an officer as mentioned in sub-paragraph (1)(b) or (1)(c) above;

(b)   as another Minister as mentioned in sub-paragraph (1)(b) above;

(c)   as a person authorised as mentioned in sub-paragraph (1)(d) above,
shall be presumed to be the officer, other Minister or authorised person, as the case may be.

(3)   Sub-paragraphs (1) and (2) of this paragraph are without prejudice to section 3 of and Schedule 1 to the Ministers of the Crown Act 1975.

(4)   Sub-paragraphs (1) to (3) of this paragraph apply in relation to the signing of an alteration made to a document as they apply in relation to the signing of a document.

(5)   Where a granter of a document is a Minister or office-holder, section 3 of and Schedule 1 to this Act shall have effect subject to the modifications set out in sub-paragraphs (6) and (7) below.

(6)   For section 3(1) there shall be substituted the following subsections—

'(1)   Subject to subsections (1A) to (7) below, where—

(a)   a document bears to have been subscribed—

(i)   by a Minister or, in a case where by virtue of any enactment or rule of law a document by a Minister may be signed by an officer

of his or by any other Minister, by that officer or by that other
Minister; or

    (ii)   by an office-holder or, in a case where by virtue of any enact-
ment or rule of law a document by an office-holder may be signed by an
officer of his, by that officer; or

    (iii)   by any other person bearing to have been authorised to sub-
scribe the document on behalf of the Minister or office-holder;

    (b)   the document bears to have been signed by a person as a witness
of the subscription mentioned in paragraph (a) above and to state the
name and address of the witness; and

    (c)   nothing in the document, or in the testing clause or its equivalent,
indicates—

    (i)   that it was not subscribed as it bears to have been subscribed;
or

    (ii)   that it was not validly witnessed for any reason specified in
paragraphs (a) to (e) of subsection (4) below,

the document shall be presumed to have been subscribed by the officer,
other Minister or authorised person and by the Minister or office-holder,
as the case may be.

    (1A)   For the purposes of subsection (1)(b) above, the name and address
of the witness may bear to be stated in the document itself or in the testing
clause or its equivalent.'.

    (7)   For paragraph 1(1) of Schedule 1 there shall be substituted the following
sub-paragraphs—

    '(1)   Subject to sub-paragraphs (1A) to (7) below, where—

    (a)   an alteration to a document bears to have been signed by—

    (i)   a Minister or, in a case where by virtue of any enactment or
rule of law a document by a Minister may be signed by an officer of
his or by any other Minister, by that officer or by that other Minister;
or

    (ii)   an office-holder or, in a case where by virtue of any enactment
or rule of law a document by an office-holder may be signed by an
officer of his, by that officer; or

    (iii)   any other person bearing to have been authorised to sign the
alteration on behalf of the Minister or office-holder;

    (b)   the alteration bears to have been signed by a person as a witness of
the signature mentioned in paragraph (a) above and to state the name and
address of the witness; and

    (c)   nothing in the document or alteration, or in the testing clause or its
equivalent, indicates—

    (i)   that the alteration was not signed as it bears to have been
signed; or

    (ii)   that the alteration was not validly witnessed for any reason
specified in paragraphs (a) to (e) of sub-paragraph (4) below,

the alteration shall be presumed to have been signed by the officer, other
Minister or authorised person and by the Minister or office-holder, as the
case may be.

    (1A)   For the purposes of sub-paragraph (1)(b) above, the name and
address of the witness may bear to be stated in the alteration itself or in the
testing clause or its equivalent.'.

SCHEDULE 3
MODIFICATIONS OF THIS ACT IN RELATION TO SUBSCRIPTION OR SIGNING BY RELEVANT PERSON UNDER SECTION 9

1. For any reference to the subscription or signing of a document by a granter there shall be substituted a reference to such subscription or signing by a relevant person under section 9(1).

2. For section 3(1) there shall be substituted the following subsection—
　'(1)　Subject to subsections (2) to (6) below, where—
　　(a)　a document bears to have been subscribed by a relevant person with the authority of a granter of it;
　　(b)　the document, or the testing clause or its equivalent, states that the document was read to that granter by the relevant person before such subscription or states that it was not so read because the granter made a declaration that he did not wish him to do so;
　　(c)　the document bears to have been signed by a person as a witness of the relevant person's subscription and the document, or the testing clause or its equivalent, bears to state the name and address of the witness; and
　　(d)　nothing in the document, or in the testing clause or its equivalent, indicates—
　　　(i)　that it was not subscribed by the relevant person as it bears to have been so subscribed;
　　　(ii)　that the statement mentioned in paragraph (b) above is incorrect; or
　　　(iii)　that it was not validly witnessed for any reason specified in paragraphs (a) to (e) of subsection (4) below (as modified by paragraph 4 of Schedule 3 to this Act),
　the document shall be presumed to have been subscribed by the relevant person and the statement so mentioned shall be presumed to be correct.'.

3. In section 3(3) for the words 'subsection (1)(b)' there shall be substituted the words 'subsection (1)(c)'.

4. For section 3(4) there shall be substituted the following subsection—
　'(4)　Where, in any proceedings relating to a document in which a question arises as to a relevant person's subscription on behalf of a granter under section 9(1) of this Act, it is established—
　　(a)　that a signature bearing to be the signature of the witness of the relevant person's subscription is not such a signature, whether by reason of forgery or otherwise;
　　(b)　that the person who signed the document as the witness of the relevant person's subscription is a person who is named in the document as a granter of it;
　　(c)　that the person who signed the document as the witness of the relevant person's subscription, at the time of signing—
　　　(i)　did not know the granter on whose behalf the relevant person had so subscribed;
　　　(ii)　was under the age of 16 years; or
　　　(iii)　was mentally incapable of acting as a witness;
　　(d)　that the person who signed the document, purporting to be the witness of the relevant person's subscription, did not see him subscribe it;
　　(dd)　that the person who signed the document as the witness of the relevant person's subscription did not witness the granting of authority by the granter concerned to the relevant person to subscribe the document on his behalf or did not witness the reading of the document to the granter by

the relevant person or the declaration that the granter did not wish him to do so;

(e)   that the person who signed the document as the witness of the relevant person's subscription did not sign the document after him or that such subscription and signature were not one continuous process;

(f)   that the name or address of such a witness was added after the document was founded on or registered as mentioned in subsection (3)(a) above or is erroneous in any material respect; or

(g)   in the case of a testamentary document consisting of more than one sheet, that a signature on any sheet bearing to be the signature of the relevant person is not such a signature, whether by reason of forgery or otherwise,

then, for the purposes of those proceedings, there shall be no presumption that the document has been subscribed by the relevant person on behalf of the granter concerned.'.

5.   In section 3(6) the words 'or acknowledgement' in both places where they occur shall be omitted.

6.   Section 3(7) shall be omitted.

7.   For section 4(1) there shall be substituted the following subsection—
'(1)   Where—

(a)   a document bears to have been subscribed by a relevant person under section 9(1) of this Act on behalf of a granter of it; but

(b)   there is no presumption under section 3 of this Act (as modified by paragraph 2 of Schedule 3 to this Act) that the document has been subscribed by that person or that the procedure referred to section 3(1)(b) of this Act as so modified was followed,

then, if the court, on an application being made to it by any person who has an interest in the document, is satisfied that the document was so subscribed by the relevant person with the authority of the granter and that the relevant person read the document to the granter before subscription or did not so read it because the granter declared that he did not wish him to do so, it shall—

(i)   cause the document to be endorsed with a certificate to that effect; or

(ii)   where the document has already been registered in the Books of Council and Session or in sheriff court books, grant decree to that effect.'.

8.   At the end of section 4(5)(a) there shall be added the following words—
'and that the procedure referred to in section 3(1)(b) of this Act as modified by paragraph 2 of Schedule 3 to this Act was followed.'.

9.   For paragraph 1(1) of Schedule 1 there shall be substituted the following sub-paragraph—
'(1)   Subject to sub-paragraphs (2) to (6) below, where—

(a)   an alteration to a document bears to have been signed by a relevant person with the authority of a granter of the document;

(b)   the document or alteration, or the testing clause or its equivalent, states that the alteration was read to that granter by the relevant person before such signature or states that the alteration was not so read because the granter made a declaration that he did not wish him to do so;

(c)   the alteration bears to have been signed by a person as a witness of the relevant person's signature and the alteration, or the testing clause or its equivalent, bears to state the name and address of the witness; and

(d)   nothing in the document or alteration, or in the testing clause or its equivalent, indicates—

    (i)   that the alteration was not signed by the relevant person as it bears to have been so signed;

    (ii)   that the statement mentioned in paragraph (b) above is incorrect; or

    (iii)   that the alteration was not validly witnessed for any reason specified in paragraphs (a) to (e) of sub-paragraph (4) below (as modified by paragraph 11 of Schedule 3 to this Act),

the alteration shall be presumed to have been signed by the relevant person and the statement so mentioned shall be presumed to be correct.'.

10. In paragraph 1(3) of Schedule 1 for the words 'sub-paragraph (1)(b)' there shall be substituted the words 'sub-paragraph (1)(c)'.

11. For paragraph 1(4) of Schedule 1 there shall be substituted the following sub-paragraph—

'(4)   Where, in any proceedings relating to an alteration to a document in which a question arises as to a relevant person's signature on behalf of a granter under section 9(1) of this Act, it is established—

    (a)   that a signature bearing to be the signature of the witness of the relevant person's signature is not such a signature, whether by reason of forgery or otherwise;

    (b)   that the person who signed the alteration as the witness of the relevant person's signature is a person who is named in the document as a granter of it;

    (c)   that the person who signed the alteration as the witness of the relevant person's signature, at the time of signing—

    (i)   did not know the granter on whose behalf the relevant person had so signed;

    (ii)   was under the age of 16 years; or

    (iii)   was mentally incapable of acting as a witness;

    (d)   that the person who signed the alteration, purporting to be the witness of the relevant person's signature, did not see him sign it;

    (dd)   that the person who signed the alteration as the witness of the relevant person's signature did not witness the granting of authority by the granter concerned to the relevant person to sign the alteration on his behalf or did not witness the reading of the alteration to the granter by the relevant person or the declaration that the granter did not wish him to do so;

    (e)   that the person who signed the alteration as the witness of the relevant person's signature did not sign the alteration after him or that the signing of the alteration by the granter and the witness was not one continuous process;

    (f)   that the name or address of such a witness was added after the alteration was founded on or registered as mentioned in sub-paragraph (3)(a) above or is erroneous in any material respect; or

    (g)   in the case of an alteration to a testamentary document consisting of more than one sheet, that a signature on any sheet of the alteration bearing to be the signature of the relevant person is not such a signature, whether by reason of forgery or otherwise,

then, for the purposes of those proceedings, there shall be no presumption that the alteration has been signed by the relevant person on behalf of the granter concerned.'.

12. In paragraph 1(6) of Schedule 1 the words 'or the acknowledgement of his signature' and the words 'or acknowledgement' shall be omitted.

13. Paragraph 1(7) of Schedule 1 shall be omitted.

14. For paragraph 2(1) of Schedule 1 there shall be substituted the following sub-paragraph—

'(1) Where—

(a) an alteration to a document bears to have been signed by a relevant person under section 9(1) of this Act on behalf of a granter of the document; but

(b) there is no presumption under paragraph 1 of Schedule 1 to this Act (as modified by paragraph 9 of Schedule 3 to this Act) that the alteration has been signed by that person or that the procedure referred to in paragraph 1(1)(b) of Schedule 1 to this Act as so modified was followed,

then, if the court, on an application being made to it by any person who has an interest in the document, is satisfied that the alteration was so signed by the relevant person with the authority of the granter and that the relevant person read the alteration to the granter before signing or did not so read it because the granter declared that he did not wish him to do so, it shall—

(i) cause the document to be endorsed with a certificate to that effect; or

(ii) where the document has already been registered in the Books of Council and Session or in sheriff court books, grant decree to that effect.'.

15. At the end of paragraph 2(5)(a) of Schedule 1 there shall be added the following words—

'and that the procedure referred to in paragraph 1(1)(b) of Schedule 1 to this Act as modified by paragraph 9 of Schedule 3 to this Act was followed.'.

CHILDREN (SCOTLAND) ACT 1995
(1995, c 36)

PART I
PARENTS, CHILDREN AND GUARDIANS

Parental responsibilities and parental rights

1 Parental responsibilities

(1) Subject to section 3(1)(b) [, and (d)] and (3) of this Act, a parent has in relation to his child the responsibility—

(a) to safeguard and promote the child's health, development and welfare;

(b) to provide, in a manner appropriate to the stage of development of the child—

(i) direction;

(ii) guidance,

to the child;

(c) if the child is not living with the parent, to maintain personal relations and direct contact with the child on a regular basis; and

(d) to act as the child's legal representative,

but only in so far as compliance with this section is practicable and in the interests of the child.

(2) 'Child' means for the purposes of—

(a) paragraphs (a), (b)(i), (c) and (d) of subsection (1) above, a person under the age of sixteen years;

(b) paragraph (b)(ii) of that subsection, a person under the age of eighteen years.

(3) The responsibilities mentioned in paragraphs (a) to (d) of subsection (1) above are in this Act referred to as 'parental responsibilities'; and the child, or any

person acting on his behalf, shall have title to sue, or to defend, in any proceedings as respects those responsibilities.

(4) The parental responsibilities supersede any analogous duties imposed on a parent at common law; but this section is without prejudice to any other duty so imposed on him or to any duty imposed on him by, under or by virtue of any other provision of this Act or of any other enactment.

6 Views of children

(1) A person shall, in reaching any major decision which involves—

(a) his fulfilling a parental responsibility or the responsibility mentioned in section 5(1) of this Act; or

(b) his exercising a parental right or giving consent by virtue of that section, have regard so far as practicable to the views (if he wishes to express them) of the child concerned, taking account of the child's age and maturity, and to those of any other person who has parental responsibilities or parental rights in relation to the child (and wishes to express those views); and without prejudice to the generality of this subsection a child twelve years of age or more shall be presumed to be of sufficient age and maturity to form a view.

(2) A transaction entered into in good faith by a third party and a person acting as legal representative of a child shall not be challengeable on the ground only that the child, or a person with parental responsibilities or parental rights in relation to the child, was not consulted or that due regard was not given to his views before the transaction was entered into.

Guardianship

. . .

10 Obligations and rights of person administering child's property

(1) A person acting as a child's legal representative in relation to the administration of the child's property—

(a) shall be required to act as a reasonable and prudent person would act on his own behalf; and

(b) subject to any order made under section 11 of this Act, shall be entitled to do anything which the child, if of full age and capacity, could do in relation to that property;

and subject to subsection (2) below, on ceasing to act as legal representative, shall be liable to account to the child for his intromissions with the child's property.

(2) No liability shall be incurred by virtue of subsection (1) above in respect of funds which have been used in the proper discharge of the person's responsibility to safeguard and promote the child's health, development and welfare.

CRIMINAL PROCEDURE (SCOTLAND) ACT 1995
(1995, c 46)

170 Damages in respect of summary proceedings

(1) No judge, clerk of court or prosecutor in the public interest shall be found liable by any court in damages for or in respect of any proceedings taken, act done, or judgment, decree or sentence pronounced in any summary proceedings under this Act, unless—

(a) the person suing has suffered imprisonment in consequence thereof; and

(b) such proceedings, act, judgment, decree or sentence has been quashed; and

(c) the person suing specifically avers and proves that such proceeding, act, judgment, decree or sentence was taken, done or pronounced maliciously and without probable cause.

(2) No such liability as aforesaid shall be incurred or found where such judge,

clerk of court or prosecutor establishes that the person suing was guilty of the offence in respect whereof he had been convicted, or on account of which he had been apprehended or had otherwise suffered, and that he had undergone no greater punishment than was assigned by law to such offence.

(3)   No action to enforce such liability as aforesaid shall lie unless it is commenced within two months after the proceeding, act, judgment, decree or sentence founded on, or in the case where the Act under which the action is brought fixes a shorter period, within that shorter period.

(4)   In this section 'judge' shall not include 'sheriff', and the provisions of this section shall be without prejudice to the privileges and immunities possessed by sheriffs.

DEFAMATION ACT 1996
(1996, c 31)

1   Responsibility for publication

(1)   In defamation proceedings a person has a defence if he shows that—

(a)   he was not the author, editor or publisher of the statement complained of,

(b)   he took reasonable care in relation to its publication, and

(c)   he did not know, and had no reason to believe, that what he did caused or contributed to the publication of a defamatory statement.

(2)   For this purpose 'author', 'editor' and 'publisher' have the following meanings, which are further explained in subsection (3)—

'author' means the originator of the statement, but does not include a person who did not intend that his statement be published at all;

'editor' means a person having editorial or equivalent responsibility for the content of the statement or the decision to publish it; and

'publisher' means a commercial publisher, that is, a person whose business is issuing material to the public, or a section of the public, who issues material containing the statement in the course of that business.

(3)   A person shall not be considered the author, editor or publisher of a statement if he is only involved—

(a)   in printing, producing, distributing or selling printed material containing the statement;

(b)   in processing, making copies of, distributing, exhibiting or selling a film or sound recording (as defined in Part I of the Copyright, Designs and Patents Act 1988) containing the statement;

(c)   in processing, making copies of, distributing or selling any electronic medium in or on which the statement is recorded, or in operating or providing any equipment, system or service by means of which the statement is retrieved, copied, distributed or made available in electronic form;

(d)   as the broadcaster of a live programme containing the statement in circumstances in which he has no effective control over the maker of the statement;

(e)   as the operator of or provider of access to a communications system by means of which the statement is transmitted, or made available, by a person over whom he has no effective control.

In a case not within paragraphs (a) to (e) the court may have regard to those provisions by way of analogy in deciding whether a person is to be considered the author, editor or publisher of a statement.

(4)   Employees or agents of an author, editor or publisher are in the same position as their employer or principal to the extent that they are responsible for the content of the statement or the decision to publish it.

(5)   In determining for the purposes of this section whether a person took reasonable care, or had reason to believe that what he did caused or contributed to the publication of a defamatory statement, regard shall be had to—

(a)   the extent of his responsibility for the content of the statement or the decision to publish it,

(b)   the nature or circumstances of the publication, and

(c)   the previous conduct or character of the author, editor or publisher.

(6)   This section does not apply to any cause of action which arose before the section came into force.

2   Offer to make amends

(1)   A person who has published a statement alleged to be defamatory of another may offer to make amends under this section.

(2)   The offer may be in relation to the statement generally or in relation to a specific defamatory meaning which the person making the offer accepts that the statement conveys ('a qualified offer').

(3)   An offer to make amends—

(a)   must be in writing

(b)   must be expressed to be an offer to make amends under section 2 of the Defamation Act 1996, and

(c)   must state whether it is a qualified offer and, if so, set out the defamatory meaning in relation to which it is made.

(4)   An offer to make amends under this section is an offer—

(a)   to make a suitable correction of the statement complained of and a sufficient apology to the aggrieved party;

(b)   to publish the correction and apology in a manner that is reasonable and practicable in the circumstances, and

(c)   to pay to the aggrieved party such compensation (if any), and such costs, as may be agreed or determined to be payable.

The fact that the offer is accompanied by an offer to take specific steps does not affect the fact that an offer to make amends under this section is an offer to do all the things mentioned in paragraphs (a) to (c).

(5)   An offer to make amends under this section may not be made by a person after serving a defence in defamation proceedings brought against him by the aggrieved party in respect of the publication in question.

(6)   An offer to make amends under this section may be withdrawn before it is accepted; and a renewal of an offer which has been withdrawn shall be treated as a new offer.

3   Accepting an offer to make amends

(1)   If an offer to make amends under section 2 is accepted by the aggrieved party, the following provisions apply.

(2)   The party accepting the offer may not bring or continue defamation proceedings in respect of the publication concerned against the person making the offer, but he is entitled to enforce the offer to make amends, as follows.

(3)   If the parties agree on the steps to be taken in fulfilment of the offer, the aggrieved party may apply to the court for an order that the other party fulfil his offer by taking the steps agreed.

(4)   If the parties do not agree on the steps to be taken by way of correction, apology and publication, the party who made the offer may take such steps as he thinks appropriate, and may in particular—

(a)   make the correction and apology by a statement in open court in terms approved by the court, and

(b)   give an undertaking to the court as to the manner of their publication.

(5)   If the parties do not agree on the amount to be paid by way of compensation, it shall be determined by the court on the same principles as damages in defamation proceedings.

The court shall take account of any steps taken in fulfilment of the offer and (so far as not agreed between the parties) of the suitability of the correction, the sufficiency of the apology and whether the manner of their publication was reasonable in the circumstances, and may reduce or increase the amount of compensation accordingly.

(6)   If the parties do not agree on the amount to be paid by way of costs, it shall be determined by the court on the same principles as costs awarded in court proceedings.

(7)   The acceptance of an offer by one person to make amends does not affect any cause of action against another person in respect of the same publication, subject as follows.

(8)   [*applies to England and Wales only*]

(9)   In Scotland—

   (a)   subsection (2) of section 3 of the Law Reform (Miscellaneous Provisions) (Scotland) Act 1940 (right of one joint wrongdoer as respects another to recover contribution towards damages) applies in relation to compensation paid under an offer to make amends as it applies in relation to damages in an action to which that section applies; and

   (b)   where another person is liable in respect of the same damage (whether jointly or otherwise), the person whose offer to make amends was accepted is not required to pay by virtue of any contribution under section 3(2) of that Act a greater amount than the amount of compensation payable in pursuance of the offer.

(10)   Proceedings under this section shall be heard and determined without a jury.

4   Failure to accept offer to make amends

(1)   If an offer to make amends under section 2, duly made and not withdrawn, is not accepted by the aggrieved party, the following provisions apply.

(2)   The fact that the offer was made is a defence (subject to subsection (3)) to defamation proceedings in respect of the publication in question by that party against the person making the offer.

A qualified offer is only a defence in respect of the meaning to which the offer related.

(3)   There is no such defence if the person by whom the offer was made knew or had reason to believe that the statement complained of—

   (a)   referred to the aggrieved party or was likely to be understood as referring to him, and

   (b)   was both false and defamatory of that party;

but it shall be presumed until the contrary is shown that he did not know and had no reason to believe that was the case.

(4)   The person who made the offer need not rely on it by way of defence, but if he does he may not rely on any other defence.

If the offer was a qualified offer, this applies only in respect of the meaning to which the offer related.

(5)   The offer may be relied on in mitigation of damages whether or not it was relied on as a defence.

. . .

The meaning of a statement

7   Ruling on the meaning of a statement

In defamation proceedings the court shall not be asked to rule whether a statement is arguably capable, as opposed to capable, of bearing a particular meaning or meanings attributed to it.

. . .

Evidence of convictions

12   Evidence of convictions

(1)   [*applies to England and Wales only*]

(2)   In section 12 of the Law Reform (Miscellaneous Provisions) (Scotland) Act 1968 (conclusiveness of convictions for purposes of defamation actions), in subsections (1) and (2) for 'a person' substitute 'the pursuer' and for 'that person' substitute 'he'; and after subsection (2) insert—

'(2A) In the case of an action for defamation in which there is more than one pursuer—

(a)   the references in subsections (1) and (2) above to the pursuer shall be construed as references to any of the pursuers, and

(b)   proof that any of the pursuers stands convicted of an offence shall be conclusive evidence that he committed that offence so far as that fact is relevant to any issue arising in relation to his cause of action or that of any other pursuer.'.

The amendments made by this subsection apply only for the purposes of an action begun after this section comes into force, whenever the cause of action arose.

(3)   [*applies to Northern Ireland only*]

Evidence concerning proceedings in Parliament

13   Evidence concerning proceedings in Parliament

(1)   Where the conduct of a person in or in relation to proceedings in Parliament is in issue in defamation proceedings, he may waive for the purposes of those proceedings, so far as concerns him, the protection of any enactment or rule of law which prevents proceedings in Parliament being impeached or questioned in any court or place out of Parliament.

(2)   Where a person waives that protection—

(a)   any such enactment or rule of law shall not apply to prevent evidence being given, questions being asked or statements, submissions, comments or findings being made about his conduct, and

(b)   none of those things shall be regarded as infringing the privilege of either House of Parliament.

(3)   The waiver by one person of that protection does not affect its operation in relation to another person who has not waived it.

(4)   Nothing in this section affects any enactment or rule of law so far as it protects a person (including a person who has waived the protection referred to above) from legal liability for words spoken or things done in the course of, or for the purposes of or incidental to, any proceedings in Parliament.

(5)   Without prejudice to the generality of subsection (4), that subsection applies to—

(a)   the giving of evidence before either House or a committee;

(b)   the presentation or submission of a document to either House or a committee;

(c)   the preparation of a document for the purposes of or incidental to the transacting of any such business;

(d)   the formulation, making or publication of a document, including a report, by or pursuant to an order of either House or a committee; and

(e)   any communication with the Parliamentary Commissioner for Standards or any person having functions in connection with the registration of members' interests.

In this subsection 'a committee' means a committee of either House or a joint committee of both Houses of Parliament.

Statutory privilege

14   Reports of court proceedings absolutely privileged

(1)   A fair and accurate report of proceedings in public before a court to which this section applies, if published contemporaneously with the proceedings, is absolutely privileged.

(2)   A report of proceedings which by an order of the court, or as a consequence of any statutory provision, is required to be postponed shall be treated as published contemporaneously if it is published as soon as practicable after publication is permitted.

(3)   This section applies to—

(a)   any court in the United Kingdom,

(b)   the European Court of Justice or any court attached to that court,

(c)   the European Court of Human Rights, and

(d)   any international criminal tribunal established by the Security Council of the United Nations or by an international agreement to which the United Kingdom is a party.

In paragraph (a) 'court' includes any tribunal or body exercising the judicial power of the State.

(4)   In section 8(6) of the Rehabilitation of Offenders Act 1974 and in Article 9(6) of the Rehabilitation of Offenders (Northern Ireland) Order 1978 (defamation actions: reports of court proceedings), for 'section 3 of the Law of Libel Amendment Act 1888' substitute 'section 14 of the Defamation Act 1996'.

15   Reports, etc protected by qualified privilege

(1)   The publication of any report or other statement mentioned in Schedule 1 to this Act is privileged unless the publication is shown to be made with malice, subject as follows.

(2)   In defamation proceedings in respect of the publication of a report or other statement mentioned in Part II of that Schedule, there is no defence under this section if the plaintiff shows that the defendant—

(a)   was requested by him to publish in a suitable manner a reasonable letter or statement by way of explanation or contradiction, and

(b)   refused or neglected to do so.

For this purpose 'in a suitable manner' means in the same manner as the publication complained of or in a manner that is adequate and reasonable in the circumstances.

(3)   This section does not apply to the publication to the public, or a section of the public, of matter which is not of public concern and the publication of which is not for the public benefit.

(4)   Nothing in this section shall be construed—

(a)   as protecting the publication of matter the publication of which is prohibited by law, or

(b)   as limiting or abridging any privilege subsisting apart from this section.

Supplementary provisions

. . .

17   Interpretation

(1)   In this Act—

'publication' and 'publish', in relation to a statement, have the meaning they have for the purposes of the law of defamation generally, but 'publisher' is specially defined for the purposes of section 1;

'statement' means words, pictures, visual images, gestures or any other method of signifying meaning; and

'statutory provision' means—

(a)   a provision contained in an Act or in subordinate legislation within the meaning of the Interpretation Act 1978,

[(aa)   a provision contained in an Act of the Scottish Parliament or in an instrument made under such an Act], or

(b)   a statutory provision within the meaning given by section 1(f) of the Interpretation Act (Northern Ireland) 1954.

(2)   In this Act as it applies to proceedings in Scotland—

'costs' means expenses; and

'plaintiff' and 'defendant' mean pursuer and defender.

General provisions

18   Extent

. . .

(2)   The following provisions of this Act extend to Scotland—

section 1 (responsibility for publication),

sections 2 to 4 (offer to make amends), except section 3(8),

section 12(2) (evidence of convictions),

section 13 (evidence concerning proceedings in Parliament),

sections 14 and 15 and Schedule 1 (statutory privilege),

section 16 and Schedule 2 (repeals) so far as relating to enactments extending to Scotland,

section 17 (interpretation),

this subsection,

section 19 (commencement) so far as relating to provisions which extend to Scotland, and

section 20 (short title and saving).

. . .

20   Short title and saving

(1)   This Act may be cited as the Defamation Act 1996.

[. . .]

SCHEDULES

SCHEDULE 1
QUALIFIED PRIVILEGE

PART I
STATEMENTS HAVING QUALIFIED PRIVILEGE WITHOUT EXPLANATION OR CONTRADICTION

1.   A fair and accurate report of proceedings in public of a legislature anywhere in the world.

2.   A fair and accurate report of proceedings in public before a court anywhere in the world.

3.   A fair and accurate report of proceedings in public of a person appointed to hold a public inquiry by a government or legislature anywhere in the world.

4.   A fair and accurate report of proceedings in public anywhere in the world of an international organisation or an international conference.

5.   A fair and accurate copy of or extract from any register or other document required by law to be open to public inspection.

6.   A notice or advertisement published by or on the authority of a court, or of a judge or officer of a court, anywhere in the world.

7.   A fair and accurate copy of or extract from matter published by or on the authority of a government or legislature anywhere in the world.

8.   A fair and accurate copy of or extract from matter published anywhere in the world by an international organisation or an international conference.

PART II
STATEMENTS PRIVILEGED SUBJECT TO EXPLANATION OR CONTRADICTION

9.   (1)   A fair and accurate copy of or extract from a notice or other matter issued for the information of the public by or on behalf of—

(a)   a legislature in any member State or the European Parliament;

(b)   the government of any member State, or any authority performing governmental functions in any member State or part of a member State, or the European Commission;

(c)   an international organisation or international conference.

(2)   In this paragraph 'governmental functions' includes police functions.

10.   A fair and accurate copy of or extract from a document made available by a court in any member State or the European Court of Justice (or any court attached to that court), or by a judge or officer of any such court.

11.   (1)   A fair and accurate report of proceedings at any public meeting or sitting in the United Kingdom of—

(a)   a local authority [, local authority committee or in the case of a local authority which are operating executive arrangements the executive of that authority or a committee of that executive];

(b)   a justice or justices of the peace acting otherwise than as a court exercising judicial authority;

(c)   a commission, tribunal, committee or person appointed for the purposes of any inquiry by any statutory provision, by Her Majesty or by a Minister of the Crown [, a member of the Scottish Executive, the Welsh Ministers or the Counsel General to the Welsh Assembly Government] or a Northern Ireland Department;

(d)   a person appointed by a local authority to hold a local inquiry in pursuance of any statutory provision;

(e)   any other tribunal, board, committee or body constituted by or under, and exercising functions under, any statutory provision.

[(1A)   In the case of a local authority which are operating executive arrangements, a fair and accurate record of any decision made by any member of the executive where that record is required to be made and available for public inspection by virtue of section 22 of the Local Government Act 2000 or of any provision in regulations made under that section.]

(2)   [In sub-paragraphs (1)(a) and (1A)]—

['executive' and 'executive arrangements' have the same meaning as in Part II of the Local Government Act 2000;]

'local authority' means—

(a)   in relation to England and Wales, a principal council within the meaning of the Local Government Act 1972, any body falling within any paragraph of section 100J(1) of that Act or an authority or body to which the Public Bodies (Admission to Meetings) Act 1960 applies,

(b)   in relation to Scotland, a council constituted under section 2 of the Local Government etc (Scotland) Act 1994 or an authority or body to which the Public Bodies (Admission to Meetings) Act 1960 applies,

(c)   in relation to Northern Ireland, any authority or body to which sections 23 to 27 of the Local Government Act (Northern Ireland) 1972 apply; and

'local authority committee' means any committee of a local authority or of local authorities, and includes—

(a)   any committee or sub-committee in relation to which sections 100A to

100D of the Local Government Act 1972 apply by virtue of section 100E of that Act (whether or not also by virtue of section 100J of that Act), and

(b)   any committee or sub-committee in relation to which sections 50A to 50D of the Local Government (Scotland) Act 1973 apply by virtue of section 50E of that Act.

(3)   A fair and accurate report of any corresponding proceedings in any of the Channel Islands or the Isle of Man or in another member State.

12.   (1)   A fair and accurate report of proceedings at any public meeting held in a member State.

(2)   In this paragraph a 'public meeting' means a meeting bona fide and lawfully held for a lawful purpose and for the furtherance or discussion of a matter of public concern, whether admission to the meeting is general or restricted.

13.   (1)   A fair and accurate report of proceedings at a general meeting of a UK public company.

(2)   A fair and accurate copy of or extract from any document circulated to members of a UK public company—

(a)   by or with the authority of the board of directors of the company,

(b)   by the auditors of the company, or

(c)   by any member of the company in pursuance of a right conferred by any statutory provision.

(3)   A fair and accurate copy of or extract from any document circulated to members of a UK public company which relates to the appointment, resignation, retirement or dismissal of directors of the company.

(4)   In this paragraph 'UK public company' means—

(a)   a public company within the meaning of [section 4(2) of the Companies Act 2006], or

(b)   a body corporate incorporated by or registered under any other statutory provision, or by Royal Charter, or formed in pursuance of letters patent.

(5)   A fair and accurate report of proceedings at any corresponding meeting of, or copy of or extract from any corresponding document circulated to members of, a public company formed under the law of any of the Channel Islands or the Isle of Man or of another member State.

14.   A fair and accurate report of any finding or decision of any of the following descriptions of association, formed in the United Kingdom or another member State, or of any committee or governing body of such an association—

(a)   an association formed for the purpose of promoting or encouraging the exercise of or interest in any art, science, religion or learning, and empowered by its constitution to exercise control over or adjudicate on matters of interest or concern to the association, or the actions or conduct of any person subject to such control or adjudication;

(b)   an association formed for the purpose of promoting or safeguarding the interests of any trade, business, industry or profession, or of the persons carrying on or engaged in any trade, business, industry or profession, and empowered by its constitution to exercise control over or adjudicate upon matters connected with that trade, business, industry or profession, or the actions or conduct of those persons;

(c)   an association formed for the purpose of promoting or safeguarding the interests of a game, sport or pastime to the playing or exercise of which members of the public are invited or admitted, and empowered by its constitution to exercise control over or adjudicate upon persons connected with or taking part in the game, sport or pastime;

(d)   an association formed for the purpose of promoting charitable objects or other objects beneficial to the community and empowered by its constitution to exercise control over or to adjudicate on matters of interest or concern to the association, or the actions or conduct of any person subject to such control or adjudication.

15. (1) A fair and accurate report of, or copy of or extract from, any adjudication, report, statement or notice issued by a body, officer or other person designated for the purposes of this paragraph—

(a) for England and Wales or Northern Ireland, by order of the Lord Chancellor, and

(b) for Scotland, by order of the Secretary of State.

(2) An order under this paragraph shall be made by statutory instrument which shall be subject to annulment in pursuance of a resolution of either House of Parliament.

PART III
SUPPLEMENTARY PROVISIONS

16. (1) In this Schedule—

'court' includes any tribunal or body exercising the judicial power of the State;

'international conference' means a conference attended by representatives of two or more governments;

'international organisation' means an organisation of which two or more governments are members, and includes any committee or other subordinate body of such an organisation; and

'legislature' includes a local legislature.

(2) References in this Schedule to a member State include any European dependent territory of a member State.

(3) In paragraphs 2 and 6 'court' includes—

(a) the European Court of Justice (or any court attached to that court) and the Court of Auditors of the European Communities,

(b) the European Court of Human Rights,

(c) any international criminal tribunal established by the Security Council of the United Nations or by an international agreement to which the United Kingdom is a party, and

(d) the International Court of Justice and any other judicial or arbitral tribunal deciding matters in dispute between States.

(4) In paragraphs 1, 3 and 7 'legislature' includes the European Parliament.

17. (1) Provision may be made by order identifying—

(a) for the purposes of paragraph 11, the corresponding proceedings referred to in sub-paragraph (3);

(b) for the purposes of paragraph 13, the corresponding meetings and documents referred to in sub-paragraph (5).

(2) An order under this paragraph may be made—

(a) for England and Wales or Northern Ireland, by the Lord Chancellor, and

(b) for Scotland, by the Secretary of State.

(3) An order under this paragraph shall be made by statutory instrument which shall be subject to annulment in pursuance of a resolution of either House of Parliament.

DAMAGES ACT 1996
(1996, c 48)

1   Assumed rate of return on investment of damages

(1)   In determining the return to be expected from the investment of a sum awarded as damages for future pecuniary loss in an action for personal injury the court shall, subject to and in accordance with rules of court made for the purposes of this section, take into account such rate of return (if any) as may from time to time be prescribed by an order made by the Lord Chancellor.

(2)   Subsection (1) above shall not however prevent the court taking a different rate of return into account if any party to the proceedings shows that it is more appropriate in the case in question.

(3)   An order under subsection (1) above may prescribe different rates of return for different classes of case.

(4)   Before making an order under subsection (1) above the Lord Chancellor shall consult the Government Actuary and the Treasury; and any order under that subsection shall be made by statutory instrument subject to annulment in pursuance of a resolution of either House of Parliament.

(5)   In the application of this section to Scotland—

(a)   for the reference to the Lord Chancellor in subsections (1) and (4) there is substituted a reference to the Scottish Ministers; and

(b)   in subsection (4)—

(i)   'and the Treasury' is omitted; and

(ii)   for 'either House of Parliament' there is substituted 'the Scottish Parliament'.

HOUSING GRANTS, CONSTRUCTION AND REGENERATION ACT 1996
(1996, c 53)

113   Prohibition of conditional payment provisions

(1)   A provision making payment under a construction contract conditional on the payer receiving payment from a third person is ineffective, unless that third person, or any other person payment by whom is under the contract (directly or indirectly) a condition of payment by that third person, is insolvent.

(2)   For the purposes of this section a company becomes insolvent—

[(a)   when it enters administration within the meaning of Schedule B1 to the Insolvency Act 1986,]

(b)   on the appointment of an administrative receiver or a receiver or manager of its property under Chapter I of Part III of that Act, or the appointment of a receiver under Chapter II of that Part,

(c)   on the passing of a resolution for voluntary winding-up without a declaration of solvency under section 89 of that Act, or

(d)   on the making of a winding-up order under Part IV or V of that Act.

(3)   For the purposes of this section a partnership becomes insolvent—

(a)   on the making of a winding-up order against it under any provision of the Insolvency Act 1986 as applied by an order under section 420 of that Act, or

(b)   when sequestration is awarded on the estate of the partnership under section 12 of the Bankruptcy (Scotland) Act 1985 or the partnership grants a trust deed for its creditors.

(4)   For the purposes of this section an individual becomes insolvent—

(a)   on the making of a bankruptcy order against him under Part IX of the Insolvency Act 1986, or

(b)   on the sequestration of his estate under the Bankruptcy (Scotland) Act 1985 or when he grants a trust deed for his creditors.

(5)   A company, partnership or individual shall also be treated as insolvent on the occurrence of any event corresponding to those specified in subsection (2), (3)

or (4) under the law of Northern Ireland or of a country outside the United Kingdom.

(6)   Where a provision is rendered ineffective by subsection (1), the parties are free to agree other terms for payment.

In the absence of such agreement, the relevant provisions of the Scheme for Construction Contracts apply.

SOCIAL SECURITY (RECOVERY OF BENEFITS) ACT 1997
(1997, c 27)

3 'The relevant period'

(1)   In relation to a person ('the claimant') who has suffered any accident, injury or disease, 'the relevant period' has the meaning given by the following subsections.

(2)   Subject to subsection (4), if it is a case of accident or injury, the relevant period is the period of five years immediately following the day on which the accident or injury in question occurred.

(3)   Subject to subsection (4), if it is a case of disease, the relevant period is the period of five years beginning with the date on which the claimant first claims a listed benefit in consequence of the disease.

(4)   If at any time before the end of the period referred to in subsection (2) or (3)—

(a)   a person makes a compensation payment in final discharge of any claim made by or in respect of the claimant and arising out of the accident, injury or disease, or

(b)   an agreement is made under which an earlier compensation payment is treated as having been made in final discharge of any such claim,

the relevant period ends at that time.

6   Liability to pay Secretary of State amount of benefits

(1)   A person who makes a compensation payment in any case is liable to pay to the Secretary of State an amount equal to the total amount of the recoverable benefits.

(2)   The liability referred to in subsection (1) arises immediately before the compensation payment or, if there is more than one, the first of them is made.

(3)   No amount becomes payable under this section before the end of the period of 14 days following the day on which the liability arises.

7   Recovery of payments due under section 6

(1)   This section applies where a person has made a compensation payment but—

(a)   has not applied for a certificate of recoverable benefits, or

(b)   has not made a payment to the Secretary of State under section 6 before the end of the period allowed under that section.

(2)   The Secretary of State may—

(a)   issue the person who made the compensation payment with a certificate of recoverable benefits, if none has been issued, or

(b)   issue him with a copy of the certificate of recoverable benefits or (if more than one has been issued) the most recent one,

and (in either case) issue him with a demand that payment of any amount due under section 6 be made immediately.

(3)   The Secretary of State may, in accordance with subsections (4) and (5), recover the amount for which a demand for payment is made under subsection (2) from the person who made the compensation payment.

(4)   If the person who made the compensation payment resides or carries on business in England and Wales and a county court so orders, any amount recover-

able under subsection (3) is recoverable [under section 85 of the County Courts Act 1984] or otherwise as if it were payable under an order of that court.

(5)   If the person who made the payment resides or carries on business in Scotland, any amount recoverable under subsection (3) may be enforced in like manner as an extract registered decree arbitral bearing a warrant for execution issued by the sheriff court of any sheriffdom in Scotland.

(6)   A document bearing a certificate which—

(a)   is signed by a person authorised to do so by the Secretary of State, and

(b)   states that the document, apart from the certificate, is a record of the amount recoverable under subsection (3),

is conclusive evidence that that amount is so recoverable.

(7)   A certificate under subsection (6) purporting to be signed by a person authorised to do so by the Secretary of State is to be treated as so signed unless the contrary is proved.

SCHEDULES

SCHEDULE 1
COMPENSATION PAYMENTS

PART I
EXEMPTED PAYMENTS

1.   Any small payment (defined in Part II of this Schedule).

2.   Any payment made to or for the injured person under section [130 of the Powers of Criminal Courts (Sentencing) Act 2000 or section 175 of the Armed Forces Act 2006] or section 249 of the Criminal Procedure (Scotland) Act 1995 (compensation orders against convicted persons).

3.   Any payment made in the exercise of a discretion out of property held subject to a trust in a case where no more than 50 per cent. by value of the capital contributed to the trust was directly or indirectly provided by persons who are, or are alleged to be, liable in respect of—

(a)   the accident, injury or disease suffered by the injured person, or

(b)   the same or any connected accident, injury or disease suffered by another.

4.   Any payment made out of property held for the purposes of any prescribed trust (whether the payment also falls within paragraph 3 or not).

5.   (1)   Any payment made to the injured person by an [insurer] under the terms of any contract of insurance entered into between the injured person and the [insurer] before—

(a)   the date on which the injured person first claims a listed benefit in consequence of the disease in question, or

(b)   the occurrence of the accident or injury in question.

[(2)   'Insurer' means—

(a)   a person who has permission under Part 4 of the Financial Services and Markets Act 2000 to effect or carry out contracts of insurance; or

(b)   an EEA firm of the kind mentioned in paragraph 5(d) of Schedule 3 to that Act which has permission under paragraph 15 of that Schedule (as a result of qualifying for authorisation under paragraph 12 of that Schedule) to effect or carry out contracts of insurance.

(3)   Sub-paragraph (2) must be read with—

(a)   section 22 of the Financial Services and Markets Act 2000;

(b)   any relevant order under that section; and

(c)   Schedule 2 to that Act.]

6.   Any redundancy payment falling to be taken into account in the assessment of damages in respect of an accident, injury or disease.

7.   So much of any payment as is referable to costs.

8.   Any prescribed payment.

PART II
POWER TO DISREGARD SMALL PAYMENTS

9.—(1) Regulations may make provision for compensation payments to be disregarded for the purposes of sections 6 and 8 in prescribed cases where the amount of the compensation payment, or the aggregate amount of two or more connected compensation payments, does not exceed the prescribed sum.

(2) A compensation payment disregarded by virtue of this paragraph is referred to in paragraph 1 as a 'small payment'.

(3) For the purposes of this paragraph—

(a) two or more compensation payments are 'connected' if each is made to or in respect of the same injured person and in respect of the same accident, injury or disease, and

(b) any reference to a compensation payment is a reference to a payment which would be such a payment apart from paragraph 1.

SCHEDULE 2
CALCULATION OF COMPENSATION PAYMENT

(1) *Head of compensation*	(2) *Benefit*
1. Compensation for earnings lost during the relevant period	. . . Disablement pension payable under section 103 of the 1992 Act [Employment and support allowance] Incapacity benefit Income support Invalidity pension and allowance Jobseeker's allowance Reduced earnings allowance Severe disablement allowance Sickness benefit Statutory sick pay Unemployability supplement Unemployment benefit
2. Compensation for cost of care incurred during the relevant period	Attendance allowance Care component of disability living allowance Disablement pension increase payable under section 104 or 105 of the 1992 Act
3. Compensation for loss of mobility during the relevant period	Mobility allowance Mobility component of disability living allowance

CONTRACT (SCOTLAND) ACT 1997
(1997, c 34)

1 Extrinsic evidence of additional contract term etc

(1) Where a document appears (or two or more documents appear) to comprise all the express terms of a contract or unilateral voluntary obligation, it shall be presumed, unless the contrary is proved, that the document does (or the documents do) comprise all the express terms of the contract or unilateral voluntary obligation.

(2) Extrinsic oral or documentary evidence shall be admissible to prove, for the purposes of subsection (1) above, that the contract or unilateral voluntary obligation includes additional express terms (whether or not written terms).

(3) Notwithstanding the foregoing provisions of this section, where one of the terms in the document (or in the documents) is to the effect that the document does (or the documents do) comprise all the express terms of the contract or unilateral voluntary obligation, that term shall be conclusive in the matter.

(4) This section is without prejudice to any enactment which makes provision as respects the constitution, or formalities of execution, of a contract or unilateral voluntary obligation.

2 Supersession

(1) Where a deed is executed in implement, or purportedly in implement, of a contract, an unimplemented, or otherwise unfulfilled, term of the contract shall not be taken to be superseded by virtue only of that execution or of the delivery and acceptance of the deed.

(2) Subsection (1) above is without prejudice to any agreement which the parties to a contract may reach (whether or not an agreement incorporated into the contract) as to supersession of the contract.

3 Damages for breach of contract of sale

Any rule of law which precludes the buyer in a contract of sale of property from obtaining damages for breach of that contract by the seller unless the buyer rejects the property and rescinds the contract shall cease to have effect.

4 Short title, extent etc

(1) This Act may be cited as the Contract (Scotland) Act 1997.

(2) This Act shall come into force at the end of that period of three months which begins with the day on which the Act is passed.

(3) Section 1 of this Act applies only for the purposes of proceedings commenced on or after, and sections 2 and 3 only as respects contracts entered into on or after, the date on which this Act comes into force.

(4) This Act extends to Scotland only.

PROTECTION FROM HARASSMENT ACT 1997
(1997, c 40)

Scotland

8 Harassment

(1) Every individual has a right to be free from harassment and, accordingly, a person must not pursue a course of conduct which amounts to harassment of another and—

(a) is intended to amount to harassment of that person; or

(b) occurs in circumstances where it would appear to a reasonable person that it would amount to harassment of that person.

[1A Subsection (1) is subject to section 8A.]

(2) An actual or apprehended breach of subsection (1) may be the subject of a claim in civil proceedings by the person who is or may be the victim of the course

of conduct in question; and any such claim shall be known as an action of harassment.

(3)   For the purposes of this section—

'conduct' includes speech;

'harassment' of a person includes causing the person alarm or distress; and

a course of conduct must involve conduct on at least two occasions.

(4)   It shall be a defence to any action of harassment to show that the course of conduct complained of—

    (a)   was authorised by, under or by virtue of any enactment or rule of law;

    (b)   was [engaged in] for the purpose of preventing or detecting crime; or

    (c)   was, in the particular circumstances, reasonable.

(5)   In an action of harassment the court may, without prejudice to any other remedies which it may grant—

    (a)   award damages;

    (b)   grant—

       (i)   interdict or interim interdict;

       (ii)   if it is satisfied that it is appropriate for it to do so in order to protect the person from further harassment, an order, to be known as a 'non-harassment order', requiring the defender to refrain from such conduct in relation to the pursuer as may be specified in the order for such period (which includes an indeterminate period) as may be so specified,

but a person may not be subjected to the same prohibitions in an interdict or interim interdict and a non-harassment order at the same time.

(6)   The damages which may be awarded in an action of harassment include damages for any anxiety caused by the harassment and any financial loss resulting from it.

(7)   Without prejudice to any right to seek review of any interlocutor, a person against whom a non-harassment order has been made, or the person for whose protection the order was made, may apply to the court by which the order was made for revocation of or a variation of the order and, on any such application, the court may revoke the order or vary it in such manner as it considers appropriate.

    [. . .]

[8A   Harassment amounting to domestic abuse

(1)   Every individual has a right to be free from harassment and, accordingly, a person must not engage in conduct which amounts to harassment of another and—

    (a)   is intended to amount to harassment of that person; or

    (b)   occurs in circumstances where it would appear to a reasonable person that it would amount to harassment of that person.

(2)   Subsection (1) only applies where the conduct referred to amounts to domestic abuse.

(3)   Subsections (2) to (7) of section 8 apply in relation to subsection (1) as they apply in relation to subsection (1) of that section but with the following modifications—

    (a)   in subsections (2) and (4), the words 'course of' are omitted;

    (b)   for subsection (3) there is substituted—

    '(3)   For the purposes of this section—

    "conduct"—

       (a)   may involve behaviour on one or more than one occasion; and

       (b)   includes—

          (i)   speech; and

          (ii)   presence in any place or area; and

    "harassment" of a person includes causing the person alarm or distress.'.]

9   Breach of non-harassment order

(1)   Any person who is [. . .] in breach of a non-harassment order made under section 8 [or section 8A] is guilty of an offence and liable—

(a)   on conviction on indictment, to imprisonment for a term not exceeding five years or to a fine, or to both such imprisonment and such fine; and

(b)   on summary conviction, to imprisonment for a period not exceeding six months or to a fine not exceeding the statutory maximum, or to both such imprisonment and such fine.

(2)   A breach of a non-harassment order shall not be punishable other than in accordance with subsection (1).

[(3)   A constable may arrest without warrant any person he reasonably believes is committing or has committed an offence under subsection (1).

(4)   Subsection (3) is without prejudice to any power of arrest conferred by law apart from that subsection.]

LATE PAYMENT OF COMMERCIAL DEBTS (INTEREST) ACT 1998
(1998, c 20)

PART I
STATUTORY INTEREST ON QUALIFYING DEBTS

1   Statutory interest

(1)   It is an implied term in a contract to which this Act applies that any qualifying debt created by the contract carries simple interest subject to and in accordance with this Part.

(2)   Interest carried under that implied term (in this Act referred to as 'statutory interest') shall be treated, for the purposes of any rule of law or enactment (other than this Act) relating to interest on debts, in the same way as interest carried under an express contract term.

(3)   This Part has effect subject to Part II (which in certain circumstances permits contract terms to oust or vary the right to statutory interest that would otherwise be conferred by virtue of the term implied by subsection (1)).

2   Contracts to which Act applies

(1)   This Act applies to a contract for the supply of goods or services where the purchaser and the supplier are each acting in the course of a business, other than an excepted contract.

(2)   In this Act 'contract for the supply of goods or services' means—

(a)   a contract of sale of goods; or

(b)   a contract (other than a contract of sale of goods) by which a person does any, or any combination, of the things mentioned in subsection (3) for a consideration that is (or includes) a money consideration.

(3)   Those things are—

(a)   transferring or agreeing to transfer to another the property in goods;

(b)   bailing or agreeing to bail goods to another by way of hire or, in Scotland, hiring or agreeing to hire goods to another; and

(c)   agreeing to carry out a service.

(4)   For the avoidance of doubt a contract of service or apprenticeship is not a contract for the supply of goods or services.

(5)   The following are excepted contracts—

(a)   a consumer credit agreement;

(b)   a contract intended to operate by way of mortgage, pledge, charge or other security.

[. . .]

(7)   In this section—

'business' includes a profession and the activities of any government department or local or public authority;

'consumer credit agreement' has the same meaning as in the Consumer Credit Act 1974;

'contract of sale of goods' and 'goods' have the same meaning as in the Sale of Goods Act 1979;

['government department' includes any part of the Scottish Administration].

'property in goods' means the general property in them and not merely a special property.

[2A   Application of the Act to advocates

The provisions of this Act apply to a transaction in respect of which fees are paid for professional services to a member of the Faculty of Advocates as they apply to a contract for the supply of services for the purpose of this Act.]

3   Qualifying debts

(1)   A debt created by virtue of an obligation under a contract to which this Act applies to pay the whole or any part of the contract price is a 'qualifying debt' for the purposes of this Act, unless (when created) the whole of the debt is prevented from carrying statutory interest by this section.

(2)   A debt does not carry statutory interest if or to the extent that it consists of a sum to which a right to interest or to charge interest applies by virtue of any enactment (other than section 1 of this Act).

This subsection does not prevent a sum from carrying statutory interest by reason of the fact that a court, arbitrator or arbiter would, apart from this Act, have power to award interest on it.

(3)   A debt does not carry (and shall be treated as never having carried) statutory interest if or to the extent that a right to demand interest on it, which exists by virtue of any rule of law, is exercised.

[. . .]

4   Period for which statutory interest runs

(1)   Statutory interest runs in relation to a qualifying debt in accordance with this section (unless section 5 applies).

(2)   Statutory interest starts to run on the day after the relevant day for the debt, at the rate prevailing under section 6 at the end of the relevant day.

(3)   Where the supplier and the purchaser agree a date for payment of the debt (that is, the day on which the debt is to be created by the contract), that is the relevant day unless the debt relates to an obligation to make an advance payment.

A date so agreed may be a fixed one or may depend on the happening of an event or the failure of an event to happen.

(4)   Where the debt relates to an obligation to make an advance payment, the relevant day is the day on which the debt is treated by section 11 as having been created.

(5)   In any other case, the relevant day is the last day of the period of 30 days beginning with—

(a)   the day on which the obligation of the supplier to which the debt relates is performed; or

(b)   the day on which the purchaser has notice of the amount of the debt or (where that amount is unascertained) the sum which the supplier claims is the amount of the debt,

whichever is the later.

(6)   Where the debt is created by virtue of an obligation to pay a sum due in respect of a period of hire of goods, subsection (5)(a) has effect as if it referred to the last day of that period.

(7)   Statutory interest ceases to run when the interest would cease to run if it were carried under an express contract term.

(8)   In this section 'advance payment' has the same meaning as in section 11.

5   Remission of statutory interest

(1)   This section applies where, by reason of any conduct of the supplier, the interests of justice require that statutory interest should be remitted in whole or part in respect of a period for which it would otherwise run in relation to a qualifying debt.

(2)   If the interests of justice require that the supplier should receive no statutory interest for a period, statutory interest shall not run for that period.

(3)   If the interests of justice require that the supplier should receive statutory interest at a reduced rate for a period, statutory interest shall run at such rate as meets the justice of the case for that period.

(4)   Remission of statutory interest under this section may be required—

(a)   by reason of conduct at any time (whether before or after the time at which the debt is created); and

(b)   for the whole period for which statutory interest would otherwise run or for one or more parts of that period.

(5)   In this section 'conduct' includes any act or omission.

[5A   Compensation arising out of late payment

(1)   Once statutory interest begins to run in relation to a qualifying debt, the supplier shall be entitled to a fixed sum (in addition to the statutory interest on the debt).

(2)   That sum shall be—

(a)   for a debt less than £1,000, the sum of £40;

(b)   for a debt of £1,000 or more, but less than £10,000, the sum of £70;

(c)   for a debt of £10,000 or more, the sum of £100.

(3)   The obligation to pay an additional fixed sum under this section in respect of a qualifying debt shall be treated as part of the term implied by section 1(1) in the contract creating the debt.]

6   Rate of statutory interest

(1)   The Secretary of State shall by order made with the consent of the Treasury set the rate of statutory interest by prescribing—

(a)   a formula for calculating the rate of statutory interest; or

(b)   the rate of statutory interest.

(2)   Before making such an order the Secretary of State shall, among other things, consider the extent to which it may be desirable to set the rate so as to—

(a)   protect suppliers whose financial position makes them particularly vulnerable if their qualifying debts are paid late; and

(b)   deter generally the late payment of qualifying debts.

PART II
CONTRACT TERMS RELATING TO LATE PAYMENT OF QUALIFYING DEBTS

7   Purpose of Part II

(1)   This Part deals with the extent to which the parties to a contract to which this Act applies may by reference to contract terms oust or vary the right to statutory interest that would otherwise apply when a qualifying debt created by the contract (in this Part referred to as 'the debt') is not paid.

(2)   This Part applies to contract terms agreed before the debt is created; after that time the parties are free to agree terms dealing with the debt.

(3)   This Part has effect without prejudice to any other ground which may affect the validity of a contract term.

8   Circumstances where statutory interest may be ousted or varied

(1)   Any contract terms are void to the extent that they purport to exclude the right to statutory interest in relation to the debt, unless there is a substantial contractual remedy for late payment of the debt.

(2)   Where the parties agree a contractual remedy for late payment of the debt that is a substantial remedy, statutory interest is not carried by the debt (unless they agree otherwise).

(3)   The parties may not agree to vary the right to statutory interest in relation to the debt unless either the right to statutory interest as varied or the overall remedy for late payment of the debt is a substantial remedy.

(4)   Any contract terms are void to the extent that they purport to—

     (a)   confer a contractual right to interest that is not a substantial remedy for late payment of the debt, or

     (b)   vary the right to statutory interest so as to provide for a right to statutory interest that is not a substantial remedy for late payment of the debt,

unless the overall remedy for late payment of the debt is a substantial remedy.

(5)   Subject to this section, the parties are free to agree contract terms which deal with the consequences of late payment of the debt.

9   Meaning of 'substantial remedy'

(1)   A remedy for the late payment of the debt shall be regarded as a substantial remedy unless—

     (a)   the remedy is insufficient either for the purpose of compensating the supplier for late payment or for deterring late payment; and

     (b)   it would not be fair or reasonable to allow the remedy to be relied on to oust or (as the case may be) to vary the right to statutory interest that would otherwise apply in relation to the debt.

(2)   In determining whether a remedy is not a substantial remedy, regard shall be had to all the relevant circumstances at the time the terms in question are agreed.

(3)   In determining whether subsection (1)(b) applies, regard shall be had (without prejudice to the generality of subsection (2)) to the following matters—

     (a)   the benefits of commercial certainty;

     (b)   the strength of the bargaining positions of the parties relative to each other;

     (c)   whether the term was imposed by one party to the detriment of the other (whether by the use of standard terms or otherwise); and

     (d)   whether the supplier received an inducement to agree to the term.

10   Interpretation of Part II

In this Part—

'contract term' means a term of the contract creating the debt or any other contract term binding the parties (or either of them);

'contractual remedy' means a contractual right to interest or any contractual remedy other than interest;

'contractual right to interest' includes a reference to a contractual right to charge interest;

'overall remedy', in relation to the late payment of the debt, means any combination of a contractual right to interest, a varied right to statutory interest or a contractual remedy other than interest;

'substantial remedy' shall be construed in accordance with section 9.

(2)   In this Part a reference (however worded) to contract terms which vary the right to statutory interest is a reference to terms altering in any way the effect of Part I in relation to the debt (for example by postponing the time at which interest starts to run or by imposing conditions on the right to interest).

(3)   In this Part a reference to late payment of the debt is a reference to late payment of the sum due when the debt is created (excluding any part of that sum which is prevented from carrying statutory interest by section 3).

PART III
GENERAL AND SUPPLEMENTARY

11 Treatment of advance payments of the contract price

(1) A qualifying debt created by virtue of an obligation to make an advance payment shall be treated for the purposes of this Act as if it was created on the day mentioned in subsection (3), (4) or (5) (as the case may be).

(2) In this section 'advance payment' means a payment falling due before the obligation of the supplier to which the whole contract price relates ('the supplier's obligation') is performed, other than a payment of a part of the contract price that is due in respect of any part performance of that obligation and payable on or after the day on which that part performance is completed.

(3) Where the advance payment is the whole contract price, the debt shall be treated as created on the day on which the supplier's obligation is performed.

(4) Where the advance payment is a part of the contract price, but the sum is not due in respect of any part performance of the supplier's obligation, the debt shall be treated as created on the day on which the supplier's obligation is performed.

(5) Where the advance payment is a part of the contract price due in respect of any part performance of the supplier's obligation, but is payable before that part performance is completed, the debt shall be treated as created on the day on which the relevant part performance is completed.

(6) Where the debt is created by virtue of an obligation to pay a sum due in respect of a period of hire of goods, this section has effect as if—

(a) references to the day on which the supplier's obligation is performed were references to the last day of that period; and

(b) references to part performance of that obligation were references to part of that period.

(7) For the purposes of this section an obligation to pay the whole outstanding balance of the contract price shall be regarded as an obligation to pay the whole contract price and not as an obligation to pay a part of the contract price.

12 Conflict of laws

(1) This Act does not have effect in relation to a contract governed by the law of a part of the United Kingdom by choice of the parties if—

(a) there is no significant connection between the contract and that part of the United Kingdom; and

(b) but for that choice, the applicable law would be a foreign law.

(2) This Act has effect in relation to a contract governed by a foreign law by choice of the parties if—

(a) but for that choice, the applicable law would be the law of a part of the United Kingdom; and

(b) there is no significant connection between the contract and any country other than that part of the United Kingdom.

(3) In this section—

'contract' means a contract falling within section 2(1); and

'foreign law' means the law of a country outside the United Kingdom.

13 Assignments, etc

(1) The operation of this Act in relation to a qualifying debt is not affected by—

(a) any change in the identity of the parties to the contract creating the debt; or

(b) the passing of the right to be paid the debt, or the duty to pay it (in whole or in part) to a person other than the person who is the original creditor or the original debtor when the debt is created.

(2) Any reference in this Act to the supplier or the purchaser is a reference to the person who is for the time being the supplier or the purchaser or, in relation to

a time after the debt in question has been created, the person who is for the time being the creditor or the debtor, as the case may be.

(3)   Where the right to be paid part of a debt passes to a person other than the person who is the original creditor when the debt is created, any reference in this Act to a debt shall be construed as (or, if the context so requires, as including) a reference to part of a debt.

(4)   A reference in this section to the identity of the parties to a contract changing, or to a right or duty passing, is a reference to it changing or passing by assignment or assignation, by operation of law or otherwise.

14   Contract terms relating to the date for payment of the contract price

(1)   This section applies to any contract term which purports to have the effect of postponing the time at which a qualifying debt would otherwise be created by a contract to which this Act applies.

(2)   Sections 3(2)(b) and 17(1)(b) of the Unfair Contract Terms Act 1977 (no reliance to be placed on certain contract terms) shall apply in cases where such a contract term is not contained in written standard terms of the purchaser as well as in cases where the term is contained in such standard terms.

(3)   In this section 'contract term' has the same meaning as in section 10(1).

15   Orders and regulations

(1)   Any power to make an order or regulations under this Act is exercisable by statutory instrument.

(2)   Any statutory instrument containing an order or regulations under this Act, other than an order under section 17(2), shall be subject to annulment in pursuance of a resolution of either House of Parliament.

16   Interpretation

(1)   In this Act—

'contract for the supply of goods or services' has the meaning given in section 2(2);

'contract price' means the price in a contract of sale of goods or the money consideration referred to in section 2(2)(b) in any other contract for the supply of goods or services;

'purchaser' means (subject to section 13(2)) the buyer in a contract of sale or the person who contracts with the supplier in any other contract for the supply of goods or services;

'qualifying debt' means a debt falling within section 3(1);

'statutory interest' means interest carried by virtue of the term implied by section 1(1); and

'supplier' means (subject to section 13(2)) the seller in a contract of sale of goods or the person who does one or more of the things mentioned in section 2(3) in any other contract for the supply of goods or services.

(2)   In this Act any reference (however worded) to an agreement or to contract terms includes a reference to both express and implied terms (including terms established by a course of dealing or by such usage as binds the parties).

17   Short title, commencement and extent

(1)   This Act may be cited as the Late Payment of Commercial Debts (Interest) Act 1998.

(2)   This Act (apart from this section) shall come into force on such day as the Secretary of State may by order appoint; and different days may be appointed for different descriptions of contract or for other different purposes.

An order under this subsection may specify a description of contract by reference to any feature of the contract (including the parties).

(3)   The Secretary of State may by regulations make such transitional, supplemental or incidental provision (including provision modifying any provision of

this Act) as the Secretary of State may consider necessary or expedient in connection with the operation of this Act while it is not fully in force.

(4)   This Act does not affect contracts of any description made before this Act comes into force for contracts of that description.

(5)   This Act extends to Northern Ireland.

HUMAN RIGHTS ACT 1998
(1998, c 42)

Introduction

1   The Convention Rights

(1)   In this Act 'the Convention rights' means the rights and fundamental freedoms set out in—

(a)   Articles 2 to 12 and 14 of the Convention,

(b)   Articles 1 to 3 of the First Protocol, and

(c)   [Article 1 of the Thirteenth Protocol],

as read with Articles 16 to 18 of the Convention.

(2)   Those Articles are to have effect for the purposes of this Act subject to any designated derogation or reservation (as to which see sections 14 and 15).

(3)   The Articles are set out in Schedule 1.

(4)   The [Secretary of State] may by order make such amendments to this Act as he considers appropriate to reflect the effect, in relation to the United Kingdom, of a protocol.

(5)   In subsection (4) 'protocol' means a protocol to the Convention—

(a)   which the United Kingdom has ratified; or

(b)   which the United Kingdom has signed with a view to ratification.

(6)   No amendment may be made by an order under subsection (4) so as to come into force before the protocol concerned is in force in relation to the United Kingdom.

2   Interpretation of Convention rights

(1)   A court or tribunal determining a question which has arisen in connection with a Convention right must take into account any—

(a)   judgment, decision, declaration or advisory opinion of the European Court of Human Rights,

(b)   opinion of the Commission given in a report adopted under Article 31 of the Convention,

(c)   decision of the Commission in connection with Article 26 or 27(2) of the Convention, or

(d)   decision of the Committee of Ministers taken under Article 46 of the Convention,

whenever made or given, so far as, in the opinion of the court or tribunal, it is relevant to the proceedings in which that question has arisen.

(2)   Evidence of any judgment, decision, declaration or opinion of which account may have to be taken under this section is to be given in proceedings before any court or tribunal in such manner as may be provided by rules.

(3)   In this section 'rules' means rules of court or, in the case of proceedings before a tribunal, rules made for the purposes of this section—

(a)   by [the Lord Chancellor or] the Secretary of State, in relation to any proceedings outside Scotland;

(b)   by the Secretary of State, in relation to proceedings in Scotland; or

(c)   by a Northern Ireland department, in relation to proceedings before a tribunal in Northern Ireland—

(i)   which deals with transferred matters; and

(ii)   for which no rules made under paragraph (a) are in force.

Legislation

3 Interpretation of legislation

(1) So far as it is possible to do so, primary legislation and subordinate legislation must be read and given effect in a way which is compatible with the Convention rights.

(2) This section—

(a) applies to primary legislation and subordinate legislation whenever enacted;

(b) does not affect the validity, continuing operation or enforcement of any incompatible primary legislation; and

(c) does not affect the validity, continuing operation or enforcement of any incompatible subordinate legislation if (disregarding any possibility of revocation) primary legislation prevents removal of the incompatibility.

4 Declaration of incompatibility

(1) Subsection (2) applies in any proceedings in which a court determines whether a provision of primary legislation is compatible with a Convention right.

(2) If the court is satisfied that the provision is incompatible with a Convention right, it may make a declaration of that incompatibility.

(3) Subsection (4) applies in any proceedings in which a court determines whether a provision of subordinate legislation, made in the exercise of a power conferred by primary legislation, is compatible with a Convention right.

(4) If the court is satisfied—

(a) that the provision is incompatible with a Convention right, and

(b) that (disregarding any possibility of revocation) the primary legislation concerned prevents removal of the incompatibility,

it may make a declaration of that incompatibility.

(5) In this section 'court' means—

(a) [the Supreme Court;]

(b) the Judicial Committee of the Privy Council;

(c) [the Court Martial Appeal Court];

(d) in Scotland, the High Court of Justiciary sitting otherwise than as a trial court or the Court of Session;

(e) in England and Wales or Northern Ireland, the High Court or the Court of Appeal;

[(f) the Court of Protection, in any matter being dealt with by the President of the Family Division, the Vice-Chancellor or a puisne judge of the High Court.]

(6) A declaration under this section ('a declaration of incompatibility')—

(a) does not affect the validity, continuing operation or enforcement of the provision in respect of which it is given; and

(b) is not binding on the parties to the proceedings in which it is made.

5 Right of Crown to intervene

(1) Where a court is considering whether to make a declaration of incompatibility, the Crown is entitled to notice in accordance with rules of court.

(2) In any case to which subsection (1) applies—

(a) a Minister of the Crown (or a person nominated by him),

(b) a member of the Scottish Executive,

(c) a Northern Ireland Minister,

(d) a Northern Ireland department,

is entitled, on giving notice in accordance with rules of court, to be joined as a party to the proceedings.

(3) Notice under subsection (2) may be given at any time during the proceedings.

(4) A person who has been made a party to criminal proceedings (other than in

Scotland) as the result of a notice under subsection (2) may, with leave, appeal to the [Supreme Court] against any declaration of incompatibility made in the proceedings.

(5)   In subsection (4)—

'criminal proceedings' includes all proceedings before the Courts-Martial Appeal Court; and

'leave' means leave granted by the court making the declaration of incompatibility or by the [Supreme Court].

Remedial action

10   Power to take remedial action

(1)   This section applies if—

(a)   a provision of legislation has been declared under section 4 to be incompatible with a Convention right and, if an appeal lies—

(i)   all persons who may appeal have stated in writing that they do not intend to do so;

(ii)   the time for bringing an appeal has expired and no appeal has been brought within that time; or

(iii)   an appeal brought within that time has been determined or abandoned; or

(b)   it appears to a Minister of the Crown or Her Majesty in Council that, having regard to a finding of the European Court of Human Rights made after the coming into force of this section in proceedings against the United Kingdom, a provision of legislation is incompatible with an obligation of the United Kingdom arising from the Convention.

(2)   If a Minister of the Crown considers that there are compelling reasons for proceeding under this section, he may by order make such amendments to the legislation as he considers necessary to remove the incompatibility.

(3)   If, in the case of subordinate legislation, a Minister of the Crown considers—

(a)   that it is necessary to amend the primary legislation under which the subordinate legislation in question was made, in order to enable the incompatibility to be removed, and

(b)   that there are compelling reasons for proceeding under this section,

he may by order make such amendments to the primary legislation as he considers necessary.

(4)   This section also applies where the provision in question is in subordinate legislation and has been quashed, or declared invalid, by reason of incompatibility with a Convention right and the Minister proposes to proceed under paragraph 2(b) of Schedule 2.

(5)   If the legislation is an Order in Council, the power conferred by subsection (2) or (3) is exercisable by Her Majesty in Council.

(6)   In this section 'legislation' does not include a Measure of the Church Assembly or of the General Synod of the Church of England.

(7)   Schedule 2 makes further provision about remedial orders.

21   Interpretation, etc

(1)   In this Act—

'amend' includes repeal and apply (with or without modifications);

'the appropriate Minister' means the Minister of the Crown having charge of the appropriate authorised government department (within the meaning of the Crown Proceedings Act 1947);

'the Commission' means the European Commission of Human Rights;

'the Convention' means the Convention for the Protection of Human Rights and Fundamental Freedoms, agreed by the Council of Europe at Rome on 4th

November 1950 as it has effect for the time being in relation to the United Kingdom;

'declaration of incompatibility' means a declaration under section 4;

'Minister of the Crown' has the same meaning as in the Ministers of the Crown Act 1975;

'Northern Ireland Minister' includes the First Minister and the deputy First Minister in Northern Ireland;

'primary legislation' means any—

(a)   public general Act;

(b)   local and personal Act;

(c)   private Act;

(d)   Measure of the Church Assembly;

(e)   Measure of the General Synod of the Church of England;

(f)   Order in Council—

(i)   made in exercise of Her Majesty's Royal Prerogative;

(ii)   made under section 38(1)(a) of the Northern Ireland Constitution Act 1973 or the corresponding provision of the Northern Ireland Act 1998; or

(iii)   amending an Act of a kind mentioned in paragraph (a), (b) or (c);

and includes an order or other instrument made under primary legislation (other-wise than by the [Welsh Ministers, the First Minister for Wales, the Counsel General to the Welsh Assembly Government], a member of the Scottish Executive, a Northern Ireland Minister or a Northern Ireland department) to the extent to which it operates to bring one or more provisions of that legislation into force or amends any primary legislation;

'the First Protocol' means the protocol to the Convention agreed at Paris on 20th March 1952;

[. . .]

'the Eleventh Protocol' means the protocol to the Convention (restructuring the control machinery established by the Convention) agreed at Strasbourg on 11th May 1994;

['the Thirteenth Protocol' means the protocol to the Convention (concerning the abolition of the death penalty in all circumstances) agreed at Vilnius on 3rd May 2002;]

'remedial order' means an order under section 10;

'subordinate legislation' means any—

(a)   Order in Council other than one—

(i)   made in exercise of Her Majesty's Royal Prerogative;

(ii)   made under section 38(1)(a) of the Northern Ireland Constitution Act 1973 or the corresponding provision of the Northern Ireland Act 1998; or

(iii)   amending an Act of a kind mentioned in the definition of primary legislation;

(b)   Act of the Scottish Parliament;

[(ba)   Measure of the National Assembly for Wales;

(bb)   Act of the National Assembly for Wales;]

(c)   Act of the Parliament of Northern Ireland;

(d)   Measure of the Assembly established under section 1 of the Northern Ireland Assembly Act 1973;

(e)   Act of the Northern Ireland Assembly;

(f)   order, rules, regulations, scheme, warrant, byelaw or other instrument made under primary legislation (except to the extent to which it operates to bring one or more provisions of that legislation into force or amends any primary legislation);

(g)   order, rules, regulations, scheme, warrant, byelaw or other instrument made under legislation mentioned in paragraph (b), (c), (d) or (e) or made under an Order in Council applying only to Northern Ireland;

(h)   order, rules, regulations, scheme, warrant, byelaw or other instrument made by a member of the Scottish Executive, [Welsh Ministers, the First Minister for Wales, the Counsel General to the Welsh Assembly Government,] a Northern Ireland Minister or a Northern Ireland department in exercise of prerogative or other executive functions of Her Majesty which are exercisable by such a person on behalf of Her Majesty;

'transferred matters' has the same meaning as in the Northern Ireland Act 1998; and

'tribunal' means any tribunal in which legal proceedings may be brought.

(2)   The references in paragraphs (b) and (c) of section 2(1) to Articles are to Articles of the Convention as they had effect immediately before the coming into force of the Eleventh Protocol.

(3)   The reference in paragraph (d) of section 2(1) to Article 46 includes a reference to Articles 32 and 54 of the Convention as they had effect immediately before the coming into force of the Eleventh Protocol.

(4)   The references in section 2(1) to a report or decision of the Commission or a decision of the Committee of Ministers include references to a report or decision made as provided by paragraphs 3, 4 and 6 of Article 5 of the Eleventh Protocol (transitional provisions).

[. . .]

22   Short title, commencement, application and extent

(1)   This Act may be cited as the Human Rights Act 1998.

. . .

SCHEDULES

SCHEDULE 1
THE ARTICLES

PART I
THE CONVENTION

Rights and Freedoms

Article 2. Right to Life

1.   Everyone's right to life shall be protected by law. No one shall be deprived of his life intentionally save in the execution of a sentence of a court following his conviction of a crime for which this penalty is provided by law.

2.   Deprivation of life shall not be regarded as inflicted in contravention of this Article when it results from the use of force which is no more than absolutely necessary:

(a)   in defence of any person from unlawful violence;

(b)   in order to effect a lawful arrest or to prevent the escape of a person lawfully detained;

(c)   in action lawfully taken for the purpose of quelling a riot or insurrection.

Article 3. Prohibition of Torture

No one shall be subjected to torture or to inhuman or degrading treatment or punishment.

Article 4. Prohibition of Slavery and Forced Labour

1.   No one shall be held in slavery or servitude.

2.   No one shall be required to perform forced or compulsory labour.

3.   For the purpose of this Article the term 'forced or compulsory labour' shall not include:

(a)   any work required to be done in the ordinary course of detention imposed according to the provisions of Article 5 of this Convention or during conditional release from such detention;

(b)   any service of a military character or, in case of conscientious objectors in countries where they are recognised, service exacted instead of compulsory military service;

(c)   any service exacted in case of an emergency or calamity threatening the life or well-being of the community;

(d)   any work or service which forms part of normal civic obligations.

Article 5. Right to Liberty and Security

1.   Everyone has the right to liberty and security of person. No one shall be deprived of his liberty save in the following cases and in accordance with a procedure prescribed by law:

(a)   the lawful detention of a person after conviction by a competent court;

(b)   the lawful arrest or detention of a person for non-compliance with the lawful order of a court or in order to secure the fulfilment of any obligation prescribed by law;

(c)   the lawful arrest or detention of a person effected for the purpose of bringing him before the competent legal authority on reasonable suspicion of having committed an offence or when it is reasonably considered necessary to prevent his committing an offence or fleeing after having done so;

(d)   the detention of a minor by lawful order for the purpose of educational supervision or his lawful detention for the purpose of bringing him before the competent legal authority;

(e)   the lawful detention of persons for the prevention of the spreading of infectious diseases, of persons of unsound mind, alcoholics or drug addicts or vagrants;

(f)   the lawful arrest or detention of a person to prevent his effecting an unauthorised entry into the country or of a person against whom action is being taken with a view to deportation or extradition.

2.   Everyone who is arrested shall be informed promptly, in a language which he understands, of the reasons for his arrest and of any charge against him.

3.   Everyone arrested or detained in accordance with the provisions of paragraph 1(c) of this Article shall be brought promptly before a judge or other officer authorised by law to exercise judicial power and shall be entitled to trial within a reasonable time or to release pending trial. Release may be conditioned by guarantees to appear for trial.

4.   Everyone who is deprived of his liberty by arrest or detention shall be entitled to take proceedings by which the lawfulness of his detention shall be decided speedily by a court and his release ordered if the detention is not lawful.

5.   Everyone who has been the victim of arrest or detention in contravention of the provisions of this Article shall have an enforceable right to compensation.

Article 6. Right to a Fair Trial

1.   In the determination of his civil rights and obligations or of any criminal charge against him, everyone is entitled to a fair and public hearing within a reasonable time by an independent and impartial tribunal established by law. Judgment shall be pronounced publicly but the press and public may be excluded from all or part of the trial in the interest of morals, public order or national security in a democratic society, where the interests of juveniles or the protection of the private life of the parties so require, or to the extent strictly necessary in the opinion of the court in special circumstances where publicity would prejudice the interests of justice.

2.   Everyone charged with a criminal offence shall be presumed innocent until proved guilty according to law.

3.   Everyone charged with a criminal offence has the following minimum rights:

(a)   to be informed promptly, in a language which he understands and in detail, of the nature and cause of the accusation against him;

(b)   to have adequate time and facilities for the preparation of his defence;

(c) to defend himself in person or through legal assistance of his own choosing or, if he has not sufficient means to pay for legal assistance, to be given it free when the interests of justice so require;

(d) to examine or have examined witnesses against him and to obtain the attendance and examination of witnesses on his behalf under the same conditions as witnesses against him;

(e) to have the free assistance of an interpreter if he cannot understand or speak the language used in court.

Article 7. No Punishment Without Law

1. No one shall be held guilty of any criminal offence on account of any act or omission which did not constitute a criminal offence under national or international law at the time when it was committed. Nor shall a heavier penalty be imposed than the one that was applicable at the time the criminal offence was committed.

2. This Article shall not prejudice the trial and punishment of any person for any act or omission which, at the time when it was committed, was criminal according to the general principles of law recognised by civilised nations.

Article 8. Right to Respect for Private and Family Life

1. Everyone has the right to respect for his private and family life, his home and his correspondence.

2. There shall be no interference by a public authority with the exercise of this right except such as is in accordance with the law and is necessary in a democratic society in the interests of national security, public safety or the economic well-being of the country, for the prevention of disorder or crime, for the protection of health or morals, or for the protection of the rights and freedoms of others.

Article 9. Freedom of Thought, Conscience and Religion

1. Everyone has the right to freedom of thought, conscience and religion; this right includes freedom to change his religion or belief and freedom, either alone or in community with others and in public or private, to manifest his religion or belief, in worship, teaching, practice and observance.

2. Freedom to manifest one's religion or beliefs shall be subject only to such limitations as are prescribed by law and are necessary in a democratic society in the interests of public safety, for the protection of public order, health or morals, or for the protection of the rights and freedoms of others.

Article 10. Freedom of Expression

1. Everyone has the right to freedom of expression. This right shall include freedom to hold opinions and to receive and impart information and ideas without interference by public authority and regardless of frontiers. This Article shall not prevent States from requiring the licensing of broadcasting, television or cinema enterprises.

2. The exercise of these freedoms, since it carries with it duties and responsibilities, may be subject to such formalities, conditions, restrictions or penalties as are prescribed by law and are necessary in a democratic society, in the interests of national security, territorial integrity or public safety, for the prevention of disorder or crime, for the protection of health or morals, for the protection of the reputation or rights of others, for preventing the disclosure of information received in confidence, or for maintaining the authority and impartiality of the judiciary.

Article 11. Freedom of Assembly and Association

1. Everyone has the right to freedom of peaceful assembly and to freedom of association with others, including the right to form and to join trade unions for the protection of his interests.

2. No restrictions shall be placed on the exercise of these rights other than such as are prescribed by law and are necessary in a democratic society in the interests

of national security or public safety, for the prevention of disorder or crime, for the protection of health or morals or for the protection of the rights and freedoms of others. This Article shall not prevent the imposition of lawful restrictions on the exercise of these rights by members of the armed forces, of the police or of the administration of the State.

Article 12. Right to Marry

Men and women of marriageable age have the right to marry and to found a family, according to the national laws governing the exercise of this right.

Article 14. Prohibition of Discrimination

The enjoyment of the rights and freedoms set forth in this Convention shall be secured without discrimination on any ground such as sex, race, colour, language, religion, political or other opinion, national or social origin, association with a national minority, property, birth or other status.

Article 16. Restrictions on Political Activity of Aliens

Nothing in Articles 10, 11 and 14 shall be regarded as preventing the High Contracting Parties from imposing restrictions on the political activity of aliens.

Article 17. Prohibition of Abuse of Rights

Nothing in this Convention may be interpreted as implying for any State, group or person any right to engage in any activity or perform any act aimed at the destruction of any of the rights and freedoms set forth herein or at their limitation to a greater extent than is provided for in the Convention.

Article 18. Limitation on Use of Restrictions on Rights

The restrictions permitted under this Convention to the said rights and freedoms shall not be applied for any purpose other than those for which they have been prescribed.

PART II
THE FIRST PROTOCOL

Article 1. Protection of Property

Every natural or legal person is entitled to the peaceful enjoyment of his possessions. No one shall be deprived of his possessions except in the public interest and subject to the conditions provided for by law and by the general principles of international law.

The preceding provisions shall not, however, in any way impair the right of a State to enforce such laws as it deems necessary to control the use of property in accordance with the general interest or to secure the payment of taxes or other contributions or penalties.

Article 2. Right to Education

No person shall be denied the right to education. In the exercise of any functions which it assumes in relation to education and to teaching, the State shall respect the right of parents to ensure such education and teaching in conformity with their own religious and philosophical convictions.

Article 3. Right to Free Elections

The High Contracting Parties undertake to hold free elections at reasonable intervals by secret ballot, under conditions which will ensure the free expression of the opinion of the people in the choice of the legislature.

[PART III
ARTICLE 1 OF THE THIRTEENTH PROTOCOL

Abolition of the Death Penalty
The death penalty shall be abolished. No one shall be condemned to such penalty or executed.]

SCHEDULE 2
REMEDIAL ORDERS

1 Orders
(1) A remedial order may—
    (a) contain such incidental, supplemental, consequential or transitional provision as the person making it considers appropriate;
    (b) be made so as to have effect from a date earlier than that on which it is made;
    (c) make provision for the delegation of specific functions;
    (d) make different provision for different cases.
(2) The power conferred by sub-paragraph (1)(a) includes—
    (a) power to amend primary legislation (including primary legislation other than that which contains the incompatible provision); and
    (b) power to amend or revoke subordinate legislation (including subordinate legislation other than that which contains the incompatible provision).
(3) A remedial order may be made so as to have the same extent as the legislation which it affects.
(4) No person is to be guilty of an offence solely as a result of the retrospective effect of a remedial order.

2 Procedure
No remedial order may be made unless—
    (a) a draft of the order has been approved by a resolution of each House of Parliament made after the end of the period of 60 days beginning with the day on which the draft was laid; or
    (b) it is declared in the order that it appears to the person making it that, because of the urgency of the matter, it is necessary to make the order without a draft being so approved.

3 Orders laid in draft
(1) No draft may be laid under paragraph 2(a) unless—
    (a) the person proposing to make the order has laid before Parliament a document which contains a draft of the proposed order and the required information; and
    (b) the period of 60 days, beginning with the day on which the document required by this sub-paragraph was laid, has ended.
(2) If representations have been made during that period, the draft laid under paragraph 2(a) must be accompanied by a statement containing—
    (a) a summary of the representations; and
    (b) if, as a result of the representations, the proposed order has been changed, details of the changes.

4 Urgent cases
(1) If a remedial order ('the original order') is made without being approved in draft, the person making it must lay it before Parliament, accompanied by the required information, after it is made.
(2) If representations have been made during the period of 60 days beginning with the day on which the original order was made, the person making it must (after the end of that period) lay before Parliament a statement containing—
    (a) a summary of the representations; and

(b)   if, as a result of the representations, he considers it appropriate to make changes to the original order, details of the changes.

(3)   If sub-paragraph (2)(b) applies, the person making the statement must—

(a)   make a further remedial order replacing the original order; and

(b)   lay the replacement order before Parliament.

(4)   If, at the end of the period of 120 days beginning with the day on which the original order was made, a resolution has not been passed by each House approving the original or replacement order, the order ceases to have effect (but without that affecting anything previously done under either order or the power to make a fresh remedial order).

5   Definitions

In this Schedule—

'representations' means representations about a remedial order (or proposed remedial order) made to the person making (or proposing to make) it and includes any relevant Parliamentary report or resolution; and

'required information' means—

(a)   an explanation of the incompatibility which the order (or proposed order) seeks to remove, including particulars of the relevant declaration, finding or order; and

(b)   a statement of the reasons for proceeding under section 10 and for making an order in those terms.

6   Calculating periods

In calculating any period for the purposes of this Schedule, no account is to be taken of any time during which—

(a)   Parliament is dissolved or prorogued; or

(b)   both Houses are adjourned for more than four days.

[7   (1)   This paragraph applies in relation to—

(a)   any remedial order made, and any draft of such an order proposed to be made,—

(i)   by the Scottish Ministers; or

(ii)   within devolved competence (within the meaning of the Scotland Act 1998) by Her Majesty in Council; and

(b)   any document or statement to be laid in connection with such an order (or proposed order).

(2)   This Schedule has effect in relation to any such order (or proposed order), document or statement subject to the following modifications.

(3)   Any reference to Parliament, each House of Parliament or both Houses of Parliament shall be construed as a reference to the Scottish Parliament.

(4)   Paragraph 6 does not apply and instead, in calculating any period for the purposes of this Schedule, no account is to be taken of any time during which the Scottish Parliament is dissolved or is in recess for more than four days.]

SCOTLAND ACT 1998
(1998, c 46)

41 Defamatory statements

(1) For the purposes of the law of defamation—

    (a) any statement made in proceedings of the Parliament, and

    (b) the publication under the authority of the Parliament of any statement,

shall be absolutely privileged.

(2) In subsection (1), 'statement' has the same meaning as in the Defamation Act 1996.

126 Interpretation

(1) In this Act—

'body' includes unincorporated association,

'constituencies' and 'regions', in relation to the Parliament, mean the constituencies and regions provided for by Schedule l,

'constituency member' means a member of the Parliament for a constituency,

'the Convention rights' has the same meaning as in the Human Rights Act 1998,

'document' means anything in which information is recorded in any form (and references to producing a document are to be read accordingly),

'enactment' includes an Act of the Scottish Parliament, Northern Ireland legislation (within the meaning of the Northern Ireland Act 1998) and an enactment comprised in subordinate legislation, and includes an enactment comprised in, or in subordinate legislation under, an Act of Parliament, whenever passed or made,

'financial year' means a year ending with 31st March,

'functions' includes powers and duties, and 'confer', in relation to functions, includes impose,

'government department' means any department of the Government of the United Kingdom,

'the Human Rights Convention' means—

    (a) the Convention for the Protection of Human Rights and Fundamental Freedoms, agreed by the Council of Europe at Rome on 4th November 1950, and

    (b) the Protocols to the Convention,

as they have effect for the time being in relation to the United Kingdom,

'Minister of the Crown' includes the Treasury,

'modify' includes amend or repeal,

'occupational pension scheme', 'personal pension scheme' and 'public service pension scheme' have the meanings given by section 1 of the Pension Schemes Act 1993, . . .

'the Parliament' means the Scottish Parliament,

'parliamentary', in relation to constituencies, elections and electors, is to be taken to refer to the Parliament of the United Kingdom,

'prerogative instrument' means an Order in Council, warrant, charter or other instrument made under the prerogative,

'the principal appointed day' means the day appointed by an order under section 130 which is designated by the order as the principal appointed day,

'proceedings', in relation to the Parliament, includes proceedings of any committee or sub-committee,

'property' includes rights and interests of any description,

'regional member' means a member of the Parliament for a region,

'Scotland' includes so much of the internal waters and territorial sea of the United Kingdom as are adjacent to Scotland,

'Scottish public authority' means any public body (except the Parliamentary corporation), public office or holder of such an office whose functions (in each case) are exercisable only in or as regards Scotland,

'the Scottish zone' means the sea within British fishery limits (that is, the limits set by or under section 1 of the Fishery Limits Act 1976) which is adjacent to Scotland,
'standing orders' means standing orders of the Parliament,
'subordinate legislation' has the same meaning as in the Interpretation Act 1978 and also includes an instrument made under an Act of the Scottish Parliament,
'tribunal' means any tribunal in which legal proceedings may be brought.

(2) Her Majesty may by Order in Council determine, or make provision for determining, for the purposes of this Act any boundary between waters which are to be treated as internal waters or territorial sea of the United Kingdom, or sea within British fishery limits, adjacent to Scotland and those which are not.

(3) For the purposes of this Act—
    (a) the question whether any function of a body, government department, office or office-holder relates to reserved matters is to be determined by reference to the purpose for which the function is exercisable, having regard (among other things) to the likely effects in all the circumstances of any exercise of the function, but
    (b) bodies to which paragraph 3 of Part III of Schedule 5 applies are to be treated as if all their functions were functions which relate to reserved matters.

(4) References in this Act to Scots private law are to the following areas of the civil law of Scotland—
    (a) the general principles of private law (including private international law),
    (b) the law of persons (including natural persons, legal persons and unincorporated bodies),
    (c) the law of obligations (including obligations arising from contract, unilateral promise, delict, unjustified enrichment and negotiorum gestio),
    (d) the law of property (including heritable and moveable property, trusts and succession), and
    (e) the law of actions (including jurisdiction, remedies, evidence, procedure, diligence, recognition and enforcement of court orders, limitation of actions and arbitration),
and include references to judicial review of administrative action.

(5) References in this Act to Scots criminal law include criminal offences, jurisdiction, evidence, procedure and penalties and the treatment of offenders.

(6) References in this Act and in any other enactment to the Scottish Administration are to the office-holders in the Scottish Administration and the members of the staff of the Scottish Administration.

(7) For the purposes of this Act—
    (a) references to office-holders in the Scottish Administration are to—
        (i) members of the Scottish Executive and junior Scottish Ministers, and
        (ii) the holders of offices in the Scottish Administration which are not ministerial offices, and
    (b) references to members of the staff of the Scottish Administration are to the staff of the persons referred to in paragraph (a).

(8) For the purposes of this Act, the offices in the Scottish Administration which are not ministerial offices are—
    (a) the Registrar General of Births, Deaths and Marriages for Scotland, the Keeper of the Registers of Scotland and the Keeper of the Records of Scotland, and
    (b) any other office of a description specified in an Order in Council made by Her Majesty under this subsection.

(9) In this Act—
    (a) all those rights, powers, liabilities, obligations and restrictions from time to time created or arising by or under the [EU] Treaties, and
    (b) all those remedies and procedures from time to time provided for by or under the [EU] Treaties,
are referred to as '[EU] law'.

(10) In this Act, 'international obligations' means any international obligations of the United Kingdom other than obligations to observe and implement [EU] law or the Convention rights.

(11) In this Act, 'by virtue of' includes 'by' and 'under'.

CONTRACTS (RIGHTS OF THIRD PARTIES) ACT 1999
(1999 c 31)

This Act does not apply to Scotland (see s 10), but is included in this volume for comparative purposes.

1 Right of third parties to enforce contractual claim

(1) Subject to the provisions of this Act, a person who is not a party to a contract (a 'third party') may in his own right enforce a term of the contract if—

    (a) the contract expressly provides that he may, or

    (b) subject to subsection (2), the term purports to confer a benefit on him.

(2) Subsection (1)(b) does not apply if on a proper construction of the contract it appears that the parties did not intend the term to be enforceable by the third party.

(3) The third party must be expressly identified in the contract by name, as a member of a class or as answering a particular description but need not be in existence when the contract is entered into.

(4) This section does not confer a right on a third party to enforce a term of a contract otherwise than subject to and in accordance with any other relevant terms of the contract.

(5) For the purpose of exercising his right to enforce a term of the contract, there shall be available to the third party any remedy that would have been available to him in an action for breach of contract if he had been a party to the contract (and the rules relating to damages, injunctions, specific performance and other relief shall apply accordingly).

(6) Where a term of a contract excludes or limits liability in relation to any matter references in this Act to the third party enforcing the term shall be construed as references to his availing himself of the exclusion or limitation.

(7) In this Act, in relation to a term of a contract which is enforceable by a third party—

'the promisor' means the party to the contract against whom the term is enforceable by the third party, and

'the promisee' means the party to the contract by whom the term is enforceable against the promisor.

2 Variation and rescission of contract

(1) Subject to the provisions of this section, where a third party has a right under section 1 to enforce a term of the contract, the parties to the contract may not, by agreement, rescind the contract, or vary it in such a way as to extinguish or alter his entitlement under that right, without his consent if—

    (a) the third party has communicated his assent to the term to the promisor,

    (b) the promisor is aware that the third party has relied on the term, or

    (c) the promisor can reasonably be expected to have foreseen that the third party would rely on the term and the third party has in fact relied on it.

(2) The assent referred to in subsection (1)(a)—

    (a) may be by words or conduct, and

    (b) if sent to the promisor by post or other means, shall not be regarded as communicated to the promisor until received by him.

(3) Subsection (1) is subject to any express term of the contract under which—

    (a) the parties to the contract may by agreement rescind or vary the contract without the consent of the third party, or

(b)   the consent of the third party is required in circumstances specified in the contract instead of those set out in subsection (1)(a) to (c).

(4)   Where the consent of a third party is required under subsection (1) or (3), the court or arbitral tribunal may, on the application of the parties to the contract, dispense with his consent if satisfied—

(a)   that his consent cannot be obtained because his whereabouts cannot reasonably be ascertained, or

(b)   that he is mentally incapable of giving his consent.

(5)   The court or arbitral tribunal may, on the application of the parties to a contract, dispense with any consent that may be required under subsection (1)(c) if satisfied that it cannot reasonably be ascertained whether or not the third party has in fact relied on the term.

(6)   If the court or arbitral tribunal dispenses with a third party's consent, it may impose such conditions as it thinks fit, including a condition requiring the payment of compensation to the third party.

(7)   The jurisdiction conferred on the court by subsections (4) to (6) is exercisable by both the High Court and a county court.

3   Defences etc available to promisor

(1)   Subsections (2) to (5) apply where, in reliance on section 1, proceedings for the enforcement of a term of a contract are brought by a third party.

(2)   The promisor shall have available to him by way of defence or set-off any matter that—

(a)   arises from or in connection with the contract and is relevant to the term, and

(b)   would have been available to him by way of defence or set-off if the proceedings had been brought by the promisee.

(3)   The promisor shall also have available to him by way of defence or set-off any matter if—

(a)   an express term of the contract provides for it to be available to him in proceedings brought by the third party, and

(b)   it would have been available to him by way of defence or set-off if the proceedings had been brought by the promisee.

(4)   The promisor shall also have available to him—

(a)   by way of defence or set-off any matter, and

(b)   by way of counterclaim any matter not arising from the contract,

that would have been available to him by way of defence or set-off or, as the case may be, by way of counterclaim against the third party if the third party had been a party to the contract.

(5)   Subsections (2) and (4) are subject to any express term of the contract as to the matters that are not to be available to the promisor by way of defence, set-off or counterclaim.

(6)   Where in any proceedings brought against him a third party seeks in reliance on section 1 to enforce a term of a contract (including, in particular, a term purporting to exclude or limit liability), he may not do so if he could not have done so (whether by reason of any particular circumstances relating to him or otherwise) had he been a party to the contract.

4   Enforcement of contract by promisee

Section 1 does not affect any right of the promisee to enforce any term of the contract.

5   Protection of promisor from double liability

Where under section 1 a term of a contract is enforceable by a third party, and the promisee has recovered from the promisor a sum in respect of—

(a)   the third party's loss in respect of the term, or

(b)   the expense to the promisee of making good to the third party the default of the promisor,

then, in any proceedings brought in reliance on that section by the third party, the court or arbitral tribunal shall reduce any award to the third party to such extent as it thinks appropriate to take account of the sum recovered by the promisee.

6   Exceptions

(1)   Section 1 confers no rights on a third party in the case of a contract on a bill of exchange, promissory note or other negotiable instrument.

(2)   Section 1 confers no rights on a third party in the case of any contract binding on a company and its members under [section 33 of the Companies Act 2006 (effect of company's constitution)].

[(2A)   Section 1 confers no rights on a third party in the case of any incorporation document of a limited liability partnership [or any agreement (express or implied) between the members of a limited liability partnership, or between a limited liability partnership and its members, that determines the mutual rights and duties of the members and their rights and duties in relation to the limited liability partnership].]

(3)   Section 1 confers no right on a third party to enforce—

(a)   any term of a contract of employment against an employee,

(b)   any term of a worker's contract against a worker (including a home worker), or

(c)   any term of a relevant contract against an agency worker.

(4)   In subsection (3)—

(a)   'contract of employment', 'employee', 'worker's contract', and 'worker' have the meaning given by section 54 of the National Minimum Wage Act 1998,

(b)   'home worker' has the meaning given by section 35(2) of that Act,

(c)   'agency worker' has the same meaning as in section 34(1) of that Act, and

(d)   'relevant contract' means a contract entered into, in a case where section 34 of that Act applies, by the agency worker as respects work falling within subsection (1)(a) of that section.

(5)   Section 1 confers no rights on a third party in the case of—

(a)   a contract for the carriage of goods by sea, or

(b)   a contract for the carriage of goods by rail or road, or for the carriage of cargo by air, which is subject to the rules of the appropriate international transport convention,

except that a third party may in reliance on that section avail himself of an exclusion or limitation of liability in such a contract.

(6)   In subsection (5) 'contract for the carriage of goods by sea' means a contract of carriage—

(a)   contained in or evidenced by a bill of lading, sea waybill or a corresponding electronic transaction, or

(b)   under or for the purposes of which there is given an undertaking which is contained in a ship's delivery order or a corresponding electronic transaction.

(7)   For the purposes of subsection (6)—

(a)   'bill of lading', 'sea waybill' and 'ship's delivery order' have the same meaning as in the Carriage of Goods by Sea Act 1992, and

(b)   a corresponding electronic transaction is a transaction within section 1(5) of that Act which corresponds to the issue, indorsement, delivery or transfer of a bill of lading, sea waybill or ship's delivery order.

(8)   In subsection (5) 'the appropriate international transport convention' means—

(a)   in relation to a contract for the carriage of goods by rail, the Convention which has the force of law in the United Kingdom under section 1 of the International Transport Conventions Act 1983,

(b)   in relation to a contract for the carriage of goods by road, the Convention which has the force of law in the United Kingdom under section 1 of the Carriage of Goods by Road Act 1965, and

    (c)   in relation to a contract for the carriage of cargo by air—

       (i) the Convention which has the force of law in the United Kingdom under section 1 of the Carriage by Air Act 1961, or

      (ii) the Convention which has the force of law under section 1 of the Carriage by Air (Supplementary Provisions) Act 1962, or

     (iii) either of the amended Conventions set out in Part B of Schedule 2 or 3 to the Carriage by Air Acts (Application of Provisions) Order 1967.

7 Supplementary provisions relating to third party

(1)   Section 1 does not affect any right or remedy of a third party that exists or is available apart from this Act.

(2)   Section 2(2) of the Unfair Contract Terms Act 1977 (restriction on exclusion etc. of liability for negligence) shall not apply where the negligence consists of the breach of an obligation arising from a term of a contract and the person seeking to enforce it is a third party acting in reliance on section 1.

(3)   In sections 5 and 8 of the Limitation Act 1980 the references to an action founded on a simple contract and an action upon a specialty shall respectively include references to an action brought in reliance on section 1 relating to a simple contract and an action brought in reliance on that section relating to a specialty.

(4)   A third party shall not, by virtue of section 1(5) or 3(4) or (6), be treated as a party to the contract for the purposes of any other Act (or any instrument made under any other Act).

8 Arbitration provisions

(1)   Where—

    (a)   a right under section 1 to enforce a term ('the substantive term') is subject to a term providing for the submission of disputes to arbitration ('the arbitration agreement'), and

    (b)   the arbitration agreement is an agreement in writing for the purposes of Part I of the Arbitration Act 1996,

the third party shall be treated for the purposes of that Act as a party to the arbitration agreement as regards disputes between himself and the promisor relating to the enforcement of the substantive term by the third party.

(2)   Where—

    (a)   a third party has a right under section 1 to enforce a term providing for one or more descriptions of dispute between the third party and the promisor to be submitted to arbitration ('the arbitration agreement'),

    (b)   the arbitration agreement is an agreement in writing for the purposes of Part I of the Arbitration Act 1996, and

    (c)   the third party does not fall to be treated under subsection (1) as a party to the arbitration agreement,

the third party shall, if he exercises the right, be treated for the purposes of that Act as a party to the arbitration agreement in relation to the matter with respect to which the right is exercised, and be treated as having been so immediately before the exercise of the right.

9 [Amends Northern Irish statutes.]

10 Short title, commencement and extent

(1)   This Act may be cited as the Contracts (Rights of Third Parties) Act 1999.

(2)   This Act comes into force on the day on which it is passed but, subject to subsection (3), does not apply in relation to a contract entered into before the end of the period of six months beginning with that day.

(3)   The restriction in subsection (2) does not apply in relation to a contract which—

    (a)   is entered into on or after the day on which this Act is passed, and

(b)   expressly provides for the application of this Act.

(4)   This Act extends as follows—

(a)   section 9 extends to Northern Ireland only;

(b)   the remaining provisions extend to England and Wales and Northern Ireland only.

ADULTS WITH INCAPACITY (SCOTLAND) ACT 2000
(2000, asp 4)

PART 5
MEDICAL TREATMENT AND RESEARCH

47   Authority of persons responsible for medical treatment

(1)   This section applies where [any of the persons mentioned in subsection (1A)]—

(a)   is of the opinion that [an adult] is incapable in relation to a decision about the medical treatment in question; and

(b)   has certified in accordance with subsection (5) that he is of this opinion.

[(1A)   The persons are—

(a)   the medical practitioner primarily responsible for the medical treatment of the adult;

(b)   a person who is—

(i)   a dental practitioner;

(ii)   an ophthalmic optician;

(iii)   a registered nurse; or

(iv)   an individual who falls within such description of persons as may be prescribed by the Scottish Ministers,

who satisfies such requirements as may be so prescribed and who is primarily responsible for medical treatment of the kind in question.]

(2)   [. . .] [T]he [person who by virtue of subsection (1) has issued a certificate for the purposes of that subsection] shall have, during the period specified in the certificate, authority to do what is reasonable in the circumstances, in relation to [the medical treatment in question], to safeguard or promote the physical or mental health of the adult.

[(2A)   Subsection (2)—

(a)   does not affect any authority conferred by any other enactment or rule of law; and

(b)   is subject to—

(i)   the following provisions of this section;

(ii)   sections 49 and 50; and

(iii)   sections 234, 237, 240, 242, 243 and 244 of the 2003 Act.]

(3)   The authority conferred by subsection (2) shall be exercisable also by any other person who is authorised by the [person on whom that authority is conferred] to carry out [the medical treatment in question] and who is acting—

(a)   on his behalf under his instructions; or

(b)   with his approval or agreement.

(4)   In this Part 'medical treatment' includes any procedure or treatment designed to safeguard or promote physical or mental health.

(5)   A certificate for the purposes of subsection (1) shall be in the prescribed form and shall specify the period during which the authority conferred by subsection (2) shall subsist, being a period which—

(a)   the [person who issues the certificate] considers appropriate to the condition or circumstances of the adult; but

(b)   [does not exceed—

(i)   one year; or

(ii) if, in the opinion of that person any of the conditions or circumstances prescribed by the Scottish Ministers applies as respects the adult, 3 years, from] the date of the examination on which the certificate is based.

(6)   If after issuing a certificate, the [person who issued it] is of the opinion that the condition or circumstances of the adult have changed he may—

(a)   revoke the certificate;

(b)   issue a new certificate specifying such period [not exceeding—

(i)   one year; or

(ii) if, in the opinion of that person any of the conditions or circumstances prescribed by the Scottish Ministers applies as respects the adult, 3 years, from] the date of revocation of the old certificate as he considers appropriate to the new condition or circumstances of the adult.

(7)   The authority conferred by subsection (2) shall not authorise—

(a)   the use of force or detention, unless it is immediately necessary and only for so long as is necessary in the circumstances;

(b)   action which would be inconsistent with any decision by a competent court;

(c)   placing an adult in a hospital for the treatment of mental disorder against his will.

[. . .]

(9)   Subject to subsection (10), where any question as to the authority of any person to provide medical treatment in pursuance of subsection (2)—

(a)   is the subject of proceedings in any court (other than for the purposes of any application to the court made under regulations made under section 48); and

(b)   has not been determined,

medical treatment authorised by subsection (2) shall not be given unless it is authorised by any other enactment or rule of law for the preservation of the life of the adult or the prevention of serious deterioration in his medical condition.

(10)   Nothing in subsection (9) shall authorise the provision of any medical treatment where an interdict has been granted and continues to have effect prohibiting the provision of such medical treatment.

[(11)   In subsection (1A)—

'dental practitioner' has the same meaning as in section 108(1) of the National Health Service (Scotland) Act 1978 (c 29);

'ophthalmic optician' means a person registered in either of the registers kept under section 7 of the Opticians Act 1989 (c 44) of ophthalmic opticians.]

ELECTRONIC COMMUNICATIONS ACT 2000
(2000, c 7)

PART II
FACILITATION OF ELECTRONIC COMMERCE, DATA STORAGE, ETC

7   Electronic signatures and related certificates

(1)   In any legal proceedings—

(a)   an electronic signature incorporated into or logically associated with a particular electronic communication or particular electronic data, and

(b)   the certification by any person of such a signature,

shall each be admissible in evidence in relation to any question as to the authenticity of the communication or data or as to the integrity of the communication or data.

(2)   For the purposes of this section an electronic signature is so much of anything in electronic form as—

(a)   is incorporated into or otherwise logically associated with any electronic communication or electronic data; and

(b)   purports to be so incorporated or associated for the purpose of being used in establishing the authenticity of the communication or data, the integrity of the communication or data, or both.

(3)   For the purposes of this section an electronic signature incorporated into or associated with a particular electronic communication or particular electronic data is certified by any person if that person (whether before or after the making of the communication) has made a statement confirming that—

(a)   the signature,

(b)   a means of producing, communicating or verifying the signature, or

(c)   a procedure applied to the signature,

is (either alone or in combination with other factors) a valid means of establishing the authenticity of the communication or data, the integrity of the communication or data, or both.

8 Power to modify legislation

(1)   Subject to subsection (3), the appropriate Minister may by order made by statutory instrument modify the provisions of—

(a)   any enactment or subordinate legislation, or

(b)   any scheme, licence, authorisation or approval issued, granted or given by or under any enactment or subordinate legislation,

in such manner as he may think fit for the purpose of authorising or facilitating the use of electronic communications or electronic storage (instead of other forms of communication or storage) for any purpose mentioned in subsection (2).

(2)   Those purposes are—

(a)   the doing of anything which under any such provisions is required to be or may be done or evidenced in writing or otherwise using a document, notice or instrument;

(b)   the doing of anything which under any such provisions is required to be or may be done by post or other specified means of delivery;

(c)   the doing of anything which under any such provisions is required to be or may be authorised by a person's signature or seal, or is required to be delivered as a deed or witnessed;

(d)   the making of any statement or declaration which under any such provisions is required to be made under oath or to be contained in a statutory declaration;

(e)   the keeping, maintenance or preservation, for the purposes or in pursuance of any such provisions, of any account, record, notice, instrument or other document;

(f)   the provision, production or publication under any such provisions of any information or other matter;

(g)   the making of any payment that is required to be or may be made under any such provisions.

(3)   The appropriate Minister shall not make an order under this section authorising the use of electronic communications or electronic storage for any purpose, unless he considers that the authorisation is such that the extent (if any) to which records of things done for that purpose will be available will be no less satisfactory in cases where use is made of electronic communications or electronic storage than in other cases.

(4)   Without prejudice to the generality of subsection (1), the power to make an order under this section shall include power to make an order containing any of the following provisions—

(a)   provision as to the electronic form to be taken by any electronic communications or electronic storage the use of which is authorised by an order under this section;

(b)   provision imposing conditions subject to which the use of electronic communications or electronic storage is so authorised;

(c)   provision, in relation to cases in which any such conditions are not satisfied, for treating anything for the purposes of which the use of such communications or storage is so authorised as not having been done;

(d)   provision, in connection with anything so authorised, for a person to be able to refuse to accept receipt of something in electronic form except in such circumstances as may be specified in or determined under the order;

(e)   provision, in connection with any use of electronic communications so authorised, for intermediaries to be used, or to be capable of being used, for the transmission of any data or for establishing the authenticity or integrity of any data;

(f)   provision, in connection with any use of electronic storage so authorised, for persons satisfying such conditions as may be specified in or determined under the regulations to carry out functions in relation to the storage;

(g)   provision, in relation to cases in which the use of electronic communications or electronic storage is so authorised, for the determination of any of the matters mentioned in subsection (5), or as to the manner in which they may be proved in legal proceedings;

(h)   provision, in relation to cases in which fees or charges are or may be imposed in connection with anything for the purposes of which the use of electronic communications or electronic storage is so authorised, for different fees or charges to apply where use is made of such communications or storage;

(i)   provision, in relation to any criminal or other liabilities that may arise (in respect of the making of false or misleading statements or otherwise) in connection with anything for the purposes of which the use of electronic communications or electronic storage is so authorised, for corresponding liabilities to arise in corresponding circumstances where use is made of such communications or storage;

(j)   provision requiring persons to prepare and keep records in connection with any use of electronic communications or electronic storage which is so authorised;

(k)   provision requiring the production of the contents of any records kept in accordance with an order under this section;

(l)   provision for a requirement imposed by virtue of paragraph (j) or (k) to be enforceable at the suit or instance of such person as may be specified in or determined in accordance with the order;

(m)   any such provision, in relation to electronic communications or electronic storage the use of which is authorised otherwise than by an order under this section, as corresponds to any provision falling within any of the preceding paragraphs that may be made where it is such an order that authorises the use of the communications or storage.

(5)   The matters referred to in subsection (4)(g) are—

(a)   whether a thing has been done using an electronic communication or electronic storage;

(b)   the time at which, or date on which, a thing done using any such communication or storage was done;

(c)   the place where a thing done using such communication or storage was done;

(d)   the person by whom such a thing was done; and

(e)   the contents, authenticity or integrity of any electronic data.

(6)   An order under this section—

(a)   shall not (subject to paragraph (b)) require the use of electronic communications or electronic storage for any purpose; but

(b)   may make provision that a period of notice specified in the order must expire before effect is given to a variation or withdrawal of an election or other decision which—

  (i) has been made for the purposes of such an order; and

  (ii) is an election or decision to make use of electronic communications or electronic storage.

(7) The matters in relation to which provision may be made by an order under this section do not include any matter under the care and management of the Commissioners of Inland Revenue or any matter under the care and management of the Commissioners of Customs and Excise.

(8) In this section references to doing anything under the provisions of any enactment include references to doing it under the provisions of any subordinate legislation the power to make which is conferred by that enactment.

9 Section 8 orders

(1) In this Part 'the appropriate Minister' means (subject to subsections (2) and (7) and section 10(1))—

  (a) in relation to any matter with which a department of the Secretary of State is concerned, the Secretary of State;

  (b) in relation to any matter with which the Treasury is concerned, the Treasury; and

  (c) in relation to any matter with which any Government department other than a department of the Secretary of State or the Treasury is concerned, the Minister in charge of the other department.

(2) Where in the case of any matter—

  (a) that matter falls within more than one paragraph of subsection (1),

  (b) there is more than one such department as is mentioned in paragraph (c) of that subsection that is concerned with that matter, or

  (c) both paragraphs (a) and (b) of this subsection apply,

references, in relation to that matter, to the appropriate Minister are references to any one or more of the appropriate Ministers acting (in the case of more than one) jointly.

(3) Subject to subsection (4) and section 10(6), a statutory instrument containing an order under section 8 shall be subject to annulment in pursuance of a resolution of either House of Parliament.

(4) Subsection (3) does not apply in the case of an order a draft of which has been laid before Parliament and approved by a resolution of each House.

(5) An order under section 8 may—

  (a) provide for any conditions or requirements imposed by such an order to be framed by reference to the directions of such persons as may be specified in or determined in accordance with the order;

  (b) provide that any such condition or requirement is to be satisfied only where a person so specified or determined is satisfied as to specified matters.

(6) The provision made by such an order may include—

  (a) different provision for different cases;

  (b) such exceptions and exclusions as the person making the order may think fit; and

  (c) any such incidental, supplemental, consequential and transitional provision as he may think fit;

and the provision that may be made by virtue of paragraph (c) includes provision modifying any enactment or subordinate legislation or any scheme, licence, authorisation or approval issued, granted or given by or under any enactment or subordinate legislation.

(7) In the case of any matter which is not one of the reserved matters within the meaning of the Scotland Act 1998 or in respect of which functions are, by virtue of section 63 of that Act, exercisable by the Scottish Ministers instead of by or concurrently with a Minister of the Crown, this section and section 8 shall apply to Scotland subject to the following modifications—

  (a) subsections (1) and (2) of this section are omitted;

(b)   any reference to the appropriate Minister is to be read as a reference to the Secretary of State;

(c)   any power of the Secretary of State, by virtue of paragraph (b), to make an order under section 8 may also be exercised by the Scottish Ministers with the consent of the Secretary of State; and

(d)   where the Scottish Ministers make an order under section 8—

(i)   any reference to the Secretary of State (other than a reference in this subsection) shall be construed as a reference to the Scottish Ministers; and

(ii)   any reference to Parliament or to a House of Parliament shall be construed as a reference to the Scottish Parliament.

[10   *Modifications in relation to Welsh matters*]

PART III
MISCELLANEOUS AND SUPPLEMENTAL

[. . .]

Supplemental

13   Ministerial expenditure etc
There shall be paid out of money provided by Parliament—

(a)   any expenditure incurred by the Secretary of State for or in connection with the carrying out of his functions under this Act; and

(b)   any increase attributable to this Act in the sums which are payable out of money so provided under any other Act.

14   Prohibition on key escrow requirements
(1)   Subject to subsection (2), nothing in this Act shall confer any power on any Minister of the Crown, on the Scottish Ministers, on the National Assembly for Wales or on any person appointed under section 3—

(a)   by conditions of an approval under Part I, or

(b)   by any regulations or order under this Act,

to impose a requirement on any person to deposit a key for electronic data with another person.

(2)   Subsection (1) shall not prohibit the imposition by an order under section 8 of—

(a)   a requirement to deposit a key for electronic data with the intended recipient of electronic communications comprising the data; or

(b)   a requirement for arrangements to be made, in cases where a key for data is not deposited with another person, which otherwise secure that the loss of a key, or its becoming unusable, does not have the effect that the information contained in a record kept in pursuance of any provision made by or under any enactment or subordinate legislation becomes inaccessible or incapable of being put into an intelligible form.

(3)   In this section 'key', in relation to electronic data, means any code, password, algorithm, key or other data the use of which (with or without other keys)—

(a)   allows access to the electronic data, or

(b)   facilitates the putting of the electronic data into an intelligible form;

and references in this section to depositing a key for electronic data with a person include references to doing anything that has the effect of making the key available to that person.

15   General interpretation
(1)   In this Act, except in so far as the context otherwise requires—

'document' includes a map, plan, design, drawing, picture or other image;

'communication' includes a communication comprising sounds or images or both and a communication effecting a payment;

'electronic communication' means a communication transmitted (whether from one person to another, from one device to another or from a person to a device or vice versa)—

(a)   by means of [an electronic communications network]; or

(b)   by other means but while in an electronic form;

'enactment' includes—

(a)   an enactment passed after the passing of this Act,

(b)   an enactment comprised in an Act of the Scottish Parliament, and

(c)   an enactment contained in Northern Ireland legislation,

but does not include an enactment contained in Part I or II of this Act;

'modification' includes any alteration, addition or omission, and cognate expressions shall be construed accordingly;

'record' includes an electronic record; and

'subordinate legislation' means—

(a)   any subordinate legislation (within the meaning of the Interpretation Act 1978);

(b)   any instrument made under an Act of the Scottish Parliament; or

(c)   any statutory rules (within the meaning of the Statutory Rules (Northern Ireland) Order 1979).

(2)   In this Act—

(a)   references to the authenticity of any communication or data are references to any one or more of the following—

(i)   whether the communication or data comes from a particular person or other source;

(ii)   whether it is accurately timed and dated;

(iii)   whether it is intended to have legal effect; and

(b)   references to the integrity of any communication or data are references to whether there has been any tampering with or other modification of the communication or data.

(3)   References in this Act to something's being put into an intelligible form include references to its being restored to the condition in which it was before any encryption or similar process was applied to it.

16   Short title, commencement, extent

(1)   This Act may be cited as the Electronic Communications Act 2000.

(2)   Part I of this Act and sections 7, 11 and 12 shall come into force on such day as the Secretary of State may by order made by statutory instrument appoint; and different days may be appointed under this subsection for different purposes.

(3)   An order shall not be made for bringing any of Part I of this Act into force for any purpose unless a draft of the order has been laid before Parliament and approved by a resolution of each House.

(4)   If no order for bringing Part I of this Act into force has been made under subsection (2) by the end of the period of five years beginning with the day on which this Act is passed, that Part shall, by virtue of this subsection, be repealed at the end of that period.

(5)   This Act extends to Northern Ireland.

ANTISOCIAL BEHAVIOUR ETC (SCOTLAND) ACT 2004
(2004, asp 8)

4 Antisocial behaviour orders

(1) On the application of a relevant authority, the sheriff may, if satisfied that the conditions mentioned in subsection (2) are met as respects the person to whom the application relates (the 'specified person'), make an antisocial behaviour order.

(2) Those conditions are—

(a) that the specified person is at least 12 years of age;

(b) that the specified person has engaged in antisocial behaviour towards a relevant person; and

(c) that an antisocial behaviour order is necessary for the purpose of protecting relevant persons from further antisocial behaviour by the specified person.

(3) For the purpose of determining whether the condition mentioned in subsection (2)(b) is met, the sheriff shall disregard any act or conduct of the specified person which that person shows was reasonable in the circumstances.

(4) Where the specified person is a child, the sheriff shall, before determining the application, require the Principal Reporter to arrange a children's hearing for the purpose of obtaining their advice as to whether the condition mentioned in subsection (2)(c) is met; and the sheriff shall, in determining whether that condition is met, have regard to that advice.

(5) Subject to subsections (6) and (7), an antisocial behaviour order is an order which prohibits, indefinitely or for such period as may be specified in the order, the specified person from doing anything described in the order.

(6) The prohibitions that may be imposed by an antisocial behaviour order are those necessary for the purpose of protecting relevant persons from further antisocial behaviour by the specified person.

(7) If an antisocial behaviour order is made on the application of a local authority the order may, in addition to imposing prohibitions that are necessary for the purpose mentioned in subsection (6), impose such prohibitions as are necessary for the purpose of protecting other persons ('affected persons') from further antisocial behaviour by the specified person.

(8) Before making an antisocial behaviour order, the sheriff shall, where the specified person is present in court, explain in ordinary language—

(a) the effect of the order and the prohibitions proposed to be included in it;

(b) the consequences of failing to comply with the order;

(c) the powers the sheriff has under sections 5 and 6; and

(d) the entitlement of the specified person to appeal against the making of the order.

(9) Failure to comply with subsection (8) shall not affect the validity of the order.

(10) An application for an antisocial behaviour order shall be made by summary application to the sheriff within whose sheriffdom the specified person is alleged to have engaged in antisocial behaviour.

(11) Before making an application under this section—

(a) a relevant authority shall consult the relevant consultees; and

(b) a registered social landlord shall—

(i) in the case where the specified person is a child, consult the local authority within whose area the specified person resides or appears to reside about the proposed application;

(ii) in the case where the specified person is not a child, notify that local authority of the proposed application.

(12) Nothing in this section shall prevent a relevant authority from instituting any legal proceedings otherwise than under this section against any person in relation to any antisocial behaviour.

(13)   In this section, 'relevant person' means—

(a)   in relation to an application by a local authority, a person within the area of the authority; and

(b)   in relation to an application by a registered social landlord—

(i)   a person residing in, or otherwise in or likely to be in, property provided or managed by that landlord; or

(ii)   a person in, or likely to be in, the vicinity of such property.

9   Breach of orders

(1)   Subject to subsection (3), a person who—

(a)   is subject to an antisocial behaviour order or an interim order; and

(b)   without reasonable excuse, does anything that the order to which the person is subject prohibits the person from doing,

shall be guilty of an offence.

(2)   A person guilty of an offence under subsection (1) shall be liable—

(a)   on summary conviction, to imprisonment for a term not exceeding 6 months or to a fine not exceeding the statutory maximum or to both; or

(b)   on conviction on indictment, to imprisonment for a term not exceeding 5 years or to a fine or to both.

(3)   If—

(a)   otherwise than under subsection (1), the thing done by the person constitutes an offence (a 'separate offence'); and

(b)   the person is charged with the separate offence,

the person shall not be liable to be proceeded against for an offence under subsection (1).

(4)   Subject to subsection (5), if a person is convicted of a separate offence, the court which sentences the person for that offence shall, in determining the appropriate sentence or disposal, have regard to—

(a)   the fact that the separate offence was committed while the person was subject to the antisocial behaviour order or, as the case may be, interim order;

(b)   the number of antisocial behaviour orders and interim orders to which the person was subject at the time of commission of the separate offence;

(c)   any previous conviction of the person for an offence under subsection (1); and

(d)   the extent to which the sentence or disposal in respect of any previous conviction of the person differed, by virtue of this subsection, from that which the court would have imposed but for this section.

(5)   The court shall not, under subsection (4)(a), have regard to the fact that the separate offence was committed while the person was subject to the antisocial behaviour order or, as the case may be, the interim order unless that fact is libelled in the indictment or, as the case may be, specified in the complaint.

(6)   The fact that the separate offence was committed while the person was subject to an antisocial behaviour order or, as the case may be, an interim order, shall, unless challenged—

(a)   in the case of proceedings on indictment, by the giving of notice of a preliminary objection in accordance with section 71(2) or 72(6)(b)(i) of the Criminal Procedure (Scotland) Act 1995; or

(b)   in summary proceedings, by preliminary objection before the person's plea is recorded,

be held as admitted.

143   Interpretation: 'antisocial behaviour' and other expressions

(1)   For the purposes of this Act (other than Parts 7 and 8), a person ('A') engages in antisocial behaviour if A—

(a)   acts in a manner that causes or is likely to cause alarm or distress; or

(b)   pursues a course of conduct that causes or is likely to cause alarm or distress,

to at least one person who is not of the same household as A; and 'antisocial behaviour' shall be construed accordingly.

(2)   In this Act, unless the context otherwise requires—

'conduct' includes speech; and a course of conduct must involve conduct on at
least two occasions;

'local authority' means a council constituted under section 2 of the Local
Government etc (Scotland) Act 1994; and 'area', in relation to a local authority,
means the local government area (within the meaning of that Act) for which the
council is constituted;

'registered social landlord' means a body registered in the register maintained
under section 57 of the Housing (Scotland) Act 2001; and

'senior police officer' has the meaning given by section 19(1).

CIVIL PARTNERSHIP ACT 2004
(2004, c 33)

128   Promise or agreement to enter into civil partnership

No promise or agreement to enter into civil partnership creates any rights or obligations under the law of Scotland; and no action for breach of such a promise or
agreement may be brought in any court in Scotland, whatever the law applicable
to the promise or agreement.

GAMBLING ACT 2005
(2005, c 19)

PART 1
INTERPRETATION OF KEY CONCEPTS

Principal concepts

3   Gambling

In this Act 'gambling' means—
  (a)   gaming (within the meaning of section 6),
  (b)   betting (within the meaning of section 9), and
  (c)   participating in a lottery (within the meaning of section 14 and subject to
section 15).

Gaming

6   Gaming & game of chance

(1)   In this Act 'gaming' means playing a game of chance for a prize.

(2)   In this Act 'game of chance'—
  (a)   includes—
      (i)   a game that involves both an element of chance and an element of
skill,
      (ii)   a game that involves an element of chance that can be eliminated by
superlative skill, and
      (iii)   a game that is presented as involving an element of chance, but
  (b)   does not include a sport.

(3)   For the purposes of this Act a person plays a game of chance if he partici-
pates in a game of chance—
  (a)   whether or not there are other participants in the game, and
  (b)   whether or not a computer generates images or data taken to represent
the actions of other participants in the game.

(4)   For the purposes of this Act a person plays a game of chance for a prize—

(a)   if he plays a game of chance and thereby acquires a chance of winning a prize, and

(b)   whether or not he risks losing anything at the game.

(5)   In this Act 'prize' in relation to gaming (except in the context of a gaming machine)—

(a)   means money or money's worth, and

(b)   includes both a prize provided by a person organising gaming and winnings of money staked.

(6)   The Secretary of State may by regulations provide that a specified activity, or an activity carried on in specified circumstances, is or is not to be treated for the purposes of this Act as—

(a)   a game;

(b)   a game of chance;

(c)   a sport.

Betting

9   Betting: general

(1)   In this Act 'betting' means making or accepting a bet on—

(a)   the outcome of a race, competition or other event or process,

(b)   the likelihood of anything occurring or not occurring, or

(c)   whether anything is or is not true.

(2)   A transaction that relates to the outcome of a race, competition or other event or process may be a bet within the meaning of subsection (1) despite the facts that—

(a)   the race, competition, event or process has already occurred or been completed, and

(b)   one party to the transaction knows the outcome.

(3)   A transaction that relates to the likelihood of anything occurring or not occurring may be a bet within the meaning of subsection (1) despite the facts that—

(a)   the thing has already occurred or failed to occur, and

(b)   one party to the transaction knows that the thing has already occurred or failed to occur.

Lottery

14   Lottery

(1)   For the purposes of this Act an arrangement is a lottery, irrespective of how it is described, if it satisfies one of the descriptions of lottery in subsections (2) and (3).

(2)   An arrangement is a simple lottery if—

(a)   persons are required to pay in order to participate in the arrangement,

(b)   in the course of the arrangement one or more prizes are allocated to one or more members of a class, and

(c)   the prizes are allocated by a process which relies wholly on chance.

(3)   An arrangement is a complex lottery if—

(a)   persons are required to pay in order to participate in the arrangement,

(b)   in the course of the arrangement one or more prizes are allocated to one or more members of a class,

(c)   the prizes are allocated by a series of processes, and

(d)   the first of those processes relies wholly on chance.

(4)   In this Act 'prize' in relation to lotteries includes any money, articles or services—

(a)   whether or not described as a prize, and

Gambling Act 2005

(b) whether or not consisting wholly or partly of money paid, or articles or services provided, by the members of the class among whom the prize is allocated.

(5) A process which requires persons to exercise skill or judgment or to display knowledge shall be treated for the purposes of this section as relying wholly on chance if—

(a) the requirement cannot reasonably be expected to prevent a significant proportion of persons who participate in the arrangement of which the process forms part from receiving a prize, and

(b) the requirement cannot reasonably be expected to prevent a significant proportion of persons who wish to participate in that arrangement from doing so.

(6) Schedule 2 makes further provision about when an arrangement is to be or not to be treated for the purposes of this section as requiring persons to pay.

(7) The Secretary of State may by regulations provide that an arrangement of a specified kind is to be or not to be treated as a lottery for the purposes of this Act; and—

(a) the power in this subsection is not constrained by subsections (1) to (6) or Schedule 2, and

(b) regulations under this subsection may amend other provisions of this section or Schedule 2.

15 National Lottery

(1) Participating in a lottery which forms part of the National Lottery is not gambling for the purposes of this Act (despite section 3(c) but subject to subsections (2) and (3) below).

(2) Participating in a lottery which forms part of the National Lottery is gambling for the purposes of—

(a) section 42, and

(b) section 335.

(3) Where participating in a lottery which forms part of the National Lottery would also constitute gaming within the meaning of section 6, it shall be treated as gaming for the purposes of this Act if and only if a person participating in the lottery is required to participate in, or to be successful in, more than three processes before becoming entitled to a prize.

(4) Participating in a lottery which forms part of the National Lottery shall not be treated as betting for the purposes of this Act where it would—

(a) satisfy the definition of pool betting in section 12, or

(b) satisfy the definition of betting in section 9 by virtue of section 11.

(5) Schedule 3 shall have effect.

PART 17

LEGALITY AND ENFORCEMENT OF GAMBLING CONTRACTS

. . .

335 Enforceability of gambling contracts

(1)   The fact that a contract relates to gambling shall not prevent its enforcement.

(2)   Subsection (1) is without prejudice to any rule of law preventing the enforcement of a contract on the grounds of unlawfulness (other than a rule relating specifically to gambling).

PART 18

MISCELLANEOUS AND GENERAL

. . .

361 Extent

(1)   The following provisions of this Act extend to England and Wales, Scotland and Northern Ireland—

    (a)   section 43,

    (b)   section 331, and

    (c)   section 340 (and the related entry in Schedule 17).

(2)   The other provisions of this Act shall extend only to—

    (a)   England and Wales, and

    (b)   Scotland.

(3)   This section is subject to section 356.

COMPENSATION ACT 2006
(2006 c 29)

3   Mesothelioma: damages

(1)   This section applies where—

    (a)   a person ('the responsible person') has negligently or in breach of statutory duty caused or permitted another person ('the victim') to be exposed to asbestos,

    (b)   the victim has contracted mesothelioma as a result of exposure to asbestos,

    (c)   because of the nature of mesothelioma and the state of medical science, it is not possible to determine with certainty whether it was the exposure mentioned in paragraph (a) or another exposure which caused the victim to become ill, and

    (d)   the responsible person is liable in tort, by virtue of the exposure mentioned in paragraph (a), in connection with damage caused to the victim by the disease (whether by reason of having materially increased a risk or for any other reason).

(2)   The responsible person shall be liable—

    (a)   in respect of the whole of the damage caused to the victim by the disease (irrespective of whether the victim was also exposed to asbestos—

        (i)   other than by the responsible person, whether or not in circumstances in which another person has liability in tort, or

        (ii)   by the responsible person in circumstances in which he has no liability in tort), and

    (b)   jointly and severally with any other responsible person.

(3)   Subsection (2) does not prevent—

    (a)   one responsible person from claiming a contribution from another, or

    (b)   a finding of contributory negligence.

(4)   In determining the extent of contributions of different responsible persons in accordance with subsection (3)(a), a court shall have regard to the relative

lengths of the periods of exposure for which each was responsible; but this subsection shall not apply—

(a)   if or to the extent that responsible persons agree to apportion responsibility amongst themselves on some other basis, or

(b)   if or to the extent that the court thinks that another basis for determining contributions is more appropriate in the circumstances of a particular case.

(5)   In subsection (1) the reference to causing or permitting a person to be exposed to asbestos includes a reference to failing to protect a person from exposure to asbestos.

(6)   In the application of this section to Scotland—

(a)   a reference to tort shall be taken as a reference to delict, and

(b)   a reference to a court shall be taken to include a reference to a jury.

(7)   The Treasury may make regulations about the provision of compensation to a responsible person where—

(a)   he claims, or would claim, a contribution from another responsible person in accordance with subsection (3)(a), but

(b)   he is unable or likely to be unable to obtain the contribution, because an insurer of the other responsible person is unable or likely to be unable to satisfy the claim for a contribution.

(8)   The regulations may, in particular—

(a)   replicate or apply (with or without modification) a provision of the Financial Services Compensation Scheme;

(b)   replicate or apply (with or without modification) a transitional compensation provision;

(c)   provide for a specified person to assess and pay compensation;

(d)   provide for expenses incurred (including the payment of compensation) to be met out of levies collected in accordance with section 213(3)(b) of the Financial Services and Markets Act 2000 (c 8) (the Financial Services Compensation Scheme);

(e)   modify the effect of a transitional compensation provision;

(f)   enable the Financial Services Authority to amend the Financial Services Compensation Scheme;

(g)   modify the Financial Services and Markets Act 2000 in its application to an amendment pursuant to paragraph (f);

(h)   make, or require the making of, provision for the making of a claim by a responsible person for compensation whether or not he has already satisfied claims in tort against him;

(i)   make, or require the making of, provision which has effect in relation to claims for contributions made on or after the date on which this Act is passed.

(9)   Provision made by virtue of subsection (8)(a) shall cease to have effect when the Financial Services Compensation Scheme is amended by the Financial Services Authority by virtue of subsection (8)(f).

(10)   In subsections (7) and (8)—

(a)   a reference to a responsible person includes a reference to an insurer of a responsible person, and

(b)   'transitional compensation provision' means a provision of an enactment which is made under the Financial Services and Markets Act 2000 and—

(i)   preserves the effect of the Policyholders Protection Act 1975 (c 75), or

(ii)   applies the Financial Services Compensation Scheme in relation to matters arising before its establishment.

(11)   Regulations under subsection (7)—

(a)   may include consequential or incidental provision,

(b)   may make provision which has effect generally or only in relation to specified cases or circumstances,

(c)   may make different provision for different cases or circumstances,

(d)   shall be made by statutory instrument, and

    (e)   may not be made unless a draft has been laid before and approved by resolution of each House of Parliament.

16 Commencement

(1), (2) *[Do not apply to Scotland.]*

(3)   Section 3 shall be treated as having always had effect.

(4)   But the section shall have no effect in relation to—

    (a)   a claim which is settled before 3rd May 2006 (whether or not legal proceedings in relation to the claim have been instituted), or

    (b)   legal proceedings which are determined before that date.

(5)   Where a claim is settled on or after that date and before the date on which this Act is passed, a party to the settlement may apply to a relevant court to have the settlement varied; and—

    (a)   a court is a relevant court for that purpose if it had, or would have had, jurisdiction to determine the claim by way of legal proceedings,

    (b)   an application shall be brought as an application in, or by way of, proceedings on the claim, and

    (c)   a court to which an application is made shall vary the settlement to such extent (if any) as appears appropriate to reflect the effect of section 3.

(6)   Where legal proceedings are determined on or after that date and before the date on which this Act is passed, a party to the proceedings may apply to the court to vary the determination; and—

    (a)   'the court' means the court which determined the proceedings,

    (b)   the application shall be treated as an application in the proceedings, and

    (c)   the court shall vary the determination to such extent (if any) as appears appropriate to reflect the effect of section 3.

17 Extent

(1)   This Act shall extend to England and Wales only.

(2)   But section 3 (and section 16(3) to (6)) shall extend to—

    (a)   England and Wales,

    (b)   Scotland, and

    (c)   Northern Ireland.

DAMAGES (ASBESTOS-RELATED CONDITIONS) (SCOTLAND) ACT 2009
(2009, asp 4)

1 Pleural plaques

(1)   Asbestos-related pleural plaques are a personal injury which is not negligible.

(2)   Accordingly, they constitute actionable harm for the purposes of an action of damages for personal injuries.

(3)   Any rule of law the effect of which is that asbestos-related pleural plaques do not constitute actionable harm ceases to apply to the extent it has that effect.

(4)   But nothing in this section otherwise affects any enactment or rule of law which determines whether and in what circumstances a person may be liable in damages in respect of personal injuries.

2 Pleural thickening and asbestosis

(1)   For the avoidance of doubt, a condition mentioned in subsection (2) which has not caused and is not causing impairment of a person's physical condition is a personal injury which is not negligible.

(2)   Those conditions are—

    (a)   asbestos-related pleural thickening; and

    (b)   asbestosis.

(3)   Accordingly, such a condition constitutes actionable harm for the purposes of an action of damages for personal injuries.

(4)   Any rule of law the effect of which is that such a condition does not constitute actionable harm ceases to apply to the extent it has that effect.

(5)   But nothing in this section otherwise affects any enactment or rule of law which determines whether and in what circumstances a person may be liable in damages in respect of personal injuries.

3   Limitation of actions

(1)   This section applies to an action of damages for personal injuries—

(a)   in which the damages claimed consist of or include damages in respect of—

(i)   asbestos-related pleural plaques; or

(ii)   a condition to which section 2 applies; and

(b)   which, in the case of an action commenced before the date this section comes into force, has not been determined by that date.

(2)   For the purposes of sections 17 and 18 of the Prescription and Limitation (Scotland) Act 1973 (limitation in respect of actions for personal injuries), the period beginning with 17 October 2007 and ending with the day on which this section comes into force is to be left out of account.

4   Commencement and retrospective effect

(1)   This Act (other than this subsection and section 5) comes into force on such day as the Scottish Ministers may, by order made by statutory instrument, appoint.

(2)   Sections 1 and 2 are to be treated for all purposes as having always had effect.

(3)   But those sections have no effect in relation to—

(a)   a claim which is settled before the date on which subsection (2) comes into force (whether or not legal proceedings in relation to the claim have been commenced); or

(b)   legal proceedings which are determined before that date.

5   Short title and Crown application

(1)   This Act may be cited as the Damages (Asbestos-related Conditions) (Scotland) Act 2009.

(2)   This Act binds the Crown.

DAMAGES (SCOTLAND) ACT 2011
(2011, asp 7)

1   Damages to injured person whose expectation of life is diminished

(1)   This section applies to an action for damages in respect of personal injuries suffered by a pursuer whose date of death is expected to be earlier than had the injuries not been suffered.

(2)   In assessing the amount of damages by way of solatium the court is, if the pursuer—

(a)   was at any time,

(b)   is, or

(c)   is likely to become,

aware of the reduced expectation of life, to have regard to the extent to which the pursuer, in consequence of that awareness, has suffered or is likely to suffer.

(3)   Subject to subsection (2), no damages by way of solatium are recoverable by the pursuer in respect of loss of expectation of life.

(4)   In making an award of damages by way of solatium, the court is not required to ascribe specifically any part of the award to loss of expectation of life.

(5)   In assessing the amount of any patrimonial loss in respect of the period after the date of decree the court is to assume that the pursuer will live until the date when death would have been expected had the injuries not been suffered (the 'notional date of death').

(6)   Such part of that amount as is attributable to the period between the expected date of death and the notional date of death (the 'lost period') is to be assessed as follows—

(a)   the court is to estimate what (if anything) the pursuer would have earned during the lost period through the pursuer's own labour or own gainful activity had the injuries not been suffered,

(b)   the court may, if it thinks fit, add to the amount so estimated (whether or not that amount is nil) an amount equivalent to all or part of what it estimates the pursuer would have received by way of relevant benefits during the lost period had the injuries not been suffered, and

(c)   the court is then to deduct, from the total amount obtained by virtue of paragraphs (a) and (b), 25% of that amount (to represent what would have been the pursuer's living expenses during the lost period had the injuries not been suffered).

(7)   But, if satisfied that it is necessary to do so for the purpose of avoiding a manifestly and materially unfair result, the court may apply a different percentage to that specified in subsection (6)(c).

(8)   In paragraph (b) of subsection (6), 'relevant benefits' means benefits in money or money's worth other than benefits—

(a)   derived from the pursuer's own estate, or

(b)   consisting of such earnings as are mentioned in paragraph (a) of that subsection.

2   Transmission of deceased's rights to executor

(1)   There are transmissible to a deceased person's executor ('E') the like rights to damages, including a right to damages for non-patrimonial loss, in respect of injuries suffered by the deceased ('A') and vested in A immediately before A's death, being—

(a)   personal injuries, or

(b)   injuries which, though not personal injuries, are—

  (i)   injuries to name or reputation, or

  (ii)   injuries resulting from harassment actionable under section 8 [or section 8A] of the Protection from Harassment Act 1997 (c 40).

(2)   The 'like rights' mentioned in subsection (1) do not include any right to damages by way of compensation for patrimonial loss attributable to any period after the date of death; and in determining the amount of damages for non-patrimonial loss payable to E by virtue of this section, the only period to which the court is to have regard is that ending immediately before A's death.

(3)   In so far as a right to damages vested in A comprises a right to damages for non-patrimonial loss in respect of such injuries as are mentioned in sub-paragraph (i) of subsection (1)(b), that right is transmissible to E only if an action to enforce the right is brought by A and is not concluded before A's death.

(4)   For the purposes of subsection (3) an action is not to be taken to be concluded—

(a)   while an appeal is competent, or

(b)   before any appeal taken is disposed of.

3   Application of sections 4 to 6

Sections 4 to 6 apply where a person ('A') dies in consequence of suffering personal injuries as the result of the act or omission of another person ('B') and the act or omission—

(a)   gives rise to liability to pay damages to A (or to A's executor), or

(b)   would have given rise to such liability but for A's death.

4   Sums of damages payable to relatives

(1)   B is liable under this subsection to pay—

(a)   to any relative of A who is a member of A's immediate family, such sums of damages as are mentioned in paragraphs (a) and (b) of subsection (3),

(b)   to any other relative of A, such sum of damages as is mentioned in paragraph (a) of that subsection.

(2)   But, except as provided for in section 5, no such liability arises if the liability to pay damages to A (or to A's executor) in respect of the act or omission—

(a)   is excluded or discharged, whether by antecedent agreement or otherwise, by A before A's death, or

(b)   is excluded by virtue of an enactment.

(3)   The sums of damages are—

(a)   such sum as will compensate for any loss of support which as a result of the act or omission is sustained, or is likely to be sustained, by the relative after the date of A's death together with any reasonable expenses incurred by the relative in connection with A's funeral, and

(b)   such sum, if any, as the court thinks just by way of compensation for all or any of the following—

(i)   distress and anxiety endured by the relative in contemplation of the suffering of A before A's death,

(ii)   grief and sorrow of the relative caused by A's death,

(iii)   the loss of such non-patrimonial benefit as the relative might have been expected to derive from A's society and guidance if A had not died.

(4)   The court, in making an award under paragraph (b) of subsection (3) is not required to ascribe any part of the award specifically to any of the sub-paragraphs of that paragraph.

(5)   For the purpose of subsection (1)(a)—

(a)   a relative of A is a member of A's immediate family if the relative falls within any of paragraphs (a) to (d) of the definition of 'relative' in section 14(1),

(b)   paragraphs (a)(i) and (b) of section 14(2) are to be disregarded.

5   Discharge of liability to pay damages: exception for mesothelioma

(1)   This section applies where—

(a)   the liability to pay damages to A (or to A's executor) is discharged, whether by antecedent agreement or otherwise, by A before A's death,

(b)   the personal injury in consequence of which A died is mesothelioma, and

(c)   the discharge and the death each occurred on or after 20th December 2006.

(2)   Liability arises under section 4(1) but is limited to the payment of such sum of damages as is mentioned in paragraph (b) of section 4(3).

6   Relative's loss of personal services

(1)   A relative entitled to damages under paragraph (a) of section 4(3) is entitled to include, as a head of damages under that paragraph, a reasonable sum in respect of the loss to the relative of A's personal services as a result of the act or omission.

(2)   In subsection (1), 'personal services' has the same meaning as in section 9(1) of the Administration of Justice Act 1982 (damages in respect of inability of injured person to render such services).

7   Assessment of compensation for loss of support

(1)   Such part of an award under paragraph (a) of section 4(3) as consists of a sum in compensation for loss of support is to be assessed applying the following paragraphs—

(a)   the total amount to be available to support A's relatives is an amount equivalent to 75% of A's net income,

(b)   in the case of any other relative than—

(i)   a person described in paragraph (a) of the definition of 'relative' in section 14(1), or

     (ii) a dependent child,

the relative is not to be awarded more in compensation for loss of support than the actual amount of that loss,

    (c) if—

     (i) no such other relative is awarded a sum in compensation for loss of support, the total amount mentioned in paragraph (a) is to be taken to be spent by A in supporting such of A's relatives as are mentioned in sub-paragraphs (i) and (ii) of paragraph (b),

     (ii) any such other relative is awarded a sum in compensation for loss of support, the total amount mentioned in paragraph (a) is, after deduction of the amount of the sum so awarded, to be taken to be spent by A in supporting such of A's relatives as are mentioned in those sub-paragraphs, and

    (d) any multiplier applied by the court—

     (i) is to run from the date of the interlocutor awarding damages, and

     (ii) is to apply only in respect of future loss of support.

(2) But, if satisfied that it is necessary to do so for the purpose of avoiding a manifestly and materially unfair result, the court may apply a different percentage to that specified in subsection (1)(a).

(3) In subsection (1)(b)(ii), 'dependent child' means a child who as at the date of A's death—

    (a) has not attained the age of 18 years, and

    (b) is owed an obligation of aliment by A.

8 Further provision as regards relative's entitlement to damages

(1) Subject to subsection (3), in assessing for the purposes of section 4 or 6 the amount of any loss of support sustained by a relative of A no account is to be taken of—

    (a) any patrimonial gain or advantage which has accrued or will or may accrue to the relative, by way of succession or settlement, from A or from any other person, or

    (b) any insurance money, benefit, pension or gratuity which has been, or will or may be, paid as a result of A's death.

(2) In subsection (1)—

'benefit' means benefit under the Social Security Contributions and Benefits Act 1992 or the Social Security Contributions and Benefits (Northern Ireland) Act 1992 and any payment by a friendly society or trade union for the relief or maintenance of a member's dependants,

'insurance money' includes a return of premiums, and

'pension' includes a return of contributions and any payment of a lump sum in respect of a person's employment.

(3) Where A has been awarded a provisional award of damages under section 12(2) of the Administration of Justice Act 1982, the making of that award does not prevent liability from arising under section 4(1); but in assessing for the purposes of section 4 or 6 the amount of any loss of support sustained by a relative the court is to take into account such part of the provisional award relating to future patrimonial loss as was intended to compensate A for a period beyond the date on which A died.

(4) In order to establish loss of support for the purposes of section 4 or 6, it is not essential for a relative to show that A was, or might have become, subject to a duty in law to provide support for, or contribute to the support of, the relative; but if any such fact is established it may be taken into account in determining whether, and if so to what extent, A would (had A not died) have been likely to provide, or contribute to, such support.

(5) Except as provided for in this Act or in any other enactment, no person is entitled by reason of relationship to damages in respect of the death of another person.

(6)   In subsection (5), 'damages' includes damages by way of solatium.

9   Transmission of relative's rights to executor

(1)   This section applies where liability to pay damages to a relative ('R') has arisen under section 4 or 6 but R dies.

(2)   If the right to damages is vested in R immediately before R's death that right is transmissible to R's executor ('E'); but in determining the amount of damages payable to E by virtue of this section, the only period to which the court is to have regard is the period ending immediately before R's death.

(3)   In a case where—

     (a)   section 5 applies, and

     (b)   R died before 27th April 2007,

any right of R to damages under that section is to be taken, for the purposes of subsection (2), to have vested in R on A's death.

10   Enforcement by executor of rights transmitted under section 2 or 9

(1)   Where a right is transmitted by virtue of section 2 or 9, the executor in question is entitled—

     (a)   to bring an action to enforce it, or

     (b)   if an action to enforce it was brought by the deceased but not concluded before the date of death, to be sisted as pursuer in that action.

(2)   For the purposes of subsection (1)(b) an action is not to be taken to be concluded—

     (a)   while an appeal is competent, or

     (b)   before any appeal taken is disposed of.

11   Executor's claim not excluded by relative's claim etc

(1)   A claim made by virtue of this Act by a deceased's executor is not excluded by a claim so made by a relative of the deceased (or by such a relative's executor).

(2)   Nor is a claim so made by a such a relative (or by such a relative's executor) excluded by a claim so made by the deceased's executor.

12   Limitation of total amount of liability

(1)   This section applies to an action directed against a defender ('B') in which, following the death of a person ('A') from personal injuries, damages are claimed—

     (a)   in respect of those injuries, by A's executor, or

     (b)   in respect of A's death, by any relative of A or by the executor of any relative of A.

(2)   If it is shown that the liability arising in relation to B from the personal injuries in question—

     (a)   had before A's death, by antecedent agreement or otherwise, been limited to damages of a specified or ascertainable amount, or

     (b)   is so limited by virtue of an enactment,

nothing in this Act makes B liable to pay damages exceeding that amount.

(3)   Accordingly, where there are two or more pursuers, any damages to which they would (but for this section) respectively be entitled under this Act are, if necessary, to be reduced pro rata.

(4)   And where two or more actions are conjoined the conjoined actions are to be treated, for the purposes of this section, as if they were a single action.

13   [Amends Administration of Justice Act 1982 s 9]

14   Interpretation

(1)   In this Act, unless the context otherwise requires—

'personal injuries' means—

     (a)   any disease, and

     (b)   any impairment of a person's physical or mental condition, and

'relative', in relation to a person who has died, means a person who—

(a)   immediately before the death is the deceased's spouse or civil partner or is living with the deceased as if married to, or in civil partnership with, the deceased,

(b)   is a parent or child of the deceased, accepted the deceased as a child of the person's family or was accepted by the deceased as a child of the deceased's family,

(c)   is the brother or sister of the deceased or was brought up in the same household as the deceased and accepted as a child of the family in which the deceased was a child,

(d)   is a grandparent or grandchild of the deceased, accepted the deceased as a grandchild of the person or was accepted by the deceased as a grandchild of the deceased,

(e)   is an ascendant or descendant of the deceased (other than a parent or grandparent or a child or grandchild of the deceased),

(f)   is an uncle or aunt of the deceased,

(g)   is a child or other issue of—

   (i)   a brother or sister of the deceased, or

   (ii)   an uncle or aunt of the deceased, or

(h)   is a former spouse or civil partner of the deceased having become so by virtue of divorce or (as the case may be) dissolution of the partnership.

(2)   In deducing a relationship for the purposes of the definition of 'relative' in subsection (1)—

(a)   any relationship—

   (i)   by affinity is to be treated as a relationship by consanguinity,

   (ii)   of the half blood is to be treated as a relationship of the whole blood,

(b)   a stepchild of a person is to be treated as the person's child.

(3)   In any enactment passed or made before this Act, unless the context otherwise requires, any reference to—

(a)   solatium in respect of the death of any person (however expressed), or

(b)   a loss of society award,

is to be construed as a reference to an award under paragraph (b) of section 4(3).

15–17   *[Amendments, repeals and savings]*

18   Transitional provision etc

(1)   The Scottish Ministers may, by order made by statutory instrument, make such incidental, supplemental, consequential, transitional, transitory or saving provision as they consider necessary or expedient for the purposes of, or in consequence of, this Act.

(2)   Subject to subsection (4), a statutory instrument containing an order under subsection (1) is subject to annulment in pursuance of a resolution of the Parliament.

(3)   An order under subsection (1) may make different provision for different cases or for different classes of case.

(4)   A statutory instrument containing an order under subsection (1) which adds to, replaces or omits any part of the text of an Act (including this Act) is not to be made unless a draft of the instrument has been—

(a)   laid before, and

(b)   approved by resolution of, the Parliament.

19   Short title, Crown application and commencement

(1)   This Act may be cited as the Damages (Scotland) Act 2011.

(2)   This Act binds the Crown.

(3)   The provisions of this Act, except section 18 and this section, come into force on such day as the Scottish Ministers may by order made by statutory instrument appoint.

(4)   An order under subsection (3) may include such transitional, transitory or saving provision as the Scottish Ministers consider necessary or expedient in connection with the commencement of this Act.

PART II
STATUTORY INSTRUMENTS

COMMERCIAL AGENTS (COUNCIL DIRECTIVE) REGULATIONS 1993
(SI 1993/3053)

PART I
GENERAL

2 Interpretation, application and extent

(1) In these Regulations—

'commercial agent' means a self-employed intermediary who has continuing authority to negotiate the sale or purchase of goods on behalf of another person (the 'principal'), or to negotiate and conclude the sale or purchase of goods on behalf of and in the name of that principal; but shall be understood as not including in particular:

(i) a person who, in his capacity as an officer of a company or association, is empowered to enter into commitments binding on that company or association;

(ii) a partner who is lawfully authorised to enter into commitments binding on his partners;

(iii) a person who acts as an insolvency practitioner (as that expression is defined in section 388 of the Insolvency Act 1986) or the equivalent in any other jurisdiction;

'commission' means any part of the remuneration of a commercial agent which varies with the number or value of business transactions;

['EEA Agreement' means the Agreement on the European Economic Area signed at Oporto on 2nd May 1992 as adjusted by the Protocol signed at Brussels on 17th March 1993;

'member State' includes a State which is a contracting party to the EEA Agreement;]

'restraint of trade clause' means an agreement restricting the business activities of a commercial agent following termination of the agency contract.

(2) These Regulations do not apply to—

(a) commercial agents whose activities are unpaid;

(b) commercial agents when they operate on commodity exchanges or in the commodity market;

(c) the Crown Agents for Overseas Governments and Administrations, as set up under the Crown Agents Act 1979, or its subsidiaries.

(3) The provisions of the Schedule to these Regulations have effect for the purpose of determining the persons whose activities as commercial agents are to be considered secondary.

(4) These Regulations shall not apply to the persons referred to in paragraph (3) above.

(5) These Regulations do not extend to Northern Ireland.

PART II
RIGHTS AND OBLIGATIONS

3 Duties of a commercial agent to his principal

(1)   In performing his activities a commercial agent must look after the interests of his principal and act dutifully and in good faith.

(2)   In particular, a commercial agent must—

(a)   make proper efforts to negotiate and, where appropriate, conclude the transactions he is instructed to take care of;

(b)   communicate to his principal all the necessary information available to him;

(c)   comply with reasonable instructions given by his principal.

4 Duties of a principal to his commercial agent

(1)   In his relations with his commercial agent a principal must act dutifully and in good faith.

(2)   In particular, a principal must—

(a)   provide his commercial agent with the necessary documentation relating to the goods concerned;

(b)   obtain for his commercial agent the information necessary for the performance of the agency contract, and in particular notify his commercial agent within a reasonable period once he anticipates that the volume of commercial transactions will be significantly lower than that which the commercial agent could normally have expected.

(3)   A principal shall, in addition, inform his commercial agent within a reasonable period of his acceptance or refusal of, and of any non-execution by him of, a commercial transaction which the commercial agent has procured for him.

5 Prohibition on derogation from regulations 3 and 4 and consequence of breach

(1)   The parties may not derogate from regulations 3 and 4 above.

(2)   The law applicable to the contract shall govern the consequence of breach of the rights and obligations under regulations 3 and 4 above.

PART III
REMUNERATION

6 Form and amount of remuneration in absence of agreement

(1)   In the absence of any agreement as to remuneration between the parties, a commercial agent shall be entitled to the remuneration that commercial agents appointed for the goods forming the subject of his agency contract are customarily allowed in the place where he carries on his activities and, if there is no such customary practice, a commercial agent shall be entitled to reasonable remuneration taking into account all the aspects of the transaction.

(2)   This regulation is without prejudice to the application of any enactment or rule of law concerning the level of remuneration.

(3)   Where a commercial agent is not remunerated (wholly or in part) by commission, regulations 7 to 12 below shall not apply.

7 Entitlement to commission on transactions concluded during agency contract

(1)   A commercial agent shall be entitled to commission on commercial transactions concluded during the period covered by the agency contract—

(a)   where the transaction has been concluded as a result of his action; or

(b)   where the transaction is concluded with a third party whom he has previously acquired as a customer for transactions of the same kind.

(2)   A commercial agent shall also be entitled to commission on transactions concluded during the period covered by the agency contract where he has an

exclusive right to a specific geographical area or to a specific group of customers and where the transaction has been entered into with a customer belonging to that area or group.

8 Entitlement to commission on transactions concluded after agency contract has terminated

Subject to regulation 9 below, a commercial agent shall be entitled to commission on commercial transactions concluded after the agency contract has terminated if—

(a) the transaction is mainly attributable to his efforts during the period covered by the agency contract and if the transaction was entered into within a reasonable period after that contract terminated; or

(b) in accordance with the conditions mentioned in regulation 7 above, the order of the third party reached the principal or the commercial agent before the agency contract terminated.

9 Apportionment of commission between new and previous commercial agents

(1) A commercial agent shall not be entitled to the commission referred to in regulation 7 above if that commission is payable, by virtue of regulation 8 above, to the previous commercial agent, unless it is equitable because of the circumstances for the commission to be shared between the commercial agents.

(2) The principal shall be liable for any sum due under paragraph (1) above to the person entitled to it in accordance with that paragraph, and any sum which the other commercial agent receives to which he is not entitled shall be refunded to the principal.

10 When commission due and date for payment

(1) Commission shall become due as soon as, and to the extent that, one of the following circumstances occurs:

(a) the principal has executed the transaction; or

(b) the principal should, according to his agreement with the third party, have executed the transaction; or

(c) the third party has executed the transaction.

(2) Commission shall become due at the latest when the third party has executed his part of the transaction or should have done so if the principal had executed his part of the transaction, as he should have.

(3) The commission shall be paid not later than on the last day of the month following the quarter in which it became due, and, for the purposes of these Regulations, unless otherwise agreed between the parties, the first quarter period shall run from the date the agency contract takes effect, and subsequent periods shall run from that date in the third month thereafter or the beginning of the fourth month, whichever is the sooner.

(4) Any agreement to derogate from paragraphs (2) and (3) above to the detriment of the commercial agent shall be void.

11 Extinction of right to commission

(1) The right to commission can be extinguished only if and to the extent that—

(a) it is established that the contract between the third party and the principal will not be executed; and

(b) that fact is due to a reason for which the principal is not to blame.

(2) Any commission which the commercial agent has already received shall be refunded if the right to it is extinguished.

(3) any agreement to derogate from paragraph (1) above to the detriment of the commercial agent shall be void.

12 Periodic supply of information as to commission due and right of inspection of principal's books

(1)   The principal shall supply his commercial agent with a statement of the commission due, not later than the last day of the month following the quarter in which the commission has become due, and such statement shall set out the main components used in calculating the amount of the commission.

(2)   A commercial agent shall be entitled to demand that he be provided with all the information (and in particular an extract from the books) which is available to his principal and which he needs in order to check the amount of the commission due to him.

(3)   Any agreement to derogate from paragraphs (1) and (2) above shall be void.

(4)   Nothing in this regulation shall remove or restrict the effect of, or prevent reliance upon, any enactment or rule of law which recognises the right of an agent to inspect the books of a principal.

PART IV

CONCLUSION AND TERMINATION OF THE AGENCY CONTRACT

13 Right to signed written statement of terms of agency contract

(1)   The commercial agent and principal shall each be entitled to receive from the other, on request, a signed written document setting out the terms of the agency contract including any terms subsequently agreed.

(2)   Any purported waiver of the right referred to in paragraph (1) above shall be void.

14 Conversion of agency contract after expiry of fixed period

An agency contract for a fixed period which continues to be performed by both parties after that period has expired shall be deemed to be converted into an agency contract for an indefinite period.

15 Minimum periods of notice for termination of agency contract

(1)   Where an agency contract is concluded for an indefinite period either party may terminate it by notice.

(2)   The period of notice shall be—
  (a)   1 month for the first year of the contract;
  (b)   2 months for the second year commenced;
  (c)   3 months for the third year commenced and for the subsequent years;
and the parties may not agree on any shorter periods of notice.

(3)   If the parties agree on longer periods than those laid down in paragraph (2) above, the period of notice to be observed by the principal must not be shorter than that to be observed by the commercial agent.

(4)   Unless otherwise agreed by the parties, the end of the period of notice must coincide with the end of a calendar month.

(5)   The provisions of this regulation shall also apply to an agency contract for a fixed period where it is converted under regulation 14 above into an agency contract for an indefinite period subject to the proviso that the earlier fixed period must be taken into account in the calculation of the period of notice.

16 Savings with regard to immediate termination

These Regulations shall not affect the application of any enactment or rule of law which provides for the immediate termination of the agency contract—
  (a)   because of the failure of one party to carry out all or part of his obligations under that contract; or
  (b)   where exceptional circumstances arise.

17   Entitlement of commercial agent to indemnity or compensation on termination of agency contract
(1)   This regulation has effect for the purpose of ensuring that the commercial agent is, after termination of the agency contract, indemnified in accordance with paragraphs (3) to (5) below or compensated for damage in accordance with paragraphs (6) and (7) below.
(2)   Except where the agency [contract] otherwise provides, the commercial agent shall be entitled to be compensated rather than indemnified.
(3)   Subject to paragraph (9) and to regulation 18 below, the commercial agent shall be entitled to an indemnity if and to the extent that—
(a)   he has brought the principal new customers or has significantly increased the volume of business with existing customers and the principal continues to derive substantial benefits from the business with such customers; and
(b)   the payment of this indemnity is equitable having regard to all the circumstances and, in particular, the commission lost by the commercial agent on the business transacted with such customers.
(4)   The amount of the indemnity shall not exceed a figure equivalent to an indemnity for one year calculated from the commercial agent's average annual remuneration over the preceding five years and if the contract goes back less than five years the indemnity shall be calculated on the average for the period in question.
(5)   The grant of an indemnity as mentioned above shall not prevent the commercial agent from seeking damages.
(6)   Subject to paragraph (9) and to regulation 18 below, the commercial agent shall be entitled to compensation for the damage he suffers as a result of the termination of his relations with his principal.
(7)   For the purpose of these Regulations such damage shall be deemed to occur particularly when the termination takes place in either or both of the following circumstances, namely circumstances which—
(a)   deprive the commercial agent of the commission which proper performance of the agency contract would have procured for him whilst providing his principal with substantial benefits linked to the activities of the commercial agent; or
(b)   have not enabled the commercial agent to amortize the costs and expenses that he had incurred in the performance of the agency contract on the advice of his principal.
(8)   Entitlement to the indemnity or compensation for damage as provided for under paragraphs (2) to (7) above shall also arise where the agency contract is terminated as a result of the death of the commercial agent.
(9)   The commercial agent shall lose his entitlement to the indemnity or compensation for damage in the instances provided for in paragraphs (2) to (8) above if within one year following termination of his agency contract he has not notified his principal that he intends pursuing his entitlement.

18   Grounds for excluding payment of indemnity or compensation under regulation 17
The [indemnity or] compensation referred to in regulation 17 above shall not be payable to the commercial agent where—
(a)   the principal has terminated the agency contract because of default attributable to the commercial agent which would justify immediate termination of the agency contract pursuant to regulation 16 above; or
(b)   the commercial agent has himself terminated the agency contract, unless such termination is justified—
(i)   by circumstances attributable to the principal, or
(ii)   on grounds of the age, infirmity or illness of the commercial agent

in consequence of which he cannot reasonably be required to continue his activities; or

(c)   the commercial agent, with the agreement of his principal, assigns his rights and duties under the agency contract to another person.

19   Prohibition on derogation from regulations 17 and 18
The parties may not derogate from regulations 17 and 18 to the detriment of the commercial agent before the agency contract expires.

20   Restraint of trade clauses
(1)   A restraint of trade clause shall be valid only if and to the extent that—

(a)   it is concluded in writing; and

(b)   it relates to the geographical area or the group of customers and the geographical area entrusted to the commercial agent and to the kind of goods covered by his agency under the contract.

(2)   A restraint of trade clause shall be valid for not more than two years after termination of the agency contract.

(3)   Nothing in this regulation shall affect any enactment or rule of law which imposes other restrictions on the validity or enforceability of restraint of trade clauses or which enables a court to reduce the obligations on the parties resulting from such clauses.

PART V

MISCELLANEOUS AND SUPPLEMENTAL

21   Disclosure of information
Nothing in these Regulations shall require information to be given where such disclosure would be contrary to public policy.

22   Service of notice etc
(1)   Any notice, statement or other document to be given or supplied to a commercial agent or to be given or supplied to the principal under these Regulations may be so given or supplied:

(a)   by delivering it to him;

(b)   by leaving it at his proper address addressed to him by name;

(c)   by sending it by post to him addressed either to his registered address or to the address of his registered or principal office;

or by any other means provided for in the agency contract.

(2)   Any such notice, statement or document may—

(a)   in the case of a body corporate, be given or served on the secretary or clerk of that body;

(b)   in the case of a partnership, be given to or served on any partner or on any person having the control or management of the partnership business.

23   Transitional provisions
(1)   Notwithstanding any provision in an agency contract made before 1st January 1994, these Regulations shall apply to that contract after that date and, accordingly any provision which is inconsistent with these Regulations shall have effect subject to them.

(2)   Nothing in these Regulations shall affect the rights and liabilities of a commercial agent or a principal which have accrued before 1st January 1994.

Regulation 2(3)   THE SCHEDULE

1   The activities of a person as a commercial agent are to be considered secondary where it may reasonably be taken that the primary purpose of the arrangement with his principal is other than as set out in paragraph 2 below.

2   An arrangement falls within this paragraph if—
    (a)   the business of the principal is the sale, or as the case may be purchase, of goods of a particular kind; and
    (b)   the goods concerned are such that—
        (i)   transactions are normally individually negotiated and concluded on a commercial basis, and
        (ii)   procuring a transaction on one occasion is likely to lead to further transactions in those goods with that customer on future occasions, or to transactions in those goods with other customers in the same geographical area or among the same group of customers, and
that accordingly it is in the commercial interests of the principal in developing the market in those goods to appoint a representative to such customers with a view to the representative devoting effort, skill and expenditure from his own resources to that end.

3   The following are indications that an arrangement falls within paragraph 2 above, and the absence of any of them is an indication to the contrary—
    (a)   the principal is the manufacturer, importer or distributor of the goods;
    (b)   the goods are specifically identified with the principal in the market in question rather than, or to a greater extent than, with any other person;
    (c)   the agent devotes substantially the whole of his time to representative activities (whether for one principal or for a number of principals whose interests are not conflicting);
    (d)   the goods are not normally available in the market in question other than by means of the agent;
    (e)   the arrangement is described as one of commercial agency.

4   The following are indications that an arrangement does not fall within paragraph 2 above—
    (a)   promotional material is supplied direct to potential customers;
    (b)   persons are granted agencies without reference to existing agents in a particular area or in relation to a particular group;
    (c)   customers normally select the goods for themselves and merely place their orders through the agent.

5   The activities of the following categories of persons are presumed, unless the contrary is established, not to fall within paragraph 2 above—
    Mail order catalogue agents for consumer goods.
    Consumer credit agents.

PROVISION AND USE OF WORK EQUIPMENT REGULATIONS 1998
(SI 1998/2306)

2   **Interpretation**
    (1)   In these Regulations, unless the context otherwise requires—
    'the 1974 Act' means the Health and Safety at Work etc Act 1974;
    'employer' except in regulation 3(2) and (3) includes a person to whom the requirements imposed by the Regulations apply by virtue of regulation 3(3)(a) and (b);
    'essential requirements' means requirements described in regulation 10(1);
    'the Executive' means the Health and Safety Executive;
    'inspection' in relation to an inspection under paragraph (1) or (2) of regulation 6—

(a)   means such visual or more rigorous inspection by a competent person as is appropriate for the purpose described in the paragraph;

(b)   where it is appropriate to carry out testing for the purpose, includes testing the nature and extent of which are appropriate for the purpose;

'power press' means a press or press brake for the working of metal by means of tools, or for die proving, which is power driven and which embodies a flywheel and clutch;

'thorough examination' in relation to a thorough examination under paragraph (1), (2), (3) or (4) of regulation 32—

(a)   means a thorough examination by a competent person;

(b)   includes testing the nature and extent of which are appropriate for the purpose described in the paragraph;

'use' in relation to work equipment means any activity involving work equipment and includes starting, stopping, programming, setting, transporting, repairing, modifying, maintaining, servicing and cleaning;

'work equipment' means any machinery, appliance, apparatus, tool or installation for use at work (whether exclusively or not);

and related expressions shall be construed accordingly.

4 Suitability of work equipment

(1)   Every employer shall ensure that work equipment is so constructed or adapted as to be suitable for the purpose for which it is used or provided.

(2)   In selecting work equipment, every employer shall have regard to the working conditions and to the risks to the health and safety of persons which exist in the premises or undertaking in which that work equipment is to be used and any additional risk posed by the use of that work equipment.

(3)   Every employer shall ensure that work equipment is used only for operations for which, and under conditions for which, it is suitable.

(4)   In this regulation 'suitable' [—

(a)   subject to subparagraph (b), means suitable in any respect which it is reasonably foreseeable will affect the health or safety of any person; . . .]

5 Maintenance

(1)   Every employer shall ensure that work equipment is maintained in an efficient state, in efficient working order and in good repair.

(2)   Every employer shall ensure that where any machinery has a maintenance log, the log is kept up to date.

6 Inspection

(1)   Every employer shall ensure that, where the safety of work equipment depends on the installation conditions, it is inspected—

(a)   after installation and before being put into service for the first time; or

(b)   after assembly at a new site or in a new location,

to ensure that it has been installed correctly and is safe to operate.

(2)   Every employer shall ensure that work equipment exposed to conditions causing deterioration which is liable to result in dangerous situations is inspected—

(a)   at suitable intervals; and

(b)   each time that exceptional circumstances which are liable to jeopardise the safety of the work equipment have occurred,

to ensure that health and safety conditions are maintained and that any deterioration can be detected and remedied in good time.

(3)   Every employer shall ensure that the result of an inspection made under this regulation is recorded and kept until the next inspection under this regulation is recorded.

(4)   Every employer shall ensure that no work equipment—

(a)   leaves his undertaking; or

(b)   if obtained from the undertaking of another person, is used in his under-taking, unless it is accompanied by physical evidence that the last inspection required to be carried out under this regulation has been carried out.

7   Specific risks

(1)   Where the use of work equipment is likely to involve a specific risk to health or safety, every employer shall ensure that—

(a)   the use of that work equipment is restricted to those persons given the task of using it; and

(b)   repairs, modifications, maintenance or servicing of that work equipment is restricted to those persons who have been specifically designated to perform operations of that description (whether or not also authorised to perform other operations).

(2)   The employer shall ensure that the persons designated for the purposes of sub-paragraph (b) of paragraph (1) have received adequate training related to any operations in respect of which they have been so designated.

8   Information and instructions

(1)   Every employer shall ensure that all persons who use work equipment have available to them adequate health and safety information and, where appro-priate, written instructions pertaining to the use of the work equipment.

(2)   Every employer shall ensure that any of his employees who supervises or manages the use of work equipment has available to him adequate health and safety information and, where appropriate, written instructions pertaining to the use of the work equipment.

(3)   Without prejudice to the generality of paragraph (1) or (2), the information and instructions required by either of those paragraphs shall include information and, where appropriate, written instructions on—

(a)   the conditions in which and the methods by which the work equipment may be used;

(b)   foreseeable abnormal situations and the action to be taken if such a situa-tion were to occur; and

(c)   any conclusions to be drawn from experience in using the work equip-ment.

(4)   Information and instructions required by this regulation shall be readily comprehensive to those concerned.

9   Training

(1)   Every employer shall ensure that all persons who use work equipment have received adequate training for purposes of health and safety, including train-ing in the methods which may be adopted when using the work equipment, any risks which such use may entail and precautions to be taken.

(2)   Every employer shall ensure that any of his employees who supervises or manages the use of work equipment has received adequate training for purposes of health and safety, including training in the methods which may be adopted when using the work equipment, any risks which such use may entail and pre-cautions to be taken.

10   Conformity with Community requirements

[(1)   Every employer shall ensure that an item of work equipment conforms at all times with any essential requirements, other than requirements which, at the time of its being first supplied or put into service in any place in which these Regulations apply, did not apply to work equipment of its type.

(2)   In this regulation 'essential requirements', in relation to an item of work equipment, means requirements relating to the design and construction of work equipment of its type in any of the instruments listed in Schedule 1 (being instru-ments which give effect to Community directives concerning the safety of products)].

(3)   This regulation applies to items of work equipment provided for use in the premises or undertaking of the employer for the first time after 31 December 1992.

11   Dangerous parts of machinery

(1)   Every employer shall ensure that measures are taken in accordance with paragraph (2) which are effective—

(a)   to prevent access to any dangerous part of machinery or to any rotating stock-bar; or

(b)   to stop the movement of any dangerous part of machinery or rotating stock-bar before any part of a person enters a danger zone.

[(2)   The measures required by paragraph (1) shall consist of—

(a)   the provision of fixed guards enclosing every dangerous part or rotating stock-bar where and to the extent that it is practicable to do so, but where or to the extent that it is not, then

(b)   the provision of other guards or protection devices where and to the extent that it is practicable to do so, but where or to the extent that it is not, then

(c)   the provision of jigs, holders, push-sticks or similar protection appliances used in conjunction with the machinery where and to the extent that it is practicable to do so, and the provision of such information, instruction, training and supervision as is necessary.]

(3)   All guards and protection devices provided under sub-paragraphs (a) or (b) of paragraph (2) shall—

(a)   be suitable for the purpose for which they are provided;

(b)   be of good construction, sound material and adequate strength;

(c)   be maintained in an efficient state, in efficient working order and in good repair;

(d)   not give rise to any increased risk to health or safety;

(e)   not be easily bypassed or disabled;

(f)   be situated at sufficient distance from the danger zone;

(g)   not unduly restrict the view of the operating cycle of the machinery, where such a view is necessary;

(h)   be so constructed or adapted that they allow operations necessary to fit or replace parts and for maintenance work, restricting access so that it is allowed only to the area where the work is to be carried out and, if possible, without having to dismantle the guard or protection device.

(4)   All protection appliances provided under sub-paragraph (c) of paragraph (2) shall comply with sub-paragraphs (a) to (d) and (g) of paragraph (3).

(5)   In this regulation—

'danger zone' means any zone in or around machinery in which a person is exposed to a risk to health or safety from contact with a dangerous part of machinery or a rotating stock-bar;

'stock-bar' means any part of a stock-bar which projects beyond the head-stock of a lathe.

12   Protection against specified hazards

(1)   Every employer shall take measures to ensure that the exposure of a person using work equipment to any risk to his health or safety from any hazard specified in paragraph (3) is either prevented, or, where that is not reasonably practicable, adequately controlled.

(2)   The measures required by paragraph (1) shall—

(a)   be measures other than the provision of personal protective equipment or of information, instruction, training and supervision, so far as is reasonably practicable; and

(b)   include, where appropriate, measures to minimise the effects of the hazard as well as to reduce the likelihood of the hazard occurring.

(3)   The hazards referred to in paragraph (1) are—

(a)   any article or substance falling or being ejected from work equipment;

(b)   rupture or disintegration of parts of work equipment;

(c)   work equipment catching fire or overheating;

(d)   the unintended or premature discharge of any article or of any gas, dust, liquid, vapour or other substance which, in each case, is produced, used or stored in the work equipment;

(e)   the unintended or premature explosion of the work equipment or any article or substance produced, used or stored in it.

(4)   For the purposes of this regulation 'adequately' means adequately having regard only to the nature of the hazard and the nature and degree of exposure to the risk.

(5)   This regulation shall not apply where any of the following Regulations apply in respect of any risk to a person's health or safety for which such Regulations require measures to be taken to prevent or control such risk, namely—

(a)   the Ionising Radiations Regulations 1985;

(b)   the Control of Asbestos at Work Regulations 1987;

(c)   the Control of Substances Hazardous to Health Regulations 1994;

(d)   the Noise at Work Regulations 1989;

(e)   the Construction (Head Protection) Regulations 1989;

(f)   the Control of Lead at Work Regulations 1998.

13   High or very low temperature

Every employer shall ensure that work equipment, parts of work equipment and any article or substance produced, used or stored in work equipment which, in each case, is at a high or very low temperature shall have protection where appropriate so as to prevent injury to any person by burn, scald or sear.

14   Controls for starting or making a significant change in operating conditions

(1)   Every employer shall ensure that, where appropriate, work equipment is provided with one or more controls for the purposes of—

(a)   starting the work equipment (including re-starting after a stoppage for any reason); or

(b)   controlling any change in the speed, pressure or other operating conditions of the work equipment where such conditions after the change result in risk to health and safety which is greater than or of a different nature from such risks before the change.

(2)   Subject to paragraph (3), every employer shall ensure that, where a control is required by paragraph (1), it shall not be possible to perform any operation mentioned in sub-paragraph (a) or (b) of that paragraph except by a deliberate action on such control.

(3)   Paragraph (1) shall not apply to re-starting or changing operating conditions as a result of the normal operating cycle of an automatic device.

15   Stop controls

(1)   Every employer shall ensure that, where appropriate, work equipment is provided with one or more readily accessible controls the operation of which will bring the work equipment to a safe condition in a safe manner.

(2)   Any control required by paragraph (1) shall bring the work equipment to a complete stop where necessary for reasons of health and safety.

(3)   Any control required by paragraph (1) shall, if necessary for reasons of health and safety, switch off all sources of energy after stopping the functioning of the work equipment.

(4)   Any control required by paragraph (1) shall operate in priority to any control which starts or changes the operating conditions of the work equipment.

16   Emergency stop controls

(1)   Every employer shall ensure that, where appropriate, work equipment is

provided with one or more readily accessible emergency stop controls unless it is not necessary by reason of the nature of the hazards and the time taken for the work equipment to come to a complete stop as a result of the action of any control provided by virtue of regulation 15(1).

(2) Any control required by paragraph (1) shall operate in priority to any control required by regulation 15(1).

17 Controls

(1) Every employer shall ensure that all controls for work equipment are clearly visible and identifiable, including by appropriate marking where necessary.

(2) Except where necessary, the employer shall ensure that no control for work equipment is in a position where any person operating the control is exposed to a risk to his health or safety.

(3) Every employer shall ensure where appropriate—

(a)   that, so far as is reasonably practicable, the operator of any control is able to ensure from the position of that control that no person is in a place where he would be exposed to any risk to his health or safety as a result of the operation of that control, but where or to the extent that it is not reasonably practicable;

(b)   that, so far as is reasonably practicable, systems of work are effective to ensure that, when work equipment is about to start, no person is in a place where he would be exposed to a risk to his health or safety as a result of the work equipment starting, but where neither of these is reasonably practicable;

(c)   that an audible, visible or other suitable warning is given by virtue of regulation 24 whenever work equipment is about to start,

(4) Every employer shall take appropriate measures to ensure that any person who is in a place where he would be exposed to a risk to his health or safety as a result of the starting or stopping of work equipment has sufficient time and suitable means to avoid that risk.

18 Control systems

(1) Every employer shall ensure, so far as is reasonably practicable, that all control systems of work equipment—

(a)   are safe; and

(b)   are chosen making due allowance for the failures, faults and constraints to be expected in the planned circumstances of use.

(2) Without prejudice to the generality of paragraph (1), a control system shall not be safe unless—

(a)   its operation does not create any increased risk to health or safety;

(b)   it ensures, so far as is reasonably practicable, that any fault in or damage to any part of the control system or the loss of supply of any source of energy used by the work equipment cannot result in additional or increased risk to health or safety;

(c)   it does not impede the operation of any control required by regulation 15 or 16.

19 Isolation from sources of energy

(1) Every employer shall ensure that where appropriate work equipment is provided with suitable means to isolate it from all its sources of energy.

(2) Without prejudice to the generality of paragraph (1), the means mentioned in that paragraph shall not be suitable unless they are clearly identifiable and readily accessible.

(3) Every employer shall take appropriate measures to ensure that re-connection of any energy source to work equipment does not expose any person using the work equipment to any risk to his health or safety.

20 Stability
Every employer shall ensure that work equipment or any part of work equipment is stabilised by clamping or otherwise where necessary for purposes of health or safety.

21 Lighting
Every employer shall ensure that suitable and sufficient lighting, which takes account of the operations to be carried out, is provided at any place where a person uses work equipment.

22 Maintenance operations
Every employer shall take appropriate measures to ensure that work equipment is so constructed or adapted that, so far as is reasonably practicable, maintenance operations which involve a risk to health or safety can be carried out while the work equipment is shut down, or in other cases—

(a) maintenance operations can be carried out without exposing the person carrying them out to a risk to his health or safety; or

(b) appropriate measures can be taken for the protection of any person carrying out maintenance operations which involve a risk to his health or safety.

23 Markings
Every employer shall ensure that work equipment is marked in a clearly visible manner with any marking appropriate for reasons of health and safety.

24 Warnings
(1) Every employer shall ensure that work equipment incorporates any warnings or warning devices which are appropriate for reasons of health and safety.

(2) Without prejudice to the generality of paragraph (1), warnings given by warning devices on work equipment shall not be appropriate unless they are unambiguous, easily perceived and easily understood.

**EMPLOYERS' LIABILITY (COMPULSORY INSURANCE)
REGULATIONS 1998
(SI 1998/2573)**

1 Citation, commencement and interpretation

. . .

(2) In these Regulations—
'the 1969 Act' means the Employers' Liability (Compulsory Insurance) Act 1969;

. . .

2 Prohibition of certain conditions in policies of insurance
(1) For the purposes of the 1969 Act, there is prohibited in any contract of insurance any condition which provides (in whatever terms) that no liability (either generally or in respect of a particular claim) shall arise under the policy, or that any such liability so arising shall cease, if—

(a) some specified thing is done or omitted to be done after the happening of the event giving rise to a claim under the policy,

(b) the policy holder does not take reasonable care to protect his employees against the risk of bodily injury or disease in the course of their employment;

(c) the policy holder fails to comply with the requirements of any enactment for the protection of employees against the risk of bodily injury or disease in the course of their employment; or

(d) the policy holder does not keep specified records or fails to provide the insurer with or make available to him information from such records.

(2) For the purposes of the 1969 Act there is also prohibited in a policy of insurance any condition which requires—

(a) a relevant employee to pay; or

(b) an insured employer to pay the relevant employee,

the first amount of any claim or any aggregation of claims.

(3) Paragraphs (1) and (2) above do not prohibit for the purposes of the 1969 Act a condition in a policy of insurance which requires the employer to pay or contribute any sum to the insurer in respect of the satisfaction of any claim made under the contract of insurance by a relevant employee or any costs and expenses incurred in relation to any such claim.

3 Limit of amount of compulsory insurance

(1) Subject to paragraph (2) below, the amount for which an employer is required by the 1969 Act to insure and maintain insurance in respect of relevant employees under one or more policies of insurance shall be, or shall in aggregate be not less than £5 million in respect of—

(a) a claim relating to any one or more of those employees arising out of any one occurrence; and

(b) any costs and expenses incurred in relation to any such claim.

UNFAIR TERMS IN CONSUMER CONTRACTS REGULATIONS 1999
(SI 1999/2083)

3 Interpretation

(1) In these Regulations—

'the Community' means the European Community;

'consumer' means any natural person who, in contracts covered by these Regulations, is acting for purposes which are outside his trade, business or profession;

'court' in relation to England and Wales and Northern Ireland means a county court or the High Court, and in relation to Scotland, the Sheriff or the Court of Session;

'Director' means the Director General of Fair Trading;*

'EEA Agreement' means the Agreement on the European Economic Area signed at Oporto on 2nd May 1992 as adjusted by the protocol signed at Brussels on 17th March 1993;

'Member State' means a State which is a contracting party to the EEA Agreement;

'notified' means notified in writing;

'qualifying body' means a person specified in Schedule 1;

'seller or supplier' means any natural or legal person who, in contracts covered by these Regulations, is acting for purposes relating to his trade, business or profession, whether publicly owned or privately owned;

'unfair terms' means the contractual terms referred to in regulation 5.

[(1A) The references—

(a) in regulation 4(1) to a seller or a supplier, and

(b) in regulation 8(1) to a seller or supplier,

include references to a distance supplier and to an intermediary.

(1B) In paragraph (1A) and regulation 5(6)—

'distance supplier' means—

(a) a supplier under a distance contract within the meaning of the Financial Services (Distance Marketing) Regulations 2004, or

---

* All references to 'the Director' have effect as if they were references to 'the OFT': Enterprise Act 2002, s 2.

(b)   a supplier of unsolicited financial services within regulation 15 of those Regulations; and

'intermediary' has the same meaning as in those Regulations.]

(2)   In the application of these Regulations to Scotland for references to an 'injunction' or an 'interim injunction' there shall be substituted references to an 'interdict' or 'interim interdict' respectively.

4   Terms to which these Regulations apply

(1)   These Regulations apply in relation to unfair terms in contracts concluded between a seller or a supplier and a consumer.

(2)   These Regulations do not apply to contractual terms which reflect—

(a)   mandatory statutory or regulatory provisions (including such provisions under the law of any Member State or in Community legislation having effect in the United Kingdom without further enactment);

(b)   the provisions or principles of international conventions to which the Member States or the Community are party.

5   Unfair terms

(1)   A contractual term which has not been individually negotiated shall be regarded as unfair if, contrary to the requirement of good faith, it causes a significant imbalance in the parties' rights and obligations arising under the contract, to the detriment of the consumer.

(2)   A term shall always be regarded as not having been individually negotiated where it has been drafted in advance and the consumer has therefore not been able to influence the substance of the term.

(3)   Notwithstanding that a specific term or certain aspects of it in a contract has been individually negotiated, these Regulations shall apply to the rest of a contract if an overall assessment of it indicates that it is a pre-formulated standard contract.

(4)   It shall be for any seller or supplier who claims that a term was individually negotiated to show that it was.

(5)   Schedule 2 to these Regulations contains an indicative and non-exhaustive list of the terms which may be regarded as unfair.

[(6)   Any contractual term providing that the consumer bears the burden of proof in respect of showing that the supplier complied with any or all of the obligations upon him resulting from the Directive and any rule or enactment implementing it shall always be regarded as unfair.

(7)   In paragraph (6)—

'the Directive' means Directive 2002/65/EC of the European Parliament and of the Council of 23 September 2002 concerning the distance marketing of consumer financial services and amending Council Directive 90/619/EEC and Directive 97/7/EC and 98/27/EC; and

'rule' means a rule made by the Financial Services Authority under the Financial Services and Markets Act 2000 or by a designated professional body within the meaning of section 326(2) of that Act.]

6   Assessment of unfair terms

(1)   Without prejudice to regulation 12, the unfairness of a contractual term shall be assessed, taking into account the nature of the goods or services for which the contract was concluded and by referring, at the time of conclusion of the contract, to all the circumstances attending the conclusion of the contract and to all the other terms of the contract or of another contract on which it is dependent.

(2)   In so far as it is in plain intelligible language, the assessment of fairness of a term shall not relate—

(a)   to the definition of the main subject matter of the contract, or

(b)   to the adequacy of the price or remuneration, as against the goods or services supplied in exchange.

7   Written contracts

(1)   A seller or supplier shall ensure that any written term of a contract is expressed in plain, intelligible language.

(2)   If there is doubt about the meaning of a written term, the interpretation which is most favourable to the consumer shall prevail but this rule shall not apply in proceedings brought under regulation 12.

8   Effect of unfair term

(1)   An unfair term in a contract concluded with a consumer by a seller or supplier shall not be binding on the consumer.

(2)   The contract shall continue to bind the parties if it is capable of continuing in existence without the unfair term.

9   Choice of law clauses

These Regulations shall apply notwithstanding any contract term which applies or purports to apply the law of a non-Member State, if the contract has a close connection with the territory of the Member States.

10   Complaints—consideration by Director

(1)   It shall be the duty of the Director to consider any complaint made to him that any contract term drawn up for general use is unfair, unless—

(a)   the complaint appears to the Director to be frivolous or vexatious; or

(b)   a qualifying body has notified the Director that it agrees to consider the complaint.

(2)   The Director shall give reasons for his decision to apply or not to apply, as the case may be, for an injunction under regulation 12 in relation to any complaint which these Regulations require him to consider.

(3)   In deciding whether or not to apply for an injunction in respect of a term which the Director considers to be unfair, he may, if he considers it appropriate to do so, have regard to any undertakings given to him by or on behalf of any person as to the continued use of such a term in contracts concluded with consumers.

11   Complaints—consideration by qualifying bodies

(1)   If a qualifying body specified in Part One of Schedule I notifies the Director that it agrees to consider a complaint that any contract term drawn up for general use is unfair, it shall be under a duty to consider that complaint.

(2)   Regulation 10(2) and (3) shall apply to a qualifying body which is under a duty to consider a complaint as they apply to the Director.

12   Injunctions to prevent continued use of unfair terms

(1)   The Director or, subject to paragraph (2), any qualifying body may apply for an injunction (including an interim injunction) against any person appearing to the Director or that body to be using, or recommending use of, an unfair term drawn up for general use in contracts concluded with consumers.

(2)   A qualifying body may apply for an injunction only where—

(a)   it has notified the Director of its intention to apply at least fourteen days before the date on which the application is made, beginning with the date on which the notification was given; or

(b)   the Director consents to the application being made within a shorter period.

(3)   The court on an application under this regulation may grant an injunction on such terms as it thinks fit.

(4)   An injunction may relate not only to use of a particular contract term drawn up for general use but to any similar term, or a term having like effect, used or recommended for use by any person.

13   Powers of the Director and qualifying bodies to obtain documents and information

(1)   The Director may exercise the power conferred by this regulation for the purpose of—

(a)   facilitating his consideration of a complaint that a contract term drawn up for general use is unfair; or

(b)   ascertaining whether a person has complied with an undertaking or court order as to the continued use, or recommendation for use, of a term in contracts concluded with consumers.

(2)   A qualifying body specified in Part One of Schedule 1 may exercise the power conferred by this regulation for the purpose of—

(a)   facilitating its consideration of a complaint that a contract term drawn up for general use is unfair; or

(b)   ascertaining whether a person has complied with—

(i)   an undertaking given to it or to the court following an application by that body, or

(ii)   a court order made on an application by that body,

as to the continued use, or recommendation for use, of a term in contracts concluded with consumers.

(3)   The Director may require any person to supply to him, and a qualifying body specified in Part One of Schedule 1 may require any person to supply to it—

(a)   a copy of any document which that person has used or recommended for use, at the time the notice referred to in paragraph (4) below is given, as a pre-formulated standard contract in dealings with consumers;

(b)   information about the use, or recommendation for use, by that person of that document or any other such document in dealings with consumers.

(4)   The power conferred by this regulation is to be exercised by a notice in writing which may—

(a)   specify the way in which and the time within which it is to be complied with; and

(b)   be varied or revoked by a subsequent notice.

(5)   Nothing in this regulation compels a person to supply any document or information which he would be entitled to refuse to produce or give in civil proceedings before the court.

(6)   If a person makes default in complying with a notice under this regulation, the court may, on the application of the Director or of the qualifying body, make such order as the court thinks fit for requiring the default to be made good, and any such order may provide that all the costs or expenses of and incidental to the application shall be borne by the person in default or by any officers of a company or other association who are responsible for its default.

14   Notification of undertakings and orders to Director

A qualifying body shall notify the Director—

(a)   of any undertaking given to it by or on behalf of any person as to the continued use of a term which that body considers to be unfair in contracts concluded with consumers,

(b)   of the outcome of any application made by it under regulation 12, and of the terms of any undertaking given to, or order made by, the court;

(c)   of the outcome of any application made by it to enforce a previous order of the court.

15   Publication, information and advice

(1)   The Director shall arrange for the publication in such form and manner as he considers appropriate, of—

(a)   details of any undertaking or order notified to him under regulation 14;

(b)   details of any undertaking given to him by or on behalf of any persons to the continued use of a term which the Director considers to be unfair in contracts concluded with consumers;

(c)   details of any application made by him under regulation 12, and of the terms of any undertaking given to, or order made by, the court;

(d)   details of any application made by the Director to enforce a previous order of the court.

(2)   The Director shall inform any person on request whether a particular term to which these Regulations apply has been—

(a)   the subject of an undertaking given to the Director or notified to him by a qualifying body; or

(b)   the subject of an order of the court made upon application by him or notified to him by a qualifying body;

and shall give that person details of the undertaking or a copy of the order, as the case may be, together with a copy of any amendments which the person giving the undertaking has agreed to make to the term in question.

(3)   The Director may arrange for the dissemination in such form and manner as he considers appropriate of such information and advice concerning the operation of these Regulations as may appear to him to be expedient to give to the public and to all persons likely to be affected by these Regulations.

[16   The functions of the Financial Services Authority

The functions of the Financial Services Authority under these Regulations shall be treated as functions of the Financial Services Authority under the [Financial Services and Markets Act 2000.]

SCHEDULE 1   Regulation 3
QUALIFYING BODIES

PART ONE

[1.   The Information Commissioner.
2.   The Gas and Electricity Markets Authority.
3.   The Director General of Electricity Supply for Northern Ireland.
4.   The Director General of Gas for Northern Ireland.
5.   [The Office of Communications].
6.   [The Water Services Regulations Authority].
7.   The Rail Regulator.
8.   Every weights and measures authority in Great Britain.
9.   The Department of Enterprise, Trade and Investment in Northern Ireland.
10.   The Financial Services Authority.

PART TWO

11.   Consumers' Association.]

Regulation 5(5)   SCHEDULE 2

INDICATIVE AND NON-EXHAUSTIVE LIST OF TERMS WHICH MAY BE REGARDED AS UNFAIR

1.   Terms which have the object or effect of—

(a)   excluding or limiting the legal liability of a seller or supplier in the event of the death of a consumer or personal injury to the latter resulting from an act or omission of that seller or supplier;

(b)   inappropriately excluding or limiting the legal rights of the consumer vis-à-vis the seller or supplier or another party in the event of total or partial non-performance or inadequate performance by the seller or supplier of any of the contractual obligations, including the option of offsetting a debt owed to the seller or supplier against any claim which the consumer may have against him;

(c) making an agreement binding on the consumer whereas provision of services by the seller or supplier is subject to a condition whose realisation depends on his own will alone;

(d) permitting the seller or supplier to retain sums paid by the consumer where the latter decides not to conclude or perform the contract, without providing for the consumer to receive compensation of an equivalent amount from the seller or supplier where the latter is the party cancelling the contract;

(e) requiring any consumer who fails to fulfil his obligation to pay a disproportionately high sum in compensation;

(f) authorising the seller or supplier to dissolve the contract on a discretionary basis where the same facility is not granted to the consumer, or permitting the seller or supplier to retain the sums paid for services not yet supplied by him where it is the seller or supplier himself who dissolves the contract;

(g) enabling the seller or supplier to terminate a contract of indeterminate duration without reasonable notice except where there are serious grounds for doing so;

(h) automatically extending a contract of fixed duration where the consumer does not indicate otherwise, when the deadline fixed for the consumer to express his desire not to extend the contract is unreasonably early;

(i) irrevocably binding the consumer to terms with which he had no real opportunity of becoming acquainted before the conclusion of the contract;

(j) enabling the seller or supplier to alter the terms of the contract unilaterally without a valid reason which is specified in the contract;

(k) enabling the seller or supplier to alter unilaterally without a valid reason any characteristics of the product or service to be provided;

(l) providing for the price of goods to be determined at the time of delivery or allowing a seller of goods or supplier of services to increase their price without in both cases giving the consumer the corresponding right to cancel the contract if the final price is too high in relation to the price agreed when the contract was concluded;

(m) giving the seller or supplier the right to determine whether the goods or services supplied are in conformity with the contract, or giving him the exclusive right to interpret any term of the contract;

(n) limiting the seller's or supplier's obligation to respect commitments undertaken by his agents or making his commitments subject to compliance with a particular formality;

(o) obliging the consumer to fulfil all his obligations where the seller or supplier does not perform his;

(p) giving the seller or supplier the possibility of transferring his rights and obligations under the contract, where this may serve to reduce the guarantees for the consumer, without the latter's agreement,

(q) excluding or hindering the consumer's right to take legal action or exercise any other legal remedy, particularly by requiring the consumer to take disputes exclusively to arbitration not covered by legal provisions, unduly restricting the evidence available to him or imposing on him a burden of proof which, according to the applicable law, should lie with another party to the contract.

2. Scope of paragraphs 1(g), (j) and (1)—

(a) Paragraph 1(g) is without hindrance to terms by which a supplier of financial services reserves the right to terminate unilaterally a contract of indeterminate duration without notice where there is a valid reason provided that the supplier is required to inform the other contracting party or parties thereof immediately.

(b) Paragraph 1(j) is without hindrance to terms under which a supplier of financial services reserves the right to alter the rate of interest payable by the consumer or due to the latter, or the amount of other charges for financial services without notice where there is a valid reason, provided that the supplier is required to inform the other contracting party or parties thereof at the earliest opportunity and that the latter are free to dissolve the contract immediately.

Paragraph 1(j) is also without hindrance to terms under which a seller or supplier reserves the right to alter unilaterally the conditions of a contract of indeterminate duration, provided that he is required to inform the consumer with reasonable notice and that the consumer is free to dissolve the contract.

(c)   Paragraphs 1(g), (j) and (l) do not apply to:

—transactions in transferable securities, financial instruments and other products or services where the price is linked to fluctuations in a stock exchange quotation or index or a financial market rate that the seller or supplier does not control;

—contracts for the purchase or sale of foreign currency, traveller's cheques or international money orders denominated in foreign currency;

(d)   Paragraph 1(1) is without hindrance to price indexation clauses, where lawful, provided that the method by which prices vary is explicitly described.

CONSUMER PROTECTION (DISTANCE SELLING) REGULATIONS 2000
(SI 2000/2334)

(as amended by The Consumer Protection (Distance Selling) (Amendment) Regulations 2005 (SI 2005/689) and The Consumer Protection from Unfair Trading Regulations 2008 (SI 2008/1277))

3   Interpretation

(1)   In these Regulations—

['the 2000 Act' means the Financial Services and Markets Act 2000;

'appointed representative' has the same meaning as in section 39(2) of the 2000 Act;

'authorised person' has the same meaning as in section 31(2) of the 2000 Act;]

'breach' means contravention by a supplier of a prohibition in, or failure to comply with a requirement of, these Regulations;

'business' includes a trade or profession;

'consumer' means any natural person who, in contracts to which these Regulations apply, is acting for purposes which are outside his business;

'court' in relation to England and Wales and Northern Ireland means a county court or the High Court, and in relation to Scotland means the Sheriff Court or the Court of Session;

'credit' includes a cash loan and any other form of financial accommodation, and for this purpose 'cash' includes money in any form;

'Director' means the Director General of Fair Trading;*

'distance contract' means any contract concerning goods or services concluded between a supplier and a consumer under an organised distance sales or service provision scheme run by the supplier who, for the purpose of the contract, makes exclusive use of one or more means of distance communication up to and including the moment at which the contract is concluded;

'EEA Agreement' means the Agreement on the European Economic Area signed at Oporto on 2 May 1992 as adjusted by the Protocol signed at Brussels on 17 March 1993;

'enactment' includes an enactment comprised in, or in an instrument made under, an Act of the Scottish Parliament;

---

* All references to 'the Director' have effect as if they were references to 'the OFT': Enterprise Act 2002, s 2.

'enforcement authority' means the Director, every weights and measures authority in Great Britain, and the Department of Enterprise, Trade and Investment in Northern Ireland;

'excepted contract' means a contract such as is mentioned in regulation 5(1);

['financial service' means any service of a banking, credit, insurance, personal pension, investment or payment nature;]

'means of distance communication' means any means which, without the simultaneous physical presence of the supplier and the consumer, may be used for the conclusion of a contract between those parties; and an indicative list of such means is contained in Schedule 1;

'Member State' means a State which is a contracting party to the EEA Agreement;

'operator of a means of communication' means any public or private person whose business involves making one or more means of distance communication available to suppliers;

'period for performance' has the meaning given by regulation 19(2);

'personal credit agreement' has the meaning given by regulation 14(8);

['regulated activity' means an activity which is a regulated activity within the meaning of section 22 of the 2000 Act, read with any relevant order under that section and Schedule 2 to that Act;]

'related credit agreement' has the meaning given by regulation 15(5);

'supplier' means any person who, in contracts to which these Regulations apply, is acting in his commercial or professional capacity; and

'working days' means all days other than Saturdays, Sundays and public holidays.

(2)   In the application of these Regulations to Scotland, for references to an 'injunction' or an 'interim injunction' there shall be substituted references to an 'interdict' or an 'interim interdict' respectively.

4   Contracts to which these Regulations apply

These Regulations apply, subject to regulation 6, to distance contracts other than excepted contracts.

5   Excepted contracts

(1)   The following are excepted contracts, namely any contract—

(a)   for the sale or other disposition of an interest in land except for a rental agreement;

(b)   for the construction of a building where the contract also provides for a sale or other disposition of an interest in land on which the building is constructed, except for a rental agreement;

(c)   relating to financial services; [. . .]

(d)   concluded by means of an automated vending machine or automated commercial premises;

(e)   concluded with a telecommunications operator through the use of a public pay-phone;

(f)   concluded at an auction.

(2)   References in paragraph (1) to a rental agreement—

(a)   if the land is situated in England and Wales, are references to any agreement which does not have to be made in writing (whether or not in fact made in writing) because of section 2(5)(a) of the Law of Property (Miscellaneous Provisions) Act 1989;

(b)   if the land is situated in Scotland, are references to any agreement for the creation, transfer, variation or extinction of an interest in land, which does not have to be made in writing (whether or not in fact made in writing) as provided for in section 1(2) and (7) of the Requirements of Writing (Scotland) Act 1995; and

(c)   if the land is situated in Northern Ireland, are references to any agreement which is not one to which section II of the Statute of Frauds, (Ireland) 1695 applies.

(3) Paragraph (2) shall not be taken to mean that a rental agreement in respect of land situated outside the United Kingdom is not capable of being a distance contract to which these Regulations apply.

[(4) Regulations 7 to 14, 17 to 20, and 22 to 29 shall not apply to any contract which is made by an authorised person, the making or performance of which constitutes or is part of a regulated activity carried on by him.

(5) Regulations 7 to 9, 17 to 20, and 22 to 29 shall not apply to any contract which is made by an appointed representative, the making or performance of which constitutes or is part of a regulated activity carried on by him.]

6 Contracts to which only part of these Regulations apply

(1) Regulations 7 to 20 shall not apply to a contract which is a 'timeshare agreement' within the meaning of the Timeshare Act 1992 and to which that Act applies.

(2) Regulations 7 to 19(1) shall not apply to—

(a) contracts for the supply of food, beverages or other goods intended for everyday consumption supplied to the consumer's residence or to his workplace by regular roundsmen; or

(b) contracts for the provision of accommodation, transport, catering or leisure services, where the supplier undertakes, when the contract is concluded, to provide these services on a specific date or within a specific period.

(3) Regulations 19(2) to (8) and 20 do not apply to a contract for a 'package' within the meaning of the Package Travel, Package Holidays and Package Tours Regulations 1992 which is sold or offered for sale in the territory of the Member States.

[(4) Regulations 7 to 14, 17 to 20 and 25 do not apply to any contract which is made, and regulation 24 does not apply to any unsolicited services which are supplied, by an unauthorised person where the making or performance of that contract or the supply of those services, as the case may be, constitutes or is part of a regulated activity carried on by him.

(5) Regulations 7 to 9, 17 to 20 and 25 do not apply to any contract which is made, and regulation 24 does not apply to any unsolicited services which are supplied, by an appointed representative where the making or performance of that contract or the supply of those services, as the case may be, constitutes or is part of a regulated activity carried on by him.]

7 Information required prior to the conclusion of the contract

(1) Subject to paragraph (4), in good time prior to the conclusion of the contract the supplier shall—

(a) provide to the consumer the following information—

(i) the identity of the supplier and, where the contract requires payment in advance, the supplier's address;

(ii) a description of the main characteristics of the goods or services;

(iii) the price of the goods or services including all taxes;

(iv) delivery costs where appropriate;

(v) the arrangements for payment, delivery or performance;

(vi) the existence of a right of cancellation except in the cases referred to in regulation 13;

(vii) the cost of using the means of distance communication where it is calculated other than at the basic rate;

(viii) the period for which the offer or the price remains valid; and

(ix) where appropriate, the minimum duration of the contract, in the case of contracts for the supply of goods or services to be performed permanently or recurrently;

(b) inform the consumer if he proposes, in the event of the goods or services

ordered by the consumer being unavailable, to provide substitute goods or services (as the case may be) of equivalent quality and price; and
    (c)   inform the consumer that the cost of returning any such substitute goods
to the supplier in the event of cancellation by the consumer would be met by the
supplier.
    (2)   The supplier shall ensure that the information required by paragraph (1) is
provided in a clear and comprehensible manner appropriate to the means of distance communication used, with due regard in particular to the principles of good
faith in commercial transactions and the principles governing the protection of
those who are unable to give their consent such as minors.
    (3)   Subject to paragraph (4), the supplier shall ensure that his commercial pur-
pose is made clear when providing the information required by paragraph (1).
    (4)   In the case of a telephone communication, the identity of the supplier and
the commercial purpose of the call shall be made clear at the beginning of the con-
versation with the consumer.

8 Written and additional information

    (1)   Subject to regulation 9, the supplier shall provide to the consumer in writ-
ing, or in another durable medium which is available and accessible to the consumer, the information referred to in paragraph (2), either—
    (a)   prior to the conclusion of the contract, or
    (b)   thereafter, in good time and in any event—
        (i)   during the performance of the contract, in the case of services;
        (ii)   at the latest at the time of delivery where goods not for delivery to
third parties are concerned;
        [(iii) in the case of a contract for the supply of services, information as to
how the right to cancel may be affected by the consumer agreeing to
performance of the services beginning before the end of the seven working
day period referred to in regulation 12.]
    (2)   The information required to be provided by paragraph (1) is—
    (a)   the information set out in paragraphs (i) to (vi) of regulation 7(1)(a);
    (b)   information about the conditions and procedures for exercising the right
to cancel under regulation 10, including—
        (i)   where a term of the contract requires (or the supplier intends that it
will require) that the consumer shall return the goods to the supplier in the
event of cancellation, notification of that requirement;
        (ii)   information as to whether the consumer or the supplier would be
responsible under these Regulations for the cost of returning any goods to the
supplier, or the cost of his recovering them, if the consumer cancels the contract
under regulation 10;
        [(iii) in the case of a contract for the supply of services, information as to
how the right to cancel may be affected by the consumer agreeing to
performance of the services beginning before the end of the seven working
day period referred to in regulation 12;]
    (c)   the geographical address of the place of business of the supplier to which
the consumer may address any complaints;
    (d)   information about any after-sales services and guarantees; and
    (e)   the conditions for exercising any contractual right to cancel the contract,
where the contract is of an unspecified duration or a duration exceeding one
year.
    [. . .]

9 Services performed through the use of a means of distance communication

    (1)   Regulation 8 shall not apply to a contract for the supply of services which
are performed through the use of a means of distance communication, where those
services are supplied on only one occasion and are invoiced by the operator of the
means of distance communication.

(2)   But the supplier shall take all necessary steps to ensure that a consumer who is a party to a contract to which paragraph (1) applies is able to obtain the supplier's geographical address and the place of business to which the consumer may address any complaints.

10   Right to cancel

(1)   Subject to regulation 13, if within the cancellation period set out in regulations 11 and 12, the consumer gives a notice of cancellation to the supplier, or any other person previously notified by the supplier to the consumer as a person to whom notice of cancellation may be given, the notice of cancellation shall operate to cancel the contract.

(2)   Except as otherwise provided by these Regulations, the effect of a notice of cancellation is that the contract shall be treated as if it had not been made.

(3)   For the purposes of these Regulations, a notice of cancellation is a notice in writing or in another durable medium available and accessible to the supplier (or to the other person to whom it is given) which, however expressed, indicates the intention of the consumer to cancel the contract.

(4)   A notice of cancellation given under this regulation by a consumer to a supplier or other person is to be treated as having been properly given if the consumer—

(a)   leaves it at the address last known to the consumer and addressed to the supplier or other person by name (in which case it is to be taken to have been given on the day on which it was left);

(b)   sends it by post to the address last known to the consumer and addressed to the supplier or other person by name (in which case, it is to be taken to have been given on the day on which it was posted);

(c)   sends it by facsimile to the business facsimile number last known to the consumer (in which case it is to be taken to have been given on the day on which it is sent); or

(d)   sends it by electronic mail, to the business electronic mail address last known to the consumer (in which case it is to be taken to have been given on the day on which it is sent).

(5)   Where a consumer gives a notice in accordance with paragraph (4)(a) or (b) to a supplier who is a body corporate or a partnership, the notice is to be treated as having been properly given if—

(a)   in the case of a body corporate, it is left at the address of, or sent to, the secretary or clerk of that body; or

(b)   in the case of a partnership, it is left with or sent to a partner or a person having control or management of the partnership business.

11   Cancellation period in the case of contracts for the supply of goods

(1)   For the purposes of regulation 10, the cancellation period in the case of contracts for the supply of goods begins with the day on which the contract is concluded and ends as provided in paragraphs (2) to (5).

(2)   Where the supplier complies with regulation 8, the cancellation period ends on the expiry of the period of seven working days beginning with the day after the day on which the consumer receives the goods.

(3)   Where a supplier who has not complied with regulation 8 provides to the consumer the information referred to in regulation 8(2), and does so in writing or in another durable medium available and accessible to the consumer, within the period of three months beginning with the day after the day on which the consumer receives the goods, the cancellation period ends on the expiry of the period of seven working days beginning with the day after the day on which the consumer receives the information.

(4)   Where neither paragraph (2) nor (3) applies, the cancellation period ends on the expiry of the period of three months and seven working days beginning with the day after the day on which the consumer receives the goods.

(5)   In the case of contracts for goods for delivery to third parties, paragraphs (2) to (4) shall apply as if the consumer had received the goods on the day on which they were received by the third party.

12   Cancellation period in the case of contracts for the supply of services

(1)   For the purposes of regulation 10, the cancellation period in the case of contracts for the supply of services begins with the day on which the contract is concluded and ends as provided in paragraphs (2) to (4).

(2)   Where the supplier complies with regulation 8 on or before the day on which the contract is concluded, the cancellation period ends on the expiry of the period of seven working days beginning with the day after the day on which the contract is concluded.

(3)   [Subject to paragraph (3A)] where a supplier who has not complied with regulation 8 on or before the day on which the contract is concluded provides to the consumer the information referred to in regulation 8(2) [. . .], and does so in writing or in another durable medium available and accessible to the consumer, within the period of three months beginning with the day after the day on which the contract is concluded, the cancellation period ends on the expiry of the period of seven working days beginning with the day after the day on which the consumer receives the information.

[(3A)   Where the performance of the contract has begun with the consumer's agreement before the expiry of the period of seven working days beginning with the day after the day on which the contract was concluded and the supplier has not complied with regulation 8 on or before the day on which performance began, but provides to the consumer the information referred to in regulation 8(2) in good time during the performance of the contract, the cancellation period ends—

(a)   on the expiry of the period of seven working days beginning with the day after the day on which the consumer receives the information; or

(b)   if the performance of the contract is completed before the expiry of the period referred to in sub-paragraph (a), on the day when the performance of the contract is completed.]

(4)   Where [none of paragraphs (2) to (3A) applies], the cancellation period ends on the expiry of the period of three months and seven working days beginning with the day after the day on which the contract is concluded.

13   Exceptions to the right to cancel

(1)   Unless the parties have agreed otherwise, the consumer will not have the right to cancel the contract by giving notice of cancellation pursuant to regulation 10 in respect of contracts—

[(a)   for the supply of services if the performance of the contract has begun with the consumer's agreement—

(i)   before the end of the cancellation period applicable under regulation 12(2); and

(ii)   after the supplier has provided the information referred to in regulation 8(2).]

(b)   for the supply of goods or services the price of which is dependent on fluctuations in the financial market which cannot be controlled by the supplier;

(c)   for the supply of goods made to the consumer's specifications or clearly personalised or which by reason of their nature cannot be returned or are liable to deteriorate or expire rapidly;

(d)   for the supply of audio or video recordings or computer software if they are unsealed by the consumer;

(e)   for the supply of newspapers, periodicals or magazines; or

(f)   for gaming, betting or lottery services.

14 Recovery of sums paid by or on behalf of the consumer on cancellation, and return of security

(1)   On the cancellation of a contract under regulation 10, the supplier shall reimburse any sum paid by or on behalf of the consumer under or in relation to the contract to the person by whom it was made free of any charge, less any charge made in accordance with paragraph (5).

(2)   The reference in paragraph (1) to any sum paid on behalf of the consumer includes any sum paid by a creditor who is not the same person as the supplier under a personal credit agreement with the consumer.

(3)   The supplier shall make the reimbursement referred to in paragraph (1) as soon as possible and in any case within a period not exceeding 30 days beginning with the day on which the notice of cancellation was given.

(4)   Where any security has been provided in relation to the contract, the security (so far as it is so provided) shall, on cancellation under regulation 10, be treated as never having had effect and any property lodged with the supplier solely for the purposes of the security as so provided shall be returned by him forthwith.

(5)   Subject to paragraphs (6) and (7), the supplier may make a charge, not exceeding the direct costs of recovering any goods supplied under the contract, where a term of the contract provides that the consumer must return any goods supplied if he cancels the contract under regulation 10 but the consumer does not comply with this provision or returns the goods at the expense of the supplier.

(6)   Paragraph (5) shall not apply where—

(a)   the consumer cancels in circumstances where he has the right to reject the goods under a term of the contract, including a term implied by virtue of any enactment, or

(b)   the term requiring the consumer to return any goods supplied if he cancels the contract is an 'unfair term' within the meaning of the Unfair Terms in Consumer Contracts Regulations 1999.

(7)   Paragraph (5) shall not apply to the cost of recovering any goods which were supplied as substitutes for the goods ordered by the consumer.

(8)   For the purposes of these Regulations, a personal credit agreement is an agreement between the consumer and any other person ('the creditor') by which the creditor provides the consumer with credit of any amount.

15 Automatic cancellation of a related credit agreement

(1)   Where a notice of cancellation is given under regulation 10 which has the effect of cancelling the contract, the giving of the notice shall also have the effect of cancelling any related credit agreement.

(2)   Where a related credit agreement is cancelled by virtue of paragraph (1), the supplier shall, if he is not the same person as the creditor under that agreement, forthwith on receipt of the notice of cancellation inform the creditor that the notice has been given.

(3)   Where a related credit agreement is cancelled by virtue of paragraph (1)—

(a)   any sum paid by or on behalf of the consumer under, or in relation to, the credit agreement which the supplier is not obliged to reimburse under regulation 14(1) shall be reimbursed, except for any sum which, if it had not already been paid, would have to be paid under sub-paragraph (b);

(b)   the agreement shall continue in force so far as it relates to repayment of the credit and payment of interest, subject to regulation 16; and

(c)   subject to sub-paragraph (b), the agreement shall cease to be enforceable.

(4)   Where any security has been provided under a related credit agreement, the security, so far as it is so provided, shall be treated as never having had effect and any property lodged with the creditor solely for the purposes of the security as so provided shall be returned by him forthwith.

(5)   For the purposes of this regulation and regulation 16, a 'related credit

agreement' means an agreement under which fixed sum credit which fully or partly covers the price under a contract cancelled under regulation 10 is granted—

(a)   by the supplier, or

(b)   by another person, under an arrangement between that person and the supplier.

(6)   For the purposes of this regulation and regulation 16—

(a)   'creditor' is a person who grants credit under a related credit agreement;

(b)   'fixed sum credit' has the same meaning as in section 10 of the Consumer Credit Act 1974;

(c)   'repayment' in relation to credit means repayment of money received by the consumer, and cognate expressions shall be construed accordingly; and

(d)   'interest' means interest on money so received.

16   Repayment of credit and interest after cancellation of a related credit agreement

(1)   This regulation applies following the cancellation of a related credit agreement by virtue of regulation 15(1).

(2)   If the consumer repays the whole or a portion of the credit—

(a)   before the expiry of one month following the cancellation of the credit agreement, or

(b)   in the case of a credit repayable by instalments, before the date on which the first instalment is due,

no interest shall be payable on the amount repaid.

(3)   If the whole of a credit repayable by instalments is not repaid on or before the date referred to in paragraph (2)(b), the consumer shall not be liable to repay any of the credit except on receipt of a request in writing, signed by the creditor, stating the amounts of the remaining instalments (recalculated by the creditor as nearly as may be in accordance with the agreement and without extending the repayment period), but excluding any sum other than principal and interest.

(4)   Where any security has been provided under a related credit agreement the duty imposed on the consumer to repay credit and to pay interest shall not be enforceable before the creditor has discharged any duty imposed on him by regulation 15(4) to return any property lodged with him as security on cancellation.

17   Restoration of goods by consumer after cancellation

(1)   This regulation applies where a contract is cancelled under regulation 10 after the consumer has acquired possession of any goods under the contract other than any goods mentioned in regulation 13(1)(b) to (e).

(2)   The consumer shall be treated as having been under a duty throughout the period prior to cancellation—

(a)   to retain possession of the goods, and

(b)   to take reasonable care of them.

(3)   On cancellation, the consumer shall be under a duty to restore the goods to the supplier in accordance with this regulation, and in the meanwhile to retain possession of the goods and take reasonable care of them.

(4)   The consumer shall not be under any duty to deliver the goods except at his own premises and in pursuance of a request in writing, or in another durable medium available and accessible to the consumer, from the supplier and given to the consumer either before, or at the time when, the goods are collected from those premises.

(5)   If the consumer—

(a)   delivers the goods (whether at his own premises or elsewhere) to any person to whom, under regulation 10(1), a notice of cancellation could have been given; or

(b)   sends the goods at his own expense to such a person,

he shall be discharged from any duty to retain possession of the goods or restore them to the supplier.

(6)   Where the consumer delivers the goods in accordance with paragraph (5)(a), his obligation to take care of the goods shall cease; and if he sends the goods in accordance with paragraph (5)(b), he shall be under a duty to take reasonable care to see that they are received by the supplier and not damaged in transit, but in other respects his duty to take care of the goods shall cease when he sends them.

(7)   Where, at any time during the period of 21 days beginning with the day notice of cancellation was given, the consumer receives such a request as is mentioned in paragraph (4), and unreasonably refuses or unreasonably fails to comply with it, his duty to retain possession and take reasonable care of the goods shall continue until he delivers or sends the goods as mentioned in paragraph (5), but if within that period he does not receive such a request his duty to take reasonable care of the goods shall cease at the end of that period.

(8)   Where—

(a)   a term of the contract provides that if the consumer cancels the contract, he must return the goods to the supplier, and

(b)   the consumer is not otherwise entitled to reject the goods under the terms of the contract or by virtue of any enactment,

paragraph (7) shall apply as if for the period of 21 days there were substituted the period of 6 months.

(9)   Where any security has been provided in relation to the cancelled contract, the duty to restore goods imposed on the consumer by this regulation shall not be enforceable before the supplier has discharged any duty imposed on him by regulation 14(4) to return any property lodged with him as security on cancellation.

(10)   Breach of a duty imposed by this regulation on a consumer is actionable as a breach of statutory duty.

18   Goods given in part-exchange

(1)   This regulation applies on the cancellation of a contract under regulation 10 where the supplier agreed to take goods in part-exchange (the 'part-exchange goods') and those goods have been delivered to him.

(2)   Unless, before the end of the period of 10 days beginning with the date of cancellation, the part-exchange goods are returned to the consumer in a condition substantially as good as when they were delivered to the supplier, the consumer shall be entitled to recover from the supplier a sum equal to the part-exchange allowance.

(3)   In this regulation the part-exchange allowance means the sum agreed as such in the cancelled contract, or if no such sum was agreed, such sum as it would have been reasonable to allow in respect of the part-exchange goods if no notice of cancellation had been served.

(4)   Where the consumer recovers from the supplier a sum equal to the part-exchange allowance, the title of the consumer to the part-exchange goods shall vest in the supplier (if it has not already done so) on recovery of that sum.

19   Performance

(1)   Unless the parties agree otherwise, the supplier shall perform the contract within a maximum of 30 days beginning with the day after the day the consumer sent his order to the supplier.

(2)   Subject to paragraphs (7) and (8), where the supplier is unable to perform the contract because the goods or services ordered are not available, within the period for performance referred to in paragraph (1) or such other period as the parties agree ('the period for performance'), he shall—

(a)   inform the consumer; and

(b)   reimburse any sum paid by or on behalf of the consumer under or in relation to the contract to the person by whom it was made.

(3)   The reference in paragraph (2)(b) to any sum paid on behalf of the con-

sumer includes any sum paid by a creditor who is not the same person as the supplier under a personal credit agreement with the consumer.

(4)   The supplier shall make the reimbursement referred to in paragraph (2)(b) as soon as possible and in any event within a period of 30 days beginning with the day after the day on which the period for performance expired.

(5)   A contract which has not been performed within the period for performance shall be treated as if it had not been made, save for any rights or remedies which the consumer has under it as a result of the non-performance.

(6)   Where any security has been provided in relation to the contract, the security (so far as it is so provided) shall, where the supplier is unable to perform the contract within the period for performance, be treated as never having had any effect and any property lodged with the supplier solely for the purposes of the security as so provided shall be returned by him forthwith.

(7)   Where the supplier is unable to supply the goods or services ordered by the consumer, the supplier may perform the contract for the purposes of these Regulations by providing substitute goods or services (as the case may be) of equivalent quality and price provided that—

(a)   this possibility was provided for in the contract;

(b)   prior to the conclusion of the contract the supplier gave the consumer the information required by regulation 7(1)(b) and (c) in the manner required by regulation 7(2).

(8)   In the case of outdoor leisure events which by their nature cannot be rescheduled, paragraph 2(b) shall not apply where the consumer and the supplier so agree.

20   Effect of non-performance on related credit agreement
Where a supplier is unable to perform the contract within the period for performance—

(a)   regulations 15 and 16 shall apply to any related credit agreement as if the consumer had given a valid notice of cancellation under regulation 10 on the expiry of the period for performance; and

(b)   the reference in regulation 15(3)(a) to regulation 14(1) shall be read, for the purposes of this regulation, as a reference to regulation 19(2).

21   Payment by card
(1)   Subject to paragraph (4), the consumer shall be entitled to cancel a payment where fraudulent use has been made of his payment card in connection with a contract to which this regulation applies by another person not acting, or to be treated as acting, as his agent.

(2)   Subject to paragraph (4), the consumer shall be entitled to be recredited, or to have all sums returned by the card issuer, in the event of fraudulent use of his payment card in connection with a contract to which this regulation applies by another person not acting, or to be treated as acting, as the consumer's agent.

(3)   Where paragraphs (1) and (2) apply, in any proceedings if the consumer alleges that any use made of the payment card was not authorised by him it is for the card issuer to prove that the use was so authorised.

(4)   Paragraphs (1) and (2) shall not apply to an agreement to which section 83(1) of the Consumer Credit Act 1974 applies.

(5)   [amends Consumer Credit Act 1974].

(6)   For the purposes of this regulation—

'card issuer' means the owner of the card; and

'payment card' includes credit cards, charge cards, debit cards and store cards.

22, 23   [Amending provisions]

24 Inertia selling
(1)   Paragraphs (2) and (3) apply if—
    (a)   unsolicited goods are sent to a person ('the recipient') with a view to his acquiring them;
    (b)   the recipient has no reasonable cause to believe that they were sent with a view to their being acquired for the purposes of a business; and
    (c)   the recipient has neither agreed to acquire nor agreed to return them.
(2)   The recipient may, as between himself and the sender, use, deal with or dispose of the goods as if they were an unconditional gift to him.
(3)   The rights of the sender to the goods are extinguished.
[. . .]
(6)   In this regulation—
    'acquire' includes hire;
    'send' includes deliver;
    'sender', in relation to any goods, includes—
        (a)   any person on whose behalf or with whose consent the goods are sent;
        (b)   any other person claiming through or under the sender or any person mentioned in paragraph (a); and
        (c)   any person who delivers the goods; and
    'unsolicited' means, in relation to goods sent or services supplied to any person, that they are sent or supplied without any prior request made by or on behalf of the recipient.
[. . .]
(10)   This regulation applies only to goods sent and services supplied after the date on which it comes into force.

25 No contracting-out
(1)   A term contained in any contract to which these Regulations apply is void if, and to the extent that, it is inconsistent with a provision for the protection of the consumer contained in these Regulations.
(2)   Where a provision of these Regulations specifies a duty or liability of the consumer in certain circumstances, a term contained in a contract to which these Regulations apply, other than a term to which paragraph (3) applies, is inconsistent with that provision if it purports to impose, directly or indirectly, an additional duty or liability on him in those circumstances.
(3)   This paragraph applies to a term which requires the consumer to return any goods supplied to him under the contract if he cancels it under regulation 10.
(4)   A term to which paragraph (3) applies shall, in the event of cancellation by the consumer under regulation 10, have effect only for the purposes of regulations 14(5) and 17(8).
(5)   These Regulations shall apply notwithstanding any contract term which applies or purports to apply the law of a non-Member State if the contract has a close connection with the territory of a Member State.

26 Consideration of complaints
(1)   It shall be the duty of an enforcement authority to consider any complaint made to it about a breach unless—
    (a)   the complaint appears to the authority to be frivolous or vexatious; or
    (b)   another enforcement authority has notified the Director that it agrees to consider the complaint.
(2)   If an enforcement authority notifies the Director that it agrees to consider a complaint made to another enforcement authority, the first mentioned authority shall be under a duty to consider the complaint.
(3)   An enforcement authority which is under a duty to consider a complaint shall give reasons for its decision to apply or not to apply, as the case may be, for an injunction under regulation 27.
(4)   In deciding whether or not to apply for an injunction in respect of a breach

an enforcement authority may, if it considers it appropriate to do so, have regard to any undertaking given to it or another enforcement authority by or on behalf of any person as to compliance with these Regulations.

27 Injunctions to secure compliance with these Regulations

(1)   The Director or, subject to paragraph (2), any other enforcement authority may apply for an injunction (including an interim injunction) against any person who appears to the Director or that authority to be responsible for a breach.

(2)   An enforcement authority other than the Director may apply for an injunction only where—

(a)   it has notified the Director of its intention to apply at least fourteen days before the date on which the application is to be made, beginning with the date on which the notification was given; or

(b)   the Director consents to the application being made within a shorter period.

(3)   The court on an application under this regulation may grant an injunction on such terms as it thinks fit to secure compliance with these Regulations.

28 Notification of undertakings and orders to the Director

An enforcement authority other than the Director shall notify the Director—

(a)   of any undertaking given to it by or on behalf of any person who appears to it to be responsible for a breach;

(b)   of the outcome of any application made by it under regulation 27 and of the terms of any undertaking given to or order made by the court;

(c)   of the outcome of any application made by it to enforce a previous order of the court.

29 Publication, information and advice

(1)   The Director shall arrange for the publication in such form and manner as he considers appropriate of—

(a)   details of any undertaking or order notified to him under regulation 28;

(b)   details of any undertaking given to him by or on behalf of any person as to compliance with these Regulations;

(c)   details of any application made by him under regulation 27, and of the terms of any undertaking given to, or order made by, the court;

(d)   details of any application made by the Director to enforce a previous order of the court.

(2)   The Director may arrange for the dissemination in such form and manner as he considers appropriate of such information and advice concerning the operation of these Regulations as it may appear to him to be expedient to give to the public and to all persons likely to be affected by these Regulations.

SCHEDULE 1   Regulation 3

INDICATIVE LIST OF MEANS OF DISTANCE COMMUNICATION

1.   Unaddressed printed matter.
2.   Addressed printed matter.
3.   Letter.
4.   Press advertising with order form.
5.   Catalogue.
6.   Telephone with human intervention.
7.   Telephone without human intervention (automatic calling machine, audio-text).
8.   Radio.
9.   Videophone (telephone with screen).

10. Videotext (microcomputer and television screen) with keyboard or touch screen.

11. Electronic mail.

12. Facsimile machine (fax).

13. Television (teleshopping).

ELECTRONIC SIGNATURES REGULATIONS 2002
(SI 2002/318)

1 Citation and commencement

These Regulations may be cited as the Electronic Signatures Regulations 2002 and shall come into force on 8th March 2002.

2 Interpretation

In these Regulations—

'advanced electronic signature' means an electronic signature—

(a) which is uniquely linked to the signatory,

(b) which is capable of identifying the signatory,

(c) which is created using means that the signatory can maintain under his sole control, and

(d) which is linked to the data to which it relates in such a manner that any subsequent change of the data is detectable;

'certificate' means an electronic attestation which links signature-verification data to a person and confirms the identity of that person;

'certification-service-provider' means a person who issues certificates or provides other services related to electronic signatures;

'Directive' means Directive 1999/93/EC of the European Parliament and of the Council on a Community framework for electronic signatures;

'electronic signature' means data in electronic form which are attached to or logically associated with other electronic data and which serve as a method of authentication;

'qualified certificate' means a certificate which meets the requirements in Schedule 1 and is provided by a certification-service-provider who fulfils the requirements in Schedule 2;

'signatory' means a person who holds a signature-creation device and acts either on his own behalf or on behalf of the person he represents;

'signature-creation data' means unique data (including, but not limited to, codes or private cryptographic keys) which are used by the signatory to create an electronic signature;

'signature-creation device' means configured software or hardware used to implement the signature-creation data;

'signature-verification data' means data (including, but not limited to, codes or public cryptographic keys) which are used for the purpose of verifying an electronic signature;

'signature-verification device' means configured software or hardware used to implement the signature-verification data;

'voluntary accreditation' means any permission, setting out rights and obligations specific to the provision of certification services, to be granted upon request by the certification-service-provider concerned by the person charged with the elaboration of, and supervision of compliance with, such rights and obligations, where the certification-service-provider is not entitled to exercise the rights stemming from the permission until he has received the decision of that person.

3 Supervision of certification-service-providers

(1) It shall be the duty of the Secretary of State to keep under review the carrying on of activities of certification-service-providers who are established in the United Kingdom and who issue qualified certificates to the public and the persons

by whom they are carried on with a view to her becoming aware of the identity of those persons and the circumstances relating to the carrying on of those activities.

(2)   It shall also be the duty of the Secretary of State to establish and maintain a register of certification-service-providers who are established in the United Kingdom and who issue qualified certificates to the public.

(3)   The Secretary of State shall record in the register the names and addresses of those certification-service-providers of whom she is aware who are established in the United Kingdom and who issue qualified certificates to the public.

(4)   The Secretary of State shall publish the register in such manner as she considers appropriate.

(5)   The Secretary of State shall have regard to evidence becoming available to her with respect to any course of conduct of a certification-service-provider who is established in the United Kingdom and who issues qualified certificates to the public and which appears to her to be conduct detrimental to the interests of those persons who use or rely on those certificates with a view to making any of this evidence as she considers expedient available to the public in such manner as she considers appropriate.

4   Liability of certification-service-providers

(1)   Where—

(a)   a certification-service-provider either—

(i)   issues a certificate as a qualified certificate to the public, or

(ii)   guarantees a qualified certificate to the public,

(b)   a person reasonably relies on that certificate for any of the following matters—

(i)   the accuracy of any of the information contained in the qualified certificate at the time of issue,

(ii)   the inclusion in the qualified certificate of all the details referred to in Schedule 1,

(iii)   the holding by the signatory identified in the qualified certificate at the time of its issue of the signature-creation data corresponding to the signature-verification data given or identified in the certificate, or

(iv)   the ability of the signature-creation data and the signature-verification data to be used in a complementary manner in cases where the certification-service-provider generates them both,

(c)   that person suffers loss as a result of such reliance, and

(d)   the certification-service-provider would be liable in damages in respect of any extent of the loss—

(i)   had a duty of care existed between him and the person referred to in sub-paragraph (b) above, and

(ii)   had the certification-service-provider been negligent,

then that certification-service-provider shall be so liable to the same extent notwithstanding that there is no proof that the certification-service-provider was negligent unless the certification-service-provider proves that he was not negligent.

(2)   For the purposes of the certification-service-provider's liability under paragraph (1) above there shall be a duty of care between that certification-service-provider and the person referred to in paragraph (1)(b) above.

(3)   Where—

(a)   a certification-service-provider issues a certificate as a qualified certificate to the public,

(b)   a person reasonably relies on that certificate,

(c)   that person suffers loss as a result of any failure by the certification-service-provider to register revocation of the certificate, and

(d)   the certification-service-provider would be liable in damages in respect of any extent of the loss—

(i)   had a duty of care existed between him and the person referred to in sub-paragraph (b) above, and
(ii)   had the certification-service-provider been negligent,
then that certification-service-provider shall be so liable to the same extent notwithstanding that there is no proof that the certification-service-provider was negligent unless the certification-service-provider proves that he was not negligent.

(4)   For the purposes of the certification-service-provider's liability under paragraph (3) above there shall be a duty of care between that certification-service-provider and the person referred to in paragraph (3)(b) above.

5   Data Protection

(1)   A certification-service-provider who issues a certificate to the public and to whom this paragraph applies in accordance with paragraph (6) below—

(a)   shall not obtain personal data for the purpose of issuing or maintaining that certificate otherwise than directly from the data subject or after the explicit consent of the data subject, and

(b)   shall not process the personal data referred to in sub-paragraph (a) above—

(i)   to a greater extent than is necessary for the purpose of issuing or maintaining that certificate, or

(ii)   to a greater extent than is necessary for any other purpose to which the data subject has explicitly consented,

unless the processing is necessary for compliance with any legal obligation, to which the certification-service-provider is subject, other than an obligation imposed by contract.

(2)   The obligation to comply with paragraph (1) above shall be a duty owed to any data subject who may be affected by a contravention of paragraph (1).

(3)   Where a duty is owed by virtue of paragraph (2) above to any data subject, any breach of that duty which causes that data subject to sustain loss or damage shall be actionable by him.

(4)   Compliance with paragraph (1) above shall also be enforceable by civil proceedings brought by the Crown for an injunction or for an interdict or for any other appropriate relief or remedy.

(5)   Paragraph (4) above shall not prejudice any right that a data subject may have by virtue of paragraph (3) above to bring civil proceedings for the contravention or apprehended contravention of paragraph (1) above.

(6)   Paragraph (1) above applies to a certification-service-provider in respect of personal data only if the certification-service-provider is established in the United Kingdom and the personal data are processed in the context of that establishment.

(7)   For the purposes of paragraph (6) above, each of the following is to be treated as established in the United Kingdom—

(a)   an individual who is ordinarily resident in the United Kingdom,

(b)   a body incorporated under the law of, or in any part of, the United Kingdom,

(c)   a partnership or other unincorporated association formed under the law of any part of the United Kingdom, and

(d)   any person who does not fall within ssub-paragraph (a), (b) or (c) above but maintains in the United Kingdom—

(i)   an office, branch or agency through which he carries on any activity, or

(ii)   a regular practice.

(8)   In this regulation—

'data subject' and 'personal data' and 'processing' shall have the same meanings as in section 1(1) of the Data Protection Act 1998, and

'obtain' shall bear the same interpretation as 'obtaining' in section 1(2) of the Data Protection Act 1998.

SCHEDULE 1 (Regulation 2)
(Annex I to the Directive)
REQUIREMENTS FOR QUALIFIED CERTIFICATES

Qualified certificates must contain:

    (a)   an indication that the certificate is issued as a qualified certificate;

    (b)   the identification of the certification-service-provider and the State in which it is established;

    (c)   the name of the signatory or a pseudonym, which shall be identified as such;

    (d)   provision for a specific attribute of the signatory to be included if relevant, depending on the purpose for which the certificate is intended;

    (e)   signature-verification data which correspond to signature-creation data under the control of the signatory;

    (f)   an indication of the beginning and end of the period of validity of the certificate;

    (g)   the identity code of the certificate;

    (h)   the advanced electronic signature of the certification-service-provider issuing it;

    (i)   limitations on the scope of use of the certificate, if applicable; and

    (j)   limits on the value of transactions for which the certificate can be used, if applicable.

SCHEDULE 2 (Regulation 2)
(Annex II to the Directive)
REQUIREMENTS FOR CERTIFICATION-SERVICE-PROVIDERS ISSUING QUALIFIED CERTIFICATES

Certification-service-providers must:

    (a)   demonstrate the reliability necessary for providing certification services;

    (b)   ensure the operation of a prompt and secure directory and a secure and immediate revocation service;

    (c)   ensure that the date and time when a certificate is issued or revoked can be determined precisely;

    (d)   verify, by appropriate means in accordance with national law, the identity and, if applicable, any specific attributes of the person to which a qualified certificate is issued;

    (e)   employ personnel who possess the expert knowledge, experience, and qualifications necessary for the services provided, in particular competence at managerial level, expertise in electronic signature technology and familiarity with proper security procedures; they must also apply administrative and management procedures which are adequate and correspond to recognised standards;

    (f)   use trustworthy systems and products which are protected against modification and ensure the technical and cryptographic security of the process supported by them;

    (g)   take measures against forgery of certificates, and, in cases where the certification-service-provider generates signature-creation data, guarantee confidentiality during the process of generating such data;

    (h)   maintain sufficient financial resources to operate in conformity with the requirements laid down in the Directive, in particular to bear the risk of liability for damages, for example, by obtaining appropriate insurance;

    (i)   record all relevant information concerning a qualified certificate for an appropriate period of time, in particular for the purpose of providing evidence of certification for the purposes of legal proceedings. Such recording may be done electronically;

(j)   not store or copy signature-creation data of the person to whom the certi-fication-service-provider provided key management services;

(k)   before entering into a contractual relationship with a person seeking a certificate to support his electronic signature inform that person by a durable means of communication of the precise terms and conditions regarding the use of the certificate, including any limitations on its use, the existence of a volun-tary accreditation scheme and procedures for complaints and dispute settlement. Such information, which may be transmitted electronically, must be in writing and in readily understandable language. Relevant parts of this information must also be made available on request to third parties relying on the certificate;

(l)   use trustworthy systems to store certificates in a verifiable form so that:

– only authorised persons can make entries and changes,

– information can be checked for authenticity,

– certificates are publicly available for retrieval in only those cases for which the certificate-holder's consent has been obtained, and

– any technical changes compromising these security requirements are apparent to the operator.

LATE PAYMENT OF COMMERCIAL DEBTS (SCOTLAND) REGULATIONS 2002 (SSI 2002/335)

3   Proceedings restraining use of grossly unfair terms

(1)   In this regulation—

(a)   'small and medium-sized enterprises' means those enterprises defined in Annex 1 to Commission Regulation (EC) No 70/2001 of 12th January 2001 on the application of Articles 87 and 88 of the EC Treaty to State aid to small and medium-sized enterprises;

(b)   'representative body' means an organisation established to represent the collective interests of small and medium-sized enterprises in general or in a par-ticular sector or area.

(2)   This regulation applies where a person acting in the course of a business has written standard terms on which he or she enters (or intends to enter) as pur-chaser into contracts to which the Late Payment of Commercial Debts (Interest) Act 1998 applies which include a term purporting to oust or vary the right to statutory interest in relation to qualifying debts created by those contracts.

(3)   If it appears to the Court of Session that in all or any circumstances the purported use of such a term in a relevant contract would be void under the Late Payment of Commercial Debts (Interest) Act 1998, the court on the application of a representative body may grant an interdict against that person prohibiting that person in those circumstances from using the offending term, on such terms as the court may think fit.

(4)   Only a representative body may apply to the Court of Session under this regulation.

4   Saving for existing contracts

These Regulations do not affect contracts made before 7th August 2002.

LATE PAYMENT OF COMMERCIAL DEBTS (RATE OF INTEREST) (SCOTLAND) ORDER 2002 (SSI 2002/336)

1   Citation, commencement and extent

(1)   This Order may be cited as the Late Payment of Commercial Debts (Rate of Interest) (Scotland) Order 2002 and shall come into force on 7th August 2002.

(2)   This Order extends to Scotland only.

2 Revocation
The Late Payment of Commercial Debts (Rate of Interest) (No 2) Order 1998 is revoked.

3 Interpretation
In this Order, 'the official dealing rate' means the rate announced from time to time by the Monetary Policy Committee of the Bank of England ('the Bank') and for the time being in force as the official dealing rate, being the rate at which the Bank is willing to enter into transactions for providing short term liquidity in the money markets.

4 Rate of statutory interest
The rate of interest for the purposes of the Late Payment of Commercial Debts (Interest) Act 1998 shall be 8 per cent per annum over the official dealing rate in force on the 30th June (in respect of interest which starts to run between 1st July and 31st December) or the 31st December (in respect of interest which starts to run between 1st January and 30th June) immediately before the day on which statutory interest starts to run.

ELECTRONIC COMMERCE (EC DIRECTIVE) REGULATIONS 2002
(SI 2002/2013)

9 Information to be provided where contracts are concluded by electronic means
(1)   Unless parties who are not consumers have agreed otherwise, where a contract is to be concluded by electronic means a service provider shall, prior to an order being placed by the recipient of a service, provide to that recipient in a clear, comprehensible and unambiguous manner the information set out in (a) to (d) below—
    (a)   the different technical steps to follow to conclude the contract;
    (b)   whether or not the concluded contract will be filed by the service provider and whether it will be accessible;
    (c)   the technical means for identifying and correcting input errors prior to the placing of the order; and
    (d)   the languages offered for the conclusion of the contract.
(2)   Unless parties who are not consumers have agreed otherwise, a service provider shall indicate which relevant codes of conduct he subscribes to and give information on how those codes can be consulted electronically.
(3)   Where the service provider provides terms and conditions applicable to the contract to the recipient, the service provider shall make them available to him in a way that allows him to store and reproduce them.
(4)   The requirements of paragraphs (1) and (2) above shall not apply to contracts concluded exclusively by exchange of electronic mail or by equivalent individual communications.

10 Other information requirements
Regulations 6, 7, 8 and 9(1) have effect in addition to any other information requirements in legislation giving effect to Community law.

11 Placing of the order
(1)   Unless parties who are not consumers have agreed otherwise, where the recipient of the service places his order through technological means, a service provider shall—
    (a)   acknowledge receipt of the order to the recipient of the service without undue delay and by electronic means; and
    (b)   make available to the recipient of the service appropriate, effective and accessible technical means allowing him to identify and correct input errors prior to the placing of the order.

(2)   For the purposes of paragraph (1)(a) above—

(a)   the order and the acknowledgement of receipt will be deemed to be received when the parties to whom they are addressed are able to access them; and

(b)   the acknowledgement of receipt may take the form of the provision of the service paid for where that service is an information society service.

(3)   The requirements of paragraph (1) above shall not apply to contracts concluded exclusively by exchange of electronic mail or by equivalent individual communications.

GENERAL PRODUCT SAFETY REGULATIONS 2005
(SI 2005/1803)

PART 1. GENERAL

1   Citation, commencement and revocation

(1)   These Regulations may be cited as the General Product Safety Regulations 2005 and shall come into force on 1st October 2005 with the exception of the reference to a civil partner in regulation 43(2) which shall come into force on 5th December 2005.

(2)   The General Product Safety Regulations 1994 are hereby revoked.

2   Interpretation

In these Regulations—

'the 1987 Act' means the Consumer Protection Act 1987;

'Community law' includes a law in any part of the United Kingdom which implements a Community obligation;

'contravention' includes a failure to comply and cognate expressions shall be construed accordingly;

'dangerous product' means a product other than a safe product;

'distributor' means a professional in the supply chain whose activity does not affect the safety properties of a product;

'enforcement authority' means the Secretary of State, any other Minister of the Crown in charge of a government department, any such department and any authority or council mentioned in regulation 10;

'general safety requirement' means the requirement that only safe products should be placed on the market;

'the GPS Directive' means Directive 2001/95/EC of the European Parliament and of the Council of 3 December 2001 on general product safety;

'magistrates' court' in relation to Northern Ireland, means a court of summary jurisdiction;

'Member State' means a Member State, Norway, Iceland or Liechtenstein;

'notice' means a notice in writing;

'officer', in relation to an enforcement authority, means a person authorised in writing to assist the authority in carrying out its functions under or for the purposes of the enforcement of these Regulations and safety notices, except in relation to an enforcement authority which is a government department where it means an officer of that department;

'producer' means—

(a)   the manufacturer of a product, when he is established in a Member State and any other person presenting himself as the manufacturer by affixing to the product his name, trade mark or other distinctive mark, or the person who reconditions the product;

(b)   when the manufacturer is not established in a Member State—

(i)   if he has a representative established in a Member State, the representative,

(ii) in any other case, the importer of the product from a state that is not a Member State into a Member State;

(c) other professionals in the supply chain, insofar as their activities may affect the safety properties of a product;

'product' means a product which is intended for consumers or likely, under reasonably foreseeable conditions, to be used by consumers even if not intended for them and which is supplied or made available, whether for consideration or not, in the course of a commercial activity and whether it is new, used or reconditioned and includes a product that is supplied or made available to consumers for their own use in the context of providing a service. 'Product' does not include equipment used by service providers themselves to supply a service to consumers, in particular equipment on which consumers ride or travel which is operated by a service provider;

'recall' means any measure aimed at achieving the return of a dangerous product that has already been supplied or made available to consumers;

'recall notice' means a notice under regulation 15;

'record' includes any book or document and any record in any form;

'requirement to mark' means a notice under regulation 12;

'requirement to warn' means a notice under regulation 13;

'safe product' means a product which, under normal or reasonably foreseeable conditions of use including duration and, where applicable, putting into service, installation and maintenance requirements, does not present any risk or only the minimum risks compatible with the product's use, considered to be acceptable and consistent with a high level of protection for the safety and health of persons. In determining the foregoing, the following shall be taken into account in particular—

(a) the characteristics of the product, including its composition, packaging, instructions for assembly and, where applicable, instructions for installation and maintenance,

(b) the effect of the product on other products, where it is reasonably foreseeable that it will be used with other products,

(c) the presentation of the product, the labelling, any warnings and instructions for its use and disposal and any other indication or information regarding the product, and

(d) the categories of consumers at risk when using the product, in particular children and the elderly.

The feasibility of obtaining higher levels of safety or the availability of other products presenting a lesser degree of risk shall not constitute grounds for considering a product to be a dangerous product;

'safety notice' means a suspension notice, a requirement to mark, a requirement to warn, a withdrawal notice or a recall notice;

'serious risk' means a serious risk, including one the effects of which are not immediate, requiring rapid intervention;

'supply' in relation to a product includes making it available, in the context of providing a service, for use by consumers;

'suspension notice' means a notice under regulation 11;

'withdrawal' means any measure aimed at preventing the distribution, display or offer of a dangerous product to a consumer;

'withdrawal notice' means a notice under regulation 14.

3 Application

(1) Each provision of these Regulations applies to a product in so far as there are no specific provisions with the same objective in rules of Community law governing the safety of the product other than the GPS Directive.

(2) Where a product is subject to specific safety requirements imposed by rules of Community law other than the GPS Directive, these Regulations shall apply

only to the aspects and risks or category of risks not covered by those requirements. This means that:

(a)   the definition of 'safe product' and 'dangerous product' in regulation 2 and regulations 5 and 6 shall not apply to such a product in so far as concerns the risks or category of risks covered by the specific rules, and

(b)   the remainder of these Regulations shall apply except where there are specific provisions governing the aspects covered by those regulations with the same objective.

4 These Regulations do not apply to a second-hand product supplied as a product to be repaired or reconditioned prior to being used, provided the supplier clearly informs the person to whom he supplies the product to that effect.

PART 2. OBLIGATIONS OF PRODUCERS AND DISTRIBUTORS

5 General safety requirement

(1)   No producer shall place a product on the market unless the product is a safe product.

(2)   No producer shall offer or agree to place a product on the market or expose or possess a product for placing on the market unless the product is a safe product.

(3)   No producer shall offer or agree to supply a product or expose or possess a product for supply unless the product is a safe product.

(4)   No producer shall supply a product unless the product is a safe product.

6 Presumption of conformity

(1)   Where, in the absence of specific provisions in rules of Community law governing the safety of a product, the product conforms to the specific rules of the law of part of the United Kingdom laying down the health and safety requirements which the product must satisfy in order to be marketed in the United Kingdom, the product shall be deemed safe so far as concerns the aspects covered by such rules.

(2)   Where a product conforms to a voluntary national standard of the United Kingdom giving effect to a European standard the reference of which has been published in the Official Journal of the European Union in accordance with Article 4 of the GPS Directive, the product shall be presumed to be a safe product so far as concerns the risks and categories of risk covered by that national standard. The Secretary of State shall publish the reference number of such national standards in such manner as he considers appropriate.

(3)   In circumstances other than those referred to in paragraphs (1) and (2), the conformity of a product to the general safety requirement shall be assessed taking into account—

(a)   any voluntary national standard of the United Kingdom giving effect to a European standard, other than one referred to in paragraph (2),

(b)   other national standards drawn up in the United Kingdom,

(c)   recommendations of the European Commission setting guidelines on product safety assessment,

(d)   product safety codes of good practice in the sector concerned,

(e)   the state of the art and technology, and

(f)   reasonable consumer expectations concerning safety.

(4)   Conformity of a product with the criteria designed to ensure the general safety requirement is complied with, in particular the provisions mentioned in paragraphs (1) to (3), shall not bar an enforcement authority from exercising its powers under these Regulations in relation to that product where there is evidence that, despite such conformity, it is dangerous.

7   Other obligations of producers

(1)   Within the limits of his activities, a producer shall provide consumers with the relevant information to enable them—

(a)   to assess the risks inherent in a product throughout the normal or reasonably foreseeable period of its use, where such risks are not immediately obvious without adequate warnings, and

(b)   to take precautions against those risks.

(2)   The presence of warnings does not exempt any person from compliance with the other requirements of these Regulations.

(3)   Within the limits of his activities, a producer shall adopt measures commensurate with the characteristics of the products which he supplies to enable him to—

(a)   be informed of the risks which the products might pose, and

(b)   take appropriate action including, where necessary to avoid such risks, withdrawal, adequately and effectively warning consumers as to the risks or, as a last resort, recall.

(4)   The measures referred to in paragraph (3) include—

(a)   except where it is not reasonable to do so, an indication by means of the product or its packaging of—

(i)   the name and address of the producer, and

(ii)   the product reference or where applicable the batch of products to which it belongs; and

(b)   where and to the extent that it is reasonable to do so—

(i)   sample testing of marketed products,

(ii)   investigating and if necessary keeping a register of complaints concerning the safety of the product, and

(iii)   keeping distributors informed of the results of such monitoring where a product presents a risk or may present a risk.

8   Obligations of distributors

(1)   A distributor shall act with due care in order to help ensure compliance with the applicable safety requirements and in particular he—

(a)   shall not expose or possess for supply or offer or agree to supply, or supply, a product to any person which he knows or should have presumed, on the basis of the information in his possession and as a professional, is a dangerous product; and

(b)   shall, within the limits of his activities, participate in monitoring the safety of a product placed on the market, in particular by—

(i)   passing on information on the risks posed by the product,

(ii)   keeping the documentation necessary for tracing the origin of the product,

(iii)   producing the documentation necessary for tracing the origin of the product, and (iv) cooperating in action taken by a producer or an enforcement authority to avoid the risks.

(2)   Within the limits of his activities, a distributor shall take measures enabling him to co-operate efficiently in the action referred to in paragraph (1)(b)(iii).

9   Obligations of producers and distributors

(1)   Subject to paragraph (2), where a producer or a distributor knows that a product he has placed on the market or supplied poses risks to the consumer that are incompatible with the general safety requirement, he shall forthwith notify an enforcement authority in writing of that information and—

(a)   the action taken to prevent risk to the consumer; and

(b)   where the product is being or has been marketed or otherwise supplied to consumers outside the United Kingdom, of the identity of each Member State in which, to the best of his knowledge, it is being or has been so marketed or supplied.

(2)   Paragraph (1) shall not apply—

(a)   in the case of a second-hand product supplied as an antique or as a product to be repaired or reconditioned prior to being used, provided the supplier clearly informed the person to whom he supplied the product to that effect,

(b)   in conditions concerning isolated circumstances or products.

(3)   In the event of a serious risk the notification under paragraph (1) shall include the following—

(a)   information enabling a precise identification of the product or batch of products in question,

(b)   a full description of the risks that the product presents,

(c)   all available information relevant for tracing the product, and

(d)   a description of the action undertaken to prevent risks to the consumer.

(4)   Within the limits of his activities, a person who is a producer or a distributor shall co-operate with an enforcement authority (at the enforcement authority's request) in action taken to avoid the risks posed by a product which he supplies or has supplied. Every enforcement authority shall maintain procedures for such co-operation, including procedures for dialogue with the producers and distributors concerned on issues related to product safety.

PART 3. ENFORCEMENT

10   Enforcement

(1)   It shall be the duty of every authority to which paragraph (4) applies to enforce within its area these Regulations and safety notices.

(2)   An authority in England or Wales to which paragraph (4) applies shall have the power to investigate and prosecute for an alleged contravention of any provision imposed by or under these Regulations which was committed outside its area in any part of England and Wales.

(3)   A district council in Northern Ireland shall have the power to investigate and prosecute for an alleged contravention of any provision imposed by or under these Regulations which was committed outside its area in any part of Northern Ireland.

(4)   The authorities to which this paragraph applies are:

(a)   in England, a county council, district council, London Borough Council, the Common Council of the City of London in its capacity as a local authority and the Council of the Isles of Scilly,

(b)   in Wales, a county council or a county borough council,

(c)   in Scotland, a council constituted under section 2 of the Local Government etc (Scotland) Act 1994,

(d)   in Northern Ireland any district council.

(5)   An enforcement authority shall in enforcing these Regulations act in a manner proportionate to the seriousness of the risk and shall take due account of the precautionary principle. In this context, it shall encourage and promote voluntary action by producers and distributors. Notwithstanding the foregoing, an enforcement authority may take any action under these Regulations urgently and without first encouraging and promoting voluntary action if a product poses a serious risk.

11   Suspension notices

(1)   Where an enforcement authority has reasonable grounds for suspecting that a requirement of these Regulations has been contravened in relation to a product, the authority may, for the period needed to organise appropriate safety evaluations, checks and controls, serve a notice ('a suspension notice') prohibiting the person on whom it is served from doing any of the following things without the consent of the authority, that is to say—

(a)   placing the product on the market, offering to place it on the market, agreeing to place it on the market or exposing it for placing on the market, or

(b)   supplying the product, offering to supply it, agreeing to supply it or exposing it for supply.

(2)   A suspension notice served by an enforcement authority in relation to a product may require the person on whom it is served to keep the authority informed of the whereabouts of any such product in which he has an interest.

(3)   A consent given by the enforcement authority for the purposes of paragraph (1) may impose such conditions on the doing of anything for which the consent is required as the authority considers appropriate.

12   Requirements to mark

(1)   Where an enforcement authority has reasonable grounds for believing that a product is a dangerous product in that it could pose risks in certain conditions, the authority may serve a notice ('a requirement to mark') requiring the person on whom the notice is served at his own expense to undertake either or both of the following, as specified in the notice—

(a)   to ensure that the product is marked in accordance with requirements specified in the notice with warnings as to the risks it may present,

(b)   to make the marketing of the product subject to prior conditions as specified in the notice so as to ensure the product is a safe product.

(2)   The requirements referred to in paragraph (1)(a) shall be such as to ensure that the product is marked with a warning which is suitable, clearly worded and easily comprehensible.

13   Requirements to warn

Where an enforcement authority has reasonable grounds for believing that a product is a dangerous product in that it could pose risks for certain persons, the authority may serve a notice ('a requirement to warn') requiring the person on whom the notice is served at his own expense to undertake one or more of the following, as specified in the notice—

(a)   where and to the extent it is practicable to do so, to ensure that any person who could be subject to such risks and who has been supplied with the product be given warning of the risks in good time and in a form specified in the notice,

(b)   to publish a warning of the risks in such form and manner as is likely to bring those risks to the attention of any such person,

(c)   to ensure that the product carries a warning of the risks in a form specified in the notice.

14   Withdrawal notices

(1)   Where an enforcement authority has reasonable grounds for believing that a product is a dangerous product, the authority may serve a notice ('a withdrawal notice') prohibiting the person on whom it is served from doing any of the following things without the consent of the authority, that is to say—

(a)   placing the product on the market, offering to place it on the market, agreeing to place it on the market or exposing it for placing on the market, or

(b)   supplying the product, offering to supply it, agreeing to supply it or exposing it for supply.

(2)   A withdrawal notice may require the person on whom it is served to take action to alert consumers to the risks that the product presents.

(3)   In relation to a product that is already on the market, a withdrawal notice may only be served by an enforcement authority where the action being undertaken by the producer or the distributor concerned in fulfilment of his obligations under these Regulations is unsatisfactory or insufficient to prevent the risks concerned to the health and safety of persons.

(4)   Paragraph (3) shall not apply in the case of a product posing a serious risk requiring, in the view of the enforcement authority, urgent action.

(5)   A withdrawal notice served by an enforcement authority in relation to

a product may require the person on whom it is served to keep the authority informed of the whereabouts of any such product in which he has an interest.

(6) A consent given by the enforcement authority for the purposes of paragraph (1) may impose such conditions on the doing of anything for which the consent is required as the authority considers appropriate.

15 Recall notices

(1) Subject to paragraph (4), where an enforcement authority has reasonable grounds for believing that a product is a dangerous product and that it has already been supplied or made available to consumers, the authority may serve a notice ('a recall notice') requiring the person on whom it is served to use his reasonable endeavours to organise the return of the product from consumers to that person or to such other person as is specified in the notice.

(2) A recall notice may require—

    (a) the recall to be effected in accordance with a code of practice applicable to the product concerned, or

    (b) the recipient of the recall notice to—

        (i) contact consumers who have purchased the product in order to inform them of the recall, where and to the extent it is practicable to do so,

        (ii) publish a notice in such form and such manner as is likely to bring to the attention of purchasers of the product the risk the product poses and the fact of the recall, or

        (iii) make arrangements for the collection or return of the product from consumers who have purchased it or for its disposal,

and may impose such additional requirements on the recipient of the notice as are reasonable and practicable with a view to achieving the return of the product from consumers to the person specified in the notice or its disposal.

(3) In determining what requirements to include in a recall notice, the enforcement authority shall take into consideration the need to encourage distributors, users and consumers to contribute to its implementation.

(4) A recall notice may only be issued by an enforcement authority where—

    (a) other action which it may require under these Regulations would not suffice to prevent the risks concerned to the health and safety of persons,

    (b) the action being undertaken by the producer or the distributor concerned in fulfilment of his obligations under these Regulations is unsatisfactory or insufficient to prevent the risks concerned to the health and safety of persons, and

    (c) the authority has given not less than seven days' notice to the person on whom the recall notice is to be served of its intention to serve such a notice and where that person has before the expiry of that period by notice required the authority to seek the advice of such person as the Institute determines on the questions of—

        (i) whether the product is a dangerous product,

        (ii) whether the issue of a recall notice is proportionate to the seriousness of the risk,

and the authority has taken account of such advice.

(5) Paragraphs (4)(b) and (c) shall not apply in the case of a product posing a serious risk requiring, in the view of the enforcement authority, urgent action.

(6) Where a person requires an enforcement authority to seek advice as referred to in paragraph (4)(c), that person shall be responsible for the fees, costs and expenses of the Institute and of the person appointed by the Institute to advise the authority.

(7) In paragraphs 4(c) and (6) 'the Institute' means the charitable organisation with registered number 803725 and known as the Chartered Institute of Arbitrators.

(8) A recall notice served by an enforcement authority in relation to a product may require the person on whom it is served to keep the authority informed of the whereabouts of any such product to which the recall notice relates, so far as he is able to do so.

(9) Where the conditions in paragraph (1) for serving a recall notice are satisfied and either the enforcement authority has been unable to identify any person on whom to serve a recall notice, or the person on whom such a notice has been served has failed to comply with it, then the authority may itself take such action as could have been required by a recall notice.

(10) Where—

(a) an authority has complied with the requirements of paragraph (4); and

(b) the authority has exercised its powers under paragraph (9) to take action following the failure of the person on whom the recall notice has been served to comply with that notice,

then the authority may recover from the person on whom the notice was served summarily as a civil debt, any costs or expenses reasonably incurred by it in undertaking the action referred to in sub-paragraph (b).

(11) A civil debt recoverable under the preceding paragraph may be recovered—

(a) in England and Wales by way of complaint (as mentioned in section 58 of the Magistrates' Courts Act 1980,

(b) in Northern Ireland in proceedings under Article 62 of the Magistrates' Courts (Northern Ireland) Order 1981.

16 Supplementary provisions relating to safety notices

(1) Whenever feasible, prior to serving a safety notice the authority shall give an opportunity to the person on whom the notice is to be served to submit his views to the authority. Where, due to the urgency of the situation, this is not feasible the person shall be given an opportunity to submit his views to the authority after service of the notice.

(2) A safety notice served by an enforcement authority in respect of a product shall—

(a) describe the product in a manner sufficient to identify it;

(b) state the reasons on which the notice is based;

(c) indicate the rights available to the recipient of the notice under these Regulations and (where applicable) the time limits applying to their exercise; and

(d) in the case of a suspension notice, state the period of time for which it applies.

(3) A safety notice shall have effect throughout the United Kingdom.

(4) Where an enforcement authority serves a suspension notice in respect of a product, the authority shall be liable to pay compensation to a person having an interest in the product in respect of any loss or damage suffered by reason of the notice if—

(a) there has been no contravention of any requirement of these Regulations in relation to the product; and

(b) the exercise by the authority of the power to serve the suspension notice was not attributable to any neglect or default by that person.

(5) Where an enforcement authority serves a withdrawal notice in respect of a product, the authority shall be liable to pay compensation to a person having an interest in the product in respect of any loss or damage suffered by reason of the notice if—

(a) the product was not a dangerous product; and

(b) the exercise by the authority of the power to serve the withdrawal notice was not attributable to any neglect or default by that person.

(6) Where an enforcement authority serves a recall notice in respect of a product, the authority shall be liable to pay compensation to the person on whom the

notice was served in respect of any loss or damage suffered by reason of the notice if—

(a)   the product was not a dangerous product; and

(b)   the exercise by the authority of the power to serve the recall notice was not attributable to any neglect or default by that person.

(7)   An enforcement authority may vary or revoke a safety notice which it has served provided that the notice is not made more restrictive for the person on whom it is served or more onerous for that person to comply with.

(8)   Wherever feasible prior to varying a safety notice the authority shall give an opportunity to the person on whom the original notice was served to submit his views to the authority.

17   Appeals against safety notices

(1)   A person on whom a safety notice has been served and a person having an interest in a product in respect of which a safety notice (other than a recall notice) has been served may, before the end of the period of 21 days beginning with the day on which the notice was served, apply for an order to vary or set aside the terms of the notice.

(2)   On an application under paragraph (1) the court or the sheriff, as the case may be, shall make an order setting aside the notice only if satisfied that—

(a)   in the case of a suspension notice, there has been no contravention in relation to the product of any requirement of these Regulations,

(b)   in the case of a requirement to mark or a requirement to warn, the product is not a dangerous product,

(c)   in the case of a withdrawal notice—

(i)   the product is not a dangerous product, or

(ii)   where applicable, regulation 14(3) has not been complied with by the enforcement authority concerned,

(d)   in the case of a recall notice—

(i)   the product is not a dangerous product, or

(ii)   regulation 15(4) has not been complied with,

(e)   in any case, the serving of the safety notice concerned was not proportionate to the seriousness of the risk.

(3)   On an application concerning the period of time specified in a suspension notice as the period for which it applies, the court or the sheriff, as the case may be, may reduce the period to such period as it considers sufficient for organising appropriate safety evaluations, checks and controls.

(4)   On an application to vary the terms of a notice, the court or the sheriff, as the case may be, may vary the requirements specified in the notice as it considers appropriate.

(5)   A person on whom a recall notice has been served and who proposes to make an application under paragraph (1) in relation to the notice may, before the end of the period of seven days beginning with the day on which the notice was served, apply to the court or the sheriff for an order suspending the effect of the notice and the court or the sheriff may, in any case where it considers it appropriate to do so, make an order suspending the effect of the notice.

(6)   If the court or the sheriff makes an order suspending the effect of a recall notice under paragraph (5) in the absence of the enforcement authority, the enforcement authority may apply for the revocation of such order.

(7)   An order under paragraph (5) shall take effect from the time it is made until—

(a)   it is revoked under paragraph (6),

(b)   where no application is made under paragraph (1) in respect of the recall notice within the time specified in that paragraph, the expiration of that time,

(c)   where such an application is made but is withdrawn or dismissed for want of prosecution, the date of dismissal or withdrawal of the application, or

(d)   where such an application is made and is not withdrawn or dismissed for want of prosecution, the determination of the application.

(8)   Subject to paragraph (6), in Scotland the sheriff's decision under paragraph (5) shall be final.

(9)   An application under this regulation may be made—

(a)   by way of complaint to any magistrates' court in which proceedings have been brought in England and Wales or Northern Ireland—

(i)   in respect of a contravention in relation to the product of a requirement imposed by or under these Regulations; or

(ii)   for the forfeiture of the product under regulation 18;

(b)   where no such proceedings have been brought, by way of complaint to any magistrates' court; or

(c)   in Scotland, by summary application to the sheriff.

(10)   A person aggrieved by an order made pursuant to an application under paragraph (1) by a magistrates' court in England, Wales or Northern Ireland, or by a decision of such a court not to make such an order, may appeal against that order or decision—

(a)   in England and Wales, to the Crown Court;

(b)   in Northern Ireland, to the county court.

[**18**   *Does not apply to Scotland*]

19   Forfeiture: Scotland

(1)   In Scotland a sheriff may make an order for forfeiture of a product on the grounds that the product is a dangerous product—

(a)   on an application by a procurator-fiscal made in the manner specified in section 134 of the Criminal Procedure (Scotland) Act 1995, or

(b)   where a person is convicted of any offence in respect of a contravention in relation to the product of a requirement imposed by or under these Regulations, in addition to any other penalty which the sheriff may impose.

(2)   The procurator-fiscal making an application under paragraph (1)(a) shall serve on any person appearing to him to be the owner of, or otherwise to have an interest in, the product to which the application relates a copy of the application, together with a notice giving him the opportunity to appear at the hearing of the application to show cause why the product should not be forfeited.

(3)   Service under paragraph (2) shall be carried out, and such service may be proved, in the manner specified for citation of an accused in summary proceedings under the Criminal Procedure (Scotland) Act 1995.

(4)   A person upon whom notice is served under paragraph (2) and any other person claiming to be the owner of, or otherwise to have an interest in, the product to which the application relates shall be entitled to appear at the hearing of the application to show cause why the product should not be forfeited.

(5)   The sheriff shall not make an order following an application under paragraph (1)(a)—

(a)   if any person on whom notice is served under paragraph (2) does not appear, unless service of the notice on that person is proved; or

(b)   if no notice under paragraph (2) has been served, unless the sheriff is satisfied that in the circumstances it was reasonable not to serve notice on any person.

(6)   The sheriff may make an order under this regulation only if he is satisfied that the product is a dangerous product.

(7)   Where an order for the forfeiture of a product is made following an application by the procurator-fiscal under paragraph (1)(a), any person who appeared, or was entitled to appear to show cause why the product should not be forfeited may, within twenty-one days of the making of the order, appeal to the High Court by Bill of Suspension on the ground of an alleged miscarriage of justice; and sec-

tion 182(5)(a) to (e) of the Criminal Procedure (Scotland) Act 1995 shall apply to an appeal under this paragraph as it applies to a stated case under Part X of that Act.

(8) An order following an application under paragraph (1)(a) shall not take effect—

(a) until the end of the period of twenty-one days beginning with the day after the day on which the order is made; or

(b) if an appeal is made under paragraph (7) within that period, until the appeal is determined or abandoned.

(9) An order under paragraph (1)(b) shall not take effect—

(a) until the end of the period within which an appeal against the order could be brought under the Criminal Procedure (Scotland) Act 1995; or

(b) if an appeal is made within that period, until the appeal is determined or abandoned.

(10) Subject to paragraph (11), a product forfeited under this regulation shall be destroyed in accordance with such directions as the sheriff may give.

(11) If he thinks fit, the sheriff may direct that the product be released to such person as he may specify, on condition that that person does not supply the product to any other person otherwise than as mentioned in paragraph (11) of regulation 18.

20 Offences

(1) A person who contravenes regulations 5 or 8(1)(a) shall be guilty of an offence and liable on conviction on indictment to imprisonment for a term not exceeding 12 months or to a fine not exceeding £20,000 or to both, or on summary conviction to imprisonment for a term not exceeding three months or to a fine not exceeding the statutory maximum or to both.

(2) A person who contravenes regulation 7(1), 7(3) (by failing to take any of the measures specified in regulation 7(4)), 8(1)(b)(i), (ii) or (iii) or 9(1) shall be guilty of an offence and liable on summary conviction to imprisonment for a term not exceeding three months or to a fine not exceeding level 5 on the standard scale or to both.

(3) A producer or distributor who does not give notice to an enforcement authority under regulation 9(1) in respect of a product he has placed on the market or supplied commits an offence where it is proved that he ought to have known that the product poses risks to consumers that are incompatible with the general safety requirement and he shall be liable on summary conviction to imprisonment for a term not exceeding three months or to a fine not exceeding level 5 on the standard scale or to both.

(4) A person who contravenes a safety notice shall be guilty of an offence and liable on conviction on indictment to imprisonment for a term not exceeding 12 months or to a fine not exceeding £20,000 or to both, or on summary conviction to imprisonment for a term not exceeding three months or to a fine not exceeding the statutory maximum or to both.

21 Test purchases

(1) An enforcement authority shall have power to organise appropriate checks on the safety properties of a product, on an adequate scale, up to the final stage of use or consumption and for that purpose may make a purchase of a product or authorise an officer of the authority to make a purchase of a product.

(2) Where a product purchased under paragraph (1) is submitted to a test and the test leads to—

(a) the bringing of proceedings for an offence in respect of a contravention in relation to the product of any requirement imposed by or under these Regulations or for the forfeiture of the product under regulation 18 or 19, or

(b) the serving of a safety notice in respect of the product, and

(c) the authority is requested to do so and it is practicable for the authority to comply with the request, then the authority shall allow the person from whom the product was purchased, a person who is a party to the proceedings, on whom the notice was served or who has an interest in the product to which the notice relates, to have the product tested.

22 Powers of entry and search etc

(1)   An officer of an enforcement authority may at any reasonable hour and on production, if required, of his credentials exercise any of the powers conferred by the following provisions of this regulation.

(2)   The officer may, for the purposes of ascertaining whether there has been a contravention of a requirement imposed by or under these Regulations, enter any premises other than premises occupied only as a person's residence and inspect any record or product.

(3)   The officer may, for the purpose of ascertaining whether there has been a contravention of a requirement imposed by or under these Regulations, examine any procedure (including any arrangements for carrying out a test) connected with the production of a product.

(4)   If the officer has reasonable grounds for suspecting that the product has not been placed on the market or supplied in the United Kingdom since it was manufactured or imported he may for the purpose of ascertaining whether there has been a contravention in relation to the product of a requirement imposed by or under these Regulations—

(a)   require a person carrying on a commercial activity, or employed in connection with a commercial activity, to supply all necessary information relating to the activity, including by the production of records,

(b)   require any record which is stored in an electronic form and is accessible from the premises to be produced in a form —

(i)   in which it can be taken away, and

(ii)   in which it is visible and legible.

(c)   for the purpose of ascertaining (by testing or otherwise) whether there has been any such contravention, seize and detain samples of the product,

(d)   take copies of, or of an entry in, any records produced by virtue of sub-paragraph (a).

(5)   If the officer has reasonable grounds for suspecting that there has been a contravention in relation to a product of a requirement imposed by or under these Regulations, he may—

(a)   for the purpose of ascertaining whether there has been any such contravention, require a person carrying on a commercial activity, or employed in connection with a commercial activity, to supply all necessary information relating to the activity, including by the production of records,

(b)   for the purpose of ascertaining whether there has been any such contravention, require any record which is stored in an electronic form and is accessible from the premises to be produced in a form—

(i)   in which it can be taken away, and

(ii)   in which it is visible and legible,

(c)   for the purpose of ascertaining (by testing or otherwise) whether there has been any such contravention, seize and detain samples of the product,

(d)   take copies of, or of an entry in, any records produced by virtue of sub-paragraph (a).

(6)   The officer may seize and detain any products or records which he has reasonable grounds for believing may be required as evidence in proceedings for an offence in respect of a contravention of any requirement imposed by or under these Regulations.

(7)   If and to the extent that it is reasonably necessary to do so to prevent a contravention of any requirement imposed by or under these Regulations, the

officer may, for the purpose of exercising his power under paragraphs (4) to (6) to seize products or records—

(a)   require any person having authority to do so to open any container or to open any vending machine; and

(b)   himself open or break open any such container or machine where a requirement made under sub-paragraph (a) in relation to the container or machine has not been complied with.

23   Provisions supplemental to regulation 22 and search warrants etc

(1)   An officer seizing any products or records shall, before he leaves the premises, provide to the person from whom they were seized a written notice—

(a)   specifying the products (including the quantity thereof) and records seized,

(b)   stating the reasons for their seizure, and

(c)   explaining the right of appeal under regulation 25.

(2)   References in paragraph (1) and regulation 25 to the person from whom something has been seized, in relation to a case in which the power of seizure was exercisable by reason of the product having been found on any premises, are references to the occupier of the premises at the time of the seizure.

(3)   If a justice of the peace—

(a)   is satisfied by written information on oath that there are reasonable grounds for believing either—

(i)   that any products or records which an officer has power to inspect under regulation 22 are on any premises and that their inspection is likely to disclose evidence that there has been a contravention of any requirement imposed by or under these Regulations, or

(ii)   that such a contravention has taken place, is taking place or is about to take place on any premises, and

(b)   is also satisfied by such information either—

(i)   that admission to the premises has been or is likely to be refused and that notice of the intention to apply for a warrant under this paragraph has been given to the occupier, or

(ii)   that an application for admission, or the giving of such a notice, would defeat the object of the entry or that the premises are unoccupied or that the occupier is temporarily absent and it might defeat the object of the entry to await his return,

the justice may by warrant under his hand, which shall continue in force for a period of one month, authorise any officer of an enforcement authority to enter the premises, if need be by force.

(4)   An officer entering premises by virtue of regulation 22 or a warrant under paragraph (3) may take with him such other persons and equipment as may appear to him necessary.

(5)   On leaving any premises which a person is authorised to enter by a warrant under paragraph (3), that person shall, if the premises are unoccupied or the occupier is temporarily absent—

(a)   leave the premises as effectively secured against trespassers as he found them,

(b)   attach a notice such as is mentioned in paragraph (1) in a prominent place at the premises.

(6)   Where a product seized by an officer of an enforcement authority under regulation 22 or 23 is submitted to a test, the authority shall inform the person mentioned in paragraph (1) of the result of the test and, if—

(a)   proceedings are brought for an offence in respect of a contravention in relation to the product of any requirement imposed by or under these Regulations or for the forfeiture of the product under regulation 18 or 19; or

(b)   a safety notice is served in respect of the product; and

(c)   the authority is requested to do so and it is practicable for him to comply with the request,

then the authority shall allow a person who is a party to the proceedings or on whom the notice was served or who has an interest in the product to which the notice relates to have the product tested.

(7)   If a person who is not an officer of an enforcement authority purports to act as such under regulation 22 or under this regulation he shall be guilty of an offence and liable on summary conviction to a fine not exceeding level 5 on the standard scale.

(8)   In the application of this section to Scotland, the reference in paragraph (3) to a justice of the peace shall include a reference to a sheriff and the reference to written information on oath shall be construed as a reference to evidence on oath.

(9)   In the application of this section to Northern Ireland, the reference in paragraph (3) to a justice of the peace shall include a reference to a lay magistrate and the references to an information on oath shall be construed as a reference to a complaint on oath.

24   Obstruction of officers

(1)   A person who—

(a)   intentionally obstructs an officer of an enforcement authority who is acting in pursuance of any provision of regulation 22 or 23; or

(b)   intentionally fails to comply with a requirement made of him by an officer of an enforcement authority under any provision of those regulations; or

(c)   without reasonable cause fails to give an officer of an enforcement authority who is so acting any other assistance or information which the officer may reasonably require of him for the purposes of the exercise of the officer's functions under any provision of those regulations,

shall be guilty of an offence and liable on summary conviction to a fine not exceeding level 5 on the standard scale.

(2)   A person shall be guilty of an offence if, in giving any information which is required by him by virtue of paragraph (1)(c)—

(a)   he makes a statement which he knows is false in a material particular; or

(b)   he recklessly makes a statement which is false in a material particular.

(3)   A person guilty of an offence under paragraph (2) shall be liable—

(a)   on conviction on indictment, to a fine;

(b)   on summary conviction, to a fine not exceeding the statutory maximum.

25   Appeals against detention of products and records

(1)   A person referred to in regulation 23(1) may apply for an order requiring any product or record which is for the time being detained under regulation 22 or 23 by an enforcement authority or by an officer of such an authority to be released to him or to another person.

(2)   An application under the preceding paragraph may be made—

(a)   to any magistrates' court in which proceedings have been brought in England and Wales or Northern Ireland—

(i)   for an offence in respect of a contravention in relation to the product of a requirement imposed by or under these Regulations, or

(ii)   for the forfeiture of the product under regulation 18,

(b)   where no such proceedings have been brought, by way of complaint to a magistrates' court;

(c)   in Scotland, by summary application to the sheriff.

(3)   On an application under paragraph (1) to a magistrates' court or to the sheriff, the court or the sheriff may make an order requiring a product or record to be released only if the court or sheriff is satisfied—

(a)   that proceedings—

(i)   for an offence in respect of any contravention in relation to the product or, in the case of a record, the product to which the record relates, of any requirement imposed by or under these Regulations; or

    (ii) for the forfeiture of the product or, in the case of a record, the product to which the record relates, under regulation 18 or 19,

have not been brought or, having been brought, have been concluded without the product being forfeited; and

    (b) where no such proceedings have been brought, that more than six months have elapsed since the product or records was seized.

(4) In determining whether to make an order under this regulation requiring the release of a product or record the court or sheriff shall take all the circumstances into account including the results of any tests on the product which have been carried out by or on behalf of the enforcement authority and any statement made by the enforcement authority to the court or sheriff as to its intention to bring proceedings for an offence in respect of a contravention in relation to the product of any requirement imposed by or under these Regulations.

(5) Where—

    (a) more than 12 months have elapsed since a product or records were seized and the enforcement authority has not commenced proceedings for an offence in respect of a contravention in relation to the product (or, in the case of records, the product to which the records relate) of any requirement imposed by or under these Regulations or for the forfeiture of the product under regulation 18 or 19, or

    (b) an enforcement authority has brought proceedings for an offence as mentioned in sub-paragraph (a) and the proceedings were dismissed and all rights of appeal have been exercised or the time for appealing has expired,

the authority shall be under a duty to return the product or records detained under regulation 22 or 23 to the person from whom they were seized.

(6) Where the authority is satisfied that some other person has a better right to a product or record than the person from whom it was seized, the authority shall, instead of the duty in paragraph (5), be under a duty to return it to that other person or, as the case may be, to the person appearing to the authority to have the best right to the product or record in question.

(7) Where different persons claim to be entitled to the return of a product or record that is required to be returned under paragraph (5), then it may be retained for as long as is reasonably necessary for the determination in accordance with paragraph (6) of the person to whom it must be returned.

(8) A person aggrieved by an order made under this regulation by a magistrates' court in England and Wales or Northern Ireland, or by a decision of such a court not to make such an order, may appeal against that order or decision—

    (a) in England and Wales, to the Crown Court;

    (b) in Northern Ireland, to the county court;

and an order so made may contain such provision as appears to the court to be appropriate for delaying the coming into force of the order pending the making and determination of any appeal (including any application under section 111 of the Magistrates' Courts Act 1980 or article 146 of the Magistrates' Courts (Northern Ireland) Order 1981 (statement of case)).

26 Compensation for seizure and detention

Where an officer of an enforcement authority exercises any power under regulation 22 or 23 to seize and detain a product, the enforcement authority shall be liable to pay compensation to any person having an interest in the product in respect of any loss or damage caused by reason of the exercise of the power if—

    (a) there has been no contravention in relation to the product of any requirement imposed by or under these Regulations, and

    (b) the exercise of the power is not attributable to any neglect or default by that person.

27   Recovery of expenses of enforcement

(1)   This regulation shall apply where a court—

(a)   convicts a person of an offence in respect of a contravention in relation to a product of any requirement imposed by or under these Regulations, or

(b)   makes an order under regulation 18 or 19 for the forfeiture of a product.

(2)   The court may (in addition to any other order it may make as to costs or expenses) order the person convicted or, as the case may be, any person having an interest in the product to reimburse an enforcement authority for any expenditure which has been or may be incurred by that authority—

(a)   in connection with any seizure or detention of the product by or on behalf of the authority, or

(b)   in connection with any compliance by the authority with directions given by the court for the purposes of any order for the forfeiture of the product.

28   Power of Secretary of State to obtain information

(1)   If the Secretary of State considers that, for the purposes of deciding whether to serve a safety notice, or to vary or revoke a safety notice which he has already served, he requires information or a sample of a product he may serve on a person a notice requiring him—

(a)   to furnish to the Secretary of State, within a period specified in the notice, such information as is specified;

(b)   to produce such records as are specified in the notice at a time and place so specified (and to produce any such records which are stored in any electronic form in a form in which they are visible and legible) and to permit a person appointed by the Secretary of State for that purpose to take copies of the records at that time and place;

(c)   to produce such samples of a product as are specified in the notice at a time and place so specified.

(2)   A person shall be guilty of an offence if he—

(a)   fails, without reasonable cause, to comply with a notice served on him under paragraph (1); or

(b)   in purporting to comply with a requirement which by virtue of paragraph (1)(a) or (b) is contained in such a notice—

(i)   furnishes information or records which he knows are false in a material particular, or

(ii)   recklessly furnishes information or records which are false in a material particular.

(3)   A person guilty of an offence under paragraph (2) shall—

(a)   in the case of an offence under sub-paragraph (a) of that paragraph, be liable on summary conviction to a fine not exceeding level 5 on the standard scale; and

(b)   in the case of an offence under sub-paragraph (b) of that paragraph, be liable—

(i)   on conviction on indictment, to a fine;

(ii)   on summary conviction, to a fine not exceeding the statutory maximum.

29   Defence of due diligence

(1)   Subject to the following provisions of this regulation, in proceedings against a person for an offence under these Regulations it shall be a defence for that person to show that he took all reasonable steps and exercised all due diligence to avoid committing the offence.

(2)   Where in any proceedings against any person for such an offence the defence provided by paragraph (1) involves an allegation that the commission of the offence was due—

(a)   to the act or default of another, or

(b)   to reliance on information given by another,

that person shall not, without the leave of the court, be entitled to rely on the defence unless, not less than seven clear days before, in England, Wales and Northern Ireland, the hearing of the proceedings or, in Scotland, the trial diet, he has served a notice under paragraph (3) on the person bringing the proceedings.

(3)   A notice under this paragraph shall give such information identifying or assisting in the identification of the person who—

(a)   committed the act or default, or

(b)   gave the information,

as is in the possession of the person serving the notice at the time he serves it.

(4)   A person may not rely on the defence provided by paragraph (1) by reason of his reliance on information supplied by another, unless he shows that it was reasonable in all the circumstances to have relied on the information, having regard in particular—

(a)   to the steps which he took, and those which might reasonably have been taken, for the purpose of verifying the information; and

(b)   to whether he had any reason to disbelieve the information.

30   Defence in relation to antiques

(1)   This regulation shall apply in proceedings against any person for an offence under regulation 20(1) in respect of the supply, offer or agreement to supply or exposure or possession for supply of second hand products supplied as antiques.

(2)   It shall be a defence for that person to show that the terms on which he supplied the product or agreed or offered to supply the product or, in the case of a product which he exposed or possessed for supply, the terms on which he intended to supply the product, contemplated the acquisition of an interest in the product by the person supplied or to be supplied.

(3)   Paragraph (2) applies only if the producer or distributor clearly informed the person to whom he supplied the product, or offered or agreed to supply the product or, in the case of a product which he exposed or possessed for supply, he intended to so inform that person, that the product is an antique.

31   Liability of person other than principal offender

(1)   Where the commission by a person of an offence under these Regulations is due to an act or default committed by some other person in the course of a commercial activity of his, the other person shall be guilty of the offence and may be proceeded against and punished by virtue of this paragraph whether or not proceedings are taken against the first-mentioned person.

(2)   Where a body corporate is guilty of an offence under these Regulations (including where it is so guilty by virtue of paragraph (1)) in respect of any act or default which is shown to have been committed with the consent or connivance of, or to be attributable to any neglect on the part of, any director, manager, secretary or other similar officer of the body corporate or any person who was purporting to act in any such capacity he, as well as the body corporate, shall be guilty of that offence and shall be liable to be proceeded against and punished accordingly.

(3)   Where the affairs of a body corporate are managed by its members, paragraph (2) shall apply in relation to the acts and defaults of a member in connection with his functions of management as if he were a director of the body corporate.

(4)   Where a Scottish partnership is guilty of an offence under these Regulations (including where it is so guilty by virtue of paragraph (1)) in respect of any act or default which is shown to have been committed with the consent or connivance of, or to be attributable to any neglect on the part of, a partner in the partnership, he, as well as the partnership, shall be guilty of that offence and shall be liable to be proceeded against and punished accordingly.

PART 4. MISCELLANEOUS

32 Reports

(1) It shall be the duty of the Secretary of State to lay before each House of Parliament a report on the exercise during the period to which the report relates of the functions which are exercisable by enforcement authorities under these Regulations.

(2) The first such report shall relate to the period beginning on the day on which these Regulations come into force and ending on 31 March 2008 and subsequent reports shall relate to a period of not more than five years beginning on the day after the day on which the period to which the previous report relates ends.

(3) The Secretary of State may from time to time prepare and lay before each House of Parliament such other reports on the exercise of those functions as he considers appropriate.

(4) The Secretary of State may direct an enforcement authority to report at such intervals as he may specify in the direction on the discharge by that authority of the functions exercisable by it under these Regulations.

(5) A report under paragraph (4) shall be in such form and shall contain such particulars as are specified in the direction of the Secretary of State.

33 Duty to notify Secretary of State and Commission

(1) An enforcement authority which has received a notification under regulation 9(1) shall immediately pass the same on to the Secretary of State, who shall immediately pass it on to the competent authorities appointed for the purpose in the Member States where the product in question is or has been marketed or otherwise supplied to consumers.

(2) Where an enforcement authority takes a measure which restricts the placing on the market of a product, or requires its withdrawal or recall, it shall immediately notify the Secretary of State, specifying its reasons for taking the action. It shall also immediately notify the Secretary of State of any modification or lifting of such a measure.

(3) On receiving a notification under paragraph (2), or if he takes a measure which restricts the placing on the market of a product, or requires its withdrawal or recall, the Secretary of State shall (to the extent that such notification is not required under article 12 of the GPS Directive or any other Community legislation) immediately notify the European Commission of the measure taken, specifying the reasons for taking it. The Secretary of State shall also immediately notify the European Commission of any modification or lifting of such a measure. If the Secretary of State considers that the effects of the risk do not or cannot go beyond the territory of the United Kingdom, he shall notify the European Commission of the measure concerned insofar as it involves information likely to be of interest to Member States from the product safety standpoint, and in particular if it is in response to a new risk which has not yet been reported in other notifications.

(4) Where an enforcement authority adopts or decides to adopt, recommend or agree with producers and distributors, whether on a compulsory or voluntary basis, a measure or action to prevent, restrict or impose specific conditions on the possible marketing or use of a product (other than a pharmaceutical product) by reason of a serious risk, it shall immediately notify the Secretary of State. It shall also immediately notify the Secretary of State of any modification or withdrawal of any such measure or action.

(5) On receiving a notification under paragraph (4), or if he adopts or decides to adopt, recommend or agree with producers and distributors, whether on a compulsory or voluntary basis, a measure or action to prevent, restrict or impose specific conditions on the possible marketing or use of a product (other than a pharmaceutical product) by reason of a serious risk, the Secretary of State shall

immediately notify the European Commission of it through the Community Rapid Information System, known as RAPEX. The Secretary of State shall also inform the European Commission without delay of any modification or withdrawal of any such measure or action.

(6) If the Secretary of State considers that the effects of the risk do not or cannot go beyond the territory of the United Kingdom, he shall notify the European Commission of the measures or action concerned insofar as they involve information likely to be of interest to Member States of the European Union from the product safety standpoint, and in particular if they are in response to a new risk which has not been reported in other notifications.

(7) Before deciding to adopt such a measure or take such an action as is referred to in paragraph (5), the Secretary of State may pass on to the European Commission any information in his possession regarding the existence of a serious risk. Where he does so, he must inform the European Commission, within 45 days of the day of passing the information to it, whether he confirms or modifies that information.

(8) Upon receipt of a notification from the European Commission under article 12(2) of the GPS Directive, the Secretary of State shall notify the Commission of the following—

(a) whether the product the subject of the notification has been marketed in the United Kingdom;

(b) what measure concerning the product the enforcement authorities in the United Kingdom may be adopting, stating the reasons, including any differing assessment of risk or any other special circumstance justifying the decision as to the measure, in particular lack of action or follow-up; and

(c) any relevant supplementary information he has obtained on the risk involved, including the results of any test or analysis carried out.

(9) The Secretary of State shall notify the European Commission without delay of any modification or withdrawal of any measures notified to it under paragraph (8)(b).

(10) In this regulation—

(a) references to a product excludes a second hand product supplied as an antique or as a product to be repaired or reconditioned prior to being used, provided the supplier clearly informs the person to whom he supplies the product to that effect;

(b) 'pharmaceutical product' means a product falling within Council Directive 2001/83/EC of the European Parliament and of the Council on the Community code relating to medicinal products for human use.

34 Provisions supplemental to regulation 33

(1) A notification under regulation 33(2) to (6), (8) or (9) to the Secretary of State or the Commission shall be in writing and shall provide all available details and at least the following information—

(a) information enabling the product to be identified,

(b) a description of the risk involved, including a summary of the results of any test or analysis and of their conclusions which are relevant to assessing the level of risk,

(c) the nature and the duration of the measures or action taken or decided on, if applicable,

(d) information on supply chains and distribution of the product, in particular on destination countries.

(2) Where a measure notified to the Commission under regulation 33 seeks to limit the marketing or use of a chemical substance or preparation, the Secretary of State shall provide to the Commission as soon as possible either a summary or the references of the relevant data relating to the substance or preparation considered and to known and available substitutes, where such information is available. The

Secretary of State shall also notify the Commission of the anticipated effects of the measure on consumer health and safety together with the assessment of the risk carried out in accordance with the general principles for the risk evaluation of chemical substances as referred to in article 10(4) of Council Regulation (EEC) No 793/93 of 23 March 1993 on the evaluation and control of the risks of existing substances, in the case of an existing substance, or in article 3(2) of Council Directive 67/548/EEC on the approximation of laws, regulations and administrative provisions relating to the classification, packaging and labelling of dangerous substances in the case of a new substance.

(3) Where the Commission carries out an investigation under paragraph 5 of Annex II to the GPS Directive, the Secretary of State shall supply the Commission with such information as it requests, to the best of his ability.

35 Implementation of Commission decisions

(1) This regulation applies where the Commission adopts a decision pursuant to article 13 of the GPS Directive.

(2) The Secretary of State shall—
    (a) take such action under these Regulations, or
    (b) direct another enforcement authority to take such action under these Regulations, as is necessary to comply with the decision.

(3) Where an enforcement authority serves a safety notice pursuant to paragraph (2), the following provisions of these Regulations shall not apply in relation to that notice, namely regulations 14(3), 15(4) to (6) and 16(1), 16(2)(c) and (d), 16(5) to (7) and 17.

(4) Unless the Commission's decision provides otherwise, export from the Community of a dangerous product which is the subject of such a decision is prohibited with effect from the date the decision comes into force.

(5) The enforcement of the prohibition in paragraph (4) shall be treated as an assigned matter within the meaning of section 1(1) of the Customs and Excise Management Act 1979.

(6) The measures necessary to implement the decision shall be taken within 20 days, unless the decision specifies a different period.

(7) The Secretary of State or, where the Secretary of State has directed another enforcement authority to take action under paragraph (2)(b), that enforcement authority shall, within one month, give the parties concerned an opportunity to submit their views and shall inform the Commission accordingly.

36 Market surveillance

In order to ensure a high level of consumer health and safety protection, enforcement authorities shall within the limits of their responsibility and to the extent of their ability undertake market surveillance of products employing appropriate means and procedures and co-operating with other enforcement authorities and competent authorities of other Member States which may include:
    (a) establishment, periodical updating and implementation of sectoral surveillance programmes by categories of products or risks and the monitoring of surveillance activities, findings and results,
    (b) follow-up and updating of scientific and technical knowledge concerning the safety of products,
    (c) the periodical review and assessment of the functioning of the control activities and their effectiveness and, if necessary, revision of the surveillance approach and organisation put in place.

37 Complaints procedures

An enforcement authority shall maintain and publish a procedure by which complaints may be submitted by any person on product safety and on surveillance and control activities, which complaints shall be followed up as appropriate.

38 Co-operation between enforcement authorities

(1) It shall be the duty of an enforcement authority to co-operate with other enforcement authorities in carrying out the functions conferred on them by these Regulations. In particular—

(a) enforcement authorities shall share their expertise and best practices with each other;

(b) enforcement authorities shall undertake collaborative working where they have a shared interest.

(2) The Secretary of State shall inform the European Commission as to the arrangements for the enforcement of these Regulations, including which bodies are enforcement authorities.

39 Information

(1) An enforcement authority shall in general make available to the public such information as is available to it on the following matters relating to the risks to consumer health and safety posed by a product—

(a) the nature of the risk,

(b) the product identification,

and the measures taken in respect of the risk, without prejudice to the need not to disclose information for effective monitoring and investigation activities.

(2) Paragraph (1) shall not apply to any information obtained by an enforcement authority for the purposes of these Regulations which, by its nature, is covered by professional secrecy, unless the circumstances require such information to be made public in order to protect the health and safety of consumers.

(3) *[Amends Enterprise Act 2002 (Part 9 Restrictions on Disclosure of Information) (Amendment and Specification) Order 2003.]*

40 Service of documents

(1) A document required or authorised by virtue of these Regulations to be served on a person may be so served—

(a) on an individual by delivering it to him or by leaving it at his proper address or by sending it by post to him at that address;

(b) on a body corporate other than a limited liability partnership, by serving it in accordance with sub-paragraph (a) on the secretary of the body;

(c) on a limited liability partnership, by serving it in accordance with sub-paragraph (a) on a member of the partnership; or

(d) on a partnership, by serving it in accordance with sub-paragraph (a) on a partner or a person having the control or management of the partnership business;

(e) on any other person by leaving it at his proper address or by sending it by post to him at that address.

(2) For the purposes of paragraph (1), and for the purposes of section 7 of the Interpretation Act 1978 (which relates to the service of documents by post) in its application to that paragraph, the proper address of a person on whom a document is to be served by virtue of these Regulations shall be his last known address except that—

(a) in the case of a body corporate (other than a limited liability partnership) or its secretary, it shall be the address of the registered or principal office of the body;

(b) in the case of a limited liability partnership or a member of the partnership, it shall be the address of the registered or principal office of the partnership;

(c) in the case of a partnership or a partner or a person having the control or management of a partnership business, it shall be the address of the principal office of the partnership,

and for the purposes of this paragraph the principal officer of a company constituted under the law of a country or territory outside the United Kingdom or of a partnership carrying on business outside the United Kingdom is its principal office within the United Kingdom.

(3)   A document required or authorised by virtue of these Regulations to be served on a person may also be served by transmitting the request by any means of electronic communication to an electronic address (which includes a fax number and an e-mail address) being an address which the person has held out as an address at which he or it can be contacted for the purposes of receiving such documents.

(4)   A document transmitted by any means of electronic communication in accordance with the preceding paragraph is, unless the contrary is proved, deemed to be received on the business day after the notice was transmitted over a public electronic communications network.

41   Extension of time for bringing summary proceedings

(1)   Notwithstanding section 127 of the Magistrates' Courts Act 1980 or article 19 of the Magistrates' Courts (Northern Ireland) Order 1981, in England, Wales and Northern Ireland a magistrates' court may try an information (in the case of England and Wales) or a complaint (in the case of Northern Ireland) in respect of an offence under these Regulations if (in the case of England and Wales) the information is laid or (in the case of Northern Ireland) the complaint is made within three years from the date of the offence or within one year from the discovery of the offence by the prosecutor whichever is the earlier.

(2)   Notwithstanding section 136 of the Criminal Procedure (Scotland) Act 1995, in Scotland summary proceedings for an offence under these Regulations may be commenced within three years from the date of the offence or within one year from the discovery of the offence by the prosecutor whichever is the earlier.

(3)   For the purposes of paragraph (2), section 136(3) of the Criminal Procedure (Scotland) Act 1995 shall apply as it applies for the purposes of that section.

42   Civil proceedings

These Regulations shall not be construed as conferring any right of action in civil proceedings in respect of any loss or damage suffered in consequence of a contravention of these Regulations.

43   Privileged information

(1)   Nothing in these Regulations shall be taken as requiring a person to produce any records if he would be entitled to refuse to produce those records in any proceedings in any court on the grounds that they are the subject of legal professional privilege or, in Scotland, that they contain a confidential communication made by or to an advocate or solicitor in that capacity, or as authorising a person to take possession of any records which are in the possession of a person who would be so entitled.

(2)   Nothing in these Regulations shall be construed as requiring a person to answer any question or give any information if to do so would incriminate that person or that person's spouse or civil partner.

44   Evidence in proceedings for offence relating to regulation 9(1)

(1)   This regulation applies where a person has given a notification to an enforcement authority pursuant to regulation 9(1).

(2)   No evidence relating to that statement may be adduced and no question relating to it may be asked by the prosecution in any criminal proceedings (other than proceedings in which that person is charged with an offence under regulation 20 for a contravention of regulation 9(1)), unless evidence relating to it is adduced, or a question relating to it is asked, in the proceedings by or on behalf of that person.

45   Transitional provisions

Where, in relation to a product, a suspension notice (within the meaning of the 1987 Act) has (by virtue of regulation 11(b) of the General Product Safety Regulations 1994) been served under section 14 of the 1987 Act and is in force immediately prior to the coming into force of these Regulations, it shall continue in force notwithstanding the revocation of the General Product Safety Regulations 1994 by these Regulations, and those Regulations shall continue to apply accordingly.

46–47   *[Amendment provisions]*

BUSINESS PROTECTION FROM MISLEADING MARKETING REGULATIONS 2008
(SI 2008/1276)

PART 1
DEFINITIONS AND PROHIBITIONS

1   Citation and Commencement

These Regulations may be cited as the Business Protection from Misleading Marketing Regulations 2008 and shall come into force on 26th May 2008.

2   Interpretation

(1)   In these Regulations—

'advertising' means any form of representation which is made in connection with a trade, business, craft or profession in order to promote the supply or transfer of a product and 'advertiser' shall be construed accordingly;

'code owner' means a trader or a body responsible for—

(a)   the formulation and revision of a code of conduct; or

(b)   monitoring compliance with the code by those who have undertaken to be bound by it;

'comparative advertising' means advertising which in any way, either explicitly or by implication, identifies a competitor or a product offered by a competitor;

'court', in relation to England and Wales and Northern Ireland, means a county court or the High Court, and, in relation to Scotland, the sheriff or the Court of Session;

'enforcement authority' means the OFT, every local weights and measures authority in Great Britain (within the meaning of section 69 of the Weights and Measure Act 1985) and the Department of Enterprise, Trade and Investment in Northern Ireland;

'goods' includes ships, aircraft, animals, things attached to land and growing crops;

'OFT' means the Office of Fair Trading;

'premises' includes any place and any stall, vehicle, ship or aircraft;

'product' means any goods or services and includes immovable property, rights and obligations;

'ship' includes any boat and any other description of vessel used in navigation; and

'trader' means any person who is acting for purposes relating to his trade, craft, business or profession and anyone acting in the name of or on behalf of a trader.

(2)   In the application of these Regulations to Scotland for references to an 'injunction' or an 'interim injunction' there shall be substituted references to an 'interdict' or an 'interim interdict' respectively.

3   Prohibition of advertising which misleads traders

(1)   Advertising which is misleading is prohibited.

(2)   Advertising is misleading which—

(a) in any way, including its presentation, deceives or is likely to deceive the traders to whom it is addressed or whom it reaches; and by reason of its deceptive nature, is likely to affect their economic behaviour; or

(b) for those reasons, injures or is likely to injure a competitor.

(3) In determining whether advertising is misleading, account shall be taken of all its features, and in particular of any information it contains concerning—

(a) the characteristics of the product (as defined in paragraph (4));

(b) the price or manner in which the price is calculated;

(c) the conditions on which the product is supplied or provided; and

(d) the nature, attributes and rights of the advertiser (as defined in paragraph (5)).

(4) In paragraph (3)(a) the 'characteristics of the product' include—

(a) availability of the product;

(b) nature of the product;

(c) execution of the product;

(d) composition of the product;

(e) method and date of manufacture of the product;

(f) method and date of provision of the product;

(g) fitness for purpose of the product;

(h) uses of the product;

(i) quantity of the product;

(j) specification of the product;

(k) geographical or commercial origin of the product;

(l) results to be expected from use of the product; or

(m) results and material features of tests or checks carried out on the product.

(5) In paragraph (3)(d) the 'nature, attributes and rights' of the advertiser include the advertiser's—

(a) identity;

(b) assets;

(c) qualifications;

(d) ownership of industrial, commercial or intellectual property rights; or

(e) awards and distinctions.

4 Comparative advertising

Comparative advertising shall, as far as the comparison is concerned, be permitted only when the following conditions are met—

(a) it is not misleading under regulation 3;

(b) it is not a misleading action under regulation 5 of the Consumer Protection from Unfair Trading Regulations 2008 or a misleading omission under regulation 6 of those Regulations;

(c) it compares products meeting the same needs or intended for the same purpose;

(d) it objectively compares one or more material, relevant, verifiable and representative features of those products, which may include price;

(e) it does not create confusion among traders—

(i) between the advertiser and a competitor, or

(ii) between the trade marks, trade names, other distinguishing marks or products of the advertiser and those of a competitor;

(f) it does not discredit or denigrate the trade marks, trade names, other distinguishing marks, products, activities, or circumstances of a competitor;

(g) for products with designation of origin, it relates in each case to products with the same designation;

(h) it does not take unfair advantage of the reputation of a trade mark, trade name or other distinguishing marks of a competitor or of the designation of origin of competing products;

  (i) it does not present products as imitations or replicas of products bearing a protected trade mark or trade name.

5 Promotion of misleading advertising and comparative advertising which is not permitted
A code owner shall not promote in a code of conduct—
  (a) advertising which is misleading under regulation 3; or
  (b) comparative advertising which is not permitted under regulation 4.

PART 2
OFFENCES

6 Misleading advertising
A trader is guilty of an offence if he engages in advertising which is misleading under regulation 3.

7 Penalty for offence under regulation 6
A person guilty of an offence under regulation 6 shall be liable—
  (a) on summary conviction, to a fine not exceeding the statutory maximum; or
  (b) on conviction on indictment, to a fine or imprisonment for a term not exceeding two years or both.

8 Offences committed by bodies of persons
  (1) Where an offence under these Regulations committed by a body corporate is proved—
  (a) to have been committed with the consent or connivance of an officer of the body, or
  (b) to be attributable to any neglect on his part,
the officer as well as the body corporate is guilty of the offence and liable to be proceeded against and punished accordingly.
  (2) In paragraph (1) a reference to an officer of a body corporate includes a reference to—
  (a) a director, manager, secretary or other similar officer; and
  (b) a person purporting to act as a director, manager, secretary or other similar officer.
  (3) Where an offence under these Regulations committed by a Scottish partnership is proved—
  (a) to have been committed with the consent or connivance of a partner, or
  (b) to be attributable to any neglect on his part,
the partner as well as the partnership is guilty of the offence and liable to be proceeded against and punished accordingly.
  (4) In paragraph (3) a reference to a partner includes a person purporting to act as a partner.

9 Offence due to the default of another person
  (1) This regulation applies where a person 'X'—
  (a) commits an offence under regulation 6, or
  (b) would have committed an offence under regulation 6 but for a defence under regulation 11 or 12,
and the commission of the offence, or of what would have been an offence but for X being able to rely on a defence under regulations 11 or 12, is due to the act or default of some other person 'Y'.
  (2) Where this regulation applies Y shall be guilty of the offence subject to regulations 11 and 12 whether or not Y is a trader and whether or not Y's act or default is advertising.
  (3) Y may be charged with and convicted of the offence by virtue of paragraph (2) whether or not proceedings are taken against X.

10　Time limit for prosecution

(1)　No proceedings for an offence under these Regulations shall be commenced after—

    (a)　the end of the period of three years beginning with the date of the commission of the offence; or

    (b)　the end of the period of one year beginning with the date of discovery of the offence by the prosecutor,

whichever is earlier.

(2)　For the purposes of paragraph (1)(b) a certificate signed by or on behalf of the prosecutor and stating the date on which the offence was discovered by him shall be conclusive evidence of that fact and a certificate stating that matter and purporting to be so signed shall be treated as so signed unless the contrary is proved.

(3)　Notwithstanding anything in section 127(1) of the Magistrates' Courts Act 1980, an information relating to an offence under these Regulations which is triable by a magistrates' court in England and Wales may be so tried if it is laid at any time before the end of the period of twelve months beginning with the date of the commission of the offence.

(4)　Notwithstanding anything in section 136 of the Criminal Procedure (Scotland) Act 1995 summary proceedings in Scotland for an offence under these Regulations may be commenced at any time before the end of the period of twelve months beginning with the date of the commission of the offence.

(5)　For the purposes of paragraph (4), section 136(3) of the Criminal Procedure (Scotland) Act 1995 shall apply as it applies for the purposes of that section.

(6)　Notwithstanding anything in Article 19(1) of the Magistrates' Courts (Northern Ireland) Order 1981 a complaint charging an offence under these Regulations which is triable by a magistrates' court in Northern Ireland may be so tried if it is made at any time before the end of the period of twelve months beginning with the date of the commission of the offence.

11　Due diligence defence

(1)　In any proceedings against a person for an offence under regulation 6 it is a defence for that person to prove—

    (a)　that the commission of the offence was due to—

        (i)　a mistake;

        (ii)　reliance on information supplied to him by another person;

        (iii)　the act or default of another person;

        (iv)　an accident; or

        (v)　another cause beyond his control; and

    (b)　that he took all reasonable precautions and exercised all due diligence to avoid the commission of such an offence by himself or any person under his control.

(2)　A person shall not be entitled to rely on the defence provided by paragraph (1) by reason of the matters referred to in paragraph (ii) or (iii) of paragraph (1)(a) without the leave of the court unless—

    (a)　he has served on the prosecutor a notice in writing giving such information identifying or assisting in the identification of that other person as was in his possession; and

    (b)　the notice is served on the prosecutor at least seven clear days before the date of the hearing.

12　Innocent publication defence

In any proceedings against a person for an offence under regulation 6 committed by the publication of advertising it is a defence for that person to prove that—

    (a)　he is a person whose business it is to publish or to arrange for the publication of advertising;

(b)   he received the advertising for publication in the ordinary course of business; and

(c)   he did not know and had no reason to suspect that its publication would amount to an offence under regulation 6.

PART 3

ENFORCEMENT

13   Duty to enforce

(1)   It shall be the duty of every enforcement authority to enforce these Regulations.

(2)   Where an enforcement authority is a local weights and measures authority the duty referred to in paragraph (1) shall apply to the enforcement of these Regulations within the authority's area.

(3)   Where the enforcement authority is the Department of Enterprise, Trade and Investment in Northern Ireland the duty referred to in paragraph (1) shall apply to the enforcement of these Regulations within Northern Ireland.

(4)   In determining how to comply with its duty of enforcement every enforcement authority shall have regard to the desirability of encouraging control of advertising which is misleading under regulation 3 and comparative advertising which is not permitted under regulation 4 by such established means as it considers appropriate having regard to all the circumstances of the particular case.

(5)   Nothing in this regulation shall authorise any enforcement authority to bring proceedings in Scotland for an offence.

14   Notice to OFT of intended prosecution

(1)   Where an enforcement authority is a local weights and measures authority in England and Wales it may bring proceedings for an offence under regulation 6 only if—

(a)   it has notified the OFT of its intention to bring proceedings at least fourteen days before the date on which proceedings are brought; or

(b)   the OFT consents to proceedings being brought in a shorter period.

(2)   The enforcement authority must also notify the OFT of the outcome of the proceedings after they are finally determined.

(3)   Such proceedings are not invalid by reason only of the failure to comply with this regulation.

15   Injunctions to secure compliance with the Regulations

(1)   This regulation applies where an enforcement authority considers that there has been or is likely to be a breach of regulation 3, 4 or 5.

(2)   Where this regulation applies an enforcement authority may, subject to paragraph (3), if it thinks it appropriate to do so, bring proceedings for an injunction (in which proceedings it may also apply for an interim injunction) against any person appearing to it to be concerned or likely to be concerned with the breach.

(3)   Where the enforcement authority is a local weights and measures authority in Great Britain it may apply for an injunction only if—

(a)   it has notified the OFT of its intention to apply for an injunction at least fourteen days before the date on which the application is made; or

(b)   the OFT consents to the application for an injunction being made within a shorter period.

(4)   Proceedings referred to in paragraph (2) are not invalid by reason only of the failure to comply with paragraph (3).

16   Undertakings

Where an enforcement authority considers that there has been or is likely to be a breach of regulation 3, 4 or 5 it may accept from the person concerned or likely to be concerned with the breach an undertaking that he will comply with those regulations.

17 Co-ordination

(1) If more than one local weights and measures authority in Great Britain is contemplating bringing proceedings under regulation 15 in any particular case, the OFT may direct which enforcement authority is to bring the proceedings or decide that only it may do so.

(2) Where the OFT directs that only it may bring such proceedings it may take into account whether compliance with regulation 3, 4 or 5 could be achieved by other means in deciding whether to bring proceedings.

18 Powers of the court

(1) The court on an application by an enforcement authority may grant an injunction on such terms as it may think fit to secure compliance with regulation 3, 4 or 5.

(2) Before granting an injunction the court shall have regard to all the interests involved and in particular the public interest.

(3) An injunction may relate not only to particular advertising but to any advertising in similar terms or likely to convey a similar impression.

(4) The court may also require any person against whom an injunction (other than an interim injunction) is granted to publish in such form and manner and to such extent as the court thinks appropriate for the purpose of eliminating any continuing effects of the advertising—

    (a) the injunction; and

    (b) a corrective statement.

(5) In considering an application for an injunction the court may require the person named in the application to provide evidence as to the accuracy of any factual claim made as part of the advertising of that person if, taking into account the legitimate interests of that person and any other party to the proceedings, it appears appropriate in the circumstances.

(6) If, having been required under paragraph (5) to provide evidence as to the accuracy of a factual claim, a person—

    (a) fails to provide such evidence, or

    (b) provides evidence as to the accuracy of the factual claim that the court considers inadequate,

the court may consider that the factual claim is inaccurate.

(7) The court may grant an injunction even where there is no evidence of proof of actual loss or damage or of intention or negligence on the part of the advertiser.

19 Notifications of undertakings and orders to the OFT

An enforcement authority, other than the OFT, shall notify the OFT—

    (a) of any undertaking given to it under regulation 16;

    (b) of the outcome of any application made by it under regulation 15 and the terms of any order made by the court; and

    (c) of the outcome of any application made by it to enforce a previous order of the court.

20 Publication, information and advice

(1) The OFT must arrange for the publication, in such form and manner as it considers appropriate, of—

    (a) details of any undertaking or order notified to it under regulation 19;

    (b) details of any undertaking given to it under regulation 16;

    (c) details of any application made by it under regulation 15 and of the terms of any undertaking given to, or order made by, the court;

    (d) details of any application made by it to enforce a previous order of the court.

(2) The OFT may arrange for the dissemination, in such form and manner as it considers appropriate, of such information and advice concerning the operation of

these Regulations as appear to it to be expedient to give to the public and to all persons likely to be affected by these Regulations.

PART 4
INVESTIGATION POWERS

21   Powers of Enforcement Authorities to obtain information

(1)   For the purpose of determining whether to bring proceedings for an injunction under regulation 15, an enforcement authority may by notice in writing require a person to provide to it such information as may be specified or described in the notice or to produce to it any documents so specified or described.

(2)   A notice under paragraph (1) may—

(a)   specify the way in which and the time within which it is to be complied with; and

(b)   be varied or revoked by a subsequent notice.

(3)   Nothing in this regulation gives an enforcement authority any power to require another person to provide or produce any information or document which the other person would be entitled to refuse to provide or produce in proceedings in the High Court on the grounds of legal professional privilege or (in Scotland) in proceedings in the Court of Session on the grounds of confidentiality of communications.

(4)   In paragraph (3) 'communications' means—

(a)   communications between a professional legal adviser and his client; or

(b)   communications made in connection with or in contemplation of legal proceedings and for the purposes of those proceedings.

(5)   Nothing in this regulation shall be construed as requiring a person to provide information if to do so might incriminate him.

(6)   If a person does not comply with a notice under paragraph (1) the court may, on the application of an enforcement authority, make such order as the court thinks fit for requiring the default to be made good, and any such order may provide that all the costs or expenses of and incidental to the application shall be borne by the person in default or by any officers of a company or other association who are responsible for its default.

22   Power to make test purchases

An enforcement authority may or may authorise any of its officers on its behalf to—

(a)   make a purchase of a product; or

(b)   enter into an agreement to secure the provision of a product,

for the purposes of determining whether these Regulations are being complied with.

23   Power of entry and investigation, etc

(1)   A duly authorised officer of an enforcement authority may at all reasonable hours exercise the following powers—

(a)   he may, for the purpose of ascertaining whether a breach of these Regulations has been committed, inspect any goods and enter any premises other than premises used only as a dwelling;

(b)   if he has reasonable cause to suspect that a breach of these Regulations has been committed, he may, for the purpose of ascertaining whether it has been committed, require any trader to produce any documents relating to his trade, business, craft or profession and may take copies of, or of any entry in, any such document;

(c)   if he has reasonable cause to believe that a breach of these Regulations has been committed, he may seize and detain any goods for the purpose of ascertaining, by testing or otherwise, whether the breach has been committed; and

(d)   he may seize and detain goods or documents which he has reason to believe may be required as evidence in proceedings for a breach of these Regulations.

(2)   If and to the extent that it is reasonably necessary to do so to secure that the provisions of these Regulations are observed, the officer may for the purpose of exercising his powers under paragraphs (1)(c) and (d) to seize goods or documents—

(a)   require any person having authority to do so to break open any container or open any vending machine; and

(b)   himself open or break open any such container or open any vending machine where a requirement made under sub-paragraph (a) in relation to the container or vending machine has not been complied with.

(3)   An officer seizing any goods or documents in exercise of his powers under this regulation shall—

(a)   inform the person from whom they are seized; and

(b)   where goods are seized from a vending machine, inform—

(i)   the person whose name and address are stated on the vending machine as being the proprietor's, or

(ii)   if there is no such name or address stated on the vending machine, the occupier of the premises on which the machine stands or to which it is affixed,

that the goods or documents have been so seized.

(4)   In this regulation 'document' includes information recorded in any form.

(5)   The reference in paragraph (1)(b) to the production of documents is, in the case of a document which contains information recorded otherwise than in legible form, a reference to the production of a copy of the information in legible form.

(6)   An officer seeking to exercise a power under this regulation must produce evidence of his identity and authority to a person (if there is one) who appears to the officer to be the occupier of the premises.

(7)   Where an officer seizes goods or documents in exercise of a power under this regulation they may not be detained—

(a)   for a period of more than 3 months; or

(b)   where the goods or documents are reasonably required by the enforcement authority in connection with the enforcement of these Regulations, for longer than they are so required.

(8)   An officer entering any premises under this regulation may take with him such other persons and such equipment as may appear to him to be necessary.

(9)   Nothing in this regulation or in regulation 24 gives any power to an officer of an enforcement authority—

(a)   to require any person to produce, or

(b)   to seize from another person,

any document which the other person would be entitled to refuse to produce in proceedings in the High Court on the grounds of legal professional privilege or (in Scotland) in proceedings in the Court of Session on the grounds of confidentiality of communications.

(10)   In paragraph (9) 'communications' means—

(a)   communications between a professional legal adviser and his client; or

(b)   communications made in connection with or in contemplation of legal proceedings and for the purposes of those proceedings.

(11)   If any person who is not an officer of an enforcement authority purports to act as such under this regulation or regulation 24 he shall be guilty of an offence and liable on summary conviction to a fine not exceeding level 5 on the standard scale.

24   Power to enter premises with a warrant

(1)   If a justice of the peace by a written information on oath is satisfied—

(a)   that there are reasonable grounds for believing that Condition A or B is met, and

(b)   that Condition C, D or E is met,

the justice may by warrant under his hand authorise an officer of an enforcement authority to enter the premises at all reasonable times, if necessary by force.

(2)   Condition A is that there are on any premises goods or documents which a duly authorised officer of the enforcement authority has power under regulation 23(1) to inspect and that their inspection is likely to disclose evidence of a breach of these Regulations.

(3)   Condition B is that a breach of these Regulations has occurred, is occurring or is about to occur on any premises.

(4)   Condition C is that the admission to the premises has been or is likely to be refused and that notice of intention to apply for a warrant under this regulation has been given to the occupier.

(5)   Condition D is that an application for admission, or the giving of a notice of intention to apply for a warrant, would defeat the object of the entry.

(6)   Condition E is that the premises are unoccupied or that the occupier is absent and it might defeat the object of the entry to await his return.

(7)   A warrant under paragraph (1)—

(a)   ceases to have effect at the end of the period of one month beginning with the day it is issued;

(b)   must be produced for inspection to the person (if there is one) who appears to the officer to be the occupier of the premises.

(8)   An officer entering any premises under this regulation may take with him such other persons and such equipment as may appear to him to be necessary.

(9)   On leaving any premises which an officer is authorised to enter by warrant under this regulation the officer shall, if the premises are unoccupied or the occupier is temporarily absent, leave the premises as effectively secured against trespassers as he found them.

(10)   In its application to Scotland, this regulation has effect as if—

(a)   the references in paragraph (1) to a justice of the peace included references to a sheriff; and

(b)   the reference in paragraph (1) to information on oath were a reference to evidence on oath.

(11)   In its application to Northern Ireland, this regulation has effect as if the references in paragraph (1) to a justice of the peace were references to a lay magistrate.

25   Obstruction of authorised officers

(1)   Any person who—

(a)   intentionally obstructs an officer of an enforcement authority acting in pursuance of these Regulations;

(b)   intentionally fails to comply with any requirement properly made of him by such an officer under regulation 23; or

(c)   without reasonable cause fails to give such an officer any other assistance or information which he may reasonably require of him for the purpose of the performance of his functions under these Regulations,

is guilty of an offence and liable, on summary conviction, to a fine not exceeding level 5 on the standard scale.

(2)   Any person who, in giving any information which is required of him under paragraph (1)(c), makes any statement which he knows to be false in a material particular is guilty of an offence and liable—

(a)   on summary conviction, to a fine not exceeding the statutory maximum; or

(b)   on conviction on indictment, to a fine or imprisonment for a term not exceeding two years or both.

(3)   Nothing in this regulation shall be construed as requiring a person to answer any question or give any information if to do so might incriminate him.

(4)   Paragraph (1)(a) does not apply in relation to the exercise by an enforcement authority of its power to require information under regulation 21.

26   Notice of test and intended proceedings

(1)   Where goods purchased by an officer pursuant to regulation 22 are submitted to a test and the test leads to the institution of any proceedings for a breach of these Regulations the officer shall inform—

(a)   the person from whom the goods were purchased; or

(b)   where the goods were sold through a vending machine, the person mentioned in regulation 23(3)(b);

of the result of the test.

(2)   Where goods seized by an officer pursuant to regulation 23 are submitted to a test then the officer shall inform the person mentioned in regulation 23(3) of the result of the test.

(3)   Where, as a result of the test, proceedings for a breach of these Regulations are taken against any person, the officer shall allow him to have the goods tested on his behalf if it is reasonably practicable to do so.

27   Compensation

(1)   Where an officer of an enforcement authority seizes and detains goods in exercise of the powers under regulation 23 the enforcement authority shall be liable to pay compensation to any person having an interest in the goods in respect of any loss or damage caused by reason of the exercise of the power if—

(a)   there has been no breach of these Regulations in relation to the goods, and

(b)   the exercise of that power is not attributable to any neglect or default by that person.

(2)   Any disputed question as to the right to or the amount of any compensation payable under this provision shall be determined by arbitration or, in Scotland, by a single arbiter appointed, failing agreement between the parties, by the sheriff.

28   Crown

(1)   The powers conferred by regulations 23 and 24 are not exercisable in relation to premises occupied by the Crown.

(2)   The Crown is not criminally liable as a result of any provision of these Regulations.

(3)   Paragraph (2) does not affect the application of any provision of these Regulations in relation to a person in the public service of the Crown.

29   Validity of agreements

An agreement shall not be void or unenforceable by reason only of a breach of these Regulations.

CONSUMER PROTECTION FROM UNFAIR TRADING REGULATIONS 2008
(SI 2008/1277)

PART 1
GENERAL

2 Interpretation

(1) In these Regulations—

'average consumer' shall be construed in accordance with paragraphs (2) to (6);

'business' includes a trade, craft or profession;

'code of conduct' means an agreement or set of rules (which is not imposed by legal or administrative requirements), which defines the behaviour of traders who undertake to be bound by it in relation to one or more commercial practices or business sectors;

'code owner' means a trader or a body responsible for—

(a)   the formulation and revision of a code of conduct; or

(b)   monitoring compliance with the code by those who have undertaken to be bound by it;

'commercial practice' means any act, omission, course of conduct, representation or commercial communication (including advertising and marketing) by a trader, which is directly connected with the promotion, sale or supply of a product to or from consumers, whether occurring before, during or after a commercial transaction (if any) in relation to a product

'consumer' means any individual who in relation to a commercial practice is acting for purposes which are outside his business;

'enforcement authority' means the OFT, every local weights and measures authority in Great Britain (within the meaning of section 69 of the Weights and Measures Act 1985) and the Department of Enterprise, Trade and Investment in Northern Ireland;

'goods' includes ships, aircraft, animals, things attached to land and growing crops;

'invitation to purchase' means a commercial communication which indicates characteristics of the product and the price in a way appropriate to the means of that commercial communication and thereby enables the consumer to make a purchase;

'materially distort the economic behaviour' means in relation to an average consumer, appreciably to impair the average consumer's ability to make an informed decision thereby causing him to take a transactional decision that he would not have taken otherwise;

'OFT' means the Office of Fair Trading;

'premises' includes any place and any stall, vehicle, ship or aircraft;

'product' means any goods or service and includes immovable property, rights and obligations;

'professional diligence' means the standard of special skill and care which a trader may reasonably be expected to exercise towards consumers which is commensurate with either—

(a)   honest market practice in the trader's field of activity, or

(b)   the general principle of good faith in the trader's field of activity;

'ship' includes any boat and any other description of vessel used in navigation;

'trader' means any person who in relation to a commercial practice is acting for purposes relating to his business, and anyone acting in the name of or on behalf of a trader;

'transactional decision' means any decision taken by a consumer, whether it is to act or to refrain from acting, concerning—

(a)   whether, how and on what terms to purchase, make payment in whole or in part for, retain or dispose of a product; or

(b)   whether, how and on what terms to exercise a contractual right in relation to a product.

(2)   In determining the effect of a commercial practice on the average consumer where the practice reaches or is addressed to a consumer or consumers account shall be taken of the material characteristics of such an average consumer including his being reasonably well informed, reasonably observant and circumspect.

(3)   Paragraphs (4) and (5) set out the circumstances in which a reference to the average consumer shall be read as in addition referring to the average member of a particular group of consumers.

(4)   In determining the effect of a commercial practice on the average consumer where the practice is directed to a particular group of consumers, a reference to the average consumer shall be read as referring to the average member of that group.

(5)   In determining the effect of a commercial practice on the average consumer—

(a)   where a clearly identifiable group of consumers is particularly vulnerable to the practice or the underlying product because of their mental or physical infirmity, age or credulity in a way which the trader could reasonably be expected to foresee, and

(b)   where the practice is likely to materially distort the economic behaviour only of that group, a reference to the average consumer shall be read as referring to the average member of that group.

(6)   Paragraph (5) is without prejudice to the common and legitimate advertising practice of making exaggerated statements which are not meant to be taken literally.

PART 2
PROHIBITIONS

3   Prohibition of unfair commercial practices

(1)   Unfair commercial practices are prohibited.

(2)   Paragraphs (3) and (4) set out the circumstances when a commercial practice is unfair.

(3)   A commercial practice is unfair if—

(a)   it contravenes the requirements of professional diligence; and

(b)   it materially distorts or is likely to materially distort the economic behaviour of the average consumer with regard to the product.

(4)   A commercial practice is unfair if—

(a)   it is a misleading action under the provisions of regulation 5;

(b)   it is a misleading omission under the provisions of regulation 6;

(c)   it is aggressive under the provisions of regulation 7; or

(d)   it is listed in Schedule 1.

4   Prohibition of the promotion of unfair commercial practices

The promotion of any unfair commercial practice by a code owner in a code of conduct is prohibited.

5   Misleading actions

(1)   A commercial practice is a misleading action if it satisfies the conditions in either paragraph (2) or paragraph (3).

(2)   A commercial practice satisfies the conditions of this paragraph—

(a)   if it contains false information and is therefore untruthful in relation to any of the matters in paragraph (4) or if it or its overall presentation in any way deceives or is likely to deceive the average consumer in relation to any of the matters in that paragraph, even if the information is factually correct; and

(b)   it causes or is likely to cause the average consumer to take a transactional decision he would not have taken otherwise.

(3)   A commercial practice satisfies the conditions of this paragraph if—

(a)   it concerns any marketing of a product (including comparative advertising) which creates confusion with any products, trade marks, trade names or other distinguishing marks of a competitor; or

(b)   it concerns any failure by a trader to comply with a commitment contained in a code of conduct which the trader has undertaken to comply with, if—

(i)   the trader indicates in a commercial practice that he is bound by that code of conduct, and

(ii)   the commitment is firm and capable of being verified and is not aspirational, and it causes or is likely to cause the average consumer to take a transactional decision he would not have taken otherwise, taking account of its factual context and of all its features and circumstances.

(4)   The matters referred to in paragraph (2)(a) are—

(a)   the existence or nature of the product;
(b)   the main characteristics of the product (as defined in paragraph 5);
(c)   the extent of the trader's commitments;
(d)   the motives for the commercial practice;
(e)   the nature of the sales process;
(f)   any statement or symbol relating to direct or indirect sponsorship or approval of the trader or the product;
(g)   the price or the manner in which the price is calculated;
(h)   the existence of a specific price advantage;
(i)   the need for a service, part, replacement or repair;
(j)   the nature, attributes and rights of the trader (as defined in paragraph 6);
(k)   the consumer's rights or the risks he may face.

(5)   In paragraph (4)(b), the 'main characteristics of the product' include—

(a)   availability of the product;
(b)   benefits of the product;
(c)   risks of the product;
(d)   execution of the product;
(e)   composition of the product;
(f)   accessories of the product;
(g)   after-sale customer assistance concerning the product;
(h)   the handling of complaints about the product;
(i)   the method and date of manufacture of the product;
(j)   the method and date of provision of the product;
(k)   delivery of the product;
(l)   fitness for purpose of the product;
(m)   usage of the product;
(n)   quantity of the product;
(o)   specification of the product;
(p)   geographical or commercial origin of the product;
(q)   results to be expected from use of the product; and
(r)   results and material features of tests or checks carried out on the product.

(6)   In paragraph (4)(j), the 'nature, attributes and rights' as far as concern the trader include the trader's—

(a)   identity;
(b)   assets;
(c)   qualifications;
(d)   status;
(e)   approval;
(f)   affiliations or connections;
(g)   ownership of industrial, commercial or intellectual property rights; and
(h)   awards and distinctions.

(7) In paragraph (4)(k) 'consumer's rights' include rights the consumer may have under Part 5A of the Sale of Goods Act 1979(5) or Part 1B of the Supply of Goods and Services Act 1982.

6 Misleading omissions

(1) A commercial practice is a misleading omission if, in its factual context, taking account of the matters in paragraph (2)—

(a) the commercial practice omits material information,

(b) the commercial practice hides material information,

(c) the commercial practice provides material information in a manner which is unclear, unintelligible, ambiguous or untimely, or

(d) the commercial practice fails to identify its commercial intent, unless this is already apparent from the context, and as a result it causes or is likely to cause the average consumer to take a transactional decision he would not have taken otherwise.

(2) The matters referred to in paragraph (1) are—

(a) all the features and circumstances of the commercial practice;

(b) the limitations of the medium used to communicate the commercial practice (including limitations of space or time); and

(c) where the medium used to communicate the commercial practice imposes limitations of space or time, any measures taken by the trader to make the information available to consumers by other means.

(3) In paragraph (1) 'material information' means—

(a) the information which the average consumer needs, according to the context, to take an informed transactional decision; and

(b) any information requirement which applies in relation to a commercial communication as a result of a Community obligation.

(4) Where a commercial practice is an invitation to purchase, the following information will be material if not already apparent from the context in addition to any other information which is material information under paragraph (3)—

(a) the main characteristics of the product, to the extent appropriate to the medium by which the invitation to purchase is communicated and the product;

(b) the identity of the trader, such as his trading name, and the identity of any other trader on whose behalf the trader is acting;

(c) the geographical address of the trader and the geographical address of any other trader on whose behalf the trader is acting;

(d) either—

(i) the price, including any taxes; or

(ii) where the nature of the product is such that the price cannot reasonably be calculated in advance, the manner in which the price is calculated;

(e) where appropriate, either—

(i) all additional freight, delivery or postal charges; or

(ii) where such charges cannot reasonably be calculated in advance, the fact that such charges may be payable;

(f) the following matters where they depart from the requirements of professional diligence—

(i) arrangements for payment,

(ii) arrangements for delivery,

(iii) arrangements for performance,

(iv) complaint handling policy;

(g) for products and transactions involving a right of withdrawal or cancellation, the existence of such a right.

7 Aggressive commercial practices

(1) A commercial practice is aggressive if, in its factual context, taking account of all of its features and circumstances—

(a) it significantly impairs or is likely significantly to impair the average consumer's freedom of choice or conduct in relation to the product concerned through the use of harassment, coercion or undue influence; and

(b)   it thereby causes or is likely to cause him to take a transactional decision he would not have taken otherwise.

(2)   In determining whether a commercial practice uses harassment, coercion or undue influence account shall be taken of—

(a)   its timing, location, nature or persistence;

(b)   the use of threatening or abusive language or behaviour;

(c)   the exploitation by the trader of any specific misfortune or circumstance of such gravity as to impair the consumer's judgment, of which the trader is aware, to influence the consumer's decision with regard to the product;

(d)   any onerous or disproportionate non-contractual barrier imposed by the trader where a consumer wishes to exercise rights under the contract, including rights to terminate a contract or to switch to another product or another trader; and

(e)   any threat to take any action which cannot legally be taken.

(3)   In this regulation—

(a)   'coercion' includes the use of physical force; and

(b)   'undue influence' means exploiting a position of power in relation to the consumer so as to apply pressure, even without using or threatening to use physical force, in a way which significantly limits the consumer's ability to make an informed decision.

PART 3
OFFENCES

8 Offences relating to unfair commercial practices

(1)   A trader is guilty of an offence if—

(a)   he knowingly or recklessly engages in a commercial practice which contravenes the requirements of professional diligence under regulation 3(3)(a); and

(b)   the practice materially distorts or is likely to materially distort the economic behaviour of the average consumer with regard to the product under regulation 3(3)(b).

(2)   For the purposes of paragraph (1)(a) a trader who engages in a commercial practice without regard to whether the practice contravenes the requirements of professional diligence shall be deemed recklessly to engage in the practice, whether or not the trader has reason for believing that the practice might contravene those requirements.

9   A trader is guilty of an offence if he engages in a commercial practice which is a misleading action under regulation 5 otherwise than by reason of the commercial practice satisfying the condition in regulation 5(3)(b).

10   A trader is guilty of an offence if he engages in a commercial practice which is a misleading omission under regulation 6.

11   A trader is guilty of an offence if he engages in a commercial practice which is aggressive under regulation 7.

12   A trader is guilty of an offence if he engages in a commercial practice set out in any of paragraphs 1 to 10, 12 to 27 and 29 to 31 of Schedule 1.

13 Penalty for offences

A person guilty of an offence under regulation 8, 9, 10, 11 or 12 shall be liable—

(a)   on summary conviction, to a fine not exceeding the statutory maximum; or

(b)   on conviction on indictment, to a fine or imprisonment for a term not exceeding two years or both.

14   Time limit for prosecution

(1)   No proceedings for an offence under these Reegulations shall be commenced after—

(a)   the end of the period of three years beginning with the date of the commission of the offence, or

(b)   the end of the period of one year beginning with the date of discovery of the offence by the prosecutor, whichever is earlier.

(2)   For the purposes of paragraph (1)(b) a certificate signed by or on behalf of the prosecutor and stating the date on which the offence was discovered by him shall be conclusive evidence of that fact and a certificate stating that matter and purporting to be so signed shall be treated as so signed unless the contrary is proved.

(3)   Notwithstanding anything in section 127(1) of the Magistrates' Courts Act 1980, an information relating to an offence under these Regulations which is triable by a magistrates' court in England and Wales may be so tried if it is laid at any time before the end of the period of twelve months beginning with the date of the commission of the offence.

(4)   Notwithstanding anything in section 136 of the Criminal Procedure (Scotland) Act 1995 summary proceedings in Scotland for an offence under these Regulations may be commenced at any time before the end of the period of twelve months beginning with the date of the commission of the offence.

(5)   For the purposes of paragraph (4), section 136(3) of the Criminal Procedure (Scotland) Act 1995 shall apply as it applies for the purposes of that subsection.

(6)   Notwithstanding anything in Article 19(1) of the Magistrates' Courts (Northern Ireland) Order 1981 a complaint charging an offence under these Regulations which is triable by a magistrates' court in Northern Ireland may be so tried if it is made at any time before the end of the period of twelve months beginning with the date of the commission of the offence.

15   Offences committed by bodies of persons

(1)   Where an offence under these Regulations committed by a body corporate is proved—

(a)   to have been committed with the consent or connivance of an officer of the body, or

(b)   to be attributable to any neglect on his part, the officer as well as the body corporate is guilty of the offence and liable to be proceeded against and punished accordingly.

(2)   In paragraph (1) a reference to an officer of a body corporate includes a reference to—

(a)   a director, manager, secretary or other similar officer; and

(b)   a person purporting to act as a director, manager, secretary or other similar officer.

(3)   Where an offence under these Regulations committed by a Scottish partnership is proved—

(a)   to have been committed with the consent or connivance of a partner, or

(b)   to be attributable to any neglect on his part, the partner as well as the partnership is guilty of the offence and liable to be proceeded against and punished accordingly.

(4)   In paragraph (3) a reference to a partner includes a person purporting to act as a partner.

16   Offence due to the default of another person

(1)   This regulation applies where a person 'X'—

(a)   commits an offence under regulation 9, 10, 11 or 12, or

(b)   would have committed an offence under those regulations but for a defence under regulation 17 or 18, and the commission of the offence, or of what would have been an offence but for X being able to rely on a defence under regulation 17 or 18, is due to the act or default of some other person 'Y'.

(2)   Where this regulation applies Y is guilty of the offence, subject to regulations 17 and 18, whether or not Y is a trader and whether or not Y's act or default is a commercial practice.

(3)   Y may be charged with and convicted of the offence by virtue of paragraph (2) whether or not proceedings are taken against X.

17   Due diligence defence

(1)   In any proceedings against a person for an offence under regulation 9, 10, 11 or 12 it is a defence for that person to prove—

    (a)   that the commission of the offence was due to—

        (i)   a mistake;

        (ii)   reliance on information supplied to him by another person;

        (iii)   the act or default of another person;

        (iv)   an accident; or

        (v)   another cause beyond his control; and

    (b)   that he took all reasonable precautions and exercised all due diligence to avoid the commission of such an offence by himself or any person under his control.

(2)   A person shall not be entitled to rely on the defence provided by paragraph (1) by reason of the matters referred to in paragraph (ii) or (iii) of paragraph (1)(a) without leave of the court unless—

    (a)   he has served on the prosecutor a notice in writing giving such information identifying or assisting in the identification of that other person as was in his possession; and

    (b)   the notice is served on the prosecutor at least seven clear days before the date of the hearing.

18   Innocent publication of advertisement defence

(1)   In any proceedings against a person for an offence under regulation 9, 10, 11 or 12 committed by the publication of an advertisement it shall be a defence for a person to prove that—

    (a)   he is a person whose business it is to publish or to arrange for the publication of advertisements;

    (b)   he received the advertisement for publication in the ordinary course of business; and

    (c)   he did not know and had no reason to suspect that its publication would amount to an offence under the regulation to which the proceedings relate.

(2)   In paragraph (1) 'advertisement' includes a catalogue, a circular and a price list.

PART 4

ENFORCEMENT

19   Duty to enforce

(1)   It shall be the duty of every enforcemennt authority to enforce these Regulations.

(2)   Where the enforcement authority is a local weights and measures authority the duty referred to in paragraph (1) shall apply to the enforcement of these Regulations within the authority's area.

(3)   Where the enforcement authority is the Department of Enterprise, Trade and Investment in Northern Ireland the duty referred to in paragraph (1) shall apply to the enforcement of these Regulations within Northern Ireland.

(4)   In determining how to comply with its duty of enforcement every enforcement authority shall have regard to the desirability of encouraging control of

unfair commercial practices by such established means as it considers appropriate having regard to all the circumstances of the particular case.

(5)   Nothing in this regulation shall authorise any enforcement authority to bring proceedings in Scotland for an offence.

20   Power to make test purchases

An enforcement authority may or may authorisse any of its officers on its behalf to—

(a)   make a purchase of a product, or

(b)   enter into an agreement to secure the provision of a product, for the purposes of determining whether these Regulations are being complied with.

21   Power of entry and investigation, etc

(1)   A duly authorised officer of an enfoorcement authority may at all reasonable hours exercise the following powers—

(a)   he may, for the purposes of ascertaining whether a breach of these Regulations has been committed, inspect any goods and enter any premises other than premises used only as a dwelling;

(b)   if he has reasonable cause to suspect that a breach of these Regulations has been committed, he may, for the purpose of ascertaining whether it has been committed, require any trader to produce any documents relating to his business and may take copies of, or of any entry in, any such document;

(c)   if he has reasonable cause to believe that a breach of these Regulations has been committed, he may seize and detain any goods for the purpose of ascertaining, by testing or otherwise, whether the breach has been committed; and

(d)   he may seize and detain goods or documents which he has reason to believe may be required as evidence in proceedings for a breach of these Regulations.

(2)   If and to the extent that it is reasonably necessary to secure that the provisions of these Regulations are observed, the officer may for the purpose of exercising his powers under paragraphs (1)(c) and (d) to seize goods or documents—

(a)   require any person having authority to do so to break open any container or open any vending machine; and

(b)   himself open or break open any such container or open any vending machine where a requirement made under sub-paragraph (a) in relation to the container or vending machine has not been complied with.

(3)   An officer seizing any goods or documents in exercise of his powers under this regulation shall—

(a)   inform the person from whom they are seized, and,

(b)   where goods are seized from a vending machine, inform—

(i)   the person whose name and address are stated on the machine as being the proprietor's; or

(ii)   if there is no such name or address stated on the machine the occupier of the ppremises on which the machinestands or to which it is affixed, that the goods or documents have been so seized.

(4)   In this regulation 'document' includes information recorded in any form.

(5)   The reference in paragraph (1)(b) to the production of documents is, in the case of a document which contains information recorded otherwise than in legible form, a reference to the production of a copy of the information in legible form.

(6)   An officer seeking to exercise a power under this regulation must produce evidence of his identity and authority to a person (if there is one) who appears to the officer to be the occupier of the premises.

(7)   Where an officer seizes goods or documents in exercise of a power under this regulation they may not be detained—

(a)   for a period of more than 3 months; or

(b)   where the goods or documents are reasonably required by the enforcement authority in connection with the enforcement of these Regulations, for longer than they are so required.

(8)   An officer entering any premises under this regulation may take with him such other persons and such equipment as may appear to him to be necessary.

(9)   Nothing in this regulation or in regulation 22 gives any power to an officer of an enforcement authority—

(a)   to require any person to produce, or

(b)   to seize from another person, any document which the other person would be entitled to refuse to produce in proceedings in the High Court on the grounds of legal professional privilege or (in Scotland) in proceedings in the Court of Session on the grounds of confidentiality of communications.

(10)   In paragraph (9) 'communications' means—

(a)   communications between a professional legal adviser and his client; or

(b)   communications made in connection with or in contemplation of legal proceedings and for the purposes of those proceedings.

(11)   If any person who is not an officer of an enforcement authority purports to act as such under this regulation or under regulation 22 he shall be guilty of an offence and liable on summary conviction to a fine not exceeding level 5 on the standard scale.

22   Power to enter premises with a warrant

(1)   If a justice of the peace by any wrritten information on oath is satisfied—

(a)   that there are reasonable grounds for believing that Condition A or B is met, and

(b)   that Condition C, D or E is met, the justice may by warrant under his hand authorise an officer of an enforcement authority to enter the premises at all reasonable times, if necessary by force.

(2)   Condition A is that there are on any premises goods or documents which a duly authorised officer of the enforcement authority has power under regulation 21(1) to inspect and that their inspection is likely to disclose evidence of a breach of these Regulations.

(3)   Condition B is that a breach of these Regulations has been, is being or is about to be committed on any premises.

(4)   Condition C is that the admission to the premises has been or is likely to be refused and that notice of intention to apply for a warrant under this regulation has been given to the occupier.

(5)   Condition D is that an application for admission, or the giving of a notice of intention to apply for a warrant, would defeat the object of the entry.

(6)   Condition E is that the premises are unoccupied or that the occupier is absent and it might defeat the object of the entry to await his return.

(7)   A warrant under paragraph (1)—

(a)   ceases to have effect at the end of the period of one month beginning with the day it is issued; (b) must be produced for inspection to the person (if there is one) who appears to the officer to be the occupier of the premises.

(8)   An officer entering any premises under this regulation may take with him such other persons and such equipment as may appear to him to be necessary.

(9)   On leaving any premises which an officer is authorised to enter by warrant under this regulation the officer shall, if the premises are unoccupied or the occupier is temporarily absent, leave the premises as effectively secured against trespassers as he found them.

(10)   In its application to Scotland, this regulation has effect as if—

(a)   the references in paragraph (1) to a justice of the peace included references to a sheriff; and

(b)   the reference in paragraph (1) to information on oath were a reference to evidence on oath.

(11)   In its application to Northern Ireland, this regulation has effect as if the references in paragraph (1) to a justice of the peace were references to a lay magistrate.

23   Obstruction of authorised officers

(1)   Any person who—

(a)   intentionally obstructs an officer of an enforcement authority acting in pursuance of these Regulations,

(b)   intentionally fails to comply with any requirement properly made of him by such an officer under regulation 21, or

(c)   without reasonable cause fails to give such an officer any other assistance or information which he may reasonably require of him for the purpose of the performance of his functions under these Regulations, is guilty of an offence and liable, on summary conviction, to a fine not exceeding level 5 on the standard scale.

(2)   Any person who, in giving any information which is required of him under paragraph (1)(c), makes any statement which he knows to be false in a material particular is guilty of an offence and liable—

(a)   on summary conviction, to a fine not exceeding the statutory maximum; or

(b)   on conviction on indictment, to a fine or imprisonment for a term not exceeding two years or both.

(3)   Nothing in this regulation shall be construed as requiring a person to answer any question or give any information if to do so might incriminate him.

24   Notice of test and intended proceedings

(1)   Where goods purchased by an officer pursuant to regulation 20 are submitted to a test and the test leads to the institution of any proceedings for a breach of these Regulations the officer shall inform—

(a)   the person from whom the goods were purchased, or

(b)   where the goods were sold through a vending machine, the person mentioned in regulation 21(3)(b), of the result of the test.

(2)   Where goods seized by an officer pursuant to regulation 21 are submitted to a test then the officer shall inform the person mentioned in regulation 21(3) of the result of the test.

(3)   Where, as a result of the test, any proceedings in respect of a breach of these Regulations are taken against any person, the officer shall allow him to have the goods tested on his behalf if it is reasonably practicable to do so.

25   Compensation

(1)   Where an officer of an enforcement authority seizes and detains goods in exercise of the powers under regulation 21 the enforcement authority shall be liable to pay compensation to any person having an interest in the goods in respect of any loss or damage caused by reason of the exercise of the power if—

(a)   there has been no breach of these Regulations in relation to the goods, and

(b)   the exercise of that power is not attributable to any neglect or default by that person.

(2)   Any disputed question as to the right to or the amount of any compensation payable under this provision shall be determined by arbitration or, in Scotland, by a single arbiter appointed, failing agreement between the parties, by the sheriff.

26–27   *[Amend the Enterprise Act 2002]*

PART 5
SUPPLEMENTARY

28   Crown

(1)   The powers conferred by regulations 21 aand 22 are not exercisable in relation to premises occupied by the Crown.

(2)   The Crown is not criminally liable as a result of any provision of these Regulations.

(3)   Paragraph (2) does not affect the application of any provision of these Regulations in relation to a person in the public service of the Crown.

29   Validity of agreements

An agreement shall not be void or unenforceablle by reason only of a breach of these Regulations.

. . .

SCHEDULE 1
COMMERCIAL PRACTICES WHICH ARE IN ALL CIRCUMSTANCES
CONSIDERED UNFAIR

1   Claiming to be a signatory to a code of conduct when the trader is not.

2   Displaying a trust mark, quality mark or equivalent without having obtained the necessary authorisation.

3   Claiming that a code of conduct has an endorsement from a public or other body which it does not have.

4   Claiming that a trader (including his commercial practices) or a product has been approved, endorsed or authorised by a public or private body when the trader, the commercial practices or the product have not or making such a claim without complying with the terms of the approval, endorsement or authorisation.

5   Making an invitation to purchase products at a specified price without disclosing the existence of any reasonable grounds the trader may have for believing that he will not be able to offer for supply, or to procure another trader to supply, those products or equivalent products at that price for a period that is, and in quantities that are, reasonable having regard to the product, the scale of advertising of the product and the price offered (bait advertising).

6   Making an invitation to purchase products at a specified price and then—

(a)   refusing to show the advertised item to consumers,

(b)   refusing to take orders for it or deliver it within a reasonable time, or

(c)   demonstrating a defective sample of it, with the intention of promoting a different product (bait and switch).

7   Falsely stating that a product will only be available for a very limited time, or that it will only be available on particular terms for a very limited time, in order to elicit an immediate decision and deprive consumers of sufficient opportunity or time to make an informed choice.

8   Undertaking to provide after-sales service to consumers with whom the trader has communicated prior to a transaction in a language which is not an official language of the EEA State where the trader is located and then making such service available only in another language without clearly disclosing this to the consumer before the consumer is committed to the transaction.

9   Stating or otherwise creating the impression that a product can legally be sold when it cannot.

10   Presenting rights given to consumers in law as a distinctive feature of the trader's offer.

11   Using editorial content in the media to promote a product where a trader has paid for the promotion without making that clear in the content or by images or sounds clearly identifiable by the consumer (advertorial).

12   Making a materially inaccurate claim concerning the nature and extent of the risk to the personal security of the consumer or his family if the consumer does not purchase the product.

13   Promoting a product similar to a product made by a particular manufacturer in such a manner as deliberately to mislead the consumer into believing that the product is made by that same manufacturer when it is not.

14   Establishing, operating or promoting a pyramid promotional scheme where a consumer gives consideration for the opportunity to receive compensation that is derived primarily from the introduction of other consumers into the scheme rather than from the sale or consumption of products.

15   Claiming that the trader is about to cease trading or move premises when he is not.

16   Claiming that products are able to facilitate winning in games of chance.

17   Falsely claiming that a product is able to cure illnesses, dysfunction or malformations.

18   Passing on materially inaccurate information on market conditions or on the possibility of finding the product with the intention of inducing the consumer to acquire the product at conditions less favourable than normal market conditions.

19   Claiming in a commercial practice to offer a competition or prize promotion without awarding the prizes described or a reasonable equivalent.

20   Describing a product as 'gratis', 'free', 'without charge' or similar if the consumer has to pay anything other than the unavoidable cost of responding to the commercial practice and collecting or paying for delivery of the item.

21   Including in marketing material an invoice or similar document seeking payment which gives the consumer the impression that he has already ordered the marketed product when he has not.

22   Falsely claiming or creating the impression that the trader is not acting for purposes relating to his trade, business, craft or profession, or falsely representing oneself as a consumer.

23   Creating the false impression that after-sales service in relation to a product is available in an EEA State other than the one in which the product is sold.

24   Creating the impression that the consumer cannot leave the premises until a contract is formed.

25   Conducting personal visits to the consumer's home ignoring the consumer's request to leave or not to return, except in circumstances and to the extent justified to enforce a contractual obligation.

26   Making persistent and unwanted solicitations by telephone, fax, e-mail or other remote media except in circumstances and to the extent justified to enforce a contractual obligation.

27   Requiring a consumer who wishes to claim on an insurance policy to produce documents which could not reasonably be considered relevant as to whether the claim was valid, or failing systematically to respond to pertinent correspondence, in order to dissuade a consumer from exercising his contractual rights.

28   Including in an advertisement a direct exhortation to children to buy advertised products or persuade their parents or other adults to buy advertised products for them.

29   Demanding immediate or deferred payment for or the return or safekeeping of products supplied by the trader, but not solicited by the consumer, except where the product is a substitute supplied in accordance with regulation 19(7) of the Consumer Protection (Distance Selling) Regulations 2000 (inertia selling).

30   Explicitly informing a consumer that if he does not buy the product or service, the trader's job or livelihood will be in jeopardy.

31   Creating the false impression that the consumer has already won, will win, or will on doing a particular act win, a prize or other equivalent benefit, when in fact either—

    (a)   there is no prize or other equivalent benefit, or

    (b)   taking any action in relation to claiming the prize or other equivalent benefit is subject to the consumer paying money or incurring a cost.

PART III
EC MATERIALS

COUNCIL DIRECTIVE OF 25 JULY 1985
on the approximation of the laws, regulations and administrative provisions
of the Member States concerning liability for defective products
(85/374/EEC)

(amended by Directive 99/34/EC)

THE COUNCIL OF THE EUROPEAN COMMUNITIES,

. . .

HAS ADOPTED THIS DIRECTIVE:

Article 1
The producer shall be liable for damage caused by a defect in his product.

[Article 2
For the purpose of this Directive 'product' means all movables even if incorporated into another movable or into an immovable. 'Product' includes electricity.]

Article 3
1. 'Producer' means the manufacturer of a finished product, the producer of any raw material or the manufacturer of a component part and any person who, by putting his name, trade mark or other distinguishing feature on the product presents himself as its producer.
2. Without prejudice to the liability of the producer, any person who imports into the Community a product for sale, hire, leasing or any form of distribution in the course of his business shall be deemed to be a producer within the meaning of this Directive and shall be responsible as a producer.
3. Where the producer of the product cannot be identified, each supplier of the product shall be treated as its producer unless he informs the injured person, within a reasonable time, of the identity of the producer or of the person who supplied him with the product. The same shall apply, in the case of an imported product, if this product does not indicate the identity of the importer referred to in paragraph 2, even if the name of the producer is indicated.

Article 4
The injured person shall be required to prove the damage, the defect and the causal relationship between defect and damage.

Article 5
Where, as a result of the provisions of this Directive, two or more persons are liable for the same damage, they shall be liable jointly and severally, without prejudice to the provisions of national law concerning the rights of contribution or recourse.

Article 6
1. A product is defective when it does not provide the safety which a person is entitled to expect, taking all circumstances into account, including:

(a)   the presentation of the product;

(b)   the use to which it could reasonably be expected that the product would be put;

(c)   the time when the product was put into circulation.

2.   A product shall not be considered defective for the sole reason that a better product is subsequently put into circulation.

Article 7

The producer shall not be liable as a result of this Directive if he proves:

(a)   that he did not put the product into circulation; or

(b)   that, having regard to the circumstances, it is probable that the defect which caused the damage did not exist at the time when the product was put into circulation by him or that this defect came into being afterwards; or

(c)   that the product was neither manufactured by him for sale or any form of distribution for economic purpose nor manufactured or distributed by him in the course of his business; or

(d)   that the defect is due to compliance of the product with mandatory regulations issued by the public authorities; or

(e)   that the state of scientific and technical knowledge at the time when he put the product into circulation was not such as to enable the existence of the defect to be discovered; or

(f)   in the case of a manufacturer of a component, that the defect is attributable to the design of the product in which the component has been fitted or to the instructions given by the manufacturer of the product.

Article 8

1.   Without prejudice to the provisions of national law concerning the right of contribution or recourse, the liability of the producer shall not be reduced when the damage is caused both by a defect in product and by the act or omission of a third party.

2.   The liability of the producer may be reduced or disallowed when, having regard to all the circumstances, the damage is caused both by a defect in the product and by the fault of the injured person or any person for whom the injured person is responsible.

Article 9

For the purpose of Article 1, 'damage' means:

(a)   damage caused by death or by personal injuries;

(b)   damage to, or destruction of, any item of property other than the defective product itself, with a lower threshold of 500 ECU, provided that the item of property:

(i)   is of a type ordinarily intended for private use or consumption, and

(ii)   was used by the injured person mainly for his own private use or consumption.

This Article shall be without prejudice to national provisions relating to non-material damage.

Article 10

1.   Member States shall provide in their legislation that a limitation period of three years shall apply to proceedings for the recovery of damages as provided for in this Directive. The limitation period shall begin to run from the day on which the plaintiff became aware, or should reasonably have become aware, of the damage, the defect and the identity of the producer.

2.   The laws of Member States regulating suspension or interruption of the limitation period shall not be affected by this Directive.

Article 11

Member States shall provide in their legislation that the rights conferred upon the injured person pursuant to this Directive shall be extinguished upon the expiry of a period of 10 years from the date on which the producer put into circulation the actual product which caused the damage, unless the injured person has in the meantime instituted proceedings against the producer.

Article 12
The liability of the producer arising from this Directive may not, in relation to the injured person, be limited or excluded by a provision limiting his liability or exempting him from liability.

Article 13
This Directive shall not affect any rights which an injured person may have according to the rules of the law of contractual or non-contractual liability or a special liability system existing at the moment when this Directive is notified.

Article 14
This Directive shall not apply to injury or damage arising from nuclear accidents and covered by international conventions ratified by the Member States.

Article 15
1.   Each Member State may:
  (a)   [. . .]
  (b)   by way of derogation from Article 7(e), maintain or, subject to the procedure set out in paragraph 2 of this Article, provide in this legislation that the producer shall be liable even if he proves that the state of scientific and technical knowledge at the time when he put the product into circulation was not such as to enable the existence of a defect to be discovered.
2.   A Member State wishing to introduce the measure specified in paragraph 1(b) shall communicate the text of the proposed measure to the Commission. The Commission shall inform the other Member States thereof.
The Member State concerned shall hold the proposed measure in abeyance for nine months after the Commission is informed and provided that in the meantime the Commission has not submitted to the Council a proposal amending this Directive on the relevant matter. However, if within three months of receiving the said information, the Commission does not advise the Member State concerned that it intends submitting such a proposal to the Council, the Member State may take the proposed measure immediately.
If the Commission does submit to the Council such a proposal amending this Directive within the aforementioned nine months, the Member State concerned shall hold the proposed measure in abeyance for a further period of 18 months from the date on which the proposal is submitted.
3.   Ten years after the date of notification of this Directive, the Commission shall submit to the Council a report on the effect that rulings by the courts as to the application of Article 7(e) and of paragraph 1(b) of this Article have on consumer protection and the functioning of the common market. In the light of this report the Council, acting on a proposal from the Commission and pursuant to the terms of Article 100 of the Treaty, shall decide whether to repeal Article 7(e).

Article 16
1.   Any Member State may provide that a producer's total liability for damage resulting from a death or personal injury and caused by identical items with the same defect shall be limited to an amount which may not be less than 70 million ECU.
2.   Ten years after the date of notification of this Directive, the Commission shall submit to the Council a report on the effect on consumer protection and the functioning of the common market of the implementation of the financial limit on liability by those Member States which have used the option provided for in paragraph 1. In the light of this report the Council, acting on a proposal from the Com-

mission and pursuant to the terms of Article 100 of the Treaty, shall decide whether to repeal paragraph 1.

Article 17
This Directive shall not apply to products put into circulation before the date on which the provisions referred to in Article 19 enter into force.

Article 18
1. For the purposes of this Directive, the ECU shall be that defined by Regulation (EEC) No 3180/78, as amended by Regulation (EEC) No 2626/84. The equivalent in national currency shall initially be calculated at the rate obtaining on the date of adoption of this Directive.

2. Every five years the Council, acting on a proposal from the Commission, shall examine and, if need be, revise the amounts in this Directive, in the light of economic and monetary trends in the Community.

Article 19
1. Member States shall bring into force, not later than three years from the date of notification of this Directive, the laws, regulations and administrative provisions necessary to comply with this Directive. They shall forthwith inform the Commission thereof.

2. The procedure set out in Article 15(2) shall apply from the date of notification of this Directive.

Article 20
Member States shall communicate to the Commission the texts of the main provisions of national law which they subsequently adopt in the field governed by this Directive.

Article 21
Every five years the Commission shall present a report to the Council on the application of this Directive and, if necessary, shall submit appropriate proposals to it.

Article 22
This Directive is addressed to the Member States.

Done at Brussels, 25 July 1985.

DIRECTIVE 2000/35/EC OF THE EUROPEAN PARLIAMENT AND OF THE COUNCIL OF 29 JUNE 2000
on combating late payment in commercial transactions

THE EUROPEAN PARLIAMENT AND THE COUNCIL OF THE EUROPEAN UNION,

. . .

HAVE ADOPTED THIS DIRECTIVE:

Article 1. Scope
This Directive shall apply to all payments made as remuneration for commercial transactions.

Article 2. Definitions
For the purposes of this Directive:
1. 'commercial transactions' means transactions between undertakings or between undertakings and public authorities which lead to the delivery of goods or the provision of services for remuneration,

'public authority' means any contracting authority or entity, as defined by the Public Procurement Directives (92/50/EEC, 93/36/EEC, 93/37/EEC and 93/38/EEC),

'undertaking' means any organisation acting in the course of its independent economic or professional activity, even where it is carried on by a single person;

2.   'late payment' means exceeding the contractual or statutory period of payment;

3.   'retention of title' means the contractual agreement according to which the seller retains title to the goods in question until the price has been paid in full;

4.   'interest rate applied by the European Central Bank to its main refinancing operations' means the interest rate applied to such operations in the case of fixed-rate tenders. In the event that a main refinancing operation was conducted according to a variable-rate tender procedure, this interest rate refers to the marginal interest rate which resulted from that tender. This applies both in the case of single-rate and variable-rate auctions;

5.   'enforceable title' means any decision, judgment or order for payment issued by a court or other competent authority, whether for immediate payment or payment by instalments, which permits the creditor to have his claim against the debtor collected by means of forced execution; it shall include a decision, judgment or order for payment that is provisionally enforceable and remains so even if the debtor appeals against it.

Article 3. Interest in case of late payment

1.   Member States shall ensure that:

(a)   interest in accordance with point (d) shall become payable from the day following the date or the end of the period for payment fixed in the contract;

(b)   if the date or period for payment is not fixed in the contract, interest shall become payable automatically without the necessity of a reminder:

(i)   30 days following the date of receipt by the debtor of the invoice or an equivalent request for payment; or

(ii)   if the date of the receipt of the invoice or the equivalent request for payment is uncertain, 30 days after the date of receipt of the goods or services; or

(iii)   if the debtor receives the invoice or the equivalent request for payment earlier than the goods or the services, 30 days after the receipt of the goods or services; or

(iv)   if a procedure of acceptance or verification, by which the conformity of the goods or services with the contract is to be ascertained, is provided for by statute or in the contract and if the debtor receives the invoice or the equivalent request for payment earlier or on the date on which such acceptance or verification takes place, 30 days after this latter date;

(c)   the creditor shall be entitled to interest for late payment to the extent that:

(i)   he has fulfilled his contractual and legal obligations; and

(ii)   he has not received the amount due on time, unless the debtor is not responsible for the delay;

(d)   the level of interest for late payment ('the statutory rate'), which the debtor is obliged to pay, shall be the sum of the interest rate applied by the European Central Bank to its most recent main refinancing operation carried out before the first calendar day of the half-year in question ('the reference rate'), plus at least seven percentage points ('the margin'), unless otherwise specified in the contract. For a Member State which is not participating in the third stage of economic and monetary union, the reference rate referred to above shall be the equivalent rate set by its national central bank. In both cases, the reference rate in force on the first calendar day of the half-year in question shall apply for the following six months;

(e)   unless the debtor is not responsible for the delay, the creditor shall be

entitled to claim reasonable compensation from the debtor for all relevant recovery costs incurred through the latter's late payment. Such recovery costs shall
respect the principles of transparency and proportionality as regards the
debt in question. Member States may, while respecting the principles referred to
above, fix maximum amounts as regards the recovery costs for different levels of
debt.

2.   For certain categories of contracts to be defined by national law, Member
States may fix the period after which interest becomes payable to a maximum of 60
days provided that they either restrain the parties to the contract from exceeding
this period or fix a mandatory interest rate that substantially exceeds the statutory
rate.

3.   Member States shall provide that an agreement on the date for payment or
on the consequences of late payment which is not in line with the provisions of
paragraphs 1(b) to (d) and 2 either shall not be enforceable or shall give rise to a
claim for damages if, when all circumstances of the case, including good commercial practice and the nature of the product, are considered, it is grossly unfair to
the creditor. In determining whether an agreement is grossly unfair to the creditor,
it will be taken, inter alia, into account whether the debtor has any objective reason
to deviate from the provisions of paragraphs 1(b) to (d) and 2. If such an agreement is determined to be grossly unfair, the statutory terms will apply, unless the
national courts determine different conditions which are fair.

4.   Member States shall ensure that, in the interests of creditors and of competi-
tors, adequate and effective means exist to prevent the continued use of terms
which are grossly unfair within the meaning of paragraph 3.

5.   The means referred to in paragraph 4 shall include provisions whereby organisations officially recognised as, or having a legitimate interest in, representing
small and medium-sized enterprises may take action according to the national law
concerned before the courts or before competent administrative bodies on the
grounds that contractual terms drawn up for general use are grossly unfair within
the meaning of paragraph 3, so that they can apply appropriate and effective
means to prevent the continued use of such terms.

Article 4. Retention of title

1.   Member States shall provide in conformity with the applicable national provisions designated by private international law that the seller retains title to goods
until they are fully paid for if a retention of title clause has been expressly agreed
between the buyer and the seller before the delivery of the goods.

2.   Member States may adopt or retain provisions dealing with down payments
already made by the debtor.

Article 5. Recovery procedures for unchallenged claims

1.   Member States shall ensure that an enforceable title can be obtained, irrespective of the amount of the debt, normally within 90 calendar days of the lodging of the creditor's action or application at the court or other competent
authority, provided that the debt or aspects of the procedure are not disputed.
This duty shall be carried out by Member States in conformity with their respective national legislation, regulations and administrative provisions.

2.   The respective national legislation, regulations and administrative provisions
shall apply the same conditions for all creditors who are established in the
European Community.

3.   The 90 calendar day period referred to in paragraph 1 shall not include the
following:

(a)   periods for service of documents;

(b)   any delays caused by the creditor, such as periods devoted to correcting
applications.

4.   This Article shall be without prejudice to the provisions of the Brussels Con-

vention on jurisdiction and enforcement of judgments in civil and commercial matters.

Article 6. Transposition

1.   Member States shall bring into force the laws, regulations and administrative provisions necessary to comply with this Directive before 8 August 2002. They shall forthwith inform the Commission thereof.

When Member States adopt these measures, they shall contain a reference to this Directive or shall be accompanied by such reference on the occasion of their official publication. The methods of making such reference shall be laid down by Member States.

2.   Member States may maintain or bring into force provisions which are more favourable to the creditor than the provisions necessary to comply with this Directive.

3.   In transposing this Directive, Member States may exclude:

(a)   debts that are subject to insolvency proceedings instituted against the debtor;

(b)   contracts that have been concluded prior to 8 August 2002; and

(c)   claims for interest of less than EUR 5.

4.   Member States shall communicate to the Commission the text of the main provisions of national law which they adopt in the field covered by this Directive.

5.   The Commission shall undertake two years after 8 August 2002 a review of, inter alia, the statutory rate, contractual payment periods and late payments, to assess the impact on commercial transactions and the operation of the legislation in practice. The results of this review and of other reviews will be made known to the European Parliament and the Council, accompanied where appropriate by proposals for improvement of this Directive.

Article 7. Entry into force

This Directive shall enter into force on the day of its publication in the Official Journal of the European Communities.

Article 8. Addressees

This Directive is addressed to the Member States.

Done at Luxembourg, 29 June 2000.

DIRECTIVE 2000/31/EC OF THE EUROPEAN PARLIAMENT AND OF THE COUNCIL OF 8 JUNE 2000
on certain legal aspects of information society services, in particular electronic commerce, in the internal market

THE EUROPEAN PARLIAMENT AND THE COUNCIL OF THE EUROPEAN UNION,

. . .

HAVE ADOPTED THIS DIRECTIVE:

CHAPTER I
GENERAL PROVISIONS

Article 1. Objective and scope

1.   This Directive seeks to contribute to the proper functioning of the internal market by ensuring the free movement of information society services between the Member States.

2.   This Directive approximates, to the extent necessary for the achievement of the objective set out in paragraph 1, certain national provisions on information

society services relating to the internal market, the establishment of service providers, commercial communications, electronic contracts, the liability of intermediaries, codes of conduct, out-of-court dispute settlements, court actions and cooperation between Member States.

3. This Directive complements Community law applicable to information society services without prejudice to the level of protection for, in particular, public health and consumer interests, as established by Community acts and national legislation implementing them in so far as this does not restrict the freedom to provide information society services.

4. This Directive does not establish additional rules on private international law nor does it deal with the jurisdiction of Courts.

5. This Directive shall not apply to:

(a) the field of taxation;

(b) questions relating to information society services covered by Directives 95/46/EC and 97/66/EC;

(c) questions relating to agreements or practices governed by cartel law;

(d) the following activities of information society services:

– the activities of notaries or equivalent professions to the extent that they involve a direct and specific connection with the exercise of public authority,

– the representation of a client and defence of his interests before the courts,

– gambling activities which involve wagering a stake with monetary value in games of chance, including lotteries and betting transactions.

6. This Directive does not affect measures taken at Community or national level, in the respect of Community law, in order to promote cultural and linguistic diversity and to ensure the defence of pluralism.

Article 2. Definitions

For the purpose of this Directive, the following terms shall bear the following meanings:

(a) 'information society services': services within the meaning of Article 1(2) of Directive 98/34/EC as amended by Directive 98/48/EC;

(b) 'service provider': any natural or legal person providing an information society service;

(c) 'established service provider': a service provider who effectively pursues an economic activity using a fixed establishment for an indefinite period. The presence and use of the technical means and technologies required to provide the service do not, in themselves, constitute an establishment of the provider;

(d) 'recipient of the service': any natural or legal person who, for professional ends or otherwise, uses an information society service, in particular for the purposes of seeking information or making it accessible;

(e) 'consumer': any natural person who is acting for purposes which are outside his or her trade, business or profession;

(f) 'commercial communication': any form of communication designed to promote, directly or indirectly, the goods, services or image of a company, organisation or person pursuing a commercial, industrial or craft activity or exercising a regulated profession. The following do not in themselves constitute commercial communications:

– information allowing direct access to the activity of the company, organisation or person, in particular a domain name or an electronic-mail address,

– communications relating to the goods, services or image of the company, organisation or person compiled in an independent manner, particularly when this is without financial consideration;

(g) 'regulated profession': any profession within the meaning of either Article 1(d) of Council Directive 89/48/EEC of 21 December 1988 on a general system for the recognition of higher-education diplomas awarded on completion of professional education and training of at least three-years' duration or of Article 1(f) of Council Directive 92/51/EEC of 18 June 1992 on a second general system for the recognition of professional education and training to supplement Directive 89/48/EEC;

(h) 'coordinated field': requirements laid down in Member States' legal systems applicable to information society service providers or information society services, regardless of whether they are of a general nature or specifically designed for them.

(i) The coordinated field concerns requirements with which the service provider has to comply in respect of:

– the taking up of the activity of an information society service, such as requirements concerning qualifications, authorisation or notification,

– the pursuit of the activity of an information society service, such as requirements concerning the behaviour of the service provider, requirements regarding the quality or content of the service including those applicable to advertising and contracts, or requirements concerning the liability of the service provider;

(ii) The coordinated field does not cover requirements such as:

– requirements applicable to goods as such,

– requirements applicable to the delivery of goods,

– requirements applicable to services not provided by electronic means.

Article 3. Internal market

1. Each Member State shall ensure that the information society services provided by a service provider established on its territory comply with the national provisions applicable in the Member State in question which fall within the coordinated field.

2. Member States may not, for reasons falling within the coordinated field, restrict the freedom to provide information society services from another Member State.

3. Paragraphs 1 and 2 shall not apply to the fields referred to in the Annex.

4. Member States may take measures to derogate from paragraph 2 in respect of a given information society service if the following conditions are fulfilled:

(a) the measures shall be:

(i) necessary for one of the following reasons:

– public policy, in particular the prevention, investigation, detection and prosecution of criminal offences, including the protection of minors and the fight against any incitement to hatred on grounds of race, sex, religion or nationality, and violations of human dignity concerning individual persons,

– the protection of public health,

– public security, including the safeguarding of national security and defence,

– the protection of consumers, including investors;

(ii) taken against a given information society service which prejudices the objectives referred to in point (i) or which presents a serious and grave risk of prejudice to those objectives;

(iii) proportionate to those objectives;

(b) before taking the measures in question and without prejudice to court proceedings, including preliminary proceedings and acts carried out in the framework of a criminal investigation, the Member State has:

– asked the Member State referred to in paragraph 1 to take measures and the latter did not take such measures, or they were inadequate,

– notified the Commission and the Member State referred to in paragraph 1 of its intention to take such measures.

5. Member States may, in the case of urgency, derogate from the conditions stipulated in paragraph 4(b). Where this is the case, the measures shall be notified

in the shortest possible time to the Commission and to the Member State referred to in paragraph 1, indicating the reasons for which the Member State considers that there is urgency.

6.   Without prejudice to the Member State's possibility of proceeding with the measures in question, the Commission shall examine the compatibility of the notified measures with Community law in the shortest possible time; where it comes to the conclusion that the measure is incompatible with Community law, the Commission shall ask the Member State in question to refrain from taking any proposed measures or urgently to put an end to the measures in question.

CHAPTER II
PRINCIPLES

Section 1: Establishment and information requirements

Article 4. Principle excluding prior authorisation

1.   Member States shall ensure that the taking up and pursuit of the activity of an information society service provider may not be made subject to prior authorisation or any other requirement having equivalent effect.

2.   Paragraph 1 shall be without prejudice to authorisation schemes which are not specifically and exclusively targeted at information society services, or which are covered by Directive 97/13/EC of the European Parliament and of the Council of 10 April 1997 on a common framework for general authorisations and individual licences in the field of telecommunications services.

Article 5. General information to be provided

1.   In addition to other information requirements established by Community law, Member States shall ensure that the service provider shall render easily, directly and permanently accessible to the recipients of the service and competent authorities, at least the following information:

(a)   the name of the service provider;

(b)   the geographic address at which the service provider is established;

(c)   the details of the service provider, including his electronic mail address, which allow him to be contacted rapidly and communicated with in a direct and effective manner;

(d)   where the service provider is registered in a trade or similar public register, the trade register in which the service provider is entered and his registration number, or equivalent means of identification in that register;

(e)   where the activity is subject to an authorisation scheme, the particulars of the relevant supervisory authority;

(f)   as concerns the regulated professions:

– any professional body or similar institution with which the service provider is registered,

– the professional title and the Member State where it has been granted,

– a reference to the applicable professional rules in the Member State of establishment and the means to access them;

(g)   where the service provider undertakes an activity that is subject to VAT, the identification number referred to in Article 22(1) of the sixth Council Directive 77/388/EEC of 17 May 1977 on the harmonisation of the laws of the Member States relating to turnover taxes—Common system of value added tax: uniform basis of assessment.

2.   In addition to other information requirements established by Community law, Member States shall at least ensure that, where information society services refer to prices, these are to be indicated clearly and unambiguously and, in particular, must indicate whether they are inclusive of tax and delivery costs.

Section 2: Commercial communications

Article 6. Information to be provided

In addition to other information requirements established by Community law, Member States shall ensure that commercial communications which are part of, or constitute, an information society service comply at least with the following conditions:

(a)   the commercial communication shall be clearly identifiable as such;

(b)   the natural or legal person on whose behalf the commercial communication is made shall be clearly identifiable;

(c)   promotional offers, such as discounts, premiums and gifts, where permitted in the Member State where the service provider is established, shall be clearly identifiable as such, and the conditions which are to be met to qualify for them shall be easily accessible and be presented clearly and unambiguously;

(d)   promotional competitions or games, where permitted in the Member State where the service provider is established, shall be clearly identifiable as such, and the conditions for participation shall be easily accessible and be presented clearly and unambiguously.

Article 7. Unsolicited commercial communication

1.   In addition to other requirements established by Community law, Member States which permit unsolicited commercial communication by electronic mail shall ensure that such commercial communication by a service provider established in their territory shall be identifiable clearly and unambiguously as such as soon as it is received by the recipient.

2.   Without prejudice to Directive 97/7/EC and Directive 97/66/EC, Member States shall take measures to ensure that service providers undertaking unsolicited commercial communications by electronic mail consult regularly and respect the opt-out registers in which natural persons not wishing to receive such commercial communications can register themselves.

Article 8. Regulated professions

1.   Member States shall ensure that the use of commercial communications which are part of, or constitute, an information society service provided by a member of a regulated profession is permitted subject to compliance with the professional rules regarding, in particular, the independence, dignity and honour of the profession, professional secrecy and fairness towards clients and other members of the profession.

2.   Without prejudice to the autonomy of professional bodies and associations, Member States and the Commission shall encourage professional associations and bodies to establish codes of conduct at Community level in order to determine the types of information that can be given for the purposes of commercial communication in conformity with the rules referred to in paragraph 1.

3.   When drawing up proposals for Community initiatives which may become necessary to ensure the proper functioning of the Internal Market with regard to the information referred to in paragraph 2, the Commission shall take due account of codes of conduct applicable at Community level and shall act in close cooperation with the relevant professional associations and bodies.

4.   This Directive shall apply in addition to Community Directives concerning access to, and the exercise of, activities of the regulated professions.

Section 3: Contracts concluded by electronic means

Article 9. Treatment of contracts

1.   Member States shall ensure that their legal system allows contracts to be concluded by electronic means. Member States shall in particular ensure that the

legal requirements applicable to the contractual process neither create obstacles for the use of electronic contracts nor result in such contracts being deprived of legal effectiveness and validity on account of their having been made by electronic means.

2.   Member States may lay down that paragraph 1 shall not apply to all or certain contracts falling into one of the following categories:

(a)   contracts that create or transfer rights in real estate, except for rental rights;

(b)   contracts requiring by law the involvement of courts, public authorities or professions exercising public authority;

(c)   contracts of suretyship granted and on collateral securities furnished by persons acting for purposes outside their trade, business or profession;

(d)   contracts governed by family law or by the law of succession.

3.   Member States shall indicate to the Commission the categories referred to in paragraph 2 to which they do not apply paragraph 1. Member States shall submit to the Commission every five years a report on the application of paragraph 2 explaining the reasons why they consider it necessary to maintain the category referred to in paragraph 2(b) to which they do not apply paragraph 1.

Article 10. Information to be provided

1.   In addition to other information requirements established by Community law, Member States shall ensure, except when otherwise agreed by parties who are not consumers, that at least the following information is given by the service provider clearly, comprehensibly and unambiguously and prior to the order being placed by the recipient of the service:

(a)   the different technical steps to follow to conclude the contract;

(b)   whether or not the concluded contract will be filed by the service provider and whether it will be accessible;

(c)   the technical means for identifying and correcting input errors prior to the placing of the order;

(d)   the languages offered for the conclusion of the contract.

2.   Member States shall ensure that, except when otherwise agreed by parties who are not consumers, the service provider indicates any relevant codes of conduct to which he subscribes and information on how those codes can be consulted electronically.

3.   Contract terms and general conditions provided to the recipient must be made available in a way that allows him to store and reproduce them.

4.   Paragraphs 1 and 2 shall not apply to contracts concluded exclusively by exchange of electronic mail or by equivalent individual communications.

Article 11. Placing of the order

1.   Member States shall ensure, except when otherwise agreed by parties who are not consumers, that in cases where the recipient of the service places his order through technological means, the following principles apply:

– the service provider has to acknowledge the receipt of the recipient's order without undue delay and by electronic means,

– the order and the acknowledgement of receipt are deemed to be received when the parties to whom they are addressed are able to access them.

2.   Member States shall ensure that, except when otherwise agreed by parties who are not consumers, the service provider makes available to the recipient of the service appropriate, effective and accessible technical means allowing him to identify and correct input errors, prior to the placing of the order.

3.   Paragraph 1, first indent, and paragraph 2 shall not apply to contracts concluded exclusively by exchange of electronic mail or by equivalent individual communications.

Section 4: Liability of intermediary service providers

Article 12. 'Mere conduit'

1.   Where an information society service is provided that consists of the transmission in a communication network of information provided by a recipient of the service, or the provision of access to a communication network, Member States shall ensure that the service provider is not liable for the information transmitted, on condition that the provider:

(a)   does not initiate the transmission;

(b)   does not select the receiver of the transmission; and

(c)   does not select or modify the information contained in the transmission.

2.   The acts of transmission and of provision of access referred to in paragraph 1 include the automatic, intermediate and transient storage of the information transmitted in so far as this takes place for the sole purpose of carrying out the transmission in the communication network, and provided that the information is not stored for any period longer than is reasonably necessary for the transmission.

3.   This Article shall not affect the possibility for a court or administrative authority, in accordance with Member States' legal systems, of requiring the service provider to terminate or prevent an infringement.

Article 13. 'Caching'

1.   Where an information society service is provided that consists of the transmission in a communication network of information provided by a recipient of the service, Member States shall ensure that the service provider is not liable for the automatic, intermediate and temporary storage of that information, performed for the sole purpose of making more efficient the information's onward transmission to other recipients of the service upon their request, on condition that:

(a)   the provider does not modify the information;

(b)   the provider complies with conditions on access to the information;

(c)   the provider complies with rules regarding the updating of the information, specified in a manner widely recognised and used by industry;

(d)   the provider does not interfere with the lawful use of technology, widely recognised and used by industry, to obtain data on the use of the information; and

(e)   the provider acts expeditiously to remove or to disable access to the information it has stored upon obtaining actual knowledge of the fact that the information at the initial source of the transmission has been removed from the network, or access to it has been disabled, or that a court or an administrative authority has ordered such removal or disablement.

2.   This Article shall not affect the possibility for a court or administrative authority, in accordance with Member States' legal systems, of requiring the service provider to terminate or prevent an infringement.

Article 14. Hosting

1.   Where an information society service is provided that consists of the storage of information provided by a recipient of the service, Member States shall ensure that the service provider is not liable for the information stored at the request of a recipient of the service, on condition that:

(a)   the provider does not have actual knowledge of illegal activity or information and, as regards claims for damages, is not aware of facts or circumstances from which the illegal activity or information is apparent; or

(b)   the provider, upon obtaining such knowledge or awareness, acts expeditiously to remove or to disable access to the information.

2.   Paragraph 1 shall not apply when the recipient of the service is acting under the authority or the control of the provider.

3.   This Article shall not affect the possibility for a court or administrative authority, in accordance with Member States' legal systems, of requiring the ser-

vice provider to terminate or prevent an infringement, nor does it affect the possibility for Member States of establishing procedures governing the removal or disabling of access to information.

Article 15. No general obligation to monitor

1. Member States shall not impose a general obligation on providers, when providing the services covered by Articles 12, 13 and 14, to monitor the information which they transmit or store, nor a general obligation actively to seek facts or circumstances indicating illegal activity.

2. Member States may establish obligations for information society service providers promptly to inform the competent public authorities of alleged illegal activities undertaken or information provided by recipients of their service or obligations to communicate to the competent authorities, at their request, information enabling the identification of recipients of their service with whom they have storage agreements.

CHAPTER III
IMPLEMENTATION

Article 16. Codes of conduct

1. Member States and the Commission shall encourage:

    (a)   the drawing up of codes of conduct at Community level, by trade, professional and consumer associations or organisations, designed to contribute to the proper implementation of Articles 5 to 15;

    (b)   the voluntary transmission of draft codes of conduct at national or Community level to the Commission;

    (c)   the accessibility of these codes of conduct in the Community languages by electronic means;

    (d)   the communication to the Member States and the Commission, by trade, professional and consumer associations or organisations, of their assessment of the application of their codes of conduct and their impact upon practices, habits or customs relating to electronic commerce;

    (e)   the drawing up of codes of conduct regarding the protection of minors and human dignity.

2. Member States and the Commission shall encourage the involvement of associations or organisations representing consumers in the drafting and implementation of codes of conduct affecting their interests and drawn up in accordance with paragraph 1(a). Where appropriate, to take account of their specific needs, associations representing the visually impaired and disabled should be consulted.

Article 17. Out-of-court dispute settlement

1. Member States shall ensure that, in the event of disagreement between an information society service provider and the recipient of the service, their legislation does not hamper the use of out-of-court schemes, available under national law, for dispute settlement, including appropriate electronic means.

2. Member States shall encourage bodies responsible for the out-of-court settlement of, in particular, consumer disputes to operate in a way which provides adequate procedural guarantees for the parties concerned.

3. Member States shall encourage bodies responsible for out-of-court dispute settlement to inform the Commission of the significant decisions they take regarding information society services and to transmit any other information on the practices, usages or customs relating to electronic commerce.

Article 18. Court actions

1. Member States shall ensure that court actions available under national law concerning information society services' activities allow for the rapid adoption of measures, including interim measures, designed to terminate any alleged infringement and to prevent any further impairment of the interests involved.

2.   The Annex to Directive 98/27/EC shall be supplemented as follows:
'11. Directive 2000/31/EC of the European Parliament and of the Council of 8 June 2000 on certain legal aspects on information society services, in particular electronic commerce, in the internal market (Directive on electronic commerce) (OJ L 178, 17.7.2000, p 1).'

Article 19. Cooperation

1.   Member States shall have adequate means of supervision and investigation necessary to implement this Directive effectively and shall ensure that service providers supply them with the requisite information.

2.   Member States shall cooperate with other Member States; they shall, to that end, appoint one or several contact points, whose details they shall communicate to the other Member States and to the Commission.

3.   Member States shall, as quickly as possible, and in conformity with national law, provide the assistance and information requested by other Member States or by the Commission, including by appropriate electronic means.

4.   Member States shall establish contact points which shall be accessible at least by electronic means and from which recipients and service providers may:

(a)   obtain general information on contractual rights and obligations as well as on the complaint and redress mechanisms available in the event of disputes, including practical aspects involved in the use of such mechanisms;

(b)   obtain the details of authorities, associations or organisations from which they may obtain further information or practical assistance.

5.   Member States shall encourage the communication to the Commission of any significant administrative or judicial decisions taken in their territory regarding disputes relating to information society services and practices, usages and customs relating to electronic commerce. The Commission shall communicate these decisions to the other Member States.

Article 20. Sanctions

Member States shall determine the sanctions applicable to infringements of national provisions adopted pursuant to this Directive and shall take all measures necessary to ensure that they are enforced. The sanctions they provide for shall be effective, proportionate and dissuasive.

CHAPTER IV
FINAL PROVISIONS

Article 21. Re-examination

1.   Before 17 July 2003, and thereafter every two years, the Commission shall submit to the European Parliament, the Council and the Economic and Social Committee a report on the application of this Directive, accompanied, where necessary, by proposals for adapting it to legal, technical and economic developments in the field of information society services, in particular with respect to crime prevention, the protection of minors, consumer protection and to the proper functioning of the internal market.

2.   In examining the need for an adaptation of this Directive, the report shall in particular analyse the need for proposals concerning the liability of providers of hyperlinks and location tool services, 'notice and take down' procedures and the attribution of liability following the taking down of content. The report shall also analyse the need for additional conditions for the exemption from liability, provided for in Articles 12 and 13, in the light of technical developments, and the possibility of applying the internal market principles to unsolicited commercial communications by electronic mail.

Article 22. Transposition

1.   Member States shall bring into force the laws, regulations and administrative

provisions necessary to comply with this Directive before 17 January 2002. They shall forthwith inform the Commission thereof.

2. When Member States adopt the measures referred to in paragraph 1, these shall contain a reference to this Directive or shall be accompanied by such reference at the time of their official publication. The methods of making such reference shall be laid down by Member States.

Article 23. Entry into force
This Directive shall enter into force on the day of its publication in the Official Journal of the European Communities.

Article 24. Addressees
This Directive is addressed to the Member States.

Done at Luxemburg, 8 June 2000.

PART IV
CODES

DRAFT RULES ON UNJUSTIFIED ENRICHMENT
(SLC Discussion Paper No 99 (1996), Appendix)

1 General principle
A person who has been enriched at the expense of another person is bound, if the enrichment is unjustified, to redress the enrichment.

2 Enrichment
(1) A person is enriched if he acquires an economic benefit.

(2) A person acquires an economic benefit if his net worth is increased or is prevented from being decreased, and accordingly a person may be enriched, among other ways, by
- (a) acquiring money or other property
- (b) having value added to property
- (c) being freed, in whole or in part, from an obligation, or
- (d) being saved from a loss or expenditure

(3) A person is treated as acquiring an economic benefit under a void contract, or under a voidable contract which has been reduced, rescinded or otherwise set aside, or under a contract which has been terminated by frustration or rescission for breach or by some other means (apart from full performance) or under any other transaction or purported transaction which does not provide legal cause for the acquisition, if he would have acquired an economic benefit but for the fact that he gave consideration, and accordingly in such circumstances both parties to the transaction or purported transaction may be regarded as being enriched.

3 At the expense of another person
(1) The enrichment of one person is at the expense of another person if it is the direct result of
- (a) a payment, grant, transfer, incurring of liability, or rendering of services by the other person
  - (i) to the enriched person
  - (ii) in fulfilment of an obligation of the enriched person
  - (iii) in adding value to the enriched person's property, or
  - (iv) in acquiring some other economic benefit for the enriched person, or
- (b) in any case not covered by paragraph (a), an interference with the patrimonial rights of the other person otherwise than by the operation of natural forces.

(2) A person interferes with the patrimonial rights of another person if, among other things, he
- (a) extinguishes those rights or acts in such a way that they are extinguished
- (b) disposes or purports to dispose of property belonging to that other person
- (c) uses property which that other person has the right to use to the exclusion of the interferer, or
- (d) actively intercepts a benefit due to the other person

but a person does not interfere with the patrimonial rights of another person merely because he breaches a contract between himself and the other person.

(3)   A person who claims redress or any unjustified enrichment resulting from an interference with his patrimonial rights is treated for the purpose of any claims by or against third parties as thereby ratifying the interference.

(4)   A person who purchases property in good faith from someone who is not the owner of the property is not treated as being enriched at the expense of the owner or of any former owner by reason only of any economic benefit derived by him from the purchase of the property; and the same rule applies to any other acquirer, in good faith and for value, of the right, or of what purports to be the right, to deal with the property or rights of another, and to anyone deriving title from such a purchaser or acquirer.

(5)   Where a person (E) has been enriched indirectly as a result of performance by another person (C) under a contract between C and a third party (T), E's enrichment is not regarded as being at the expense of C, even if C is unable to recover under his contract with T.

(6)   This rule is subject to rule 8 (which deals with certain exceptional cases where redress is due for indirect enrichment).

4   Unjustified
An enrichment is unjustified unless it is justified under rules 5 or 6.

5   Enrichment justified by legal cause
(1)   An enrichment is justified if the enriched person is entitled to it by virtue of
   (a)   an enactment
   (b)   a rule of law
   (c)   a court decree
   (d)   a contract (whether or not the person claiming redress is a party) or unilateral voluntary obligation
   (e)   a will or trust
   (f)   a gift, or
   (g)   some other legal cause.

(2)   The reference to an enactment or rule of law in rule 5(1) is to an enactment or rule of law which confers rights directly and not to an enactment or rule of law in so far as it operates indirectly by regulating the effects of court decrees, contracts, wills, trusts, gifts or other legal causes.

(3)   A purported or apparent legal cause does not justify an enrichment if it is void or if, being voidable, it has been reduced, rescinded or otherwise set aside.

(4)   An acquisition of property is not a justified enrichment merely because legal title to the property has been acquired.

6   Enrichment justified by public policy
(1)   An enrichment is justified if it is the result of
   (a)   work or expenditure which was undertaken or incurred by the other person for his own benefit, or for the benefit of a third party or the public at large, which has incidentally conferred a benefit on the enriched person, and which was undertaken or incurred when the person knew or could reasonably have been expected to know that there would be a benefit to the enriched person and accepted, or could reasonably be supposed to have accepted, the risk that the enriched person would not pay for the benefit
   (b)   the voluntary and deliberate conferring by the other person of a benefit on the enriched person, in the knowledge that it is not due and in acceptance of the risk that the enriched person may choose not to pay or do anything in return
   (c)   a voluntary performance by the other person of an obligation which has prescribed, even if he erroneously believed that the obligation was still due, provided that any due counter-performance has been given
   (d)   a voluntary performance by the other person of an obligation which is

invalid for some formal reason only, even if he erroneously believed that the obligation was valid, provided that any due counter-performance has been given or if there is some other consideration of public policy which requires it to be regarded as justified.

(2) For the purpose of rule 6(1)(a) 'benefit', in relation to a person who has done work or provided services in tendering for a contract or in the anticipation of obtaining a contract, includes the benefit to the person of having, or improving, the chance of obtaining the contract.

7 Exceptions to rules 5 and 6

(1) Rule 5(1)(b) does not apply in so far as the enrichment is the result of any rule of law on the acquisition of property by accession or specification, or any analogous rule whereby one person may acquire another's property when it becomes attached to or mixed with his own.

(2) Rule 5(1)(d) does not apply in so far as the contract or obligation,

(a) is unenforceable because of an enactment or rule of law (whether or not it is also illegal), unless allowing redress for the enrichment would contravene the policy underlying the enactment or rule of law,

(b) has been terminated by rescission or frustration or some other means (apart from full performance) and the contract or obligation does not, expressly or impliedly, exclude redress in respect of the benefit in question.

(3) For the purpose of rule 7(2)(b) a contract which provides for performance in several parts or stages is presumed, unless the contract indicates the contrary, to exclude redress in so far as performance by one party under, and substantially in accordance with, the contract has been met by performance by the other party under, and substantially in accordance with, the contract.

(4) Rule 5(1)(f) does not apply where the gift

(a) was made in error, whether of fact or law, or

(b) was subject to a condition, which has been met, that it would be returned.

(5) Rule 6(1)(a) and (b) do not apply where the other person has, in circumstances where it was reasonable to do so,

(a) paid a monetary debt due by the enriched person

(b) fulfilled an alimentary obligation due by the enriched person

(c) incurred expenditure or performed services necessary for preserving the life, health or welfare of the enriched person, or

(d) incurred expenditure or performed services urgently necessary for preserving the property of the enriched person or preventing it from being dangerous.

8 Redress for indirect enrichment

(1)(a) Where a person (E) has acquired money or money's worth from a third party (T) by disposing or purporting to dispose of property belonging to another person (C), or by otherwise interfering with C's patrimonial rights, or by disposing of property acquired by him from C under a transaction voidable at C's instance, E's enrichment is treated, notwithstanding anything in the preceding rules, as being at the expense of C and as not being justified by any contract between himself and T.

(b) Paragraph (a) does not apply if E was a purchaser in good faith of the property in question, or had otherwise acquired, in good faith and for value, the right, or what purported to be the right, to deal with the property or rights in question, or had derived title from such a purchaser or acquirer.

(2) Where a person (T) has been enriched at the expense of another person (C) and T has transferred to another person (E) any benefit arising out of the enrichment then, notwithstanding anything in the preceding rules, E is taken to be enriched at the expense of C and neither the transfer by T to E, nor any voluntary obligation underlying the transfer, justifies the enrichment if

(a)   T's enrichment at the expense of C was unjustified or was justified only by a transaction voidable at C's instance

(b)   C is unable to recover from T, or cannot reasonably be expected to attempt to recover from T, and

(c)   the acquisition by E from T was not in good faith and for value.

(3)   Where a person (E) has been enriched by receiving a benefit from a trust estate or from the estate of a deceased person, the fact that E's enrichment is the result of a transfer from a trustee or executor does not prevent him from being liable to make redress to

(a)   a creditor of the estate to the extent that the creditor, because of the transfer to the beneficiary, has been unable to recover from the trustee or executor, or

(b)   a person (the true beneficiary) who is legally entitled to the benefit in question.

(4)   Where a debtor pays the wrong person, that person is enriched at the expense of the true creditor in so far as the payment extinguishes the liability of the debtor to the true creditor.

(5)   Nothing in these rules affects any procedural rule designed to avoid duplication of proceedings.

9   Redress due

(1)   The redress due by an enriched person under these rules is such transfer of property or payment of money, or both, as is required to redress the enriched person's unjustified enrichment at the expense of the claimant.

(2)   The redress due is assessed in accordance with the rules in the schedule in any case where those rules are applicable.

(3)   Where the enriched person has been enriched at the expense of the claimant in more than one way, the rules in the schedule apply cumulatively unless there would be double redress in respect of the same enrichment.

(4)   This rule is subject to the provisions of rule 10.

10   Court's powers to refuse or modify award

(1)   Where, in an action for unjustified enrichment, it appears to the court that each party is bound to make redress to the other, the court may

(a)   refuse to grant decree against the defender until satisfied that the pursuer has made, or will make, the redress due by him, or

(b)   where both obligations are to pay money, set off one entitlement against the other and grant decree for the difference.

(2)   Where, in an action for unjustified enrichment based on the passive receipt of a benefit by the enriched person, it appears to the court

(a)   that the enriched person had no reasonable opportunity to refuse the benefit

(b)   that the enriched person would have refused the benefit if he had had such an opportunity

(c)   that the enriched person cannot, or cannot reasonably be expected to, convert the value of the benefit into money or money's worth, and

(d)   that it would be inequitable to make a full award

the court may refuse or modify the award accordingly.

(3)   Where, in an action for unjustified enrichment based on the defender's acquisition of the pursuer's property by accession or specification or any analogous rule, it appears to the court that the pursuer has acted in good faith and that, having regard to the respective values of the properties involved, the conduct of the parties and all other relevant factors, the most appropriate and equitable solution would be for the defender to be ordered to sell to the pursuer such property at such a price as would enable the pursuer to regain his property without prejudice to the defender, the court may grant decree accordingly.

(4)   Notwithstanding anything in the preceding rules, a court deciding an

action for unjustified enrichment may refuse to make an award, or may make a reduced award, or may grant decree subject to conditions, if it considers

(a) that the person enriched, where he did not know, and could not reasonably be expected to know, that redress was due, changed his position (whether by spending money, disposing of property, consuming property or its fruits, abandoning rights, failing to exercise rights in time, or otherwise) in reliance on his enrichment, and it would for that reason be inequitable to make a full award or grant decree unconditionally

(b) that the claimant was so culpable or negligent in causing the unjustified enrichment that it would be inequitable or contrary to public policy to make a full award or grant decree unconditionally

(c) that the claimant would be unjustly enriched if a full award were made or if decree were granted unconditionally, or

(d) that, for any other reason, it would be inequitable or contrary to public policy to make a full award or grant decree unconditionally.

11 Bars to proceedings

(1)(a) An action for unjustified enrichment cannot be brought under these rules if there is, or was,

    (i) a special statutory or contractual procedure for dealing with the situation giving rise to the enrichment or

    (ii) another legal remedy for the enrichment

and if the claimant could reasonably have been expected to use that procedure or remedy.

(b) Paragraph (a) does not apply if the enactment or contract providing the other procedure or remedy indicates expressly or impliedly that it is intended to be in addition to any remedy available under the general law on unjustified enrichment.

(c) The availability of damages for loss does not preclude an action for redress of unjustified enrichment but, without prejudice to his right to claim damages for any consequential or other loss, the claimant cannot claim both redress of the other party's unjustified enrichment and damages for his corresponding loss.

(2)(a) A person who, before a court decision in proceedings to which he was not a party, has made a payment or transfer which was apparently due under the law as it was commonly supposed to be at that time cannot bring an action for unjustified enrichment in respect of that payment or transfer on the ground that the decision has shown that the law was not as it was commonly supposed to be and that the payment or transfer was accordingly not in fact due.

(b) In the preceding paragraph, 'decision' in any case where a decision is affirmed or restored on appeal means the decision so affirmed or restored and not the decision affirming or restoring it.

(3) The bars mentioned in this rule are in addition to any bar resulting from the operation of the general law on personal bar.

12 Areas of law not affected

(1) These rules replace the existing Scottish common law on unjustified enrichment, including

(a) the common law on restitution in so far as it is part of the law on unjustified enrichment

(b) the common law on repetition and recompense, and

(c) the *condictio indebiti*; the *condictio causa data causa non secuta*; the *condictio ob turpem vel iniustam causam*; the *condictio ob non causam*; the *condictio sine causa*; the *actio in quantum locupletior factus est*; and the *actio de in rem verso* in so far as they form part of the existing law.

(2) Nothing in these rules affects

(a) any enacted law

(b)   the law on rights of relief of cautioners and co-obligants

(c)   the law on subrogation of insurers or those who have paid an indemnity

(d)   the law derived from the case of *Walker v Milne* (whereby loss suffered or expenditure incurred in the expectation of a contract may in certain circumstances be recovered)

(e)   the law on the rights of a defrauded person as against the creditors of the person who defrauded him

(f)   the law on the recovery by a person of the possession or control of his own property or of any other property to the possession or control of which he is entitled

(g)   the law on the special obligations of those in a fiduciary position

(h)   the law on general average or salvage

(i)   the law on *negotiorum gestio*.

13   Interpretation

(1)   In these rules, and in the schedule where applicable,

(a)   'court decree' includes the decision of any tribunal, quasi-judicial body or arbiter having jurisdiction

(b)   'enactment' includes subordinate legislation

(c)   'gift' includes a gratuitous waiver, renunciation or discharge of a right

(d)   'he' means he, she or it; 'him' means him, her or it; and 'his' means his, hers or its

(e)   'patrimonial rights' include rights flowing from the ownership of property, rights to protect confidential information and other rights having an economic value but do not include purely personal rights, such as the rights to life, liberty, bodily integrity or reputation, and

(f)   'property' means property of any kind, corporeal or incorporeal, heritable or moveable.

(2)   Any reference in these rules to a contract which has been terminated by rescission or frustration includes a reference to a contract which has been substantially terminated by rescission or frustration and a reference to a severable part of a contract which has been terminated by rescission or frustration.

SCHEDULE. REDRESS DUE

PART I

E acquires benefit directly from C

1.   This part of the schedule applies where the enriched person (E) has been enriched by acquiring a benefit directly from the claimant (C).

2(1)   Where the unjustified enrichment resulted from the acquisition of money by E from C, the redress due by E to C is the amount acquired, with interest from the time of acquisition.

(2)   Where the unjustified enrichment resulted from the acquisition of other property by E from C, the redress due by E to C is

(a)   if the property is corporeal and can be returned in substantially the same condition as it was in at the time of the acquisition, the return of the property in that condition along with a sum of money to take account of any benefit derived by E from the ownership, use or possession of the property and interest on that sum where appropriate

(b)   if the property is corporeal and cannot be returned in substantially the same condition as it was in at the time of the acquisition, the amount which it would have been reasonable to expect E to pay C for the property at the time of its acquisition by E, with interest on that amount from the time of acquisition

(c)   if the property is incorporeal, the return of the property where possible and, whether or not return is possible, a sum of money to take account of any benefit derived by E from the ownership of the property and interest on that sum where appropriate.

3. Where the unjustified enrichment resulted from the addition of value by C to E's property, the redress due by E to C is the amount which it would have been reasonable to expect E to pay C for his work or expenditure in adding that value, or the amount of value added (at the time when the addition was made), if less, with interest where appropriate.

4. Where the unjustified enrichment resulted from the discharge or reduction of any liability of E by means of a payment by C, the redress due by E to C is the amount paid, with interest from the date of payment.

5. Where the unjustified enrichment resulted from E's being saved a loss or expenditure by receiving C's services, the redress due by E to C is the amount which it would have been reasonable to expect E to pay for those services, or the amount of loss or expenditure saved, if less, with interest where appropriate.

6(1) Where the unjustified enrichment resulted from E's being saved a loss or expenditure by using or possessing C's property, the redress due by E to C is the amount which it would have been reasonable to expect E to pay for that use or possession, or the amount of loss or expenditure saved, if less, with interest where appropriate.

(2) Where the unjustified enrichment resulted from E's being saved a loss or expenditure by consuming C's property, the redress due by E to C is the amount which it would have been reasonable to expect E to pay for the property at the time of consumption, or the amount of loss or expenditure saved, if less, with interest where appropriate.

(3) Where the unjustified enrichment resulted from E's being saved a loss or expenditure by interfering with C's patrimonial rights in any other way, the redress due by E to C is the amount which it would have been reasonable to expect E to pay C, at the time of the interference, for permission to interfere with those rights in that way in the circumstances, or the amount of loss or expenditure saved, if less, with interest where appropriate.

7. Where the unjustified enrichment resulted from the acquisition of any other benefit by E from C, the redress due by E to C is the amount which it would have been reasonable to expect E to pay C for the benefit at the time or acquisition, or the amount of E's actual enrichment, if less, with interest where appropriate.

PART II

E acquires benefit from T at indirect expense of C

8. This part of the schedule applies where the enriched person (E) has been enriched indirectly at the expense of the claimant (C).

9. Where E has enriched himself by using or disposing of C's property, or otherwise interfering with C's patrimonial rights, in order to obtain money or money's worth from a third party (T) the redress due by E to C is the amount which it would have been reasonable for E to pay C at the time of the use, disposal or interference for permission to use or dispose of C's property or to interfere with his rights in that way, or the amount of E's actual enrichment attributable to the use, disposal or interference, if less, with interest where appropriate.

10. Where E has been indirectly enriched at the expense of C as a result of the transfer of a benefit from a third party (T) in the circumstances covered by rule 8(2) (transfer of benefit arising from unjustified enrichment to person taking otherwise than in good faith and for value) T is treated as if he had been acting as E's agent and accordingly the redress due by E to C is the same, and is due on the same conditions, as it would have been if E had acquired the benefit directly from C.

11.   Where E has been indirectly enriched at the expense of C in the circumstances covered by rule 8(3) (transfers from trusts or executries) the redress due by E to C is

(1)   where C is a creditor claiming under rule 8(3)(a) the amount of the debt due to C out of the estate or the amount of E's enrichment out of the estate, whichever is the less, with interest where appropriate

(2)   where C is a true beneficiary claiming under rule 8(3)(b), and the benefit due to him out of the estate and received by E was a special legacy, the transfer of the subject matter of the legacy along with a sum to take account of any benefit derived by E from its use or possession or, if the subject matter of the legacy cannot be transferred in substantially the same condition as it was in when acquired by E, an amount representing its value when acquired by E, with interest from that date

(3)   where C is a true beneficiary claiming under rule 8(3)(b), and the benefit due to him out of the estate and received by E was not a special legacy, the amount of the benefit due to C out of the estate or the amount of E's unjustified enrichment out of the estate, whichever is the less, with interest where appropriate.

PART III

General

12.   Any reference in this schedule to the return of property includes a reference to a return by reconveyance or by any other means by which ownership can be restored to the other person.

13.   For the purposes of paragraph 2(2) corporeal property acquired by the enriched person by accession or specification, or any analogous rule whereby one person may acquire another's property when it becomes attached to or mixed with his own, is treated as property which cannot be returned in substantially the same condition as it was in at the time of acquisition.

14.   Where property is to be returned or transferred to the claimant by the enriched person under these rules, the expenses of the return or transfer are to be borne

(1)   by the claimant if the enrichment was in good faith, or

(2)   by the enriched person if the enrichment was in bad faith unless a court dealing with the claim orders otherwise.

15.   In assessing what it would have been reasonable for E to pay C for any interference with C's rights or for permission to interfere with those rights regard may be had to any factors which would have made C reluctant or unwilling to permit the interference.

UNIDROIT PRINCIPLES FOR INTERNATIONAL COMMERCIAL CONTRACTS 2010*

PREAMBLE

(Purpose of the Principles)
These Principles set forth general rules for international commercial contracts.

They shall be applied when the parties have agreed that their contract be governed by them.†)

They may be applied when the parties have agreed that their contract be governed by general principles of law, the *lex mercatoria* or the like.

They may be applied when the parties have not chosen any law to govern their contract.

They may be used to interpret or supplement international uniform law instruments.

They may be used to interpret or supplement domestic law.

They may serve as a model for national and international legislators.

CHAPTER 1. GENERAL PROVISIONS

Article 1.1   Freedom of contract
The parties are free to enter into a contract and to determine its content.

Article 1.2   No form required
Nothing in these Principles requires a contract, statement or any other act to be made in or evidenced by a particular form. It may be proved by any means, including witnesses.

Article 1.3   Binding character of contract
A contract validly entered into is binding upon the parties. It can only be modified or terminated in accordance with its terms or by agreement or as otherwise provided in these Principles.

Article 1.4   Mandatory rules
Nothing in these Principles shall restrict the application of mandatory rules, whether of national, international or supranational origin, which are applicable in accordance with the relevant rules of private international law.

Article 1.5   Exclusion or modification by the parties
The parties may exclude the application of these Principles or derogate from or vary the effect of any of their provisions, except as otherwise provided in the Principles.

---

*The reader is reminded that the complete version of the Unidroit Principles contains not only the black-letter rules reproduced hereunder, but also detailed comments on each article and, where appropriate, illustrations. The complete version can be obtained from Unidroit (see http://www.unidroit.org). For international case law relating to the Unidroit Principles see the Unilex database at http://www.unilex.info.

† Parties wishing to provide that their agreement be governed by the Principles might use the following words, adding any desired exceptions or modifications: 'This contract shall be governed by the Unidroit Principles (2010) [except as to Articles . . .]'.

   Parties wishing to provide in addition for the application of the law of a particular jurisdiction might use the following words: 'This contract shall be governed by the Unidroit Principles (2010) [except as to Articles . . .]', supplemented when necessary by the law of [jurisdiction X].

Article 1.6   Interpretation and supplementation of the Principles
(1)   In the interpretation of these Principles, regard is to be had to their international character and to their purposes including the need to promote uniformity in their application.

(2)   Issues within the scope of these Principles but not expressly settled by them are as far as possible to be settled in accordance with their underlying general principles.

Article 1.7   Good faith and fair dealing
(1)   Each party must act in accordance with good faith and fair dealing in international trade.

(2)   The parties may not exclude or limit this duty.

Article 1.8   Inconsistent behaviour
A party cannot act inconsistently with an understanding it has caused the other party to have and upon which that other party reasonably has acted in reliance to its detriment.

Article 1.9   Usages and practices
(1)   The parties are bound by any usage to which they have agreed and by any practices which they have established between themselves.

(2)   The parties are bound by a usage that is widely known to and regularly observed in international trade by parties in the particular trade concerned except where the application of such a usage would be unreasonable.

Article 1.10   Notice
(1)   Where notice is required it may be given by any means appropriate to the circumstances.

(2)   A notice is effective when it reaches the person to whom it is given.

(3)   For the purpose of paragraph (2) a notice 'reaches' a person when given to that person orally or delivered at that person's place of business or mailing address.

(4)   For the purpose of this article 'notice' includes a declaration, demand, request or any other communication of intention.

Article 1.11   Definitions
In these Principles
   – 'court' includes an arbitral tribunal;
   – where a party has more than one place of business the relevant 'place of business' is that which has the closest relationship to the contract and its performance, having regard to the circumstances known to or contemplated by the parties at any time before or at the conclusion of the contract;
   – 'obligor' refers to the party who is to perform an obligation and 'obligee' refers to the party who is entitled to performance of that obligation.
   – 'writing' means any mode of communication that preserves a record of the information contained therein and is capable of being reproduced in tangible form.

Article 1.12   Computation of time set by parties
(1)   Official holidays or non-business days occurring during a period set by parties for an act to be performed are included in calculating the period.

(2)   However, if the last day of the period is an official holiday or a non-business day at the place of business of the party to perform the act, the period is extended until the first business day which follows, unless the circumstances indicate otherwise.

(3)   The relevant time zone is that of the place of business of the party setting the time, unless the circumstances indicate otherwise.

CHAPTER 2 — FORMATION AND AUTHORITY OF AGENTS

Section 1: Formation

Article 2.1.1   Manner of formation
A contract may be concluded either by the acceptance of an offer or by conduct of the parties that is sufficient to show agreement.

Article 2.1.2   Definition of offer
A proposal for concluding a contract constitutes an offer if it is sufficiently definite and indicates the intention of the offeror to be bound in case of acceptance.

Article 2.1.3   Withdrawal of offer
(1)   An offer becomes effective when it reaches the offeree.
(2)   An offer, even if it is irrevocable, may be withdrawn if the withdrawal reaches the offeree before or at the same time as the offer.

Article 2.1.4   Revocation of offer
(1)   Until a contract is concluded an offer may be revoked if the revocation reaches the offeree before it has dispatched an acceptance.
(2)   However, an offer cannot be revoked
   (a)   if it indicates, whether by stating a fixed time for acceptance or other-wise, that it is irrevocable; or
   (b)   if it was reasonable for the offeree to rely on the offer as being irrevoc-able and the offeree has acted in reliance on the offer.

Article 2.1.5   Rejection of offer
An offer is terminated when a rejection reaches the offeror.

Article 2.1.6   Mode of acceptance
(1)   A statement made by or other conduct of the offeree indicating assent to an offer is an acceptance. Silence or inactivity does not in itself amount to acceptance.
(2)   An acceptance of an offer becomes effective when the indication of assent reaches the offeror.
(3)   However, if, by virtue of the offer or as a result of practices which the parties have established between themselves or of usage, the offeree may indicate assent by performing an act without notice to the offeror, the acceptance is effec-tive when the act is performed.

Article 2.1.7   Time of acceptance
An offer must be accepted within the time the offeror has fixed or, if no time is fixed, within a reasonable time having regard to the circumstances, including the rapidity of the means of communication employed by the offeror. An oral offer must be accepted immediately unless the circumstances indicate otherwise.

Article 2.1.8   Acceptance within a fixed period of time
A period of acceptance fixed by the offeror begins to run from the time that the offer is dispatched. A time indicated in the offer is deemed to be the time of dis-patch unless the circumstances indicate otherwise.

Article 2.1.9   Late acceptance. Delay in transmission
(1)   A late acceptance is nevertheless effective as an acceptance if without undue delay the offeror so informs the offeree or gives notice to that effect.
(2)   If a communication containing a late acceptance shows that it has been sent in such circumstances that if its transmission had been normal it would have reached the offeror in due time, the late acceptance is effective as an acceptance unless, without undue delay, the offeror informs the offeree that it considers the offer as having lapsed.

Article 2.1.10   Withdrawal of acceptance

An acceptance may be withdrawn if the withdrawal reaches the offeror before or at the same time as the acceptance would have become effective.

Article 2.1.11   Modified acceptance

(1)   A reply to an offer which purports to be an acceptance but contains additions, limitations or other modifications is a rejection of the offer and constitutes a counter-offer.

(2)   However, a reply to an offer which purports to be an acceptance but contains additional or different terms which do not materially alter the terms of the offer constitutes an acceptance, unless the offeror, without undue delay, objects to the discrepancy. If the offeror does not object, the terms of the contract are the terms of the offer with the modifications contained in the acceptance.

Article 2.1.12   Writings in confirmation

If a writing which is sent within a reasonable time after the conclusion of the contract and which purports to be a confirmation of the contract contains additional or different terms, such terms become part of the contract, unless they materially alter the contract or the recipient, without undue delay, objects to the discrepancy.

Article 2.1.13   Conclusion of contract dependent on agreement on specific matters or in particular form

Where in the course of negotiations one of the parties insists that the contract is not concluded until there is agreement on specific matters or in a particular form, no contract is concluded before agreement is reached on those matters or in that form.

Article 2.1.14   Contract with terms deliberately left open

(1)   If the parties intend to conclude a contract, the fact that they intentionally leave a term to be agreed upon in further negotiations or to be determined by a third person does not prevent a contract from coming into existence.

(2)   The existence of the contract is not affected by the fact that subsequently

   (a)   the parties reach no agreement on the term; or

   (b)   the third person does not determine the term,

provided that there is an alternative means of rendering the term definite that is reasonable in the circumstances, having regard to the intention of the parties.

Article 2.1.15   Negotiations in bad faith

(1)   A party is free to negotiate and is not liable for failure to reach an agreement.

(2)   However, a party who negotiates or breaks off negotiations in bad faith is liable for the losses caused to the other party.

(3)   It is bad faith, in particular, for a party to enter into or continue negotiations when intending not to reach an agreement with the other party.

Article 2.1.16   Duty of confidentiality

Where information is given as confidential by one party in the course of negotiations, the other party is under a duty not to disclose that information or to use it improperly for its own purposes, whether or not a contract is subsequently concluded. Where appropriate, the remedy for breach of that duty may include compensation based on the benefit received by the other party.

Article 2.1.17   Merger clauses

A contract in writing which contains a clause indicating that the writing completely embodies the terms on which the parties have agreed cannot be contradicted or supplemented by evidence of prior statements or agreements. However, such statements or agreements may be used to interpret the writing.

Article 2.1.18   Modification in a particular form

A contract in writing which contains a clause requiring any modification or termination by agreement to be in a particular form may not be otherwise modified or terminated. However, a party may be precluded by its conduct from asserting such a clause to the extent that the other party has reasonably acted in reliance on that conduct.

Article 2.1.19   Contracting under standard terms

(1)   Where one party or both parties use standard terms in concluding a contract, the general rules on formation apply, subject to Articles 2.1.20–2.1.22.

(2)   Standard terms are provisions which are prepared in advance for general and repeated use by one party and which are actually used without negotiation with the other party.

Article 2.1.20   Surprising terms

(1)   No term contained in standard terms which is of such a character that the other party could not reasonably have expected it, is effective unless it has been expressly accepted by that party.

(2)   In determining whether a term is of such a character regard shall be had to its content, language and presentation.

Article 2.1.21   Conflict between standard terms and non-standard terms

In case of conflict between a standard term and a term which is not a standard term the latter prevails.

Article 2.1.22   Battle of forms

Where both parties use standard terms and reach agreement except on those terms, a contract is concluded on the basis of the agreed terms and of any standard terms which are common in substance unless one party clearly indicates in advance, or later and without undue delay informs the other party, that it does not intend to be bound by such a contract.

Section 2: Authority of Agents

Article 2.2.1   Scope of the Section

(1)   This Section governs the authority of a person ('the agent'), to affect the legal relations of another person ('the principal'), by or with respect to a contract with a third party, whether the agent acts in its own name or in that of the principal.

(2)   It governs only the relations between the principal or the agent on the one hand, and the third party on the other.

(3)   It does not govern an agent's authority conferred by law or the authority of an agent appointed by a public or judicial authority.

Article 2.2.2   Establishment and scope of the authority of the agent

(1)   The principal's grant of authority to an agent may be express or implied.

(2)   The agent has authority to perform all acts necessary in the circumstances to achieve the purposes for which the authority was granted.

Article 2.2.3   Agency disclosed

(1)   Where an agent acts within the scope of its authority and the third party knew or ought to have known that the agent was acting as an agent, the acts of the agent shall directly affect the legal relations between the principal and the third party and no legal relation is created between the agent and the third party.

(2)   However, the acts of the agent shall affect only the relations between the agent and the third party, where the agent with the consent of the principal undertakes to become the party to the contract.

Article 2.2.4   Agency undisclosed

(1)   Where an agent acts within the scope of its authority and the third party neither knew nor ought to have known that the agent was acting as an agent, the

acts of the agent shall affect only the relations between the agent and the third party.

(2)   However, where such an agent, when contracting with the third party on behalf of a business, represents itself to be the owner of that business, the third party, upon discovery of the real owner of the business, may exercise also against the latter the rights it has against the agent.

Article 2.2.5   Agent acting without or exceeding its authority

(1)   Where an agent acts without authority or exceeds its authority, its acts do not affect the legal relations between the principal and the third party.

(2)   However, where the principal causes the third party reasonably to believe that the agent has authority to act on behalf of the principal and that the agent is acting within the scope of that authority, the principal may not invoke against the third party the lack of authority of the agent.

Article 2.2.6   Liability of agent acting without or exceeding its authority

(1)   An agent that acts without authority or exceeds its authority is, failing ratification by the principal, liable for damages that will place the third party in the same position as if the agent had acted with authority and not exceeded its authority.

(2)   However, the agent is not liable if the third party knew or ought to have known that the agent had no authority or was exceeding its authority.

Article 2.2.7   Conflict of interests

(1)   If a contract concluded by an agent involves the agent in a conflict of interests with the principal of which the third party knew or ought to have known, the principal may avoid the contract. The right to avoid is subject to Articles 3.2.9 and 3.2.11 to 3.2.15.

(2)   However, the principal may not avoid the contract
    (a)   if the principal had consented to, or knew or ought to have known of, the agent's involvement in the conflict of interests; or
    (b)   if the agent had disclosed the conflict of interests to the principal and the latter had not objected within a reasonable time.

Article 2.2.8   Sub-agency

An agent has implied authority to appoint a sub-agent to perform acts which it is not reasonable to expect the agent to perform itself. The rules of this Section apply to the sub-agency.

Article 2.2.9   Ratification

(1)   An act by an agent that acts without authority or exceeds its authority may be ratified by the principal. On ratification the act produces the same effects as if it had initially been carried out with authority.

(2)   The third party may by notice to the principal specify a reasonable period of time for ratification. If the principal does not ratify within that period of time it can no longer do so.

(3)   If, at the time of the agent's act, the third party neither knew nor ought to have known of the lack of authority, it may, at any time before ratification, by notice to the principal indicate its refusal to become bound by a ratification.

Article 2.2.10   Termination of authority

(1)   Termination of authority is not effective in relation to the third party unless the third party knew or ought to have known of it.

(2)   Notwithstanding the termination of its authority, an agent remains authorised to perform the acts that are necessary to prevent harm to the principal's interests.

CHAPTER 3 — VALIDITY

Section 1: General Provisions

Article 3.1.1   Matters not covered
This Chapter does not deal with lack of capacity.

Article 3.1.2   Validity of mere agreement
A contract is concluded, modified or terminated by the mere agreement of the parties, without any further requirement.

Article 3.1.3   Initial impossibility
(1)   The mere fact that at the time of the conclusion of the contract the performance of the obligation assumed was impossible does not affect the validity of the contract.
(2)   The mere fact that at the time of the conclusion of the contract a party was not entitled to dispose of the assets to which the contract relates does not affect the validity of the contract.

Article 3.1.4   Mandatory character of the provision
The provisions on fraud, threat, gross disparity and illegality contained in this Chapter are mandatory.

Section 2: Grounds for Avoidance

Article 3.2.1   Definition of mistake
Mistake is an erroneous assumption relating to facts or to law existing when the contract was concluded.

Article 3.2.2   Relevant mistake
(1)   A party may only avoid the contract for mistake if, when the contract was concluded, the mistake was of such importance that a reasonable person in the same situation as the party in error would only have concluded the contract on materially different terms or would not have concluded it at all if the true state of affairs had been known, and
    (a)   the other party made the same mistake, or caused the mistake, or knew or ought to have known of the mistake and it was contrary to reasonable commercial standards of fair dealing to leave the mistaken party in error; or
    (b)   the other party had not at the time of avoidance reasonably acted in reliance on the contract.
(2)   However, a party may not avoid the contract if
    (a)   it was grossly negligent in committing the mistake; or
    (b)   the mistake relates to a matter in regard to which the risk of mistake was assumed or, having regard to the circumstances, should be borne by the mistaken party.

Article 3.2.3   Error in expression or transmission
An error occurring in the expression or transmission of a declaration is considered to be a mistake of the person from whom the declaration emanated.

Article 3.2.4   Remedies for non-performance
A party is not entitled to avoid the contract on the ground of mistake if the circumstances on which that party relies afford, or could have afforded, a remedy for non-performance.

Article 3.2.5   Fraud
A party may avoid the contract when it has been led to conclude the contract by the other party's fraudulent representation, including language or practices, or fraudulent non-disclosure of circumstances which, according to reasonable commercial standards of fair dealing, the latter party should have disclosed.

Article 3.2.6   Threat

A party may avoid the contract when it has been led to conclude the contract by the other party's unjustified threat which, having regard to the circumstances, is so imminent and serious as to leave the first party no reasonable alternative. In particular, a threat is unjustified if the act or omission with which a party has been threatened is wrongful in itself, or it is wrongful to use it as a means to obtain the conclusion of the contract.

Article 3.2.7   Gross disparity

(1)   A party may avoid the contract or an individual term of it if, at the time of the conclusion of the contract, the contract or term unjustifiably gave the other party an excessive advantage. Regard is to be had, among other factors, to

(a)   the fact that the other party has taken unfair advantage of the first party's dependence, economic distress or urgent needs, or of its improvidence, ignorance, inexperience or lack of bargaining skill, and

(b)   the nature and purpose of the contract.

(2)   Upon the request of the party entitled to avoidance, a court may adapt the contract or term in order to make it accord with reasonable commercial standards of fair dealing.

(3)   A court may also adapt the contract or term upon the request of the party receiving notice of avoidance, provided that that party informs the other party of its request promptly after receiving such notice and before the other party has reasonably acted in reliance on it. The provisions of Article 3.2.10(2) apply accordingly.

Article 3.2.8   Third persons

(1)   Where fraud, threat, gross disparity or a party's mistake is imputable to, or is known or ought to be known by, a third person for whose acts the other party is responsible, the contract may be avoided under the same conditions as if the behaviour or knowledge had been that of the party itself.

(2)   Where fraud, threat or gross disparity is imputable to a third person for whose acts the other party is not responsible, the contract may be avoided if that party knew or ought to have known of the fraud, threat or disparity, or has not at the time of avoidance reasonably acted in reliance on the contract.

Article 3.2.9   Confirmation

If the party entitled to avoid the contract expressly or impliedly confirms the contract after the period of time for giving notice of avoidance has begun to run, avoidance of the contract is excluded.

Article 3.2.10   Loss of right to avoid

(1)   If a party is entitled to avoid the contract for mistake but the other party declares itself willing to perform or performs the contract as it was understood by the party entitled to avoidance, the contract is considered to have been concluded as the latter party understood it. The other party must make such a declaration or render such performance promptly after having been informed of the manner in which the party entitled to avoidance had understood the contract and before that party has reasonably acted in reliance on a notice of avoidance.

(2)   After such a declaration or performance the right to avoidance is lost and any earlier notice of avoidance is ineffective.

Article 3.2.11   Notice of avoidance

The right of a party to avoid the contract is exercised by notice to the other party.

Article 3.2.12   Time limits

(1)   Notice of avoidance shall be given within a reasonable time, having regard to the circumstances, after the avoiding party knew or could not have been unaware of the relevant facts or became capable of acting freely.

(2)   Where an individual term of the contract may be avoided by a party under

Article 3.2.7, the period of time for giving notice of avoidance begins to run when that term is asserted by the other party.

Article 3.2.13   Partial avoidance

Where a ground of avoidance affects only individual terms of the contract, the effect of avoidance is limited to those terms unless, having regard to the circumstances, it is unreasonable to uphold the remaining contract.

Article 3.2.14   Retroactive effect of avoidance

Avoidance takes effect retroactively.

Article 3.2.15   Restitution

(1)   On avoidance either party may claim restitution of whatever it has supplied under the contract, or the part of it avoided, provided that the party concurrently makes restitution of whatever it has received under the contract, or the part of it avoided.

(2)   If restitution in kind is not possible or appropriate, an allowance has to be made in money whenever reasonable.

(3)   The recipient of the performance does not have to make an allowance in money if the impossibility to make restitution in kind is attributable to the other party.

(4)   Compensation may be claimed for expenses reasonably required to preserve or maintain the performance received.

Article 3.2.16   Damages

Irrespective of whether or not the contract has been avoided, the party who knew or ought to have known of the ground for avoidance is liable for damages so as to put the other party in the same position in which it would have been if it had not concluded the contract.

Article 3.2.17   Unilateral declarations

The provisions of this Chapter apply with appropriate adaptations to any communication of intention addressed by one party to the other.

Section 3: Illegality

Article 3.3.1   Contracts infringing mandatory rules

(1)   Where a contract infringes a mandatory rule, whether of national, international or supranational origin, applicable under Article 1.4 of these Principles, the effects of that infringement upon the contract are the effects, if any, expressly prescribed by that mandatory rule.

(2)   Where the mandatory rule does not expressly prescribe the effects of an infringement upon a contract, the parties have the right to exercise such remedies under the contract as in the circumstances are reasonable.

(3)   In determining what is reasonable regard is to be had in particular to:
   (a)   the purpose of the rule which has been infringed;
   (b)   the category of persons for whose protection the rule exists;
   (c)   any sanction that may be imposed under the rule infringed;
   (d)   the seriousness of the infringement;
   (e)   whether one or both parties knew or ought to have known of the infringement;
   (f)   whether the performance of the contract necessitates the infringement; and
   (g)   the parties' reasonable expectations.

Article 3.3.2   Restitution

(1)   Where there has been performance under a contract infringing a mandatory rule under Article 3.3.1, restitution may be granted where this would be reasonable in the circumstances.

(2)   In determining what is reasonable, regard is to be had, with the appropriate adaptations, to the criteria referred to in Article 3.3.1(3).

(3)   If restitution is granted, the rules set out in Article 3.2.15 apply with appropriate adaptations.

CHAPTER 4 — INTERPRETATION

Article 4.1   Intention of the parties
(1)   A contract shall be interpreted according to the common intention of the parties.

(2)   If such an intention cannot be established, the contract shall be interpreted according to the meaning that reasonable persons of the same kind as the parties would give to it in the same circumstances.

Article 4.2   Interpretation of statements and other conduct
(1)   The statements and other conduct of a party shall be interpreted according to that party's intention if the other party knew or could not have been unaware of that intention.

(2)   If the preceding paragraph is not applicable, such statements and other conduct shall be interpreted according to the meaning that a reasonable person of the same kind as the other party would give to it in the same circumstances.

Article 4.3   Relevant circumstances
In applying Articles 4.1 and 4.2, regard shall be had to all the circumstances, including

(a)   preliminary negotiations between the parties;

(b)   practices which the parties have established between themselves;

(c)   the conduct of the parties subsequent to the conclusion of the contract;

(d)   the nature and purpose of the contract;

(e)   the meaning commonly given to terms and expressions in the trade concerned;

(f)   usages.

Article 4.4   Reference to contract or statement as a whole
Terms and expressions shall be interpreted in the light of the whole contract or statement in which they appear.

Article 4.5   All terms to be given effect
Contract terms shall be interpreted so as to give effect to all the terms rather than to deprive some of them of effect.

Article 4.6   Contra proferentem rule
If contract terms supplied by one party are unclear, an interpretation against that party is preferred.

Article 4.7   Linguistic discrepancies
Where a contract is drawn up in two or more language versions which are equally authoritative there is, in case of discrepancy between the versions, a preference for the interpretation according to a version in which the contract was originally drawn up.

Article 4.8   Supplying an omitted term
(1)   Where the parties to a contract have not agreed with respect to a term which is important for a determination of their rights and duties, a term which is appropriate in the circumstances shall be supplied.

(2)   In determining what is an appropriate term regard shall be had, among other factors, to

(a)   the intention of the parties;

(b)   the nature and purpose of the contract;

(c)   good faith and fair dealing;

(d)   reasonableness.

CHAPTER 5 — CONTENT AND THIRD PARTY RIGHTS

Section 1: Content

Article 5.1.1   Express and implied obligations
The contractual obligations of the parties may be express or implied.

Article 5.1.2   Implied obligations
Implied obligations stem from
    (a)   the nature and purpose of the contract;
    (b)   practices established between the parties and usages;
    (c)   good faith and fair dealing;
    (d)   reasonableness.

Article 5.1.3   Co-operation between the parties
Each party shall co-operate with the other party when such co-operation may reasonably be expected for the performance of that party's obligations.

Article 5.1.4   Duty to achieve a specific result. Duty of best efforts
(1)   To the extent that an obligation of a party involves a duty to achieve a specific result, that party is bound to achieve that result.
(2)   To the extent that an obligation of a party involves a duty of best efforts in the performance of an activity, that party is bound to make such efforts as would be made by a reasonable person of the same kind in the same circumstances.

Article 5.1.5   Determination of kind of duty involved
In determining the extent to which an obligation of a party involves a duty of best efforts in the performance of an activity or a duty to achieve a specific result, regard shall be had, among other factors, to
    (a)   the way in which the obligation is expressed in the contract;
    (b)   the contractual price and other terms of the contract;
    (c)   the degree of risk normally involved in achieving the expected result;
    (d)   the ability of the other party to influence the performance of the obligation.

Article 5.1.6   Determination of quality of performance
Where the quality of performance is neither fixed by, nor determinable from, the contract a party is bound to render a performance of a quality that is reasonable and not less than average in the circumstances.

Article 5.1.7   Price determination
(1)   Where a contract does not fix or make provision for determining the price, the parties are considered, in the absence of any indication to the contrary, to have made reference to the price generally charged at the time of the conclusion of the contract for such performance in comparable circumstances in the trade concerned or, if no such price is available, to a reasonable price.
(2)   Where the price is to be determined by one party and that determination is manifestly unreasonable, a reasonable price shall be substituted notwithstanding any contract term to the contrary.
(3)   Where the price is to be fixed by a third person, and that person cannot or will not do so, the price shall be a reasonable price.
(4)   Where the price is to be fixed by reference to factors which do not exist or have ceased to exist or to be accessible, the nearest equivalent factor shall be treated as a substitute.

Article 5.1.8   Contract for an indefinite period
A contract for an indefinite period may be ended by either party by giving notice a reasonable time in advance.

Article 5.1.9   Release by agreement

(1)   An obligee may release its right by agreement with the obligor.

(2)   An offer to release a right gratuitously shall be deemed accepted if the obligor does not reject the offer without delay after having become aware of it.

Section 2: Third Party Rights

Article 5.2.1   Contracts in favour of third parties

(1)   The parties (the 'promisor' and the 'promisee') may confer by express or implied agreement a right on a third party (the 'beneficiary').

(2)   The existence and content of the beneficiary's right against the promisor are determined by the agreement of the parties and are subject to any conditions or other limitations under the agreement.

Article 5.2.2   Third party identifiable

The beneficiary must be identifiable with adequate certainty by the contract but need not be in existence at the time the contract is made.

Article 5.2.3   Exclusion and limitation clauses

The conferment of rights in the beneficiary includes the right to invoke a clause in the contract which excludes or limits the liability of the beneficiary.

Article 5.2.4   Defences

The promisor may assert against the beneficiary all defences which the promisor could assert against the promisee.

Article 5.2.5   Revocation

The parties may modify or revoke the rights conferred by the contract on the bene-ficiary until the beneficiary has accepted them or reasonably acted in reliance on them.

Article 5.2.6   Renunciation

The beneficiary may renounce a right conferred on it.

Section 3: Conditions

Article 5.3.1   Types of condition

A contract or a contractual obligation may be made conditional upon the occur-rence of a future uncertain event, so that the contract or the contractual obligation only takes effect if the event occurs (suspensive condition) or comes to an end if the event occurs (resolutive condition).

Article 5.3.2   Effect of conditions

Unless the parties otherwise agree:

(a)   the relevant contract or contractual obligation takes effect upon fulfil-ment of a suspensive condition;

(b)   the relevant contract or contractual obligation comes to an end upon ful-filment of a resolutive condition.

Article 5.3.3   Interference with conditions

(1)   If fulfilment of a condition is prevented by a party, contrary to the duty of good faith and fair dealing or the duty of co-operation, that party may not rely on the non-fulfilment of the condition.

(2)   If fulfilment of a condition is brought about by a party, contrary to the duty of good faith and fair dealing or the duty of co-operation, that party may not rely on the fulfilment of the condition

Article 5.3.4   Duty to preserve rights

Pending fulfilment of a condition, a party may not, contrary to the duty to act in accordance with good faith and fair dealing, act so as to prejudice the other party's rights in case of fulfilment of the condition.

Article 5.3.5   Restitution in case of fulfilment of a resolutive condition
(1)   On fulfilment of a resolutive condition, the rules on restitution set out in Articles 7.3.6 and 7.3.7 apply with appropriate adaptations.

(2)   If the parties have agreed that the resolutive condition is to operate retro-actively, the rules on restitution set out in Article 3.2.15 apply with appropriate adaptations.

CHAPTER 6 — PERFORMANCE

Section 1: Performance in General

Article 6.1.1   Time of performance
A party must perform its obligations:

    (a)   if a time is fixed by or determinable from the contract, at that time;

    (b)   if a period of time is fixed by or determinable from the contract, at any time within that period unless circumstances indicate that the other party is to choose a time;

    (c)   in any other case, within a reasonable time after the conclusion of the contract.

Article 6.1.2   Performance at one time or in instalments
In cases under Article 6.1.1(b) or (c), a party must perform its obligations at one time if that performance can be rendered at one time and the circumstances do not indicate otherwise.

Article 6.1.3   Partial performance
(1)   The obligee may reject an offer to perform in part at the time performance is due, whether or not such offer is coupled with an assurance as to the balance of the performance, unless the obligee has no legitimate interest in so doing.

(2)   Additional expenses caused to the obligee by partial performance are to be borne by the obligor without prejudice to any other remedy.

Article 6.1.4   Order of performance
(1)   To the extent that the performances of the parties can be rendered simul-taneously, the parties are bound to render them simultaneously unless the circum-stances indicate otherwise.

(2)   To the extent that the performance of only one party requires a period of time, that party is bound to render its performance first, unless the circumstances indicate otherwise.

Article 6.1.5   Earlier performance
(1)   The obligee may reject an earlier performance unless it has no legitimate interest in so doing.

(2)   Acceptance by a party of an earlier performance does not affect the time for the performance of its own obligations if that time has been fixed irrespective of the performance of the other party's obligations.

(3)   Additional expenses caused to the obligee by earlier performance are to be borne by the obligor, without prejudice to any other remedy.

Article 6.1.6   Place of performance
(1)   If the place of performance is neither fixed by, nor determinable from, the contract, a party is to perform:

    (a)   a monetary obligation, at the obligee's place of business;

    (b)   any other obligation, at its own place of business.

(2)   A party must bear any increase in the expenses incidental to performance which is caused by a change in its place of business subsequent to the conclusion of the contract.

Article 6.1.7   Payment by cheque or other instrument

(1)   Payment may be made in any form used in the ordinary course of business at the place for payment.

(2)   However, an obligee who accepts, either by virtue of paragraph (1) or voluntarily, a cheque, any other order to pay or a promise to pay, is presumed to do so only on condition that it will be honoured.

Article 6.1.8   Payment by funds transfer

(1)   Unless the obligee has indicated a particular account, payment may be made by a transfer to any of the financial institutions in which the obligee has made it known that it has an account.

(2)   In case of payment by a transfer the obligation of the obligor is discharged when the transfer to the obligee's financial institution becomes effective.

Article 6.1.9   Currency of payment

(1)   If a monetary obligation is expressed in a currency other than that of the place for payment, it may be paid by the obligor in the currency of the place for payment unless

(a)   that currency is not freely convertible; or

(b)   the parties have agreed that payment should be made only in the currency in which the monetary obligation is expressed.

(2)   If it is impossible for the obligor to make payment in the currency in which the monetary obligation is expressed, the obligee may require payment in the currency of the place for payment, even in the case referred to in paragraph (1)(b).

(3)   Payment in the currency of the place for payment is to be made according to the applicable rate of exchange prevailing there when payment is due.

(4)   However, if the obligor has not paid at the time when payment is due, the obligee may require payment according to the applicable rate of exchange prevailing either when payment is due or at the time of actual payment.

Article 6.1.10   Currency not expressed

Where a monetary obligation is not expressed in a particular currency, payment must be made in the currency of the place where payment is to be made.

Article 6.1.11   Costs of performance

Each party shall bear the costs of performance of its obligations.

Article 6.1.12   Imputation of payments

(1)   An obligor owing several monetary obligations to the same obligee may specify at the time of payment the debt to which it intends the payment to be applied. However, the payment discharges first any expenses, then interest due and finally the principal.

(2)   If the obligor makes no such specification, the obligee may, within a reasonable time after payment, declare to the obligor the obligation to which it imputes the payment, provided that the obligation is due and undisputed.

(3)   In the absence of imputation under paragraphs (1) or (2), payment is imputed to that obligation which satisfies one of the following criteria in the order indicated:

(a)   an obligation which is due or which is the first to fall due;

(b)   the obligation for which the obligee has least security;

(c)   the obligation which is the most burdensome for the obligor;

(d)   the obligation which has arisen first.

If none of the preceding criteria applies, payment is imputed to all the obligations proportionally.

Article 6.1.13   Imputation of non-monetary obligations

Article 6.1.12 applies with appropriate adaptations to the imputation of performance of non-monetary obligations.

Article 6.1.14   Application for public permission
Where the law of a State requires a public permission affecting the validity of the contract or its performance and neither that law nor the circumstances indicate otherwise
(a)   if only one party has its place of business in that State, that party shall take the measures necessary to obtain the permission;
(b)   in any other case the party whose performance requires permission shall take the necessary measures.

Article 6.1.15   Procedure in applying for permission
(1)   The party required to take the measures necessary to obtain the permission shall do so without undue delay and shall bear any expenses incurred.
(2)   That party shall whenever appropriate give the other party notice of the grant or refusal of such permission without undue delay.

Article 6.1.16   Permission neither granted nor refused
(1)   If, notwithstanding the fact that the party responsible has taken all measures required, permission is neither granted nor refused within an agreed period or, where no period has been agreed, within a reasonable time from the conclusion of the contract, either party is entitled to terminate the contract.
(2)   Where the permission affects some terms only, paragraph (1) does not apply if, having regard to the circumstances, it is reasonable to uphold the remaining contract even if the permission is refused.

Article 6.1.17   Permission refused
(1)   The refusal of a permission affecting the validity of the contract renders the contract void. If the refusal affects the validity of some terms only, only such terms are void if, having regard to the circumstances, it is reasonable to uphold the remaining contract.
(2)   Where the refusal of a permission renders the performance of the contract impossible in whole or in part, the rules on non-performance apply.

Section 2: Hardship

Article 6.2.1   Contract to be observed
Where the performance of a contract becomes more onerous for one of the parties, that party is nevertheless bound to perform its obligations subject to the following provisions on hardship.

Article 6.2.2   Definition of hardship
There is hardship where the occurrence of events fundamentally alters the equilibrium of the contract either because the cost of a party's performance has increased or because the value of the performance a party receives has diminished, and
(a)   the events occur or become known to the disadvantaged party after the conclusion of the contract;
(b)   the events could not reasonably have been taken into account by the disadvantaged party at the time of the conclusion of the contract;
(c)   the events are beyond the control of the disadvantaged party; and
(d)   the risk of the events was not assumed by the disadvantaged party.

Article 6.2.3   Effects of hardship
(1)   In case of hardship the disadvantaged party is entitled to request renegotiations. The request shall be made without undue delay and shall indicate the grounds on which it is based.
(2)   The request for renegotiation does not in itself entitle the disadvantaged party to withhold performance.
(3)   Upon failure to reach agreement within a reasonable time either party may resort to the court.

(4)   If the court finds hardship it may, if reasonable,
    (a)   terminate the contract at a date and on terms to be fixed, or
    (b)   adapt the contract with a view to restoring its equilibrium.

CHAPTER 7 — NON-PERFORMANCE

Section 1: Non-Performance in General

Article 7.1.1   Non-performance defined
Non-performance is failure by a party to perform any of its obligations under the contract, including defective performance or late performance.

Article 7.1.2   Interference by the other party
A party may not rely on the non-performance of the other party to the extent that such non-performance was caused by the first party's act or omission or by another event for which the first party bears the risk.

Article 7.1.3   Withholding performance
(1)   Where the parties are to perform simultaneously, either party may withhold performance until the other party tenders its performance.

(2)   Where the parties are to perform consecutively, the party that is to perform later may withhold its performance until the first party has performed.

Article 7.1.4   Cure by non-performing party
(1)   The non-performing party may, at its own expense, cure any non-performance, provided that
    (a)   without undue delay, it gives notice indicating the proposed manner and timing of the cure;
    (b)   cure is appropriate in the circumstances;
    (c)   the aggrieved party has no legitimate interest in refusing cure; and
    (d)   cure is effected promptly.

(2)   The right to cure is not precluded by notice of termination.

(3)   Upon effective notice of cure, rights of the aggrieved party that are inconsistent with the non-performing party's performance are suspended until the time for cure has expired.

(4)   The aggrieved party may withhold performance pending cure.

(5)   Notwithstanding cure, the aggrieved party retains the right to claim damages for delay as well as for any harm caused or not prevented by the cure.

Article 7.1.5   Additional period for performance
(1)   In a case of non-performance the aggrieved party may by notice to the other party allow an additional period of time for performance.

(2)   During the additional period the aggrieved party may withhold performance of its own reciprocal obligations and may claim damages but may not resort to any other remedy. If it receives notice from the other party that the latter will not perform within that period, or if upon expiry of that period due performance has not been made, the aggrieved party may resort to any of the remedies that may be available under this Chapter.

(3)   Where in a case of delay in performance which is not fundamental the aggrieved party has given notice allowing an additional period of time of reasonable length, it may terminate the contract at the end of that period. If the additional period allowed is not of reasonable length it shall be extended to a reasonable length. The aggrieved party may in its notice provide that if the other party fails to perform within the period allowed by the notice the contract shall automatically terminate.

(4)   Paragraph (3) does not apply where the obligation which has not been performed is only a minor part of the contractual obligation of the non-performing party.

Article 7.1.6   Exemption clauses
A clause which limits or excludes one party's liability for non-performance or which permits one party to render performance substantially different from what the other party reasonably expected may not be invoked if it would be grossly unfair to do so, having regard to the purpose of the contract.

Article 7.1.7   Force majeure
(1)   Non-performance by a party is excused if that party proves that the non-performance was due to an impediment beyond its control and that it could not reasonably be expected to have taken the impediment into account at the time of the conclusion of the contract or to have avoided or overcome it or its consequences.

(2)   When the impediment is only temporary, the excuse shall have effect for such period as is reasonable having regard to the effect of the impediment on the performance of the contract.

(3)   The party who fails to perform must give notice to the other party of the impediment and its effect on its ability to perform. If the notice is not received by the other party within a reasonable time after the party who fails to perform knew or ought to have known of the impediment, it is liable for damages resulting from such non-receipt.

(4)   Nothing in this article prevents a party from exercising a right to terminate the contract or to withhold performance or request interest on money due.

Section 2: Right to Performance

Article 7.2.1   Performance of monetary obligation
Where a party who is obliged to pay money does not do so, the other party may require payment.

Article 7.2.2   Performance of non-monetary obligation
Where a party who owes an obligation other than one to pay money does not perform, the other party may require performance, unless
  (a)   performance is impossible in law or in fact;
  (b)   performance or, where relevant, enforcement is unreasonably burdensome or expensive;
  (c)   the party entitled to performance may reasonably obtain performance from another source;
  (d)   performance is of an exclusively personal character; or
  (e)   the party entitled to performance does not require performance within a reasonable time after it has, or ought to have, become aware of the non-performance.

Article 7.2.3   Repair and replacement of defective performance
The right to performance includes in appropriate cases the right to require repair, replacement, or other cure of defective performance. The provisions of Articles 7.2.1 and 7.2.2 apply accordingly.

Article 7.2.4   Judicial penalty
(1)   Where the court orders a party to perform, it may also direct that this party pay a penalty if it does not comply with the order.

(2)   The penalty shall be paid to the aggrieved party unless mandatory provisions of the law of the forum provide otherwise. Payment of the penalty to the aggrieved party does not exclude any claim for damages.

Article 7.2.5   Change of remedy
(1)   An aggrieved party who has required performance of a non-monetary obligation and who has not received performance within a period fixed or otherwise within a reasonable period of time may invoke any other remedy.

(2)   Where the decision of a court for performance of a non-monetary obligation cannot be enforced, the aggrieved party may invoke any other remedy.

Section 3: Termination

Article 7.3.1   Right to terminate the contract

(1)   A party may terminate the contract where the failure of the other party to perform an obligation under the contract amounts to a fundamental non-performance.

(2)   In determining whether a failure to perform an obligation amounts to a fundamental non-performance regard shall be had, in particular, to whether

(a)   the non-performance substantially deprives the aggrieved party of what it was entitled to expect under the contract unless the other party did not foresee and could not reasonably have foreseen such result;

(b)   strict compliance with the obligation which has not been performed is of essence under the contract;

(c)   the non-performance is intentional or reckless;

(d)   the non-performance gives the aggrieved party reason to believe that it cannot rely on the other party's future performance;

(e)   the non-performing party will suffer disproportionate loss as a result of the preparation or performance if the contract is terminated.

(3)   In the case of delay the aggrieved party may also terminate the contract if the other party fails to perform before the time allowed it under Article 7.1.5 has expired.

Article 7.3.2   Notice of termination

(1)   The right of a party to terminate the contract is exercised by notice to the other party.

(2)   If performance has been offered late or otherwise does not conform to the contract the aggrieved party will lose its right to terminate the contract unless it gives notice to the other party within a reasonable time after it has or ought to have become aware of the offer or of the non-conforming performance.

Article 7.3.3   Anticipatory non-performance

Where prior to the date for performance by one of the parties it is clear that there will be a fundamental non-performance by that party, the other party may terminate the contract.

Article 7.3.4   Adequate assurance of due performance

A party who reasonably believes that there will be a fundamental non-performance by the other party may demand adequate assurance of due performance and may meanwhile withhold its own performance. Where this assurance is not provided within a reasonable time the party demanding it may terminate the contract.

Article 7.3.5   Effects of termination in general

(1)   Termination of the contract releases both parties from their obligation to effect and to receive future performance.

(2)   Termination does not preclude a claim for damages for non-performance.

(3)   Termination does not affect any provision in the contract for the settlement of disputes or any other term of the contract which is to operate even after termination.

Article 7.3.6   Restitution with respect to contracts to be performed at one time

(1)   On termination of a contract to be performed at one time either party may claim restitution of whatever it has supplied under the contract, provided that such party concurrently makes restitution of whatever it has received under the contract.

(2)   If restitution in kind is not possible or appropriate, an allowance has to be made in money whenever reasonable.

(3)   The recipient of the performance does not have to make an allowance in money if the impossibility to make restitution in kind is attributable to the other party.

(4)   Compensation may be claimed for expenses reasonably required to preserve or maintain the performance received.

Article 7.3.7   Restitution with respect to contracts to be performed over a period of time

(1)   On termination of a contract to be performed over a period of time restitution can only be claimed for the period after termination has taken effect, provided the contract is divisible.

(2)   As far as restitution has to be made, the provisions of Article 7.3.6 apply.

Section 4: Damages

Article 7.4.1   Right to damages

Any non-performance gives the aggrieved party a right to damages either exclusively or in conjunction with any other remedies except where the non-performance is excused under these Principles.

Article 7.4.2   Full compensation

(1)   The aggrieved party is entitled to full compensation for harm sustained as a result of the non-performance. Such harm includes both any loss which it suffered and any gain of which it was deprived, taking into account any gain to the aggrieved party resulting from its avoidance of cost or harm.

(2)   Such harm may be non-pecuniary and includes, for instance, physical suffering or emotional distress.

Article 7.4.3   Certainty of harm

(1)   Compensation is due only for harm, including future harm, that is established with a reasonable degree of certainty.

(2)   Compensation may be due for the loss of a chance in proportion to the probability of its occurrence.

(3)   Where the amount of damages cannot be established with a sufficient degree of certainty, the assessment is at the discretion of the court.

Article 7.4.4   Foreseeability of harm

The non-performing party is liable only for harm which it foresaw or could reasonably have foreseen at the time of the conclusion of the contract as being likely to result from its non-performance.

Article 7.4.5   Proof in harm in case of replacement transaction

Where the aggrieved party has terminated the contract and has made a replacement transaction within a reasonable time and in a reasonable manner it may recover the difference between the contract price and the price of the replacement transaction as well as damages for any further harm.

Article 7.4.6   Proof of harm by current price

(1)   Where the aggrieved party has terminated the contract and has not made a replacement transaction but there is a current price for the performance contracted for, it may recover the difference between the contract price and the price current at the time the contract is terminated as well as damages for any further harm.

(2)   Current price is the price generally charged for goods delivered or services rendered in comparable circumstances at the place where the contract should have been performed or, if there is no current price at that place, the current price at such other place that appears reasonable to take as a reference.

Article 7.4.7   Harm due in part to aggrieved party

Where the harm is due in part to an act or omission of the aggrieved party or to another event for which that party bears the risk, the amount of damages shall be reduced to the extent that these factors have contributed to the harm, having regard to the conduct of each of the parties.

Article 7.4.8   Mitigation of harm

(1)   The non-performing party is not liable for harm suffered by the aggrieved party to the extent that the harm could have been reduced by the latter party's taking reasonable steps.

(2)   The aggrieved party is entitled to recover any expenses reasonably incurred in attempting to reduce the harm.

Article 7.4.9   Interest for failure to pay money

(1)   If a party does not pay a sum of money when it falls due the aggrieved party is entitled to interest upon that sum from the time when payment is due to the time of payment whether or not the non-payment is excused.

(2)   The rate of interest shall be the average bank short-term lending rate to prime borrowers prevailing for the currency of payment at the place for payment, or where no such rate exists at that place, then the same rate in the State of the currency of payment. In the absence of such a rate at either place the rate of interest shall be the appropriate rate fixed by the law of the State of the currency of payment.

(3)   The aggrieved party is entitled to additional damages if the non-payment caused it a greater harm.

Article 7.4.10   Interest on damages

Unless otherwise agreed, interest on damages for non-performance of non-monetary obligations accrues as from the time of non-performance.

Article 7.4.11   Manner of monetary redress

(1)   Damages are to be paid in a lump sum. However, they may be payable in instalments where the nature of the harm makes this appropriate.

(2)   Damages to be paid in instalments may be indexed.

Article 7.4.12   Currency in which to assess damages

Damages are to be assessed either in the currency in which the monetary obligation was expressed or in the currency in which the harm was suffered, whichever is more appropriate.

Article 7.4.13   Agreed payment for non-performance

(1)   Where the contract provides that a party who does not perform is to pay a specified sum to the aggrieved party for such non-performance, the aggrieved party is entitled to that sum irrespective of its actual harm.

(2)   However, notwithstanding any agreement to the contrary the specified sum may be reduced to a reasonable amount where it is grossly excessive in relation to the harm resulting from the non-performance and to the other circumstances.

CHAPTER 8 — SET-OFF

Article 8.1   Conditions of set-off

(1)   Where two parties owe each other money or other performances of the same kind, either of them ('the first party') may set off its obligation against that of its obligee ('the other party') if at the time of set-off,

  (a)   the first party is entitled to perform its obligation;

  (b)   the other party's obligation is ascertained as to its existence and amount and performance is due.

(2)   If the obligations of both parties arise from the same contract, the first party may also set off its obligation against an obligation of the other party which is not ascertained as to its existence or to its amount.

Article 8.2   Foreign currency set-off

Where the obligations are to pay money in different currencies, the right of set-off may be exercised, provided that both currencies are freely convertible and the parties have not agreed that the first party shall pay only in a specified currency.

Article 8.3   Set-off by notice
The right of set-off is exercised by notice to the other party.

Article 8.4   Content of notice
(1)   The notice must specify the obligations to which it relates.

(2)   If the notice does not specify the obligation against which set-off is exercised, the other party may, within a reasonable time, declare to the first party the obligation to which set-off relates. If no such declaration is made, the set-off will relate to all the obligations proportionally.

Article 8.5   Effect of set-off
(1)   Set-off discharges the obligations.

(2)   If obligations differ in amount, set-off discharges the obligations up to the amount of the lesser obligation.

(3)   Set-off takes effect as from the time of notice.

CHAPTER 9 — ASSIGNMENT OF RIGHTS, TRANSFER OF OBLIGATIONS, ASSIGNMENT OF CONTRACTS

Section 1: Assignment of rights

Article 9.1.1   Definitions
'Assignment of a right' means the transfer by agreement from one person (the 'assignor') to another person (the 'assignee'), including transfer by way of security, of the assignor's right to payment of a monetary sum or other performance from a third person ('the obligor').

Article 9.1.2   Exclusions
This Section does not apply to transfers made under the special rules governing the transfers:

(a)   of instruments such as negotiable instruments, documents of title or financial instruments, or

(b)   of rights in the course of transferring a business.

Article 9.1.3   Assignability of non-monetary rights
A right to non-monetary performance may be assigned only if the assignment does not render the obligation significantly more burdensome.

Article 9.1.4   Partial assignment
(1)   A right to the payment of a monetary sum may be assigned partially.

(2)   A right to other performance may be assigned partially only if it is divisible, and the assignment does not render the obligation significantly more burdensome.

Article 9.1.5   Future rights
A future right is deemed to be transferred at the time of the agreement, provided the right, when it comes into existence, can be identified as the right to which the assignment relates.

Article 9.1.6   Rights assigned without individual specification
A number of rights may be assigned without individual specification, provided such rights can be identified as rights to which the assignment relates at the time of the assignment or when they come into existence.

Article 9.1.7   Agreement between assignor and assignee sufficient
(1)   A right is assigned by mere agreement between the assignor and the assignee, without notice to the obligor.

(2)   The consent of the obligor is not required unless the obligation in the circumstances is of an essentially personal character.

Article 9.1.8   Obligor's additional costs
The obligor has a right to be compensated by the assignor or the assignee for any additional costs caused by the assignment.

Article 9.1.9   Non-assignment clauses
(1)   The assignment of a right to the payment of a monetary sum is effective notwithstanding an agreement between the assignor and the obligor limiting or prohibiting such an assignment. However, the assignor may be liable to the obligor for breach of contract.

(2)   The assignment of a right to other performance is ineffective if it is contrary to an agreement between the assignor and the obligor limiting or prohibiting the assignment. Nevertheless, the assignment is effective if the assignee, at the time of the assignment, neither knew nor ought to have known of the agreement. The assignor may then be liable to the obligor for breach of contract.

Article 9.1.10   Notice to the obligor
(1)   Until the obligor receives a notice of the assignment from either the assignor or the assignee, it is discharged by paying the assignor.

(2)   After the obligor receives such a notice, it is discharged only by paying the assignee.

Article 9.1.11   Successive assignments
If the same right has been assigned by the same assignor to two or more successive assignees, the obligor is discharged by paying according to the order in which the notices were received.

Article 9.1.12   Adequate proof of assignment
(1)   If notice of the assignment is given by the assignee, the obligor may request the assignee to provide within a reasonable time adequate proof that the assignment has been made.

(2)   Until adequate proof is provided, the obligor may withhold payment.

(3)   Unless adequate proof is provided, notice is not effective.

(4)   Adequate proof includes, but is not limited to, any writing emanating from the assignor and indicating that the assignment has taken place.

Article 9.1.13   Defences and rights of set-off
(1)   The obligor may assert against the assignee all defences that the obligor could assert against the assignor.

(2)   The obligor may exercise against the assignee any right of set-off available to the obligor against the assignor up to the time notice of assignment was received.

Article 9.1.14   Rights related to the right assigned
The assignment of a right transfers to the assignee:

(a)   all the assignor's rights to payment or other performance under the contract in respect of the right assigned, and

(b)   all rights securing performance of the right assigned.

Article 9.1.15   Undertakings of the assignor
The assignor undertakes towards the assignee, except as otherwise disclosed to the assignee, that:

(a)   the assigned right exists at the time of the assignment, unless the right is a future right;

(b)   the assignor is entitled to assign the right;

(c)   the right has not been previously assigned to another assignee, and it is free from any right or claim from a third party;

(d)   the obligor does not have any defences;

(e)   neither the obligor nor the assignor has given notice of set-off concerning the assigned right and will not give any such notice;

(f)   the assignor will reimburse the assignee for any payment received from the obligor before notice of the assignment was given.

Section 2: Transfer of obligations

Article 9.2.1   Modes of transfer
An obligation to pay money or render other performance may be transferred from one person (the 'original obligor') to another person (the 'new obligor') either
(a)   by an agreement between the original obligor and the new obligor subject to Article 9.2.3, or
(b)   by an agreement between the obligee and the new obligor, by which the new obligor assumes the obligation.

Article 9.2.2   Exclusion
This Section does not apply to transfers of obligations made under the special rules governing transfers of obligations in the course of transferring a business.

Article 9.2.3   Requirement of obligee's consent to transfer
The transfer of an obligation by an agreement between the original obligor and the new obligor requires the consent of the obligee.

Article 9.2.4   Advance consent of obligee
(1)   The obligee may give its consent in advance.
(2)   If the obligee has given its consent in advance, the transfer of the obligation becomes effective when a notice of the transfer is given to the obligee or when the obligee acknowledges it.

Article 9.2.5   Discharge of original obligor
(1)   The obligee may discharge the original obligor.
(2)   The obligee may also retain the original obligor as an obligor in case the new obligor does not perform properly.
(3)   Otherwise the original obligor and the new obligor are jointly and severally liable.

Article 9.2.6   Third party performance
(1)   Without the obligee's consent, the obligor may contract with another person that this person will perform the obligation in place of the obligor, unless the obligation in the circumstances has an essentially personal character.
(2)   The obligee retains its claim against the obligor.

Article 9.2.7   Defences and rights of set-off
(1)   The new obligor may assert against the obligee all defences which the original obligor could assert against the obligee.
(2)   The new obligor may not exercise against the obligee any right of set-off available to the original obligor against the obligee.

Article 9.2.8   Rights related to the obligation transferred
(1)   The obligee may assert against the new obligor all its rights to payment or other performance under the contract in respect of the obligation transferred.
(2)   If the original obligor is discharged under Article 9.2.5(1), a security granted by any person other than the new obligor for the performance of the obligation is discharged, unless that other person agrees that it should continue to be available to the obligee.
(3)   Discharge of the original obligor also extends to any security of the original obligor given to the obligee for the performance of the obligation, unless the security is over an asset which is transferred as part of a transaction between the original obligor and the new obligor.

Section 3: Assignment of contracts

Article 9.3.1 Definitions

'Assignment of a contract' means the transfer by agreement from one person (the 'assignor') to another person (the 'assignee') of the assignor's rights and obligations arising out of a contract with another person (the 'other party').

Article 9.3.2 Exclusion

This Section does not apply to the assignment of contracts made under the special rules governing transfers of contracts in the course of transferring a business.

Article 9.3.3 Requirement of consent of the other party

The assignment of a contract requires the consent of the other party.

Article 9.3.4 Advance consent of the other party

(1)   The other party may give its consent in advance.

(2)   If the other party has given its consent in advance, the assignment of the contract becomes effective when a notice of the assignment is given to the other party or when the other party acknowledges it.

Article 9.3.5 Discharge of the assignor

(1)   The other party may discharge the assignor.

(2)   The other party may also retain the assignor as an obligor in case the assignee does not perform properly.

(3)   Otherwise the assignor and the assignee are jointly and severally liable.

Article 9.3.6 Defences and rights of set-off

(1)   To the extent that the assignment of a contract involves an assignment of rights, Article 9.1.13 applies accordingly.

(2)   To the extent that the assignment of a contract involves a transfer of obligations, Article 9.2.7 applies accordingly.

Article 9.3.7 Rights transferred with the contract

(1)   To the extent that the assignment of a contract involves an assignment of rights, Article 9.1.14 applies accordingly.

(2)   To the extent that the assignment of a contract involves a transfer of obligations, Article 9.2.8 applies accordingly.

CHAPTER 10 — LIMITATION PERIODS

Article 10.1 Scope of the Chapter

(1)   The exercise of rights governed by the Principles is barred by the expiration of a period of time, referred to as 'limitation period', according to the rules of this Chapter.

(2)   This Chapter does not govern the time within which one party is required under the Principles, as a condition for the acquisition or exercise of its right, to give notice to the other party or to perform any act other than the institution of legal proceedings.

Article 10.2 Limitation periods

(1)   The general limitation period is three years beginning on the day after the day the obligee knows or ought to know the facts as a result of which the obligee's right can be exercised.

(2)   In any event, the maximum limitation period is ten years beginning on the day after the day the right can be exercised.

Article 10.3 Modification of limitation periods by the parties

(1)   The parties may modify the limitation periods.

(2)   However they may not

  (a)   shorten the general limitation period to less than one year;

(b)   shorten the maximum limitation period to less than four years;

(c)   extend the maximum limitation period to more than fifteen years.

Article 10.4   New limitation period by acknowledgement

(1)   Where the obligor before the expiration of the general limitation period acknowledges the right of the obligee, a new general limitation period begins on the day after the day of the acknowledgement.

(2)   The maximum limitation period does not begin to run again, but may be exceeded by the beginning of a new general limitation period under Article 10.2(1).

Article 10.5   Suspension by judicial proceedings

(1)   The running of the limitation period is suspended

(a)   when the obligee performs any act, by commencing judicial proceedings or in judicial proceedings already instituted, that is recognised by the law of the court as asserting the obligee's right against the obligor;

(b)   in the case of the obligor's insolvency when the obligee has asserted its rights in the insolvency proceedings; or

(c)   in the case of proceedings for dissolution of the entity which is the obligor when the obligee has asserted its rights in the dissolution proceedings.

(2)   Suspension lasts until a final decision has been issued or until the proceedings have been otherwise terminated.

Article 10.6   Suspension by arbitral proceedings

(1)   The running of the limitation period is suspended when the obligee performs any act, by commencing arbitral proceedings or in arbitral proceedings already instituted, that is recognised by the law of the arbitral tribunal as asserting the obligee's right against the obligor. In the absence of regulations for arbitral proceedings or provisions determining the exact date of the commencement of arbitral proceedings, the proceedings are deemed to commence on the date on which a request that the right in dispute should be adjudicated reaches the obligor.

(2)   Suspension lasts until a binding decision has been issued or until the proceedings have been otherwise terminated.

Article 10.7   Alternative dispute resolution

The provisions of Articles 10.5 and 10.6 apply with appropriate modifications to other proceedings whereby the parties request a third person to assist them in their attempt to reach an amicable settlement of their dispute.

Article 10.8   Suspension in case of force majeure, death or incapacity

(1)   Where the obligee has been prevented by an impediment that is beyond its control and that it could neither avoid nor overcome, from causing a limitation period to cease to run under the preceding Articles, the general limitation period is suspended so as not to expire before one year after the relevant impediment has ceased to exist.

(2)   Where the impediment consists of the incapacity or death of the obligee or obligor, suspension ceases when a representative for the incapacitated or deceased party or its estate has been appointed or a successor has inherited the respective party's position. The additional one-year period under paragraph (1) applies accordingly.

Article 10.9   Effects of expiration of limitation period

(1)   The expiration of the limitation period does not extinguish the right.

(2)   For the expiration of the limitation period to have effect, the obligor must assert it as a defence.

(3)   A right may still be relied on as a defence even though the expiration of the limitation period for that right has been asserted.

Article 10.10   Right of set-off
The obligee may exercise the right of set-off until the obligor has asserted the expiration of the limitation period.

Article 10.11   Restitution
Where there has been performance in order to discharge an obligation, there is no right of restitution merely because the limitation period has expired.

CHAPTER 11—PLURALITY OF OBLIGORS AND OF OBLIGEES

Section 1: Plurality of Obligors

Article 11.1.1   Definitions
When several obligors are bound by the same obligation towards an obligee:
    (a)   the obligations are joint and several when each obligor is bound for the whole obligation;
    (b)   the obligations are separate when each obligor is bound only for its share.

Article 11.1.2   Presumption of joint and several obligations
When several obligors are bound by the same obligation towards an obligee, they are presumed to be jointly and severally bound, unless the circumstances indicate otherwise.

Article 11.1.3   Obligee's rights against joint and several obligors
When obligors are jointly and severally bound, the obligee may require performance from any one of them, until full performance has been received.

Article 11.1.4   Availability of defences and rights of set-off
A joint and several obligor against whom a claim is made by the obligee may assert all the defences and rights of set-off that are personal to it or that are common to all the co-obligors, but may not assert defences or rights of set-off that are personal to one or several of the other co-obligors.

Article 11.1.5   Effect of performance or set-off
Performance or set-off by a joint and several obligor or set-off by the obligee against one joint and several obligor discharges the other obligors in relation to the obligee to the extent of the performance or set-off.

Article 11.1.6   Effect of release or settlement
    (1)   Release of one joint and several obligor, or settlement with one joint and several obligor, discharges all the other obligors for the share of the released or settling obligor, unless the circumstances indicate otherwise.
    (2)   When the other obligors are discharged for the share of the released obligor, they no longer have a contributory claim against the released obligor under Article 11.1.10.

Article 11.1.7   Effect of expiration or suspension of limitation period
    (1)   Expiration of the limitation period of the obligee's rights against one joint and several obligor does not affect:
    (a)   the obligations to the obligee of the other joint and several obligors; or
    (b)   the rights of recourse between the joint and several obligors under Article 11.1.10.
    (2)   If the obligee initiates proceedings under Articles 10.5, 10.6 or 10.7 against one joint and several obligor, the running of the limitation period is also suspended against the other joint and several obligors.

Article 11.1.8   Effect of judgment
    (1)   A decision by a court as to the liability to the obligee of one joint and several obligor does not affect:

(a)   the obligations to the obligee of the other joint and several obligors; or

(b)   the rights of recourse between the joint and several obligors under Article 11.1.10.

(2)   However, the other joint and several obligors may rely on such a decision, except if it was based on grounds personal to the obligor concerned. In such a case, the rights of recourse between the joint and several obligors under Article 11.1.10 are affected accordingly.

Article 11.1.9   Apportionment among joint and several obligors

As among themselves, joint and several obligors are bound in equal shares, unless the circumstances indicate otherwise.

Article 11.1.10   Extent of contributory claim

A joint and several obligor who has performed more than its share may claim the excess from any of the other obligors to the extent of each obligor's unperformed share.

Article 11.1.11   Rights of the obligee

(1)   A joint and several obligor to whom Article 11.1.10 applies may also exercise the rights of the obligee, including all rights securing their performance, to recover the excess from all or any of the other obligors to the extent of each obligor's unperformed share.

(2)   An obligee who has not received full performance retains its rights against the co-obligors to the extent of the unperformed part, with precedence over co-obligors exercising contributory claims.

Article 11.1.12   Defences in contributory claims

A joint and several obligor against whom a claim is made by the co-obligor who has performed the obligation:

(a)   may raise any common defences and rights of set-off that were available to be asserted by the co-obligor against the obligee;

(b)   may assert defences which are personal to itself;

(c)   may not assert defences and rights of set-off which are personal to one or several of the other co-obligors.

Article 11.1.13   Inability to recover

If a joint and several obligor who has performed more than that obligor's share is unable, despite all reasonable efforts, to recover contribution from another joint and several obligor, the share of the others, including the one who has performed, is increased proportionally.

Section 2: Plurality of Obligees

Article 11.2.1   Definitions

When several obligees can claim performance of the same obligation from an obligor:

(a)   the claims are separate when each obligee can only claim its share;

(b)   the claims are joint and several when each obligee can claim the whole performance;

(c)   the claims are joint when all obligees have to claim performance together.

Article 11.2.2   Effects of joint and several claims

Full performance of an obligation in favour of one of the joint and several obligees discharges the obligor towards the other obligees.

Article 11.2.3   Availability of defences against joint and several obligees

(1)   The obligor may assert against any of the joint and several obligees all the defences and rights of set-off that are personal to its relationship to that obligee or that it can assert against all the co-obligees, but may not assert defences and rights

of set-off that are personal to its relationship to one or several of the other co-obligees.

(2)   The provisions of Articles 11.1.5, 11.1.6, 11.1.7 and 11.1.8 apply, with appropriate adaptations, to joint and several claims.

Article 11.2.4   Allocation between joint and several obligees

(1)   As among themselves, joint and several obligees are entitled to equal shares, unless the circumstances indicate otherwise.

(2)   An obligee who has received more than its share must transfer the excess to the other obligees to the extent of their respective shares.

PRINCIPLES, DEFINITIONS AND MODEL RULES OF EUROPEAN PRIVATE LAW

DRAFT COMMON FRAME OF REFERENCE (DCFR)*
Outline Edition

BOOK I
GENERAL PROVISIONS

I.—1:101: Intended field of application

(1)   These rules are intended to be used primarily in relation to contracts and other juridical acts, contractual and non-contractual rights and obligations and related property matters.

(2)   They are not intended to be used, or used without modification or supplementation, in relation to rights and obligations of a public law nature or, except where otherwise provided, in relation to:

(a)   the status or legal capacity of natural persons;

(b)   wills and succession;

(c)   family relationships, including matrimonial and similar relationships;

(d)   bills of exchange, cheques and promissory notes and other negotiable instruments;

(e)   employment relationships;

(f)   the ownership of, or rights in security over, immovable property;

(g)   the creation, capacity, internal organisation, regulation or dissolution of companies and other bodies corporate or unincorporated;

(h)   matters relating primarily to procedure or enforcement.

(3)   Further restrictions on intended fields of application are contained in later Books.

I.—1:102: Interpretation and development

(1)   These rules are to be interpreted and developed autonomously and in accordance with their objectives and the principles underlying them.

(2)   They are to be read in the light of any applicable instruments guaranteeing human rights and fundamental freedoms and any applicable constitutional laws.

(3)   In their interpretation and development regard should be had to the need to promote:

(a)   uniformity of application;

(b)   good faith and fair dealing; and

(c)   legal certainty.

(4)   Issues within the scope of the rules but not expressly settled by them are so far as possible to be settled in accordance with the principles underlying them.

(5)   Where there is a general rule and a special rule applying to a particular situation within the scope of the general rule, the special rule prevails in any case of conflict.

I.—1:103: Good faith and fair dealing
(1)   The expression 'good faith and fair dealing' refers to a standard of conduct characterised by honesty, openness and consideration for the interests of the other party to the transaction or relationship in question.
(2)   It is, in particular, contrary to good faith and fair dealing for a party to act inconsistently with that party's prior statements or conduct when the other party has reasonably relied on them to that other party's detriment.

I.—1:104: Reasonableness
Reasonableness is to be objectively ascertained, having regard to the nature and purpose of what is being done, to the circumstances of the case and to any relevant usages and practices.

I.—1:105: 'Consumer' and 'business'
(1)   A 'consumer' means any natural person who is acting primarily for purposes which are not related to his or her trade, business or profession.
(2)   A 'business' means any natural or legal person, irrespective of whether publicly or privately owned, who is acting for purposes relating to the person's self-employed trade, work or profession, even if the person does not intend to make a profit in the course of the activity.
(3)   A person who is within both of the preceding paragraphs is regarded as falling exclusively within paragraph (1) in relation to a rule which would provide protection for that person if that person were a consumer, and otherwise as falling exclusively within paragraph (2).

I.—1:107: 'Signature' and similar expressions
(1)   A reference to a person's signature includes a reference to that person's handwritten signature, electronic signature or advanced electronic signature, and references to anything being signed by a person are to be construed accordingly.
(2)   A 'handwritten signature' means the name of, or sign representing, a person written by that person's own hand for the purpose of authentication.
(3)   An 'electronic signature' means data in electronic form which are attached to or logically associated with other electronic data, and which serve as a method of authentication.
(4)   An 'advanced electronic signature' means an electronic signature which is:
    (a)   uniquely linked to the signatory;
    (b)   capable of identifying the signatory;
    (c)   created using means which can be maintained under the signatory's sole control; and
    (d)   linked to the data to which it relates in such a manner that any subsequent change of the data is detectable.
(5)   In this Article, 'electronic' means relating to technology with electrical, digital, magnetic, wireless, optical, electromagnetic, or similar capabilities.

I.—1:108: Definitions in Annex
(1)   The definitions in the Annex apply for all the purposes of these rules unless the context otherwise requires.
(2)   Where a word is defined, other grammatical forms of the word have a corresponding meaning.

BOOK II
CONTRACTS AND OTHER JURIDICAL ACTS

Chapter 1: General provisions

II.—1:101: Meaning of 'contract' and 'juridical act'
(1)   A contract is an agreement which is intended to give rise to a binding legal relationship or to have some other legal effect. It is a bilateral or multilateral juridical act.

(2)   A juridical act is any statement or agreement, whether express or implied from conduct, which is intended to have legal effect as such. It may be unilateral, bilateral or multilateral.

II.—1:102: Party autonomy
(1)   Parties are free to make a contract or other juridical act and to determine its contents, subject to any applicable mandatory rules.

(2)   Parties may exclude the application of any of the following rules relating to contracts or other juridical acts, or the rights and obligations arising from them, or derogate from or vary their effects, except as otherwise provided.

(3)   A provision to the effect that parties may not exclude the application of a rule or derogate from or vary its effects does not prevent a party from waiving a right which has already arisen and of which that party is aware.

II.—1:103: Binding effect
(1)   A valid contract is binding on the parties.

(2)   A valid unilateral undertaking is binding on the person giving it if it is intended to be legally binding without acceptance.

(3)   This Article does not prevent modification or termination of any resulting right or obligation by agreement between the debtor and creditor or as provided by law.

II.—1:104: Usages and practices
(1)   The parties to a contract are bound by any usage to which they have agreed and by any practice they have established between themselves.

(2)   The parties are bound by a usage which would be considered generally applicable by persons in the same situation as the parties, except where the application of such usage would be unreasonable.

(3)   This Article applies to other juridical acts with any necessary adaptations.

II.—1:109: Standard terms
A 'standard term' is a term which has been formulated in advance for several transactions involving different parties and which has not been individually negotiated by the parties.

II.—1:110: Terms 'not individually negotiated'
(1)   A term supplied by one party is not individually negotiated if the other party has not been able to influence its content, in particular because it has been drafted in advance, whether or not as part of standard terms.

(2)   If one party supplies a selection of terms to the other party, a term will not be regarded as individually negotiated merely because the other party chooses that term from that selection.

(3)   If it is disputed whether a term supplied by one party as part of standard terms has since been individually negotiated, that party bears the burden of proving that it has been.

(4)   In a contract between a business and a consumer, the business bears the burden of proving that a term supplied by the business has been individually negotiated.

(5)   In contracts between a business and a consumer, terms drafted by a third

person are considered to have been supplied by the business, unless the consumer introduced them to the contract.

Chapter 3: Marketing and pre-contractual duties

Section 3: Negotiation and confidentiality duties

II.—3:301: Negotiations contrary to good faith and fair dealing
(1)   A person is free to negotiate and is not liable for failure to reach an agreement.

(2)   A person who is engaged in negotiations has a duty to negotiate in accordance with good faith and fair dealing and not to break off negotiations contrary to good faith and fair dealing. This duty may not be excluded or limited by contract.

(3)   A person who is in breach of the duty is liable for any loss caused to the other party by the breach.

(4)   It is contrary to good faith and fair dealing, in particular, for a person to enter into or continue negotiations with no real intention of reaching an agreement with the other party.

II.—3:302: Breach of confidentiality
(1)   If confidential information is given by one party in the course of negotiations, the other party is under a duty not to disclose that information or use it for that party's own purposes whether or not a contract is subsequently concluded.

(2)   In this Article, 'confidential information' means information which, either from its nature or the circumstances in which it was obtained, the party receiving the information knows or could reasonably be expected to know is confidential to the other party.

(3)   A party who reasonably anticipates a breach of the duty may obtain a court order prohibiting it.

(4)   A party who is in breach of the duty is liable for any loss caused to the other party by the breach and may be ordered to pay over to the other party any benefit obtained by the breach.

Section 5: Damages for breach of duty under this Chapter

II.—3:501: Liability for damages
(1)   Where any rule in this Chapter makes a person liable for loss caused to another person by a breach of a duty, the other person has a right to damages for that loss.

(2)   The rules on III.—3:704 (Loss attributable to creditor) and III.—3:705 (Reduction of loss) apply with the adaptation that the reference to non-performance of the obligation is to be taken as a reference to breach of the duty.

Chapter 4: Formation

Section 1: General provisions

II.—4:101: Requirements for the conclusion of a contract
A contract is concluded, without any further requirement, if the parties:

(a)   intend to enter into a binding legal relationship or bring about some other legal effect; and

(b)   reach a sufficient agreement.

II.—4:102: How intention is determined
The intention of a party to enter into a binding legal relationship or bring about some other legal effect is to be determined from the party's statements or conduct as they were reasonably understood by the other party.

II.—4:103: Sufficient agreement

(1)   Agreement is sufficient if:

(a)   the terms of the contract have been sufficiently defined by the parties for the contract to be given effect; or

(b)   the terms of the contract, or the rights and obligations of the parties under it, can be otherwise sufficiently determined for the contract to be given effect.

(2)   If one of the parties refuses to conclude a contract unless the parties have agreed on some specific matter, there is no contract unless agreement on that matter has been reached.

Section 2: Offer and acceptance

II.—4:201: Offer

(1)   A proposal amounts to an offer if:

(a)   it is intended to result in a contract if the other party accepts it; and

(b)   it contains sufficiently definite terms to form a contract.

(2)   An offer may be made to one or more specific persons or to the public.

(3)   A proposal to supply goods from stock, or a service, at a stated price made by a business in a public advertisement or a catalogue, or by a display of goods, is treated, unless the circumstances indicate otherwise, as an offer to supply at that price until the stock of goods, or the business's capacity to supply the service, is exhausted.

II.—4:202: Revocation of offer

(1)   An offer may be revoked if the revocation reaches the offeree before the offeree has dispatched an acceptance or, in cases of acceptance by conduct, before the contract has been concluded.

(2)   An offer made to the public can be revoked by the same means as were used to make the offer.

(3)   However, a revocation of an offer is ineffective if:

(a)   the offer indicates that it is irrevocable;

(b)   the offer states a fixed time for its acceptance; or

(c)   it was reasonable for the offeree to rely on the offer as being irrevocable and the offeree has acted in reliance on the offer.

(4)   Paragraph (3) does not apply to an offer if the offeror would have a right under any rule in Books II to IV to withdraw from a contract resulting from its acceptance. The parties may not, to the detriment of the offeror, exclude the application of this rule or derogate from or vary its effects.

II.—4:203: Rejection of offer

When a rejection of an offer reaches the offeror, the offer lapses.

II.—4:204: Acceptance

(1)   Any form of statement or conduct by the offeree is an acceptance if it indicates assent to the offer.

(2)   Silence or inactivity does not in itself amount to acceptance.

II.—4:205: Time of conclusion of the contract

(1)   If an acceptance has been dispatched by the offeree the contract is concluded when the acceptance reaches the offeror.

(2)   In the case of acceptance by conduct, the contract is concluded when notice of the conduct reaches the offeror.

(3)   If by virtue of the offer, of practices which the parties have established between themselves, or of a usage, the offeree may accept the offer by doing an act without notice to the offeror, the contract is concluded when the offeree begins to do the act.

II.—4:206: Time limit for acceptance

(1)   An acceptance of an offer is effective only if it reaches the offeror within the time fixed by the offeror.

(2)   If no time has been fixed by the offeror the acceptance is effective only if it reaches the offeror within a reasonable time.

(3)   Where an offer may be accepted by performing an act without notice to the offeror, the acceptance is effective only if the act is performed within the time for acceptance fixed by the offeror or, if no such time is fixed, within a reasonable time.

II.—4:207: Late acceptance

(1)   A late acceptance is nonetheless effective as an acceptance if without undue delay the offeror informs the offeree that it is treated as an effective acceptance.

(2)   If a letter or other communication containing a late acceptance shows that it has been dispatched in such circumstances that if its transmission had been normal it would have reached the offeror in due time, the late acceptance is effective as an acceptance unless, without undue delay, the offeror informs the offeree that the offer is considered to have lapsed.

II.—4:208: Modified acceptance

(1)   A reply by the offeree which states or implies additional or different terms which materially alter the terms of the offer is a rejection and a new offer.

(2)   A reply which gives a definite assent to an offer operates as an acceptance even if it states or implies additional or different terms, provided these do not materially alter the terms of the offer. The additional or different terms then become part of the contract.

(3)   However, such a reply is treated as a rejection of the offer if:

(a)   the offer expressly limits acceptance to the terms of the offer;

(b)   the offeror objects to the additional or different terms without undue delay; or

(c)   the offeree makes the acceptance conditional upon the offeror's assent to the additional or different terms, and the assent does not reach the offeree within a reasonable time.

II.—4:209: Conflicting standard terms

(1)   If the parties have reached agreement except that the offer and acceptance refer to conflicting standard terms, a contract is nonetheless formed. The standard terms form part of the contract to the extent that they are common in substance.

(2)   However, no contract is formed if one party:

(a)   has indicated in advance, explicitly, and not by way of standard terms, an intention not to be bound by a contract on the basis of paragraph (1); or

(b)   without undue delay, informs the other party of such an intention.

II.—4:211: Contracts not concluded through offer and acceptance

The rules in this Section apply with appropriate adaptations even though the process of conclusion of a contract cannot be analysed into offer and acceptance.

Chapter 7: Grounds of invalidity

Section 1: General provisions

II.—7:101: Scope

(1)   This Chapter deals with the effects of:

(a)   mistake, fraud, threats, or unfair exploitation; and

(b)   infringement of fundamental principles or mandatory rules.

(2)   It does not deal with lack of capacity.

(3)   It applies in relation to contracts and, with any necessary adaptations, other juridical acts.

II.—7:102: Initial impossibility or lack of right or authority to dispose
A contract is not invalid, in whole or in part, merely because at the time it is concluded performance of any obligation assumed is impossible, or because a party has no right or authority to dispose of any assets to which the contract relates.

Section 2: Vitiated consent or intention

II.—7:201: Mistake
(1) A party may avoid a contract for mistake of fact or law existing when the contract was concluded if:
    (a)   the party, but for the mistake, would not have concluded the contract or would have done so only on fundamentally different terms and the other party knew or could reasonably be expected to have known this; and
    (b)   the other party;
        (i) caused the mistake;
        (ii) caused the contract to be concluded in mistake by leaving the mistaken party in error, contrary to good faith and fair dealing, when the other party knew or could reasonably be expected to have known of the mistake;
        (iii) caused the contract to be concluded in mistake by failing to comply with a pre-contractual information duty or a duty to make available a means of correcting input errors; or
        (iv) made the same mistake.
(2)   However a party may not avoid the contract for mistake if:
    (a)   the mistake was inexcusable in the circumstances; or
    (b)   the risk of the mistake was assumed, or in the circumstances should be borne, by that party.

II.—7:202: Inaccuracy in communication may be treated as mistake
An inaccuracy in the expression or transmission of a statement is treated as a mistake of the person who made or sent the statement.

II.—7:203: Adaptation of contract in case of mistake
(1) If a party is entitled to avoid the contract for mistake but the other party performs, or indicates a willingness to perform, the obligations under the contract as it was understood by the party entitled to avoid it, the contract is treated as having been concluded as that party understood it. This applies only if the other party performs, or indicates a willingness to perform, without undue delay after being informed of the manner in which the party entitled to avoid it understood the contract and before that party acts in reliance on any notice of avoidance.
(2) After such performance or indication the right to avoid is lost and any earlier notice of avoidance is ineffective.
(3) Where both parties have made the same mistake, the court may at the request of either party bring the contract into accordance with what might reasonably have been agreed had the mistake not occurred.

II.—7:204: Liability for loss caused by reliance on incorrect information
(1) A party who has concluded a contract in reasonable reliance on incorrect information given by the other party in the course of negotiations has a right to damages for loss suffered as a result if the provider of the information:
    (a)   believed the information to be incorrect or had no reasonable grounds for believing it to be correct; and
    (b)   knew or could reasonably be expected to have known that the recipient would rely on the information in deciding whether or not to conclude the contract on the agreed terms.
(2) This Article applies even if there is no right to avoid the contract.

II.—7:205: Fraud
(1) A party may avoid a contract when the other party has induced the con-

clusion of the contract by fraudulent misrepresentation, whether by words or conduct, or fraudulent non-disclosure of any information which good faith and fair dealing, or any pre-contractual information duty, required that party to disclose.

(2) A misrepresentation is fraudulent if it is made with knowledge or belief that the representation is false and is intended to induce the recipient to make a mistake. A non-disclosure is fraudulent if it is intended to induce the person from whom the information is withheld to make a mistake.

(3) In determining whether good faith and fair dealing required a party to disclose particular information, regard should be had to all the circumstances, including:

    (a) whether the party had special expertise;

    (b) the cost to the party of acquiring the relevant information;

    (c) whether the other party could reasonably acquire the information by other means; and

    (d) the apparent importance of the information to the other party.

II.—7:206: Coercion or threats

(1) A party may avoid a contract when the other party has induced the conclusion of the contract by coercion or by the threat of an imminent and serious harm which it is wrongful to inflict, or wrongful to use as a means to obtain the conclusion of the contract.

(2) A threat is not regarded as inducing the contract if in the circumstances the threatened party had a reasonable alternative.

II.—7:207: Unfair exploitation

(1) A party may avoid a contract if, at the time of the conclusion of the contract:

    (a) the party was dependent on or had a relationship of trust with the other party, was in economic distress or had urgent needs, was improvident, ignorant, inexperienced or lacking in bargaining skill; and

    (b) the other party knew or could reasonably be expected to have known this and, given the circumstances and purpose of the contract, exploited the first party's situation by taking an excessive benefit or grossly unfair advantage.

(2) Upon the request of the party entitled to avoidance, a court may if it is appropriate adapt the contract in order to bring it into accordance with what might have been agreed had the requirements of good faith and fair dealing been observed.

(3) A court may similarly adapt the contract upon the request of a party receiving notice of avoidance for unfair exploitation, provided that this party informs the party who gave the notice without undue delay after receiving it and before that party has acted in reliance on it.

II.—7:208: Third persons

(1) Where a third person for whose acts a party is responsible or who with a party's assent is involved in the making of a contract:

    (a) causes a mistake, or knows of or could reasonably be expected to know of a mistake; or

    (b) is guilty of fraud, coercion, threats or unfair exploitation,

remedies under this Section are available as if the behaviour or knowledge had been that of the party.

(2) Where a third person for whose acts a party is not responsible and who does not have the party's assent to be involved in the making of a contract is guilty of fraud, coercion, threats or unfair exploitation, remedies under this Section are available if the party knew or could reasonably be expected to have known of the relevant facts, or at the time of avoidance has not acted in reliance on the contract.

II.—7:212: Effects of avoidance

(1) A contract which may be avoided under this Section is valid until avoided but, once avoided, is retrospectively invalid from the beginning.

(2) The question whether either party has a right to the return of whatever has been transferred or supplied under a contract which has been avoided under this Section, or a monetary equivalent, is regulated by the rules on unjustified enrichment.

(3) The effect of avoidance under this Section on the ownership of property which has been transferred under the avoided contract is governed by the rules on the transfer of property.

II.—7:213: Partial avoidance

If a ground of avoidance under this Section affects only particular terms of a contract, the effect of an avoidance is limited to those terms unless, giving due consideration to all the circumstances of the case, it is unreasonable to uphold the remaining contract.

II.—7:214: Damages for loss

(1) A party who has the right to avoid a contract under this Section (or who had such a right before it was lost by the effect of time limits or confirmation) is entitled, whether or not the contract is avoided, to damages from the other party for any loss suffered as a result of the mistake, fraud, coercion, threats or unfair exploitation, provided that the other party knew or could reasonably be expected to have known of the ground for avoidance.

(2) The damages recoverable are such as to place the aggrieved party as nearly as possible in the position in which that party would have been if the contract had not been concluded, with the further limitation that, if the party does not avoid the contract, the damages are not to exceed the loss caused by the mistake, fraud, coercion, threats or unfair exploitation.

(3) In other respects the rules on damages for non-performance of a contractual obligation apply with any appropriate adaptation.

II.—7:216: Overlapping remedies

A party who is entitled to a remedy under this Section in circumstances which afford that party a remedy for non-performance may pursue either remedy.

Chapter 8: Interpretation

Section 1: Interpretation of contracts

II.—8:101: General rules

(1) A contract is to be interpreted according to the common intention of the parties even if this differs from the literal meaning of the words.

(2) If one party intended the contract, or a term or expression used in it, to have a particular meaning, and at the time of the conclusion of the contract the other party was aware, or could reasonably be expected to have been aware, of the first party's intention, the contract is to be interpreted in the way intended by the first party.

(3) The contract is, however, to be interpreted according to the meaning which a reasonable person would give to it:

(a) if an intention cannot be established under the preceding paragraphs; or

(b) if the question arises with a person, not being a party to the contract or a person who by law has no better rights than such a party, who has reasonably and in good faith relied on the contract's apparent meaning.

II.—8:102: Relevant matters

(1) In interpreting the contract, regard may be had, in particular, to:

(a) the circumstances in which it was concluded, including the preliminary negotiations;

(b)   the conduct of the parties, even subsequent to the conclusion of the contract;

(c)   the interpretation which has already been given by the parties to terms or expressions which are the same as, or similar to, those used in the contract and the practices they have established between themselves;

(d)   the meaning commonly given to such terms or expressions in the branch of activity concerned and the interpretation such terms or expressions may already have received;

(e)   the nature and purpose of the contract;

(f)   usages; and

(g)   good faith and fair dealing.

(2)   In a question with a person, not being a party to the contract or a person such as an assignee who by law has no better rights than such a party, who has reasonably and in good faith relied on the contract's apparent meaning, regard may be had to the circumstances mentioned in sub-paragraphs (a) to (c) above only to the extent that those circumstances were known to, or could reasonably be expected to have been known to, that person.

II.—8:103: Interpretation against supplier of term or dominant party

(1)   Where there is doubt about the meaning of a term not individually nego-tiated, an interpretation of the term against the party who supplied it is to be preferred.

(2)   Where there is doubt about the meaning of any other term, and that term has been established under the dominant influence of one party, an interpretation of the term against that party is to be preferred.

II.—8:104: Preference for negotiated terms

Terms which have been individually negotiated take preference over those which have not.

II.—8:105: Reference to contract as a whole

Terms and expressions are to be interpreted in the light of the whole contract in which they appear.

II.—8:106: Preference for interpretation which gives terms effect

An interpretation which renders the terms of the contract lawful, or effective, is to be preferred to one which would not.

II.—8:107: Linguistic discrepancies

Where a contract document is in two or more language versions none of which is stated to be authoritative, there is, in case of discrepancy between the versions, a preference for the interpretation according to the version in which the contract was originally drawn up.

Chapter 9: Contents and effects of contracts

Section 1: Contents

II.—9:101: Terms of a contract

(1)   The terms of a contract may be derived from the express or tacit agreement of the parties, from rules of law or from practices established between the parties or usages.

(2)   Where it is necessary to provide for a matter which the parties have not foreseen or provided for, a court may imply an additional term, having regard in particular to:

(a)   the nature and purpose of the contract;

(b)   the circumstances in which the contract was concluded; and

(c)   the requirements of good faith and fair dealing.

(3)   Any term implied under paragraph (2) should, where possible, be such as

to give effect to what the parties, had they provided for the matter, would probably have agreed.

(4)   Paragraph (2) does not apply if the parties have deliberately left a matter unprovided for, accepting the consequences of so doing.

II.—9:102: Certain pre-contractual statements regarded as contract terms

(1)   A statement made by one party before a contract is concluded is regarded as a term of the contract if the other party reasonably understood it as being made on the basis that it would form part of the contract terms if a contract were concluded. In assessing whether the other party was reasonable in understanding the statement in that way account may be taken of:

(a)   the apparent importance of the statement to the other party;

(b)   whether the party was making the statement in the course of business; and

(c)   the relative expertise of the parties.

(2)   If one of the parties to a contract is a business and before the contract is concluded makes a statement, either to the other party or publicly, about the specific characteristics of what is to be supplied by that business under the contract, the statement is regarded as a term of the contract unless:

(a)   the other party was aware when the contract was concluded, or could reasonably be expected to have been so aware, that the statement was incorrect or could not otherwise be relied on as such a term; or

(b)   the other party's decision to conclude the contract was not influenced by the statement.

(3)   For the purposes of paragraph (2), a statement made by a person engaged in advertising or marketing on behalf of the business is treated as being made by the business.

(4)   Where the other party is a consumer then, for the purposes of paragraph (2), a public statement made by or on behalf of a producer or other person in earlier links of the business chain between the producer and the consumer is treated as being made by the business unless the business, at the time of conclusion of the contract, did not know and could not reasonably be expected to have known of it.

(5)   In the circumstances covered by paragraph (4) a business which at the time of conclusion of the contract did not know and could not reasonably be expected to have known that the statement was incorrect has a right to be indemnified by the person making the statement for any liability incurred as a result of that paragraph.

(6)   In relations between a business and a consumer the parties may not, to the detriment of the consumer, exclude the application of this Article or derogate from or vary its effects.

II.—9:103: Terms not individually negotiated

(1)   Terms supplied by one party and not individually negotiated may be invoked against the other party only if the other party was aware of them, or if the party supplying the terms took reasonable steps to draw the other party's attention to them, before or when the contract was concluded.

(2)   If a contract is to be concluded by electronic means, the party supplying any terms which have not been individually negotiated may invoke them against the other party only if they are made available to the other party in textual form.

(3)   For the purposes of this Article

(a)   'not individually negotiated' has the meaning given by II.—1:110 (Terms 'not individually negotiated'); and

(b)   terms are not sufficiently brought to the other party's attention by a mere reference to them in a contract document, even if that party signs the document.

Section 3: Effect of stipulation in favour of a third party

II.—9:301: Basic rules

(1) The parties to a contract may, by the contract, confer a right or other benefit on a third party. The third party need not be in existence or identified at the time the contract is concluded.

(2) The nature and content of the third party's right or benefit are determined by the contract and are subject to any conditions or other limitations under the contract.

(3) The benefit conferred may take the form of an exclusion or limitation of the third party's liability to one of the contracting parties.

II.—9:302: Rights, remedies and defences

Where one of the contracting parties is bound to render a performance to the third party under the contract, then, in the absence of provision to the contrary in the contract:

(a) the third party has the same rights to performance and remedies for non-performance as if the contracting party was bound to render the performance under a binding unilateral undertaking in favour of the third party; and

(b) the contracting party may assert against the third party all defences which the contracting party could assert against the other party to the contract.

II.—9:303: Rejection or revocation of benefit

(1) The third party may reject the right or benefit by notice to either of the contracting parties, if that is done without undue delay after being notified of the right or benefit and before it has been expressly or impliedly accepted. On such rejection, the right or benefit is treated as never having accrued to the third party.

(2) The contracting parties may remove or modify the contractual term conferring the right or benefit if this is done before either of them has given the third party notice that the right or benefit has been conferred. The contract determines whether and by whom and in what circumstances the right or benefit can be revoked or modified after that time.

(3) Even if the right or benefit conferred is by virtue of the contract revocable or subject to modification, the right to revoke or modify is lost if the parties have, or the party having the right to revoke or modify has, led the third party to believe that it is not revocable or subject to modification and if the third party has reasonably acted in reliance on it.

Section 4: Unfair terms

II.—9:401: Mandatory nature of following provisions

The parties may not exclude the application of the provisions in this Section or derogate from or vary their effects.

II.—9:402: Duty of transparency in terms not individually negotiated

(1) A person who supplies terms which have not been individually negotiated has a duty to ensure that they are drafted and communicated in plain, intelligible language.

(2) In a contract between a business and a consumer a term which has been supplied by the business in breach of the duty of transparency imposed by paragraph (1) may on that ground alone be considered unfair.

II.—9:403: Meaning of 'unfair' in contracts between a business and a consumer

In a contract between a business and a consumer, a term [which has not been individually negotiated] is unfair for the purposes of this Section if it is supplied by the business and if it significantly disadvantages the consumer, contrary to good faith and fair dealing.

II.—9:404: Meaning of 'unfair' in contracts between non-business parties

In a contract between parties neither of whom is a business, a term is unfair for the purposes of this Section only if it is a term forming part of standard terms supplied by one party and significantly disadvantages the other party, contrary to good faith and fair dealing.

II.—9:405: Meaning of 'unfair' in contracts between businesses

A term in a contract between businesses is unfair for the purposes of this Section only if it is a term forming part of standard terms supplied by one party and of such a nature that its use grossly deviates from good commercial practice, contrary to good faith and fair dealing.

II.—9:406: Exclusions from unfairness test

(1) Contract terms are not subjected to an unfairness test under this Section if they are based on:

(a) provisions of the applicable law;

(b) international conventions to which the Member States are parties, or to which the European Union is a party; or

(c) these rules.

(2) For contract terms which are drafted in plain and intelligible language, the unfairness test extends neither to the definition of the main subject matter of the contract, nor to the adequacy of the price to be paid.

II.—9:407: Factors to be taken into account in assessing unfairness

(1) When assessing the unfairness of a contractual term for the purposes of this Section, regard is to be had to the duty of transparency under II.—9:402 (Duty of transparency in terms not individually negotiated), to the nature of what is to be provided under the contract, to the circumstances prevailing during the conclusion of the contract, to the other terms of the contract and to the terms of any other contract on which the contract depends.

(2) For the purposes of II.—9:403 (Meaning of 'unfair' in contracts between a business and a consumer) the circumstances prevailing during the conclusion of the contract include the extent to which the consumer was given a real opportunity to become acquainted with the term before the conclusion of the contract.

II.—9:408: Effects of unfair terms

(1) A term which is unfair under this Section is not binding on the party who did not supply it.

(2) If the contract can reasonably be maintained without the unfair term, the other terms remain binding on the parties.

II.—9:410: Terms which are presumed to be unfair in contracts between a business and a consumer

(1) A term in a contract between a business and a consumer is presumed to be unfair for the purposes of this Section if it is supplied by the business and if it:

(a) excludes or limits the liability of a business for death or personal injury caused to a consumer through an act or omission of that business;

(b) inappropriately excludes or limits the remedies, including any right to set-off, available to the consumer against the business or a third party for non-performance by the business of obligations under the contract;

(c) makes binding on a consumer an obligation which is subject to a condition the fulfilment of which depends solely on the intention of the business;

(d) permits a business to keep money paid by a consumer if the latter decides not to conclude the contract, or perform obligations under it, without providing for the consumer to receive compensation of an equivalent amount from the business in the reverse situation;

(e)   requires a consumer who fails to perform his or her obligations to pay a disproportionately high amount of damages;

(f)   entitles a business to withdraw from or terminate the contractual relationship on a discretionary basis without giving the same right to the consumer, or entitles a business to keep money paid for services not yet supplied in the case where the business withdraws from or terminates the contractual relationship;

(g)   enables a business to terminate a contractual relationship of indeterminate duration without reasonable notice, except where there are serious grounds for doing so; this does not affect terms in financial services contracts where there is a valid reason, provided that the supplier is required to inform the other contracting party thereof immediately;

(h)   automatically extends a contract of fixed duration unless the consumer indicates otherwise, in cases where such terms provide for an unreasonably early deadline;

(i)   enables a business to alter the terms of the contract unilaterally without a valid reason which is specified in the contract; this does not affect terms under which a supplier of financial services reserves the right to change the rate of interest to be paid by, or to, the consumer, or the amount of other charges for financial services without notice where there is a valid reason, provided that the supplier is required to inform the consumer at the earliest opportunity and that the consumer is free to terminate the contractual relationship with immediate effect; neither does it affect terms under which a business reserves the right to alter unilaterally the conditions of a contract of indeterminate duration, provided that the business is required to inform the consumer with reasonable notice, and that the consumer is free to terminate the contractual relationship;

(j)   enables a business to alter unilaterally without a valid reason any characteristics of the goods, other assets or services to be provided;

(k)   provides that the price of goods or other assets is to be determined at the time of delivery or supply, or allows a business to increase the price without giving the consumer the right to withdraw if the increased price is too high in relation to the price agreed at the conclusion of the contract; this does not affect price-indexation clauses, where lawful, provided that the method by which prices vary is explicitly described;

(l)   gives a business the right to determine whether the goods, other assets or services supplied are in conformity with the contract, or gives the business the exclusive right to interpret any term of the contract;

(m)   limits the obligation of a business to respect commitments undertaken by its agents, or makes its commitments subject to compliance with a particular formality;

(n)   obliges a consumer to fulfil all his or her obligations where the business fails to fulfil its own;

(o)   allows a business to transfer its rights and obligations under the contract without the consumer's consent, if this could reduce the guarantees available to the consumer;

(p)   excludes or restricts a consumer's right to take legal action or to exercise any other remedy, in particular by referring the consumer to arbitration proceedings which are not covered by legal provisions, by unduly restricting the evidence available to the consumer, or by shifting a burden of proof on to the consumer;

(q)   allows a business, where what has been ordered is unavailable, to supply an equivalent without having expressly informed the consumer of this possibility and of the fact that the business must bear the cost of returning what the consumer has received under the contract if the consumer exercises a right to withdraw.

(2) Subparagraphs (g), (i) and (k) do not apply to:
   (a) transactions in transferable securities, financial instruments and other products or services where the price is linked to fluctuations in a stock exchange quotation or index or a financial market rate beyond the control of the business;
   (b) contracts for the purchase or sale of foreign currency, traveller's cheques or international money orders denominated in foreign currency

BOOK III
OBLIGATIONS AND CORRESPONDING RIGHTS

Chapter 1: General

III.—1:101: Scope of Book
This Book applies, except as otherwise provided, to all obligations within the scope of these rules, whether they are contractual or not, and to corresponding rights to performance.

III.—1:102: Definitions
(1) An obligation is a duty to perform which one party to a legal relationship, the debtor, owes to another party, the creditor.
(2) Performance of an obligation is the doing by the debtor of what is to be done under the obligation or the not doing by the debtor of what is not to be done.
(3) Non-performance of an obligation is any failure to perform the obligation, whether or not excused, and includes delayed performance and any other performance which is not in accordance with the terms regulating the obligation.
(4) An obligation is reciprocal in relation to another obligation if:
   (a) performance of the obligation is due in exchange for performance of the other obligation;
   (b) it is an obligation to facilitate or accept performance of the other obligation; or
   (c) it is so clearly connected to the other obligation or its subject matter that performance of the one can reasonably be regarded as dependent on performance of the other.
(5) The terms regulating an obligation may be derived from a contract or other juridical act, the law or a legally binding usage or practice, or a court order; and similarly for the terms regulating a right.

III.—1:103: Good faith and fair dealing
(1) A person has a duty to act in accordance with good faith and fair dealing in performing an obligation, in exercising a right to performance, in pursuing or defending a remedy for non-performance, or in exercising a right to terminate an obligation or contractual relationship.
(2) The duty may not be excluded or limited by contract or other juridical act.
(3) Breach of the duty does not give rise directly to the remedies for non-performance of an obligation but may preclude the person in breach from exercising or relying on a right, remedy or defence which that person would otherwise have.

III.—1:104: Co-operation
The debtor and creditor are obliged to co-operate with each other when and to the extent that this can reasonably be expected for the performance of the debtor's obligation.

III.—1:105: Non-discrimination
Chapter 2 (Non-discrimination) of Book II applies with appropriate adaptations to:
   (a) the performance of any obligation to provide access to, or supply, goods, other assets or services which are available to members of the public;

(b)   the exercise of a right to performance of any such obligation or the pursuing or defending of any remedy for non-performance of any such obligation; and

(c)   the exercise of a right to terminate any such obligation.

III.—1:110: Variation or termination by court on a change of circumstances

(1)   An obligation must be performed even if performance has become more onerous, whether because the cost of performance has increased or because the value of what is to be received in return has diminished.

(2)   If, however, performance of a contractual obligation or of an obligation arising from a unilateral juridical act becomes so onerous because of an exceptional change of circumstances that it would be manifestly unjust to hold the debtor to the obligation a court may:

(a)   vary the obligation in order to make it reasonable and equitable in the new circumstances; or

(b)   terminate the obligation at a date and on terms to be determined by the court.

(3)   Paragraph (2) applies only if:

(a)   the change of circumstances occurred after the time when the obligation was incurred;

(b)   the debtor did not at that time take into account, and could not reasonably be expected to have taken into account, the possibility or scale of that change of circumstances;

(c)   the debtor did not assume, and cannot reasonably be regarded as having assumed, the risk of that change of circumstances; and

(d)   the debtor has attempted, reasonably and in good faith, to achieve by negotiation a reasonable and equitable adjustment of the terms regulating the obligation.

Chapter 2: Performance

III.—2:101: Place of performance

(1)   If the place of performance of an obligation cannot be otherwise determined from the terms regulating the obligation it is:

(a)   in the case of a monetary obligation, the creditor's place of business;

(b)   in the case of any other obligation, the debtor's place of business.

(2)   For the purposes of the preceding paragraph:

(a)   if a party has more than one place of business, the place of business is that which has the closest relationship to the obligation; and

(b)   if a party does not have a place of business, or the obligation does not relate to a business matter, the habitual residence is substituted.

(3)   If, in a case to which paragraph (1) applies, a party causes any increase in the expenses incidental to performance by a change in place of business or habitual residence subsequent to the time when the obligation was incurred, that party is obliged to bear the increase.

III.—2:102: Time of performance

(1)   If the time at which, or a period of time within which, an obligation is to be performed cannot otherwise be determined from the terms regulating the obligation it must be performed within a reasonable time after it arises.

(2)   If a period of time within which the obligation is to be performed can be determined from the terms regulating the obligation, the obligation may be performed at any time within that period chosen by the debtor unless the circumstances of the case indicate that the creditor is to choose the time.

(3)   Unless the parties have agreed otherwise, a business must perform the obligations incurred under a contract concluded at a distance for the supply of goods,

other assets or services to a consumer no later than 30 days after the contract was concluded.

(4) If a business has an obligation to reimburse money received from a consumer for goods, other assets or services supplied, the reimbursement must be made as soon as possible and in any case no later than 30 days after the obligation arose.

Chapter 3: Remedies for non-performance

Section 1: General

III.—3:101: Remedies available

(1) If an obligation is not performed by the debtor and the non-performance is not excused, the creditor may resort to any of the remedies set out in this Chapter.

(2) If the debtor's non-performance is excused, the creditor may resort to any of those remedies except enforcing specific performance and damages.

(3) The creditor may not resort to any of those remedies to the extent that the creditor caused the debtor's non-performance.

III.—3:102: Cumulation of remedies

Remedies which are not incompatible may be cumulated. In particular, a creditor is not deprived of the right to damages by resorting to any other remedy.

III.—3:103: Notice fixing additional period for performance

(1) In any case of non-performance of an obligation the creditor may by notice to the debtor allow an additional period of time for performance.

(2) During the additional period the creditor may withhold performance of the creditor's reciprocal obligations and may claim damages, but may not resort to any other remedy.

(3) If the creditor receives notice from the debtor that the debtor will not perform within that period, or if upon expiry of that period due performance has not been made, the creditor may resort to any available remedy.

III.—3:104: Excuse due to an impediment

(1) A debtor's non-performance of an obligation is excused if it is due to an impediment beyond the debtor's control and if the debtor could not reasonably be expected to have avoided or overcome the impediment or its consequences.

(2) Where the obligation arose out of a contract or other juridical act, non-performance is not excused if the debtor could reasonably be expected to have taken the impediment into account at the time when the obligation was incurred.

(3) Where the excusing impediment is only temporary the excuse has effect for the period during which the impediment exists. However, if the delay amounts to a fundamental non-performance, the creditor may treat it as such.

(4) Where the excusing impediment is permanent the obligation is extinguished. Any reciprocal obligation is also extinguished. In the case of contractual obligations any restitutionary effects of extinction are regulated by the rules in Chapter 3, Section 5, Sub-section 4 (Restitution) with appropriate adaptations.

(5) The debtor has a duty to ensure that notice of the impediment and of its effect on the ability to perform reaches the creditor within a reasonable time after the debtor knew or could reasonably be expected to have known of these circumstances. The creditor is entitled to damages for any loss resulting from the non-receipt of such notice.

III.—3:107: Failure to notify non-conformity

(1) If, in the case of an obligation to supply goods, other assets or services, the debtor supplies goods, other assets or services which are not in conformity with the terms regulating the obligation, the creditor may not rely on the lack of con-

formity unless the creditor gives notice to the debtor within a reasonable time specifying the nature of the lack of conformity.

(2)   The reasonable time runs from the time when the goods or other assets are supplied or the service is completed or from the time, if it is later, when the creditor discovered or could reasonably be expected to have discovered the non-conformity.

(3)   The debtor is not entitled to rely on paragraph (1) if the failure relates to facts which the debtor knew or could reasonably be expected to have known and which the debtor did not disclose to the creditor.

(4)   This Article does not apply where the creditor is a consumer.

Section 2: Cure by debtor of non-conforming performance

III.—3:201: Scope
This Section applies where a debtor's performance does not conform to the terms regulating the obligation.

III.—3:202: Cure by debtor: general rules
(1)   The debtor may make a new and conforming tender if that can be done within the time allowed for performance.

(2)   If the debtor cannot make a new and conforming tender within the time allowed for performance but, promptly after being notified of the lack of conformity, offers to cure it within a reasonable time and at the debtor's own expense, the creditor may not pursue any remedy for non-performance, other than withholding performance, before allowing the debtor a reasonable period in which to attempt to cure the nonconformity.

(3)   Paragraph (2) is subject to the provisions of the following Article.

III.—3:203: When creditor need not allow debtor an opportunity to cure
The creditor need not, under paragraph (2) of the preceding Article, allow the debtor a period in which to attempt cure if:

(a)   failure to perform a contractual obligation within the time allowed for performance amounts to a fundamental non-performance;

(b)   the creditor has reason to believe that the debtor's performance was made with knowledge of the non-conformity and was not in accordance with good faith and fair dealing;

(c)   the creditor has reason to believe that the debtor will be unable to effect the cure within a reasonable time and without significant inconvenience to the creditor or other prejudice to the creditor's legitimate interests; or

(d)   cure would be inappropriate in the circumstances.

III.—3:204: Consequences of allowing debtor opportunity to cure
(1)   During the period allowed for cure the creditor may withhold performance of the creditor's reciprocal obligations, but may not resort to any other remedy.

(2)   If the debtor fails to effect cure within the time allowed, the creditor may resort to any available remedy.

(3)   Notwithstanding cure, the creditor retains the right to damages for any loss caused by the debtor's initial or subsequent non-performance or by the process of effecting cure.

III.—3:205: Return of replaced item
(1)   Where the debtor has, whether voluntarily or in compliance with an order under III.—3:302 (Enforcement of non-monetary obligations), remedied a non-conforming performance by replacement, the debtor has a right and an obligation to take back the replaced item at the debtor's expense.

(2)   The creditor is not liable to pay for any use made of the replaced item in the period prior to the replacement.

Section 3: Right to enforce performance

III.—3:301: Enforcement of monetary obligations
(1)   The creditor is entitled to recover money payment of which is due.

(2)   Where the creditor has not yet performed the reciprocal obligation for which payment will be due and it is clear that the debtor in the monetary obligation will be unwilling to receive performance, the creditor may nonetheless proceed with performance and may recover payment unless:

(a)   the creditor could have made a reasonable substitute transaction without significant effort or expense; or

(b)   performance would be unreasonable in the circumstances.

III.—3:302: Enforcement of non-monetary obligations
(1)   The creditor is entitled to enforce specific performance of an obligation other than one to pay money.

(2)   Specific performance includes the remedying free of charge of a performance which is not in conformity with the terms regulating the obligation.

(3)   Specific performance cannot, however, be enforced where:

(a)   performance would be unlawful or impossible;

(b)   performance would be unreasonably burdensome or expensive; or

(c)   performance would be of such a personal character that it would be unreasonable to enforce it.

(4)   The creditor loses the right to enforce specific performance if performance is not requested within a reasonable time after the creditor has become, or could reasonably be expected to have become, aware of the non-performance.

(5)   The creditor cannot recover damages for loss or a stipulated payment for non-performance to the extent that the creditor has increased the loss or the amount of the payment by insisting unreasonably on specific performance in circumstances where the creditor could have made a reasonable substitute transaction without significant effort or expense.

III.—3:303: Damages not precluded
The fact that a right to enforce specific performance is excluded under the preceding Article does not preclude a claim for damages.

Section 4: Withholding performance

III.—3:401: Right to withhold performance of reciprocal obligation
(1)   A creditor who is to perform a reciprocal obligation at the same time as, or after, the debtor performs has a right to withhold performance of the reciprocal obligation until the debtor has tendered performance or has performed.

(2)   A creditor who is to perform a reciprocal obligation before the debtor performs and who reasonably believes that there will be non-performance by the debtor when the debtor's performance becomes due may withhold performance of the reciprocal obligation for as long as the reasonable belief continues. However, the right to withhold performance is lost if the debtor gives an adequate assurance of due performance.

(3)   A creditor who withholds performance in the situation mentioned in paragraph (2) has a duty to give notice of that fact to the debtor as soon as is reasonably practicable and is liable for any loss caused to the debtor by a breach of that duty.

(4)   The performance which may be withheld under this Article is the whole or part of the performance as may be reasonable in the circumstances.

Section 5: Termination

III.—3:501: Scope and definition
(1)   This Section applies only to contractual obligations and contractual relation-ships.
(2)   In this Section 'termination' means the termination of the contractual re-lationship in whole or in part and 'terminate' has a corresponding meaning.

Sub-section 1: Grounds for termination

III.—3:502: Termination for fundamental non-performance
(1)   A creditor may terminate if the debtor's non-performance of a contractual obligation is fundamental.
(2)   A non-performance of a contractual obligation is fundamental if:
   (a)   it substantially deprives the creditor of what the creditor was entitled to expect under the contract, as applied to the whole or relevant part of the perfor-mance, unless at the time of conclusion of the contract the debtor did not foresee and could not reasonably be expected to have foreseen that result; or
   (b)   it is intentional or reckless and gives the creditor reason to believe that the debtor's future performance cannot be relied on.

III.—3:503: Termination after notice fixing additional time for performance
(1)   A creditor may terminate in a case of delay in performance of a contractual obligation which is not in itself fundamental if the creditor gives a notice fixing an additional period of time of reasonable length for performance and the debtor does not perform within that period.
(2)   If the period fixed is unreasonably short, the creditor may terminate only after a reasonable period from the time of the notice.

III.—3:504: Termination for anticipated non-performance
A creditor may terminate before performance of a contractual obligation is due if the debtor has declared that there will be a non-performance of the obliga-tion, or it is otherwise clear that there will be such a non-performance, and if the non-performance would have been fundamental.

III.—3:505: Termination for inadequate assurance of performance
A creditor who reasonably believes that there will be a fundamental non-performance of a contractual obligation by the debtor may terminate if the creditor demands an adequate assurance of due performance and no such assurance is pro-vided within a reasonable time.

Sub-section 2: Scope, exercise and loss of right to terminate

III.—3:506: Scope of right to terminate
(1)   Where the debtor's obligations under the contract are not divisible the creditor may only terminate the contractual relationship as a whole.
(2)   Where the debtor's obligations under the contract are to be performed in separate parts or are otherwise divisible, then:
   (a)   if there is a ground for termination under this Section of a part to which a counter-performance can be apportioned, the creditor may terminate the con-tractual relationship so far as it relates to that part;
   (b)   the creditor may terminate the contractual relationship as a whole only if the creditor cannot reasonably be expected to accept performance of the other parts or there is a ground for termination in relation to the contractual relation-ship as a whole.

III.—3:507: Notice of termination

(1)   A right to terminate under this Section is exercised by notice to the debtor.

(2)   Where a notice under III.—3:503 (Termination after notice fixing additional time for performance) provides for automatic termination if the debtor does not perform within the period fixed by the notice, termination takes effect after that period or a reasonable length of time from the giving of notice (whichever is longer) without further notice.

III.—3:508: Loss of right to terminate

(1)   If performance has been tendered late or a tendered performance otherwise does not conform to the contract the creditor loses the right to terminate under this Section unless notice of termination is given within a reasonable time.

(2)   Where the creditor has given the debtor a period of time to cure the non-performance under III.—3:202 (Cure by debtor: general rules) the time mentioned in paragraph (1) begins to run from the expiry of that period. In other cases that time begins to run from the time when the creditor has become, or could reasonably be expected to have become, aware of the tender or the non-conformity.

(3)   A creditor loses a right to terminate by notice under III.—3:503 (Termination after notice fixing additional time for performance), III.—3:504 (Termination for anticipated non-performance) or III.—3:505 (Termination for inadequate assurance of performance) unless the creditor gives notice of termination within a reasonable time after the right has arisen.

Sub-section 3: Effects of termination

III.—3:509: Effect on obligations under the contract

(1)   On termination under this Section, the outstanding obligations or relevant part of the outstanding obligations of the parties under the contract come to an end.

(2)   Termination does not, however, affect any provision of the contract for the settlement of disputes or other provision which is to operate even after termination.

(3)   A creditor who terminates under this Section retains existing rights to damages or a stipulated payment for non-performance and in addition has the same right to damages or a stipulated payment for non-performance as the creditor would have had if there had been non-performance of the now extinguished obligations of the debtor. In relation to such extinguished obligations the creditor is not regarded as having caused or contributed to the loss merely by exercising the right to terminate.

Section 6: Price reduction

III.—3:601: Right to reduce price

(1)   A creditor who accepts a performance not conforming to the terms regulating the obligation may reduce the price. The reduction is to be proportionate to the decrease in the value of what was received by virtue of the performance at the time it was made compared to the value of what would have been received by virtue of a conforming performance.

(2)   A creditor who is entitled to reduce the price under the preceding paragraph and who has already paid a sum exceeding the reduced price may recover the excess from the debtor.

(3)   A creditor who reduces the price cannot also recover damages for the loss thereby compensated but remains entitled to damages for any further loss suffered.

(4)   This Article applies with appropriate adaptations to a reciprocal obligation of the creditor other than an obligation to pay a price.

Section 7: Damages and interest

III.—3:701: Right to damages

(1)   The creditor is entitled to damages for loss caused by the debtor's non-performance of an obligation, unless the non-performance is excused.

(2)   The loss for which damages are recoverable includes future loss which is reasonably likely to occur.

(3)   'Loss' includes economic and non-economic loss. 'Economic loss' includes loss of income or profit, burdens incurred and a reduction in the value of property. 'Non-economic loss' includes pain and suffering and impairment of the quality of life.

III.—3:702: General measure of damages

The general measure of damages for loss caused by non-performance of an obligation is such sum as will put the creditor as nearly as possible into the position in which the creditor would have been if the obligation had been duly performed. Such damages cover loss which the creditor has suffered and gain of which the creditor has been deprived.

III.—3:703: Foreseeability

The debtor in an obligation which arises from a contract or other juridical act is liable only for loss which the debtor foresaw or could reasonably be expected to have foreseen at the time when the obligation was incurred as a likely result of the non-performance, unless the non-performance was intentional, reckless or grossly negligent.

III.—3:704: Loss attributable to creditor

The debtor is not liable for loss suffered by the creditor to the extent that the creditor contributed to the non-performance or its effects.

III.—3:705: Reduction of loss

(1)   The debtor is not liable for loss suffered by the creditor to the extent that the creditor could have reduced the loss by taking reasonable steps.

(2)   The creditor is entitled to recover any expenses reasonably incurred in attempting to reduce the loss.

III.—3:706: Substitute transaction

A creditor who has terminated a contractual relationship in whole or in part under Section 5 and has made a substitute transaction within a reasonable time and in a reasonable manner may, in so far as entitled to damages, recover the difference between the value of what would have been payable under the terminated relationship and the value of what is payable under the substitute transaction, as well as damages for any further loss.

III.—3:707: Current price

Where the creditor has terminated a contractual relationship in whole or in part under Section 5 and has not made a substitute transaction but there is a current price for the performance, the creditor may, in so far as entitled to damages, recover the difference between the contract price and the price current at the time of termination as well as damages for any further loss.

III.—3:712: Stipulated payment for non-performance

(1)   Where the terms regulating an obligation provide that a debtor who fails to perform the obligation is to pay a specified sum to the creditor for such non-performance, the creditor is entitled to that sum irrespective of the actual loss.

(2)   However, despite any provision to the contrary, the sum so specified in a contract or other juridical act may be reduced to a reasonable amount where it is grossly excessive in relation to the loss resulting from the non-performance and the other circumstances.

III.—3:713: Currency by which damages to be measured
Damages are to be measured by the currency which most appropriately reflects the creditor's loss.

ANNEX
DEFINITIONS

Note: Only selected definitions from the Annex are reproduced here; they have been chosen on the basis of their relevance to the subjects covered in this volume.

Avoidance—'Avoidance' of a juridical act or legal relationship is the process whereby a party or, as the case may be, a court invokes a ground of invalidity so as to make the act or relationship, which has been valid until that point, retrospectively ineffective from the beginning.

Business—'Business' means any natural or legal person, irrespective of whether publicly or privately owned, who is acting for purposes relating to the person's self-employed trade, work or profession, even if the person does not intend to make a profit in the course of the activity. (I. –1:106(2))

Claim—A 'claim' is a demand for something based on the assertion of a right.

Claimant—A 'claimant' is a person who makes, or who has grounds for making, a claim.

Compensation—'Compensation' means reparation in money. (VI.—6:101(2))

Condition—A 'condition' is a provision which makes a legal relationship or effect depend on the occurrence or non-occurrence of an uncertain future event. A condition may be suspensive or resolutive. (III. –1:106)

Conduct—'Conduct' means voluntary behaviour of any kind, verbal or nonverbal: it includes a single act or a number of acts, behaviour of a negative or passive nature (such as accepting something without protest or not doing something) and behaviour of a continuing or intermittent nature (such as exercising control over something).

Confidential information—'Confidential information' means information which, either from its nature or the circumstances in which it was obtained, the party receiving the information knows or could reasonably be expected to know is confidential to the other party. (II.—2:302(2))

Consumer—A 'consumer' means any natural person who is acting primarily for purposes which are not related to his or her trade, business or profession. (I.—1:106(1))

Contract—A 'contract' is an agreement which is intended to give rise to a binding legal relationship or to have some other legal effect. It is a bilateral or multilateral juridical act. (II.—1:101(1))

Contractual obligation—A 'contractual obligation' is an obligation which arises from a contract, whether from an express term or an implied term or by operation of a rule of law imposing an obligation on a contracting party as such.

Contractual relationship—A 'contractual relationship' is a legal relationship resulting from a contract.

Costs—'Costs' includes expenses.

Counter-performance—A 'counter-performance' is a performance which is due in exchange for another performance.

Creditor—A 'creditor' is a person who has a right to performance of an obligation, whether monetary or non-monetary, by another person, the debtor.

Damage—'Damage' means any type of detrimental effect.

Damages—'Damages' means a sum of money to which a person may be entitled, or which a person may be awarded by a court, as compensation for some specified type of damage.

Debtor—A 'debtor' is a person who has an obligation, whether monetary or non-monetary, to another person, the creditor.

Default—'Default', in relation to proprietary security, means any non-performance by the debtor of the obligation covered by the security; and any other event or set of circumstances agreed by the secured creditor and the security provider as entitling the secured creditor to have recourse to the security. (IX.—1:201(5))

Defence—A 'defence' to a claim is a legal objection or a factual argument, other than a mere denial of an element which the claimant has to prove which, if well-founded, defeats the claim in whole or in part.

Delivery—'Delivery' to a person, for the purposes of any obligation to deliver goods, means transferring possession of the goods to that person or taking such steps to transfer possession as are required by the terms regulating the obligation. For the purposes of Book VIII (Acquisition and loss of ownership of goods) delivery of the goods takes place only when the transferor gives up and the transferee obtains possession of the goods: if the contract or other juridical act, court order or rule of law under which the transferee is entitled to the transfer of ownership involves carriage of the goods by a carrier or a series of carriers, delivery of the goods takes place when the transferor's obligation to deliver is fulfilled and the carrier or the transferee obtains possession of the goods. (VIII.—2:104)

Discrimination—'Discrimination' means any conduct whereby, or situation where, on grounds such as sex or ethnic or racial origin, (a) one person is treated less favourably than another person is, has been or would be treated in a comparable situation; or (b) an apparently neutral provision, criterion or practice would place one group of persons at a particular disadvantage when compared to a different group of persons. (II.—2:102(1))

Duty—A person has a 'duty' to do something if the person is bound to do it or expected to do it according to an applicable normative standard of conduct. A duty may or may not be owed to a specific creditor. A duty is not necessarily an aspect of a legal relationship. There is not necessarily a sanction for breach of a duty. All obligations are duties, but not all duties are obligations.

Fraudulent—A misrepresentation is fraudulent if it is made with knowledge or belief that it is false and is intended to induce the recipient to make a mistake to the recipient's prejudice. A non-disclosure is fraudulent if it is intended to induce the person from whom the information is withheld to make a mistake to that person's prejudice. (II. –7:205(2))

Fundamental non-performance—A non-performance of a contractual obligation is fundamental if (a) it substantially deprives the creditor of what the creditor was entitled to expect under the contract, as applied to the whole or relevant part of the performance, unless at the time of conclusion of the contract the debtor did not foresee and could not reasonably be expected to have foreseen that result or (b) it is intentional or reckless and gives the creditor reason to believe that the debtor's future performance cannot be relied on. (III.—3:502(2))

Good faith—'Good faith' is a mental attitude characterised by honesty and an absence of knowledge that an apparent situation is not the true situation.

Good faith and fair dealing—'Good faith and fair dealing' is a standard of conduct characterised by honesty, openness and consideration for the interests of the other party to the transaction or relationship in question. (I.—1:103)

Goods—'Goods' means corporeal movables. It includes ships, vessels, hovercraft or aircraft, space objects, animals, liquids and gases. See also 'movables'.

Indemnify—To 'indemnify' means to make such payment to a person as will ensure that that person suffers no loss.

Ineffective—'Ineffective' in relation to a contract or other juridical act means having no effect, whether that state of affairs is temporary or permanent, general or restricted.

Interest—'Interest' means simple interest without any assumption that it will be capitalised from time to time.

Invalid—'Invalid' in relation to a juridical act or legal relationship means that the act or relationship is void or has been avoided.

Juridical act—A 'juridical act' is any statement or agreement, whether express or implied from conduct, which is intended to have legal effect as such. It may be unilateral, bilateral or multilateral. (II.—1:101(2))

Loss—'Loss' includes economic and non-economic loss. 'Economic loss' includes loss of income or profit, burdens incurred and a reduction in the value of property. 'Non-economic loss' includes pain and suffering and impairment of the quality of life. (III.—3:701(3) and VI.—2:101(4))

Not individually negotiated—A term supplied by one party is not individually negotiated if the other party has not been able to influence its content, in particular because it has been drafted in advance, whether or not as part of standard terms. (II.—1:110)

Obligation—An obligation is a duty to perform which one party to a legal relationship, the debtor, owes to another party, the creditor. (III.—1:101(1))

Performance—'Performance', in relation to an obligation, is the doing by the debtor of what is to be done under the obligation or the not doing by the debtor of what is not to be done. (III.—1:101(2))

Person—'Person' means a natural or legal person.

Possession—Possession, in relation to goods, means having physical control over the goods. (VIII.—1:205)

Price—The 'price' is what is due by the debtor under a monetary obligation, in exchange for something supplied or provided, expressed in a currency which the law recognises as such.

Proceeds—'Proceeds', in relation to proprietary security, is every value derived from an encumbered asset, such as value realised by sale, collection or other disposition; damages or insurance payments in respect of defects, damage or loss; civil and natural fruits, including distributions; and proceeds of proceeds. (IX.—1:201(11))

Reasonable—What is 'reasonable' is to be objectively ascertained, having regard to the nature and purpose of what is being done, to the circumstances of the case and to any relevant usages and practices. (I.—1:104)

Reparation—'Reparation' means compensation or another appropriate measure to reinstate the person suffering damage in the position that person would have been in had the damage not occurred. (VI.—6:101)

Resolutive—A condition is 'resolutive' if it causes a legal relationship or effect to come to an end when the condition is satisfied. (III.—1:106)

Right—'Right', depending on the context, may mean (a) the correlative of an obligation or liability (as in 'a significant imbalance in the parties' rights and obligations arising under the contract'); (b) a proprietary right (such as the right of ownership); (c) a personality right (as in a right to respect for dignity, or a right to liberty and privacy); (d) a legally conferred power to bring about a particular result (as in 'the right to avoid' a contract); (e) an entitlement to a particular remedy (as in a right to have performance of a contractual obligation judicially ordered) or (f) an entitlement to do or not to do something affecting another person's legal position without exposure to adverse consequences (as in a 'right to withhold performance of the reciprocal obligation').

Standard terms—'Standard terms' are terms which have been formulated in advance for several transactions involving different parties, and which have not been individually negotiated by the parties. (II.—1:109)

Supply—To 'supply' goods or other assets means to make them available to another person, whether by sale, gift, barter, lease or other means: to 'supply' services means to provide them to another person, whether or not for a price. Unless otherwise stated, 'supply' covers the supply of goods, other assets and services.

Suspensive—A condition is 'suspensive' if it prevents a legal relationship or effect from coming into existence until the condition is satisfied. (III. –1:106)

Term—'Term' means any provision, express or implied, of a contract or other juridical act, of a law, of a court order or of a legally binding usage or practice: it includes a condition.

Termination—'Termination', in relation to an existing right, obligation or legal relationship, means bringing it to an end with prospective effect except in so far as otherwise provided.

Valid—'Valid', in relation to a juridical act or legal relationship, means that the act or relationship is not void and has not been avoided.

Void—'Void', in relation to a juridical act or legal relationship, means that the act or relationship is automatically of no effect from the beginning.

Voidable—'Voidable', in relation to a juridical act or legal relationship, means that the act or relationship is subject to a defect which renders it liable to be avoided and hence rendered retrospectively of no effect.

Withdraw—A right to 'withdraw' from a contract or other juridical act is a right, exercisable only within a limited period, to terminate the legal relationship arising from the contract or other juridical act, without having to give any reason for so doing and without incurring any liability for non-performance of the obligations arising from that contract or juridical act. (II.—5:101 to II.—5:105)

Withholding performance—'Withholding performance', as a remedy for non-performance of a contractual obligation, means that one party to a contract may decline to render due counter-performance until the other party has tendered performance or has performed. (III.—3:401)

PART V
DRAFT MATERIAL

UNFAIR CONTRACT TERMS BILL*

[DRAFT]

PART 1
BUSINESS LIABILITY FOR NEGLIGENCE

1 Business liability for negligence

(1) Business liability for death or personal injury resulting from negligence cannot be excluded or restricted by a contract term or a notice.

(2) Business liability for other loss or damage resulting from negligence cannot be excluded or restricted by a contract term or a notice unless the term or notice is fair and reasonable.

(3) 'Business liability' means liability arising from—

   (a) anything that was or should have been done for purposes related to a business, or

   (b) the occupation of premises used for purposes related to the occupier's business.

(4) The reference in subsection (3)(a) to anything done for purposes related to a business includes anything done by an employee of that business within the scope of his employment.

(5) 'Negligence' means the breach of—

   (a) an obligation to take reasonable care or exercise reasonable skill in the performance of a contract where the obligation arises from an express or implied term of the contract,

   (b) a common law duty to take reasonable care or exercise reasonable skill,

   (c) the common duty of care imposed by the Occupiers' Liability Act 1957 (c 31) or the Occupiers' Liability Act (Northern Ireland) 1957 (c 25 NI), or

   (d) the duty of reasonable care imposed by section 2(1) of the Occupiers' Liability (Scotland) Act 1960 (c 30).

(6) It does not matter—

   (a) whether a breach of obligation or duty was, or was not, inadvertent, or

   (b) whether liability for it arises directly or vicariously.

2 Exceptions to section 1

(1) Section 1 does not prevent an employee from excluding or restricting his liability for negligence to his employer.

(2) Section 1 does not apply to the business liability of an occupier of premises

*This Bill is appended to the joint Law Commissions' *Report on Unfair Terms in Contracts* (Law Com No 292; Scot Law Com No 199 (2005)).

to a person who obtains access to the premises for recreational or educational purposes if—

    (a)   that person suffers loss or damage because of the dangerous state of the premises, and

    (b)   allowing that person access to those premises for those purposes is not within the purposes of the occupier's business.

(3)   Subsection (2) does not extend to Scotland.

3 Voluntary acceptance of risk

The defence that a person voluntarily accepted a risk cannot be used against him just because he agreed to or knew about a contract term, or a notice, appearing to exclude or restrict business liability for negligence in the case in question.

PART 2

CONSUMER CONTRACTS

Contracts in general

4 Terms of no effect unless fair and reasonable

(1)   If a term of a consumer contract is detrimental to the consumer, the business cannot rely on the term unless the term is fair and reasonable.

(2)   But subsection (1) does not apply to a term which defines the main subject matter of a consumer contract, if the definition is—

    (a)   transparent, and

    (b)   substantially the same as the definition the consumer reasonably expected.

(3)   Nor does subsection (1) apply to a term in so far as it sets the price payable under a consumer contract, if the price is—

    (a)   transparent,

    (b)   payable in circumstances substantially the same as those the consumer reasonably expected, and

    (c)   calculated in a way substantially the same as the way the consumer reasonably expected.

(4)   Nor does subsection (1) apply to a term which—

    (a)   is transparent, and

    (b)   leads to substantially the same result as would be produced as a matter of law if the term were not included.

(5)   The reference to the price payable under a consumer contract does not include any amount, payment of which would be incidental or ancillary to the main purpose of the contract.

(6)   'Price' includes remuneration.

Sale or supply of goods

5 Sale or supply to consumer

(1)   This section applies to a consumer contract for the sale or supply of goods to the consumer.

(2)   In the case of a contract for the sale of the goods, the business cannot rely on a term of the contract to exclude or restrict liability arising under any of the following sections of the 1979 Act—

    (a)   section 12 (implied term that seller entitled to sell),

    (b)   section 13 (implied term that goods match description),

    (c)   section 14 (implied term that goods satisfactory and fit for the purpose),

    (d)   section 15 (implied term that goods match sample).

(3)   In the case of a contract for the hire-purchase of the goods, the business cannot rely on a term of the contract to exclude or restrict liability arising under any of the following sections of the 1973 Act—

    (a)   section 8 (implied term that supplier entitled to supply),

    (b)   section 9 (implied term that goods match description),

    (c)   section 10 (implied term that goods satisfactory and fit for the purpose),

    (d)   section 11 (implied term that goods match sample).

(4)   In the case of any other contract for the transfer of property in the goods, the business cannot rely on a term of the contract to exclude or restrict liability arising under any of the following sections of the 1982 Act—

    (a)   section 2 or 11B (implied term that supplier entitled to supply),

    (b)   section 3 or 11C (implied term that goods match description),

    (c)   section 4 or 11D (implied term that goods satisfactory and fit for the purpose),

    (d)   section 5 or 11E (implied term that goods match sample).

(5)   In the case of a contract for the hire of the goods, the business cannot rely on a term of the contract to exclude or restrict liability arising under any of the following sections of the 1982 Act—

    (a)   section 8 or 11I (implied term that goods match description),

    (b)   section 9 or 11J (implied term that goods satisfactory and fit for the purpose),

    (c)   section 10 or 11K (implied term that goods match sample).

(6)   Subsection (2)(b) to (d) does not apply if the contract is—

    (a)   for the sale of second-hand goods, and

    (b)   made at a public auction which the consumer had the opportunity to attend in person.

6 Sale or supply to business

(1)   This section applies to a consumer contract for the sale or supply of goods to the business.

(2)   In the case of a contract for the sale of the goods, the consumer cannot rely on a term of the contract to exclude or restrict liability—

    (a)   arising under section 12 of the 1979 Act (implied term that seller entitled to sell), or

    (b)   unless the term is fair and reasonable, arising under either of the following sections of that Act—

        (i)   section 13 (implied term that goods match description),

        (ii) section 15 (implied term that goods match sample).

(3)   In the case of a contract for the hire-purchase of the goods, the consumer cannot rely on a term of the contract to exclude or restrict liability—

    (a)   arising under section 8 of the 1973 Act (implied term that supplier entitled to supply), or

    (b)   unless the term is fair and reasonable, arising under either of the following sections of that Act—

        (i)   section 9 (implied term that goods match description),

        (ii) section 11 (implied term that goods match sample).

Supplemental

7 Regulation and enforcement

Schedule 1 confers functions on the OFT and regulators in relation to—

    (a)   consumer contract terms,

    (b)   terms drawn up or proposed for use as consumer contract terms,

    (c)   terms which a trade association recommends for use as consumer contract terms, and

    (d)   notices relating to the rights conferred or duties imposed by consumer contracts.

8 Ambiguity

(1)   If it is reasonable to read a written term of a consumer contract in two (or

more) ways, the term is to be read in whichever of those ways it is reasonable to think the more (or the most) favourable to the consumer.

(2)   This section does not apply in relation to proceedings under Schedule 1 (regulation and enforcement of consumer contract terms, etc).

PART 3
NON-CONSUMER CONTRACTS

Business contracts

9   Written standard terms

(1)   This section applies where one party to a business contract ('A') deals on the written standard terms of business of the other ('B').

(2)   Unless the term is fair and reasonable, B cannot rely on any of those terms to exclude or restrict its liability to A for breach of the contract.

(3)   Unless the term is fair and reasonable, B cannot rely on any of those terms to claim that it has the right—

   (a)   to carry out its obligations under the contract in a way substantially different from the way in which A reasonably expected them to be carried out, or

   (b)   not to carry out all or part of those obligations.

10   Sale or supply of goods

(1)   In the case of a business contract for the sale of goods, the seller cannot rely on a term of the contract to exclude or restrict liability arising under section 12 of the 1979 Act (implied term that seller entitled to sell).

(2)   In the case of a business contract for the hire-purchase of goods, the supplier cannot rely on a term of the contract to exclude or restrict liability arising under section 8 of the 1973 Act (implied term that supplier entitled to supply).

(3)   In the case of any other business contract for the transfer of property in goods, the supplier cannot rely on a term of the contract to exclude or restrict liability arising under section 2 or 11B of the 1982 Act (implied term that supplier entitled to supply).

Small business contracts

11   Non-negotiated terms

(1)   This section applies where there is a small business contract and—

   (a)   the terms on which one party ('A') deals include a term which the other party ('B') put forward during the negotiation of the contract as one of its written standard terms of business,

   (b)   the substance of the term was not, as a result of negotiation, changed in favour of A, and

   (c)   at the time the contract is made, A is a small business.

(2)   If that term is detrimental to A, B cannot rely on the term unless the term is fair and reasonable.

(3)   But subsection (2) does not apply to a term which defines the main subject matter of a small business contract, if the definition is—

   (a)   transparent, and

   (b)   substantially the same as the definition A reasonably expected.

(4)   Nor does subsection (2) apply to a term in so far as it sets the price payable under a small business contract, if the price is—

   (a)   transparent,

   (b)   payable in circumstances substantially the same as those A reasonably expected, and

   (c)   calculated in a way substantially the same as the way A reasonably expected.

(5)   Nor does subsection (2) apply to a term which—

(a)   is transparent, and

(b)   leads to substantially the same result as would be produced as a matter of law if the term were not included.

(6)   The reference to the price payable under a small business contract does not include any amount, payment of which would be incidental or ancillary to the main purpose of the contract.

(7)   'Price' includes remuneration.

Employment contracts

12   Written standard terms

(1)   This section applies in relation to an employment contract under which an individual ('the employee') is employed by a business on its written standard terms of employment.

(2)   Unless the term is fair and reasonable, the business cannot rely on any of those terms to exclude or restrict its liability for breach of the contract.

(3)   Unless the term is fair and reasonable, the business cannot rely on any of those terms to claim it has the right—

(a)   to carry out its obligations under the contract in a way substantially different from the way in which the employee reasonably expected them to be carried out, or

(b)   not to carry out all or part of those obligations.

Private contracts

13   Sale or supply of goods

(1)   This section applies if neither party to a contract for the sale or supply of goods enters into it for purposes related to a business of his.

(2)   In the case of a contract for the sale of the goods, the seller cannot rely on a term of the contract to exclude or restrict liability—

(a)   arising under section 12 of the 1979 Act (implied term that seller entitled to sell), or

(b)   unless the term is fair and reasonable, arising under either of the following sections of that Act—

(i)   section 13 (implied term that goods match description),

(ii)   section 15 (implied term that goods match sample).

(3)   In the case of a contract for the hire-purchase of the goods, the supplier cannot rely on a term of the contract to exclude or restrict liability—

(a)   arising under section 8 of the 1973 Act (implied term that supplier entitled to supply), or

(b)   unless the term is fair and reasonable, arising under either of the following sections of that Act—

(i)   section 9 (implied term that goods match description),

(ii)   section 11 (implied term that goods match sample).

PART 4

THE 'FAIR AND REASONABLE' TEST

The test

14   The test

(1)   Whether a contract term is fair and reasonable is to be determined by taking into account—

(a)   the extent to which the term is transparent, and

(b)   the substance and effect of the term, and all the circumstances existing at the time it was agreed.

(2)   Whether a notice is fair and reasonable is to be determined by taking into account—

    (a)   the extent to which the notice is transparent, and

    (b)   the substance and effect of the notice, and all the circumstances existing at the time when the liability arose (or, but for the notice, would have arisen).

(3)   'Transparent' means—

    (a)   expressed in reasonably plain language,

    (b)   legible,

    (c)   presented clearly, and

    (d)   readily available to any person likely to be affected by the contract term or notice in question.

(4)   Matters relating to the substance and effect of a contract term, and to all the circumstances existing at the time it was agreed, include the following—

    (a)   the other terms of the contract,

    (b)   the terms of any other contract on which the contract depends,

    (c)   the balance of the parties' interests,

    (d)   the risks to the party adversely affected by the term,

    (e)   the possibility and probability of insurance,

    (f)   other ways in which the interests of the party adversely affected by the term might have been protected,

    (g)   the extent to which the term (whether alone or with others) differs from what would have been the case in its absence,

    (h)   the knowledge and understanding of the party adversely affected by the term,

    (i)   the strength of the parties' bargaining positions,

    (j)   the nature of the goods or services to which the contract relates.

(5)   Subsection (4) applies, with any necessary modifications, in relation to a notice as it applies in relation to a contract term.

(6)   Schedule 2 contains an indicative and non-exhaustive list of consumer contract terms and small business contract terms which may be regarded as not being fair and reasonable.

(7)   The Secretary of State may by order amend Schedule 2 so as to add, modify or omit an entry.

Burden of proof

15   Business liability for negligence
It is for a person wishing to rely on a contract term or a notice which purports to exclude or restrict liability of the kind mentioned in section 1(2) (business liability for negligence other than in case of death or personal injury) to prove that the term or notice is fair and reasonable.

16   Consumer contracts
(1)   If an issue is raised as to whether a term in a consumer contract is fair and reasonable, it is for the business to prove that it is.

(2)   But in proceedings under Schedule 1 (regulation and enforcement of consumer contracts) it is for a person claiming that a term in a consumer contract, or a notice, is not fair and reasonable to prove that it is not.

(3)   It is for a person wishing to rely on a contract not being a consumer contract to prove that it is not.

17   Business contracts
(1)   It is for a person wishing to rely on a term of a business contract to prove that the term is fair and reasonable.

(2)   But in relation to a term to which section 11(2) (non-negotiated terms in small business contracts) applies, it is for a person claiming that the term is not fair and reasonable to prove that it is not.

PART 5
CHOICE OF LAW

18 Consumer contracts

(1)   Where a term of a consumer contract applies (or appears to apply) the law of somewhere outside the United Kingdom, this Act has effect in relation to the contract if—

(a)   the consumer was living in the United Kingdom when the contract was made, and

(b)   all the steps which the consumer had to take for the conclusion of the contract were taken there by him or on his behalf.

(2)   Subsection (3) applies where—

(a)   a consumer contract has a close connection with the territory of the member States, and

(b)   subsection (1) does not apply.

(3)   This Act has effect in relation to the contract unless, according to the law of the forum, the provisions of the law of a member State (other than the United Kingdom) which give effect to the Directive have effect in relation to the contract.

(4)   A court is not, for the purposes of this section, to treat a consumer contract as having a close connection with the territory of the member States if—

(a)   the contract provides for goods to be supplied, or services to be performed, outside the European Union, and

(b)   all the steps which the consumer had to take for the conclusion of the contract were taken outside the European Union by him or on his behalf.

(5)   Subsection (4) does not apply if it nevertheless appears to the court from all the circumstances of the case that the contract does have a close connection with the territory of the member States.

(6)   'Territory of the member States' means the same as it does for the purposes of the Treaty establishing the European Community (and, for the avoidance of doubt, any reference in this section to the territory of the member States is to be read as including a part of that territory).

(7)   'The Directive' means Council Directive 93/13/EEC on unfair terms in consumer contracts.

19 Business contracts

(1)   Part 1 (business liability for negligence) does not apply to a business contract term, and sections 9 to 11 (business contracts) do not apply to a business contract, if—

(a)   the law applicable to the term, or contract, is the law of a part of the United Kingdom,

(b)   it is the applicable law only by the choice of the parties, and

(c)   were it not for that choice, the applicable law would be the law of somewhere outside the United Kingdom.

(2)   This Act has effect in relation to a business contract despite a term of the contract which applies (or appears to apply) the law of somewhere outside the United Kingdom if the contract is in every other respect wholly connected with the United Kingdom.

20 Small business contracts

(1)   This Act has effect in relation to a small business contract despite a term of the contract which applies (or appears to apply) the law of somewhere outside the United Kingdom if—

(a)   A had a place of business in the United Kingdom when the contract was made, and

(b)   either of the following conditions applies in relation to the contract.

(2)   The first condition is that—

(a)   the making of the contract was preceded in the United Kingdom by an invitation addressed specifically to A, or by advertising, about the main subject-matter of the contract, and

(b)   all the steps which A had to take for the making of the contract were taken in the United Kingdom by A through A's place of business there or on A's behalf.

(3)   The second is that A's order was received by B in the United Kingdom.

(4)   'A' and 'B' mean, respectively, the persons referred to as A and B in section 11.

PART 6
MISCELLANEOUS AND SUPPLEMENTARY

Miscellaneous

21   Unfairness issue raised by court
A court may, in proceedings before it, raise an issue about whether a contract term or a notice is fair and reasonable even if none of the parties to the proceedings has raised the issue or indicated that it intends to raise it.

22   Exceptions
Schedule 3 sets out types of contract, and of contract term, to which this Act does not apply or to which specified provisions of this Act do not apply.

23   Secondary contracts
(1)   A term of a contract ('the secondary contract') which reduces the rights or remedies, or increases the obligations, of a person under another contract ('the main contract') is subject to the provisions of this Act that would apply to the term if it were in the main contract.

(2)   It does not matter for the purposes of this section whether the parties to the secondary contract are the same as the parties to the main contract.

(3)   This section does not apply if the secondary contract is a settlement of a claim arising under the main contract.

24   Effect of unfair term on contract
Where a contract term cannot be relied on by a person as a result of this Act, the contract continues, so far as practicable, to have effect in every other respect.

Interpretation, etc

25   Preliminary
Sections 26 to 32 define or otherwise explain expressions for the purposes of this Act.

26   'Consumer contract' and 'business contract'
(1)   'Consumer contract' means a contract (other than one of employment) between—

(a)   an individual ('the consumer') who enters into it wholly or mainly for purposes unrelated to a business of his, and

(b)   a person ('the business') who enters into it wholly or mainly for purposes related to his business.

(2)   'Business contract' means a contract between two persons, each of whom enters into it wholly or mainly for purposes related to his business.

27   'Small business'
(1)   'Small business' means a person in whose business the number of employees does not exceed—

(a)   nine, or

(b)   where the Secretary of State specifies by order another number for the purposes of this section, that number.

(2)   But a person is not a small business if adding the number of employees in his business to the number of employees in any other business of his, or in any business of an associated person, gives a total exceeding the number which for the time being applies for the purposes of subsection (1).

(3)   A reference to the number of employees in a business is to the number calculated according to Schedule 4.

28   'Associated person'

(1)   For the purposes of this Act, two persons are associated if—
    (a)   one controls the other, or
    (b)   both are controlled by the same person.

(2)   A person ('A') controls a body corporate ('B') if A can secure that B's affairs are conducted according to A's wishes, directions or instructions.

(3)   The reference in subsection (2) to wishes, directions or instructions does not include advice given in a professional capacity.

(4)   Subsection (2) applies, with any necessary modifications, in relation to an unincorporated association (other than a partnership) as it applies in relation to a body corporate.

(5)   A person controls a partnership if he has the right to a share of more than half the assets or income of the partnership.

(6)   For the purposes of this section, one person does not control another just because he grants that other person a right to supply goods or services.

29   'Small business contract'

(1)   'Small business contract' means a business contract—
    (a)   to which at least one of the parties is, at the time the contract is made, a small business, and
    (b)   which does not come within any of four exceptions.

(2)   The first exception is that the price payable under the contract exceeds £500,000.

(3)   The second is that—
    (a)   the transaction provided for by the contract forms part of a larger transaction, or part of a scheme or arrangement, and
    (b)   the total price payable in respect of the larger transaction, or the scheme or arrangement, exceeds £500,000.

(4)   The third is that—
    (a)   a person agrees to carry on a regulated activity under the contract, and
    (b)   he is an authorised person or, in relation to that activity, an exempt person.

(5)   The fourth is that the contract is a series contract.

(6)   A contract is a series contract if—
    (a)   the transaction provided for by the contract forms part of a series, and
    (b)   during the period of two years ending with the date of the contract, the total price payable under contracts providing for transactions in the series exceeds £500,000.

(7)   A contract is also a series contract if, at the time the contract was made, both parties intended that—
    (a)   the transaction provided for by the contract would form part of a series, and
    (b)   the total price payable under contracts providing for transactions in the series and made during any period of two years, would exceed £500,000.

(8)   Where a contract is a series contract, every subsequent contract providing for a transaction in the series is a series contract.

(9)   The Secretary of State may by order vary the amount specified in subsections (2), (3), (6) and (7).

(10)   'Authorised person', 'exempt person' and 'regulated activity' have the same meaning as in the Financial Services and Markets Act 2000 (c 8).

30 'Excluding or restricting liability'

(1)   A reference to excluding or restricting a liability includes—

   (a)   making a right or remedy in respect of the liability subject to a restrictive or onerous condition;

   (b)   excluding or restricting a right or remedy in respect of the liability;

   (c)   putting a person at a disadvantage if he pursues a right or remedy in respect of the liability;

   (d)   excluding or restricting rules of evidence or procedure.

(2)   A reference in Part 1 or section 5, 6, 10 or 13 to excluding or restricting a liability includes preventing an obligation or duty arising or limiting its extent.

(3)   A written agreement to submit current or future differences to arbitration is not to be regarded as excluding or restricting the liability in question.

31 'Hire-purchase' and 'hire'

(1)   A reference to a contract for the hire-purchase of goods is to a hire-purchase agreement within the meaning of the Consumer Credit Act 1974 (c 39).

(2)   A reference to a contract for the hire of goods is to be read with the 1982 Act.

32   General interpretation

(1)   In this Act—

'the 1973 Act' means the Supply of Goods (Implied Terms) Act 1973 (c 13),

'the 1979 Act' means the Sale of Goods Act 1979 (c 54),

'the 1982 Act' means the Supply of Goods and Services Act 1982 (c 29),

'associated person' has the meaning given in section 28,

'business contract' has the meaning given in section 26(2),

'business liability' has the meaning given in section 1(3) and (4),

'consumer', in relation to a party to a consumer contract, has the meaning given by section 26(1)(a),

'consumer contract' has the meaning given in section 26(1),

'court' means—

   (a)   in England and Wales and Northern Ireland, the High Court or a county court, and

   (b)   in Scotland, the Court of Session or a sheriff,

and, except in Schedule 1, includes a tribunal, arbitrator or arbiter,

'enactment' includes—

   (a)   a provision of, or of an instrument made under, an Act of the Scottish Parliament or Northern Ireland legislation, and

   (b)   a provision of subordinate legislation (within the meaning of the Interpretation Act 1978 (c 30)),

'fair and reasonable', in relation to a contract term or a notice, has the meaning given in section 14,

'goods' has the same meaning as in the 1979 Act,

'injunction' includes interim injunction,

'interdict' includes interim interdict,

'negligence' has the meaning given in section 1(5),

'notice' includes an announcement, whether or not in writing, and any other communication,

'the OFT' means the Office of Fair Trading,

'personal injury' includes any disease and any impairment of physical or mental condition,

'public authority' has the same meaning as in section 6 of the Human Rights Act 1998 (c 42),

'regulator' has the meaning given in paragraph 10 of Schedule 1,

'small business' has the meaning given in section 27,

'small business contract' has the meaning given in section 29,

'statutory' means conferred by an enactment,

'supplier', in relation to a contract for the hire-purchase of goods or a contract for the hire of goods, means the person by whom goods are bailed or (in Scotland) hired to another person under the contract, and

'transparent' has the meaning given in section 14(3).

(2)   A reference to a business includes a profession and the activities of a public authority.

(3)   A reference to excluding or restricting liability is to be read with section 30.

(4)   A reference to a contract for the hire-purchase or hire of goods is to be read with section 31.

Final provisions

33   Orders

(1)   Any power of the Secretary of State to make an order under this Act is exercisable by statutory instrument.

(2)   A statutory instrument containing an order under this Act, other than one containing an order under section 35 (commencement), is subject to annulment in pursuance of a resolution of either House of Parliament.

34   Consequential amendments and repeals, etc.

(1)   Schedule 5 contains minor and consequential amendments.

(2)   Schedule 6 contains repeals and revocations.

35   Short title, commencement and extent

(1)   This Act may be cited as the Unfair Contract Terms Act 2005.

(2)   The preceding provisions come into force on such day as the Secretary of State may by order appoint.

(3)   Different days may be appointed for different provisions.

(4)   No provision of this Act applies in relation to a contract term agreed before the commencement of the provision (except in so far as the term has been varied after that commencement).

(5)   An amendment, repeal or revocation contained in Schedule 5 or 6 has the same
extent as the enactment to which it relates.

(6)   This Act extends to Northern Ireland.

Section 7   SCHEDULES

SCHEDULE 1
CONSUMER CONTRACT TERMS, ETC: REGULATION AND ENFORCEMENT

Cases where this Schedule applies

1.—(1)   This Schedule applies to a complaint about—
      (a)   a consumer contract term,
      (b)   a term drawn up or proposed for use as a consumer contract term, or
      (c)   a term which a trade association recommends for use as a consumer contract term.

(2)   This Schedule also applies to a complaint about—
      (a)   a notice relating to the rights conferred or duties imposed by a consumer contract on the parties, or
      (b)   any other notice purporting to exclude or restrict liability for negligence.

Consideration of complaints

2.—(1)   If the OFT receives a complaint to which this Schedule applies, it must consider the complaint unless—

(a)   it thinks that the complaint is frivolous or vexatious,

(b)   it is notified by a regulator that that regulator intends to consider the complaint, or

(c)   in the case of a complaint under paragraph 1(2)(b), it thinks that sub-paragraph (2) applies in relation to the notice.

(2)   This sub-paragraph applies in relation to a notice which—

(a)   does not exclude or restrict business liability for negligence, or

(b)   excludes or restricts such liability only in relation to a person who, at the time when the liability arises, is acting for purposes related to a business.

(3)   If the regulator intends to consider a complaint to which this Schedule applies, it must—

(a)   notify the OFT that it intends to consider the complaint, and

(b)   consider the complaint.

Application for injunction or interdict

3.—(1)   The OFT (or a regulator) may apply for an injunction or interdict against such persons as it considers appropriate if it thinks that the term or notice to which the complaint relates comes within this paragraph.

(2)   A term or notice comes within this paragraph if it purports to exclude or restrict liability of the kind mentioned in—

(a)   section 1(1) (business liability for death or personal injury resulting from negligence), or

(b)   section 5 (implied terms in supply of goods to consumer).

(3)   A term or notice also comes within this paragraph if it—

(a)   is drawn up for general use, and

(b)   is not fair and reasonable.

(4)   A term also comes within this paragraph if—

(a)   however it is expressed, it is in its effect a term of a kind which the business usually seeks to include in the kind of consumer contract in question, and

(b)   it is not fair and reasonable.

(5)   A term which comes within paragraph 1(b) or (c) (but not within paragraph 1(a)) is to be treated for the purposes of section 14 (the 'fair and reasonable' test) as if it were a contract term.

Notification of application

4.—(1)   If a regulator intends to make an application under paragraph 3—

(a)   it must notify the OFT of its intention, and

(b)   it may make the application only if this paragraph applies.

(2)   This paragraph applies if—

(a)   the period of 14 days beginning with the date of the notification to the OFT has ended, or

(b)   before the end of that period, the OFT allows the regulator to make the application.

(3)   Where the OFT (or a regulator), having considered a complaint to which this Schedule applies, decides not to make an application under paragraph 3 in response to the complaint, it must give its reasons to the person who made the complaint.

Determination of application

5.—(1)   On an application under paragraph 3, the court may grant an injunction or interdict on such conditions, and against such of the respondents, as it thinks appropriate.

(2)   The injunction or interdict may include provision about—

(a)   a term or notice to which the application relates;

(b)   any consumer contract term, or any notice, of a similar kind or like effect.

(3)   It is not a defence to show that, because of a rule of law, a term to which the application relates is not, or could not be, an enforceable contract term.

(4)   If a regulator makes the application, it must notify the OFT of—

(a)   the outcome of the application, and

(b)   if an injunction or interdict is granted, the conditions on which, and the identity of any person against whom, it is granted.

Undertakings

6.—(1)   The OFT (or a regulator) may accept from a relevant person an undertaking that he will comply with such conditions about the use of specified terms or notices, or of terms or notices of a specified kind, as he and the OFT (or the regulator) may agree.

(2)   If a regulator accepts an undertaking under this paragraph, it must notify the OFT of—

(a)   the conditions on which the undertaking is accepted, and

(b)   the identity of the person who gave it.

(3)   'Relevant person', in relation to the OFT or a regulator, means a person against whom it has applied, or thinks it is entitled to apply, for an injunction or interdict under paragraph 3.

(4)   'Specified', in relation to an undertaking, means specified in the undertaking.

Power to obtain information

7.—(1)   The OFT (or a regulator which is a public authority) may, for a purpose mentioned in sub-paragraph (2)(a) or (b), give notice to a person requiring him to provide it with specified information.

(2)   The purposes are—

(a)   to facilitate the exercise of the OFT's (or the regulator's) functions for the purposes of this Schedule,

(b)   to find out whether a person has complied, or is complying, with—

(i)   an injunction or interdict granted under paragraph 5 on an application by the OFT (or the regulator), or

(ii)   an undertaking accepted by it under paragraph 6.

(3)   The notice must—

(a)   be in writing,

(b)   specify the purpose for which the information is required, and

(c)   specify how and when the notice is to be complied with.

(4)   The notice may require the production of specified documents or documents of a specified description.

(5)   The OFT (or the regulator) may take copies of any documents produced in compliance with the notice.

(6)   The notice may be varied or revoked by a subsequent notice under this paragraph.

(7)   The notice may not require a person to provide information or produce documents which he would be entitled to refuse to provide or produce—

(a)   in proceedings in the High Court, on the grounds of legal professional privilege;

(b)   in proceedings in the Court of Session, on the grounds of confidentiality of communication.

(8)   'Specified', in relation to a notice under this paragraph, means specified in the notice.

Notices under paragraph 7: enforcement

8.—(1) If the OFT (or the regulator) thinks that a person (a 'defaulter') has failed, or is failing, to comply with a notice given under paragraph 7, it may apply to the court for an order under this paragraph (a 'compliance order').

(2) If the court thinks that the defaulter has failed to comply with the notice, it may make a compliance order.

(3) A compliance order—
    (a) must specify such things as the court thinks it reasonable for the defaulter to do to ensure compliance with the notice;
    (b) must require the defaulter to do those things;
    (c) may require the defaulter to pay some or all of the costs or expenses of the application for the order ('the application costs').

(4) If the defaulter is a company or association, the court may, when acting under sub-paragraph (3)(c), require payment of some or all of the application costs by an officer of the company or association whom the court thinks responsible for the failure.

(5) If a regulator applies for a compliance order, it must notify the OFT of—
    (a) the outcome of the application, and
    (b) if the order is made, the conditions on which, and the identity of any person against whom, it is made.

(6) 'Officer'—
    (a) in relation to a company, means a director, manager, secretary or other similar officer of the company,
    (b) in relation to a partnership, means a partner,
    (c) in relation to any other association, means an officer of the association or a member of its governing body.

Publication, information and advice

9.—(1) The OFT must arrange to publish details of any—
    (a) application it makes for an injunction or interdict under paragraph 3;
    (b) injunction or interdict granted on an application by it under paragraph 3;
    (c) injunction or interdict notified to it under paragraph 5(4)(b);
    (d) undertaking it accepts under paragraph 6(1);
    (e) undertaking notified to it under paragraph 6(2);
    (f) application it makes for a compliance order under paragraph 8(1);
    (g) compliance order made under paragraph 8(2);
    (h) compliance order notified to it under paragraph 8(5)(b).

(2) Sub-paragraph (3) applies where a person tells the OFT about a term or notice and asks the OFT whether that term or notice, or one of a similar kind or like effect, is or has been the subject of an injunction, interdict or undertaking under this Schedule.

(3) The OFT must reply; and if it replies that the term or notice, or one of a similar kind or like effect, is or has been the subject of an injunction, interdict or undertaking under this Schedule, the OFT must give the person—
    (a) a copy of the injunction or interdict or details of the undertaking, and
    (b) if the person giving the undertaking has agreed to amend the term or notice concerned, a copy of the amendments.

(4) The OFT may arrange to publish advice and information about the provisions of this Act.

(5) A reference to an injunction or interdict under this Schedule is to an injunction or interdict—
    (a) granted on an application by the OFT under paragraph 3, or
    (b) notified to it under paragraph 5(4)(b).

(6) A reference to an undertaking under this Schedule is to an undertaking—

(a)   accepted by the OFT under paragraph 6(1), or

(b)   notified to it under paragraph 6(2).

Meaning of 'regulator'

10.—(1)   For the purposes of this Schedule, 'regulator' means—

(a)   the Financial Services Authority,

(b)   the Office of Communications,

(c)   the Information Commissioner,

(d)   the Gas and Electricity Markets Authority,

(e)   the Water Services Regulation Authority,

(f)   the Office of Rail Regulation,

(g)   the Northern Ireland Authority for Energy Regulation,

(h)   the Department of Enterprise, Trade and Investment in Northern Ireland,

(i)   a local weights and measures authority in Great Britain, or

(j)   a body designated as a regulator under sub-paragraph (3).

(2)   The Secretary of State may by order amend sub-paragraph (1) so as to add, modify or omit an entry.

(3)   Where the Secretary of State thinks that a body which is not a public authority represents the interests of consumers (or consumers of a particular description), he may by order designate the body as a regulator.

(4)   The Secretary of State may cancel the designation if he thinks that the body has failed, or is likely to fail, to comply with a duty imposed on it under this Act.

(5)   The Secretary of State must publish (and may from time to time vary) other criteria to be applied by him in deciding whether to make or cancel a designation under this paragraph.

The Financial Services Authority

11.   Any function that the Financial Services Authority has under this Act is to be regarded, for the purposes of the Financial Services and Markets Act 2000 (c 8), as a function that it has under that Act.

Section 14(6)   SCHEDULE 2
    CONTRACT TERMS WHICH MAY BE REGARDED AS NOT FAIR AND
                          REASONABLE

PART 1
INTRODUCTION

1.—(1)   A term of a consumer contract or small business contract may be regarded as not being fair and reasonable if it—

(a)   has the object or effect of a term listed in Part 2, and

(b)   does not come within an exception mentioned in Part 3.

(2)   In this Schedule—

(a)   in relation to a consumer contract, 'A' means the consumer and 'B' means the business, and

(b)   in relation to a small business contract, 'A' and 'B' mean, respectively, the persons referred to as A and B in section 11.

PART 2
LIST OF TERMS

2.   A term excluding or restricting liability to A for breach of contract.

3.   A term imposing obligations on A in circumstances where B's obligation to perform depends on the satisfaction of a condition wholly within B's control.

4.   A term entitling B, if A exercises a right to cancel the contract or if B terminates the contract as a result of A's breach, to keep sums that A has paid, the amount of which is unreasonable.

5.   A term requiring A, when in breach of contract, to pay B a sum significantly above the likely loss to B.

6. A term entitling B to cancel the contract without incurring liability, unless there is also a term entitling A to cancel it without incurring liability.

7.   A term entitling B, if A exercises a right to cancel the contract, to keep sums A has paid in respect of services which B has yet to supply.

8.   A term in a fixed-term contract or a contract of indefinite duration entitling B to terminate the contract without giving A reasonable advance notice (except in an urgent case).

9.   A term—

(a)   providing for a contract of fixed duration to be renewed unless A indicates otherwise, and

(b)   requiring A to give that indication a disproportionately long time before the contract is due to expire.

10.   A term binding A to terms with which A did not have an opportunity to become familiar before the contract was made.

11.   A term entitling B, without a good reason which is specified in the contract, to vary the terms of the contract.

12.   A term entitling B, without a good reason, to vary the characteristics of the goods or services concerned.

13.   A term requiring A to pay whatever price is set for the goods at the time of delivery (including a case where the price is set by reference to a list price), unless there is also a term entitling A to cancel the contract if that price is higher than the price indicated to A when the contract was made.

14.   A term entitling B to increase the price specified in the contract, unless there is also a term entitling A to cancel the contract if the business does increase the price.

15.   A term giving B the exclusive right (and, accordingly, excluding any power of a court) to determine—

(a)   whether the goods or services supplied match the definition of them given in the contract, or

(b)   the meaning of any term in the contract.

16.   A term excluding or restricting B's liability for statements or promises made by B's employees or agents, or making B's liability for statements or promises subject to formalities.

17.   A term requiring A to carry out its obligations in full (in particular, to pay the whole of the price specified in the contract) in circumstances where B has failed to carry out its obligations in full.

18.   A term entitling B to transfer its obligations without A's consent.

19.   A term entitling B to transfer its rights in circumstances where A's position might be weakened as a result.

20.   A term excluding or restricting A's right—

(a)   to bring or defend any action or other legal proceedings, or

(b)   to exercise other legal remedies.

21.   A term restricting the evidence on which A may rely.

PART 3
EXCEPTIONS

Financial services contracts

22.—(1)   Sub-paragraph (2) applies where a term in a financial services contract of indefinite duration provides that B may terminate the contract—

(a)   by giving A relatively short advance notice, or

(b)   if B has a good reason for terminating the contract, without giving A any advance notice.

(2)   Paragraph 8 (termination without reasonable notice) does not apply to the term if the contract also provides that B must immediately inform A of the termination.

(3)   Sub-paragraph (4) applies where a term in a financial services contract of indefinite duration provides that B may vary the interest rate or other charges payable under it—

(a)   by giving A relatively short advance notice, or

(b)   if B has a good reason for making the variation, without giving A any advance notice.

(4)   Paragraph 11 (variation without good reason) does not apply to a term if the contract also provides that—

(a)   B must as soon as practicable inform A of the variation, and

(b)   A may then cancel the contract, without incurring liability.

(5)   'Financial services contract' means a contract for the supply by B of financial services to A.

Contracts of indefinite duration

23.   Paragraph 11 (variation without good reason) does not apply to a term in a contract of indefinite duration if the contract also provides that—

(a)   B must give reasonable notice of the variation, and

(b)   A may then cancel the contract, without incurring liability.

Contracts for sale of securities, foreign currency, etc

24.—(1)   None of the following paragraphs applies to a contract term if sub-paragraph (2) or (3) applies—

(a)   paragraph 8 (termination without reasonable notice),

(b)   paragraph 11 (variation without good reason),

(c)   paragraph 13 (determination of price at time of delivery),

(d)   paragraph 14 (increase in price).

(2)   This sub-paragraph applies if the contract is for the transfer of securities, financial instruments or anything else, the price of which is linked to—

(a)   fluctuations in prices quoted on a stock exchange, or

(b)   a financial index or market rate that B does not control.

(3)   This sub-paragraph applies if the contract is for the sale of foreign currency (and, for this purpose, that includes foreign currency in the form of traveller's cheques or international money orders).

Price index clauses

25.   Neither paragraph 13 nor paragraph 14 (determination of price at time of delivery or increase in price) applies to a contract term if—

(a)   the term provides for the price of the goods or services to be varied by reference to an index of prices, and

(b)   the contract specifies how a change to the index is to affect the price.

SCHEDULE 3   Section 22
EXCEPTIONS

Legal requirements

1.—(1)   This Act does not apply to a contract term—
    (a)   required by an enactment or a rule of law,
    (b)   required or authorised by a provision in an international convention to which the United Kingdom or the European Community is a party, or
    (c)   required by, or incorporated as a result of a decision or ruling of, a competent authority acting in the exercise of its statutory jurisdiction or any of its functions.
(2)   Sub-paragraph 1(c) does not apply if the competent authority is itself a party to the contract.
(3)   'Competent authority' means a public authority other than a local authority.

Settlements of claims

2.—(1)   This Act does not apply to a contract term in so far as it is, or forms part of—
    (a)   a settlement of a claim in tort;
    (b)   a discharge or indemnity given by a person in consideration of the receipt by him of compensation in settlement of any claim which he has.
(2)   In sub-paragraph (1)—
    (a)   paragraph (a) does not extend to Scotland, and
    (b)   paragraph (b) extends only to Scotland.

Insurance

3.   The following sections do not apply to an insurance contract (including a contract to pay an annuity on human life)—
    (a)   section 1 (exclusion of business liability for negligence),
    (b)   section 9 (exclusion of liability for breach of business contract where one party deals on written standard terms of the other),
    (c)   section 11 (non-negotiated terms in small business contracts),
    (d)   section 12 (exclusion of employer's liability under employment contract).

Land

4.   The following sections do not apply to a contract term in so far as it relates to the creation, transfer, variation or termination of an interest or real right in land—
    (a)   section 1 (exclusion of business liability for negligence),
    (b)   section 9 (exclusion of liability for breach of business contract where one party deals on written standard terms of the other),
    (c)   section 11 (non-negotiated terms in small business contracts).

Intellectual property

5.   Nor do those sections apply to a contract term in so far as it relates to the creation, transfer, variation or termination of a right or interest in any patent, trade mark, copyright or design right, registered design, technical or commercial information or other intellectual property.

Company formation, etc

6.   Nor do those sections apply to a contract term in so far as it relates to—

(a) the formation or dissolution of a body corporate or unincorporated association (including a partnership),

(b) its constitution, or

(c) the rights and obligations of its members.

Securities

7. Nor do those sections apply to a contract term in so far as it relates to the creation or transfer of securities or of a right or interest in securities.

International supply contracts

8. The following provisions do not apply to a business contract for the supply of goods where the supply is to be made to a place outside the United Kingdom—

(a) section 1(2) (business liability for negligence other than in case of death or personal injury),

(b) sections 9 to 11 (unfair terms in business contracts),

(c) sections 19 and 20 (choice of law in business contracts).

Shipping

9.—(1) Section 1(2) does not apply to a shipping contract unless it is also a consumer contract.

(2) Sections 9 and 11 do not apply to a shipping contract.

(3) 'Shipping contract' means—

(a) a contract of marine salvage or towage,

(b) a charterparty of a ship or hovercraft, or

(c) a contract for the carriage of goods by ship or hovercraft.

10.—(1) This paragraph applies where goods are carried by ship or hovercraft under a contract which—

(a) specifies that as the means of transport for part of the journey, or

(b) does not specify a means of transport but does not exclude that one.

(2) Section 1(2) does not apply to the contract, unless it is also a consumer contract, in so far as it relates to the carriage of the goods by that means of transport.

(3) Sections 9 and 11 do not apply to the contract in so far as it relates to the carriage of the goods by that means of transport.

Section 27   SCHEDULE 4
CALCULATING THE NUMBER OF EMPLOYEES IN A BUSINESS

Introduction

1.—(1) This Schedule sets out how to calculate the number of employees that a party to a business contract, or an associated person, has in its business.

(2) 'The business period' means a continuous period for which—

(a) the party to the business contract has been carrying on the business to which the contract relates, or

(b) an associated person has been carrying on business.

Calculation for established business

2. Where the business period is at least twelve months ending on the last day of the month immediately before the month including the contract date—

(a) work out how many full-time employees there are in the business on the last day of each of the twelve months ending with the last complete month before the contract date,

(b) add together the numbers for those twelve days, and

(c) divide the total by twelve.

Calculation for new business

3.   Where the business period is at least one complete month ending on the last day of the month immediately before the month including the contract date (but paragraph 2 does not apply)—

(a) work out how many full-time employees there are in the business on the last day of each complete month,

(b) add together the numbers for those days, and

(c) divide the total by the number of complete months.

4.   Where the business period is less than one complete month, but more than one day, before the contract date—

(a) work out how many full-time employees there are in the business on each day,

(b) add together the numbers for those days, and

(c) divide that total by the number of days.

5.   Where the party to the contract enters into it on the first day on which it carries on the business to which the contract relates, or an associated person has been carrying on business for only one day, work out how many fulltime employees there are in the business on the day in question.

The number of full-time employees in a business

6.—(1)   This paragraph sets out how to work out how many full-time employees there are in a business.

(2)   An employee who works for at least 35 hours a week for a business counts as one full-time employee.

(3)   An employee who works for under 35 hours a week for a business (a 'part-time employee') counts as a fraction of one full-time employee, with the fraction being calculated as—

$$\frac{A}{B}$$

where A and B are defined as follows.

(4)   A is the number of hours a week which the part-time employee works for the business.

(5)   B is—

(a) the number of hours a week which a full-time employee of the same description as the part-time employee works for the business, or

(b) if there are no full-time employees of that description, 35 hours a week.

(6)   The number of hours a week which an employee works for a business is—

(a) the number of hours a week which he is contractually required to work for the business, or

(b) if he ordinarily works for a longer period than that, or his contract does not specify for how many hours a week he is to work, the number of hours a week he ordinarily works for the business,

but does not include any meal break, or rest period, exceeding 15 minutes.

Interpretation

7. 'Contract date', in relation to a business contract, means the date on which the contract is made.

8. 'Employee'—
(a) in relation to any business, means an individual who works in the business under a contract of employment or a contract for services;
(b) in relation to a business carried on by a partnership (or other unincorporated association), includes a partner (or member);
(c) in relation to a business carried on by only one individual, includes that individual.

[Schedules 5 and 6 contain amendments and repeals.]

INTEREST (SCOTLAND) BILL[1]

[CONSULTATION DRAFT]

An Act of the Scottish Parliament to make provision for the creation of an entitlement to interest in certain circumstances; to change the law on entitlement to interest on damages payments; to make provision about interest and tenders in proceedings; and for connected purposes

1   Entitlement to interest

(1) A person entitled to payment of a sum of money is entitled to interest on that sum in accordance with the provisions of this Act.

(2) Interest to which a person is entitled under subsection (1) is in this Act referred to as 'statutory interest'.

2   Circumstances in which interest not payable

Where a person (in this section referred to as 'the creditor') is entitled to payment of a sum of money from another person (in this section referred to as 'the debtor'), statutory interest is not due on that sum if—
(a) there is express or implied agreement between the creditor and the debtor—
(i) that interest is to be due on that sum on a basis different from that provided for in this Act; or
(ii) that no interest is to be due on that sum;
(b) the payment represents a fine, penalty or tax due to a public authority;
(c) any enactment (other than this Act or the Late Payment of Commercial Debts (Interest) Act 1998 (c.20))—
(i) makes provision for interest to be due on that sum; or
(ii) provides that no interest is due on that sum;
(d) interest is due on that sum by virtue of that Act of 1998 and is claimed as so due by the creditor; or
(e) the payment is of a type specified by the Scottish Ministers by order.

3   Starting date generally

(1) In a case where a starting date falls to be ascertained in accordance with section 4, 5, 6, 7 or 8, statutory interest runs for the period beginning on the day after that date and ending on the day or days on which the principal sum is paid.

---

[1] This is the Bill as published on the Scottish Government website on 25 January 2008 (http://www.scotland.gov.uk/Publications/2008/01).

(2)   In any other case, statutory interest runs for the period beginning on the day after the date on which the principal sum is due and ending on the day or days on which that sum is paid.

4   Starting date: certain obligations where provision is made for date of payment of principal sum

(1)   Where a contract (other than a contract of loan or a contract of cautionry) makes provision as to the date on which any payment under the contract is due, that date is the starting date in respect of that payment.

(2)   In the case of a cautionary obligation, where provision is made as to the date on which any payment due in satisfaction of the cautioner's right of relief against the principal debtor or any co-cautioner is due, that date is the starting date in respect of that payment.

5   Starting date: certain obligations where no such provision is made

(1)   Where—

(a)   a contract of a type referred to in subsection (2) makes no provision; or

(b)   in the case of an obligation of a type referred to in subsection (3) no provision is made,

as to the date on which any payment due under the contract, or the obligation, and mentioned in that subsection is due, the starting date in respect of that payment is to be ascertained in accordance with whichever of those subsections is applicable.

(2)   In the case of a contract for the supply of goods or services (other than a contract of employment or apprenticeship), the starting date in respect of any payment due under the contract is the date 30 days after whichever is the later of—

(a)   the day on which the supplier's obligation is performed; and

(b)   the day on which the other party has notice of—

(i)   the amount of the debt; or

(ii)   where that amount is unascertained, the sum which the supplier claims is the amount of the debt.

(3)   In the case of a cautionary obligation, the starting date in respect of any payment due in satisfaction of the cautioner's right of relief against the principal debtor or any co-cautioner is the day on which the payment in respect of which the right of relief arises is made by the cautioner.

6   Starting date: contracts of loan

In the case of a contract of loan, the starting date is the day on which the loan is made.

7   Starting date: damages

(1)   Where statutory interest is due on a sum of money payable as damages, the starting date in respect of any part of that sum representing a head of loss is the day on which the loss in question is sustained.

(2)   Nothing in this section prevents a court from treating a loss (including non-patrimonial loss) in respect of which an award of damages is made as having been sustained over a period of time.

8   Starting date: fees and outlays in proceedings

Where a party to proceedings is liable to pay any fees or outlays incurred by another party to those proceedings, the starting date is the day on which they are paid by the other party.

9   Calculation of interest

(1)   Subject to section 10, statutory interest in respect of any period runs at the statutory rate for that period.

(2)   Subject to subsection (3), statutory interest is simple interest.

(3)   Where a court orders payment of a sum of money on which statutory interest is to run, interest starts to run on the day after the date of the order on both—

(a)   the principal sum; and

(b)   any interest accrued on that sum as at that date.

(4)   Subsection (3) does not apply in respect of—

(a)   an order authorising execution in Scotland of a foreign judgment; or

(b)   any order made in connection with, or in consequence of—

(i)   the registration of a document for execution; or

(ii)   a bill protested for non-payment by a notary public.

10   Principal sum payable in foreign currency

(1)   Where a principal sum is payable in a foreign currency, statutory interest on that sum runs at—

(a)   the rate 1.5% per year over such rate as is, in relation to the foreign currency in question, that currency's nearest equivalent to the official dealing rate; or

(b)   if it is not possible to identify such an equivalent, such rate as best meets the interests of justice.

(2)   The Scottish Ministers may by order amend paragraph (a) of subsection (1) so as to substitute a different percentage for the percentage for the time being specified there.

11   Power of court to waive or reduce interest

(1)   If a court considers that it would be in the interests of justice to do so, having regard in particular to any conduct which it considers relevant of the person to whom statutory interest would be payable, it may decide that—

(a)   statutory interest which, but for this section, would be payable is not to be payable;

(b)   an amount payable as statutory interest is to be less than, but for this section, it would be.

(2)   In subsection (1), 'conduct' includes any act or omission (whether before or after the time when the principal sum fell due for payment).

12   Tenders

(1)   Where a tender is made in the course of any proceedings, the tender is, unless it states otherwise, in full satisfaction of any claim for interest in the action by any person in whose favour the tender is made.

(2)   Where a court is considering whether a sum of money payable under an order made by it is equal to or greater than an amount tendered in the proceedings, it is to leave out of account any element of the sum which represents interest in respect of the period between the making of the tender and the date of the order.

13   Application of Act

This Act binds the Crown.

14   Ancillary provision

(1)   The Scottish Ministers may by order make such incidental, supplemental, consequential, transitional, transitory or saving provision as they consider necessary or expedient for the purposes, or in consequence, of this Act or for giving full effect to any of its provisions.

(2)   An order under subsection (1) may modify any enactment.

15   Modification and repeal of enactments

(1)   Schedule 1, which modifies enactments, has effect.

(2)   The enactments mentioned in the first column of schedule 2 are repealed to the extent specified in the second column.

16   Orders

(1)   Any power conferred by this Act on the Scottish Ministers to make orders—

(a)   must be exercised by statutory instrument;

(b)   may be exercised so as to make different provision for different purposes.

(2)   A statutory instrument containing an order made under this Act (except an order made under section 18(2)) is, subject to subsection (3), subject to annulment in pursuance of a resolution of the Scottish Parliament.

(3)   A statutory instrument containing—

(a)   an order under section 2(e);

(b)   an order under section 14 containing provisions which add to, replace or omit any part of the text of an Act,

is not to be made unless a draft of the instrument has been laid before, and approved by resolution of, the Scottish Parliament.

17 Interpretation

(1)   In this Act—

'court' includes any tribunal, arbiter or adjudicator;

'the official dealing rate' means the rate announced from time to time by the Monetary Policy Committee of the Bank of England ('the Bank') and for the time being in force as the official dealing rate, being the rate at which the Bank is willing to enter into transactions for providing short term liquidity in the money markets;

'principal sum' means a sum of money on which statutory interest is payable;

'starting date' means the date on which statutory interest on a sum of money begins to run;

'statutory interest' has the meaning given by section 1(2);

'the statutory rate' means the rate 1.5% per year over the official dealing rate;

'supply' includes 'sale' and 'supplier' includes 'seller'.

(2)   The Scottish Ministers may by order amend the definition of 'the statutory rate' in subsection (1) so as to substitute a different percentage for the percentage for the time being specified there.

18 Short title and commencement

(1)   This Act may be cited as the Interest (Scotland) Act 2007.

(2)   This Act (other than sections 14, 16, 17 and this section) comes into force in accordance with provision made by the Scottish Ministers by order.

INDEX

INDEX OF MATERIALS